P9-AOU-445

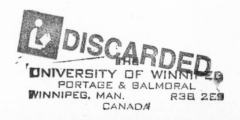

THE

HISTORY OF SCOTLAND

THE
HISTORY OF SCOTLAND

DURING THE REIGNS OF

QUEEN MARY, AND OF KING JAMES VI.

TILL HIS ACCESSION TO THE CROWN OF ENGLAND.

WITH

A REVIEW OF THE SCOTTISH HISTORY

PREVIOUS TO THAT PERIOD:

AND

AN APPENDIX, CONTAINING ORIGINAL PAPERS.

———

BY WILLIAM ROBERTSON, D.D.

PRINCIPAL OF THE UNIVERSITY OF EDINBURGH, ETC.

———

A NEW AND COMPLETE EDITION.

———

ABERDEEN:

PUBLISHED BY GEORGE CLARK AND SON.

IPSWICH:—J. M. BURTON.
———
MDCCCXLVII.
KRAUS REPRINT CO.
Millwood, New York
1976

Library of Congress Cataloging in Publication Data

Robertson, William, 1721-1793.
    The history of Scotland during the reigns of Queen
Mary and of King James VI till his accession to the
Crown of England.

    Reprint of the new and complete ed. published in
1847 by G. Clark, Aberdeen.
    1. Scotland—History—Mary Stuart, 1542-1567.
2. Scotland—History—James VI, 1567-1625.
I. Title: The history of Scotland during the reigns
of Queen Mary and of King James VI . . .
DA785.R64   1976   941.105   76-40980
ISBN 0-527-75915-5

PREFACE

TO THE FIRST EDITION.

———

I DELIVER this book to the world with all the diffidence and anxiety natural to an author on publishing his first performance. The time I have employed, and the pains I have taken, in order to render it worthy of the public approbation, it is perhaps, prudent to conceal, until it be known whether that approbation shall ever be bestowed upon it.

But as I have departed, in many instances from former historians, as I have placed facts in a different light, and have drawn characters with new colours, I ought to account for this conduct to my readers; and to produce the evidence on which, at the distance of two centuries, I presume to contradict the testimony of less remote, or even of contemporary historians.

The transactions in Mary's reign gave rise to two parties, which were animated against each other with the fiercest political hatred, embittered by religious zeal. Each of these produced historians of considerable merit, who adopted all their sentiments, and defended all their actions. Truth was not the sole object of these authors. Blinded by prejudices, and heated by the part which they themselves had acted in the scenes they describe, they wrote an apology for a faction, rather than the history of their country. Succeeding historians have followed these guides almost implicitly, and have repeated their errors and misrepresentations. But as the same passions which inflamed parties in that age have descended to their posterity; as almost every event in Mary's reign has become the object of doubt or of dispute; the eager spirit of controversy soon discovered, that without some evidence more authentic and more impartial than that of such historians, none of the points in question could be decided with certainty. Records have therefore been searched, original papers have been produced, and public archives, as well as the repositories of private men, have been ransacked by the zeal and curiosity of writers of different parties. The attention of Cecil to collect whatever related to that period, in which he acted so conspicuous a part, hath provided such an immense store of original papers for illustrating this part of the English and Scottish history, as are almost sufficient to satisfy the utmost avidity of an antiquary. Sir Robert Cotton (whose library is now the property of the public) made great and valuable additions to Cecil's collection; and from this magazine,

Digges, the compilers of the Cabbala, Anderson, Keith, Haynes, Forbes, have drawn most of the papers which they have printed. No History of Scotland, that merits any degree of attention, has appeared since these collections were published. By consulting them, I have been enabled, in many instances, to correct the inaccuracies of former historians, to avoid their mistakes, and to detect their misrepresentations.

But many important papers have escaped the notice of those industrious collectors; and, after all they produced to light, much still remained in darkness, unobserved or unpublished. It was my duty to search for these; and I found this unpleasant task attended with considerable utility.

The library of the Faculty of Advocates of Edinburgh, contains not only a large collection of original papers relating to the affairs of Scotland, but copies of others no less curious, which have been preserved by Sir Robert Cotton, or are extant in the public offices in England. Of all these the curators of that library were pleased to allow me the perusal.

Though the British Museum be not yet open to the public, Dr. Birch, whose obliging disposition is well known, procured me access to that noble collection, which is worthy of the magnificence of a great and polished nation.

That vast and curious collection of papers relating to the reign of Elizabeth, which was made by Dr. Forbes, and of which he published only two volumes, having been purchased since his death by Lord Viscount Royston, his lordship was so good as to allow me the use of fourteen volumes in quarto, containing that part of them which is connected with my subject.

Sir Alexander Dick communicated to me a very valuable collection of original papers, in two large volumes. They relate chiefly to the reign of James. Many of them are marked with Archbishop Spotiswood's hand; and it appears from several passages in the History, that he had perused them with great attention.

Mr. Calderwood, an eminent Presbyterian clergyman of the last century, compiled a History of Scotland from the beginning of the reign of James V. to the death of James the VI. in six large volumes: wherein he has inserted many papers of consequence, which are no where else to be found. This History has not been published, but a copy of it, which still remains in manuscript, in the possession of the church of Scotland, was put into my hands by my worthy friend the Reverend Dr. George Wishart, principal clerk of the church.

Sir David Dalrymple not only communicated to me the papers which he has collected relating to Gowrie's conspiracy; but, by explaining to me his sentiments with regard to that problematical passage in the Scottish history, has enabled me to place that transaction in a light which dispels much of the darkness and confusion in which it has been hitherto involved.

Mr. Goodall, though he knew my sentiments with regard to the conduct and character of Queen Mary to be extremely different from his own, communicated to me a volume of manuscripts in his possession, which contains a great number of valuable papers copied from the originals in the Cottonian Library and Paper Office, by the late Reverend Mr. Crawford, Regius Professor of Church History in the University of Edinburgh. I likewise received from him the original Register of letters kept by the Regent Lennox during his administration.

I have consulted all these papers, as far as I thought they could be of any use towards illustrating that period of which I write the history. With what success I have employed them to confirm what was already known, to ascertain what was dubious, or to determine what was controverted, the Public must judge.

I might easily have drawn, from the different repositories to which I had access, as many papers as would have rendered my Appendix equal in size to the most bulky collection of my predecessors. But I have satisfied myself with publishing a few of the most curious among them, to which I found it necessary to appeal as vouchers for my own veracity. None of these, as far as I can recollect, ever appeared in any former collection.

I have added a "Critical Dissertation concerning the Murder of King Henry, and the Genuineness of the Queen's Letters to Bothwell." The facts and observations which relate to Mary's letters, I owe to my friend Mr. John Davidson, one of the Clerks to the Signet, who hath examined this point with his usual acuteness and industry.

PREFACE

TO THE ELEVENTH EDITION.

———

IT is now twenty-eight years since I published the History of Scotland. During that time I have been favoured by my friends with several remarks upon it; and various strictures have been made by persons who entertained sentiments different from mine, with respect to the transactions of the reign of Queen Mary. From whatever quarter information came, in whatever mode it has been communicated, I have considered it calmly and with attention. Wherever I perceived that I had erred, either in relating events, or in delineating characters, I have, without hesitation, corrected those errors. Wherever I am satisfied that my original ideas were just and well founded, I adhere to them; and resting upon their conformity to evidence already produced, I enter into no discussion or controversy in order to support them. Wherever the opportunity of consulting original papers, either in print or in manuscript, to which I had formerly access, has enabled me to throw new light upon any part of the History, I have made alterations and additions, which, I flatter myself, will be found to be of some importance.

COLLEGE OF EDINBURGH,
March 5, 1787.

LIFE OF DR. ROBERTSON.

WILLIAM ROBERTSON, the eldest son of the Rev. William Robertson, was born on the 8th of September, 1721, at Borthwick, in the shire of Mid Lothian, of which parish his father was the minister. By the paternal line he descended from a respectable family in the county of Fife, a branch of that which, for many generations, possessed the estate of Struan, in Perthshire. His mother was the daughter of David Pitcairn, Esq. of Dreghorn. He had one brother and six sisters; all of whom were well settled in life, and most of whom lived to an advanced age.

At the parochial School of Borthwick Robertson received the initiatory part of his education; but when he was sufficiently forward to enter on the study of the learned languages, he was removed to the school of Dalkeith. The latter seminary was then superintended by Mr. Leslie, whose eminence as a teacher, attracted pupils from all parts of Scotland.

When Robertson was twelve years old, his father was transferred from Borthwick to one of the churches of Edinburgh. In the autumn of 1733 he joined his parents; and, in October, he was admitted into the college and university of the northern capital.

Among the men of eminence, by whose instructions he profited at the university, were Sir John Pringle, afterwards President of the Royal Society, but then Professor of Moral Philosophy; Maclaurin, justly celebrated for the extent of his mathematical skill and the purity of his style; and Dr. Stevenson, the learned and indefatigable Professor of Logic. To the masterly prelections of the latter, especially to his illustrations of the Poetics of Aristotle, and of Longinus on the Sublime, Robertson often declared that he considered himself more deeply indebted than to any circumstance in the course of his academical career. It was not towards the abstract sciences that the bent of his genius was directed. Neither was he remarkable for metaphysical acuteness. He delighted to elucidate moral and religious truths, to apply the process of reasoning to subjects more immediately connected with the every-day business of existence, to search into the causes and effects of historical events, and, by meditating on the great models of oratorical art, to render himself master of all the powerful resources of a ready and persuasive eloquence.

During the last years, therefore, of his residing at college, he

A 5

joined with some of his contemporaries in establishing a society, the avowed purpose of which, as we are told by Mr. Stewart, was "to cultivate the study of elocution, and to prepare themselves, by the habits of extemporary discussion and debate, for conducting the business of popular assemblies."

Of the colleagues of Robertson in this society many ultimately rose, like himself, to high reputation. Among them were Cleghorn, subsequently Professor of Moral Philosophy at Edinburgh; Dr. John Blair, who became a member of the Royal Society, and a prebendary of Westminster, and who gave to the public "The Chronology and History of the World;" Wilkie, the author of the Epigoniad, a faulty poem, but above contempt; Home, the author of Douglas; and Dr. Erskine, who, in after life, was at once the coadjutor, rival, opponent, and friend of Robertson.

Having completed his academic course, and richly stored his mind, he quitted the university, and, in 1741, before he was twenty, a license to preach the gospel was given to him by the Presbytery of Dalkeith. This license, does not authorize to administer the sacraments, or to undertake the cure of souls, and is granted to laymen.

After two years, from his leaving the university, (when he was yet little more than twenty-two,) he was presented, by the Earl of Hopetoun, to the living of Gladsmuir, of the yearly value of about one hundred pounds. He had not long resided at Gladsmuir, when an unexpected and melancholy event occurred, which put to the trial at once his firmness and benevolence. His father and mother expired within a few hours of each other, leaving behind them a family of six daughters and one son, without the means of providing for their education and maintenance. On this occasion, Robertson acted in a manner which bore testimony to the goodness of his heart, and which was also, as Mr. Stewart justly observes, "strongly marked with that manly decision in his plans, and that persevering steadiness in their execution, which were the characteristic features of his mind." Regardless of any privations or interruptions to his literary and other projects, he received his father's family into his house at Gladsmuir, and educated his sisters under his own roof, retaining them there till opportunities arose of settling them respectably in the world. His merit is enhanced by the circumstance of his fraternal affection having imposed on him a sacrifice more painful than that of riches or fame. He was tenderly attached to his cousin Miss Mary Nesbit, daughter of the Rev. J. Nesbit, one of the ministers of Edinburgh, and his attachment was returned; but it was not till 1751, when his family had ceased to need his protecting care, that he felt himself at liberty to complete a union which had, for several years, been the object of his ardent wishes.

While he was laudably occupied in promoting the welfare of his orphan relatives, the rebellion broke out in Scotland. "It afforded him," says Mr. Stewart, "an opportunity of evincing the sincerity of that zeal for the civil and religious liberties of his country, which he had imbibed with the first principles of his education; and which afterwards, at the distance of forty years, when he was called on to employ his eloquence in the national commemoration of the Revolution, seemed to rekindle the fires of his youth. His situation as a country clergyman confined indeed his patriotic exertions within a narrow sphere; but even here his conduct was guided by a mind superior to the scene in which he acted. On one occasion, (when the capital was in danger of falling into the hands of the rebels,) the present state of public affairs appeared so critical that he thought himself justified in laying aside, for a time, the pacific habits of his profession, and in quitting his parochial residence at Gladsmuir to join the volunteers of Edinburgh. And when, at last, it was determined that the city should be surrendered, he was one of the small band who repaired to Haddington, and offered their services to the commander of His Majesty's forces."

With the exception of this one troubled interval, he remained many years in the tranquil performance of his pastoral duties. The hours of his leisure were devoted to literary researches and to laying the foundation of future eminence. He rose early, and read and wrote much before breakfast. The remainder of the day he devoted to the claims of his profession. As a minister of the gospel he was conscientious and active, endeavouring by every means to extend the comforts and influence of religion. In the summer months, previous to the commencement of church-service, he usually assembled the youthful part of his flock, for the purpose of explaining to them the doctrines of the catechism. By his zeal, and the suavity of his behaviour, he won the love of his parishioners; so that, in all their difficulties, it was to him that they resorted for consolation and for counsel.

The time at length arrived when Robertson was to assume a leading share in the government of the Scottish church. He did not, however, come forward among his colleagues until he had attained the age of thirty, and had thoroughly prepared himself to sustain his new and important part with vigour and effect. It was on the subject of patronage that he first exerted his eloquence in a deliberative assembly.

The history of clerical patronage in Scotland since the overthrow of catholicism, and of the struggles to which it has given rise, has been traced with great clearness by Dr. Gleig, and I shall therefore give it in his own words. "The Reformation of Scotland," says he, "was irregular and tumultuous; and the great object of the powerful aristocracy of that kingdom seems to have been rather to get possession of the tithes, and the lands of the dignified clergy, than to purify the doctrine and reform the worship of the church. Of this Knox and the other reformed clergymen complained bitterly; and their complaints were extorted from them by their own sufferings. Never, I believe, were the established clergy of any Christian country reduced to such indigence as were those zealous and well meaning men during the disastrous reign of Queen Mary, and the minority of her son and successor; whilst the pittance that was promised to them, instead of being regularly paid, was often seized by the rapacity of the regents and the powerful barons who adhered to their cause, and the ministers left to depend for their subsistance on the generosity of the people.

"As nearly the whole of the ecclesiastical patronage of the kingdom had come into the possession of those barons, partly by inheritance from their ancestors, and partly with the church lands which, on the destruction of the monasteries, they had appropriated to themselves, it is not wonderful, that in an age when men were very apt to confound the illegal and mischievous conduct of him who exercised an undoubted right with the natural consequences of that right itself, strong prejudices were excited in the minds of the clergy and more serious part of the people against the law which vested in such sacrilegious robbers the right of presentation to parish churches. It is not indeed very accurately known by whom ministers were nominated to vacant churches for thirty years after the commencement of the Reformation, when there was hardly any settled government in the church or in the state In some parishes they were probably called by the general voice of the people; in others, obtruded on them by the violence of the prevailing faction, to serve some political purpose of the day; and in others again appointed by the superintendent and his council; whilst in a few the legal patron may have exercised his right, without making any simoniacal contract with the presentee; which, however, there is reason to suspect was no uncommon practice.

"Hitherto the government of the Protestant church of Scotland had fluctuated from one form to another, sometimes assuming the appearance of episcopacy under superintendents, and at other times being presbyterian in the strictest sense of the word. In the month of June, 1592, an act was passed, giving a legal sanction to the presbyterian form of government, and restoring the ancient law of patronage. By that act the patron of a vacant parish was authorized to present, to the presbytery comprehending that parish, a person properly qualified to be intrusted with the cure of souls; and the presbytery was enjoined, after subjecting the presentee to certain trials and examinations, of which its members were constituted the judges, 'to ordain and settle him as minister of the parish, provided no relevant objection should be stated to his life, doctrine, or qualifications.'

"Though we are assured by the highest authority* that this right of patronage, thus conferred by the fundamental charter of Presbyterian government in Scotland, was early complained of as a grievance, it appears to have been regularly exercised until the era of the rebellion against Charles I. during the establishment as well of the presbyterian as of the episcopal church. It was indeed abolished by the usurping powers, which in 1649 established in its stead what was then called 'the gospel right of popular election;' but at the Restoration it was re-established together with episcopacy, and was regularly exercised until the Revolution, when episcopacy was finally overthrown, and, by an act passed on the 26th of May, 'the presbyterian church, government, and discipline, by kirk sessions, presbyteries, provincial synods, and general assemblies,' established in its stead. The act of James VI. in 1592 was 'revived and confirmed in every head thereof, except

* Dr. Hill, Principal of St. Mary's College, in the University of St. Andrews.

in that part of it relating to patronages,' which were utterly abolished, though nothing was substituted in their stead until the 19th of July immediately succeeding.

"It was then statuted and declared, to use the language of the act, 'that, in the vacancy of any particular church, and for supplying the same with a minister, the Protestant heritors and elders are to name and propose the person to the whole congregation, to be either approven or disapproven by them; and if they disapprove, they are to give in their reasons, to the effect the affairs may be cognesced by the presbytery of the bounds; at whose judgment, and by whose determination, the calling and entry of every particular minister is to be ordered and concluded. In recompense of which rights of presentation the heritors of every parish were to pay to the patron six hundred marks (£33. 6s. 8d. sterling), against a certain time, and under certain proportions.'

"Whether this sum, which at that period was very considerable, was actually paid to the patrons of the several parishes, I know not; but if it was, or indeed whether it was or not, had it been the intention of the legislature to produce dissension in the country, it could not have devised any thing better calculated to effect its purpose than the mode of appointing ministers to vacant churches. The heritors or landholders, if the price was paid, would naturally contend for the uncontrolled exercise of the right which they, and they only, had purchased; but it is not by any means probable that at such a period they could often agree in their choice of a minister for a vacant parish. The elders, who were men of inferior rank and inferior education, would by the envy of the low, when comparing themselves with the high, be prompted to thwart the wishes of their landlords, which the act of parliament enabled them to do effectually; and the consequence must have been that two or three candidates for every vacant church were at once proposed to the people of the parish for their approbation or disapprobation. The people might either give the preference to one of the candidates proposed, or reject them all, for reasons of which the members of the presbytery were constituted the judges; and as it appears that the presbytery generally took part with the people, a source of everlasting contention was thus established between the country gentlemen and the parochial clergy; an evil than which a greater cannot easily be conceived. For these, and other reasons, this ill digested law was repealed in the tenth year of the reign of Queen Anne, and the right of patronage restored as in all other established churches.

"By many of the clergy, however, patronage seems to have been considered as an appendage of prelacy; though it has obviously no greater connexion with that form of ecclesiastical polity than with any other that is capable of being allied with the state; and, till after the year 1730, ministers continued to be settled in vacant parishes in the manner prescribed by the act of King William and Queen Mary. 'Even then,' says Dr. Hill, 'the church courts, although they could not entirely disregard the law, continued, in many instances, to render it ineffectual, and by their authority sanctioned the prevailing prejudices of the people against it. T 1» admitted, as an incontrovertible principle in presbyterian church government, that a presentee, although perfectly well qualified, and unexceptionable in his life and doctrine, was nevertheless inadmissible to his clerical office, till the concurrence of the people who were to be under his ministry had been regularly ascertained.' The form of expressing this concurrence was by the subscription of a paper termed 'a call;' to which many of the old ministers paid greater respect than to the deed of presentation by the patron of the church.

" To render the call good, however, the unanimous consent of the landholders, elders, and people was not considered as necessary, nor indeed ever looked for. Nay, it appears that even a majority was not in all cases deemed indispensable; for the presbytery often admitted to his charge, and proceeded to ordain the presentee whose call, by whatever number of parishioners, appeared to them to afford a reasonable prospect of his becoming, by prudent conduct, a useful parish minister. On the other hand, presbyteries sometimes set aside the presentation, altogether, when they were not satisfied with the call; and when the patron insisted on his right, and the presbytery continued inflexible, the general assembly was, in such cases, under the necessity either of compelling the members of the presbytery, by ecclesiastical censures, to do their duty, or of appointing a committee of its own body to relieve them from that duty, by ordaining the presentee, and inducting him into the vacant church. To compulsion recourse had seldom been had; and the consequence was that individuals openly claimed a right to disobey the injunctions of the assembly, whenever they conceived their disobedience justified by a principle of conscience.

" Such also was the state of ecclesiastical discipline in Scotland when Mr. Robertson first took an active part in the debates of the general assembly; and he very justly thought that its tendency was to overturn the presbyterian establishment, and introduce in its stead a number of independent congregational churches. He therefore supported the law of patronage, not merely because it was part of the law of the land, but because he thought it the most expedient method of filling the vacant churches. It did not appear to him that the people at large are competent judges of those qualities which a minister should possess in order to be a useful teacher of the truth as it is in Jesus, or of the precepts of a sound morality. He more than suspected that if the candidates for churches were taught to consider their success in obtaining a settlement as depending on a popular election, many of them would be tempted to adopt a manner of preaching calculated rather to please the people than to promote their edification. He thought that there is little danger to be apprehended from the abuse of the law of patronage; because the presentee must be chosen from amongst those whom the church had approved, and licensed as qualified for the office of a parish minister; because a presentee cannot be admitted to the benefice if any relevant objection to his life or doctrine be proved against him; and because, after ordination and admission, he is liable to be deposed for improper conduct, and the church declared vacant."

Whatever may be thought of the merits of the cause which Robertson espoused, he was certainly a conscientious supporter of it. To undertake its defence some strength of nerve was, indeed, required. The first time that he came forward in the Assembly was in May, 1751, when a debate arose on the conduct of a minister, who had disobeyed the sentence of a former assembly. Seizing this opportunity to enforce his principles of church discipline, Robertson, in an eloquent speech, contended that if subordination were not strictly maintained the Presbyterian establishment would ultimately be overthrown, and, therefore, an exemplary punishment should be inflicted on the offending party. But, though he was heard with attention, his arguments produced little effect, and on the house being divided, he was left in a minority of no more than eleven against two hundred.

Though this decision was not encouraging, he determined to persist, and he was soon enabled to renew the contest. The presbytery of Dumferline having been guilty of disobedience, in refusing to admit a minister to the church of Inverkeithing, the commission of the assembly, ordered them to cease from their opposition, and threatened that, if they continued to be refractory, they should be subjected to a high censure. Notwithstanding this, the presbytery again disobeyed the mandate of the superior court. Yet, instead of carrying its threat into effect, the commission came to a resolution that no censure should be inflicted.

This resolution, after the commission had gone so far as to resort to threats, seemed absurd. Robertson therefore drew up a protest, intituled, "Reasons of Dissent from the Judgment and Resolution of the Commission." This protest, which was signed by himself, Dr. Blair, Home, and a few other friends, is an able production. It boldly declares the sentence of the commission to be inconsistent with the nature and first principles of society; charges the commission itself with having, by that sentence, gone beyond its powers, and betrayed the privileges and deserted the doctrines of the constitution; considers the impunity thus granted as encouraging contumacy; insists on the lawfulness of ecclesiastical censures, and on the absolute necessity of preserving obedience in the church; and, maintains that he who becomes a member of a church ought to conform to its decrees, or, "if he hath rashly joined himself, that he is bound, as an honest man and a good Christian, to withdraw, and to keep his conscience pure and undefiled."

When the assembly met, in 1752, the question was brought before it; and Robertson supported the protest with such cogency of argument, that he obtained a majority to his side, and achieved a complete triumph. The judgment of the commission was reversed, Mr. Gillespie, (one of the ministers of the presbytery of Dumferline,) was deposed from his pastoral office, and ejected from his living, and three other individuals were suspended from their judicative capacity in the superior ecclesiastical courts.

From this time, Robertson was at the head of the assembly; which during his ascendancy, he contrived to keep steady to his principles. It was not, however, without many struggles that he retained his pre-eminence. From what is mentioned by Sir Henry Wellwood, in his "Memoirs of Dr. Erskine," it appears that the exertions of Robertson were unremitting, and that for his victory he was partly indebted to cautious management, and untiring patience. "During Dr. Robertson's time says he, "the struggle with the people was perpetual; and the opposition to presentees so extremely pertinacious, as in a great measure to engross the business of the assemblies. The parties in the church were then more equally balanced than they have ever been since that period. The measures which were adopted, in the face of such perpetual opposition, it required no common talents to manage or defend; especially considering that the leaders in opposition were such men as Dr. Dick, Dr. Macqueen, Dr. Erskine, Mr. Stevenson of St. Madois, Mr. Freebairn of Dumbarton, Mr. Andrew Crosbie, &c. &c.; men of the first ability in the country, and some of them possessed of an eloquence for a popular assembly to which there was nothing superior in the church or in the state.

"Dr. Robertson's firmness was not easily shaken, but his caution and prudence never deserted him. He held it for a maxim never wantonly to offend the prejudices of the people, and rather to endeavour to manage than directly to combat them. Some of the settlements in dispute were protracted for eight or ten years together; and though the general assemblies steadily pursued their system, and uniformly appointed the presentees to be inducted, their strongest sentences were not vindictive, and seldom went beyond the leading points to which they were directed."

In 1757 an event happened, which afforded him an opportunity of exercising his influence over his colleagues, and moderate the vengeance which seemed about to be hurled at some of his brethren, for having been guilty of an act which was considered most profane. The chief offender was his friend Home, who was then minister of Athelstaneford. The crime consisted in Home having produced the tragedy of Douglas, and being present at the acting of it on the Edinburgh theatre. With him were involved several of his clerical intimates, who had been induced to accompany him to the theatre on the first night of the performance. The storm which this circumstance raised among the Scottish clergy can hardly be imagined. The presbytery of Edinburgh summoned before its tribunal such members as had committed this heinous offence, and dispatched circulars to the presbyteries in the vicinity, recommending rigorous steps against all clergymen who had desecrated themselves by appearing in the polluted region of the theatre. Home, and his friend Carlyle, of Inveresk, were cited to answer for their misconduct.

Throughout the whole of the proceedings, which on this occasion were instituted, Robertson exerted himself with great ardour and eloquence on behalf of his friends. Though, being restrained by a promise which he had given to his father, he had himself never been within the walls of a theatre, he scrupled not to avow his belief that no culpability attached to the persons who were under prosecution. "The promise," said he, "which was exacted by the most indulgent of parents, I have hitherto religiously kept, and it my intention to keep it till the day of my death. I am at the same time free to declare, that I perceive nothing sinful or inconsistent with the spirit of Christianity in writing : tragedy, which gives no encouragement to baseness or vice, and that I cannot concur in censuring my brethren for being present at the representation of such a tragedy, from which I was kept back by a promise, which, though sacred to me, is not obligatory on them."

To his persuasive eloquence is attributed, and no doubt justly, the comparative mildness of the sentence which was ultimately pronounced. A declaratory act was passed by the assembly, prohibiting the writing of plays. Some of the offending ministers, were rebuked by the presbyteries to which they belonged, others suspended from their office for a few weeks. Home, however, resigned his living at Athelstaneford in June, 1757, and fixed his residence in London.

By the departure of Home, the Select Society, lost an able member. This society was instituted at Edinburgh, in 1754, by Allan Ramsay, the painter, (son of the poet of the same name.) Its object was philosophical and literary inquiry, and the improvement of the members in the art of speaking. It held its meetings in the Advocates' Library, and met every Friday evening, during the sittings of the Court of Session. At the first it consisted of only fifteen persons, of whom Robertson was one; but it soon acquired such high reputation, that its list of associates was swelled to upwards of a hundred and thirty names; including Hume, Adam Smith, Wedderburn, afterwards Lord Chancellor, Sir Hilbert Elliot, Lord Elibank, Lord Monboddo, Lord Kames, Lord Woodhouselee, Adam Ferguson, Wilkie, Dr. Cullen, and many other talented persons. This society flourished for some years : and is said by professor Stewart, to have "produced such debates as have not often been heard in modern assemblies;—debates, where the dignity of the speakers was not lowered by the intrigues of policy, or the intemperance of faction; and where the most splendid talents that have ever adorned this country were roused to their best exertions, by the liberal and ennobling discussions of literature and philosophy." That such an assemblage of learning and genius must have done much towards diffusing through Scotland a taste for letters, there cannot be the shadow of a doubt. Robertson took an active part, and was one of its presidents. As a speaker, it was remarked of him, that "whereas most of the others in their previous discourses exhausted the subject so much that there was no room for debate, he gave only such brief but artful sketches, as served to suggest ideas, without leading to a decision."

Robertson had long been sedulously engaged on the History of Scotland, the plan of which he is said to have formed soon after his settling at Gladsmuir. It appears that as early as 1753 he had commenced his labours, and that by the summer of 1757 he had advanced as far as the narrative of Gowrie's conspiracy. In the spring of 1758 he visited London, to concert measures for publishing; and the History, in two volumes quarto, was given to the world on the first of February, 1759, about three months subsequent to the completion of it. While the last sheets were in the press, the author received, by diploma, the degree of Doctor of Divinity from the University of Edinburgh.

The popularity which the History of Scotland soon acquired, it yet retains. Fourteen editions were published during the lifetime of the author, and the editions since his decease have been still more numerous. It has undoubtedly established itself as a classical English production.

Dr. Robertson was no sooner known to the world than preferment was rapidly bestowed on him. In the autumn of 1755, while his work was in the hands of the printer, he was translated from Gladsmuir to one of the churches of the Scottish metropolis. On the History issuing from the press, he was appointed Chaplain of Stirling Castle, and, in 1761, one of his Majesty's Chaplains in Ordinary for Scotland. The dignity of Principal of the College of Edinburgh was conferred on him in 1762; and, two years subsequently to this, the office of Historiographer for Scotland, which, since the death of Crawford, in 1726, had been disused, was revived in his favour, with an annual stipend of two hundred pounds.

By the remuneration which he had received for his History, and the salaries which arose from his various appointments, Dr. Robertson now possessed an income far greater than had ever before been possessed by any Scotch presbyterian minister, and not short of that which had been enjoyed by some bishops when the church of Scotland was under episcopal government.

Having resolved to remain in Scotland, and rely mainly on his pen for the advancement of his fortune, Dr. Robertson had now to choose another theme on which his talents could be profitably employed. To the composition of history, in which he had met with such success, he wisely determined to adhere; and at length, notwithstanding the objections which were urged by Hume and Horace Walpole, he made choice of the reign of Charles the Fifth as the subject of his second attempt; and, early in 1769, it appeared in three volumes quarto. It had been perused, while in the press, by Hume, and probably by other friends, and had gained the highest praise. "I got yesterday from Strahan," says Hume, in one of his letters, "about thirty sheets of your History, to be sent over to Suard, and last night and this morning have run them over with great avidity. I could not deny myself the satisfaction (which I hope also will not displease you), of expressing presently my extreme approbation of them. To say only they are very well written is by far too faint an expression, and much inferior to the sentiments I feel; they are composed with nobleness, with dignity, with elegance, and with judgment, to which there are few equals. They even excel, and I think in a sensible degree, your History of Scotland. I propose to myself great pleasure in being the only man in England, during some months, who will be in the situation of doing you justice, after which you may certainly expect that my voice will be drowned in that of the public."

Hume's anticipation was correct. Soon after the work appeared, he wrote to his friend, in the following terms: "The success has answered my expectations, and I, who converse with the great, the fair, and the learned, have scarcely heard an opposite voice, or even whisper, to the general sentiments. Only I have heard that the Sanhedrim at Mrs. Macaulay's condemns you as little less a friend to government and monarchy than myself." Horace Walpole was equally laudatory; and Lord Lyttelton testified his admiration. Voltaire, also, paid a flattering tribute. "It is to you and to Mr. Hume," said he, "that it belongs to write history. You are eloquent, learned, and impartial. I unite with Europe in esteeming you." Nor was the fame of the author limited to his native island. M. Suard translated the work into French, and the new translation is said to have established his own literary character, and to have been the means of his obtaining a seat in the French Academy. The remuneration received by the author was magnificent; particularly in an age when it was not usual to give a large sum of money for the purchase of copy right. It is said to have been four thousand five hundred pounds.

The next work undertaken by Dr. Robertson was a narrative of the Spanish discoveries, conquests, and proceedings of America.

To the first part of his subject, that which relates to the discovery of the New World, and the conquests and policy of the Spaniards, eight years of studious toil were devoted by Dr. Robertson. At length, early in 1771, he put forth, in two quartos, the result of his labours. The public again received him with enthusiasm, and his literary friends again pressed forward to congratulate and praise him. Hume was no longer in existence; but Gibbon testified his entire approbation of the volumes, even before he had wholly perused them. "I have said enough," said he, "to convince me that the present publication will support, and, if possible, extend the fame of the author; and the materials are collected with care, and arranged with skill; and the progress of discovery is displayed with learning and perspicuity; that the dangers, the achievements, and the views of the Spanish Adventurers, are related with a temperate spirit; and that the most original, perhaps the most curious portions of human manners, is at length rescued from the hands of sophists and declaimers."

The labours of Dr. Robertson, as a writer, were closed by a work which entered largely into antiquarian investigation, as connected with history. In 1791 he published a quarto volume, containing his "Historical Disquisitions concerning the Knowledge which the Ancients had of India; and the Progress of Trade with that Country prior to the Discovery of the Passage to it by the Cape of Good Hope."

About the end of the year 1791 the health of Dr. Robertson began to decline. Strong symptoms of jaundice shortly appeared, his constitution was sapped, and a lingering and fatal illness ensued. His spirits, however, remained unbroken. Till within a few months of his death, he persisted in officiating as a minister. When his decaying strength no longer permitted him to perform his clerical duties, he retired to Grange House, in the neighbourhood of Edinburgh, that he might have the advantage of more quiet, a pure air, and the sight of those picturesque objects in which he had ever delighted. "While he was able to walk abroad," says Mr. Stewart, "he commonly passed a part of the day

in a small garden, enjoying the simple gratifications it afforded
with all his wonted relish. Some who now hear me will long remember,—among the trivial yet interesting incidents which
marked these last weeks of his memorable life—his daily visits to
the fruit trees (which were then in blossom), and the smile with
which he, more than once, contrasted the interest he took in their
progress, with the event which was to happen before their maturity." It was while he was thus lingering on the verge of the
grave, that he was visited by two gentlemen from New York, who
were very anxious for an interview with him. He rallied all his
powers to entertain his guests; and, on their rising to take leave,
he said to them, in accents at once dignified and pathetic. "When
you go home, tell your countrymen that you saw the wreck of Dr.
Robertson." In less than two months that wreck disappeared in the
ocean of eternity. He expired, with the fortitude which became
him, on the 11th of July, 1793, in the seventy-first year of his age,
and the fiftieth of his ministry.

THE

HISTORY OF SCOTLAND.

BOOK I.

CONTAINING A REVIEW OF THE SCOTTISH HISTORY PREVIOUS TO THE
DEATH OF JAMES V.

THE first ages of the Scottish History are dark and fabulous. Nations, as well as men, arrive at maturity by degrees, and the events which happened during their infancy or early youth cannot be recollected, and deserves not to be remembered. The gross ignorance which anciently covered all the north of Europe, the continual migrations of its inhabitants, and the frequent and destructive revolutions which these occasioned, render it impossible to give any authentic account of the origin of the different kingdoms now established there. Every thing beyond that short period to which well attested annals reach is obscure; an immense space is left for invention to occupy; each nation, with a vanity inseparable from human nature, hath filled that void with events calculated to display its own antiquity and lustre. History, which ought to record truth and to teach wisdom, often sets out with retailing fictions and absurdities.

The Scots carry their pretensions to antiquity as high as any of their neighbours. Relying upon uncertain legends, and the traditions of their bards, still more uncertain, they reckon up a series of Kings several ages before the birth of Christ; and give a particular detail of the occurrences which happened in their reigns. But with regard to the Scots, as well as the other northern nations we receive the earliest accounts on which we can depend, not from their own, but from the Roman authors. [81]. When the Romans under Agricola, first carried their arms into the northern parts of Britain, they found it possessed by the Caledonians, a fierce and warlike people; and having repulsed rather than conquered them, they erected a strong wall between the Firths of Forth and Clyde, and there fixed the boundaries of their empire. [121]. Adrian, on account of the difficulty of defending such a distant frontier, contracted the limits of the Roman province in Britain, by building a second wall, which ran between Newcastle and Carlisle. The ambition of succeeding Emperors endeavoured to recover what Adrian had abandoned; and the country between the two walls was alternately under the dominion of the Romans and that of the

Caledonians. About the beginning of the fifth century, the inroads of the Goths and other barbarians obliged the Romans, in order to defend the centre of their empire, to recall those legions which guarded the frontier provinces; and at that time they quitted all their conquests in Britain.

421]. Their long residence in the island had polished, in some degree, the rude inhabitants; and the Britons were indebted to their intercourse with the Romans, for the art of writing and the use of numbers, without which it is impossible long to preserve the memory of past events.

North Britain was, by their retreat, left under the dominion of the Scots and Picts. The former, who are not mentioned by any Roman author before the end of the fourth century, were probably a colony of the Celtæ or Gauls; their affinity to whom appears from their language, their manners, and religious rites; circum-stances more decisive with regard to the origin of nations than either fabulous traditions or the tales of ill informed or credulous annalists. The Scots, if we may believe the common accounts, settled at first in Ireland; and extending themselves by degrees, landed at last on the coast opposite to that island, and fixed their habitations there. Fierce and bloody wars were, during several ages, carried on between them and the Picts. [838]. At length, Kenneth II., the sixty-ninth king of the Scots (according to their own fabulous authors), obtained a complete victory over the Picts, and united under one monarchy all the country from the wall of Adrian to the Northern Ocean. The kingdom henceforward be-came known by its present name, which is derived from a people who at first settled there as strangers, and remained long obscure and inconsiderable.

From this period the History of Scotland would merit some at-tention, were it accompanied with any certainty. But as our re-mote antiquities are involved in the same darkness with those of other nations, a calamity peculiar to ourselves has thrown almost an equal obscurity over our more recent transactions. This was occasioned by the malicious policy of Edward I. of England. To-wards the end of the thirteenth century, this monarch called in question the independence of Scotland; pretending that the king-dom was held as a fief of the crown of England, and subjected to all the conditions of a feudal tenure. In order to establish his claim, he seized the public archives, he ransacked churches and monasteries, and getting possession, by force or fraud, of many his-torical monuments, which tended to prove the antiquity or free-dom of the kingdom, he carried some of them into England, and commanded the rest to be burned. A universal oblivion of past transactions might have been the effect of this fatal event, but some imperfect chronicles had escaped the rage of Edward; foreign writers had recorded some important facts relating to Scotland; and the traditions concerning recent occurrences were fresh and worthy of credit. These broken fragments John de Fordun, who lived in the fourteenth century, collected with a pious industry, and from them gleaned materials which he formed into a regula history. His work was received by his countrymen with applause and, as no recourse could be had to more ancient records, it supplied the place of the authentic annals of the kingdom. It was copied in many monasteries, and the thread of the narrative was continued, by different monks, through the subsequent reigns. In the beginning of the sixteenth century, John Major, and Hector Boethius published their Histories of Scotland, the former a succinct and dry writer, the latter a copious and florid one, and both equally credulous. Not many years after, Buchanan undertook the same work; and if his accuracy and impartiality had been, in any degree, equal to the elegance of his taste, and to the purity and vigour of his style, his History might be placed on a level with the most admired compositions of the ancients. But, instead of rejecting the improbable tales of chronicle writers, he was at the utmost pains to adorn them; and hath clothed, with all the beauties and graces of fiction, those legends, which formerly had only its wildness and extravagance.

The History of Scotland may probably be divided into four periods. The first reaches from the origin of the monarchy to the reign of Kenneth II. The second, from Kenneth's conquest of the Picts to the death of Alexander III. The third extends to the death of James V. The last, from thence to the accession of James VI. to the crown of England.

The first period is the region of pure fable and conjecture, and ought to be totally neglected, or abandoned to the industry and credulity of antiquaries. Truth begins to dawn in the second period, with a light, feeble at first, but gradually increasing, and the events which then happened may be slightly touched, but merit no particular or laborious inquiry. In the third period, the History of Scotland, chiefly by means of records preserved in England, becomes more authentic : not only are events related, but their causes and effects explained ; the characters of the actors are displayed ; the manners of the age described ; the revolutions in the constitution pointed out : and here every Scotsman should begin not to read only, but to study the history of his country. During the fourth period, the affairs of Scotland were so mingled with those of other nations, its situation in the political state of Europe was so important, its influence on the operations of the neighbouring kingdoms was so visible, that its history becomes an object of attention to foreigners ; and without some knowledge of the various and extraordinary revolutions which happened there, they cannot form a just notion with respect either to the most illustrious events, or to the characters of the most distinguished personages in the sixteenth century.

The following history is confined to the last of these periods : to give a view of the political state of the kingdom during that which immediately preceded it is the design of this preliminary Book. The imperfect knowledge which strangers have of the affairs of Scotland, and the prejudices Scotsmen themselves have imbibed, with regard to the various revolutions in the government of their country, render such an introduction equally necessary to both.

The period from the death of Alexander III. to the death of

James V. contains upwards of two centuries and a half, from the year 1286, to the year 1542.

It opens with the famous controversy concerning the independence of Scotland. Before the union of the two kingdoms, this was a question of much importance. If the one crown had been considered, not as imperial and independent, but as feudatory to the other, a treaty of union could not have been concluded on equal terms, and every advantage which the dependent kingdom procured must have been deemed the concession of a sovereign to his vassal. Accordingly, about the beginning of the present century, and while a treaty of union between the two kingdoms was negociating, this controversy was agitated with all the heat which national animosities naturally inspire. What was then the subject of serious concern, the union of the two kingdoms had rendered a matter of mere curiosity. But though the objects which at that time warmed and interested both nations exist no longer, a question which appeared so momentous to our ancestors cannot be altogether indifferent or uninstructive to us.

Some of the northern counties of England were early in the hands of the Scottish Kings, who, as far back as the feudal customs can be traced, held these possessions of the Kings of England, and did homage to them on that account. This homage, due only for the territories which they held in England, was nowise derogatory from their royal dignity. Nothing is more suitable to feudal ideas than that the same person should be both a lord and a vassal, independent in one capacity, and dependent in another. The crown of England was, without doubt, imperial and independent, though the Princes who wore it, were, for many ages, the vassals of the Kings of France; and, in consequence of their possessions in that kingdom, bound to perform all the services which a feudal sovereign has a right to exact. The same was the condition of the monarchs of Scotland; free and independent as Kings of their own country, but, as possessing English territories, vassals to the King of England. The English Monarchs, satisfied with their legal and uncontroverted rights, were, during a long period, neither capable, nor had any thoughts of, usurping more. England when conquered by the Saxons being divided by them into many small kingdoms, was in no condition to extend its dominion over Scotland, united at that time under one monarch. And though these petty principalities were gradually formed into one kingdom, the reigning Princes, exposed to continual invasions of the Danes, and often subjected to the yoke of these formidable pirates, seldom turned their arms towards Scotland, and were little able to establish new rights in that country. The first Kings of the Norman race, busied with introducing their own laws and manners into the kingdom which they had conquered, or with maintaining themselves on the throne which some of them possessed by a very dubious title, were as little solicitous to acquire new authority, or to form new pretensions in Scotland. An unexpected calamity that befell one of the Scottish Kings first encouraged the English to think of bringing his kingdom under dependence. William, surnamed the Lion, being taken prisoner at Alnwick, Henry II., as the price of his liberty, not only extorted from him an exorbitant ransom, and a promise to surrender the places of greatest strength in his dominions, but compelled him to do homage for his whole kingdom. Richard I., a generous prince, solemnly renounced this claim of homage; and absolved William from the hard conditions which Henry had imposed. Upon the death of Alexander III., nearly a century after, Edward I., availing himself of the situation of affairs in Scotland, acquired an influence in that kingdom which no English Monarch before him ever possessed, and imitating the interested policy of Henry, rather than the magnanimity of Richard revived the claim of sovereignty to which the former had pretended.

Margaret of Norway, granddaughter of Alexander, and heir to his crown, did not long survive him. The right of succession belonged to the descendants of David Earl of Huntingdon, third son of King David I. Among these, Robert Bruce, and John Baliol two illustrious competitors for the crown, appeared. Bruce was the son of Isabel, Earl David's second daughter; Baliol, the grandson of Margaret the eldest daughter. According to the rules of succession which are now established, the right of Baliol was preferable; and notwithstanding Bruce's plea of being nearer in blood to Earl David, Baliol's claim, as the representative of his mother and grandmother, would be deemed incontestable. But in that age the order of succession was not ascertained with the same precision. The question appeared to be no less intricate than it was important. Although the prejudices of the people, and perhaps the laws of the kingdom, favoured Bruce, each of the rivals was supported by a very powerful faction. Arms alone, it was much feared, must terminate a dispute too weighty for the laws to decide. But, in order to avoid the miseries of a civil war, Edward was chosen umpire, and both parties agreed to acquiesce in his decree. This had well nigh proved fatal to the independence of Scotland; and the nation, by its eagerness to guard against a civil war, was not only exposed to that calamity, but almost subjected to a foreign yoke. Edward was artful, brave, enterprising, and commanded a powerful and martial people, at peace with the whole world. The anarchy which prevailed in Scotland, and the ambition of competitors ready to sacrifice their country in order to obtain even a dependent crown, invited him first to seize and then to subject the kingdom. The authority of an umpire, which had been unwarily bestowed upon him, and from which the Scots dreaded no dangerous consequences, enabled him to execute his schemes with the greater facility. Under pretence of examining the question with the utmost solemnity, he summoned all the Scottish Barons to Norham; and, having gained some and intimidated others, he prevailed on all who were present, not excepting Bruce and Baliol, the competitors, to acknowledge Scotland to be a fief of the English Crown, and to swear fealty to him as their *Sovereign* or *Liege Lord*. This step led to another still more important. As it was vain to pronounce a sentence which he had not power to execute, Edward demanded possession of the kingdom, that he might be able to deliver it to him whose right should be found preferable; and such was the pusillanimity of the nobles, and the impatient ambition of the competitors, that both assented to this strange demand, and Gilbert de Umfraville, Earl of Angus, was the only man who refused to surrender the castles in his custody to the enemy of his country. Edward, finding Baliol the most obsequious and the least formidable of the two competitors, soon after gave judgment in his favour. Baliol once more professed himself the vassal of England, and submitted to every condition which the sovereign whom he had now acknowledged was pleased to prescribe.

Edward, having thus placed a creature of his own upon the throne of Scotland, and compelled the nobles to renounce the ancient liberties and independence of their country, had reason to conclude that his dominion was now fully established. But he began too soon to assume the master: his new vassals, fierce and independent, bore with impatience a yoke to which they were not accustomed. Provoked by his haughtiness, even the passive spirit of Baliol began to mutiny. But Edward, who had no longer use for such a pageant king, forced him to resign the crown, and openly attempted to seize it as fallen to himself by the rebellion of his vassal. At that critical period arose Sir William Wallace, a hero, to whom the fond admiration of his countrymen hath ascribed many fabulous acts of prowess, though his real valour, as well as integrity and wisdom, are such as need not the heightenings of fiction. He, almost single, ventured to take arms in defence of the kingdom, and his boldness revived the spirit of his countrymen. At last, Robert Bruce, the grandson of him who stood in competition with Baliol, appeared to assert his own rights, and to vindicate the honour of his country. The nobles, ashamed of their former baseness, and enraged at the many indignities offered to the nation, crowded to his standard. In order to crush him at once, the English Monarch entered Scotland at the head of a mighty army. Many battles were fought, and the Scots, though often vanquished, were not subdued. The ardent zeal with which the nobles contended for the independence of the kingdom, the prudent valour of Bruce, and, above all, a national enthusiasm inspired by such a cause, baffled the repeated efforts of Edward, and counterbalanced all the advantages which he derived from the number and wealth of his subjects. Though the war continued with little intermission upwards of seventy years, Bruce and his posterity kept possession of the throne of Scotland, and reigned with an authority not inferior to that of its former monarchs.

But while the sword, the ultimate judge of all disputes between contending nations, was employed to terminate this controversy, neither Edward nor the Scots seemed to distrust the justice of their cause; and both appealed to history and records, and from these produced, in their own favour, such evidence as they pretended to be unanswerable. The letters and memorials addressed by each party to the Pope, who was then reverenced as the common father, and often appealed to as the common judge of all Christian

Princes, are still extant. The fabulous tales of the early British history, the partial testimony of ignorant chroniclers, supposititious treaties and charters, are the proofs on which Edward founded his title to the sovereignty of Scotland; and the homage done by the Scottish monarchs for their lands in England is preposterously supposed to imply the subjection of their whole kingdom. Ill founded, however, as their right was, the English did not fail to revive it, in all the subsequent quarrels between the two kingdoms; while the Scots disclaimed it with the utmost indignation. To this we must impute the fierce and implacable hatred to each other, which long inflamed both. Their national antipathies were excited, not only by the usual circumstances of frequent hostilities, and reciprocal injuries; but the English considered the Scots as vassals who had presumed to rebel; and the Scots, in their turn, regarded the English as usurpers who aimed at enslaving their country.

1306.] At the time when Robert Bruce began his reign in Scotland, the same form of government was established in all the kingdoms of Europe. This surprising similarity in their constitution and laws demonstrates that the nations which overturned the Roman empire, and erected these kingdoms, though divided into different tribes and distinguished by different names, were either derived originally from the same source, or had been placed in similar situations. When we take a view of the feudal system of laws and policy, that stupendous and singular fabric erected by them, the first object that strikes us is the King. And when we are told that he is the sole proprietor of all the lands within his dominions, that all his subjects derive their possessions from him, and in return consecrate their lives to his service; when we hear that all marks of distinction and titles of dignity flow from him as the only fountain of honour; when we behold the most potent peers, on their bended knees, and with folded hands, swearing fealty at his feet, and acknowleding him to to be their *Sovereign* and their *Liege Lord;* we are apt to pronounce him a powerful, nay an absolute monarch. No conclusion, however, would be more rash, or worse founded. The genius of the feudal government was purely aristocratical. With all the ensigns of royalty, and with many appearances of despotic power, a feudal King was the most limited of all Princes.

Before they sallied out of their own habitations to conquer the world, many of the northern nations seemed not to have been subject to the government of Kings; and even where monarchical government was established, the Prince possessed but little authority. A General, rather than a King, his military command was extensive, his civil jurisdiction almost nothing. The army which he led was not composed of soldiers, who could be compelled to serve, but of such as voluntarily followed his standard. These conquered not for their leader, but for themselves; and, being free in their own country, renounced not their liberty when they acquired new settlements. They did not exterminate the ancient inhabitants of the countries which they subdued; but, seizing the greater part of their lands, they took their persons under protection. The difficulty of maintaining a new conquest, as well as the danger of being attacked by new invaders, rendering it necessary to be always in a posture of defence, the form of government which they established was altogether military, and nearly resembled that to which they had been accustomed in their native country.   Their General still continuing to be the head of the colony, part of the conquered lands were allotted to him; the remainder, under the name of *beneficia* or *fiefs*, was divided among his principal officers. As the common safety required that these officers should, upon all occasions, be ready to appear in arms for the common defence, and should continue obedient to their General, they bound themselves to take the field, when called, and to serve him with a number of men, in proportion to the extent of their territory These great officers again parcelled out their lands among their followers, and annexed the same condition to the grant. A feudal kingdom was properly the encampment of a great army; military ideas predominated, military subordination was established, and the possession of land was the pay which soldiers received for their personal service. In consequence of these notions, the possession of land was granted during pleasure only, and Kings were elective. In other words, an officer disagreeable to his General was deprived of his pay, and the person who was most capable of conducting an army was chosen to command it. Such were the first rudiments or infancy of feudal government.

But long before the beginning of the fourteenth century, the feudal system had undergone many changes, of which the following were the most considerable. Kings, formerly elective, were then hereditary; and fiefs, granted at first during pleasure, descended from father to son, and were become perpetual. Those changes, not less advantageous to the nobles than to the prince, made no alteration in the aristocratical spirit of the feudal constitution. The King, who at a distance seemed to be invested with majesty and power, appears on a nearer view to possess almost none of those advantages which bestow on monarchs their grandeur and authority.   His revenues were scanty; he had not a standing army; and the jurisdiction he possessed was circumscribed within very narrow limits.

At a time when pomp and splendour were little known, even in the palaces of kings; when the officers of the crown received scarcely any salary besides the fees and perquisites of their office; when embassies to foreign courts were rare; when armies were composed of soldiers who served without pay; it was not necessary that a King should possess a great revenue; nor did the condition of Europe, in those ages, allow its Princes to be opulent. Commerce made little progress in the kingdoms where the feudal government was established. Institutions which had no other object but to inspire a martial spirit, to train men to be soldiers, and to make arms the only honourable profession, naturally discouraged the commercial arts. The revenues, arising from the taxes imposed on the different branches of commerce, were by consequence inconsiderable; and the Prince's treasury received little supply from a source, which, among a trading people, flows with such abundance as is almost inexhaustible. A fixed tax was not levied even on land: such a burden would have appeared intolerable to men who received their estates as the reward of their valour, and who considered their service in the field as a full retribution for what they possessed. The King's *demesnes*, or the portion of land which he still retained in his own hands unalienated, furnished subsistence to his court, and defrayed the ordinary expense of government. The only stated taxes which the feudal law obliged vassals to pay to the King, or to those of whom they held their lands, were three: one when his eldest son was made a knight; another, when his eldest daughter was married; and a third, in order to ransom him if he should happen to be taken prisoner. Besides these, the King received the feudal casualties of the ward, marriage, &c. of his own vassals. And, on some extraordinary occasions, his subjects granted him an aid, which they distinguished by the name of a *benevolence*, in order to declare that he received it not in consequence of any right, but as a gift flowing from their good will. All these added together produced a revenue so scanty and precarious as naturally incited a feudal monarch to aim at diminishing the exorbitant power and wealth of the nobility, which, instead of enabling him to carry on his schemes with full effect, kept him in continual indigence, anxiety, and dependence.

Nor could the King supply the defect of his revenues by the terror of his arms. Mercenary troops and standing armies were unknown as long as the feudal government subsisted in vigour. Europe was peopled with soldiers. The vassals of the King, and the sub-vassals of the barons. were all obliged to carry arms. While the poverty of the Princes prevented them from fortifying their frontier towns, while a campaign continued but a few weeks, and while a fierce and impetuous courage was impatient to bring every quarrel to the decision of a battle, an army without pay, and with little discipline, was sufficient for all the purposes both of the security and of the glory of the nation. Such an army, however, far from being an engine at the King's disposal, was often no less formidable to him than to his enemies. The more warlike any people were, the more independent they became; and the same persons being both soldiers and subjects, civil privileges and immunities were the consequence of their victories, and the reward of their martial exploits. Conquerors, whom mercenary armies, under our present forms of government, often render the tyrants of their own people, as well as the scourges of mankind, were commonly under the feudal constitution the most indulgent of all Princes to their subjects, because they stood most in need of their assistance. A Prince, whom even war and victories did not render the master of his own army, possessed hardly any shadow of military power during time of peace. His disbanded soldiers mingled with his other subjects; not a single man received pay from him; many ages elapsed before a guard was appointed to defend his person; and destitute of that great instrument of dominion, a standing army, the authority of the King continued always feeble, and was often contemptible.

Nor were these the only circumstances which contributed to-

wards depressing the regal power. By the feudal system, as has
been already observed, the King's judicial authority was extremely
circumscribed. At first, Princes seem to have been the supreme
judges of their people, and, in person, heard and determined all
controversies among them. The multiplicity of causes soon made
it necessary to appoint judges, who, in the King's name, decided
matters that belonged to the royal jurisdiction. But the barbarians, who overran Europe, having destroyed most of the great
cities, and the countries which they seized being cantoned out
among powerful chiefs, who were blindly followed by numerous
dependants, whom, in return, they were bound to protect from
every injury; the administration of justice was greatly interrupted, and the execution of any legal sentence became almost
impracticable. Theft, rapine, murder, and disorder of all kinds
prevailed in every kingdom of Europe, to a degree almost incredible with the subsistence of civil society. Every offender sheltered
himself under the protection of some powerful chieftain, who
screened him from the pursuits of justice. To apprehend and
to punish a criminal often required the union and effort of half a
kingdom*. In order to remedy these evils, many persons of distinction were intrusted with the administration of justice within
their own territories. But what we may presume was, at first, only
a temporary grant of a personal privilege, the encroaching spirit of
the nobles gradually converted into a right, and rendered hereditary. The lands of some were, in process of time, erected into
Baronies, those of others into *Regalities*. The jurisdiction of the
former was extensive; that of the latter, as the name implies,
royal and almost unbounded. All causes, whether civil or criminal,
were tried by judges, whom the lord of the regality appointed;
and if the King's courts called any person within his territory before them, the lord of regality might put a stop to their proceedings, and, by the privilege of *repleading*, remove the cause to his
own court, and even punish his vassal if he submitted to a foreign
jurisdiction. Thus almost every question, in which any person
who resided on the lands of the nobles was interested, being determined by judges appointed by the nobles themselves, their vassals
were hardly sensible of being in any degree subject to the crown.

* A remarkable instance of this occurs in the following history, so late as the
year 1561. Mary having appointed a court of justice to be held on the borders,
the inhabitants of no less than eleven counties were summoned to guard the
person who was to act as judge, and to enable him to enforce his decisions. The
words of a proclamation, which afford such convincing proof of the feebleness of
the feudal government, deserve our notice—" And because it is necessary for the
execution of Her Highness' commandments and service, that her justice be well
accompanied, and her authority sufficiently fortified, by the concurrence of a good
power of her faithful subjects—Therefore commands and charges all and sundry
Earls, Lords, Barons, Freeholders, Landed men, and other gentlemen, dwelling
within the said counties, and that they and every one of them, with their kin,
friends, servants, and household men, well bodin in feir of war in the most substantial manner, [i. e. completely armed and provided], and with twenty days'
victuals, to meet and to pass forward with him to the borough of Jedburgh, and
there to remain during the said space of twenty days, and to receive such dire. tion
and commands as shall be given by him to them in our Sovereign Lady's name, for
quietness of the country : and to put the same in execution under the pain of
losing their life, lands, and goods." Keith's History of Scotland, 198.

A feudal kingdom was split into many small principalities, almost independent, and held together by a feeble and commonly an imperceptible bond of union. The King was not only stripped of the authority annexed to the person of a supreme judge, but his revenue suffered no small diminution by the loss of those pecuniary emoluments which were in that age due to the person who administered justice.

In the same proportion that the King sunk in power, the nobles rose towards independence. Not satisfied with having obtained an hereditary right to their fiefs, which they formerly held during pleasure, their ambition aimed at something bolder, and, by introducing *entails*, endeavoured, as far as human ingenuity and invention can reach that end, to render their possessions unalienable and everlasting. As they had full power to aid to the inheritance transmitted to them from their ancestors, but none to diminish it, time alone, by means of marriages, legacies, and other accidents, brought continued accessions of wealth and dignity; a great family, like a river, became considerable from the length of its course, and, as it rolled on, new honours and new property flowed successively into it. Whatever influence is derived from titles of honour, the feudal barons likewise possessed in an ample manner. These marks of distinction are, in their own nature, either official or personal, and being annexed to a particular charge, or bestowed by the admiration of mankind upon illustrious characters, ought to be appropriated to these. But the son, however unworthy, could not bear to be stripped of that appellation by which his father had been distinguished. His presumption claimed what his virtue did not merit; titles of honour became hereditary, and added new lustre to nobles already in possession of too much power. Something more audacious and more extravagant still remained. The supreme direction of all affairs, both civil and military, being committed to the great officers of the crown, the fame and safety of princes, as well as of their people, depended upon the fidelity and abilities of these officers. But such was the preposterous ambition of the nobles, and so successful even in their wildest attempts to aggrandize themselves, that in all the kingdoms where the feudal institutions prevailed, most of the chief offices of state were annexed to great families, and held, like fiefs, by hereditary right. A person whose undutiful behaviour rendered him odious to his Prince, or whose incapacity exposed him to the contempt of the people, often held a place of power and trust of the greatest importance to both. In Scotland, the offices of Lord Justice General, Great Chamberlain, High Steward, High Constable, Earl Marshal, and High Admiral, were all hereditary; and, in many counties, the office of Sheriff was held in the same manner.

Nobles whose property was so extensive, and whose power was so great, could not fail of being turbulent and formidable. Nor did they want instruments for executing their boldest designs. That portion of their lands, which they parceled out among their followers, supplied them with a numerous band of faithful and determined vassals; while that which they retained in their own hands enabled them to live with a princely splendour. The great hall of an ambitious baron was often more crowded than the court of his sovereign. The strong castles, in which they resided, afforded a secure retreat to the discontented and seditious. A great part of their revenue was spent upon multitudes of indigent but bold retainers. And if at the time they left their retreat to appear in the court of their sovereign, they were accompanied, even in times of peace, with a vast train of armed followers. The usual retinue of William, the sixth Earl of Douglas, consisted of two thousand horse. Those of the other nobles were magnificent and formidable, in proportion. Impatient of subordination, and forgetting their proper rank, such potent and haughty barons were the rivals rather than the subjects of their prince. They often despised his orders, insulted his person, and wrested from him his crown. The history of Europe, during several ages, contains little else but the accounts of the wars and revolutions occasioned by their exorbitant ambition.

But, if the authority of the barons far exceeded its proper bounds in the other nations of Europe, we may affirm that the balance which ought to be preserved between a King and his nobles was almost entirely lost in Scotland. The Scottish nobles enjoyed, in common with those of other nations, all the means for extending their authority which arise from the aristocratical genius of the feudal government. Besides these, they possessed advantages peculiar to themselves : the accidental sources of their power were considerable ; and singular circumstances concurred with the spirit of the constitution to aggrandize them. To enumerate the most remarkable state of these will serve both to explain the political state of the kingdom, and to illustrate many important occurrences in the period now under our review.

I. the nature of their country was no cause of the power and independence of the Scottish nobility. Level and open countries are formed for servitude. The authority of the supreme magistrate reaches with ease to the most distant corners; and when nature has erected no barrier, and affords no retreat, the guilty or obnoxious are soon detected and punished. Mountains, and fens, and rivers, set bounds to despotic power, and amidst these is the natural seat of freedom and independence. In such places did the Scottish nobles usually fix their residence. By retiring to his own castle, a mutinous baron could defy the power of his sovereign, it being almost impracticable to lead an army, through a barren country, to places of difficult access to a single man. The same causes which checked the progress of the Roman arms, and rendered all the efforts of Edward I. abortive, often protected the Scottish nobles from the vengeance of their Prince ; and they owed their personal independence to those very mountains and marshes which saved their country from being conquered.

II. The want of great cities in Scotland contributed not a little to increase the power of the nobility, and to weaken that of the Prince. Wherever numbers of men assembled together, order must be established, and a regular form of government instituted ; the authority of the magistrate must be recognised, and his decisions meet with prompt and full obedience. Laws and subordination take rise in cities; and where there are few cities, as in Poland, or none, as in Tartary, there are few or no traces of a well arranged police. But under the feudal governments, commerce, the chief means of assembling mankind, was neglected; the nobles, in order to strengthen their influence over their vassals, resided among them, and seldom appeared at court, where they found a superior, or dwelt in cities, where they met with equals. In Scotland, the fertile counties in the South lying open to the English, no town situated there could rise to be great or populous, amidst continual inroads and alarms; the residence of our monarchs was not fixed to any particular place; many parts of the country were barren and uncultivated; and in consequence of these peculiar circumstances, adding to the general causes flowing from the nature of the feudal institutions, the towns in Scotland were extremely few, and very inconsiderable. The vassals of every baron occupied a distinct portion of the kingdom, and formed a separate and almost independent society. Instead of giving aid towards reducing to obedience their seditious chieftain, or any whom he took under his protection, they were all in arms for his defence, and obstructed the operations of justice to the utmost. The Prince was obliged to connive at criminals whom he could not reach; the nobles, conscious of this advantage, were not afraid to offend; and the difficulty of punishing almost assured them of impunity.

III. The division of the country into clans had no small effect in rendering the nobles considerable. The nations which overran Europe were originally divided into many small tribes; and when they came to parcel out the lands which they had conquered, it was natural for every chieftain to bestow a portion, in the first place, upon those of his own tribe or family. These all held their lands of him; and as the safety of each individual depended on the general union, these small societies clung together, and were distinguished by some common appellation, either patronymical or local, long before the introduction of surnames, or *ensigns armorial.* But when these became common, the descendants and relations of every chieftain assumed the same name and arms with him; other vassals were proud to imitate their example, and by degrees they were communicated to all those who held of the same superior. Thus clanships were formed; and in a generation or two, that consanguinity, which was at first in a great measure imaginary, was believed to be real. An artificial union was converted into a natural one; men willingly followed a leader, whom they regarded both as the superior of their lands and the chief of their blood, and served him not only with the fidelity of vassals, but with the affection of friends. In the other feudal kingdoms, we may observe such unions as we have described, imperfectly formed; but in Scotland, whether they were the production of chance, or the effect of policy, or introduced by the Irish colony above mentioned, and strengthened by carefully preserving their genealogies both genuine and fabulous, clanships were universal. Such a confederacy might be overcome, it could not be broken: and no change of manners or of government has been able, in some parts of the

ingdom, to dissolve associations which are founded upon prejudices so natural to the human mind. How formidable were nobles
at the head of followers, who, counting that cause just and honourable which the chief approved, rushed into the field at his command, ever ready to sacrifice their lives in defence of his person or
of his fame! Against such men a King contended with great disadvantage; and that cold service which money purchases, or authority extorts, was not an equal match for their ardour and zeal.

IV. The smallness of the number may be mentioned among the
causes of the grandeur of the Scottish nobles. Our annals reach not
back to the first division of property in the kingdom; but so far as we
can trace the matter, the original possessions of the nobles seem to
have been extensive. The ancient Thanes were the equals and rivals
of their Prince. Many of the earls and barons, who succeeded them,
were masters of territories no less ample. France and England,
countries wide and fertile, afforded settlements to a numerous and
powerful nobility. Scotland, a kingdom neither extensive nor rich
could not contain many such overgrown proprietors. But the power
of an aristocracy always diminishes in proportion to the increase
of its numbers; feeble if divided among a multitude, irresistible if
centered in a few. When nobles are numerous, their operations
nearly resemble those of the people: they are roused only by what
they apprehend; and submit to many arbitrary and oppressive
acts, before they take arms against their sovereign. A small body,
on the contrary, is more sensible and more impatient; quick in
discerning and prompt in repelling dangers, all its motions are as
sudden as those of the other are slow. Hence proceeded the extreme jealousy with which the Scottish nobles observed their monarchs, and the fierceness with which they opposed their encroachments. Even the virtue of a prince did not render them less vigilant, or less eager to defend their rights; and Robert Bruce, notwithstanding the splendour of his victories, and the glory of his
name, was upon the point of experiencing the vigour of their resistance, no less than his unpopular descendant James III. Besides this, the near alliance of the great families, by frequent inter-
marriage, was the natural consequence of their small number; and
as consanguinity was, in those ages, a powerful bond of union, all
the kindred of a nobleman interested themselves in his quarrel as a
common cause; and every contest the King had, though with a
single baron, soon drew upon him the arms of a whole confederacy.

V. Those natural connexions, both with their equals and with
their inferiors, the Scottish nobles strengthened by a device, which,
if not peculiar to themselves, was at least more frequent among
them than in any other nation. Even in times of profound peace,
they formed associations, which, when made with their equals,
were called *leagues of mutual defence;* and when with their inferiors, *bonds of manrent.* By the former, the contracting parties
bound themselves mutually to assist each other, in all causes and
against all persons. By the latter, protection was stipulated on
the one hand, and fidelity and personal service promised on the
other. Self-preservation, it is probable, forced men at first into
these confederacies; and, while disorder and rapine were universal,

while government was unsettled, and the authority of laws little known or regarded, near neighbours found it necessary to unite in this manner for their security ; and the weak were obliged to court the patronage of the strong. By degrees, these associations became so many alliances offensive and defensive against the throne ; and as their obligation was held to be more sacred than any tie whatever, they gave much umbrage to our kings, and contributed not a little to the power and independence of the nobility. In the reign of James II. William, the eighth earl of Douglas, entered into a league of this kind with the Earls of Crawford, Ross, Murray, Ormond, the Lords Hamilton, Balveny, and other powerful barons ; and so formidable was this combination to the king, that he had recourse to a measure no less violent than unjust, in order to dissolve it.

VI. The frequent wars between England and Scotland proved another cause of augmenting the power of the nobility. Nature has placed no barrier between the two kingdoms ; a river, almost every where fordable, divides them towards the east ; on the west they are separated by an imaginary line. The slender revenues of our Kings prevented them from fortifying or placing garrisons in the towns on the frontier ; nor would the jealousy of their subjects have permitted such a method of defence. The barons, whose estates lay near the borders, considered themselves as bound, both in honour and in interest, to repel the enemy. The *wardenships* of the different *marches*, offices of great power and dignity, were generally bestowed on them. This gained them the leading of the warlike counties in the south : and their vassals, living in a state of perpetual hostility, or enjoying at best an insecure peace, became more inured to war than even the rest of their countrymen, and more willing to accompany their chieftain in his most hardy and dangerous enterprises. It was the valour, no less than the number of their followers, that rendered the Douglases great. The nobles in the northern and midland counties were often dutiful and obsequious to the crown, but our Monarchs always found it impracticable to subdue the mutinous and ungovernable spirit of the borderers. In all our domestic quarrels, those who could draw to their side the inhabitants of the southern counties were almost sure of victory : and conscious of this advantage, the lords who possessed authority were there apt to forget the duty which they owed their sovereign, and to aspire beyond the rank of subjects.

VII. The calamities which befel our kings contributed more than any other cause to diminish the royal authority. Never was any race of monarchs so unfortunate as the Scottish. Of six successive Princes, from Robert III. to James VI., not one died a natural death ; and the minorities, during that time, were longer and more frequent than ever happened in any other kingdom. From Robert Bruce to James VI. we reckon ten Princes ; and seven of these were called to the throne while they were minors, and almost infants. Even the most regular and best established governments feel sensibly the pernicious effects of a minority, and either become languid and inactive, or are thrown into violent and unnatural convulsions. But under the imperfect and ill-adjusted system of government in Scotland these effects were still more fatal; the fierce and mutinous spirit of the nobles, unrestrained by the authority of a King, scorned all subjection to the delegated jurisdiction of a Regent, or to the feeble commands of a minor. The royal authority was circumscribed within narrower limits than ever; the prerogatives of the crown, naturally inconsiderable, were reduced almost to nothing; and the aristocratical power gradually rose upon the ruins of the monarchial. Lest the personal power of a Regent should enable him to act with too much vigour, the authority annexed to that office was sometimes rendered inconsiderable by being divided; or, if a single Regent was chosen, the greater nobles, and the heads of the more illustrious families, were seldom raised to that dignity. It was often conferred upon men who possessed little influence, and excited no jealousy. They, conscious of their own weakness, were obliged to overlook some irregularities, and to permit others; and, in order to support their authority, which was destitute of real strength, they endeavoured to gain the most powerful and active barons, by granting them possessions and immunities, which raised them to still greater power. When the King himself came to assume the reins of government, he found his revenues wasted or alienated, the crown lands seized or given away, and the nobles so accustomed to independence that, after the struggles of a whole reign, he was seldom able to reduce them to the same state in which they had been at the beginning of his minority, or to wrest from them what they had usurped during that time. If we take a view of what happened to each of our Kings, who was so unfortunate as to be placed in this situation, the truth and importance of this observation will fully appear.

The minority of David II. the son of Robert Bruce, was disturbed by the pretensions of Edward Baliol, who, relying on the aid of England, and on the support of some of the disaffected barons among the Scots, invaded the kingdom. The success which at first attended his arms obliged the young King to retire to France; and Baliol took possession of the throne. A small body of the nobles, however, continuing faithful to their exiled Prince, drove Baliol out of Scotland; and after an absence of nine years David returned from France, and took the government of the kingdom into his own hands. But nobles, who were thus wasting their blood and treasure in defence of the crown, had a right to the undisturbed possession of their ancient privileges; and even some title to arrogate new ones. It seems to have been a maxim in that age [1329], that every leader might claim as his own the territory which his sword had won from the enemy. Great acquisitions were gained by the nobility in that way: and to these the gratitude and liberality of David added, by distributing among such as adhered to him the vast possessions which fell to the crown by the forfeiture of his enemies. The family of Douglas, which began to rise above the other nobles in the reign of his father, augmented both its power and its property during his minority.

1405]. James I. was seized by the English during the continuance of a truce, and ungenerously detained a prisoner almost nineteen years. During that period the kingdom was governed, first by his uncle Robert, Duke of Albany, and then by Murdo, the son of Robert. Both these noblemen aspired to the crown; and their unnatural ambition, if we may believe most of our historians, not only cut short the days of Prince David, the King's eldest brother, but prolonged the captivity of James. They flattered themselves that they might step with less opposition into a throne, when almost vacant; and dreading the King's return as the extinction of their authority and the end of their hopes, they carried on the negotiations for obtaining his liberty with extreme remissness. At the same time they neglected nothing that could either soothe or bribe the nobles to approve of their scheme. They slackened the reins of government; they allowed the prerogative to be encroached upon; they suffered the most irregular acts of power, and even wanton instances of oppression, to pass with impunity; they dealt out the patrimony of the crown among those whose enmity they dreaded or whose favour they had gained; and reduced the royal authority to a state of imbecility, from which succeeding monarchs laboured in vain to raise it.

1437]. During the minority of James II. the administration of affairs, as well as the custody of the King's person, were committed to Sir William Crichton and Sir Alexander Livingston. Jealousy and discord were the effects of their conjunct authority, and each of them, in order to strengthen himself, bestowed new power and privileges upon the great men whose aid he courted; while the young Earl of Douglas, encouraged by their divisions, erected a sort of independent principality within the kingdom; and, forbidding his vassals to acknowledge any authority but his own, he created knights, appointed a privy council, named officers civil and military, assumed every ensign of royalty but the title of King, and appeared in public with a magnificence more than royal.

1460]. Eight persons were chosen to govern the kingdom during the minority of James III. Lord Boyd, however, by seizing the young King, and by the ascendant which he gained over him, soon engrossed the whole authority. He formed the ambitious project of raising his family to the same pitch of power and grandeur with those of the prime nobility; and he effected it. While intent on this, he relaxed the vigour of government, and the barons became accustomed once more to anarchy and independence. The power which Boyd had been at so much pains to acquire was of no long continuance, and the fall of his family, according to the fate of favourites, was sudden and destructive; but upon its ruins the family of Hamilton rose, which soon attained the highest rank in the kingdom.

As the minority of James V. was longer, it was likewise more turbulent than that of the preceding Kings. And the contending nobles, encouraged or protected either by the King of France or of England, formed themselves into more regular factions, and disregarded more than ever the restraints of order and authority. The French had the advantage of seeing one, devoted to their interest, raised to be Regent. This was the Duke of Albany, a native of France, and a grandson of James II. But Alexander Lord Home, the most eminent of all Scottish peers who survived the fatal field of Flodden, thwarted all his measures during the first years of his administration ; and the intrigues of the Queen Dowager, sister of Henry VIII., rendered the latter part of it no less feeble. Though supported by French auxiliaries, the nobles despised his authority, and, regardless either of his threats or his entreaties, peremptorily refused two several times to enter England, to the borders of which kingdom he had led them. Provoked by these repeated instances of contempt, the Regent abandoned his troublesome station, and, retiring to France, preferred the tranquillity of a private life to an office destitute of real authority. Upon his retreat, Douglas, Earl of Angus, became master of the King's person, and governed the kingdom in his name. Many efforts were made to deprive him of his usurped authority. But the numerous vassals and friends of his family adhered to him, because he divided with them the power and emoluments of his office ; the people reverenced and loved the name of Douglas ; he exercised, without the title of Regent, a fuller and more absolute authority than any who had enjoyed that dignity : and the ancient but dangerous pre-eminence of the Douglasses seemed to be restored.

To these, and to many other causes, omitted or unobserved by us, did the Scottish nobility owe that exorbitant and uncommon power, of which instances occur so frequently in our history. Nothing, however, demonstrates so fully the extent of their power as the length of its duration. Many years after the declension of the feudal system in other kingdoms of Europe, and when the arms or policy of Princes had, every where, shaken it or laid it in ruins, the foundation of that ancient fabric remained, in a great measure, firm and untouched in Scotland.

The powers which the feudal institutions vested in the nobles soon became intolerable to all the Princes of Europe, who longed to possess something more than a nominal and precarious authority.— Their impatience to obtain this precipitated Henry III. of England, Edward II., and some other weak Princes, into rash and premature attempts against the privileges of the barons, in which they were disappointed or perished. Princes of greater abilities were content to mitigate evils which they could not cure ; they sought occupation for the turbulent spirit of their nobles in frequent wars ; and allowed their fiery courage to evaporate in foreign expeditions, which, if they brought no other advantage, secured at least domestic tranquillity. But time and accident ripened the feudal governments for destruction. Towards the end of the fifteenth century, and beginning of the sixteenth, all the Princes of Europe attacked, as if by concert, the power of their nobles. Men of genius then undertook with success what their unskilful predecessors had attempted in vain. Louis XI. of France, the most profound and adventurous genius of that age, began, and in a single reign almost completed, the scheme of their destruction. The sure but concealed policy of Henry VII. of England produced the same effect. The means, indeed, employed by these monarchs were very different. The blow which Louis struck was sudden and fatal. The artifices of Henry resembled those slow poisons which waste the constitution, but become not mortal till some distant period. Nor did they produce consequences less opposite. Louis boldly added to the crown whatever he wrested from the nobles. Henry undermined his barons by encouraging them to sell their lands, which enriched the commons, and gave them a weight in the legislature unknown to their predecessors. But while these great revolutions were carrying on in two kingdoms with which Scotland was intimately connected, little alteration happened there; our Kings could neither extend their own prerogative, nor enable the commons to encroach upon the aristocracy; the nobles not only retained most of their ancient privileges and possessions, but continued to make new acquisitions.

This was not owing to the inattention of our Princes, or to their want of ambition. They were abundantly sensible of the exorbitant power of the nobility, and extremely solicitous to humble that order. They did not, however, possess means sufficient for accomplishing this end. The resources of our monarchs were few, and the progress which they made was of course inconsiderable. But as the number of their followers, and the extent of their jurisdiction, were the two chief circumstances which rendered the nobles formidable, in order to counterbalance the one, and restrain the other, all our Kings had recourse to nearly the same expedients.

I. Among nobles of a fierce courage and of unpolished manners, surrounded with vassals bold and licentious, whom they were bound by interest and honour to protect, the causes of discord were many and unavoidable. As the contending parties could seldom agree in acknowledging the authority of any common superior or judge, and their impatient spirit would seldom wait the slow decisions of justice, their quarrels were usually terminated by the sword. The offended baron assembled his vassals, and wasted the lands or shed the blood of his enemies. To forgive an injury was mean; to forbear revenge infamous or cowardly. Hence quarrels were transmitted from father to son, and under the name of *deadly feuds*, subsisted for many generations with unmitigated rancour. It was the interest of the crown to foment rather than to extinguish these quarrels; and by scattering or cherishing the seeds of discord among the nobles, that union, which would have rendered the aristocracy invincible, and which must at once have annihilated the prerogative, was effectually prevented. To the same cause our Kings were indebted for the success with which they sometimes attacked the most powerful chieftains. They employed private revenge to aid the impotence of public laws, and arming against the person who had incurred their displeasure those rival families which wished his fall, they rewarded their service by sharing among them the spoils of the vanquished. But this expedient, though it served to humble individuals, did not weaken the body of the nobility. Those who were now the instruments of their Prince's vengeance became, in a short time, the objects of his fear. Having acquired power and wealth by serving the crown, they, in their turn, set up for independence; and though their might be a fluctuation of power and of property; though old families fell, and new ones rose upon their ruins; the rights of the aristocracy remained entire, and its vigour unbroken.

II. As the administration of justice is one of the most powerful

ties between a King and his subjects, all our monarchs were at the
utmost pains to circumscribe the jurisdiction of the barons, and to
extend that of the crown. The external forms of subordination
natural to the feudal system favoured this attempt. An appeal
lay from the judges and courts of the barons to those of the King.
The right, however, of judging in the first instance belonged to the
nobles, and they easily found means to defeat the effects of appeals,
as well as of many other feudal regulations. The royal jurisdiction was almost confined within the narrow limits of the King's
demesnes, beyond which his judges claimed indeed much authority,
but possessed next to none. Our Kings were sensible of these limitations, and bore them with impatience. But it was impossible to
overturn in a moment what was so deeply rooted; or to strip the
nobles at once of privileges which they had held so long, and which
were wrought almost into the frame of the feudal constitution. To
accomplish this, however, was an object of uniform and anxious attention to all our Princes. James I. led the way here, as well as in
other instances, towards a more regular and perfect police. He
made choice, among the estates of parliament, of a certain number
of persons, whom he distinguished by the names of *Lords of Session*, and appointed them to hold courts for determining civil
causes three times in the year, and forty days at a time, in whatever place he pleased to name. Their jurisdiction extended to all
matters which formerly came under the cognizance of the King's
council, and being a committee of parliament, their decisions were
final. James II. obtained a law, annexing all regalities which
should be forfeited to the crown, and declaring the right of jurisdiction to be unalienable for the future. James III. imposed severe penalties upon those judges appointed by the barons, whose
decisions should be found on a review to be unjust; and, by many
other regulations, endeavoured to extend the authority of his own
court. James IV., on pretence of remedying the inconveniences
arising from the short terms of the Court of Session, appointed
other judges called *Lords of Daily Council*. The *Session* was an
ambulatory court, and met seldom; the *Daily Council* was fixed,
and sat constantly at Edinburgh; and, though not composed of
members of parliament, the same powers which the Lords of Session enjoyed were vested in it. At last James V. erected a new
court that still subsists, and which he named the *College of Justice*,
the judges or *Senators* of which were called *Lords of Council and
Session*. This court not only exercised the same jurisdiction which
formerly belonged to the Session and Daily Council, but new rights
were added. Privileges of great importance were granted to its
members, its forms were prescribed, its terms fixed, and regularity,
power, and splendour conferred upon it. The persons constituted
judges in all these different courts had, in many respects, the advantage of those who presided in the courts of the barons; they
were more eminent for their skill in law, their rules of proceeding
were more uniform, and their decisions more consistent. Such judicatories became the objects of confidence and of veneration.
Men willingly submitted their property to their determination,
and their encroachments on the jurisdictions of the nobles were

popular, and for that reason successful. By devices of a similar nature, the jurisdiction of the nobles in criminal causes was restrained, and the authority of the Court of *Justiciary* extended. The crown, in this particular, gaining insensibly upon the nobles, recovered more ample authority; and the King, whose jurisdiction once resembled that of a baron rather than that of a sovereign*, came more and more to be considered as the head of the community, and the supreme dispenser of justice to his people. These acquisitions of our Kings, however, though comparatively great, were in reality inconsiderable; and, notwithstanding all their efforts, many of the separate jurisdictions possessed by the nobles remained in great vigour; and their final abolition was reserved to a distant and more happy period.

But besides these methods of defending their prerogative and humbling the aristocracy, which may be considered as common to all our Princes, we shall find, by taking a view of their reigns, that almost every one of our Kings, from Robert Bruce to James V. had formed some particular system for depressing the authority of the nobles, which was the object both of their jealousy and terror. This conduct of our monarchs, if we rest satisfied with the accounts of their historians, must be considered as flowing entirely from their resentment against particular noblemen; and all their attempts to humble them must be viewed as the sallies of private passion, not as the consequences of any general plan of policy. But though some of their actions may be imputed to those passions, though the different genius of the men, the temper of the times, and the state of the nation, necessarily occasioned great variety in their schemes;

* The most perfect idea of the feudal system of government may be attained by attending to the state of Germany, and to the History of France. In the former, the feudal institutions still subsist with great vigour; and though altogether abolished in the latter, the public records have been so carefully preserved, that the French lawyers and antiquaries have been enabled, with more certainty and precision than those of any other country in Europe, to trace its rise, its progress, and revolutions. In Germany, every principality may be considered as a fief, and all its great princes as vassals, holding of the Emperor. They possess all the feudal privileges; their fiefs are perpetual; their jurisdictions within their own territories separate and extensive; and the great offices of the empire are all hereditary, and annexed to particular families. At the same time the Emperor retains many of the prerogatives of the feudal monarchs. Like them, his claims and pretensions are innumerable, and his power small; his jurisdiction within his own demesnes or hereditary countries is complete; beyond the bounds of these it is almost nothing: and so permanent are feudal principles, that although the feudal system be overturned in almost every particular state in Germany, and although the greater part of its princes have become absolute, the original feudal constitution of the Empire still remains, and ideas peculiar to that form of government direct all its operations, and determine the rights of all its princes. Our observations, with regard to the limited jurisdictions of kings under the feudal governments, are greatly illustrated by what happened in France. The feebleness and dotage of the descendants of Charlemagne encouraged the peers to usurp an independent jurisdiction. Nothing remained in the hands of the crown; all was seized by them. When Hugh Capet ascended the throne, A. D. 978, he kept possession of his private patrimony, the Comte of Paris; and all the jurisdiction of the Kings his successors exercised for some time, was within its territories. There were only four towns in France where he could establish Grands Baillis, or royal judges: all the other lands, towns, and bailiages, belonged to the nobles. The methods to which the French monarchs had recourse for extending their jurisdiction were exactly similar to those employed by our princes. Henault's Abrege, p. 617, &c. De l'Esprit des Loix, liv. xxx. ch. 20, &c.

yet, without being chargeable with excessive refinement, we may affirm that their end was uniformly the same; and that the project of reducing the power of the aristocracy, sometimes avowed and pursued with vigour, sometimes concealed or seemingly suspended, was never altogether abandoned.

No Prince was ever more indebted to his nobles than Robert Bruce. Their valour conquered the kingdom, and placed him on the throne. His gratitude and generosity bestowed on them the lands of the vanquished. Property has seldom undergone greater or more sudden revolutions than those to which it was subject at that time in Scotland. Edward I. having forfeited the estates of most of the ancient Scottish barons, granted them to his English subjects. These were expelled by the Scots, and their lands seized by new masters. Amidst such rapid changes confusion was unavoidable; and many possessed their lands by titles extremely defective. During one of those truces between the two nations, occasioned rather by their being weary of war than desirous of peace, Robert formed a scheme for checking the growing power and wealth of the nobles. He summoned them to appear and to show by what rights they held their lands. They assembled accordingly; and the question being put, they started up at once, and drew their swords: "By these," said they, "we acquired our lands, and with these we will defend them." The King, intimidated by their boldness, prudently dropped the project. But so deeply did they resent this attack upon their order, that, notwithstanding Robert's popular and splendid virtues, it occasioned a dangerous conspiracy against his life.

David, his son, at first an exile in France, afterward a prisoner in England, and involved in continual war with Edward III., had not leisure to attend to the internal police of his kingdom, or to think of retrenching the privileges of the nobility.

Our historians have been more careful to relate the military than the civil transactions of the reign of Robert II. Skirmishes and inroads of little consequence they describe minutely: but with regard to every thing that happened during several years of tranquillity, they are altogether silent.

The feeble administration of Robert III. must likewise be passed over slightly. A Prince of a mean genius, and of a frail and sickly constitution, was not a fit person to enter the lists with active and martial barons, or to attempt wresting from them any of their rights.

The civil transactions in Scotland are better known since the beginning of the reign of James I.; and a complete series of our laws supplies the defects of our historians. The English made some amends for their injustice in detaining that Prince a prisoner, by their generous care of his education. During his long residence in England, he had an opportunity of observing the feudal system in a more advanced state, and refined from many of the imperfections which still adhered to it in his own kingdom. He saw there, nobles great, but not independent; a king powerful, though far from absolute: he saw a regular administration of government; wise laws enacted; and a nation flourishing and happy, because all ranks of men were accustomed to obey them. Full of these ideas, he returned into his native country, which presented to him a very different scene. The royal authority, never great, was now contemptible, by having been so long delegated to Regents. The ancient patrimony and revenues of the crown were almost totally alienated. During his long absence the name of King was little known, and less regarded. The licence of many years had rendered the nobles independent. Universal anarchy prevailed. The weak were exposed to the rapine and oppression of the strong. In every corner some barbarous chieftain ruled at pleasure, and neither feared the King nor pitied the people.

James was too wise a Prince to employ open force to correct such inveterate evils. Neither the men nor the times would have borne it. He applied the gentler and less offensive remedy of laws and statutes. In a parliament held immediately after his return, he gained the confidence of his people by many wise laws, tending visibly to re-establish order, tranquillity, and justice in the kingdom. But at the same time that he endeavoured to secure these blessings to his subjects, he discovered his intention to recover those possessions of which the crown had been unjustly bereaved; and for that purpose obtained an act by which he was empowered to to summon such as had obtained crown lands during the three last reigns, to produce the rights by which they held them.* As this statute threatened the property of the nobles, another which passed in a subsequent parliament aimed a dreadful blow at their powers. By it the leagues and combinations which we have already described, and which rendered the nobles so formidable to the crown, were declared unlawful.† Encouraged by this success in the beginning of his enterprise, James's next step was still bolder and more decisive. During the sitting of parliament he seized, at once, his cousin Murdo, Duke of Albany, and his sons; the Earls of Douglas, Lennox, Angus, March, and above twenty other peers and barons of prime rank. To all of them, however, he was immediately reconciled, except to Albany and his sons, and Lennox. These were tried by their peers, and condemned; for what crime is now unknown. Their execution struck the whole order with terror, and their forfeiture added considerable possessions to the crown. He seized, likewise, the earldoms of Buchan and Strathern, upon different pretexts; and that of Mar fell to him by inheritance. The patience and inactivity of the nobles, while the King was proceeding so rapidly towards aggrandizing the crown, are amazing. The only obstruction he met with was from a slight insurrection headed by the Duke of Albany's youngest son, and that was easily suppressed. The splendour and presence of a King, to which the great men had been long unaccustomed, inspired reverence: James was a Prince of great abilities, conducted his operations with much prudence. He was in friendship with England, and closely allied with the French King: he was adored by the people, who enjoyed unusual security and happiness under his administration: and all his acquisitions, however fatal to the body of the nobles, had been

* Act 9. P. 1424.   † Act 30. P. 1424.

gained by attacks upon individuals; were obtained by decisions of law, and, being founded on circumstances peculiar to the persons who suffered, might excite murmurs and apprehensions, but afforded no colourable pretext for a general rebellion. It was not so with the next attempt which the King made. Encouraged by the facility with which he had hitherto advanced, he ventured upon a measure that irritated the whole body of the nobility, and which the events show either to have been entered into with too much precipitancy, or to have been carried on with too much violence. The father of George Dunbar, Earl of March, had taken arms against Robert III. the King's father; but that crime had been pardoned, and his lands restored by Robert Duke of Albany. James, on pretext that the Regent had exceeded his power, and that it was the prerogative of the King alone to pardon treason or to alienate lands annexed to the crown, obtained a sentence declaring the pardon to be void, and depriving Dunbar of the earldom. Many of the great men held lands by no other right than what they derived from grants of the two Dukes of Albany. Such a decision, though they had reason to expect it in consequence of the statute which the King had obtained, occasioned a general alarm. Though Dunbar was at present the only sufferer, the precedent might be extended, and their titles to possessions which they considered as the rewards of their valour, might be subjected to the review of courts of law, whose forms of proceeding and jurisdiction were in a martial age little known, and extremely odious. Terror and discontent spread fast upon this discovery of the King's intentions; the common danger called on the whole order to unite, and to make one bold stand before they were stripped successively of their acquisitions, and reduced to a state of poverty and insignificance. The prevalence of these sentiments among the nobles encouraged a few desperate men, the friends or followers of those who had been the chief sufferers under the King's administration, to form a conspiracy against his life. The first uncertain intelligence of this was brought him while he lay in his camp before Roxburgh Castle. He durst not confide in nobles, to whom he had given so many causes of disgust, but instantly dismissed them and their vassals, and retiring to a monastery near Perth, was soon after murdered there in the most cruel manner. All our historians mention with astonishment this circumstance, of the King's disbanding his army at a time when it was so necessary for his preservation. A King, say they, surrounded with his barons, is secure from secret treason, and may defy open rebellion. But those very barons were the persons whom he chiefly dreaded; and it is evident, from this review of his administration, that he had greater reason to apprehend danger than to expect defence from their hands. It was the misfortune of James, that his maxims and manners were too refined for the age in which he lived. Happy! had he reigned in a kingdom more civilized; his love of peace, of justice, and of elegance would have rendered his schemes successful; and instead of perishing because he had attempted too much, a grateful people would have applauded and seconded his efforts to reform and improve them.

Crichton, the most able man of those who had the direction of affairs during the minority of James II., had been the minister of James I., and well acquainted with his resolution of humbling the nobility. He did not relinquish the design, and he endeavoured to inspire his pupil with the same sentiments. But what James had attempted to effect slowly and by legal means, his son and Crichton pursued with the impetuosity natural to Scotsmen, and with the fierceness peculiar to that age. William, the sixth Earl of Douglas, was the first victim to their barbarous policy. That young noble-man (as we have already observed), contemning the authority of an infant Prince, almost openly renounced his allegiance, and aspired to independence. Crichton, too high spirited to bear such an in-sult, but too weak to curb or bring to justice so powerful an of-fender, decoyed him, by many promises, to an interview in the castle of Edinburgh, and, notwithstanding these, murdered both him and his brother. Crichton, however, gained little by this act of treachery, which rendered him universally odious. William, the eighth Earl of Douglas, was no less powerful, and no less formidable to the crown. By forming the league which we already mentioned, with the Earl of Crawford and other barons, he had united against his sovereign almost one half of his kingdom. But his credulity led him into the same snare which had been fatal to the former Earl. Relying on the King's promises, who had now attained to the years of manhood, and having obtained a safe conduct under the great seal, he ventured to meet him in Stirling Castle. James urged him to dissolve that dangerous confederacy into which he had entered; the Earl obstinately refused. "If you will not," said the enraged Monarch, drawing his dagger, "this shall!" and stabbed him to the heart. An action, so unworthy of a King, filled the na-tion with astonishment and with horror. The Earl's vassals ran to arms with the utmost fury, and dragging the safe conduct, which the King had granted and violated, at a horse's tail, they marched towards Stirling, burned the town, and threatened to besiege the castle. An accommodation, however, ensued; but on what terms is not known. But the King's jealousy, and the new Earl's power and resentment, prevented it from being of long continuance. Both took the field at the head of their armies, and met near Aber-corn. That of the Earl, composed chiefly of borderers, was far su-perior to the King's, both in number and in valour; and a single battle must, in all probability, have decided whether the house of Stuart or of Douglas was henceforth to possess the throne of Scot-land. But while his troops impatiently expected the signal to en-gage, the Earl ordered them to retire to their camp; and Sir James Hamilton of Cadyow, the person in whom he placed the greatest confidence, convinced of his want of genius to improve an opportu-nity, or of his want of courage to seize a crown, deserted him that very night. This example was followed by many; and the Earl, despised or forsaken by all, was soon driven out of the kingdom, and obliged to depend for his subsistence on the friendship of the King of England. The ruin of this great family, which had so long rivaled and overawed the crown, and the terror with which such an example of unsuccessful ambition filled the nobles, secured the King, for some time, from opposition; and the royal authority re-

mained uncontrolled and almost absolute. James did not suffer
this favourable interval to pass unimproved; he procured the consent of parliament to laws more advantageous to the prerogative,
and more subversive of the privileges of the aristocracy, than were
ever obtained by any former or subsequent monarch of Scotland.

By one of these, not only all the vast possessions of the Earl of
Douglass were annexed to the crown, but all prior and future alienations of crown lands were declared to be void; and the King
was empowered to seize them at pleasure, without any process or
form of law, and oblige the possessors to refund whatever they had
received from them. A dreadful instrument of oppression in the
hands of a Prince !

Another law prohibited the wardenship of the marches to be
granted hereditarily; restrained, in several instances, the jurisdiction of that office; and extended the authority of the King's courts.

By a third, it was enacted that no *Regality*, or exclusive right of
administering justice within a man's own lands, should be granted
in time to come, without the consent of parliament; a condition
which implied almost an express prohibition. Those nobles who
already possessed that great privilege would naturally be solicitous
to prevent it from becoming common, by being bestowed on many.
Those who had not themselves attained it would envy others the
acquisition of such a flattering distinction, and both would concur
in rejecting the claims of new pretenders.

By a fourth act, all new grants of hereditary offices were prohibited, and those obtained since the death of the last King were revoked.

Each of these statutes undermined some of the great pillars on
which the power of the aristocracy rested. During the remainder
of his reign, this Prince pursued the plan which he had begun
with the utmost vigour; and had not a sudden death, occasioned
by the splinter of a cannon which burst near him at the siege of
Roxburgh, prevented his progress, he wanted neither genius nor
courage to perfect it; and Scotland might, in all probability, have
been the first kingdom in Europe which would have seen the subversion of the feudal system.

James III. discovered no less eagerness than his father or grandfather to humble the nobility; but far inferior to either of them in
abilities and address, he adopted a plan extremely impolitic, and
his reign was disastrous, as well as his end tragical. Under the
feudal governments, the nobles were not only the King's ministers,
and possessed of all the great offices of power or of trust; they were
likewise his companions and favourites, and hardly any but them
approached his person or were entitled to his regard. But James,
who both feared and hated his nobles, kept them at an unusual
distance, and bestowed every mark of confidence and affection upon
a few mean persons, of professions so dishonourable as ought to
have rendered them unworthy of his presence. Shut up with these
in his castle of Stirling, he seldom appeared in public, and amused
himself in architecture, music, and other arts, which were then
little esteemed. The nobles beheld the power and favour of these
minions with indignation. Even the sanguinary measures of his

father provoked them less than his neglect. Individuals alone suffered by the former; by the latter, every man thought himself injured because all were contemned. Their discontent was much heightened by the King's recalling all rights to crown lands, hereditary offices, regalities, and every other concession which was detrimental to his prerogative, and which had been extorted during his minority. Combinations among themselves, secret intrigues with England, and all the usual preparatives for civil war, were the consequences of their resentment. Alexander Duke of Albany and John Earl of Mar, the King's brothers, two young men of turbulent and ambitious spirits, and incensed against James, who treated them with the same coldness as he did the other great men, entered deeply into all their cabals. The King detected their designs before they were ripe for execution, and, seizing his two brothers, committed the Duke of Albany to Edinburgh Castle. The Earl of Mar, having remonstrated with too much boldness against the King's conduct, was murdered, if we may believe our historians, by his command. Albany, apprehensive of the same fate, made his escape out of the castle and fled into France. Concern for the King's honour, or indignation at his measures, were perhaps the motives which first induced him to join the malcontents. But James's attachment to favourites rendering him every day more odious to the nobles, the prospect of the advantages which might be derived from their general disaffection, added to the resentment which he felt on account of his brother's death and his own injuries, soon inspired Albany with more ambitious and criminal thoughts. He concluded a treaty with Edward IV. of England, in which he assumed the name of Alexander King of Scots; and, in return for the assistance which was promised him towards dethroning his brother, he bound himself, as soon as he was put in possession of the kingdom, to swear fealty and do homage to the English monarch; to renounce the ancient alliance with France; to contract a new one with England; and to surrender some of the strongest castles and most valuable counties in the kingdom of Scotland. That aid, which the Duke so basely purchased at the price of his own honour and the independence of his country, was punctually granted him, and the Duke of Gloucester, with a powerful army, conducted him towards Scotland. The danger of a foreign invasion obliged James to implore the assistance of those nobles whom he had so long treated with contempt. Some of them were in close confederacy with the Duke of Albany, and approved of all his pretensions. Others were impatient for any event which would restore their order to its ancient pre-eminence. They appeared, however, to enter with zeal into the measures of their sovereign for the defence of the kingdom against its invaders, and took the field at the head of a powerful army of their followers, but with a stronger disposition to redress their own grievances than to annoy the enemy; and with a fixed resolution of punishing those minions whose insolence they could no longer tolerate. This resolution they executed in the camp near Lauder, with a military dispatch and rigour. Having previously concerted their plan, the Earls of Angus, Huntly, Lennox, followed by almost all the barons

of chief note in the army, forcibly entered the apartment of their
sovereign, seized all his favourites except one Ramsay, whom they
could not tear from the King, in whose arms he took shelter, and
without any form of trial, hanged them instantly over a bridge.
Among the most remarkable of those who had engrossed the King's
affection, were Cochran, a mason; Hommil, a tailor; Leonard, a
smith; Rogers, a musician; and Torsifan, a fencing-master. So
despicable a retinue discovers the capriciousness of James's character, and accounts for the indignation of the nobles when they beheld the favour due to them bestowed on such unworthy objects.

James had no reason to confide in an army so little under his
command, and dismissing it, shut himself up in the castle of Edinburgh. After various intrigues, Albany's lands and honours were
at length restored to him, and he seemed to have gained his brother's favour by some important services. But their friendship
was not of long duration. James abandoned himself once more to
the guidance of favourites; and the fate of those who had suffered
at Lauder did not deter others from seeking that dangerous pre-
eminence. Albany, on pretext that an attempt had been made to
take away his life by poison, fled from court, and retiring to his
castle at Dunbar, drew thither a greater number of barons than
attended on the King himself. At the same time he renewed his
former confederacy with Edward; the Earl of Angus openly nego-
tiated that infamous treaty; other barons were ready to concur
with it; and if the sudden death of Edward had not prevented
Albany's receiving any aid from England, the crown of Scotland
would probably have been the reward of this unworthy combination with the enemies of his country. But, instead of any hopes
of reigning in Scotland, he found, upon the death of Edward, that
he could not reside there in safety; and flying first to England, and
then to France, he seems from that time to have taken no part in
the affairs of his native country. Emboldened by his retreat, the
King and his ministers multiplied the insults which they offered
to the nobility. A standing guard, a thing unknown under the
feudal governments, and inconsistent with the familiarity and
confidence with which monarchs then lived amidst their nobles,
was raised for the King's defence, and the command of it given to
Ramsay, lately created Earl of Bothwell, the same person who had
so narrowly escaped when his companions were put to death at Lauder. As if this precaution had not been sufficient, a proclamation
was issued, forbidding any person to to appear in arms within the
precincts of the court; which, at a time when no man left his own
house without a numerous retinue of armed followers, was, in effect,
debarring the nobles from all access to the King. James, at the
same time, became fonder of retirement than ever, and sunk into
indolence or superstition, or, attentive only to amusements, devolved his whole authority upon his favourites. So many injuries
provoked the most considerable nobles to take arms; and having
persuaded or obliged the Duke of Rothesay, the King's eldest
son, a youth of fifteen, to set himself at their head, they openly
declared their intention of depriving James of a crown, of which
he had discovered himself to be so unworthy. Roused by this

danger, the King quitted his retirement, took the field, and encountered them near Bannockburn : but the valour of the borderers, of whom the army of the malecontents was chiefly composed, soon put his troops to flight, and he himself was slain in the pursuit. Suspicion, indolence, immoderate attachment to favourites, and all the vices of a feeble mind, are visible in his whole conduct; but the character of a cruel and unrelenting tyrant seems to be unjustly affixed to him by our historians. His neglect of the nobles irritated, but did not weaken them; and their discontent, the immoderate ambition of his two brothers, and their unnatural confederacies with England, were sufficient to have disturbed a more vigorous administration, and to have rendered a prince of superior talents unhappy.

The indignation which many persons of rank expressed against the conduct of the conspirators, together with the terror of the sentence of excommunication which the Pope pronounced against them, obliged them to use their victory with great moderation and humanity. Being conscious how detestable the crime of imbruing their hands in the blood of their Sovereign appeared, they endeavoured to regain the good opinion of their countrymen, and to atone for the treatment of the father by their loyalty and duty towards the son. They placed him instantly on the throne, and the whole kingdom soon united in acknowledging his authority.

James IV. was naturally generous and brave; he felt in a high degree all the passions which animate a young and noble mind.— He loved magnificence, he delighted in war, and was eager to obtain fame. During his reign the ancient and hereditary enmity between the King and nobles seem almost entirely to have ceased. He envied not their splendour, because it contributed to the ornament of his court; nor did he dread their power, which he considered as the security of his kingdom, not as an object of terror to himself. This confidence on his part met with the proper return of duty and affection on theirs; and, in his war with England, experienced how much a king beloved by his nobles is able to perform. Though the ardour of his courage and the spirit of chivalry, rather than the prospect of any national advantage, induced·him to declare war against England, such was the zeal of his subjects for the King's glory, that he was followed by as gallant an army as ever any of his ancestors had led upon English ground. But though James himself formed no scheme dangerous or detrimental to the aristocracy, his reign was distinguished by an event extremely fatal to it; and one accidental blow humbled it more than all the premeditated attacks of the preceding Kings. In the rash and unfortunate battle of Flowden, a brave nobility chose rather to die than to desert their sovereign. Twelve earls, thirteen lords, five eldest sons of noblemen, and an incredible number of barons, fell with the King. The whole body of the nobles long and sensibly felt this disaster; and if a Prince of full age had then ascended the throne, their consternation and feebleness would have afforded him advantages which no former monarch ever possessed.

But James V., who succeeded his father, was an infant of a year old; and though the office of Regent was conferred upon his cousin the Duke of Albany, a man of genius and enterprise, a native of France, and accustomed to a government where the power of the King was already great; though he made many bold attempts to extend the royal authority; though he put to death Lord Home, and banished the Earl of Angus, the two noblemen of greatest influence in the kingdom, the aristocracy lost no ground under his administration. A stranger to the manners, the laws, and the language of the people whom he was called to rule, he acted, on some occasions, rather like a Viceroy of the French King, than the Governor of Scotland; but the nobles asserted their own privileges, and contended for the interest of their country with a boldness which convinced him of their independence, and of the impotence of their own authority. After several unsuccessful struggles, he voluntarily retired to France; and the King being then in his thirteenth year, the nobles agreed that he should assume the government, and that eight persons should be appointed to attend him by turns, and to advise and assist him in the administration of public affairs. The Earl of Angus, who was one of that number, did not long remain satisfied with such divided power. He gained some of his colleagues, removed others, and intimidated the rest. When the term of his attendance expired, he still retained authority, to which all were obliged to submit, because none of them was in a condition to dispute it. The affection of the young King was the only thing wanting to fix and perpetuate his power. But an active and high-spirited prince submitted with great impatience to the restraint in which he was kept. · It ill suited his years or his disposition to be confined as a prisoner within his own palace; to be treated with no respect, and to be deprived of all power. He could not on some occasions conceal his resentment and indignation.— Angus foresaw that he had much to dread from these; and as he could not gain the King's heart, he resolved to make sure of his person. James was continually surrounded by the Earl's spies and confidants; many eyes watched all his motions, and observed every step he took. But the King's eagerness to obtain liberty eluded all their vigilance. He escaped from Falkland, and fled to the castle of Stirling, the residence of the Queen his mother, and the only place of strength in the kingdom which was not in the hands of the Douglases. The nobles, of whom some were influenced by their hatred to Angus, and others by their respect for the King, crowded to Stirling, and his court was soon filled with persons of the greatest distinction, The Earl, though astonished at this unexpected revolution, resolved at first to make one bold push for recovering his authority, by marching to Stirling at the head of his followers; but he wanted either courage or strength to execute this resolution. In a parliament held soon after, he and his adherents were attainted, and after escaping from many dangers, and enduring much misery, he was at length obliged to fly into England for refuge.

James had now not only the name, but, though extremely young, the full authority of a King. He was inferior to no Prince of that age in gracefulness of person or vigour of mind. His understanding was good, and his heart warm; the former capable of great im-

provement, and the latter susceptible of the best impressions.—
But, according to the usual fate of Princes who are called to the
throne in their infancy, his education had been neglected. His
private preceptors were more ready to flatter than to instruct him.
It was the interest of those who governed the kingdom, to prevent
him from knowing too much. The Earl of Angus, in order to divert him from business, gave him an early taste for such pleasures
as afterwards occupied and engrossed him more than became a
King. Accordingly, we discover in James all the features of a great
but uncultivated spirit. On the one hand, violent passions, implacable resentment, an immoderate desire of power, and the utmost
rage at disappointment. On the other, love to his people, zeal for
the punishment of private oppressors, confidence in his favourites,
and the most engaging openness and affability of behaviour.

What he himself had suffered from the exorbitant power of the
nobles, led him early to imitate his predecessors in their attempts
to humble them. The plan he formed for that purpose was more
profound, more systematic, and pursued with greater constancy and
steadiness, than that of any of his ancestors : and the influence
of the events in his reign and those of the subsequent period,
renders it necessary to explain his conduct at greater length, and to
enter into a more minute detail of his actions. He had penetration
enough to discover those defects in the schemes adopted by former
Kings, which occasioned their miscarriage. The examples of James
I. had taught him that wise laws operate slowly on a rude people,
and that the fierce spirit of the feudal nobles was not to be subdued
by these alone. The effects of the violent measures of James II.
convinced him that that the oppression of one great family is apt
either to excite the suspicion and resentment of the other nobles,
or to enrich with its spoils some new family, who would soon adopt
the same sentiments, and become equally formidable to the crown.
He saw, from the fatal end of James III., that neglect was still
more intolerable to the nobles than oppression, and that the ministry of new men and favourites was both dishonourable and dangerous to a Prince. At the same time, he felt that the authority of
the crown was not sufficient to counterbalance the power of the
aristocracy, and that without some new accession of strength he
could expect no better success in the struggle than his ancestors.—
In this extremity he applied himself to the clergy, hoping that
they would both relish his plan, and concur, with all their influence, in enabling him to put it into execution. Under the feudal
government, the church, being reckoned a third estate, had its representatives in parliament; the number of these was considerable,
and they possessed great influence in that assembly. The superstition of former Kings, and the zeal of many ages of ignorance, had
bestowed on ecclesiastics a portion of the national wealth ; and the
authority which they acquired by the reverence of the people was
superior even to that which they derived from their riches. This
powerful body, however, depended entirely on the crown. The
Popes, notwithstanding their attention to extend their usurpations,
had neglected Scotland as a distant and poor kingdom, and permitted its Kings to exercise powers which they disputed with more

considerable Princes. The Scottish monarchs had the sole right of
nomination to vacant bishoprics and abbeys;* and James naturally
concluded, that men who expected preferment from his favour,
would be more willing to merit it by promoting his designs. Happily for him, the nobles had not yet recovered the blow which fell
on their order at Flowden: and if we may judge, either from their
conduct, or from the character given of them by Sir Ralph Sadler,
the English envoy in Scotland, they were men of little genius, of
no experience in business, and incapable of acting either with unanimity or with vigour. Many of the clergy, on the other hand,
were distinguished by their great abilities, and no less by their ambition.   Various causes of disgust subsisted between them and the
martial nobles, who were apt to view the pacific character of ecclesiastics with some degree of contempt, and who envied their power
and wealth.   By acting in concert with the King, they not only
would gratify him, but avenge themselves, and hoped to aggrandize
their own order by depressing those who were their sole rivals.—
Secure of so powerful a concurrence, James ventured to proceed
with greater boldness. In the first heat of resentment he had
driven the Earl of Angus out of the kingdom ; and sensible that a
person so far superior to the other nobles in abilities, might create
many obstacles which would retard or render ineffectual all his
schemes, he solemnly swore that he would never permit him to return into Scotland ; and, notwithstanding the repeated solicitations
of the King of England, he adhered to his own vow with unrelenting obstinacy. He then proceeded to repair the fortifications of
Edinburgh, Stirling, and other castles, and to fill his magazines with
arms and ammunition. Having taken these precautions by way of
defence, he began to treat the nobility with the utmost coldness
and reserve. Those offices which they were apt from long possession to consider as appropriated to their order, were now bestowed
on ecclesiastics, who alone possessed the King's ear, and, together
with a few gentlemen of inferior rank, to whom he communicated
his schemes, were intrusted with the management of all public
affairs. These ministers were chosen with judgment; and Cardinal
Beatoun, who soon became the most eminent among them, was a
man of superior genius. They served the King with fidelity ; they
carried on his measures with vigour, with reputation, and with
success.   James no longer concealed his distrust of the nobles,
and suffered no opportunity of mortifying them to escape.—
Slight offences were aggravated into real crimes, and punished
with severity. Every accusation against persons of rank was heard
with pleasure ; every appearance of guilt was examined with
rigour; and every trial proved fatal to those who were accused :
the banishing of Hepburn, Earl of Bothwell, for reasons extremely
frivolous, beheading the eldest son of Lord Forbes without sufficient evidence of his guilt, and the condemning Lady Glamis, a
sister of the Earl of Angus, to be burned for the crime of witchcraft, of which even that credulous age believed her innocent, are
monuments both of the King's hatred of the nobility, of the seve-

* Epist. Reg. Scot. l. 197, &c. Act 125. P. 1540.

rity of his government, and of the stretches he made towards absolute power. By these acts of authority he tried the spirit of the
nobles, and how much they were willing to bear. Their patience
increased his contempt for them, and added to the ardour and boldness with which he pursued his plan. Meanwhile they observed
the tendency of his schemes with concern and resentment; but the
King's sagacity, the vigilance of his ministers, and the want of a
proper leader, made it dangerous to concert any measures for their
defence, and impossible to act with becoming vigour. James and
his counsellors, by a false step which they took, presented to them,
at length, an advantage which they did not fail to improve.

Motives which are well known had prompted Henry VIII. to disclaim the Pope's authority, and to seize the revenues of the regular
clergy. His system of reformation satisfied none of his subjects.—
Some were enraged because he had proceeded so far, others murmured because he proceeded no farther. By his imperious temper,
and alternate persecutions of the zealots for Popery and the converts to the Protestant opinions, he was equally formidable to both.
Henry was afraid that this general dissatisfaction of his people
might encourage his enemies on the continent to invade his kingdom. He knew that both the Pope and the Emperor courted the
friendship of the King of Scots, and endeavoured to engage him
in an alliance against England. He resolved, therefore, to disappoint the effects of their negotiations, by entering into a closer
union with his nephew. In order to accomplish this, he transmitted to James an elaborate memorial, presenting the numerous encroachments of the See of Rome upon the rights of sovereigns :
and that he might the more effectually adopt the same measures
for abolishing Papal usurpation, which had proved so efficacious in
England, he sent ambassadors into Scotland, to propose a personal
interview with him at York. It was plainly James's interest to accept this invitation ; the assistance of so powerful an ally, the high
honours which were promised him, and the liberal subsidies he
might have obtained, would have added no little dignity to his domestic government and must have greatly facilitated the execution
of his favourite plan. On the other hand, a war with England,
which he had reason to apprehend if he rejected Henry's offers of
friendship, was inconsistent with all his views. This would bring
him to depend on his barons ; an army could not be raised without
their assistance : to call nobles incensed against their Prince into
the field was to unite his enemies, to make them sensible of their
own strength, and to afford them an opportunity of redressing
their wrongs. James, who was not ignorant that all these consequences might follow a breach with England, listened at first to
Henry's proposal, and consented to the interview at York. But
the clergy dreaded a union which must have been established on
the ruins of the Church. Henry had taken great pains to infuse
into his nephew his own sentiments concerning religion, and had
frequently solicited him, by ambassadors, to renounce the usurped
dominion of the Pope, which was no less dishonourable to Princes,
than grievous to their subjects. The clergy had hitherto, with
great address, diverted the King from regarding these solicitations.

But in an amicable conference Henry expected, and they feared, that James would yield to his entreaties, or be convinced by his arguments. They knew that the revenues of the church were an alluring object to a Prince who wanted money, and who loved it; that the pride and ambition of ecclesiastics raised the indignation of the nobles; that their indecent lives gave offence to the people; that the Protestant opinions were spreading fast throughout the nation; and that a universal defection from the established church would be the consequence of giving the smallest degree of encouragement to these principles. For these reasons they employed all their credit with the King, and had recourse to every artifice and insinuation, in order to divert him from a journey which must have been so fatal to their interest. They endeavoured to inspire him with fear, by magnifying the danger to which he should expose his person, by venturing so far into England without any security but the word of a Prince, who, having violated every thing venerable and sacred in religion, was no longer to be trusted; and by way of compensation for the sums which he might have received from Henry, they offered an annual donative of fifty thousand crowns; they promised to contribute liberally towards carrying on a war with England, and flattered him with the prospect of immense riches, arising from the forfeiture of persons who were to be tried and condemned as heretics. Influenced by these considerations, James broke his agreement with Henry, who, in expectation of meeting him, had already come to York; and that haughty and impatient monarch resented the affront, by declaring war against Scotland. His army was soon ready to invade the kingdom. James was obliged to have recourse to the nobles for the defence of his dominions. At his command they assembled their followers, but with the same dispositions which had animated their ancestors in the reign of James III,, and with a full resolution of imitating their example by punishing those to whom they imputed the grievances of which they had reason to complain; and if the King's ministers had not been men of abilities, superior to those of James III., and of considerable interest even with their enemies, who could not agree among themselves what victims to sacrifice, the camp of Fala would have been as remarkable as that of Lauder, for the daring encroachments of the nobility on the prerogative of the Prince. But though his ministers were saved by this accident, the nobles had soon another opportunity of discovering to the King their dissatisfaction with his government, and their contempt of his authority. Scarcity of provisions, and the rigour of the season, having obliged the English army which had invaded Scotland to retire, James imagined that he could attack them with great advantage in their retreat: but the principal barons, with an obstinacy and disdain which greatly aggravated their disobedience, refused to advance a step beyond the limits of their own country. Provoked by this insult to himself, and suspicious of a new conspiracy against his ministers, the King instantly disbanded an army which paid so little regard to his orders, and returned abruptly into the heart of the kingdom.

An ambitious and high-spirited Prince could not brook such a mortifying affront. His hopes of success had been rash, and his despair upon a disappointment was excessive. He felt himself engaged in an unnecessary war with England, which, instead of yielding him the laurels and triumphs that he expected, had begun with such circumstances as encouraged the insolence of his subjects, and exposed him to the scorn of his enemies. He saw how vain and ineffectual all his projects to humble the nobles had been; and that, though in times of peace a Prince may endeavour to depress them, they will rise during war to their former importance and dignity. Impatience, resentment, indignation, filled his bosom by turns. The violence of these passions altered his temper, and perhaps impaired his reason. He became pensive, sullen and retired. He seemed through the day to be swallowed up in profound meditation, and through the night he was disturbed with those visionary terrors which make impression upon a weak understanding only, or a disordered fancy. In order to revive the King's spirits, an inroad on the western borders was concerted by his ministers, who prevailed upon the barons in the neighbouring provinces to raise as many troops as were thought necessary, and to enter the enemy's country. But nothing could remove the King's aversion to his nobility, or diminish his jealousy of their power. He would not even intrust them with the command of the forces which they had assembled; that was reserved for Oliver Sinclair his favourite, who no sooner appeared to take possession of the dignity conferred upon him, than rage and indignation occasioned a universal mutiny in the army. Five hundred English, who happened to be drawn up in sight, attacked the Scots in this disorder. Hatred to the King and contempt to their general produced an effect to which there is no parallel in history. They overcame the fear of death, and the love of liberty; and ten thousand men fled before a number so far inferior, without striking a single blow. No man was desirous of a victory which would have been acceptable to the King and to his favourite; few endeavoured to save themselves by flight; the English had the choice of what prisoners they pleased to take; and almost every person of distinction who was engaged in the expedition remained in their hands.* This astonishing event was a new proof to the King of the general disaffection of the nobility, and a new discovery of his own weakness and want of authority. Incapable of bearing these repeated insults, he found himself unable to revenge them. The deepest melancholy and despair succeeded to the furious transports of rage, which the first account of the rout of his army occasioned. All the violent passions which are the enemies of life preyed upon his mind, and wasted and consumed a youthful and vigorous constitution. Some authors of that age impute his untimely death to poison; but the diseases of the mind, when they rise to a height are often mortal; and the known effects of disappointment, anger, and resentment upon a sanguine and impetuous temper sufficiently account for his unhappy fate. "His

* According to an account of this event in the Hamilton MSS. about thirty were killed, above a thousand were taken prisoners; and among them a hundred and fifty persons of condition. Vol. ii. 286. The small number of English prevented their taking more prisoners.

death (says Drummond) proveth his mind to have been raised to a high strain, and above mediocrity; he could die, but could not digest a disaster." Had James survived this misfortune, one of two things must have happened; either the violence of his temper would have engaged him openly to attack the nobles, who would have found in Henry a willing and powerful protector, and have derived the same assistance from him which the malecontents, in the succeeding reign, did from his daughter Elizabeth; in that case, a dangerous civil war must have been the certain consequence. Or, perhaps, necessity might have obliged him to accept of Henry's offers, and be reconciled to his nobility. In that event, the church would have fallen a sacrifice to their union, a reformation upon Henry's plan, would have been established by law; a great part of the temporalities of the church would have been seized; and the friendship of the King and Barons would have been cemented by dividing its spoils.

Such were the efforts of our Kings towards reducing the exorbitant power of the nobles. If they were not attended with success, we must not for that reason conclude that they were not conducted with prudence. Every circumstance seems to have combined against the crown. Accidental events concurred with political causes, in rendering the best concerted measures abortive. The assassination of one King, the sudden death of another, and the fatal despair of a third, contributed, no less than its own natural strength, to preserve the aristocracy from ruin.

Amidst these struggles, the influence which our Kings possessed in their parliaments is a circumstance seemingly inexplicable, and which merits particular attention. As these assemblies were composed chiefly of the nobles, they, we are apt to imagine, must have dictated all their decisions; but, instead of this, every King found them obsequious to his will, and obtained such laws as he deemed necessary for extending his authority. All things were conducted there with dispatch and unanimity; and in none of our historians do we find an instance of any opposition formed against the court in parliament, or mention of any difficulty in carrying through the measures which were agreeable to the King. In order to account for this singular fact, it is necessary to inquire into the origin and constitution of parliament.

The genius of the feudal government, uniform in all its operations, produced the same effects in small as in great societies; and the territory of a baron was, in miniature, the model of a kingdom. He possessed the right of jurisdiction; but those who depended on him being free men, and not slaves, could be tried by their peers only; and, therefore, his vassals were bound to attend his courts, and to assist both in passing and executing his sentences. When assembled on these occasions, they established, by mutual consent such regulations as tended to the welfare of their small society; and often granted, voluntarily, such supplies to their *Superior* as his necessities required. Change now a single name; in place of baron substitute king, and we behold a parliament in its first rudiments, and observe the first exertions of those powers which its members now possess as judges, as legislators, and as dispensers of the public revenues. Suitable to this idea, are the appellations of the *King's Court*, and of the *King's Great Council*, by which parliaments were anciently distinguished; and suitable to this, likewise, were the constituent members of which it was composed. In all the feudal kingdoms, such as held of the King *in chief* were bound, by the condition of their tenure, to attend and to assist in his courts. Nor was this esteemed a privilege, but a service. It was exacted likewise of bishops, abbots, and the greater ecclesiastics, who, holding vast possessions of the crown, were deemed subject to the same burden. Parliaments did not continue long in this state. Cities gradually acquired wealth, a considerable share of the public taxes were levied on them, the inhabitants grew into estimation, and, being enfranchised by the sovereign, a place in parliament was the consequence of their liberty, and of their importance. But as it would have been absurd to confer such a privilege, or to impose such a burden on a whole community, every borough was permitted to choose one or two of its citizens to appear in the name of the corporation; and the idea of *representation* was first introduced in this manner. An innovation still more important naturally followed. The vassals of the crown were originally few in number, and extremely powerful; but as it is impossible to render property fixed and permanent, many of their possessions came gradually, and by various methods of alienations, to be split and parcelled out into different hands. Hence arose the distinction between the *Greater* and the *Lesser Barons*. The former were those who retained their original fiefs undivided, the latter were the new and less potent vassals of the crown. Both were bound, however, to perform all feudal services, and, of consequence, to give attendance in parliament. To the lesser barons, who formed no inconsiderable body, this was an intolerable grievance. Barons sometimes denied their tenure, boroughs renounced their right of electing, charters were obtained containing an exemption from attendance; and the anxiety with which our ancestors endeavoured to get free from the obligation of sitting in parliament is surpassed by that only with which their posterity solicit to be admitted there. In order to accommodate both parties at once, to secure to the King a sufficient number of members in his great council, and to save his vassals from an unnecessary burden, an easy expedient was found out. The obligation to personal attendance was continued upon the greater barons, from which the lesser barons were exempted, on condition of their electing in each county a certain number of *representatives*, to appear in their name. Thus a parliament became complete in all its members, and was composed of lords spiritual and temporal, of knights of the shires, and of burgesses. As many causes contributed to bring government earlier to perfection in England than in Scotland; as the rigour of the feudal institutions abated sooner, and its defects were supplied with greater facility in the one kingdom than in the other; England led the way in all these changes, and burgesses and knights of the shire appeared in the parliaments of that nation before they were heard of in ours. [1326] Burgesses were first admitted into the Scottish parliaments by Robert Bruce;

e 5

and in the preamble to the laws of Robert III. they are ranked among the constituent members of that assembly. [1427] The lesser barons were indebted to James I. for a statute exempting them from personal attendance, and permitting them to elect representatives: the exemption was eagerly laid hold on; but the privilege was so little valued that, except one or two instances, it lay neglected during one hundred and sixty years; and James VI. first obliged them to send representatives regularly to parliament.

A Scottish parliament, then, consisted anciently of great barons, of ecclesiastics, and a few representatives of boroughs. Nor were these divided as in England into two houses, but composed one assembly, in which the Lord Chancellor presided*. In rude ages, when the science of government was extremely imperfect among a martial people, unacquainted with the arts of peace, strangers to the talents which make a figure in debate, and despising them, parliaments were not held in the same estimation as at present; nor did haughty barons love those courts in which they appeared with such evident marks of inferiority. Parliaments were often hastily assembled, and it was probably in the King's power, by the manner in which he issued his writs for that purpose, to exclude such as were averse from his measures. At a time when deeds of violence were common, and the restraints of law and decency were little regarded, no man could venture with safety to oppose the King in his own court. The great barons, or lords of parliament, were extremely few; even so late as the beginning of the reign of James VI. they amounted only to fifty-three. The ecclesiastics equalled them in number, and being devoted implicitly to the crown, for reasons which have been already explained, rendered all hopes of victory in any struggle desperate. Nor were the nobles themselves so anxious as might be imagined, to prevent acts of parliaments favourable to the royal prerogative; conscious of their own strength, and of the King's inability to carry these acts into execution without their concurrence, they trusted that they might either elude or venture to contemn them; and the statue revoking the King's property, and annexing alienated jurisdictions to the crown, repeated in every reign, and violated and despised as often, is a standing proof of the impotence of laws when opposed to power. So many concurring causes are sufficient, perhaps, to account for the ascendant which our Kings acquired in parliament. But without having recourse to any of these, a single circumstance, peculiar to the constitution of the Scottish parliament, the mention.

* In England, the peers and commons seem early to have met in separate houses; and James I., who was fond of imitating the English in all their customs, had probably an intention of introducing some considerable distinction between the greater and lesser barons in Scotland: at least he determined that their consultations should not be carried on under the direction of the same president: for by his law, A. D. 1327, it is provided, "that out of the commis-ioners of all the shires shall be chosen a wise and expert man, called the common speaker of the parliament, who shall propose all and sundry needs and causes pertaining to the commons in the parliament or general council." No such speaker, it would seem, was ever chosen; and by a subsequent law the Chancellor was declared perpetual president of parliament.

ing of which we have hitherto avoided, will abundantly explain this fact, seemingly so repugnant to all our reasonings concerning the weakness of the king, and the power of the nobles.

As far back as our records enable us to trace the constitution of our parliaments, we find a committee distinguished by the name of *Lords of Articles.* It was their business to prepare and to digest all matters which were to be laid before the parliament. There was rarely any business introduced into parliament, but what had passed through the channel of this committee; every motion for a new law was first made there, and approved of or rejected by the members of it; what they approved was formed into a bill, and presented to parliament: and it seems probable, that what they rejected could not be introduced into the house. This committee owed the extraordinary powers vested in it to the military genius of the ancient nobles: too impatient to submit to the drudgery of civil business, too impetuous to observe the forms or to enter into the details necessary in conducting it, they were glad to lay that burden upon a small number, while they themselves had no other labour than simply to give or to refuse their assent to the bills which were presented to them. The lords of articles, then, not only directed all the proceedings of parliaments but possessed a negative before debate. That committee was chosen and constituted in such a manner as to put this valuable privilege entirely into the King's hands. It is extremely probable, that our Kings once had the sole right of nominating the lords of articles. They came afterwards to be elected by the parliament, and consisted of an equal number out of each estate, and most commonly of eight temporal and eight spiritual lords, of eight representatives of boroughs, and of the eight great officers of the crown. Of this body, the eight ecclesiastics, together with the officers of the crown, were entirely at the King's devotion; and it was scarce possible that the choice could fall on such temporal lords and burgesses as would unite in opposition to his measures. Capable either of influencing their election, or of gaining them when elected, the King commonly found the lords of articles no less obsequious to his will than his own privy council; and, by means of his authority with them, he could put a negative upon his parliament before debate, as well as after it; and, what may seem altogether incredible, the most limited Prince in Europe actually possessed, in one instance, a prerogative which the most absolute could never attain.

To this account of the internal constitution of Scotland, it will not be improper to add a view of the political state of Europe at that period, where the following history commences. A thorough knowledge of that general system, of which every kingdom in Europe forms a part, is not less requisite towards understanding the history of a nation than an acquaintance with its peculiar government and laws. The latter may enable us to comprehend domestic occurrences and revolutions; but without the former, foreign transactions must be altogether mysterious and unintelligible. By attending to this, many dark passages in our history may be placed in a clear light; and where the bulk of historians have seen only the effect, we may be able to discover the cause.

The subversion of the feudal government in France, and its declension in the neighbouring kingdoms, occasioned a remarkable
alteration in the political state of Europe. Kingdoms, which were
inconsiderable when broken, and parcelled out among nobles,
acquired firmness and strength by being united into a regular
monarchy. Kings became conscious of their own power and importance. They meditated schemes of conquest, and engaged in
wars at a distance. Numerous armies were raised, and great taxes
imposed for their subsistence. Considerable bodies of infantry were
kept in constant pay ; that service grew to be honourable : and
cavalry, in which the strength of European armies had hitherto
consisted, though proper enough for the short and voluntary excursions of barons who served at their own expense, were found to be
unfit either for making or defending any important conquest.

It was in Italy that the powerful monarchs of France and Spain
and Germany first appeared to make a trial of their new strength.
The division of that country into many small states, the luxury of
the people, and their effeminate aversion to arms, invited their
more martial neighbours to an easy prey. The Italians, who had
been accustomed to mock battles only, and to decide their interior
quarrels by innocent and bloodless victories, were astonished, when
the French invaded their country, at the sight of real war ; and, as
they could not resist the torrent, they suffered it to take its course,
and to spend its rage. Intrigue and policy supplied the want of
strength. Necessity and self-preservation led that ingenious people
to the great secret of modern politics, by teaching them how to
balance the power of one Prince, by throwing that of another into
the opposite scale. By this happy device, the liberty of Italy was
long preserved. The scales were poised by very skilful hands ; the
smallest variations were attended to, and no Prince was allowed to
retain any superiority that could be dangerous.

A system of conduct, pursued with so much success in Italy, was
not long confined to that country of political refinement. The
maxim of preserving a balance of power is founded so much upon
obvious reasoning, and the situation of Europe rendered it so necessary that it soon became a matter of chief attention to all wise
politicians. Every step any Prince took was observed by all his
neighbours. Ambassadors, a kind of honourable spies, authorized
by the mutual jealousy of Kings, resided almost constantly at every
different court, and had it in charge to watch all his motions.
Dangers were foreseen at a greater distance, and prevented with
more ease. Confederacies were formed to humble any power which
rose above its due proportion. Revenge or self-defence were no
longer the only causes of hostility, it became common to take arms
out of policy ; and war, both in its commencement and in its operations, was more an exercise of the judgment than of the passions of
men. Almost every war in Europe became general, and the most
inconsiderable states acquired importance, because they could add
weight to either scale.

Francis I., who mounted the throne of France in the year 1515,
and Charles V., who obtained the imperial crown in the year 1519,
divided between them the strength and affections of all Europe.

Their perpetual enmity was not owing solely either to personal jealousy, or to the caprice of private passion, but was founded so much in nature and true policy that it subsisted between their posterity for several ages. Charles succeeded to all the dominions of the house of Austria. No family had ever gained so much by wise and fortunate marriages. By acquisitions of this kind, the Austrian Princes rose, in a short time, from obscure Counts of Hapsbourg, to be Archdukes of Austria and Kings of Bohemia, and were in possession of the Imperial dignity by a sort of hereditary right. Besides these territories in Germany, Charles was heir to the crown of Spain, and to all the dominions which belonged to the house of Burgundy. The Burgundian provinces engrossed, at that time, the riches and commerce of one half of Europe; and he drew from them, on many occasions, those immense sums, which no people without trade and liberty are able to contribute. Spain furnished him a gallant and hardy infantry, to whose discipline he was indebted for all his conquests. At the same time, by the discovery of the new world, a vein of wealth was opened to him, which all the extravagance of ambition could not exhaust. These advantages rendered Charles the first Prince in Europe; but he wished to be more, and openly aspired to universal monarchy. His genius was of that kind which ripens slowly, and lies long concealed; but it grew up, without observation, to an unexpected height and vigour. He possessed, in an eminent degree, the characteristic virtues of all the different races of Princes to whom he was allied. In forming his schemes, he discovered all the subtlety and penetration of Ferdinand his grandfather; he pursued them with that obstinate and inflexible perseverance which has ever been peculiar to the Austrian blood; and in executing them he could employ the magnanimity and boldness of his Burgundian ancestors. His abilities were equal to his power; and neither of them would have been inferior to his designs, had not Providence, in pity to mankind, and in order to preserve them from the worst of all evils, Universal Monarchy, raised up Francis I. to defend the liberty of Europe. His dominions were less extensive, but more united than the Emperor's. His subjects were numerous, active, and warlike lovers of glory, and lovers of their King. To Charles, power was the only object of desire, and he pursued it with an unwearied and joyless industry. Francis could mingle pleasure and elegance with his ambition; and, though he neglected some advantages, which a more phlegmatic or more frugal prince would have improved, an active and intrepid courage supplied all his defects, and checked or defeated many of the Emperor's designs.

The rest of Europe observed all the motions of these mighty rivals with a jealous attention. On the one side, the Italians saw the danger which threatened Christendom, and in order to avert it, had recourse to the expedient which they had often employed with success. They endeavoured to divide the power of the two contending monarchs into equal scales, and by the union of several small estates, to counterpoise him whose power became too great. But what they concerted with much wisdom, they were able to execute with little vigour; and intrigue and refinement were feeble fences against the encroachments of military power.

On the other side, Henry VIII. of England held the balance with less delicacy, but with a stronger hand. He was the third Prince of the age in dignity and in power; and the advantageous situation of his dominions, his domestic tranquillity, his immense wealth, and absolute authority, rendered him the natural guardian of the liberty of Europe. Each of the rivals courted him with emulation; he knew it to be his interest to keep the balance even, and to restrain both by not joining entirely with either of them. But he was seldom able to reduce his ideas to practice; he was governed by caprice more than by principle; and the passions of the man were an overmatch for the maxims of the King. Vanity and resentment were the great springs of all his undertakings, and his neighbours easily found the way, by touching these, to force him upon many rash and inconsistent enterprises. His reign was a perpetual series of blunders in politics; and while he esteemed himself the wisest Prince in Europe, he was a constant hope to those who found it necessary, and could submit, to flatter him.

In this situation of Europe, Scotland, which had hitherto wasted her strength in the quarrels between France and England, emerged from her obscurity, took her station in the system, and began to have some influence upon the fate of distant nations. Her assistance was frequently of consequence to the contending parties, and the balance was often so nicely adjusted that it was in her power to make it lean to either side. The part assigned her, at this juncture, was to divert Henry from carrying his arms into the continent. That Prince having routed the French at Guinegat and invested Teronünne, France attempted to divide his forces, by engaging James IV. in that unhappy expedition which ended with his life. For the same reason Francis encouraged and assisted the Duke of Albany to ruin the families of Angus and Home, which were in the interest of England, and would willingly have persuaded the Scots to revenge the death of their King, and to enter into a new war with that kingdom. Henry and Francis having united not long after against the Emperor, it was the interest of both Kings that the Scots should continue inactive; and a long tranquillity was the effect of their union. Charles endeavoured to break this, and to embarrass Henry by another inroad of the Scots. For this end he made great advances to James V., flattering the vanity of the young monarch by electing him a Knight of the Golden Fleece, and by offering him a match in the imperial family; while, in return for these empty honours, he demanded for him to renounce his alliance with France, and to declare war against England. But James, who had much to lose, and who could gain little by closing with the Emperor's proposals, rejected them with decency, and, keeping firm to his ancient allies, left Henry at full liberty to act upon the continent with his whole strength.

Henry himself began his reign by imitating the example of his ancestors with regard to Scotland. He held its power in such extreme contempt that he was at no pains to gain its friendship;

but, on the contrary, he irritated the whole nation, by reviving the antiquated pretensions of the crown of England to the sovereignty over Scotland. But his own experience, and the examples of his enemies, give him a higher idea of its importance. It was impossible to defend an open and extensive frontier against the incursions of an active and martial people. During any war on the continent, this obliged him to divide the strength of his kingdom. It was necessary to maintain a kind of army of observation in the north of England; and, after all precautions, the Scottish borderers, who were superior to all mankind in the practice of irregular war, often made successful inroads, and spread terror and desolation over many counties. He fell, at last, upon the true secret of policy, with respect to Scotland, which his predecessors had too little penetration to discover, or too much pride to employ. The situation of the country, and the bravery of the people, made the conquest of Scotland impossible; but the national poverty, and the violence of faction, rendered it an easy matter to divide and to govern it. He abandoned, therefore, the former design, and resolved to employ his utmost address in executing the latter. It had not yet become honourable for one Prince to receive pay from another, under the more decent name of a subsidy. But, in all ages, the same arguments have been good in courts, and of weight with ministers, factious leaders, and favourites. What were the arguments by which Henry brought over so many to his interest during the minority of James V. we know by the original warrant still extant, for remitting considerable sums into Scotland. By a proper distribution of these, many persons of note were gained to his party; and a faction, which held secret correspondence with England, and received all its directions from thence, appears henceforward in our domestic contests. In the sequel of the history, we shall find Henry labouring to extend his influence in Scotland. His successors adopted the same plan, and improved upon it. The affairs of the two kingdoms became interwoven, and their interests were often the same. Elizabeth divided her attention almost equally between them; and the authority which she inherited in the one was not greater than that which she acquired in the other.

BOOK II.

1542.

MARY, Queen of Scots, the daughter of James V. and Mary of Guise, was born [Dec. 8], a few days before the death of her father. The situation in which he left the kingdom alarmed all ranks of men with the prospect of a turbulent and disastrous reign. A war against England had been undertaken without necessity, and carried on without success. Many persons of the first rank had fallen into the hands of the English, in the unfortunate rout near the firth of Solway, and were still prisoners at London. Among the

rest of the nobles there was little union either in their views
or in their affections; and the religious disputes, occasioned by
the opinions of the Reformers, growing every day more violent,
added to the rage of those factions which are natural to a form of
government nearly aristocratical.

The government of a Queen was unknown in Scotland, and did
not imprint much reverence in the minds of a martial people.
The government of an infant Queen was still more destitute of real
authority; and the prospect of a long and feeble minority invited
to faction by the hope of impunity. James had not even provided
the common remedy against the disorders of a minority, by committing to proper persons the care of his daughter's education,
and the administration of affairs in her name. Though he saw the
clouds gathering, and foretold that they would quickly burst into
a storm, he was so little able to disperse them, or to defend his
daughter and kingdom against the imminent calamities, that, in
mere despair, he abandoned them both to the mercy of fortune,
and left open to every pretender the office of Regent, which he
could not fix to his own satisfaction.

Cardinal Beatoun, who had for many years been considered as
prime minister, was the first that claimed that high dignity; and,
in support of his pretensions, he produced a testament, which he
himself had forged in the name of the late King; and, without
any other right, instantly assumed the title of Regent. He hoped
by the assistance of the clergy, the countenance of France, the connivance of the Queen Dowager, and the support of the whole Popish faction, to hold by force what he had seized on by fraud.
But Beatoun had enjoyed power too long to be a favourite of the
nation. Those among the nobles who wished for a reformation in
religion dreaded his severity, and others considered the elevation
of a churchman to the highest office in the kingdom as a depres-
sion of themselves. At their instigation, James Hamilton, Earl of
Arran, and next heir to the Queen, roused himself from his inactivity, and was prevailed on to aspire to that station to which
proximity of blood gave him a natural title. The nobles, who
were assembled for that purpose, unanimously conferred on him
the office of Regent; and the public voice applauded their choice.

No two men ever differed more widely in disposition and character than the Earl of Arran and Cardinal Beatoun. The Cardinal
was, by natue, of immoderate ambition: by long experience he
had acquired address and refinement; and insolence grew upon
him from continual success. His high station in the chuch placed
him in the way of great civil employments; his abilities were
equal to the greatest of these: nor did he reckon any of them
to be above his merit. As his own eminence was founded upon
the power of the church of Rome, he was a zealous defender of
that superstition, and for the same reason an avowed enemy to the
doctrines of the Reformers. Political motives alone determined
him to support the one or to oppose the other. His early application to public business kept him unacquainted with the learning
and controversies of the age; he gave judgment, however, upon all

points in dispute, with a precipitancy, violence, and rigour, which contemporary historians mention with indignation.

The character of the Earl of Arran was, in almost every thing, the reverse of Beatoun's. He was neither infected with ambition nor inclined to cruelty : the love of ease extinguished the former, the gentleness of his temper preserved him from the latter. Timidity and irresolution were his predominant failings; the one occasioned by his natural constitution, and the other arising from a consciousness that his abilities were not equal to his station. With these dispositions he might have enjoyed and adorned private life : but his public conduct was without courage, or dignity, or consistence; the perpetual slave of his own fears, and, by consequence, the perpetual tool of those who found their advantage in practising upon them. But, as no other person could be set in opposition to the Cardinal, with any probability of success, the nation declared in his favour with such general consent that the artifices of his rival could not withstand its united strength.

The Earl of Arran had scarce taken possession of his new dignity, when a negotiation was opened with England, which gave birth to events of the most fatal consequence to himself and to the kingdom. After the death of James, Henry VIII. was no longer afraid of any interruption from Scotland to his designs against France; and immediately conceived hopes of rendering this security perpetual, by the marriage of Edward his only son with the young Queen of Scots. He communicated his intentions to the prisoners taken at Solway, and prevailed on them to favour it, by the promise of liberty as the reward of their success. In the mean time he permitted them to return into Scotland, that, by their presence in the parliament which the Regent had called, they might be the better able to persuade their countrymen to fall in with his proposals. A cause intrusted to such able and zealous advocates, could not well miss of coming to a happy issue. All those who feared the Cardinal, or who desired a change in religion, were fond of an alliance, which afforded protection to the doctrine which they had embraced, as well as to their own persons, against the rage of that powerful and haughty prelate.

But Henry's rough and impatient temper was incapable of improving this favourable conjuncture. Address and delicacy in managing the fears, and follies, and interests of men, were arts with which he was utterly unacquainted. The designs he had formed upon Scotland were obvious from the marriage which he had proposed, and he had not dexterity enough to disguise or to conceal them. Instead of yielding to the fear or jealousy of the Scots, what time and accident would soon have enabled him to recover, he at once alarmed and irritated the whole nation, by demanding that the Queen's person should be immediately committed to his custody, and that the government of the kingdom should be put into his hands during her minority.

Henry could not have prescribed more ignominious conditions to a conquered people; and it is no wonder they were rejected, with indignation, by men who scorned to purchase an alliance with England at the price of their own liberty. [1543]. The parliament of Scotland, however influenced by the nobles who returned from England; desirous of peace with that kingdom; and delivered, by the Regent's confining the Cardinal as a prisoner, from an opposition to which he might have given rise; consented to a treaty of marriage and union, but upon terms somewhat more equal [March 12]. After some dark and unsuccessful intrigues, by which his ambassador endeavoured to carry off the young Queen and Cardinal Beatoun into England, Henry was obliged to give up his own proposals, and to accept of theirs. On his side he consented that the Queen should continue to reside in Scotland, and himself remain excluded from any share in the government of the kingdom. On the other hand, the Scots agreed to send their Sovereign into England as soon as she attained the full age of ten years, and instantly to deliver six persons of the first rank to be kept as hostages by Henry till the Queen's arrival at his court.

The treaty was still so manifestly of advantage to England that the Regent lost much of the public confidence by consenting to it. The Cardinal, who had now recovered liberty, watched for such an opportunity of regaining credit, and he did not fail to cultivate and improve this to the utmost. He complained loudly that the Regent had betrayed the kingdom to its most inveterate enemies, and sacrificed its honour to his own ambition. He foretold the extinction of the true Catholic religion, under the tyranny of an excommunicated heretic; but, above all, he lamented to see an ancient kingdom consenting to its own servitude, descending into the ignominious station of a dependent province; and, in one hour, the weakness or treachery of a single man surrendering every thing for which the Scottish nation had struggled and fought during so many ages. These remonstrances of the Cardinal were not without effect. They were addressed to prejudices and passions which are deeply rooted in the human heart. The same hatred to the ancient enemies of their country, the same jealousy of national honour, and pride of independence, which, at the beginning of the present century, went near to prevent the Scots from consenting to a union with England, upon terms of great advantage, did, at that time, induce the whole nation to declare against the alliance which had been concluded. In the one period, a hundred and fifty years of peace between the two nations, the habit of being subjected to the same King, and governed by the same maxims, had considerably abated old animosities, and prepared both people for incorporating. In the other, injuries were still fresh, the wounds on both sides were open, and in the warmth of resentment, it was natural to seek revenge, and to be averse from reconcilement. At the union in 1707, the wisdom of Parliament despised the groundless murmurs occasioned by antiquated prejudices: but in 1543, the complaints of the nation were better founded, and urged with a zeal and unanimity, which it is neither just nor safe to disregard. A rash measure of the English Monarch added greatly to the violence of this national animosity. The Scots, relying on the treaty of marriage and union, fitted out several ships for France, with which their trade had been interrupted for some time. These were driven by stress of weather to take refuge in different ports of England; and Henry, under pretext that they were carrying provisions to a kingdom with which he was at war, ordered them to be seized and condemned as lawful prizes. The Scots, astonished at this proceeding of a Prince whose interest it was manifestly at that juncture to court and to sooth them, felt it not only as an injury but as an insult, and expressed all the resentment natural to a high-spirited people. Their rage rose to such a height, that the English ambassador could hardly be protected from it. One spirit seemed now to animate all orders of men. The clergy offered to contribute a great sum towards preserving the church from the dominion of a Prince, whose system of reformation was so fatal to their power. The nobles, after having mortified the Cardinal so lately in such a cruel manner, were now ready to applaud and to second him, as the defender of the honour and liberty of his country.

Argyll, Huntly, Bothwell, and other powerful barons declared openly against the alliance with England. By their assistance, the Cardinal seized on the persons of the young Queen and her mother, and added to his party the splendour and authority of the royal name. He received, at the same time, a more real accession to his strength, by the arrival of Matthew Stewart Earl of Lennox, whose return from France he had earnestly solicited. This young nobleman was the hereditary enemy of the house of Hamilton. He had many claims upon the Regent, and pretended a right to exclude him, not only from succeeding to the crown, but to deprive him of the possession of his private fortune. The Cardinal flattered his vanity with the prospect of marrying the Queen Dowager, and affected to treat him with so much respect that the Regent became jealous of him as a rival in power.

This suspicion was artfully heightened by the Abbot of Paisley, who returned into Scotland some time before the Earl of Lennox, and acted in concert with the Cardinal. He was a natural brother of the Regent, with whom he had great credit; a warm partisan of France, and a zealous defender of the established religion. He took hold of the Regent by the proper handle, and endeavoured to bring about a change in his sentiments by working upon his fears. The desertion of the nobility, the disaffection of the clergy, and the rage of the people; the resentment of France, the power of the Cardinal, and the pretensions of Lennox, were all represented with aggravation, and with their most threatening aspect.

Meanwhile the day appointed for the ratification of the treaty with England, and the delivery of the hostages, approached, and the Regent was still undetermined in his own mind. He acted to the last with that irresolution and inconsistence which is peculiar to weak men when they are so unfortunate as to have the chief part in the conduct of difficult affairs. On the 25th of August he ratified a treaty with Henry, and proclaimed the Cardinal, who still continued to oppose it, an enemy to his country. On the 3d of September he secretly withdrew from Edinburgh, met with the Cardinal at Callendar, renounced the friendship of England, and declared for the interests of France.

Henry, in order to gain the Regent, had not spared the most

magnificent promises. He had offered to give the Princess Elizabeth in marriage to his eldest son, and to constitute him King of that part of Scotland which lies beyond the river Forth. But upon finding his interest in the kingdom to be less considerable than he had imagined, the English Monarch began to treat him with little respect. The young Queen was now in the custody of the enemies, who grew every day more numerous and more popular. They formed a separate court of Stirling, and threatened to elect another Regent. The French King was ready to afford them his protection, and the nation, out of hatred to the English, would have united in their defence. In this situation the Regent could not retain his authority without a sudden change of his measures; and though he endeavoured, by ratifying the treaty, to preserve the appearances of good faith with England, he was obliged to throw himself into the arms of the party which adhered to France.

Soon after this sudden revolution in his political principles, the Regent changed his sentiments concerning religion. The spirit of controversy was then new and warm; books of that kind were eagerly read by men of every rank; the love of novelty, or the conviction of truth, had led the Regent to express great esteem for the writings of the Reformers; and having been powerfully supported by those who had embraced their opinions, he, in order to gratify them, entertained, in his own family, two of the most noted preachers of the Protestant doctrine, and, in his first parliament, consented to an act, by which the laity were permitted to read the scriptures in a language which they understood. Truth needed only a fair hearing to be an overmatch for error. Absurdities, which had long imposed on the ignorance and credulity of mankind, were detected and exposed to public ridicule; and, under the countenance of the Regent, the Reformation made great advances. The Cardinal observed its progress with concern, and was at the utmost pains to obstruct it. He represented to the Regent his great imprudence in giving encouragement to opinions so favourable to Lennox's pretensions; that his own legitimacy depended upon the validity of a sentence of divorce, founded on the Pope's authority; and that, by suffering it to be called in question, he weakened his own title to the succession, and furnished his rival with the only argument by which it could be rendered doubtful.* These insinuations made a deep impression on the Regent's timorous spirit, who, at the prospect of such imaginary danger, was as much startled as the Cardinal could have wished; and his zeal for the Protestant religion was not long proof against his fear. He publicly adjured the doctrine of the Reformers in the Franciscan

---

*The pretensions of the Earl of Lennox to the succession were thus founded. Mary, the daughter of James II., was married to James Lord Hamilton, whom James III. created Earl of Arran on that account. Elizabeth, a daughter of that marriage, was the wife of Matthew Earl of Lennox, and the present Earl was her grandson. The Regent was likewise the grandson of the Princess Mary. But his father having married Janet Beatoun the Regent's mother, after he had obtained a divorce from Elizabeth Home his former wife. Lennox pretended that the sentence of divorce was unjust, and that the Regent, being born while Elizabeth Home, was still alive, ought to be considered as illegitimate. Crawf. Peer. 193.

church at Stirling, and declared not only for the political but the religious opinions of his new confidants.

The Protestant doctrine did not suffer much by his apostasy. It had already taken so deep root in the kingdom that no discouragement or severity could extirpate it. The Regent indeed consented to every thing that the zeal of the Cardinal thought necessary for the preservation of the established religion. The Reformers were persecuted with all the cruelty which superstition inspires into a barbarous people. Many were condemned to that dreadful death which the church has appointed for the punishment of its enemies; but they suffered with a spirit so nearly resembling the patience and fortitude of the primitive martyrs that more were converted than terrified by such spectacles.

The Cardinal, however, was now in possession of every thing his ambition could desire; and exercised all the authority of a Regent, without the envy of the name. He had nothing to fear from the Earl of Arran, who, having by his inconsistency forfeited the public esteem, was contemned by one half the nation, and little trusted by the other. The pretensions of the Earl of Lennox were the only thing which remained to embarrass him. He had very successfully made use of that nobleman to work upon the Regent's jealousy and fear; but as he no longer stood in need of such an instrument, he was willing to get rid of him with decency. Lennox soon began to suspect his intention; promises, flattery, and respect were the only returns he had hitherto received for substantial services: but at last the Cardinal's artifices could no longer be concealed; and Lennox, instead of attaining power and dignity himself, saw that he had been employed only to procure these for another. Resentment and disappointed ambition urged him to seek revenge on that cunning prelate, who, by sacrificing his interest, had so ungenerously purchased the Earl of Arran's friendship. He withdrew, for that reason, from court, and declared for the party at enmity with the Cardinal, which, with open arms, received a convert who added so much lustre to their cause.

The two factions which divided the kingdom were still the same, without any alterations in their views or principles; but, by one of those strange revolutions which were frequent in that age, they had in the course of a few weeks changed their leaders. The Regent was at the head of the partisans of France and the defenders of popery, and Lennox in the same station with the advocates for the English alliance and a reformation in religion. The one laboured to pull down his own work, which the other upheld with the same hand that had hitherto endeavoured to destroy it.

Lennox's impatience for revenge got the start of the Cardinal's activity. He surprised both him and the Regent by a sudden march to Edinburgh with a numerous army; and might easily have crushed them before they could prepare for their defence. But he was weak enough to listen to proposals for an accommodation; and the Cardinal amused him so artfully, and spun out the treaty to such a length, that the greater part of the Earl's troops, who served, as is usual wherever the feudal institutions prevailed, at their own expense, deserted him; and in concluding a peace, instead of giving the law, he was obliged to receive it. A second attempt to retrieve his affairs ended yet more unfortunately. One body of his troops was cut to pieces, and the rest dispensed; and with the poor remains of a ruined party, he must either have submitted to the conqueror, or have fled out of the kingdom, if the approach of an English army had not brought him a short relief.

Henry was not of a temper to bear tamely the indignity with which he had been treated, both by the Regent and Parliament of Scotland, who, at the time when they renounced their alliance with him, had entered into a new and stricter confederacy with France. The rigour of the season retarded for some time the execution of his vengeance. But, in the spring [1544], a considerable body of infantry, which was destined for France, received orders to sail for Scotland, and a proper number of cavalry was appointed to join it by land. The Regent and Cardinal little expected such a visit. They had trusted that the French war would find employment for all Henry's forces, and, from an unaccountable security, were wholly unprovided for the defence of the kingdom. The Earl of Hertford, a leader fatal to the Scots in that age, commanded this army, and landed it, without opposition, a few miles from Leith. He was quickly master of that place [May 3]; and, marching directly to Edinburgh, entered it with the same ease. After plundering the adjacent country, the richest and most open in Scotland, he set on fire both these towns, and, upon the approach of some troops gathered together by the Regent, put his booty on board the fleet, and with his land forces retired safely to the English borders; delivering the kingdom in a few days from the terror of an invasion, concerted with little policy, carried on at great expense, and attended with no advantage. If Henry aimed at the conquest of Scotland, he gained nothing by this expedition; if the marriage he had proposed was still in his view, he lost a great deal. Such a rough courtship, as the Earl of Huntly humorously called it, disgusted the whole nation; their aversion for the match grew into abhorrence; and, exasperated by so many indignities, the Scots were never at any period more attached to France, or more alienated from England.

The Earl of Lennox alone, in spite of the Regent and French King, continued a correspondence with England, which ruined his own interest, without promoting Henry's. Many of his own vassals, preferring their duty to their country before their affection to him, refused to concur in any design to favour the public enemy. After a few feeble and unsuccessful attempts to disturb the Regent's administration, he was obliged to fly for safety to the court of England, where Henry rewarded services which he had the inclination but not the power to perform, by giving him in marriage his niece the Lady Margaret Douglas. This unhappy exile, however, was destined to be the father of a race of Kings. He saw his son Lord Darnley mount the throne of Scotland, to the perpetual exclusion of that rival who now triumphed in his ruin. From that time his posterity have held the sceptre in two kingdoms, by one of which he was cast out as a criminal, and by the other received as a fugitive.

Meanwhile hostilities were continued by both nations, but with little vigour on either side. The historians of that age relate minutely the circumstances of several skirmishes and inroads, which, as they did not produce any considerable effect, at this distance of time deserve no remembrance. At last an end was put to this languid and inactive war, by a peace, in which England, France, and Scotland were comprehended. Henry laboured to exclude the Scots from the benefit of this treaty, and to reserve them for that vengeance which his attention to the affairs of the continent had hitherto delayed. But although a peace with England was of the last consequence to Francis I., whom the Emperor was preparing to attack with all his forces, he was too generous to abandon allies who had served him with fidelity, and he chose rather to purchase Henry's friendship with disadvantage to himself than to leave them exposed to danger. By yielding some things to the interest, and more to the vanity of that haughty Prince; by sub ission, flattery, and address, he at length prevailed to have the Scots included in the peace agreed upon.

An event which happened a short time before the conclusion of this peace rendered it more acceptable to the whole nation. Cardinal Beatoun had not used his power with moderation equal to the prudence by which he attained it. Notwithstanding his great abilities, he had too many of the passions and prejudices of an angry leader of a faction to govern a divided people with temper. His resentment against one party of the nobility, his insolence towards the rest, his severity to the Reformers, and, above all, the barbarous and illegal execution of the famous George Wishart, a man of honourable birth and of primitive sanctity, wore out the patience of a fierce age; and nothing but a bold hand was wanting to gratify the public wish by his destruction. Private revenge inflamed and sanctified by a false zeal for religion, quickly supplied this want. Norman Lesly, the eldest son of the Earl of Rothes, had been treated by the Cardinal with injustice and contempt. It was not the temper of the man, or the spirit of the times, quietly to digest an affront. As the profession of his adversary screened him from the effects of what is called an honourable resentment, he resolved to take that satisfaction which he could not demand. This resolution deserves as much censure as the singular courage and conduct with which he put it in execution excite wonder. St. Andrew's, which he had fortified at great expense, and, in the opinion of the age, had rendered it impregnable. His retinue was numerous, the town at his devotion, and the neighbouring country full of his dependents. In this situation sixteen persons undertook to surprise his castle, and to assassinate himself: and their success was equal to the boldness of the attempt. [May 20, 1546.] Early in the morning they seized on the gate of the castle, which was set open to the workmen who were employed in finishing the fortifications; and having placed sentries at the door of the Cardinal's apartment, they awakened his numerous domestics one by one; and turning them out of the castle, they without noise or tumult, or violence to any other person, delivered their country, though by a most unjustifiable action, from an ambitious man whose pride was insupportable to the nobles, as his cruelty and cunning were great checks to the Reformation.

His death was fatal to the Catholic religion, and to the French interest in Scotland. The same zeal for both continued among a great party in the nation, but, when deprived of the genius and authority of so skilful a leader, operated with less effect. Nothing can equal the consternation which a blow so unexpected occasioned among such as were attached to him; while the Regent secretly enjoyed an event which removed out of his way a rival, who had not only eclipsed his greatness, but almost extinguished his power. Decency, however, the honour of the church, the importunity of the Queen Dowager and her adherents, his engagements with France, and, above all these, the desire of recovering his eldest son, whom the Cardinal had detained for some time at St. Andrew's in pledge of his fidelity, and who, together with the castle, had fallen into the hands of the conspirators, induced him to take arms in order to revenge the death of a man whom he hated.

He threatened vengeance, but was unable to execute it. One part of military science, the art of attacking fortified places, was then imperfectly understood in Scotland. The weapons, the discipline, and impetuosity of the Scots, rendered their armies as unfit for sieges as they were active in the field. A hundred and fifty men, which was the greatest number the conspirators ever assembled, resisted all the efforts of the Regent for five months, in a place which a single battalion, with a few battering cannon, would now reduce in a few hours. This tedious siege was concluded by a truce. The Regent undertook to procure for the conspirators an absolution from the Pope, and a pardon in parliament; and upon obtaining these, they engaged to surrender the castle, and to set his son at liberty.

It is probable, that neither of them was sincere in this treaty. On both sides they sought only to amuse, and to gain time. The Regent had applied to France for assistance, and expected soon to have the conspirators at mercy. On the other hand, if Lesly and his associates were not at first incited by Henry to murder the Cardinal, they were in the sequel powerfully supported by him. Notwithstanding the silence of contemporary historians, there are violent presumptions of the former; of the latter there is undoubted certainty. During the siege, the conspirators had received from England supplies both of money and provisions; and as Henry was preparing to renew his proposals concerning the marriage and the union he had projected, and to second his negotiations with a numerous army, they hoped, by concurring with him, to be in a situation in which they would no longer need a pardon, but might claim a reward.

Jan. 28, 1547.] The death of Henry blasted all these hopes. It happened in the beginning of next year, after a reign of greater splendour than true glory; bustling, rather than active; oppressive in domestic government, and in foreign politics wild and irregular. But the vices of this Prince were more beneficial to mankind than the virtues of others. His rapaciousness, his profusion, and even his tyranny, by depressing the ancient nobility, and by adding new

property and power to the Commons, laid or strengthened the
foundations of the English liberty. His other passions contributed
no less towards the downfal of popery, and the establishment of
religious freedom in the nation. His resentment led him to abolish
the power, and his covetousness to seize the wealth, of the church ;
and, by withdrawing these supports, made it easy, in the following
reign, to overturn the whole fabric of superstition.

Francis I. did not long survive a Prince who had been alternately
his rival and his friend; but his successor Henry II. was not neglectful of the French interest in Scotland. He sent a considerable
body of men, under the command of Leon Strozzi, to the Regent's
assistance. By their long experience in the Italian and German
wars, the French had become as dexterous in the conduct of sieges
as the Scots were ignorant ; and as the boldness and despair of the
conspirators could not defend them against the superior art of these
new assailants, they, after a short resistance, surrendered to Strozzi,
who engaged, in the name of the King his master, for the security
of their lives ; and, as his prisoners, transported them into France.
The castle itself, the monument of Beatoun's power and vanity,
was demolished, in obedience to the canon law, which, with admirable policy, denounces its anathemas even against the houses in
which the sacred blood of a Cardinal happens to be shed, and
ordains them to be laid in ruins.

The archbishopric of St. Andrew's was bestowed by the Regent
upon his natural brother John Hamilton, Abbot of Paisley.

The delay of a few weeks would have saved the conspirators.
Those ministers of Henry VIII. who had the chief direction of
affairs during the minority of his son Edward VI. conducted themselves, with regard to Scotland, by the maxims of their late master,
and resolved to frighten the Scots into a treaty which they had
not abilities or address to bring about by any other method.

But before we proceed to relate the events which their invasion
of Scotland occasioned, we shall stop to take notice of a circumstance unobserved by contemporary historians, but extremely
remarkable for the discovery it makes of the sentiments and spirit
which then prevailed among the Scots. The conspirators against
Cardinal Beatoun found the Regent's eldest son in the castle of St.
Andrew's; and as they needed the protection of the English, it was
to be feared that they might endeavour to purchase it, by delivering to them this important prize. The presumptive heir to the
crown in the hands of the avowed enemies of the kingdom was a
dreadful prospect. In order to avoid it, the Parliament fell upon
a very extraordinary expedient. By an act made on purpose, they
excluded "the Regent's eldest son from all right of succession,
public or private, so long as he should be detained a prisoner, and
substituted in his place his other brothers, according to their
seniority, and in failure of them, those who were next heirs to the
Regent." Succession by hereditary right is an idea so obvious and
so popular, that a nation seldom ventures to make a breach in it,
but in cases of extreme necessity. Such a necessity did the Parliament discover in the present situation. Hatred to England, founded

D

on the memory of past hostilities, and heightened by the smart of recent injuries, was the national passion. This dictated that uncommon statute, by which the order of lineal succession was so remarkably broken. The modern theories, which represent this right as divine and unalienable, and that ought not to be violated upon any consideration whatsoever, seem to have been then altogether unknown.

In the beginning of September, the Earl of Hertford, now Duke of Somerset, and Protector of England, entered Scotland at the head of eighteen thousand men ; and, at the same time, a fleet of sixty ships appeared on the coast to second his land forces. The Scots had for some time observed this storm gathering, and were prepared for it. Their army was almost double to that of the enemy, and posted to the greatest advantage on a rising ground above Mussleburgh, not far from the banks of the river Eske. Both these circumstances alarmed the Duke of Somerset, who saw his danger, and would willingly have extricated himself out of it, by a new overture of peace, on conditions extremely reasonable. But this moderation being imputed to fear, his proposals were rejected with the scorn which the confidence of success inspires ; and if the conduct of the Regent, who commanded the Scottish army, had been, in any degree, equal to his confidence, the destruction of the English must have been inevitable. They were in a situation precisely similar to that of their countrymen under Oliver Cromwell in the following century. The Scots had chosen their ground so well that it was impossible to force them to give battle ; a few days had exhausted the forage and provision of a narrow country ; the fleet could only furnish a scanty and precarious subsistence : a retreat, therefore, was necessary : but disgrace, and perhaps ruin, were the consequences of retreating.

On both these occasions, the national heat and impetuosity of the Scots saved the English, and precipitated their own country into the utmost danger. The undisciplined courage of the private men became impatient at the sight of the enemy. The General was afraid of nothing, but that the English might escape from him by flight; and [Sept. 10], leaving his strong camp, he attacked the Duke of Somerset near Pinkey, with no better success than his rashness deserved. The Protector had drawn up his troops on a gentle eminence, and had now the advantage of ground on his side. The Scottish army consisted almost entirely of infantry, whose chief weapon was a long spear, and for that reason their files were very deep, and their ranks close. They advanced towards the enemy in three great bodies, and, as they passed the river, were considerably exposed to the fire of the English fleet, which lay in the bay of Mussleburgh, and had drawn near the shore. The English cavalry, flushed with an advantage which they had gained in a skirmish some days before, began the attack with more impetuosity than good conduct. A body so firm and compact as the Scots easily resisted the impression of cavalry, broke them, and drove them off the field. The English infantry, however, advanced ; and the Scots were at once exposed to a flight of arrows, to a fire in flank from four hundred fusileers, who served the enemy, and to their cannon, which were planted behind the infantry on the highest part of the eminence. The depth and closeness of their order making it impossible for the Scots to stand long in this situation, the Earl of Angus, who commanded the vanguard, endeavoured to change his ground, and to retire towards the main body. But his friends unhappily, mistook his motion for a flight, and fell into confusion. At that very instant the broken cavalry, having rallied, returned to the charge; the foot pursued the advantage they had gained; the prospect of victory redoubled the ardour of both; and, in a moment, the rout of the Scottish army became universal and irretrievable. The encounter in the field was not long or bloody; but, in the pursuit, the English discovered all the rage and fierceness which national antipathy, kindled by long emulation and inflamed by reciprocal injuries, is apt to inspire. The pursuit was continued for five hours, and to a great distance. All the three roads by which the Scots fled, were strewed with spears, and swords, and targets, and covered with the bodies of the slain. Above ten thousand men fell on this day, one of the most fatal Scotland had ever seen. A few were taken prisoners, and among these some persons of distinction. The Protector had it now in his power to become master of a kingdom, out of which, not many hours before, he was almost obliged to retire with infamy.

But this victory, however great, was of no real utility, for want of skill or of leisure to improve it. Every new injury rendered the Scots more averse from a union with England; and the Protector neglected the only measure which would have made it necessary for them to have given their consent to it. He amused himself in wasting the open country, and in taking or building several petty castles; whereas, by fortifying a few places which were accessible by sea, he would have laid the kingdom open to the English, and in a short time the Scots must either have accepted of his terms, or have submitted to his power. By such an improvement of it, the victory at Dunbar gave Cromwell the command of Scotland. The battle of Pinkey had no other effect but to precipitate the Scots into new engagements with France. The situation of the English court may, indeed, be pleaded in excuse for the Duke of Somerset's conduct. That cabal of his enemies, which occasioned his tragical end, was already formed; and while he triumphed in Scotland, they secretly undermined his power and credit at home. Self-preservation, therefore, obliged him to prefer his safety before his fame, and to return without reaping the fruits of his victory. At this time, however, the cloud blew over; the conspiracy by which he fell was not ripe for execution; and his presence suspended its effects for some time. The supreme power still remaining in his hands, he employed it to recover the opportunity which he had lost. [April, 1584]. A body of troops, by his command, seized and fortified Haddingtoun, a place which, on account of its distance from the sea, and from any English garrison, could not be defended without great expense and danger.

Meanwhile the French gained more by the defeat of their allies than the English by their victory. After the death of Cardinal Beatoun, Mary of Guise, the Queen Dowager, took a considerable share in the direction of affairs. She was warmly attached by blood and by inclination, to the French interest; and, in order to promote it, improved with great dexterity every event which occurred. The spirit and strength of the Scots were broken at Pinkey; and in an assembly of nobles which met at Stirling to consult upon the situation of the kingdom, all eyes were turned towards France, no prospect of safety appearing but in assistance from that quarter. But Henry II. being then at peace with England, the Queen represented that they could not expect him to take a part in their quarrel, but upon views of personal advantage; and that, without extraordinary concessions in his favour, no assistance, in proportion to their present exigencies, could be obtained. The prejudices of the nation powerfully seconded these representations of the Queen. What often happens to individuals took place among the nobles in this convention; they were swayed entirely by their passions; and in order to gratify them, they deserted their former principles, and disregarded their true interest. In the violence of resentment, they forgot their zeal for the independence of Scotland, which had prompted them to reject the proposals of Henry VIII.; and, by offering, voluntarily, their young Queen in marriage to the Dauphin, eldest son of Henry II.; and, which was still more, by proposing to send her immediately into France to be educated at his court, they granted, from a thirst of vengeance, what formerly they would not yield upon any consideration of their own safety. To gain at once such a kingdom as Scotland was a matter of no small consequence to France. Henry, without hesitation, accepted the offers of the Scottish ambassadors, and prepared for the vigorous defence of his new acquisition. Six thousand veteran soldiers, under the command of Monsieur Dessé, assisted by some of the best officers who were formed in the long wars of Francis I., arrived at Leith. They served two campaigns in Scotland, with a spirit equal to their former fame. But their exploits were not considerable. The Scots, soon becoming jealous of their designs, neglected to support them with proper vigour. The caution of the English, in acting wholly upon the defensive, prevented the French from attempting any enterprise of consequence; and obliged them to exhaust their strength in tedious sieges, undertaken under many disadvantages. Their efforts, however, were not without some benefit to the Scots, by compelling the English to evacuate Haddingtoun, and to surrender several small forts which they possessed in different parts of the kingdom.

But the effects of these operations of his troops were still of greater importance to the French king. The diversion which they occasioned enabled him to wrest Boulogne out of the hands of the English; and the influence of his army in Scotland obtained the concurrence of parliament with the overtures which had been made to him, by the assembly of nobles at Stirling, concerning the Queen's marriage with the Dauphin, and her education in the court of France. In vain did a few patriots remonstrate against such extravagant concessions, by which Scotland was reduced to be a province of France; and Henry, from an ally, raised to be master of the kingdom; by which the friendship of France became more fatal than the enmity of England; and every thing was fondly given up to the one, that had been bravely defended against the other. A point of so much consequence was hastily decided in a parliament assembled [June 5] in the camp before Haddingtoun; the intrigues of the Queen Dowager, the zeal of the clergy, and resentment against England, had prepared a great party in the nation for such a step; the French general and ambassador, by their liberality and promises, gained over many more. The Regent himself was weak enough to stoop to the offer of a pension from France, together with the title of Duke Chatelherault in that kingdom. A considerable majority declared for the treaty, and the interest of a faction was preferred before the honour of the nation.

Having hurried the Scots into this rash and fatal resolution, the source of many calamities to themselves and to their sovereign, the French allowed them no time for reflection or repentance. The fleet which had brought over their forces was still in Scotland, and without delay conveyed the Queen to France. Mary was then six years old, and by her education in that court, one of the politest but most corrupted in Europe, she acquired every accomplishment that could add to her charms as a woman, and contracted many of those prejudices which occasioned her misfortunes as a Queen.

From the time that Mary was put into their hands, it was the interest of the French to suffer war in Scotland to languish. The recovery of the Boulonnois was the object which the French king had most at heart; but a slight diversion in Britain was sufficient to divide the attention and strength of the English, whose domestic factions deprived both their arms and councils of their accustomed vigour. The government of England had undergone a great revolution. The Duke of Somerset's power had been acquired with too much violence, and was exercised with too little moderation to be of long continuance. Many good qualities, added to great love of his country, could not atone for his ambition in usurping the sole direction of affairs. Some of the most eminent courtiers combined against him; and the Earl of Warick their leader, no less ambitious but more artful than Somerset, conducted his measures with so much dexterity as to raise himself upon the ruins of his rival. Without the invidious name of Protector, he succeeded to all the power and influence of which Somerset was deprived, and he quickly found peace to be necessary for the establishment of his new authority, and the execution of the vast designs he had conceived.

Henry was no stranger to Warwick's situation, and improved his knowledge of it to good purpose, in conducting the negotiations for a general peace. He prescribed what terms he pleased to the English minister, who scrupled at nothing, however advantageous to that monarch and his allies. [March 24, 1550], England consented to restore Boulogne and its dependencies to France, and give up all pretensions to a treaty of marriage with the Queen of Scots, or to the conquest of her country. A few small forts, of which the English troops had hitherto kept possession, were razed; and peace between the two kingdoms was established on its ancient foundation.

Both the British nations lost power, as well as reputation, by this unhappy quarrel. It was on both sides a war of emulation and resentment, rather than of interest; and was carried on under the influence of national animosities, which were blind to all advantages. The French, who entered into it with greater coolness, conducted it with more skill; and, by dexterously availing themselves of every circumstance which occurred, recovered possession of an important territory which they had lost, and added to their monarchy a new kingdom. The ambition of the English minister betrayed to them the former; the inconsiderate rage of the Scots against their ancient enemies bestowed on them the latter; their own address and good policy merited both.

Immediately after the conclusion of the peace the French forces left Scotland, as much to their own satisfaction as to that of the nation. The Scots soon found that the calling to their assistance a people more powerful than themselves was a dangerous expedient. They beheld, with the utmost impatience, those who had come over to protect the kingdom taking upon them to command in it; and on many occasions they repented the rash invitation which they had given. The peculiar genius of the French nation heightened this disgust, and prepared the Scots to throw off the yoke, before they had well begun to feel it. The French were in that age, what they are in the present, one of the most polished nations in Europe. But it is to be observed, in all their expeditions into foreign countries, whether towards the south or north, that their manners have been remarkably incompatible with the manners of every other people. Barbarians are tenacious of their own customs, because they want knowledge and taste to discover the reasonableness and propriety of customs which differ from them, Nations which hold the first rank in politeness are frequently no less tenacious out of pride. The Greeks were so in the ancient world; and the French are the same in the modern. Full of themselves; flattered by the imitation of their neighbours; and accustomed to consider their own modes as the standard of elegance; they scorn to disguise, or to lay aside, the distinguishing manners of their own nation, or to make any allowance for what may differ from them among others. For this reason the behaviour of their armies has, on every occasion, been insupportable to strangers, and has always exposed them to hatred, and often to destruction. In that age they overran Italy four several times by their valour, and lost it as often by their insolence. The Scots, naturally an irascible and high spirited people, and who, of all nations, can least bear the most distant insinuation of contempt, were not of a temper to admit all the pretensions of such assuming guests. The symptoms of alienation were soon visible; they seconded the military operations of the French troops with the utmost coldness; their disgust grew insensibly to a degree of indignation that could hardly be restrained; and on occasion of a very slight accident, broke out with fatal violence. A private French soldier engaging in an idle quarrel with a citizen of Edinburgh, both nations took arms with equal rage, in defence of their countrymen. The Provost of Edinburgh, his son, and several citizens of distinction were killed in the fray; and the French were obliged to avoid the fury of the inhabitants by retiring out of the city. Notwithstanding the ancient alliance of France and Scotland, and the long intercourse of good offices between the two nations, an aversion for the French took its rise at this time among the Scots, the effects whereof were deeply felt, and operated powerfully through the subsequent period.

From the death of Cardinal Beatoun, nothing has been said of the state of religion. While the war with England continued, the clergy had no leisure to molest the Protestants; and they were not yet considerable enough to expect any thing more than connivance and impunity. The new doctrines were still in their infancy; but during this short interval of tranquillity they acquired strength, and advanced by large and firm steps towards a full establishment in the kingdom. The first preachers against Popery in Scotland, of whom several had appeared during the reign of James V., were more eminent for zeal and piety than for learning. Their acquaintance with the principles of the Reformation was partial, and at second hand; some of them had been educated in England; all of them had borrowed their notions from the books published there: and the first dawn of the new light, they did not venture far before their leaders. But in a short time the doctrines and writings of the foreign reformers became generally known; the inquisitive genius of the age pressed forward in quest of truth; the discovery of one error opened the way to others; the downfall of one impostor drew many after it; the whole fabric, which ignorance and superstition had erected in times of darkness, began to totter; and nothing was wanting to complete its ruin, but a daring and active leader to direct the attack. Such was the famous John Knox, who with better qualifications of learning, and more extensive views than any of his predecessors in Scotland, possessed a natural intrepidity of mind, which set him above fear. He began his public ministry at St. Andrew's in the year 1547, with that success which always accompanies a bold and popular eloquence. Instead of amusing himself with lopping the branches, he struck directly at the root of Popery, and attacked both the doctrine and discipline of the established church with a vehemence peculiar to himself, but admirably suited to the temper and wishes of the age.

An adversary so formidable as Knox would not have easily escaped the rage of the clergy, who observed the tendency and progress of his opinions with the utmost concern. But, at first he retired for safety into the Castle of St. Andrew's, and, while the conspirators kept possession of it, preached publicly under their protection. The great revolution in England, which followed upon the death of Henry VIII. contributed no less than the zeal of Knox towards demolishing the Popish church in Scotland. Henry had loosened the chains and lightened the yoke of Popery. The ministers of his son Edward VI. cast them off altogether, and established the Protestant religion upon almost the same footing whereon it now stands in that kingdom. The influence of this example reached Scotland, and the happy effects of ecclesiastical liberty in one nation inspired the other with an equal desire of recovering it. The reformers had, hitherto, been obliged to conduct themselves with the utmost caution, and seldom ventured to preach, but in private houses, and at a distance from court; they gained credit, as happens on the first publication of every new religion, chiefly among persons in the lower and middle rank of life.   But several noblemen, of the greatest distinction, having, about this time, openly espoused their principles, they were no longer under the necessity of acting with the same reserve; and, with more security and encouragement, they had likewise greater success.—The means of acquiring and spreading knowledge became more common, and the spirit of innovation, peculiar to that period, grew every day bolder and more universal.

Happily for the Reformation this spirit was still under some restraint.   It had not yet attained firmness and vigour sufficient to overturn a system founded on the deepest policy, and supported by the most formidable power.   Under the present circumstances, any attempt towards action must have been fatal to the Protestant doctrines; and it is no small proof of the authority as well as penetration of the heads of the party, that they were able to restrain the zeal of a fiery and impetuous people, until that critical and mature juncture when every step they took was decisive and successful.

Meanwhile their cause received reinforcement from two different quarters whence they never could have expected it.   The ambition of the house of Guise, and the bigotry of Mary of England, hastened the subversion of the Papal throne in Scotland; and, by a singular disposition of Providence, the persons who opposed the Reformation in every other part of Europe with the fiercest zeal were made instruments for advancing it in that kingdom.

Mary of Guise possessed the same bold and aspiring spirit which distinguished her family.   But in her it was softened by the female character, and accompanied with great temper and address.   Her brothers, in order to attain the high objects at which they aimed, ventured upon such daring measures as suited their great courage. Her designs upon the supreme power were concealed with the utmost care, and advanced by address and refinements more natural to her sex.   By a dexterous application of those talents, she had acquired a considerable influence on the councils of a nation hitherto unacquainted with the government of women; and, without the smallest right to any share in the administration of affairs, had engrossed the chief direction of them into her own hands.   But she did not long rest satisfied with the enjoyment of this precarious power, which the fickleness of the Regent, or the ambition of those who governed him, might so easily disturb; and she began to set on foot new intrigues, with a design of undermining him, and of opening to herself a way to succeed him in that high dignity.   Her brothers entered warmly into this scheme, and supported it with all their credit at the court of France.   The French King willingly concurred in a measure, by which he hoped to bring Scotland entirely under management, and, in any future broil with England, to turn its whole force against that kingdom.

In order to arrive at the desired elevation, the Queen Dowager had only one of two ways to choose; either violently to wrest the power out of the hands of the Regent, or to obtain it by his consent.

Under a minority, and among a warlike and factious people, the former was a very uncertain and dangerous experiment. The latter appeared to be no less impracticable. To persuade a man voluntarily to abdicate the supreme power; to descend to a level with those above whom he was raised; and to be content with the second place where he hath held a first, may well pass for a wild and chimerical project. This, however, the Queen attempted; and the prudence of the attempt was sufficiently justified by its success.

The Regent's inconstancy and irresolution, together with the calamities which had befallen the kingdom under his administration, raised the prejudices both of the nobles and of the people against him to a great height: and the Queen secretly fomented these with much industry. All who wished for a change met with a gracious reception in her court, and their spirit of disaffection was nourished by such hopes and promises as in every age impose on the credulity of the factious. The favourers of the Reformation being the most numerous and spreading body of the Regent's enemies, she applied to them with a particular attention; and the gentleness of her disposition, and seeming indifference to the religious points in dispute, made all her promises of protection and indulgence pass upon them for sincere. Finding so great a part of the nation willing to fall in with her measures [Oct.], the Queen set out for France, under pretence of visiting her daughter, and took along with her those noblemen who possessed the greatest power and credit among their countrymen. Softened by the pleasures of an elegant court, flattered by the civilities of the French King and the caresses of the house of Guise, and influenced by the seasonable distribution of a few favours, and the liberal promise of many more, they were brought to approve of all the Queen's pretensions.

While she advanced by these slow but sure steps, the Regent either did not foresee the danger which threatened him, or neglected to provide against it. The first discovery of the train which was laid came from two of his own confidants, Carnegie of Kinnaird, and Panter Bishop of Ross, whom the Queen had gained over to her interest, and then employed as the most proper instruments for obtaining his consent. The overture was made to him in the name of the French King, enforced by proper threatenings, in order to work upon his natural timidity, and sweetened by every promise that could reconcile him to a proposal so disagreeable. On the one hand, the confirmation of his French title, together with a considerable pension, the parliamentary acknowledgment of his right of succession to the crown, and a public ratification of his conduct during his regency, were offered him. On the other hand, the displeasure of the French King, the power and popularity of the Queen Dowager, the disaffection of the nobles, with the danger of an after reckoning, were represented in the strongest colours.

It was not possible to agree to a proposal so extraordinary and unexpected, without some previous struggle; and, had the Archbishop of St. Andrew's been present to fortify the irresolute and passive spirit of the Regent, he, in all probability, would have rejected it with disdain. Happily for the Queen, the sagacity and ambition of that prelate could, at this time, be no obstruction to her views. He was lying at the point of death, and in his absence the influence of the Queen's agents on a flexible temper counterbalanced several of the strongest passions of the human mind, and obtained his consent to a voluntary surrender of the supreme power.

Dec. 1551.] After gaining a point of such difficulty with so much ease, the Queen returned into Scotland, in full expectation of taking immediate possession of her new dignity. But by this time the Archbishop of St. Andrew's had recovered of that distemper which the ignorance of the Scottish physicians had pronounced to be incurable. This he owed to the assistance of the famous Cardan, one of those irregular adventurers in philosophy, of whom Italy produced so many about this period. A bold genius led him to some useful discoveries, which merit the esteem of a more discerning age; a wild imagination engaged him in those chimerical sciences which drew the admiration of his contemporaries. As a pretender to astrology and magic, he was revered and consulted by all Europe; as a proficient in natural philosophy, he was but little known. The Archbishop, it is probable, considered him as a powerful magician, when he applied to him for relief; but it was his knowledge as a philosopher, which enabled him to cure his disease.

Together with his health, the Archbishop recovered the entire government of the Regent, and quickly persuaded him to recal that dishonourable promise which he had been seduced by the artifices of the Queen to grant. However great her surprise and indignation were, at this fresh instance of his inconstancy, she was obliged to dissemble, that she might have leisure to renew her intrigues with all parties; with the Protestants, whom she favoured and courted more than ever; with the nobles, to whom she rendered herself agreeable by various arts; and with the Regent himself, in order to gain whom she employed every argument. But, whatever impressions her emissaries might have made on the Regent, it was no easy matter to over-reach or to intimidate the Archbishop. Under his management the negotiations were spun out to a great length, and his brother maintained his station with that address and firmness which its importance so well merited. The universal defection of the nobility, the growing power of the Protestants, who all adhered to the Queen Dowager, the reiterated solicitations of the French King, and, above all, the interposition of the young Queen, who was now entering the twelfth year of her age, and claimed a right of nominating whom she pleased to be Regent, obliged him at last to resign that high office, which he had held many years. He obtained, however, the same advantageous terms for himself, which had been formerly stipulated.

It was in the parliament which met on the 12th of April, 1554, that the Earl of Arran executed this extraordinary resignation; and at the same time Mary of Guise was raised to that dignity, which had been so long the object of her wishes. Thus, with their own approbation, a woman and a stranger was advanced to the supreme authority over a fierce and turbulent people, who seldom submitted, without reluctance, to the legal and ancient government of their native monarchs.

1553.] While the Queen Dowager of Scotland contributed so much towards the progress of the Reformation by the protection which she afforded it, from motives of ambition, the Englis Queen by her indiscreet zeal, filled the kingdom with persons active in promoting the same cause. Mary ascended the throne of England on the death of her brother Edward [July 6], and soon after married Philip II. of Spain. To the persecuting spirit of the Romish superstition, and the fierceness of that age, she added the private resentment of her own and of her mother's sufferings, with which she loaded the reformed religion ; and the peevishness and severity of her natural temper carried the acrimony of all these passions to the utmost extreme. The cruelty of her persecution equalled the deeds of those tyrants who have been the greatest reproach to human nature. The bigotry of her clergy could scarce keep pace with the impetuosity of her zeal. Even the unrelenting Philip was obliged, on some occasions, to mitigate the rigour of her proceedings. Many among the most eminent Reformers suffered for the doctrines which they had taught ; others fled from the storm. To the greater part of these Switzerland and Germany opened a secure asylum ; and not a few, out of choice or necessity, fled into Scotland. What they had seen and felt in England did not abate the warmth and zeal of their indignation against Popery. Their attacks were bolder and more successful than ever ; and their doctrines made a rapid progress among all ranks of men.

These doctrines, calculated to rectify the opinions and to reform the manners of mankind, had hitherto produced no other effects ; but they soon began to operate with greater violence, and proved the occasion, not only of subverting the established religion, but of shaking the throne and endangering the kingdom. The causes which facilitated the introduction of these new opinion into Scotland, and which disseminated them so fast through the nation, merit, on that account, a particular and careful inquiry. The Re, formation is one of the greatest events in the history of mankind and, in whatever point of light we view it, it is instructive and interesting.

The revival of learning in the fifteenth and sixteenth centuries roused the world from that lethargy in which it had been sunk for many ages. The human mind felt its own strength, broke the fetters of authority by which it had been so long restrained, and, venturing to move in a larger sphere, pushed its inquiries into every subject with great boldness and surprising success.

No sooner did mankind recover the capacity of exercising their reason than religion was one of the first objects which drew their attention. Long before Luther published his famous Theses, which shook the Papal throne, science and philosophy had laid open to many of the Italians the imposture and absurdity of the established superstition. That subtle and refined people, satisfied with enjoying those discoveries in secret, were little disposed to assume the dangerous character of Reformers, and concluded the knowledge of truth to be the prerogative of the wise, while vulgar minds must be overawed and governed by popular errors. But, animated with a more noble and disinterested zeal, the German theologian boldly erected the standard of truth, and upheld it with an unconquerable intrepidity, which merits the admiration and gratitude of all succeeding ages.

The occasion of Luther's being first disgusted with the tenets of the Romish church, and how, from a small rapture, the quarrel widened into an irreparable breach, is known to every one who has been the least conversant in history. From the heart of Germany his opinions spread, with astonishing rapidity, all over Europe; and, wherever they came, endangered or overturned the ancient but ill founded system. The vigilance and address of the court of Rome, co-operating with the power and bigotry of the Austrian family, suppressed these notions on their first appearance in the southern kingdoms of Europe. But the fierce spirit of the north, irritated by multiplied impositions, could neither be mollified by the same arts nor subdued by the same force; and, encouraged by some Princes from piety, and by others out of avarice, it easily bore down the feeble opposition of an illiterate and immoral clergy.

The superstition of Popery seems to have grown to the most extravagant height in those countries which are situated towards the different extremities of Europe. The vigour of imagination, and sensibility of frame, peculiar to the inhabitants of southern climates rendered them susceptible of the deepest impressions of superstitious terror and credulity. Ignorance and barbarity were no less favourable to the progress of the same spirit among the northern nations. They knew little, and were disposed to believe every thing. The most glaring absurdities did not shock their gross understandings, and the most improbable fictions were received with implicit assent and admiration.

Accordingly, that form of Popery which prevailed in Scotland was of the most bigoted and illiberal kind. Those doctrines which are most apt to shock the human understanding, and those legends which furthest exceed belief, were proposed to the people without any attempt to palliate or disguise them; nor did they ever call in question the reasonableness of the one, or the truth of the other.

The power and wealth of the church kept pace with the progress of superstition; for it is the nature of that spirit to observe no bounds in its respect and liberality towards those whose character it esteems sacred. The Scottish Kings early demonstrated how much they were under its influence, by their vast additions to the immunities and riches of the clergy. The profuse piety of David I., who acquired on that account the name of Saint, transferred almost the whole crown lands, which were at that time of great extent, into the hands of ecclesiastics. The example of that virtuous Prince was imitated by his successors. The spirit spread among all orders of men, who daily loaded the priesthood with new possessions. The riches of the church all over Europe were exorbitant; but Scotland was one of those countries wherein they had furthest exceeded the just proportion. The Scottish clergy paid one-half of every tax imposed on land; and as there is no reason to think that in that age they would be loaded with an unequal share of the burden, we may conclude that, by the time of the Reformation, little less than one-half of the national property had fallen into the hands of a society, which is acquiring, and can never lose.

The nature, too, of a considerable part of their property extended the influence of the clergy.—Many estates throughout the kingdom, held of the church; church lands were let in lease at an easy rent, and were possessed by the sons and descendants of the best families. The connexion between *superior* and *vassal*, between landlord and tenant, created dependencies, and gave rise to a union of great advantage to the church; and, in estimating the influence of the Popish ecclesiastics over the nation, these, as well as the real amount of their revenues, must be attended to, and taken into the account.

This extraordinary share in the national property was accompanied with proportionable weight in the supreme council of the kingdom. At a time when the number of the temporal peers was extremely small and when the lesser barons and representatives of boroughs seldom attended parliaments, the ecclesiastics formed a considerable body there. It appears from the ancient rolls of parliament, and from the manner of choosing the lords of articles, that the proceedings of that high court must have been, in a great measure, under their direction.

The reverence due to their sacred character, which was often carried incredibly far, contributed not a little towards the growth of their power. The dignity, the titles, and precedence of the Popish clergy are remarkable, both as causes and effects of that dominion which they had acquired over the rest of mankind. They were regarded by the credulous laity as beings of a superior species; they were neither subject to the same laws, nor tried by the same judges. Every guard that religion could supply was placed around their power, their possessions, and their persons; and endeavours were used, not without success, to represent them all as equally sacred.

The reputation for learning, which, however inconsiderable, was wholly engrossed by the clergy, added to the reverence which they derived from religion. The principles of sound philosophy and of a just taste were altogether unknown; in place of these were substituted studies barbarous and uninstructive: but as the ecclesiastics alone were conversant in them, this procured them esteem; and a very slender portion of knowledge drew the admiration of rude ages, which knew little. War was the sole profession of the nobles, and hunting their chief amusement; they divided their time between these: unacquainted with the arts, and unimproved by science, they disdained any employment foreign from military affairs, or which required rather penetration and address than bodily vigour. Wherever the former were necessary the clergy were intrusted; because they alone were properly qualified for the trust. Almost all the high offices in civil government devolved, on this account, into their hands. The Lord Chancellor was the first subject in the kingdom, both in dignity and in power. From the earliest ages of the monarchy to the death of Cardinal Beatoun, fifty-four persons had held that high office; and of these forty-three had been ecclesiastics. The lords of session were supreme judges in all matters of civil right; and, by its original constitution, the president and one half of the senators in this court were churchmen.

To all this we may add, that the clergy being separated from the rest of mankind by the law of celibacy, and undistracted by those cares, and unincumbered with those burdens which occupy and oppress other men, the interest of their order became their only object, and they were at full leisure to pursue it.

The nature of their functions gave them access to all persons, and at all seasons. They could employ all the motives of fear and of hope, of terror and of consolation, which operate most powerfully on the human mind. They haunted the weak and the credulous; they besieged the beds of the sick and of the dying; they suffered few to go out of the world without leaving marks of their liberality to the church, and taught them to compound with the Almighty for their sins, by bestowing riches upon those who called themselves his servants.

When their own industry, or the superstition of mankind, failed of producing this effect, the ecclesiastics had influence enough to call in the aid of law. When a person died *intestate*, the disposal of his effects was vested in the bishop of the diocese, after paying his funeral charges and debts, and distributing among his kindred the sums to which they were respectively entitled; it being presumed that no Christian would have chosen to leave the world without destining some part of his substance to pious uses. As men are apt to trust to the continuance of life with a fond confidence, and childishly shun everything that forces them to think of their mortality, many die without settling their affairs by will; and the right of administration in that event, acquired by the clergy, must have proved a considerable source both of wealth and of power to the church.

At the same time, no matrimonial or testamentary cause could be tried but in the spiritual courts, and by laws which the clergy themselves had framed. The penalty, too, by which the decisions of these courts were enforced, added to their authority. A sentence of excommunication was no less formidable than a sentence of outlawry. It was pronounced on many occasions, and against various crimes: and, besides excluding those upon whom it fell from Christian privileges, it deprived them of all their rights as men or as citizens; and the aid of the secular power concurred with the superstition of mankind, in rendering the thunders of the church no less destructive than terrible.

To these general causes may be attributed the immense growth both of the wealth and power of the Popish church; and, without entering into any more minute detail, this may serve to discover the foundations on which a structure so stupendous was erected.

But though the laity had contributed, by their own superstition and profuseness, to raise the clergy from poverty and obscurity to riches and eminence, they began, by degrees, to feel and to murmur at their encroachments. No wonder haughty and martial barons should view the power and possessions of the church with envy; and regard the lazy and inactive character of churchmen with the utmost contempt; while, at the same time, the indecent and licentious lives of the clergy gave great and just offence to the people, and considerably abated the veneration which they were accustomed to yield to that order of men.

Immense wealth, extreme indolence, gross ignorance, and, above all, the severe injunction of celibacy, had concurred to introduce this corruption of morals among many of the clergy, who, presuming too much upon the submission of the people, were at no pains either to conceal or to disguise their own vices. According to the accounts of the Reformers, confirmed by several Popish writers, the most open and scandalous dissoluteness of manners prevailed among the Scottish clergy. Cardinal Beatoun, with the same public pomp which is due to a legitimate child, celebrated the marriage of his natural daughter with the Earl of Crawford's son; and, if we may believe Knox, he publicly continued to the end of his days a criminal correspondence with her mother, who was a woman of rank. The other prelates seem not to have been more regular and exemplary than their primate.*

Men of such characters, ought, in reason, to have been alarmed at the first clamours raised against their own morals, and the doctrines of the church, by the Protestant preachers; but the Popish ecclesiastics, either out of pride or ignorance, neglected the proper methods for silencing them. Instead of reforming their lives, or disguising their vices, they affected to despise the censures of the people. While the Reformers, by their mortifications and austerities, endeavoured to resemble the first propagators of Christianity, the Popish clergy were compared to all those persons who are most infamous in history for the enormity and scandal of their crimes.

On the other hand, instead of mitigating the rigour, or colouring over the absurdity, of the established doctrines; instead of attempting to found them upon Scripture, or to reconcile them to reason; they left them without any other support or recommendation than the authority of the church, and the decrees of councils. The fables concerning purgatory, the virtues of pilgrimage, and the merits of the saints, were the topics on which they insisted in their discourses to the people; and the duty of preaching being left wholly to monks of the lowest and most illiterate orders, their compositions were still more wretched and contemptible than the subjects on which they insisted. While the Reformers were attended by crowded and admiring audiences, the Popish preachers were either universally deserted, or listened to with scorn.

The only device which they employed, in order to recover their declining reputation or to confirm the wavering faith of the people,

* A remarkable proof of the dissolute manners of the clergy is found in the public records. A greater number of letters of legitimation was granted during the first thirty years after the Reformation than during the whole period that has elapsed since that time. These were obtained by the sons of the Popish clergy. The ecclesiastics who were allowed to retain their benefices alienated them to their children: who, when they acquired wealth, were desirous that the stain of illegitimacy might no longer remain upon their families. In Keith's "Catalogue of Scottish Bishops," we find several instances of such alienations of church lands by the Popish incumbents to their natural children.

was equally imprudent and unsuccessful. As many doctrines of their church had derived their credit at first from the authority of false miracles, they now endeavoured to call in these to their aid. But such lying wonders, as were beheld with unsuspicious admiration, or heard with implicit faith, in times of darkness and of ignorance, met with a very different reception in a more enlightened period. The vigilance of the Reformers detected these impostures, and exposed not only them, but the cause which needed the aid of such artifices, to ridicule.

As the Popish ecclesiastics became more and more the objects of hatred and of contempt, the discourses of the Reformers were listened to as so many calls to liberty; and, besides the pious indignation which they excited against those corrupt doctrines which had perverted the nature of true Christianity; besides the zeal which they inspired for the knowledge of truth and the purity of religion; they gave rise also, among the Scottish nobles, to other views and passions. They hoped to shake off the yoke of ecclesiastical dominion, which they now discovered to be unchristian. They expected to recover possession of the church revenues, which they were now taught to consider as alienations made by their ancestors with a profusion no less undiscerning than unbounded. They flattered themselves, that a check would be given to the pride and luxury of the clergy, who would be obliged, henceforward, to confine themselves within the sphere peculiar to their sacred character. An aversion from the established church, which flowed from so many concurring causes, which was raised by considerations of religion, heightened by motives of policy, and instigated by prospects of private advantage, spread fast through the nation, and excited a spirit that burst out, at last, with irresistible violence.

Religious considerations alone were sufficient to have roused this spirit. The points in controversy with the church of Rome were of so much importance to the happiness of mankind, and so essential to Christianity, that they merited all the zeal with which the Reformers contended in order to establish them. But the Reformation having been represented as the effect of some wild and enthusiastic frenzy in the human mind, this attempt to account for the eagerness and zeal with which our ancestors embraced and propagated the Protestant doctrines, by taking a view of the political motives alone which influenced them, and by showing how naturally these prompted them to act with so much ardour, will not, perhaps, be deemed an unnecessary digression. We now return to the course of the history.

1554]. The Queen's elevation to the office of Regent seems to have transported her, at first, beyond the known prudence and moderation of her character. She began her administration by conferring upon foreigners several offices of trust and of dignity; a step which, both from the inability of strangers to discharge these offices with propriety, and from the envy which their preferment excites among the natives, is never attended with good consequences. Vilmort was made comptroller, and intrusted with the management of the public revenues; Bonot was appointed Governor of Orkney; and Rubay honoured with the custody of the great seal, and the title of Vice-chancellor. It was with the highest indignation that the Scots beheld offices of the greatest eminence and authority dealt out among strangers*. By these promotions they conceived the Queen to have offered an insult both to their understandings and to their courage : to the former, by supposing them unfit for those stations which their ancestors had filled with so much dignity; to the latter, by imagining that they were tame enough not to complain of an affront, which, in no former age, would have been tolerated with impunity.

While their minds were in this disposition, an incident happened which inflamed their aversion from French councils to the highest degree. Ever since the famous contest between the houses of Valois and Plantagenet, the French had been accustomed to embarrass the English, and to divide their strength by the sudden and formidable incursions of their allies, the Scots. But, as these inroads were seldom attended with any real advantage to Scotland, and exposed it to the dangerous resentment of a powerful neighbour, the Scots began to grow less tractable than formerly, and scrupled any longer to serve an ambitious ally at the price of their own quiet and security. The change too, which was daily introducing in the art of war, rendered the assistance of the Scottish forces of less importance to the French Monarch. For these reasons, Henry having resolved upon a war with Philip II., and foreseeing that the Queen of England would take part in her husband's quarrel, was extremely solicitous to secure in Scotland the assistance of some troops, which would be more at his command than an undisciplined army led by chieftains who were almost independent. In prosecution of this design, but under pretence of relieving the nobles from the expense and danger of defending the borders, the Queen Regent proposed in parliament [1555], to register the value of lands throughout the kingdom, to impose on them a small tax, and to apply that revenue towards maintaining a body of regular troops in constant pay. A fixed tax upon land, which the growing expense of government hath introduced into almost every part of Europe, was unknown at that time, and seemed altogether inconsistent with the genius of feudal policy. Nothing could be more shocking to a generous and brave nobility than the intrusting to mercenary hands the defence of those territories which had been acquired or preserved by the blood of their ancestors. They received this proposal with the utmost dissatisfaction. About three hundred of the lesser barons repaired in a body to the Queen Regent, and represented their sense of the intended innovation with that manly and determined boldness which is natural to a free people in a martial age. Alarmed at a remonstrance delivered in so firm a tone, and supported by such formidable numbers, the Queen prudently abandoned a scheme which she found to be universally odious. As the Queen herself was known perfectly to understand the circumstances and temper of the nation,

* The resentment of the nation against the French rose to such a height, that an act of parliament was passed on purpose to restrain or moderate it. Parl. 6 Q. Mary, c. 60.

this measure was imputed wholly to the suggestions of her foreign counsellors; and the Scots were ready to proceed to the most violent extremities against them.

The French, instead of extinguishing, added fuel to the flame. They had now commenced hostilities against Spain, and Philip had prevailed on the Queen of England to reinforce his army with a considerable body of her troops. In order to deprive him of this aid, Henry had recourse, as he projected, to the Scots; and attempted to excite them to invade England. But as Scotland had nothing to dread from a Princess of Mary's character, who, far from any ambitious scheme of disturbing her neighbours, was wholly occupied in endeavouring to reclaim her heretical subjects; the nobles who were assembled by the Queen Regent at Newbattle, listened to the solicitations of the French monarch with extreme coldness, and prudently declined engaging the kingdom in an enterprise so dangerous and unnecessary. What she could not obtain by persuasion, the Queen Regent brought about by a stratagem. Notwithstanding the peace which subsisted between the two kingdoms, she commanded her French soldiers to rebuild a small fort near to Berwick, which was appointed, by the last treaty, to be razed. The garrison of Berwick sallied out, interrupted the work, and ravaged the adjacent country. This insult roused the fiery spirit of the Scots, and their promptness to revenge the least appearance of national injury dissipated, in a moment, the wise and pacific resolutions which they had so lately formed. War was determined, and orders instantly given for raising a numerous army. But before their forces could assemble, the ardour of their indignation had time to cool; and the English having discovered no intention to push the war with vigour, the nobles resumed their pacific system, and resolved to stand altogether upon the defensive. [1556]. They marched to the banks of the Tweed, they prevented the incursions of the enemy; and having done what they thought sufficient for the safety and honour of their country, the Queen could not induce them, either by her entreaties or by her artifice to advance another step.

While the Scots persisted in their inactivity, D'Oysel, the commanded of the French troops, who possessed entirely the confidence of the Queen Regent, endeavoured, with her connivance, to engage the two nations in hostilities. Contrary to the orders of the Scottish general, he marched over the Tweed with his own soldiers, and invested Wark Castle, a garrison of the English. The Scots, instead of seconding his attempt, were enraged at his presumption. The Queen's partiality towards France had long been suspected; but it was now visible that she wantonly sacrificed the peace and safety of Scotland to the interest of that ambitious and assuming ally. Under the feudal governments, it was in camps that subjects were accustomed to address the boldest remonstrances to their sovereigns. While arms were in their hands they felt their own strength; and, at that time, all their representations of grievances carried the authority of commands. On this occasion the resentment of the nobles broke out with such violence that the Queen, perceiving all attempts to engage them in action to be vain, abruptly dismissed her army, and retired with the utmost shame and disgust; having discovered the impotence of her own authority, without effecting anything which could be of advantage to France.

It is observable that this first instance of contempt for the Regent's authority can, in no degree, be imputed to the influence of the new opinions in religion. As the Queen's pretensions to the Regency had been principally supported by those who favoured the Reformation, and as she still needed them for a counterpoise to the Archbishop of St. Andrew's, and the partisans of the house of Hamilton; she continued to treat them with great respect, and admitted them to no inconsiderable share in her favour and confidence. Kircaldy of Grange, and the other surviving conspirators against Cardinal Beatoun were about this time recalled by her from banishment; and, through her connivance, the Protestant preachers enjoyed an interval of tranquillity, which was of great advantage to their cause. Soothed by these instances of the Queen's moderation and humanity, the Protestants left to others the office of remonstrating; and the leaders of the opposite factions set them the first example of disputing the will of their sovereign.

As the Queen Regent felt how limited and precarious her authority was, while it depended on the poise of these contrary factions, she endeavoured to establish it on a broader and more secure foundation, by hastening the conclusion of her daughter's marriage with the Dauphin. Amiable as the Queen of Scots then was, in the bloom of youth, and considerable as the territories were, which she would have added to the French monarchy; reasons were not wanting to dissuade Henry from completing his first plan of marrying her to his son. The Constable Montmorency had employed all his interest to defeat an alliance which reflected so much lustre on the Princes of Lorrain. He had represented the impossibility of maintaining order and tranquillity among a turbulent people, during the absence of their sovereign; and for that reason had advised Henry to bestow the young Queen upon one of the Princes of the blood, who, by residing in Scotland, might preserve that kingdom a useful ally to France, which, by a nearer union to the crown, would become a mutinous and ungovernable province. But at this time the Constable was a prisoner in the hands of the Spaniards; the Princes of Lorrain were at the height of their power; and their influence, seconded by the charms of the young Queen, triumphed over the prudent but envious remonstrances of their rival.

Dec. 14, 1557.] The French King accordingly applied to the Parliament of Scotland, which appointed eight of its members* to represent the whole body of the nation, at the marriage of the Queen. Among the persons on whom the public choice conferred this honourable character were some of the most avowed and most zealous advocates for the Reformation; by which may be estimated the degree of respect and popularity which that party had now at-

* Viz. The Archbishop of Glasgow, the Bishop of Ross, the Bishop of Orkney, the Earls of Rothes and Cassils, Lord Fleming, Lord Seaton, the Prior of St. Andrew's, and John Erskine of Dun.

tained in the kingdom. The instructions of the parliament to these commissioners still remain, and do honour to the wisdom and integrity of that assembly. At the same time that they manifested with respect to the articles of marriage, a laudable concern for the dignity and interest of their sovereign, they employed every precaution which prudence could dictate, for preserving the liberty and independence of the nation, and for securing the succession of the crown in the house of Hamilton.

With regard to each of these, the Scots obtained whatever satisfaction their fears or jealousy could demand. The young Queen, the Dauphin, and the King of France ratified every article with the most solemn oaths, and confirmed them by deeds in form under hands and seals. But, on the part of France, all this was one continued scene of studied and elaborate deceit. Previous to these public transactions with the Scottish deputies, Mary had been persuaded to subscribe privately three deeds, equally unjust and invalid; by which, failing the heirs of her own body, she conferred the kingdom of Scotland, with whatever inheritance or succession might accrue to it, in free gift upon the throne of France, declaring all promises to the contrary, which the necessity of her affairs, and the solicitations of her subjects, had extorted, or might extort from her, to be void and of no obligation. As it gives us a proper idea of the character of the French court under Henry II., we may observe that the King himself, the keeper of the great seals, the Duke of Guise, and the Cardinal of Lorrain were the persons engaged in conducting this perfidious and dishonourable project. The Queen of Scots was the only innocent actor in that scene of iniquity. Her youth, her inexperience, her education in a foreign country, and her deference to the will of her uncles, must go far in vindicating her, in the judgment of every impartial person, from any imputation of blame on that account.

This grant, by which Mary bestowed the inheritance of her kingdom upon strangers, was concealed with the utmost care from her subjects. They seem, however, not to have been unacquainted with the intention of the French to overturn the settlement of the succession in favour of the Duke of Chatelherault. The zeal with which the Archbishop of St. Andrew's opposed all the measures of the Queen Regent, evidently proceeded from the fears and suspicions of that prudent prelate on this head.

April 14, 1558.] The marriage, however, was celebrated with great pomp; and the French, who had hitherto affected to draw a veil over their designs upon Scotland, began now to unfold their intentions without any disguise. In the treaty of marriage, the deputies had agreed that the Dauphin should assume the name of King of Scotland. This they considered only as an honorary title; but the French laboured to annex to it some solid privileges and power. They insisted that the Dauphin's title should be publicly recognised; that the *Crown Matrimonial* should be conferred upon him; and that all the rights pertaining to the husband of a Queen, should be vested in his person. By the laws of Scotland, a person, who married an heiress, kept possession of her estate during his own life, if he happened to survive her and the children born of the marriage. This was called the *courtesy of Scotland.* The French aimed at applying this rule, which takes place in private inheritances, to the succession of the kingdom; and that seems to be implied in their demand of the *Crown Matrimonial*, a phrase peculiar to the Scottish historians, and which they have neglected to explain. As the French had reason to expect difficulties in carrying through this measure, they began with sounding the deputies who were then at Paris. The English, in the marriage articles between their Queen and Philip of Spain, had set an example to the age, of that prudent jealousy and reserve with which a foreigner should be admitted so near the throne. Full of the same ideas, the Scottish deputies had, in their oath of allegiance to the Dauphin, expressed themselves with remarkable caution. Their answer was in the same spirit, respectful but firm; and discovered a fixed resolution of consenting to nothing that tended to introduce any alteration in the order of succession to the crown.

Four of the deputies* happening to die before they returned into Scotland, this accident was universally imputed to the effects of poison, which was supposed to have been given them by the emissaries of the House of Guise. The historians of all nations discover an amazing credulity with respect to rumours of this kind, which are so well calculated to please the malignity of some men, and to gratify the love of the marvellous which is natural to all, that in every age they have been swallowed without examination, and believed contrary to reason. No wonder the Scots should easily give credit to a suspicion which received such strong colours of probability, both from their own resentment and from the known character of the Princes of Lorrain, so little scrupulous about the justice of the ends which they pursued, or of the means which they employed. For the honour of human nature, however it must be observed, that as we can discover no motive which could induce any man to perpetrate such a crime, so there appears no evidence to prove that it was committed. But the Scots of that age, influenced by their national animosities and prejudices, were incapable of examining the circumstances of the case with calmness, or of judging concerning them with candour. All parties agreed in believing the French guilty of this detestable action; and it is obvious how much this tended to increase the aversion for them, which was growing among all ranks of men.

Notwithstanding the cold reception which their proposals concerning the *Crown Matrimonial* met with from the Scottish deputies, the French ventured to move it in parliament. The partisans of the house of Hamilton, suspicious of their designs upon the succession, opposed it with great zeal. But a party, which the feeble and unsteady conduct of their leader had brought under such disreputation, was little able to withstand the influence of France, and the address of the Queen Regent, seconded on this occasion, by all the numerous adherents of the Reformation. Besides, that artful Princess dressed out the French demands in a less offensive garb, and threw in so many limitations as seemed to

*The Bishop of Orkney, the Earl of Rothes, the Earl of Cassils, and Lor Fleming.

render them of small consequence.—These either deceived the
Scots, or removed their scruples; and in compliance to the Queen
they passed an act, conferring the *Crown Matrimonial* on the
Dauphin; and with the fondest credulity trusted to the frail
security of words and statues, against the dangerous encroachments
of power.*

The concurrence of the Protestants with the Queen Regent, in
promoting a measure so acceptable to France, while the Popish
clergy, under the influence of the Archbishop of St. Andrew's,
opposed it with such violence, is one of those singular circumstances in the conduct of parties, for which this period is remarkable. It may be ascribed, in some degree, to the dexterous management of the Queen, but chiefly to the moderation of those who
favoured the Reformation. The Protestants were by this time almost equal to the Catholics, both in power and in number; and,
conscious of their own strength, they submitted with impatience
to that tyrannical authority with which the ancient laws armed
the ecclesiastics against them. They longed to be exempted
from the oppressive jurisdiction, and publicly to enjoy the liberty
of professing those opinions, and of exercising that worship,
which so great a part of the nation deemed to be founded
in truth and to be acceptable to the Deity. This indulgence, to
which the whole weight of priestly authority was opposed, there
were only two ways of obtaining. Either violence must ex-
hort it from the reluctant hand of their sovereign, or by prudent
compliances they might expect it from her favour or her gratitude.
The former is an expedient for the redress of grievances, to which
no nation has recourse suddenly; and subjects seldom venture upon
resistance, which is their last remedy, but in case of extreme
necessity. On this occasion the Reformers wisely held the opposite
course, and by their zeal in forwarding the Queen's designs they
hoped to merit her protection. This disposition the Queen encouraged to the utmost, and amused them so artfully with many
promises, and some concessions, that, by their assistance, she surmounted in parliament the force of a national and laudable jealousy, which would otherwise have swayed with the greater number.

Another circumstance contributed somewhat to acquire the
Regent such considerable influence in this parliament. In Scotland, all the bishoprics, and those abbeys which conferred a title
to a seat in parliament, were in the gift of the crown†. From the
time of her accession to the regency, the Queen had kept in her
own hands almost all those which became vacant, except such as
were to the great disgust of the nation, bestowed upon foreigners.
Among, these, her brother the Cardinal of Lorrain had obtained
the abbeys of Kelso and Melross, two of the most wealthy foundations in the kingdom. By this conduct she thinned the eclesias-

---

* The act of parliament is worded with the utmost care, with a view to guard
against any breach of the order of succession. But the duke, not relying on this
alone, entered on a solemn protestation to secure his own right. Keith 76. It is
plain that he suspected the French of having intention to set aside his right of
succession; and, indeed, if they had no design of that kind, the eagerness with
which they urged their demand was childish.

tical bench*, which was entirely under the influence of the Archbishop of St. Andrew's, and which, by its numbers and authority,
usually had great weight in the house, so as to render any opposition it could give at that time of little consequence.

The Earl of Argyll, and James Stewart, Prior of St. Andrew's,
one the most powerful, and the other the most popular leader of
the Protestants, were appointed to carry the crown and other ensigns of the royalty to the Dauphin. But from this they were
diverted by the part they were called to act in a more interesting
scene, which now begins to open.

Before we turn towards this, it is necessary to observe, that on
the 17th of November, 1558, Mary of England finished her short
and inglorious reign. Her sister Elizabeth took possession of the
throne without opposition : and the Protestant religion was once
more established by law in England. The accession of a Queen,
who, under very difficult circumstances, had given strong indications of those eminent qualities which, in the sequel, rendered her
reign so illustrious, attracted the eye of all Europe. Among the
Scots, both parties observed her first motions with the utmost
solicitude, as they easily foresaw she would not remain long an indifferent spectator of their transactions.

Under many discouragements and much oppression the Reformation advanced towards a full establishment in Scotland. All the
lower country, the most populous, and at that time the most warlike part of the kingdom, was deeply tinctured with the Protestant
opinions ; and if the same impressions were not made in the more
distant counties, it was owing to no want of the same dispositions
among the people, but to the scarcity of preachers, whose most
indefatigable zeal could not satisfy the avidity of those who desired their instructions. Among a people bred to arms, and as
prompt as the Scots to act with violence ; and in an age when
religious passions had taken such strong possession of the human
mind, and moved and agitated it with so much violence, the peaceable and regular demeanour of so numerous a party is astonishing.
From the death of Mr. Patrick Hamilton, the first who suffered in
Scotland for the Protestant religion, thirty years had elapsed, and
during so long a period no violation of public order or tranquillity
had proceeded from that sect† ; and though roused and irritated by
the most cruel excesses of ecclesiastical tyranny, they did in no
instance transgress those bounds of duty which the law prescribes
to subjects. Besides the prudence of their own leaders, and the
protection which the Queen Regent, from political motives, afforded
them, the moderation of the Archbishop of St. Andrew's encouraged this pacific disposition. That prelate, whose private life
contemporary writers tax with great irregularities, governed the
church, for some years, with a temper and prudence of which there
are few examples in that age. But some time before the meeting

---

* It appears from the rolls of this parliament, which Lesly calls a very full one,
that only seven bishops and sixteen abbots were present.
† The murder of Cardinal Beatoun was occasioned by private revenge ; and
being contrived and executed by sixteen persons only, cannot with justice be imputed to the whole Protestant party.

of the last parliament, the Archbishop departed from those humane maxims by which he had hitherto regulated his conduct: and whether in spite to the Queen, who had entered into so close a union with the Protestants, or in compliance with the importunities of his clergy, he let loose all the rage of persecution against the reformed; sentenced to the flames an aged priest, who had been convicted of embracing the Protestant opinions; and summoned several others, suspected of the same crime, to appear before a synod of the clergy, which was soon to convene at Edinburgh.

Nothing could equal the horror of the Protestants at this unexpected and barbarous execution, but the zeal with which they espoused the defence of a cause that now seemed devoted to destruction. They had immediate recourse to the Queen Regent; and as her success in the parliament, which was then about to meet, depended on their concurrence, she not only sheltered them from the impeding storm, but permitted them the exercise of their religion with more freedom than they had hitherto enjoyed. Unsatisfied with this precarious tenure by which they held their religious liberty, the Protestants laboured to render their possession of it more secure and independent. With this view they determined to petition the Parliament for some legal protection against the exorbitant and oppressive jurisdiction of the ecclesiastical courts, which, by their arbitary method of proceeding, founded in the canon law, were led to sentences the most shocking to humanity, by maxims the most repugnant to justice. But the Queen, who dreaded the effect of a debate on this delicate subject, which could not fail of exciting high and dangerous passions, prevailed on the leaders of the party, by new and more solemn promises of her protection, to desist from any application to parliament, where their numbers and influence would, in all probability, have procured them, if not entire redress, at least some mitigation of their grievances.

They applied to another assembly, to a convocation of the Popish clergy, but with the same ill success which hath always attended every proposal for reformation addressed to that order of men. To abandon usurped power, to renounce lucrative error, are sacrifices which the virtue of individuals has, on some occasions, offered to truth; but from any society of men no such effort can be expected. The corruptions of a society recommended by common utility, and justified by universal practice, are viewed by its members without shame or horror; and reformation never proceeds from themselves, but is always forced upon them by some foreign hand. Suitable to this unfeeling and inflexible spirit was the behaviour of the convocation in the present conjuncture. All the demands of the Protestants were rejected with contempt; and the Popish clergy, far from endeavouring, by any prudent concessions, to sooth and to reconcile such a numerous body, asserted the doctrines of their church, concerning some of the most exceptionable articles, with an ill-timed rigour, which gave new offence.

1559.] During the sitting of the convocation, the Protestants first began to suspect some change in the Regent's disposition towards them. Though joined with them for many years by interest, and united, as they conceived, by the strongest ties of affection and of gratitude, she discovered, on this occasion, evident symptoms, not only of coldness, but of a growing disgust and aversion. In order to account for this, our historians do little more than produce the trite observations concerning the influence of prosperity to alter the character and to corrupt the heart. The Queen, say they, having reached the utmost point to which her ambition aspired, no longer preserved her accustomed moderation, but, with an insolence usual to the fortunate, looked down upon those by whose assistance she had been enabled to rise so high. But it is neither in the depravity of the human heart nor in the ingratitude of the Queen's disposition that we must search for the motives of her present conduct. These were derived from another and more remote source, which, in order to clear the subsequent transactions, we shall endeavour to open with some care.

The ambition of the Princes of Lorrain had been no less successful than daring; but all their schemes were distinguished by being vast and unbounded. Though strangers at the court of France, their eminent qualities had raised them, in a short time, to a height of power superior to that of all other subjects, and had placed them on a level even with the Princes of the blood themselves. The church, the army, the revenue, were under their direction. Nothing but the royal dignity remained unattained; and they were elevated to a near alliance with it, by the marriage of the Queen of Scots to the Dauphin. In order to gratify their own vanity, and to render their niece more worthy the heir of France, they set on foot her claim to the crown of England, which was founded on pretences not unplausible.

The tragical amours and marriages of Henry VIII. are known to all the world. Moved by the caprices of his love or of his resentment, that impatient and arbitrary monarch had divorced or beheaded four of the six Queens whom he married. In order to gratify him, both his daughters had been declared illigitimate by act of parliament; and yet, with that fantastic inconsistence which distinguishes his character, he, in his last will, whereby he was empowered to settle the order of succession, called both of them to the throne upon the death of their brother Edward; and, at the same time, passing by the posterity of his eldest sister Margaret Queen of Scotland, he appointed the line of succession to continue in the descendants of his younger sister, the Duchess of Suffolk.

In consequence of this destination, the validity whereof was admitted by the English, but never recognised by foreigners, Mary had reigned in England without the least complaint of neighbouring Princes. But the same causes which facilitated her accession to the throne were obstacles to the elevation of her sister Elizabeth, and rendered her possession of it precarious and insecure. Rome trembled for the Catholic faith under a Protestant Queen of such eminent abilities. The same superstitious fears alarmed the court of Spain. France beheld with concern a throne, to which the Queen of Scots could form so many pretensions, occupied by a rival, whose birth, in the opinion of all good Catholics, excluded her from any

E

legal right of succession. The impotent hatred of the Roman
Pontiff, or the slow councils of Philip II. would have produced no
sudden or formidable effect. The ardent and impetuous ambition
of the Princes of Lorrain, who at that time governed the court of
France, was more decisive, and more to be dreaded. Instigated by
them, Henry, soon after the death of Mary, persuaded his daughter-
in law and her husband to assume the title of King and Queen of
England. They affected to publish this to all Europe. They used
that style and appellation in public papers, some of which still remain. The arms of England were engraved on their coin and plate,
and borne by them on all occasions. No preparations, however,
were made to support this impolitic and premature claim. Elizabeth
was already seated on her throne : she possessed all the intrepidity
of spirit, and all the arts of policy, which were necessary for maintaining that station. England was growing into reputation for naval
power. The marine of France had been utterly neglected; and
Scotland remained the only avenue by which the territories of
Elizabeth could be approached. It was on that side, therefore, that
the Princes of Lorrain determined to make their attack ; and by
using the name and pretensions of the Scottish Queen, they hoped
to rouse the English Catholics, formidable at that time by their
zeal and numbers, and exasperated to the utmost against Elizabeth
on account of the change which she had made in the national religion.

It was in vain to expect the assistance of the Scottish Protestants
to dethrone a Queen whom all Europe began to consider the most
powerful guardian and defender of the reformed faith. To break
the power and reputation of that party in Scotland became, for
this reason, a necessary step towards the invasion of England. With
this the Princes of Lorrain resolved to open their scheme. And as
persecution was the only method for suppressing religious opinions
known in that age, or dictated by the despotic and sanguinary spirit
of the Romish superstition, this, in its utmost violence, they determined to employ. The Earl of Argyll, the Prior of St. Andrew's,
and other leaders of the party, were marked out by them for immediate destruction; and they hoped, by punishing them, to intimidate their followers. Instructions for this purpose were sent from
France to the Queen Regent. That humane and sagacious Princess
condemned a measure which was equally violent and impolitic. By
long residence in Scotland, she had become acquainted with the
eager and impatient temper of the nation ; she well knew the
power, the number, and popularity of the Protestant leaders ; and
had been a witness to the intrepid and unconquerable resolution
which religious fervour could inspire. What then could be gained
by rousing this dangerous spirit, which hitherto all the arts of
policy had scarcely been able to restrain ? If it once broke loose,
the authority of a Regent would be little capable to subdue, or even
to moderate its rage. If, in order to quell it, foreign forces were
called in, this would give the alarm to the whole nation, irritated
already at the excessive power which the French possessed in the
kingdom, and suspicious of all their designs. Amidst the shock
which this might occasion, far from hoping to exterminate the Pro-

testant doctrine, it would be well if the whole fabric of the established church were not shaken, and perhaps overturned from the foundation. These prudent remonstrances made no impression on her brothers; precipitant, but inflexible in all their resolutions, they insisted on the full rigorous execution of their plan. Mary, passionately devoted to the interest of France, and ready, on all occasions, to sacrifice her own opinions to the inclinations of her brothers, prepared to execute their commands with implicit submission; and, contrary to her own judgment and to all the rules of sound policy, she became the instrument of exciting civil commotions in Scotland, the fatal termination of which she foresaw and dreaded.

From the time of the Queen's competition for the regency with the Duke of Chatelherault, the Popish clergy, under the direction of the Archbishop of St. Andrew's, had set themselves in opposition to all her measures. Her first step towards the execution of her new scheme was to regain their favour. Nor was this reconcilement a matter of difficulty. The Popish ecclesiastics, separated from the rest of mankind by the law of celibacy, one of the closest and most sacred union, have been accustomed, in every age, to sacrifice all private and particular passions to the dignity and interest of their order. Delighted on this occasion with the prospect of triumphing over a faction, the encroachments of which they had long dreaded, and animated with the hopes of re-establishing their declining grandeur on a firmer basis, they at once canceled the memory of past injuries, and engaged to second the Queen in all her attempts to check the progress of the Reformation. The Queen, being secure of their assistance, openly approved of the decrees of the convocation, by which the principles of the Reformers were condemned; and at the same time she issued a proclamation, enjoining all persons to observe the approaching festival of Easter according to the Romish ritual.

As it was no longer possible to mistake the Queen's intentions, the Protestants, who saw danger approach, in order to avert it, employed the Earl of Glencairn, and Sir Hugh Campbell of London, to expostulate with her concerning this change towards severity, which their former services had so little merited, and which her reiterated promises gave them no reason to expect. She, without disguise or apology, avowed to them her resolution of extirpating the reformed religion out of the kingdom. And, upon their urging her former engagements with an uncourtly but honest boldness, she so far forgot her usual moderation, as to utter a sentiment, which, however apt those of royal condition may be to entertain it, prudence should teach them to conceal as much as possible. "The promises of Princes," says she, "ought not to be too carefully remembered, nor the performance of them exacted, unless it suits their own conveniency."

The indignation which betrayed the Queen into this rash expression was nothing in comparison of that with which she was animated upon hearing that the public exercise of the reformed religion had been introduced into the town of Perth. At once she threw off the mask, and issued a mandate, summoning all the Protestant preachers in the kingdom to a court of justice, which was to be held at Stirling on the tenth of May. The Protestants, who, from their union, began about this time to be distinguished by the name of the CONGREGATION, were alarmed, but not intimidated, by this danger; and instantly resolved not to abandon the men to whom they were indebted for the most valuable of all blessings, the knowledge of the truth. At that time there prevailed in Scotland, with respect to criminal trials, a custom, introduced at first by the institutions of vassalage and clanship, and tolerated afterwards under a feeble government : persons accused of any crime were accompanied to the place of trial by a retinue of their friends and adherents, assembled for that purpose from every quarter of the kingdom. Authorized by this ancient practice, the reformed convened in great numbers to attend their pastors to Stirling. The Queen dreaded their approach with a train so numerous, though unarmed; and in order to prevent them from advancing, she empowered John Erskine of Dun, a person of eminent authority with the party, to promise in her name that she would put a stop to the intended trial, on condition the preachers and their retinue advanced no nearer to Stirling. Erskine, being convinced himself of the Queen's sincerity, served her with the utmost zeal; and the Protestants, averse from proceeding to any act of violence, listened with pleasure to so pacific a proposition. The preachers, with a few leaders of the party, remained at Perth; the multitude which had gathered from different parts of the kingdom dispersed, and retired to their own habitations.

But, notwithstanding this solemn promise, the Queen, on the tenth of May, proceeded to call to trial the persons who had been summoned, and, upon their non-appearance, the rigour of justice took place, and they were pronounced outlaws. By this ignoble artifice, so incompatible with regal dignity, and so inconsistent with that integrity which should prevail in all transactions between sovereigns and their subjects, the Queen forfeited the esteem and confidence of the whole nation. The Protestants, shocked no less at the indecency with which she violated the public faith than at the danger which threatened themselves, prepared boldly for their own defence. Erskine, enraged at having been made the instrument for deceiving his party, instantly abandoned Stirling, and repairing to Perth, added to the zeal of his associates, by his representations of the Queen's inflexible resolution to suppress religion.

The popular rhetoric of Knox powerfully seconded his representations; he having been carried a prisoner into France, together with the other persons taken in the castle of St. Andrew's, soon made his escape out of that country; and residing sometimes in England, sometimes in Scotland, had at last been driven out of both kingdoms by the rage of the Popish clergy, and was obliged to retire to Geneva. Thence he was called by the leaders of the Protestants in Scotland; and, in compliance with their solicitations, he set out for his native country, where he arrived a few days before the trial appointed at Stirling. He hurried instantly to Perth, to share with his brethren in the common danger, or to assist them in the common cause. While their minds were in that ferment which the Queen's perfidiousness and their own dangers occasioned, he mounted the pulpit, and by a vehement harangue against idolatry, inflamed the multitude with the utmost rage. The indiscretion of a priest, who, immediately after Knox's sermon, was preparing to celebrate mass, and began to decorate the altar for that purpose, precipitated them into immediate action. With tumultuary but irresistible violence they fell upon the churches in that city, overturned the altars, defaced the pictures, broke in pieces the images, and proceeding next to the monasteries, they in a few hours laid those sumptuous fabrics almost level with the ground. This riotous insurrection was not the effect of any concert or previous deliberation: censured by the reformed preachers, and publicly condemned by persons of most power and credit with the party, it must be regarded merely as an accidental eruption of popular rage.

But to the Queen Dowager these proceedings appeared in a very different light. Besides their manifest contempt for her authority, the Protestants had violated every thing in religion which she deemed venerable or holy; and on both these accounts she determined to inflict the severest vengeance on the whole party. She had already drawn the troops in French pay to Stirling; with these, and what Scottish forces she could levy of a sudden, she marched directly to Perth, in hopes of surprising the Protestant leaders before they could assemble their followers, whom, out of confidence in her disingenuous promises, they had been rashly induced to dismiss. Intelligence of these preparations and menaces was soon conveyed to Perth. The Protestants would gladly have soothed the Queen, by addresses both to herself and to the persons of greatest credit in her court; but, finding her inexorable, they with great vigour took measures for their own defence. Their adherents, animated with zeal for religion, and eager to expose themselves in so good a cause, flocked in such numbers to Perth that they not only secured the town from danger, but within a few days were in a condition to take the field, and to face the Queen, who advanced with an army seven thousand strong.

Neither party, however, was impatient to engage. The Queen dreaded the event of a battle with men whom the fervour of religion raised above the sense of fear or danger. The Protestants beheld with regret the Earl of Argyll, the Prior of St. Andrew's, and other eminent persons of their party, still adhering to the Queen; and, destitute of their aid and counsel, declined hazarding an action, the ill success of which might have proved the ruin of their cause. The prospect of an accommodation was for these reasons highly acceptable to both sides; Argyll and the Prior, who were the Queen's commissioners for conducting the negotiation, seem to have been sincerely desirous of reconciling the contending factions; and the Earl of Glencairn arriving unexpectedly with a powerful reinforcement to the Congregation, augmented the Queen's eagerness for peace. A treaty was accordingly concluded, in which it was stipulated that both armies should be disbanded, and the gates of Perth set open to the Queen; that indemnity should be granted to the inhabitants of that city, and to all others concerned in the late insurrection; that no French garrison should be left in

Perth, and no French soldier should approach within three miles of that place ; and that a parliament should immediately be held in order to compose whatever differences might still remain.

May 29.] The leaders of the Congregation, distrustful of the Queen's sincerity, and sensible that concessions, flowing not from inclination, but extorted by the necessity of her affairs, could not long remain in force, entered into a new association, by which they bound themselves, on the first infringement of the present treaty, or on the least appearance of danger to their religion, to reassemble their followers, and to take arms in defence of what they deemed the cause of God and of their country.

The Queen, by her conduct, demonstrated these precautions to be the result of no groundless or unnecessary fear. No sooner were the Protestant forces dismissed than she broke every article in the treaty. She introduced French troops into Perth, fined some of the inhabitants, banished others, removed the magistrates out of office ; and on her retiring to Stirling, she left behind her a garrison of six hundred men, with orders to allow the exercise of no other religion than the Roman Catholic.—The situation of Perth, a place at that time of some strength, and a town among the most proper of any in the kingdom for the station of a garrison, seems to have allured the Queen to this unjustifiable and ill judged breach of public faith ; which she endeavoured to colour by alleging that the body of men left at Perth was entirely composed of native Scots, though kept in pay by the King of France.

The Queen's scheme began gradually to unfold ; it was now apparent that not only the religion but the liberties of the kingdom were threatened ; and that the French troops were to be employed as instruments for subduing the Scots, and wreathing the yoke about their necks. Martial as the genius of the Scots then was, the poverty of their country made it impossible to keep their armies long assembled ; and even a very small body of regular troops might have proved formidable to the nation, though consisting wholly of soldiers. But what number of French soldiers were then in Scotland, at what times and under what pretext they returned, after having left the kingdom in 1550, we cannot with any certainty determine. Contemporary historians often select with little judgment the circumstances which they transmit to posterity : and with respect to matters of the greatest curiosity and importance, leave succeeding ages altogether in the dark. We may conjecture, however, from some passages in Buchanan, that the French and Scots in French pay, amounted at least to three thousand men, under the command of Monsieur D'Oysel, a creature of the House of Guise ; and they were soon augmented to a much more formidable number.

The Queen, encouraged by having so considerable a body of well disciplined troops at her command, and instigated by the violent counsels of D'Oysel, had ventured, as we have observed, to violate the treaty of Perth, and by that rash action once more threw the nation into the most dangerous convulsions. The Earl of Argyll and the Prior of St. Andrew's instantly deserted a court where faith and honour seemed to them to be no longer regarded and joined the leaders of the Congregation, who had retreated to the eastern part of Fife. The barons from the neighbouring counties repaired to them, the preachers roused the people to arms, and wherever they came, the same violent operations, which accident had occasioned at Perth, were now encouraged out of policy. The enraged multitude was let loose, and churches and monasteries, the monuments of ecclesiastical pride and luxury, were sacrificed to their zeal.

In order to check their career, the Queen, without losing a moment, put her troops in motion; but the zeal of the Congregation got the start once more of her vigilance and activity. In that warlike age, when all men were accustomed to arms, and on the least prospect of danger were ready to run to them, the leaders of the Protestants found no difficulty to raise an army. Though they set out from St. Andrew's with a slender train of a hundred horse, crowds flocked to their standards from every corner of the country through which they marched; and before they reached Falkland, a village only ten miles distant, they were able to meet the Queen with superior force.

The Queen, surprised at the approach of so formidable a body, which was drawn up by its leaders in such a manner as added greatly in appearance to its numbers, had again recourse to negociation. She found, however, that the preservation of the Protestant religion, their zeal for which had at first roused the leaders of the Congregation to take arms, was not the only object they had now in view. They were animated with the warmest love of civil liberty, which they conceived to be in imminent danger from the attempts of the French forces: and these two passions mingling, added reciprocally to each other's strength. Together with more enlarged notions in religion, the Reformation filled the human mind with more liberal and generous sentiments concerning civil government. The genius of Popery is extremely favourable to the power of Princes. The implicit submission to all her decrees, which is exacted by the Romish church, prepares and breaks the mind for political servitude; and the doctrines of the Reformers, by overturning the establishment of superstition, weakening the firmest foundations of civil tyranny. That bold spirit of inquiry, which led men to reject theological errors, accompanied them in other sciences, and discovered every where the same manly zeal for truth. A new study, introduced at the same time, added greater force to the spirit of liberty. Men became more acquainted with the Greek and Roman authors, who described exquisite models of free government, far superior to the inaccurate and oppressive system established by the feudal law; and produced such illustrious examples of public virtue as wonderfully suited both the circumstances and spirit of that age. Many among the most eminent Reformers were themselves considerable masters in ancient learning; and all of them eagerly adopted the maxims and spirit of the ancients with regard to government[*]. The most ardent love of

* The excessive admiration of ancient policy was the occasion of Knox's famous book concerning the government of women, wherein, conformable to the maxims of the ancient legislators, which modern experience has proved to be ill

liberty accompanied the Protestant religion throughout all its progress; and wherever it was embraced, it roused an independent spirit, which rendered men attentive to their privileges as subjects, and jealous of the encroachments of their sovereigns. Knox and the other preachers of the Reformation infused generous sentiments concerning government in the mind of their hearers; and the Scottish barons, naturally free and bold, were prompted to assert their rights with more freedom and boldness than ever. Instead of obeying the Queen Regent, who had enjoined them to lay down their arms, they demanded not only the redress of their religious grievances, but, as a preliminary towards settling the nation, and securing its liberties, required the immediate expulsion of the French troops out of Scotland. It was not in the Queen's power to make so important a concession without the concurrence of the French Monarch; and as some time was requisite in order to obtain that, she hoped during this interval to receive such reinforcements from France, as would ensure the accomplishment of that design which she had twice attempted with unequal strength. [June 13.] Meanwhile, she agreed to a cessation of arms for eight days, and before the expiration of these, engaged to transport the French troops to the south side of the Forth; and to send commissioners to St. Andrew's, who should labour to bring all differences to an accommodation. As she hoped, by means of the French troops, to overawe the Protestants in the southern counties, the former article in the treaty was punctually executed; the latter, having been inserted merely to amuse the Congregation, was no longer remembered.

By these reiterated and wanton instances of perfidy, the Queen lost all credit with her adversaries; and no safety appearing in any other cause, they again took arms with more inflamed resentment, and with bolder and more extended views. The removing of the French forces had laid open to them all the country situated between the Forth and Tay. The inhabitants of Perth alone remaining subjected to the insolence and actions of the garrison which the Queen had left there, implored the assistance of the Congregation for their relief. Thither they marched, and having without effect required the Queen to evacuate the town in terms of the former treaty, they prepared to besiege it in form. The Queen employed the Earl of Huntly and Lord Erskine to divert them from this enterprise. But her wonted artifices were now of no avail; repeated so often, they could deceive no longer; and, without listening to her offers, the Protestants continued the siege, and soon obliged the garrison to capitulate.

After the loss of Perth, the Queen endeavoured to seize Starling, a place of some strength, and, from its command of the only bridge over the Forth, of great importance. But the leaders of the Congregation, having intelligence of her design, prevented the execu-

founded, he pronounces the elevation of women to the supreme authority to be utterly destructive of good government. His principles, authorities, and examples were all drawn from ancient writers. The same observation may be made with regard to Buchanan's Dialogue, De Jure Regni apud Scotos. It is founded, not on the maxims of feudal, but of ancient republican government.

tion of it by a hasty march thither with part of their forces. The inhabitants, heartily attached to the cause, set open to them the gates of their town. Thence they advanced, with the same rapidity, towards Edinburgh, which the Queen, on their approach, abandoned with precipitation, and retired to Dunbar.

The Protestant army, wherever it came, kindled or spread the ardour of Reformation, and the utmost excesses of violence were committed upon churches and monasteries. The former were spoiled of every decoration, which was then eteemed sacred; the latter were laid in ruins. We are apt, at this distance of time, to condemn the furious zeal of the Reformers, and to regret the overthrow of so many stately fabrics, the monuments of our ancestors' magnificence, and among the noblest ornaments of the kingdom. But amidst the violence of a Reformation, carried on in opposition to legal authority, some irregularities were unavoidable; and perhaps no one could have been permitted more proper to allure and interest the multitude, or more fatal to the grandeur of the established church. How absurd soever and ill founded the speculative errors of Popery may be, some inquiry and attention are requisite towards discovering them. The abuses and corruptions which had crept into the public worship of that church lay more open to observation, and by striking the senses excited more universal disgust. Under the long reign of heathenism, superstition seemed to have exhausted its talent of invention, so that when a superstitious spirit seized Christians, they were obliged to imitate the heathens in the pomp and magnificence of their ceremonies, and to borrow from them the ornaments and decorations of their temples. To the pure and simple worship of the primitive Christians there succeeded a species of splendid idolatry, nearly resembling those Pagan originals whence it had been copied. The contrariety of such observances to the spirit of Christianity was almost the first thing in the Romish system, which awakened the indignation of the Reformers, who, applying to these the denunciations in the Old Testament against idolatry, imagined that they could not endeavour at suppressing them with too much zeal. No task could be more acceptable to the multitude than to overturn those seats of superstition; they ran with emulation to perform it, and happy was the man whose hand was most adventurous and successful in executing a work deemed so pious. Nor did their leaders labour to restrain this impetuous spirit of Reformation. Irregular and violent as its sallies were, they tended directly to that end which they had in view; for, by demolishing the monasteries throughout the kingdom, and setting at liberty their wretched inhabitants, they hoped to render it impossible ever to rebuild the one, or to re-assemble the other.

But amidst these irregular proceedings, a circumstance which does honour to the conduct and humanity of the leaders of the Congregation deserves notice. They so far restrained the rage of their followers, and were able so to temper their heat and zeal, that few of the Roman Catholics were exposed to any personal insult, and not a single man suffered death,

E 5

At the same time we discover, by the facility with which these great revolutions were effected, how violently the current of national favour ran towards the Reformation. No more than three hundred men marched out of Perth, under the Earl of Argyll and Prior of St. Andrew's; with this inconsiderable force they advanced. But wherever they came the people joined them in a body; their army was seldom less numerous than five thousand men; the gates of every town were thrown open to receive them [June 29]; and, without striking a single blow, they took possession of the capital of the kingdom.

This rapid and astonishing success seems to have encouraged the Reformers to extend their views, and to rise in their demands. Not satisfied with their first claims of toleration for their religion, they now openly aimed at establishing the Protestant doctrine on the ruins of Popery. For this reason they determined to fix their residence at Edinburgh; and, by their appointment, Knox, and some other preachers, taking possession of the pulpits, which had been abandoned by the affrighted clergy, declaimed against the errors of Popery with such fervent zeal as could not fail of gaining many proselytes.

In the mean time the Queen, who had prudently given way to a torrent which she could not resist, observed with pleasure that it now began to subside. The leaders of the Congregation had been above two months in arms, and by the expenses of a campaign, protracted so long beyond the usual time of service in that age, had exhausted all the money which a country, where riches did not abound, had been able to supply. The multitude, dazzled with their success, and concluding the work to be already done, retired to their own habitations. A few only of the more zealous or wealthy barons remained with their preachers at Edinburgh. As intelligence is procured in civil wars with little difficulty, whatever was transacted at Edinburgh was soon known at Dunbar. The Queen, regulating her own conduct by the situation of her adversaries, artfully amused them with the prospect of an immediate accommodation; while, at the same time, she by studied delays spun out the negotiations for that purpose to such a length that, in the end, the party dwindled to an inconsiderable number; and, as if peace had been already established, became careless of military discipline. The Queen, who watched for such an opportunity, advanced unexpectedly, by a sudden march in the night, with all her forces, and, appearing before Edinburgh, filled that city with the utmost consternation. The Protestants, weakened by the imprudent dispersion of their followers, durst not encounter the French troops in the open field; and were even unable to defend an ill fortified town against their assaults. Unwilling, however, to abandon the citizens to the Queen's mercy, they endeavoured, by facing the enemy's army, to gain time for collecting their own associates. But the Queen, in spite of all their resistance, would have easily forced her way into the town, if the seasonable conclusion of a truce had not procured her admission without the effusion of blood.

Their dangerous situation easily induced the leaders of the Congregation to listen to any overtures of peace; and as the Queen was looking daily for the arrival of a strong reinforcement from France, and expected great advantages from a cessation of arms, she also agreed to it upon no unequal conditions. Together with a suspension of hostilities, from the twenty-fourth of July to the tenth of January, it was stipulated in this treaty that on the one hand the Protestants should open the gates of Edinburgh next morning to the Queen Regent; remain in dutiful subjection to her government; abstain from all future violation of religious houses; and give no interruption to the established clergy, either in the discharge of their functions, or the enjoyment of their benefices. On the other hand, the Queen agreed to give no molestation to the preachers or professors of the Protestant religion; to allow the citizens of Edinburgh, during the cessation of hostilities, to enjoy the exercise of religious worship according to the form most agreeable to the conscience of each individual; and to permit the free and public profession of the Protestant faith in every part of the kingdom. The Queen, by these liberal concessions in behalf of their religion, hoped to soothe the Protestants, and expected, from indulging their favourite passion, to render them more compliant with respect to other articles, particularly the expulsion of the French troops out of Scotland. The anxiety which the Queen expressed for retaining this body of men rendered them more and more the objects of national jealousy and aversion. The immediate expulsion of them was therefore demanded anew, and with greater warmth; but the Queen, taking advantage of the adverse party, eluded the request, and would consent to nothing more than that a French garrison should not be introduced into Edinburgh.

The desperate state of their affairs imposed on the Congregation the necessity of agreeing to this article, which, however, was very far from giving them satisfaction. Whatever apprehensions the Scots had conceived, from retaining the French forces in the kingdom, were abundantly justified during the late commotions. A small body of those troops maintained in constant pay, and rendered formidable by regular discipline, had checked the progress of a martial people, though animated with zeal both for religion and liberty. The smallest addition to their number, and a considerable one was expected, might prove fatal to the public liberty, and Scotland might be exposed to the danger of being reduced from an independent kingdom, to the mean condition of a province annexed to the dominions of its powerful ally.

In order to provide against this imminent calamity, the Duke of Chatelherault and the Earl of Huntly, immediately after concluding the truce, desired an interview with the chiefs of the Congregation. These two noblemen, the most potent at that time in Scotland, were the leaders of the party which adhered to the established church. They had followed the Queen during the late commotions; and, having access to observe more narrowly the dangerous tendency of her councils, their abhorrence of the yoke which was preparing for their country surmounted all other considerations, and determined them rather to endanger the religion which they professed than to give their aid towards the execution of her pernicious designs. They proceeded further, and promised to Argyll, Glencairn, and the Prior of St. Andrew's, who were appointed to meet them, that if the Queen should, with her usual insincerity, violate any article in the treaty of truce, or refuse to gratify the wishes of the whole nation, by dismissing her French troops, they would then instantly join with their countrymen in compelling her to a measure, which the public safety and the preservation of their liberties rendered necessary.

July 8.] About this time died Henry II. of France; just when he had adopted a system, with regard to the affairs of Scotland, which would, in all probability, have restored union and tranquillity to that kingdom. Towards the close of his reign, the Princes of Lorrain began visibly to decline in favour, and the Constable Montmorency, by the assistance of the Duchess of Valentinois, recovered that ascendant over the spirit of his master, which his great experience, and his faithful though often unfortunate services, seemed justly to merit. That prudent minister imputed the insurrections in Scotland wholly to the Duke of Guise and the Cardinal of Lorrain, whose violent and precipitate counsels could not fail of transporting beyond all bounds of moderation men whose minds were possessed with that jealousy which is inseparable from the love of civil liberty, or inflamed with that ardour which accompanies religious zeal. Montmorency, in order to convince Henry that he did not load his rivals with any groundless accusation, prevailed to have Melvil,* a Scottish gentleman of his retinue, dispatched into his native country, with instructions to observe the motions both of the Regent and of her adversaries; and the King agreed to regulate his future proceedings in that kingdom by Melvil's report.

Did history indulge herself in these speculations, it would be amusing to inquire what a different direction might have been given by this resolution to the national sprit; and to what a different issue Melvil's report, which would have set the conduct of the malecontents in the most favourable light, might have conducted the public disorders. Perhaps, by gentle treatment and artful policy, the progress of the Reformation might have been checked, and Scotland brought to depend upon France. Perhaps, by gaining possession of this avenue, the French might have made their way into England; and, under colour of supporting Mary's title to the crown, they might not only have defeated all Elizabeth's measures in favour of the Reformation, but have re-established the Roman Catholic religion, and destroyed the liberties of that kingdom. But into this boundless field of fancy and conjecture the historian must make no excursions; to relate real occurrences, and to explain their real causes and effects, is his peculiar and only province.

The tragical and untimely death of the French Monarch put an end to all moderate and pacific measures with regard to Scotland. The Duke of Guise, and the Cardinal his brother, upon the accession of Francis II., a Prince void of genius and without experience, assumed the chief direction of French affairs. Allied so nearly to the throne, by the marriage of their niece the Queen of Scots with

* The author of the Memoirs.

the young King, they now wanted but little of regal dignity, and nothing of regal power. This power did not long remain inactive in their hands. The same vast schemes of ambition, which they had planned out under the former reign, were again resumed; and they were enabled, by possessing such ample authority, to pursue them with more vigour and greater probability of success. They beheld, with infinite regret, the progress of the Protestant religion in Scotland; and sensible what an unsurmountable obstacle it would prove to their designs, they bent all their strength to check its growth before it rose to any great height. For this purpose they carried on their preparations with all possible expedition, and encouraged the Queen their sister to expect, in a short time, the arrival of an army so powerful as the zeal of their adversaries, however, desperate, would not venture to oppose.

Nor were the Lords of the Congregation either ignorant of those violent counsels which prevailed in the court of France since the death of Henry, or careless of providing against the danger which threatened them from that quarter. The success of their cause, as well as their personal safety, depending entirely on the unanimity and vigour of their own resolutions, they endeavoured to guard against division, and to cement together more closely by entering into a stricter bond of confederacy and mutual defence. Two persons concurred in this new association, who brought a great accession both of reputation and of power to the party. These were the Duke of Chatelherault, and his eldest son the Earl of Arran. This young nobleman, having resided some years in France, where he commanded the Scottish guards, had imbibed the Protestant opinions concerning religion. Hurried along by the heat of youth and the zeal of a proselyte, he had uttered sentiments with respect to the points in controversy which did not suit the temper of a bigoted court, intent at that juncture on the extinction of the Protestant religion; in order to accomplish which the greatest excesses of violence were committed. The church was suffered to wreck its utmost fury upon all who were suspected of heresy. Courts were erected in different parts of France to take cognizance of this crime; and by their sentences several persons of distinction were condemned to the flames.

But, in order to inspire more universal terror, the Princes of Lorrain resolved to select, for a sacrifice, some persons whose fall might convince all ranks of men that neither splendour of birth or eminence in station could exempt from punishment those who should be guilty of this unpardonable transgression. The Earl of Arran was the person destined to be the unhappy victim. As he was allied to one throne, and the presumptive heir to another; as he possessed the first rank in his own country, and enjoyed an honourable station in France; his condemnation could not fail of making the desired impression on the whole kingdom. But the Cardinal of Lorrain having let fell some expressions which raised Arran's suspicions of the design, he escaped the intended blow by a timely flight. Indignation, zeal, resentment, all prompted him to seek revenge upon these persecutors of himself and of the religion which he professed; and as he passed through England on his return to his native country, Elizabeth, by hopes and promises, inflamed those passions, and sent him back into Scotland animated with the same implacable aversion to France which possessed a great part of his countrymen. He quickly communicated these sentiments to his father the Duke of Chatelherault, who was already extremely disgusted with the measures carrying on in Scotland; and as it was the fate of that nobleman to be governed in every instance by those about him, he now suffered himself to be drawn from the Queen Regent; and, having joined the Congregation, was considered from that time as the head of the party.

But with respect to him, this distinction was merely nominal. James Stewart, Prior of St. Andrew's. was the person who moved and actuated the whole body of the Protestants, among whom he possessed that unbounded confidence which his strenuous adherence to their interest and his great abilities so justly merited. He was the natural son of James V. by a daughter of Lord Erskine; and as that amorous monarch had left several others a burden upon the crown, they were all destined for the church, where they could be placed in stations of dignity and affluence. In consequence of this resolution the priory of St. Andrew's had been conferred upon James : but, during so busy a period, he soon became disgusted with the indolence and retirement of a monastic life ; and his enterprising genius called him forth to act a principal part on a more public and conspicuous theatre. The scene in which he appeared required talents of different kinds : military virtue and political discernment were equally necessary in order to render him illustrious. These he possessed in an eminent degree. To the most unquestionable personal bravery he added great skill in the art of war, and in every enterprise his arms were crowned with success. His sagacity and penetration in civil affairs enabled him, amidst the reeling and turbulence of factions, to hold a prosperous course ; while his boldness in defence of the Reformation, together with the decency and even severity of his manners, secured him the reputation of being sincerely attached to religion, without which it was impossible in that age to gain an ascendant over mankind.

It was not without reason that the Queen dreaded the enmity of a man so capable to obstruct her designs. As she could not, with all her address, make the least impression on his fidelity to his associates, she endeavoured to lessen his influence, and to scatter among them the seeds of jealousy and distrust, by insinuating that the ambition of the Prior aspired beyond the condition of a subject, and aimed at nothing less than the crown itself.

An accusation so improbable gained but little credit. Whatever thoughts of this kind the presumption of unexpected success, and his elevation to the highest dignity in the kingdom, may be alleged to have inspired at any subsequent period, it is certain that at this juncture he could form no such vast design. To dethrone a Queen, who was lineal heir to an ancient race of Monarchs ; who had been guilty of no action by which she could forfeit the esteem and affection of her subjects ; who could employ, in defence of her rights, the forces of a kingdom much more powerful than her own ; and to substitute in her place a person whom the illegitimacy of his birth, by the practice of all civilized nations, rendered incapable of any inheritance either public or private; was a project so chimerical as the most extravagant ambition would hardly entertain, and could never conceive to be practicable. The promise too, which the Prior made to Melvil, of residing constantly in France, on condition the public grievances were redressed; the confidence reposed in him by the Duke of Chatelherault and his son, the presumptive heirs to the crown; and the concurrence of almost all the Scottish nobles in promoting the measures by which he gave offence to the French court, go far towards his vindication from those illegal and criminal designs, with the imputation of which the Queen endeavoured at that time to load him.

The arrival of a thousand French soldiers compensated, in some degree, for the loss which the Queen sustained by the defection of the Duke of Chatelherault. These were immediately commanded to fortify Leith, in which place, on account of its commodious harbour, and its situation in the neighbourhood of Edinburgh, and in a plentiful country, the Queen resolved to fix the head-quarters of her foreign forces. This unpopular measure, by the manner of executing it, was rendered still more unpopular. In order to bring the town entirely under their command, the French turned out a great part of the ancient inhabitants, and, taking possession of the houses which they had obliged them to abandon, presented to the view of the Scots two objects equally irritating and offensive: on the one hand, a number of their countrymen expelled their habitations by violence, and wandering without any certain abode; on the other, a colony of foreigners settling with their wives and children in the heart of Scotland, growing into strength by reinforcements, and openly preparing a yoke, to which, without some timely exertion of national spirit, the whole kingdom must of necessity submit.

It was with deep concern that the Lords of the Congregation beheld this bold and decisive step taken by the Queen Regent; nor did they hesitate a moment, whether they should employ their whole strength in one generous effort, to rescue their religion and liberty from impending destruction. But, in order to justify their own conduct, and to throw the blame entirely on their adversaries, they resolved to preserve the appearances of decency and respect towards their superiors, and to have no recourse to arms without the most urgent and apparent necessity. [Sept. 29.] They joined, with this view, in an address to the Regent, representing, in the strongest terms, their dissatisfaction with the measures she was pursuing, and beseeching her to quiet the fears and jealousies of the nation by desisting from fortifying Leith. The Queen, conscious of her present advantageous situation, and elated with the hopes of fresh succours, was in no disposition for listening to demands utterly inconsistent with her views, and urged with that bold importunity which is so little acceptable to Princes.

The suggestions of her French counsellors contributed, without doubt, to alienate her still further from any scheme of accommodation. As the Queen was ready on all occasions to discover an ex-

traordinary deference to the opinions of her countrymen, her brothers, who knew her secret disapprobation of the violent measures
they were driving on, took care to place near her such persons as
betrayed her, by their insinuations, into many actions, which her
own unbiased judgment would have highly condemned. As their
success in the present juncture, when all things were hastening towards a crisis, depended entirely on the Queen's firmness, the
Princes of Lorrain did not trust wholly to the influence of their
ordinary agents ; but, in order to add the greater weight to their
counsels, they called in aid the ministers of religion ; and, by the
authority of their sacred character, they hoped effectually to recommend to their sister that system of severity which they had
espoused. With this view, but under pretence of confounding the
Protestants by the skill of such able masters in controversy, they
appointed several French divines to reside in Scotland. At the
head of these, and with the character of legate from the Pope, was
Pelleve, Bishop of Amiens, and afterwards Archbishop and Cardinal of Sens, a furious bigot, servilely devoted to the house of Guise,
and a proper instrument for recommending or executing the most
outrageous measures.

Amidst the noise and danger of civil arms, these doctors had
little opportunity to display their address in the use of their theological weapons. But they gave no small offence to the nation by
one of their actions. They persuaded the Queen to seize the church
of St. Giles in Edinburgh, which had remained ever since the late
truce in the hands of the Protestants ; and having, by a new and
solemn consecration, purified the fabric from the pollution with
which they supposed the profane ministrations of the Protestants to
have defiled it, they, in direct contradiction to one article in the
late treaty, re-established there the rites of the Romish church.
This, added to the indifference, and even contempt, with which the
Queen received their remonstrances, convinced the Lords of the
Congregation, that it was not only vain to expect any redress of
their grievances at her hands, but absolutely necessary to take arms
in their own defence.

The eager and impetuous spirit of the nation, as well as every
consideration of good policy, prompted them to take this bold step
without delay. It was but a small part of the French auxiliaries
which had as yet arrived. The fortifications of Leith, though ad
vancing fast, were still far from being complete. Under these circumstances of disadvantage, they conceived it possible to surprise
the Queen's party, and by one sudden and decisive blow, to prevent
all future bloodshed and contention. [Oct. 6.] Full of these expectations. they advanced rapidly towards Edinburgh with a
numerous army. But it was no easy matter to deceive an adversary
as vigilant and attentive as the Queen Regent. With her usual
sagacity, she both foresaw the danger, and took the only proper
course to avoid it. Instead of keeping the field against enemies
superior in number, and formidable on a day of battle by the ardour of their courage, she retired into Leith, and determined
patiently to wait the arrival of new reinforcements. Slight
and unfinished as the fortifications of that town then were, she

did not dread the efforts of an army provided neither with heavy cannon nor with military stores, and little acquainted with the method of attacking any place fortified with more art than those ancient towers erected all over the kingdom in defence of private property against the incursions of banditti.

Nor did the Queen meanwhile neglect to have recourse to those arts which she had often employed to weaken or divide her adversaries. By private solicitations and promises she shook the fidelity or abated the ardour of some. By open reproach and accusation she blasted the reputation and diminished the authority of others. Her emissaries were every where at work; and, notwithsanding the zeal for religion and liberty which then animated the nation, they seem to have laboured not without success. We find Knox, about this period, a bounding in complaints of the lukewarm and languid spirit which had begun to spread among his party. But if their zeal slackened a little, and suffered a momentary intermission, it soon blazed up with fresh vigour, and rose to a greater height than ever.

The Queen herself gave occasion to this, by the reply which she made to a new remonstrance from the Lords of the Congregation. Upon their arrival at Edinburgh, they once more represented to her the dangers arising from the increase of the French troops, the fortifying of Leith, and her other measures which they conceived to be destructive to the peace and liberty of the kingdom; and in this address they spoke in a firmer tone, and avowed more openly than ever their resolution of proceeding to the utmost extremities, in order to put a stop to such dangerous encroachments. To a remonstrance of this nature, and urged with so much boldness, the Queen replied in terms no less vigorous and explicit. She pretended that she was not accountable to the confederate lords for any part of her conduct; and upon no representation of theirs would she either abandon measures which she deemed necessary, or dismiss forces which she found useful, or demolish a fortification which might prove of advantage. At the same time she required them, on pain of treason, to disband the forces which they had assembled.

This haughty and imperious style sounded harshly to Scottish nobles, impatient, from their national character, of the slightest appearance of injury; accustomed, even from their own monarchs, to the most respectful treatment; and possessing, under an aristocratical form of government, such a share of power, as equalled at all times, and often controlled, that of the sovereign. They were sensible at once of the indignity offered to themselves, and alarmed with this plain declaration of the Queen's intentions; and as there now remained but one step to take, they wanted neither public spirit nor resolution to take it.

But, that they might not seem to depart from the established forms of the constitution, for which, even amidst their most violent operations, men always retain the greatest reverence, [Oct. 21] they assembled all the peers, barons, and representatives of boroughs, who adhered to their party. These formed a convention, which exceeded in number, and equalled in dignity, the usual meetings of parliament. The leaders of the Congregation laid before them the declaration which the Queen had given in answer to their remonstrance; represented the unavoidable ruin which the measures she therein avowed and justified would bring upon the kingdom; and requiring their direction with regard to the obedience due to an administration so unjust and oppressive, they submitted to their decision a question, one of the most delicate and interesting that can possibly fall under the consideration of subjects.

This assembly proceeded to decide with no less dispatch than unanimity. Strangers to those forms which protract business, unacquainted with the arts which make a figure in debate, and much more fitted for action than discourse, a warlike people always hasten to a conclusion, and bring their deliberations to the shortest issue. It was the work but of one day to examine and to resolve this nice problem, concerning the behaviour of subjects towards a ruler who abuses his power. But, however abrupt their proceedings may appear, they were not destitute of solemnity. As the determination of the point in doubt was conceived to be no less the office of divines than of laymen, the former were called to assist with their opinion. Knox and Willox appeared for the whole order, and pronounced, without hesitation, both from the precepts and examples in Scripture, that it was lawful for subjects not only to resist tyrannical Princes, but to deprive them of that authority which, in their hands, becomes an instrument for destroying those whom the Almighty ordained them to protect. The decision of persons revered so highly for their sacred character, but more for their zeal and their piety, had great weight with the whole assembly. Not satisfied with the common indiscriminate manner of signifying consent, every person present was called in his turn to declare his sentiments; and rising up in order, all gave their suffrages, without one dissenting voice, for depriving the Queen of the office of Regent, which she exercised so much to the detriment of the kingdom.

This extraordinary sentence was owing no less to the love of liberty than to zeal for religion. In the act of deprivation, religious grievances are slightly mentioned; and the dangerous encroachments of the Queen upon the civil constitution are produced by the Lords of the Congregation, in order to prove their conduct to have been not only just but necessary. The introducing foreign troops into a kingdom at peace with all the world; the seizing and fortifying towns in different parts of the country; the promoting strangers to offices of great power and dignity; the debasing the current coin*; the subverting the ancient laws; the imposing of new and burdensome taxes; and the attempting to subdue the kingdom, and to oppress its liberties, by open and repeated acts of

* The standard of money in Scotland was continually varying. In the 16th of James V., A.D. 1529, a pound weight of gold, when coined, produced 108 pounds of current money. But under the Queen Regent's administration, A.D. 1556, a pound weight of gold, although the quantity of alloy was considerably increased, produced 144l. current money. In 1529, a pound weight of silver, when coined, produced 91. 2s.; but in 1556, it produced 13l. current money. Ruddiman. Prefat. ad Anders. Diplomat. Scotiæ. p. 80, 81; from which it appears, that this complaint, which the malecontents often repeated, was not altogether destitute of foundation.

violence, are enumerated at great length, and placed in the strongest light. On all these accounts, the Congregation maintained, that the nobles, as counsellors by birthright to their monarchs, and the guardians and defenders of the constitution, had a right to interpose; and therefore, by virtue of this right, in the name of the King and Queen, and with many expressions of duty and submission towards them, they deprived the Queen Regent of her office, and ordained that, for the future, no obedience should be given to her commands.*

Violent as this action may appear, there wanted not principles in the constitution, nor precedents in the history of Scotland, to justify and to authorize it. Under the aristocratical form of government established among the Scots, the power of the sovereign was extremely limited. The more considerable nobles were themselves petty Princes, possessing extensive jurisdictions, almost independent of the crown, and followed by numerous vassals, who, in every contest, always espoused their chieftain's quarrel in opposition to the King. Hence the many instances of the impotence of regal authority, which are to be found in the Scottish history. In every age, the nobles not only claimed, but exercised, the right of controlling the King. Jealous of their privileges, and ever ready to take the field in defence of them, every error in administration was observed, every encroachment upon the rights of the aristocracy excited indignation, and no Prince ever ventured to transgress the boundaries which the law had prescribed to prerogative, without meeting resistance, which shook or overturned his throne. Encouraged by the spirit of the constitution, and countenanced by the example of their ancestors, the Lords of the Congregation thought it incumbent on them, at this juncture, to inquire into the maladministration of the Queen Regent, and to preserve their country from being enslaved or conquered, by depriving her of the power to execute such a pernicious scheme.

The act of deprivation, and a letter from the Lords of the Congregation to the Queen Regent, are still extant. They discover not only that masculine and undaunted spirit, natural to men capable of so bold a resolution; but are remarkable for a precision and vigour of expression, which we are surprised to meet with in an age so unpolished. The same observation may be made with respect to the other public papers of that period. The ignorance or bad taste of any age may render the compositions of authors by profession obscure, or affected, or absurd: but the language of business is nearly the same at all times; and wherever men think clearly, and are thoroughly interested, they express themselves with perspicuity and force.

* M. Castelnau, after condemning the dangerous counsels of the Princes of Lorrain, with regard to the affairs of Scotland, acknowledges with his usual candour, that the Scots declared war against the Queen Regent, rather from a desire of vindicating their civil liberties than from any motive of religion. Mem. 446.

BOOK III.

1559.

THE Lords of the Congregation soon found that their zeal had engaged them in an undertaking which it was beyond their utmost ability to accomplish. The French garrison, despising their numerous but irregular forces, refused to surrender Leith, and to depart out of the kingdom ; nor were these sufficiently skilful in the art of war, to reduce the place by force, or possessed of the artillery or magazines requisite for that purpose ; and their followers, though of undaunted courage, yet, being accustomed to decide every quarrel by a battle, were strangers to the fatigues of a long campaign, and soon became impatient of the severe and constant duty which a siege requires. The Queen's emissaries, who found it easy to mingle with their countrymen, were at the utmost pains to heighten their disgust, which discovered itself first in murmurs and complaints, but, on occasion of the want of money for paying the army, broke out into open mutiny. The most eminent leaders were hardly secure from the unbridled insolence of the soldiers ; while some of inferior rank, interposing too rashly in order to quell them, fell victims to their rage. Discord, consternation, and perplexity reigned in the camp of the reformers. The Duke, their General, sunk, with his usual timidity, under the terror of approaching danger, and discovered manifest symptoms of repentance for his rashness in espousing such a desperate cause.

In this situation of their affairs, the Congregation had recourse to Elizabeth, from whose protection they could derive their only reasonable hope of success. Some of their more sagacious leaders, having foreseen that the party might probably be involved in great difficulties, had early endeavoured to secure a resource in any such exigency, by entering into a secret correspondence with the court of England. Elizabeth, aware of the dangerous designs which the Princes of Lorrain had formed against her crown, was early sensible of how much importance it would be, not only to check the progress of the French in Scotland, but to extend her own influence in that kingdom ;* and perceiving how effectually the present insurrections would contribute to retard or defeat the schemes formed against England, she listened with pleasure to these applications of the malcontents, and gave them private assurances of powerful support to their cause. Randolph, an agent extremely proper for conducting any dark intrigue, was dispatched into Scotland, and residing secretly among the Lords of the Congregation, observed and quickened their motions. Money seemed to be the only thing they wanted at that time ; and it was owing to a seasonable remittance from England, that the Scottish nobles had been enabled to take the field, and to advance towards Leith. But as

* See Appendix, No. I.

Elizabeth was distrustful of the Scots, and studious to preserve appearances with France, her subsidies were bestowed at first with extreme frugality. The subsistence of an army, and the expenses of a siege, soon exhausted this penurious supply, to which the Lords of the Congregation could make little addition from their own funds; and the ruin and dispersion of the party must have instantly followed.

In order to prevent this, Cockburn of Ormiston was sent, with the utmost expedition, to the governors of the town and castle of Berwick. As Berwick was at that time the town of greatest importance on the Scottish frontier, Sir Ralph Sadler and Sir James Crofts, persons of considerable figure, were employed to command there, and were intrusted with a discretionary power of supplying the Scottish malcontents, according to the exigency of their affairs. From them Cockburn received four thousand crowns, but little to to the advantage of his associates. The Earl of Bothwell, by the Queen's instigation, lay in wait for him on his return, dispersed his followers, wounded him, and carried off the money.

This unexpected disappointment proved fatal to the party. In mere despair, some of the more zealous attempted to assault Leith; but the French beat them back with disgrace, seized their cannon, and, pursuing them to the gates of Edinburgh, were on the point of entering along with them. All the terror and confusion which the prospect of pillage or of massacre can excite in a place taken by storm, filled the city on this occasion. The inhabitants fled from the enemy by the opposite gate; the forces of the Congregation were irresolute and dismayed; and the Queen's partisans in the town openly insulted both. At last, a few of the nobles ventured to face the enemy, who, after plundering some houses in the suburbs, retired with their booty, and delivered the city from this dreadful alarm.

A second skirmish, which happened a few days after, was no less unfortunate. The French sent out a detachment to intercept a convoy of provisions which was designed for Edinburgh. The Lords of the Congregation, having intelligence of this, marched in all haste with a considerable body of their troops, and falling upon the enemy between Restalrig and Leith, with more gallantry than good conduct, were almost surrounded by a second party of French, who advanced in order to support their own men. In this situation a retreat was the only thing which could save the Scots; but a retreat over marshy ground, and in the face of an enemy superior in number, could not long be conducted with order. A body of the enemy hung upon their rear, horse and foot fell into the utmost confusion, and it was entirely owing to the overcaution of the French that any of the party escaped being cut in pieces.

On this second blow, the hopes and spirits of the Congregation sunk altogether. They did not think themselves secure even within the walls of Edinburgh, but instantly determined to retire to some place at a great distance from the enemy. In vain did the Prior of St. Andrew's, and a few others, oppose this cowardly and ignomious flight. The dread of the present danger prevailed over both the sense of honour and zeal for the cause. [Nov. 6.] At midnight they set out from Edinburgh in great confusion, and marched without halting till they arrived at Stirling.

During this last insurrection, the great body of the Scottish nobility joined the Congregation. The Lords Seton and Borthwick were the only persons of rank who took arms for the Queen, and assisted her in defending Leith. Bothwell openly favoured her cause, but resided at his own house. The Earl of Huntly, conformable to the crafty policy which distinguished his character, amused the leaders of the Congregation, whom he had engaged to assist, with many fair promises, but never joined them with a single man. The Earl of Morton, a member of the Congregation, fluctuated in a state of irresolution, and did not act heartily for the common cause. Lord Erskine, governor of Edinburgh castle, though a Protestant, maintained a neutrality, which he deemed becoming the dignity of his office; and having been intrusted by parliament with the command of the principal fortress in the kingdom, he resolved that neither faction should get it into their hands.

A few days before the retreat of the Congregation, the Queen suffered an irreparable loss by the defection of her principal secretary, William Maitland of Lethington. His zeal for the reformed religion, together with his warm remonstraces against the violent measures which the Queen was carrying on, exposed him so much to her resentment, and to that of her French councillors, that he, suspecting his life to be in danger, withdrew secretly from Leith, and fled to the Lords of the Congregation; and they with open arms received a convert, whose abilities added both strength and reputation to their cause. Maitland had early applied to public business admirable natural talents, improved by an acquaintance with the liberal arts; and, at a time of life when his countrymen of the same quality were following the pleasures of the chase, or serving as adventurers in the armies of France, he was admitted into all the secrets of the cabinet, and put upon a level with persons of the most consummate experience in the management of affairs. He possessed, in an eminent degree, that intrepid spirit which delights in pursuing bold designs, and was no less master of that political dexterity which is necessary for carrying them on with success. But these qualities were deeply tinctured with the neighbouring vices. His address sometimes degenerated into cunning; his acuteness bordered upon excess; his invention, over fertile, suggested to him, on some occasions, chimerical systems of policy, too refined for the genius of his age or country; and his enterprising spirit engaged him in projects vast and splendid, but beyond his utmost power to execute. All the contemporary writers, to whatever faction they belong, mention him with an admiration which nothing could have excited but the greatest superiority of penetration and abilities.

The precipitate retreat of the Congregation increased to such a degree the terror and confusion which had seized the party at Edinburgh, that before the army reached Stirling it dwindled to an inconsiderable number. The spirit of Knox however still remained undaunted and erect; and having mounted the pulpit, he addressed to his desponding hearers an exhortation, which wonderfully animated and revived them. The heads of this discourse are inserted in his History, and afford a striking example of the boldness and freedom of reproof assumed by the first reformers, as well as a specimen of his own skill in choosing the topics most fitted to influence and rouse his audience.

A meeting of the leaders being called, to consider what course they should hold, now that their own resources were all exhausted, and that their destruction appeared to be unaviodable without foreign aid, they turned their eyes once more to England, and resolved to implore the assistance of Elizabeth towards finishing an enterprize, in which they had so fatally experienced their own weakness, and the strength of their adversaries. Maitland, as the most able negotiator of the party, was employed in this embassy. In his absence, and during the inactive season of the year, it was agreed to dismiss their followers, worn out by the fatigues of a campaign which had so far exceeded the usual time of service. But, in order to preserve the counties most devoted to their interest, the Prior of St. Andrew's, with part of their leaders, retired into Fife. The Duke of Chatelherault with the rest, fixed his residence at Hamilton. There was little need of Maitland's address or eloquence to induce Elizabeth to take his country under her protection. She observed the prevalence of the French counsels, and the progress of their arms in Scotland, with great concern ; and as she well foresaw the dangerous tendency of their schemes in that kingdom, she had already come to a resolution with regard to the part she herself would act, if their power there should grow still more formidable.

In order to give the Queen and her privy council a full and distinct view of any important matter which might come before them, it seems to have been the practice of Elizabeth's ministers to prepare memorials, in which they clearly stated the point under deliberation, laid the grounds of the conduct which they held to be most reasonable and purposed a method for carrying their plan into execution. Two papers of this kind written by Sir William Cecil with his own hand, and submitted by the Queen to the consideration of her privy council, still remain ; they are entitled, "A short Discussion of the weighty Matter of Scotland," and do honour to the industry and penetration of that great minister. The motives which determined the Queen to espouse so warmly the defence of the Congregation, are represented with perspicuity and force; and the consequences of suffering the French to establish themselves in Scotland are predicted with great accuracy and discernment.

He lays it down as a principle, agreeably to the laws both of God and of nature, that every society hath a right to defend itself, not only from present dangers, but from such as may probably ensue ; to which he adds, that nature and reason teach every prince to defend himself by the same means which his adversaries employ to distress him. Upon these grounds he establishes the right of England to interpose in the affairs of Scotland, and to prevent the conquest of that kingdom, at which the French openly aimed. The French, he observes, are the ancient and implacable enemies of England. Hostilities had subsisted between the two nations for many centuries. No treaty of peace into which they entered had ever been cordial or sincere. No good effect was therefore to be expected from the peace lately agreed upon, which, being extorted by present necessity, would be negligently observed, and broken on the slightest pretences. In a very short time France would recover its former opulence: and though now drained of men and money by a tedious and unsuccessful war, it would quickly be in a condition for acting, and the restless and martial genius of the people render action necessary. The Princes of Lorrain, who at that time had the entire direction of French affairs, were animated with the most virulent hatred against the English nation. They openly called in question the legitimacy of the Queen's birth, and, by advancing the title and pretensions of their neice the Queen of Scotland studied to deprive Elizabeth of her crown. With this view they had laboured to exclude the English from the treaty of Chateau en Cambresis, and endeavoured to conclude a separate peace with Spain. They had persuaded Henry II. to permit his daughter-in-law to assume the title and arms of Queen of England; and even since the conclusion of peace, they had solicited at Rome, and obtained a bull, declaring Elizabeth's birth to be illegitimate. Though the wisdom and moderation of the Constable Montmorency had for some time checked their career, yet these restraints being now removed by the death of Henry II. and the disgrace of his minister, the utmost excesses of violence were to be dreaded from their furious ambition, armed with sovereign power. Scotland is the quarter where they can attack England with most advantage. A war on the borders of that country exposes France to no danger; but one unsuccessful action there may hazard the crown, and overturn the government of England. In political conduct, it is childish to wait till the designs of an enemy be ripe for execution. The Scottish nobles, after their utmost efforts, have been obliged to quit the field; and, far from expelling the invaders of their liberties, they behold the French power daily increasing, and must at last cease from struggling any longer in a contest so unequal. The invading of England will immediately follow the reduction of the Scottish malecontents, by the abandoning of whom to the mercy of the French, Elizabeth will open a way for her enemies into the heart of her own kingdom, and expose it to the calamities of war and the danger of conquest. Nothing therefore remained but to meet the enemy while yet at a distance from England, and, by supporting the Congregation with a powerful army, to render Scotland the theatre of the war, to crush the designs of the Princes of Lorrain in their infancy, and, by such an early and unexpected effort, to expel the French out of Britain, before their power had time to take root and grow up to any formidable height. But as the matter was of as much importance as any which could fall under the consideration of an English monarch, wisdom and mature counsel were necessary in the first place, and afterwards vigour and expedition in conduct; the danger was urgent, and by losing a single moment might become unavoidable.*

* The arguments which the Scots employed, in order to obtain Elizabeth's assistance, are urged with great force in a paper of Maitland's. See Append. No. II.

These arguments produced their full effect upon Elizabeth, who was jealous, in an extreme degree, of every pretender to her crown, and no less anxious to preserve the tranquillity and happiness of her subjects. From these motives she had acted in granting the Congregation an early supply of money; and from the same principles she determined, in their present exigency, to afford them more effectual aid. One of Maitland's attendants was instantly dispatched into Scotland with the strongest assurances of her protection, and the Lords of the Congregation were desired to send Commissioners into England to conclude a treaty, and to settle the operations of the campaign with the Duke of Norfolk.

Meanwhile the Queen Regent, from whom no motion of the Congregation could long be concealed, dreaded the success of this negotiation with the court of England, and foresaw how little she would be able to resist the united efforts of the two kingdoms. For this reason she determined, if possible, to get the start of Elizabeth; and by venturing, notwithstanding the inclemency of the winter season, to attack the malcontents in their present dispersed and helpless situation, she hoped to put an end to the war before the arrival of their English allies.

A considerable body of her French forces, who were augmented about this time by the arrival of the Count de Martigues, with a thousand veteran foot, and some cavalry, were commanded to march to Stirling. Having there crossed the Forth, they proceeded along the coast of Fife, destroying and plundering, with excessive outrage, the houses and lands of those they deemed their enemies. Fife was the most populous and powerful county in the kingdom, and most devoted to the Congregation, who had hitherto drawn from thence their most considerable supplies, both of men and provisions; and therefore, besides punishing the disaffection of the inhabitants by pillaging the country, the French proposed to seize and fortify St. Andrew's, and to leave in it a garrison sufficient to bridle the mutinous spirit of the province, and to keep possession of a port situated on the main ocean.

But on this occasion the Prior of St. Andrew's, Lord Ruthven, Kirkaldy of Grange, and a few of the most active leaders of the Congregation, performed, by their bravery and good conduct, a service of the utmost importance to their party. Having assembled six hundred horse they infested the French with continual incursions, beat up their quarters, intercepted their convoys of provisions, cut off their straggling parties, and so harrassed them with perpetual alarms that they prevented them for more than three weeks from advancing.

1560.] At last the Prior, with his feeble party, was constrained to retire, and the French set out from Kirkaldy, and began to move along the coast towards St. Andrew's. [Jan. 23.] They had advanced but a few miles when, from an eminence, they descried a powerful fleet steering its course up the Frith of Forth. As they knew that the Marquis D'Elbeuf was at that time preparing to sail for Scotland with a numerous army, they hastily concluded that these ships belonged to them, and gave way to the most immoderate transports of joy on the prospect of this long expected succour. Their great guns were already fired to welcome their friends, and to spread the tidings and terror of their arrival among their enemies, when a small boat from the opposite coast landed, and blasted their premature and short-lived triumph, by informing them that it was the fleet of England which was in sight, intended for the aid of the Congregation, and was soon to be followed by a formidable land army.

Throughout her whole reign Elizabeth was cautious but decisive; and, by her promptitude in executing her resolutions, joined to the deliberation with which she formed them, her administration became remarkable no less for its vigour than for its wisdom. No sooner did she determine to afford her protection to the Lords of the Congregation, than they experienced the activity as well as the extent of her power. The season of the year would not permit her land army to take the field; but, lest the French should, in the mean time, receive new reinforcements, she instantly ordered a strong squadron to cruise in the Frith of Forth. She seems, by her instructions to Winter her Admiral, to have been desirous of preserving the appearances of friendship towards the French. But these were only appearances; if any French fleet should attempt to land, he was commanded to prevent it by every act of hostility and violence. It was the sight of this squadron which occasioned at first so much joy among the French, but soon inspired them with such terror as saved Fife from the effects of their vengeance. Apprehensive of being cut off from their companions on the opposite shore, they retreated towards Stirling with the utmost precipitation, and in a dreadful season, and through roads almost impassable, arrived at Leith, harassed and exhausted with fatigue.

The English fleet cast anchor in the road of Leith, and continuing in that station till the conclusion of the peace, both prevented the garrison of Leith from receiving succours of any kind, and considerably facilitated the operations of their own forces by land.

Feb. 27.] Soon after the arrival of the English squadron, the Commissioners of the Congregation repaired to Berwick, and concluded with the Duke of Norfolk a treaty, the bond of that union with Elizabeth which was of so great advantage to the cause. To give a check to the dangerous and rapid progress of the French arms in Scotland was the professed design of the contracting parties. In order to this the Scots engaged never to suffer any closer union of their country with France; and to defend themselves to the uttermost against all attempts of conquest. Elizabeth, on her part, promised to employ in Scotland a powerful army for their assistance, which the Scots undertook to join with all their forces; no place in Scotland was to remain in the hands of the English; whatever should be taken from the enemy was either to be razed or kept by the Scots at their choice; if any invasion should be made upon England, the Scots were obliged to assist Elizabeth with part of their forces; and, to ascertain their faithful observance of the treaty, they bound themselves to deliver hostages to Elizabeth, before the march of her army into Scotland: in conclusion, the Scots made many protestations of obedience and loyalty towards their own Queen, in every thing not inconsistent with their religion and the liberties of their country..

The English army, consisting of six thousand foot and two thousand horse, under the command of Lord Gray of Wilton, entered Scotland early in the spring. The members of the Congregation assembled from all parts of the kingdom to meet their new allies; and having joined them, they advanced together towards Leith [April 2]. The French were little able to keep the field against an enemy so much superior in number. A strong body of troops, destined for their relief, had been scattered by a violent storm, and had either perished on the coast of France, or with difficulty had recovered the ports of that kingdom. But they hoped to be able to defend Leith till the Princes of Lorrain should make good the magnificent promises of assistance with which they daily encouraged them; or till scarcity of provisions should constrain the English to retire into their own country. In order to hasten this latter event, they did not neglect the usual though barbarous precaution for distressing an invading enemy, by burning and laying waste all the adjacent country. The zeal, however, of the nation frustrated their intentions: eager to contribute towards removing their oppressors, the people produced their hidden stores to support their friends; the neighbouring counties supplied every thing necessary; and, far from wanting subsistence, the English found in their camp all sorts of provisions at a cheaper rate than had for some time been known in that part of the kingdom.

On the approach of the English army the Queen Regent retired into the castle of Edinburgh. Her health was now in a declining state, and her mind broken and depressed by the misfortunes of her administration. To avoid the danger and fatigue of a siege, she committed herself to the protection of Lord Erskine. This nobleman still preserved his neutrality, and by his integrity and love of his country merited equally the esteem of both parties. He received the Queen herself with the utmost honour and respect, but took care to admit of no such retinue as might endanger his command of the castle.

April 6.] A few days after they arrived in Scotland, the English invested Leith. The garrison shut up within the town was almost half as numerous as the army which sat before it, and by an obstinate defence protracted the siege to a great length. The circumstances of this siege, related by contemporary historians, men without knowledge or experience in the art of war, are often obscure and imperfect, and at this distance of time are not considerable enough to be entertaining.

At first the French endeavoured to keep possession of the Hawk Hill, a rising ground not far distant from the town, but were beat from it with great slaughter [April 15], chiefly by the furious attack of the Scottish cavalry. Within a few days the French had their full revenge; having sallied out with a strong body, they entered the English trenches, broke their troops, nailed part of their cannon, and killed at least double the number they had lost in the former skirmish. Nor were the English more fortunate in an attempt which they made to take the place by assault [May 7]; they were met with equal courage, and repulsed with considerable loss. From the detail of these circumstances by the writers of that age, it is easy to observe the different characters of the French and English troops. The former, trained to war during the active reigns of Francis I. and Henry II., defended themselves not only with the bravery but with the skill of veterans. The latter, who had been more accustomed to peace, still preserved the intrepid and desperate valour peculiar to the nation, but discovered few marks of military genius or experience in the practice of war. Every misfortune or disappointment during the siege must be imputed to manifest errors in conduct. The success of the besieged in their sally was owing entirely to the security and negligence of the English; many of their officers were absent; their soldiers had left their stations; and their trenches were almost without a guard. The ladders, which had been provided for the assault, wanted a great deal of necessary length; and the troops employed in that service were ill supported. The trenches were opened at first in an improper place; and as it was found expedient to change the ground, both time and labour was lost. The inability of their own generals, no less than the strength of the French garrison, rendered the progress of the English wonderfully slow. The long continuance, however, of the siege, and the loss of part of their magazines by an accidental fire, reduced the French to extreme distress for want of provisions, which the prospect of relief made them bear with admirable fortitude.

While the hopes and courage of the French protracted the siege so far beyond expectation, the leaders of the Congregation were not idle. By new associations and confederacies they laboured to unite their party more perfectly. By publicly ratifying the treaty concluded at Berwick, they endeavoured to render the alliance with England firm and indissoluble. Among the subscribers of these papers we find the Earl of Huntly, and some others, who had not hitherto concurred with the Congregation in any of their measures. Several of these Lords, particularly the Earl of Huntly, still adhered to the Popish church; but on this occasion, neither their religious sentiments nor their former cautious maxims were regarded; the torrent of national resentment and indignation against the French hurried them on.*

June 10.] The Queen Regent, the instrument rather than the cause of involving Scotland in those calamities under which it groaned at that time, died during the heat of the siege. No Princess ever possessed qualities more capable of rendering her administration illustrious, or the kingdom happy. Of much discernment

---

* The dread of the French power did on many occasions surmount the zeal which the Catholic nobles had for their religion. Besides the presumptive evidence for this, arising from the memorial mentioned by Burnet, Hist. of the Reformation, vol. iii., 281, and published by him, Append. p. 278, the instructions of Elizabeth to Randolph her agent put it beyond all doubt that many zealous Papists thought the alliance with England to be necessary for preserving the liberty and independence of the kingdom. Keith, 158. Huntly himself begun a correspondence with Elizabeth's ministers, before the march of the English army into Scotland. Haynes's State Papers, 261, 263. See Append. No. III.

and no less address; of great intrepidity and equal prudence; gentle and humane, without weakness; zealous for her religion, without bigotry; a lover of justice, without rigour. One circumstance, however, and that, too, the excess of a virtue, rather than any vice, poisoned all these great qualities, and rendered her government unfortunate and her name odious. Devoted to the interest of France, her native country, and attached to the Princes of Lorrain, her brothers, with most passionate fondness, she departed, in order to gratify them, from every maxim which her own wisdom or humanity would have approved. She outlived, in a great measure, that reputation and popularity, which had smoothed her way to the highest station in the kingdom; and many examples of falsehood, and some of severity, in the latter part of her administration, alienated from her the affections of a people who had once placed in her an unbounded confidence. But, even by her enemies, these unjustifiable actions were imputed to the facility, not to the malignity of her nature; and while they taxed her brothers and French counsellors with rashness and cruelty, they still allowed her the praise of prudence and of lenity. A few days before her death, she desired an interview with the Prior of St. Andrew's, the Earl of Argyle, and other chiefs of the Congregation. To them she lamented the fatal issue of those violent counsels which she had been obliged to follow; and with the candour natural to a generous mind, confessed the errors of her own administration, and begged forgiveness of those to whom she had been hurtful; but at the same time she warned them, amidst their struggles for liberty and the shock of arms, not to lose sight of the loyalty and subjection which were due to their sovereign. The remainder of her time she employed in religious meditations and exercises. She even invited the attendance of Willox, one of the most eminent of the reformed preachers, listened to his instructions with reverence and attention, and prepared for the approach of death with a decent fortitude.

Nothing could now save the French troops shut up in Leith but the immediate conclusion of a peace, or the arrival of a powerful army from the continent. The Princes of Lorrain amused their party in Scotland with continual expectations of the latter, and had thereby kept alive their hopes and their courage; but, at last, the situation of France, rather than the terror of the English arms, or the remonstrances of the Scottish malcontents, constrained them, though with reluctance, to turn their thoughts towards pacific counsels. The Protestants in France were at that time a party formidable by their number, and more by the valour and enterprising genius of their leaders. Francis II. had treated them with extreme rigour, and discovered, by every step he took, a settled resolution to extirpate their religion, and to ruin those who professed it. At the prospect of this danger to themselves and to their cause, the Protestants were alarmed, but not terrified. Animated with zeal, and inflamed with resentment, they not only prepared for their own defence, but resolved, by some bold action, to antici pate the schemes of their enemies; and as the Princes of Lorrain were deemed the authors of all the King's violent measures, they

marked them out to be the first victims of their indignation.
[March 15.] Hence, and not from disloyalty to the King, proceeded
the famous conspiracy of Amboise; and though the vigilance and
good fortune of the Princes of Lorrain discovered and disappointed
that design, it was easy to observe new storms gathering in every
province in the kingdom, and ready to burst out with all the fury
and outrage of civil war. In this situation the ambition of the
house of Lorrain was called off from the thoughts of foreign conquests, to defend the honour and dignity of the French crown;
and, instead of sending new reinforcements into Scotland, it became
necessary to withdraw the veteran troops already employed in that
kingdom.

In order to conduct an affair of so much importance and delicacy, the Princes of Lorrain made choice of Monluc, Bishop of
Valence, and of the Sieur de Randan. As both these, especially
the former, were reckoned inferior to no persons of that age in address and political refinement, Elizabeth opposed to them ambassadors of equal abilities; Cecil, her prime minister, a man perhaps
of the greatest capacity who had ever held that office; and Wotton,
Dean of Canterbury, grown old in the art of negotiating under
three successive monarchs. The interest of the French and English courts were soon adjusted by men of so great dexterity in business; and as France easily consented to withdraw those forces
which had been the chief occasion of the war, the other points in
dispute between that kingdom and England were not matters of
tedious or of difficult discussion.

The grievances of the Congregation, and their demands upon
their own sovereigns for redress, employed longer time, and required
to be treated with a more delicate hand. After so many open attempts, carried on by command of the King and Queen, in order
to overturn the ancient constitution, and to suppress the religion
which they embraced, the Scottish nobles could not think themselves secure without fixing some new barrier against the future encroachments of regal power. But the legal steps towards accomplishing this were not so obvious. The French ambassadors considered the entering into any treaty with subjects, and with rebels,
as a condescension unsuitable to the dignity of a sovereign; and
their scruples on this head might have put an end to the treaty, if
the impatience of both parties for peace had not suggested an expedient, which seemed to provide for the security of the subject,
without derogating from the honour of the Prince. The Scottish
nobles agreed, on this occasion, to pass from the point of right and
privilege, and to accept the redress of their grievances as a matter
of favour. Whatever additional security their anxiety for personal
safety or their zeal for public liberty prompted them to demand
was granted in the name of Francis and Mary, as acts of their
royal favour and indulgence. And, lest concessions of this kind
should seem precarious, and liable to be retracted by the same
power which had made them, the French ambassador agreed to in-
sert them in the treaty with Elizabeth, and thereby to bind the
King and Queen inviolably to observe them.

In relating this transaction, contemporary historians have con-

founded the concessions of Francis and Mary to their Scottish subjects, with the treaty between France and England; the latter, besides the ratification of former treaties between the two kingdoms,
and stipulations with regard to the time and manner of removing
both armies out of Scotland, contained an article to which, as the
source of many important events, we shall often have occasioned to
refer. The right of Elizabeth to her crown is thereby acknowledged in the strongest terms; and Francis and Mary solemnly engaged neither to assume the title nor to bear the arms of King and
Queen of England in any time to come.

July 6.] Honourable as this article was for Elizabeth herself, the
conditions she obtained for her allies the Scots were no less advantageous to them. Monluc and Randan consented, in the name
of Francis and Mary, that the French forces in Scotland should instantly be sent back into their own country, and no foreign troops
be hereafter introduced into the kingdom without the knowledge
and consent of Parliament; that the fortifications of Leith and
Dunbar should immediately be razed, and no new fort be erected
without the permission of Parliament; that a Parliament should be
held on the first day of August, and that assembly be deemed as
valid in all respects as if it had been called by the express commandment of the King and Queen; that, comformable to the ancient laws and customs of the country, the King and Queen should
not declare war or conclude peace without the concurrence of Parliament; that, during the Queen's absence, the administration of
government should be vested in a council of twelve persons, to be
chosen out of twenty-four named by Parliament, seven of which
counsel to be elected by the Queen, and five by the Parliament;
that hereafter the King and Queen should not advance foreigners to
places of trust or dignity in the kingdom, nor confer the offices of
treasurer or comptroller of the revenues upon any ecclesiastics;
that an act of oblivion, abolishing the guilt and memory of all offences committed since the 6th of March, 1558, should be passed in
the ensuing Parliament, and be ratified by the King and Queen;
that the King and Queen should not, under the colour of punishing
any violation of their authority during that period, seek to deprive
any of their subjects of the offices, benefices, or estates which they
now hold; that the redress due to churchmen, for the injuries
which they had sustained during the late insurrections, should be
left entirely to the cognizance of Parliament. With regard to religious controversies, the ambassadors declared that they would not
presume to decide, but permitted the Parliament, at their first
meeting, to examine the points in difference, and to represent their
sense of them to the King and Queen.

To such a memorable period did the Lords of the Congregation,
by their courage and perseverance, conduct an enterprise which at
first promised a very different issue. From beginnings extremely
feeble, and even contemptible, the party grew by degrees to great
power; and, being favoured by many fortunate incidents, baffled
all the efforts of their own Queen, aided by the forces of a more
considerable kingdom. The sovereign authority was by this treaty
transferred wholly into the hands of the Congregation; that limited

prerogative which the crown had hitherto possessed, was almost entirely annihilated : and the aristocratical power, which always predominated in the Scottish government, became supreme and incontrolable.   By this treaty, too, the influence of France, which had long been of much weight in the affairs of Scotland, was greatly diminished ; and not only were the present encroachments of that ambitious ally restrained, but, by confederating with England, protection was provided against any future attempt from the same quarter.   At the same time, the controversies in religion being left to the consideration of Parliament, the Protestants might reckon upon obtaining whatever decision was most favourable to the opinions which they professed.

A few days after the conclusion of the treaty, both the French and English armies quitted Scotland.

The eyes of every man in that kingdom were turned towards the approaching Parliament.   A meeting, summoned in a manner so extraordinary, at such a critical juncture, and to deliberate upon matters of so much consequence, was expected with the utmost anxiety.

A Scottish Parliament suitable to the aristocratical genius of the government, was properly an assembly of the nobles.   It was composed of bishops, abbots, barons, and a few commissioners of boroughs, who met all together in one house.   The lesser barons, though possessed of a right to be present, either in person or by their representatives, seldom exercised it.   The expense of attending, according to the fashion of the times, with a numerous train of vassals and dependants ; the inattention of a martial age to the forms and detail of civil government ; but, above all, the exorbitant authority of the greater nobles, who had drawn the whole power into their own hands, made this privilege of so little value as to be almost neglected.   It appears from the ancient rolls that, during times of tranquillity, few commissioners of boroughs, and almost none of the lesser barons, appeared in Parliament.   The ordinary administration of government was abandoned, without scruple or jealousy, to the King and to the greater barons.   But in extraordinary conjunctures, when the struggle for liberty was violent, and the spirit of opposition to the crown rose to a height, the burgesses and lesser barons were roused from their inactivity, and stood forth to vindicate the rights of their country.   The turbulent reign of James III. affords examples in proof of this observation.   The public indignation, against the rash designs of that weak and ill-advised Prince, brought into Parliament, besides the greater nobles and prelates, a considerable number of the lesser barons.

The same causes occasioned the unusual confluence of all orders of men to the Parliament, which met on the first of August.   The universal passion for liberty, civil and religious, which had seized the nation, suffered few persons to remain unconcerned spectators of an assembly, whose acts were likely to prove decisive with respect to both.   From all corners of the kingdom men flocked in, eager and determined to aid, with their voices in the senate, the same cause which they had defended with their swords in the field.   Besides a full convention of peers, temporal and spiritual, there appeared the representatives of almost all the boroughs, and above a hundred barons, who, though of the lesser order, were gentlemen of the first rank and fortune in the nation.

The Parliament was ready to enter on business with the utmost zeal, when a difficulty was started concerning the lawfulness of the meeting. No commissioner appeared in the name of the King and Queen, and no signification of their consent and approbation was yet received. These were deemed by many essential to the very being of a Parliament. But in opposition to this sentiment, the express words of the treaty of Edinburgh were urged, by which this assembly was declared to be as valid, in all respects, as if it had been called and appointed by the express command of the King and Queen. As the adherents of the Congregation greatly outnumbered their adversaries, the latter opinion prevailed. Their boldest leaders, and those of most approved zeal, were chosen to be lords of the articles, who formed a committee of ancient use and of great importance in the Scottish Parliament.* The deliberations of the lords of the articles were carried on with the most unanimous and active zeal. The act of oblivion, the nomination of twenty-four persons, out of whom the council, intrusted with supreme authority, was to be elected; and every other thing prescribed by the late treaty, or which seemed necessary to render it effectual, passed without dispute or delay. The article of religion employed longer time, and was attended with greater difficulty. It was brought into Parliament by a petition from those who adopted the principles of the Reformation. Many doctrines of the Popish church was a contradiction to reason, and a disgrace to religion; its discipline had become corrupt and oppressive; and its revenues were both exorbitant and ill applied. Against all these the Protestants remonstrated with the utmost asperity of style, which indignation at their absurdity, or experience of their pernicious tendency, could inspire; and, encouraged by the number as well as zeal of their friends, to improve such a favourable juncture, they aimed the blow at the whole fabric of popery, and besought the Parliament to interpose its authority for rectifying these multiplied abuses.†

Several prelates, zealously attached to the ancient superstition, were present in this Parliament. But, during these vigorous proceedings of the Protestants, they stood confounded and at gaze; and persevered in a silence which was fatal to their cause. They deemed it impossible to resist or divert that torrent of religious zeal, which was still in its full strength; they dreaded that their opposition would irritate their adversaries and excite them to new acts of violence; they hoped that the King and Queen would soon be at leisure to put a stop to the career of their insolent subjects, and that, after the rage and havoc of the present storm, the former tranquillity and order would be restored to the church and kingdom.

* From an original letter of Hamilton, Archbishop of St. Andrew's, it appears that the lords of articles were chosen in the manner afterwards appointed by an act of parliament, 163 ..—Keith. p. 487. Spotswood seems to consider this to have been the common practice. Hist. 149.

† Knox, 257.

They were willing, perhaps, to sacrifice the doctrine, and even the power of the church, in order to ensure the safety of their own persons, and to preserve the possession of those revenues which were still in their hands. From whatever motives they acted, their silence, which was imputed to the consciousness of a bad cause, afforded matter of great triumph to the Protestants, and encouraged them to proceed with more boldness and alacrity.

The Parliament did not think it enough to condemn those doctrines mentioned in the petition of the Protestants; they moreover gave the sanction of their approbation to a Confession of Faith presented to them by the reformed teachers; and composed, as might be expected from such a performance at that juncture, on purpose to expose the absurd tenets and practices of the Romish church. By another act the jurisdiction of the ecclesiastical courts was abolished, and the causes which formerly came under their cognizance were transferred to the decision of civil judges. By a third statute, the exercise of religious worship, according to the rites of the Romish church, was prohibited. The manner in which the Parliament enforced the observation of this law discovers the zeal of that assembly; the first transgression subjected the offender to the forfeiture of his goods, and to a corporeal punishment at the discretion of the judge; banishment was the penalty of the second violation of the law : and a third act of disobedience was declared to be capital. Such strangers were men at that time to the spirit of toleration, and to the laws of humanity; and with such indecent haste did the very persons who had just escaped the rigour of ecclesiastical tyranny, proceed to imitate those examples of severity of which they themselves had so justly complained.

The vigorous zeal of the Parliament overturned in a few days the ancient system of religion, which had been established so many ages. In reforming the doctrine and discipline of the church the nobles kept pace with the ardour and expectations even of Knox himself. But their proceedings with respect to these were not more rapid and impetuous than they were slow and dilatory when they entered on the consideration of ecclesiastical revenues. Among the lay members, some were already enriched with the spoils of the church, and others devoured in expectation the wealthy benefices which still remained untouched. The alteration in religion had afforded many of the dignified ecclesiastics themselves an opportunity of gratifying their avarice or ambition. The demolition of the monasteries having set the monks at liberty from their confinement, they instantly dispersed all over the kingdom, and commonly betook themselves to some secular employment. The abbot, if he had been so fortunate as to embrace the principles of the Reformation from conviction, or so cunnning as to espouse them out of policy, seized the whole revenues of the fraternity; and, except what he allowed for the subsistence of a few superannuated monks, applied them entirely to his own use. The proposal made by the reformed teachers, for applying these revenues towards the maintenance of ministers, the education of youth, and the support of the poor, was equally dreaded by all these orders of men. They opposed it with the utmost warmth, and by their numbers and authority easily prevailed on Parliament to give no ear to such a disagreeable demand. Zealous as the first reformers were, and animated with a spirit superior to the low considerations of interest, they beheld these early symptoms of selfishness and avarice among their adherents with amazement and sorrow; and we find Knox expressing the utmost sensibility of that contempt with which they were treated by many from whom he expected a more generous concern for the success of religion and the honour of its ministers.

A difficulty hath been started with regard to the acts of this parliament concerning religion. This difficulty, which at such a distance of time is of no importance, is founded on the words of the treaty of Edinburgh. By that the parliament were permitted to take into consideration the state of religion, and to signify their sentiments of it to the King and Queen. But, instead of presenting their desires to their sovereign in the humble form of a supplication or address, the parliament converted them into so many acts; which, although they never received the royal assent, obtained all over the kingdom the weight and authority of laws. In compliance with their injunctions, the established system of religion was every where overthrown, and that recommended by the reformers introduced in its place. The partiality and zeal of the people overlooked or supplied any defect in the form of these acts of parliament, or rather the nation, violated the last article in the treaty of Edinburgh, and even exceeded the powers which belong to subjects.— But when men have been accustomed to break through the common boundaries of subjection, and their minds are inflamed with the passions which civil war inspires, it is mere pedantry or ignorance to measure their conduct by those rules which can be applied only where government is in a state of order and tranquillity. A nation, when obliged to employ such extraordinary efforts in defence of its liberties, avails itself of every thing which can promote this great end; and the necessity of the case, as well as the importance of the object, justify any departure from the common and established rules of the constitution.

In consequence of the treaty of Edinburgh, as well as by the ordinary forms of business, it became necessary to lay the proceedings of parliament before the King and Queen. For this purpose Sir James Sandilands of Calder, Lord St. John, was appointed to repair to the court of France. After holding a course so irregular, the leaders of the Congregation had no reason to flatter themselves that Francis and Mary would ever approve their conduct, or confirm it by their royal assent. The reception of their ambassador was no other than they might have expected. He was treated by the King and Queen with the utmost coldness, and dismissed without obtaining the ratification of the parliament's proceedings. From the Princes of Lorrain, and their partisans, he endured all the scorn and insult which it was natural for them to pour upon the party he represented.

Though the Earls of Morton, Glencairn, and Maitland of Lethington, the ambassadors of the parliament to Elizabeth their protectress, met with a very different reception, they were not more sus-

cessful in one part of the negotiation intrusted to their care. The
Scots, sensible of the security which they derived from their union
with England, were desirous of rendering it indissoluble. With
this view, they empowered these eminent leaders of their party to
testify to Elizabeth their gratitude for that seasonable and effectual
aid which she had afforded them ; and at the same time to beseech
her to render the friendship between the nations perpetual, by condescending to marry the Earl of Arran, who, though a subject, was
nearly allied to the royal family of Scotland, and, after Mary, the
undoubted heir to the crown.

To the former part of this commission Elizabeth listened with
the utmost satisfaction, and encouraged the Scots, in any future
exigency, to hope for the continuance of her good offices ; with regard to the latter, she discovered those sentiments to which she adhered throughout her whole reign. Averse from marriage, as some
maintain through choice, but most probably out of policy, that
ambitious Princess would never admit any partner to the throne ;
but delighted with the entire and uncontrolled exercise of power,
she sacrificed to the enjoyment of that the hopes of transmitting
her crown to her own posterity. The marriage with the Earl of
Arran could not be attended with any such extraordinary advantage as to shake this resolution ; she declined, it, therefore, but with
many expressions of good will towards the Scottish nation, and of
respect for Arran himself.

Towards the conclusion of this year, distinguished by so many
remarkable events, there happened one of great importance. On
the fourth of December died Francis II., a Prince of a feeble constitution, and of a mean understanding. As he did not leave any
issue by the Queen, no incident could have been more fortunate to
those who, during the late commotions in Scotland, had taken
part with the Congregation. Mary, by the charms of her beauty,
had acquired an entire ascendant over her husband ; and as she
transferred all her influence to her uncles, the Princes of Lorrain,
Francis followed them implicitly in whatever track they were
pleased to lead him. The power of France, under such direction,
alarmed the Scottish malecontents with apprehensions of danger no
less formidable than well founded. The intestine disorders which
raged in France, and the seasonable interposition of England on
behalf of the Congregation, had hitherto prevented the Princes of
Lorrain from carrying their designs upon Scotland into execution.
But, under their vigorous and decisive administrations, it was impossible that the commotions in France could be of long continuance, and many things might fall in to divert Elizabeth's attention,
for the future, from the affairs of Scotland. In either of these
events, the Scots would stand exposed to all the vengeance
which the resentment of the French court could inflict. The
blow, however long suspended, was unavoidable, and must fall at
last with redoubled weight. From this prospect and expectation
of danger, the Scots were delivered by the death of Francis ; the
ancient confederacy of the two kingdoms had already been broken,
and by this event the chief bond of union which remained was
dissolved. Catherine of Medicis, who, during the minority of

Charles IX., her eldest son, engrossed the entire direction of the French councils, was far from any thoughts of vindicating the Scottish Queen's authority. Catherine and Mary had been rivals in power during the reign of Francis II., and had contended for the government of that weak and inexperienced Prince; but as the charms of the wife easily triumphed over the authority of the mother, Catherine could never forgive such a disappointment in her favourite passion, and beheld now, with secret pleasure, the diffi-cult and perplexing scene on which her daughter-in-law was now about to enter. Mary, overwhelmed with all the sorrow which so sad a reverse of fortune could occasion, slighted by the Queen-mother, and forsaken by the tribe of courtiers, who appear only in the sunshine of prosperity, retired to Rheims, and there in solitude indulged her grief, or hid her indignation. Even the Princes of Lorrain were obliged to contract their views: to turn them from foreign to domestic objects; and, instead of forming vast projects with regard to Britain, they found it necessary to think of acquir-ing and establishing an interest with the new administration.

It is impossible to describe the emotions of joy which, on all these accounts, the death of the French monarch excited among the Scots. They regarded it as the only event which could give firmness and stability to that system of religion and government which was now introduced : and it is no wonder contemporary his-torians should ascribe it to the immediate care of Providence, which, by unforeseen expedients, can secure the peace and happi-ness of kingdoms, in those situations where human prudence and invention would utterly despair.

About this time the Protestant church of Scotland began to as-sume a regular form. Its principles had assumed the sanction of public authority, and some fixed external policy became necessary for the government and preservation of the infant society. The model introduced by the reformers differed extremely from that which had been long established. The motives which induced them to depart so far from the ancient system deserves to be explained.

The licentious lives of the clergy, as has been already observed, seem to have been among the first things that excited any suspicion concerning the truth of the doctrines which they taught, and roused that spirit of inquiry which proved fatal to the popish sys-tem. As this disgust of the vices of ecclesiastics was soon trans-ferred to their persons, and shifting from them, by no violent tran-sition, settled at last upon the offices which ¦they enjoyed ; the ef-fects of the Reformation would naturally have extended not only to the doctrine, but to the form of government in the popish church; and the same spirit which abolished the former would¬have over-turned the latter. But in the arrangements which took place in the different kingdoms and states of Europe, in consequence of the Reformation, we may observe something similar to what happened upon the first establishment of Christianity in the Roman empire. In both periods, the form of ecclesiastical policy was modelled, in some measure, upon that of the civil government. When the Christian Church was patronised and established by the state, the jurisdiction of the various orders of the ecclesiastics, distinguished

by the names of Patriarchs, Archbishops, and Bishops, was made to
correspond with the various divisions of the empire; and the eccle-
siastic of chief eminence in each of these possessed authority, more
or less extensive, in proportion to that of the civil magistrate who
presided over the same district. When the Reformation took place,
the episcopal form of government, with its various ranks and degrees of subordination, appearing to be most consistent with the
genius of monarchy, it was continued, with a few limitations, in
several provinces of Germany, in England, and in the northern
kingdoms. But in Switzerland and some parts of the Low Countries, where the popular form of government allowed more full
scope to the innovating genius of the Reformation, all pre-eminence
of order in the church was destroyed, and an equality established
more suitable to the spirit of republican policy. As the mode of
episcopal government was copied from that of the Christian church
as established in the Roman empire, the situation of the primitive
church, prior to its establishment by civil authority, seems to have
suggested the idea, and furnished the model, of the latter system,
which has since been denominated *Presbyterian.* The first Ch s-
tians, oppressed by continual persecutions, and obliged to hold their
religious assemblies by stealth and in corners, were contented with
a form of government extremely simple. The influence of religion
concurred with the sense of danger, in extinguishing among them
the spirit of ambition, and in preserving a parity of rank, the
effect of their sufferings, and the cause of many of their virtues.
Calvin, whose decisions were received among many Protestants of
that age with indescribable submission, was the patron and restorer of this scheme of ecclesiastical policy. The church of Geneva, formed under his eye and under his direction, was deemed
the most perfect model of this government; and Knox, who, during
his residence in that city, had studied and admired it, warmly recommended it to the imitation of his countrymen.

Among the Scottish nobility, some hated the persons, and others
coveted the wealth, of the dignified clergy. By abolishing that order of men, the former indulged their resentment, and the latter
hoped to gratify their avarice. The people, inflamed with the most
violent aversion to popery, and approving of every scheme that departed farthest from the practice of the Roman church, were delighted with a system so admirably suited to their predominant
passion : while the friends of civil liberty beheld with pleasure the
Protestant clergy pulling down with their own hands that fabric of
ecclesiastical power which their own predecessors had reared with
so much art and industry; and flattered themselves that, by lending their aid to strip churchmen of their dignity and wealth, they
might entirely deliver the nation from their exorbitant and oppressive jurisdiction. The new mode of government easily made
its way among men thus prepared, by their various interests and
passions, for its reception.

But, on the first introduction of his system, Knox did not deem
it expedient to depart altogether from the ancient form. Instead
of bishops he proposed to establish ten or twelve superintendents
in different parts of the kingdom. These, as the name implies,

were empowered to inspect the life and doctrine of the other clergy. They presided in the inferior judicatories of the church, and performed several other parts of the episcopal functions. Their jurisdiction, however, extended to sacred things only; they claimed no seat in parliament, and pretended no right to the dignity of the former bishops.

The number of inferior clergy, to whom the care of parochial duty could be committed, was still extremely small; they had embraced the principles of the Reformation at different times, and from various motives; during the public commotions, they were scattered, merely by chance, over the different provinces of the kingdom, and in a few places only were formed into regular classes or societies. [Dec. 20.] The first general assembly of the church, which was held this year, bears all the marks of an infant and unformed society. The members were but few in number, and of no considerable rank; no uniform or consistent rule seems to have been observed in electing them. From a great part of the kingdom no representatives appeared. In the name of some entire counties, but one person was present; while, in other places, a single town or church sent several members. A convention so feeble and irregular, could not possess extensive authority; and, conscious of their own weakness, the members put an end to their debates, without venturing upon any decision of much importance.

1561.] In order to give greater strength and consistence to the Presbyterian plan, Knox, with the assistance of his brethren, composed the first book of discipline, which contains the model or platform of the intended policy. [Jan 15.] They presented it to a convention of estates, which was held in the beginning of this year. Whatever regulations were proposed, with regard to ecclesiastical discipline and jurisdiction, would have easily obtained the sanction of that assembly; but a design to recover the patrimony of the church, which is there insinuated, met with a very different reception.

In vain did the clergy display the advantages which would accrue to the public by a proper application of ecclesiastical revenues. In vain did they propose, by an impartial distribution of this fund, to promote true religion, to encourage learning, and to support the poor. In vain did they even intermingle threatenings of the divine displeasure against the unjust detainers of what was appropriated to a sacred use. The nobles held fast the prey which they had seized; and, bestowing upon the proposal the name of a *devout imagination*, they affected to consider it as a project altogether visionary, and treated it with the utmost scorn.

This convention appointed the Prior of St. Andrew's to repair to the Queen, and to invite her to return into her native country, and to assume the reins of government, which had been too long committed to other hands. Though some of her subjects dreaded her return, and others foresaw dangerous consequences with which it might be attended*, the bulk of them desired it with so much ardour that the invitation was given with the greatest appearance of

See Append. No. V.

unanimity. But the zeal of the Roman Catholics got the start of the Prior in paying court to Mary; and Lesly, afterwards Bishop of Ross, who was commissioned by them, arrived before him at the place of her residence. Lesly endeavoured to infuse into the Queen's mind suspicions of her Protestant subjects, and to persuade her to throw herself entirely into the arms of those who adhered to her own religion. For this purpose, he insisted that she should land at Aberdeen; and, as the Protestant doctrines had made no considerable progress in that part of the kingdom, he gave her assurance of being joined in a few days by twenty thousand men; and flattered her that, with such an army, encouraged by her presence and authority, she might easily overturn the reformed church, before it was firmly settled on its foundations.

But, at this juncture, the Princes of Lorrain were not disposed to listen to this extravagant and dangerous proposal. Intent on defending themselves against Catherine of Medicis, whose insidious policy was employed in undermining their exorbitant powers, they had no leisure to attend to the affairs of Scotland, and wished their niece to take possession of her kingdom with as little disturbance as possible. The French officers too, who had served in Scotland, dissuaded Mary from all violent measures; and, by representing the power and number of the Protestants to be irresistible, determined her to court them by every art; and rather to employ the leading men of that party as ministers than to provoke them by a fruitless opposition, to become her enemies. Hence proceeded the confidence and affection with which the Prior of St. Andrew's was received by the Queen. His representation of the state of the kingdom gained great credit; and Lesly beheld with regret the new channel in which court favour was likely to run.

Another convention of estates was held in May. The arrival of an ambassador from France seems to have been the occasion of this meeting. He was instructed to solicit the Scots to renew their ancient alliance with France, to break their new confederacy with England, and to restore the popish ecclesiastics to the possession of their revenues and the exercise of their functions. It is no easy matter to form any conjecture concerning the intentions of the French court in making these extraordinary and ill timed propositions. They were rejected with that scorn which might well have been expected from the temper of the nation.

In this convention, the Protestant clergy did not obtain a more favourable audience than formerly, and their prospect of recovering the patrimony of the church still remained as distant and uncertain as ever. But with regard to another point, they found the zeal of the nobles in no degree abated. The book of discipline seemed to require that the monuments of popery, which still remained in the kingom, should be demolished; and, though neither the same pretence of policy, nor the same ungovernable rage of the people, remained to justify or excuse this barbarous fabric as a relic of idolatry, passed sentence upon them by an act in form; and persons the most remarkable for the activity of their zeal were appointed to put it in execution. Abbeys, cathedrals, churches, libraries, records, and even the sepulchres of the dead, perished in one common ruin. The storm of popular insurrection, though impetuous and irresistible, had extended only to a few counties, and soon spent its rage; but now a deliberate and universal rapine completed the devastation of every thing venerable and magnificent which had escaped its violence.

In the meantime Mary was in no haste to return into Scotland. Accustomed to the elegance, splendour, and gaiety of a polite court, she still fondly lingered in France, the scene of all these enjoyments, and contemplated with horror the barbarism of her own country, and the turbulence of her subjects, which presented her with a very different face of things. The impatience, however, of her people, the persuasions of her uncles, but, above all, the studied and mortifying neglect with which she was treated by the Queen-mother, forced her to think of beginning this disagreeable voyage. But while she was preparing for it, there were sown between her and Elizabeth the seeds of that personal jealousy and discord which imbittered the life and shortened the days of the Scottish Queen.

The ratification of the late treaty of Edinburgh was the immediate occasion of this fatal animosity; the true cause of it lay much deeper. Almost every article in that treaty had been executed by both parties with a scrupulous exactness. The fortifications of Leith were demolished, and the armies of France and England withdrawn within the appointed time. The grievances of the malcontents were redressed, and they had obtained whatever they could demand for their future security. With regard to all these, Mary could have little reason to decline, or Elizabeth to urge, the ratification of the treaty.

The sixth article remained the only source of contest and difficulty. No minister ever entered more deeply into schemes of his sovereign, or pursued them with more dexterity or success, than Cecil. In the conduct of the negotiation at Edinburgh, the sound understanding of this able politician had proved greatly an overmatch for Monluc's refinements in intrigue, and had artfully induced the French ambassadors, not only to acknowledge that the crowns of England and Ireland did of right belong to Elizabeth alone, but also to promise, that in all times to come Mary should abstain from using the title or bearing the arms of those kingdoms.

The ratification of this article would have been of the most fatal consequence to Mary. The crown of England was an object worthy of her ambition. Her pretensions to it gave her dignity and importance in the eyes of all Europe. By many, her title was esteemed preferable to that of Elizabeth. Among the English themselves, the Roman Catholics, who formed at that time a numerous and active party, openly espoused this opinion; and even the Protestants, who supported Elizabeth's throne, could not deny the Queen of Scots to be her immediate heir. A proper opportunity to avail herself of all these advantages could not, in the course of things, be far distant, and many incidents might fall in, to bring this opportunity nearer than was expected. In these circumstances, Mary, ratifying the article in dispute, would have lost the rank she

had hitherto held among neighbouring princes; the zeal of her adherents must have gradually cooled; and she might have renounced,
from that moment, all hopes of ever wearing the English crown.

None of these beneficial consequences escaped the penetrating
eye of Elizabeth, who, for this reason, had recourse to every thing
by which she could hope either to soothe or frighten the Scottish
Queen into a compliance with her demands; and if that Princess
had been so unadvised as to ratify the rash concessions of her
ambassadors, Elizabeth, by that deed, would have acquired an advantage which, under her management, must have turned to great
account. By such a renunciation, the question with regard to the
right of succession would have been left altogether open and undecided; and by means of that, Elizabeth might either have kept
her rival in perpetual anxiety and dependence, or, by the authority
of her parliament, she might have broken in upon the order of
lineal succession, and transferred the crown to some other descendant of the royal blood. The former conduct she observed
towards James VI., whom during his whole reign she held in perpetual fear and subjection. The latter and more rigorous method of
proceeding would, in all probability, have been employed against
Mary, whom for many reasons she both envied and hated.

Nor was this step beyond her power, unprecedented in the
history, or inconsistent with the constitution of England. Though
succession by hereditary right be an idea so natural and so popular
that it has been established in almost every civilized nation, yet
England affords many memorable instances of deviation from that
rule. The crown of that kingdom having once been seized by the
hand of a conqueror, this invited the bold and enterprising in every
age to imitate such an illustrious example of fortunate ambition.
From the time of William the Norman, the regular course of
descent has seldom continued through three successive reigns.
Those princes, whose intrigues or valour opened to them a way to
the throne, called in the authority of the great council of the
nation to confirm their dubious titles. Hence parliamentary and
hereditary right became in England of equal consideration. That
great assembly claimed and actually possessed a power of altering
the order of legal succession; and even so late as Henry VIII. an
act of parliament had authorized that capricious monarch to settle
the order of succession at his pleasure. The English, jealous of
their religious liberty, and averse from the dominion of strangers,
would have eagerly adopted the passions of their sovereign, and
might have been easily induced to exclude the Scottish line from
the right of succeding to the crown. These seem to have been the
views of both Queens, and these were the difficulties which retarded
the ratification of the treaty of Edinburgh.

But, if the sources of their discord were to be traced no higher
than this treaty, an inconsiderable alteration in the words of it
might have brought the present question to an amicable issue.
The indefinite and ambiguous expression which Cecil had inserted
into the treaty, might have been changed into one more limited
but more precise; and Mary, instead of promising to abstain from

bearing the title of Queen of England in all times to come, might have engaged not to assume that title during the life of Elizabeth, or the lives of her lawful posterity.*

Such an amendment, however, did not suit the views of either Queen. Though Mary had been obliged to suspend for some time the prosecution of her title to the English crown, she had not, however relinquished it. She determined to revive her claim on the first prospect of success, and was unwilling to bind herself, by a positive engagement, not to take advantage of any such fortunate occurrence. Nor would the alteration have been more acceptable to Elizabeth, who, by agreeing to it, would have tacitly recognised the right of her rival to ascend the throne after her decease. But neither the Scottish nor English Queen durst avow these secret sentiments of their hearts. Any open discovery of an inclination to disturb the tranquillity of England, or to wrest the sceptre out of Elizabeth's hands, might have proved fatal to Mary's pretensions. Any suspicion of a design to alter the order of succession, and to set aside the claim of the Scottish Queen, would have exposed Elizabeth to much and deserved censure, and have raised up against her many and dangerous enemies. These, however carefully concealed or artfully disguised, were, in all probability, the real motives which determined the one Queen to solicit, and the other to refuse, the ratification of the treaty in its original form; while neither had recourse to that explication of it, which, to a heart unwarped by political interest, and sincerely desirous of union and concord, would have appeared so obvious and natural.

But, though considerations of interest first occasioned this rupture between the British Queens, rivalship of another kind contributed to widen the breach, and female jealousy increased the violence of their political hatred. Elizabeth, with all those extraordinary qualities, by which she equalled or surpassed such of her sex as have merited the greatest renown, discovered an admiration of her own person, to a degree which women of ordinary understandings either do not entertain, or prudently endeavour to conceal. Her attention to dress, her solicitude to display her charms, her love of flattery, were all excessive. Nor were those weaknesses

---

* This expedient for terminating the difference between Elizabeth and Mary was so obvious that it could not fail of presenting itself to the view of the English ministers.

"There hath been a matter secretly thought of (says Cecil in a letter to Throkmorton, July 14, 1561), which I dare communicate to you, although I mean never to be an author thereof; and that is, if an accord might be made betwixt our Mistress and the Scottish Queen, that this should by parliament in Scotland, &c. surrender unto the Queen's Majesty all matters of claim, and unto the heirs of her body; and in consideration thereof, the Scottish Queen's interest should be acknowledged in default of heirs of the body of the Queen's Majesty. Well, God send our Mistress a husband, and by time a son, that we may hope our posterity shall have a masculine succession. This matter is too big for weak folks, and too deep for simple. The Queen's Majesty knoweth of it." Hardw. State Pap. 1. 174. But with regard to every point relating to the succession, Elizabeth was so jealous and so apt to take offence that her most confidential ministers durst not urge her to advance one step farther than she herself chose to go. Cecil, mentioning some scheme about the succession, if the Queen should not marry or leave issue, adds, with his usual caution: "This song hath many parts; but, for my part, I have no skill but in plain song." Ibid. 175.

confined to that period of life when they are more pardonable. Even in very advanced years, the wisest woman of that, or perhaps of any other age, wore the garb and affected the manners of a girl. Though Elizabeth was as much inferior to Mary in beauty and gracefulness of person, as she excelled her in political abilities and in the arts of government, she was weak enough to compare herself with the Scottish Queen; and as it was impossible she could be altogether ignorant how much Mary gained by the comparison, she envied and hated her as a rival by whom she was eclipsed. In judging of the conduct of Princes, we are apt to ascribe too much to political motives, and too little to the passions which they feel in common with the rest of mankind. In order to account for Elizabeth's present as well as subsequent conduct towards Mary, we must not always consider her as a Queen, we must sometimes regard her merely as a woman.

Elizabeth, though no stranger to Mary's difficulties with respect to the treaty, continued to urge her, by repeated applications, to ratify it. Mary, under various pretences, still contrived to gain time, and to elude the request. But while the one Queen solicited with persevering importunity, and the other evaded with artful delay, they both studied an extreme politeness of behaviour, and loaded each other with professions of sisterly love, with reciprocal declarations of unchangeable esteem and amity.

It was not long before Mary was convinced, that among princes these expressions of friendship are commonly far distant from the heart. In sailing from France to Scotland, the course lies along the English coast. In order to be safe from the insults of the English fleet, or, in case of tempestuous weather, to secure a retreat in the harbours of that kingdom, Mary sent M. D'Oysel to demand of Elizabeth a safe conduct during her voyage. This request, which decency alone obliged one prince to grant to another, Elizabeth rejected, in such a manner as gave rise to no slight suspicion of a design, either to obstruct the passage or to intercept the person of the Scottish Queen.

Mary, in a long conference with Throkmorton, the English ambassador in France, explained her sentiments concerning this ungenerous behaviour of his mistress, in a strain of dignified expostulation, which conveys an idea of her abilities, address, and spirit, as advantageous as any transaction in her reign. Mary was at that time only in her eighteenth year; and as Thorkmorton's account of what passed in his interview with her, is addressed directly to Elizabeth, that dexterous courtier, we may be well assured, did not embellish the discourse of the Scottish Queen with any colouring too favourable.

Whatever resentment Mary might feel, it did not retard her departure from France. She was accompanied to Calais, the place where she embarked, in a manner suitable to her dignity, as the Queen of two powerful kingdoms. Six princes of Lorrain, her uncles, with many of the most eminent among the French nobles, were in her retinue. Catherine, who secretly rejoiced at her departure, graced it with every circumstance of magnificence and respect. After bidding adieu to her mourning attendants, with a sad heart, and eyes bathed in tears, Mary left that kingdom, the short but only scene of her life in which fortune smiled upon her. While the French coast continued in sight, she intently gazed upon it, and musing, in a thoughtful posture, on that height of fortune whence she had fallen, and presaging, perhaps the disasters and calamities which imbittered the remainder of her days, she sighed often, and cried out, " Farewell, France ! Farewell, beloved country which I shall never more behold !" Even when the darkness of the night had hid the land from her view, she would neither retire to the cabin, nor taste food, but commanding a couch to be placed on the deck, she there waited the return of day with the utmost impatience. Fortune soothed her on this occasion ; the galley made little way during the night. In the morning, the coast of France was still within sight, and she continued to feed her melancholy with the prospect ; and, as long as her eyes could distinguish it, to utter the same expressions of regret*. At last a brisk gale arose, by the favour of which for some days, and afterwards under the cover of a thick fog, Mary escaped the English fleet, which, as she apprehended, lay in wait in order to intercept her † ; and on the nineteenth of August, after an absence of near thirteen years, landed safely at Leith in her native kingdom.

Mary was received by her subjects with shouts and acclamations of joy, and with every demonstration of welcome and regard. But as her arrival was unexpected, and no suitable preparation had been made for it, they could not, with all their efforts, hide from her the poverty of the country, and were obliged to conduct her to the palace of Holyrood-house with little pomp. The Queen, accustomed from her infancy to splendour and magnificence, and fond of them, as was natural to her age, could not help observing the change in her situation, and seemed to be deeply affected with it.

Never did any Prince ascend the throne at a juncture which called for more wisdom in council, or more courage and steadiness in action. The rage of religious controversy was still unabated. The memory of past oppression exasperated the Protestants ; the smart of ancient injuries rendered the Papists desperate ; both were zealous, fierce, and irreconcilable. The absence of their sovereign had accustomed the nobles to independence ; and, during the late commotions, they had acquired such an increase of wealth, by the spoils of the church, as threw great weight into the scale of the aristocracy, which stood not in need of any accession of power. The kingdom had long been under the government of regents, who

---

* Brantome, 488. He himself was in the same galley with the Queen.

† Goodal, vol. i. 175. Camden insinuates, rather than affirms, that it was the object of the English fleet to intercept Mary. This, however, seems to be doubtful. Elizabeth positively asserts that, at the request of the King of Spain, she had fitted out a few ships of slender force, in order to clear the narrow seas of pirates, which infested them : and she appeals for the truth of this to Mary's own ministers. App. No. VI. Cecil, in a letter to Thorkmorton, Aug. 26, 1561, informs him, that " the Queen's ships, which were upon the seas to cleanse them of pirates, saw her [i. e. Mary], and saluted her galleys, and staying her ships examined them of pirates, and dismissed them gently. One Scottish ship they detained as vehemently suspected of piracy." Hard. State Papers, i. 176. Castelnau who accompanied Mary in this voyage, confirms the circumstance of her galleys being in sight of of the English fleet. Mem. ap. Jebb. xi. 455.

exercised a delegated jurisdiction, attended with little authority, and which inspired no reverence. A state of pure anarchy had prevailed for the two last years, without a regent, without a supreme council, without the power, or even the form, of a regular government. A licentious spirit, unacquainted with subordination, and disdaining the restraints of law and justice, had spread through all ranks of men. The influence of France, the ancient ally of the kingdom, was withdrawn or despised. The English, of enemies became confederates, had grown into confidence with the nation, and had gained an ascendant over all its councils. The Scottish monarchs did not derive more splendour or power from the friendship of the former than they had reason to dread injury and diminution from the interposition of the latter. Every consideration, whether of interest or of self-preservation, obliged Elizabeth to depress the royal authority of Scotland, and to create the Prince perpetual difficulties, by fomenting the spirit of dissatisfaction among the people.

In this posture were the affairs of Scotland when the administration fell into the hands of a young Queen, not nineteen years of age, unacquainted with the manners and laws of her country, a stranger to her subjects, without experience, without allies, and almost without a friend.

On the other hand, in Mary's situation we find some circumstances which, though they did not balance these disadvantages, contributed however to alleviate them; and, with skilful management, might have produced great effects. Her subjects, unacquainted so long to the residence of their Prince, were not only dazzled by the novelty and splendour of the royal presence, but inspired with awe and reverence. Besides the places of power and profit bestowed by the favour of a prince, his protection, his familiarity, and even his smiles, confer honour and win the hearts of men. From all corners of the kingdom the nobles crowded to testify their duty and affection to their sovereign, and studied by every art to wipe out the memory of past misconduct, and to lay in a stock of future merit. The amusements and gaiety of her court, which was filled with the most accomplished of the French nobility, who had attended her, began to soften and polish the rude manners of the nation. Mary herself possessed many of those qualifications which raise affection and procure esteem. The beauty and gracefulness of her person drew universal admiration, the elegance and politeness of her manners commanded general respect. To all the charms of her own sex she added many of the accomplishments of the other. The progress she had made in all the arts and sciences, which were then deemed necessary or ornamental, as far beyond what is commonly attained by princes; and all her other qualities were rendered more agreeable by a courteous affability, which, without lessening the dignity of a prince, steals on the hearts of subjects with a bewitching insinuation.

From these circumstances, notwithstanding the threatening aspect of affairs at Mary's return into Scotland; notwithstanding the clouds which gathered on every hand, a political observer would have predicted a very different issue of her reign; and, whatever sudden gusts of faction he might have expected, he would never have dreaded the destructive violence of that storm which followed.

While all parties were contending who should discover the most dutiful attachment to the Queen, the zealous and impatient spirit of the age broke out in a remarkable instance. On the Sunday after her arrival the Queen commanded mass to be celebrated in the chapel of her palace. The first rumour of this occasioned a secret murmuring among the Protestants who attended the court; complaints and threatenings soon followed; the servants belonging to the chapel were insulted and abused; and, if the Prior of St. Andrew's had not seasonably interposed, the rioters might have proceeded to the utmost excesses.

It is impossible, at this distance of time, and under circumstances so very different, to conceive the violence of that zeal against Popery which then possessed the nation. Every instance of condescension to the Papists was deemed an act of apostacy, and the toleration of a single mass pronounced to be more formidable to the nation, than the invasion of ten thousand armed men. Under the influence of these opinions many Protestants would have ventured to go dangerous lengths; and, without attempting to convince their sovereign by argument, or to reclaim her by indulgence, would have abruptly denied her the liberty of worshiping God in that manner which alone she thought acceptable to him. But the Prior of St. Andrew's, and other leaders of the party, not only restrained this impetuous spirit, but, in spite of the murmurs of the people and the exclamations of the preachers, obtained for the Queen and her domestics the undisturbed exercise of the Catholic religion. Near a hundred years after this period, when the violence of religious animosities had begun to subside, when time and the progress of learning had enlarged the views of the human mind, an English House of Commons refused to indulge the wife of their sovereign in the private use of the mass. The Protestant leaders deserve, on this occasion, the praise both of wisdom and of moderation for conduct so different. But, at the same time, whoever reflects upon the encroaching and sanguinary spirit of popery in that age, will be far from treating the fears and caution of the more zealous reformers as altogether imaginary, and destitute of any real foundation.

The leaders of the Protestants, however, by this prudent compliance with the prejudices of their sovereign, obtained from her a proclamation highly favourable to their religion, which was issued six days after her arrival in Scotland [Aug. 25.] The reformed doctrine, though established over all the kingdom by the parliament, which met in consequence of the treaty of pacification, had never received the countenance or sanction of royal authority. In order to quiet the minds of those who had embraced that doctrine, and to remove any dread of molestation which they might entertain, Mary declared, "that until she should take final orders concerning religion, with advice of Parliament, any attempt to alter or subvert the religion which she found universally practised in the realm, should be deemed a capital crime." Next year a second proclamation to the same effect was published.

The Queen, conformably to the plan which had been concerted in France, committed the administration of affairs entirely to Protestants. Her council was filled with the most eminent persons of that party; not a single Papist was admitted into any degree of confidence. The Prior of St. Andrew's and Maitland of Lethington seemed to hold the first place in the Queen's affection, and possessed all the power as well as reputation of favourite ministers. Her choice could not have fallen upon persons more acceptable to her people; and, by their prudent advice, Mary conducted herself with so much moderation, and deference to the sentiments of the nation, as could not fail of gaining the affection of her subjects, the firmest foundation of a prince's power, and the only genuine source of his happiness and glory. A cordial reconcilement with Elizabeth was another object of great importance to Mary; and though she seems to have had it much at heart, in the beginning of her administration, to accomplish such a desirable conjunction, yet many events occurred to widen rather than to close the breach. The formal offices of friendship, however, are seldom neglected among princes; and Elizabeth, who had attempted so openly to obstruct the Queen's voyage into Scotland, did not fail, a few days after her arrival, to command Randolph to congratulate her safe return. Mary, that she might be on equal terms with her, sent Maitland to the English court, with many ceremonious expressions of regard for Elizabeth. Both the ambassadors were received with the utmost civility; and on each side the professions of kindness, as they were made with little sincerity, were listened to with proportionable credit.

Both were intrusted, however, with something more than mere matter of ceremony. Randolph urged Mary with fresh importunity, to ratify the treaty of Edinburgh. Maitland endeavoured to amuse Elizabeth, by apologizing for the dilatory conduct of his mistress with regard to that point. The multiplicity of public affairs since her arrival in Scotland, the importance of the question in dispute, and the absence of many noblemen, with whom she was obliged in decency to consult, were the pretences offered in excuse for her conduct; the real causes of it were those which have already been mentioned. But in order to extricate herself out of these difficulties, into which the treaty of Edinburgh had led her, Mary was brought to yield a point, which formerly she seemed determined never to give up. She instructed Maitland to signify her willingness to disclaim any right to the crown of England, during the life of Elizabeth, and the lives of her posterity; if, in failure of these, she were declared next heir by an act of parliament.

Reasonable as this proposal might appear to Mary, who thereby precluded herself from disturbing Elizabeth's possession of the throne, nothing could be more inconsistent with Elizabeth's interest, or more contradictory to a passion which predominated in the character of that Princess. Notwithstanding all the great qualities which threw such lustre on her reign, we may observe, that she was tinctured with a jealousy of her right to the crown, which often betrayed her into mean and ungenerous actions. The peculiarity of her situation heightened, no doubt, and increased, but did not infuse, this passion. It descended to her from Henry VII., her grandfather, whom, in several features of his character she nearly resembled. Like him, she suffered the title by which she held the crown to remain ambiguous and controverted, rather than submit it to a parliamentary discussion, or derive any addition to her right from such authority. Like him, she observed every pretender to the succession, not only with that attention which prudence prescribes, but with that aversion which suspicion inspires. The present uncertainty with regard to the right of succession operated for Elizabeth's advantage, both on her subjects and on her rivals. Among the former, every lover of his country regarded her life as the great security of the national tranquillity; and chose rather to acknowledge a title which was dubious than to search for one that was unknown. The latter, while nothing was decided, were held in dependence, and obliged to court her. The manner in which she received the ill-timed proposal of the Scottish Queen was no other than might have been expected. She rejected it in a peremptory tone, with many expressions of a resolution never to permit a point of so much delicacy to be touched.

Sept. 1.] About this time the Queen made her public entry into Edinburgh with great pomp. Nothing was neglected that could express the duty and affection of the citizens towards their sovereign. But, amidst these demonstrations of regard, the genius and sentiments of the nation discovered themselves in a circumstance, which, though inconsiderable, ought not to be overlooked. As it was the mode of the times to exhibit many pageants at every public solemnity, most of these, on this occasion, were contrived to be representations of the vengeance which the Almighty had inflicted upon idolaters. Even while they studied to amuse and to flatter the Queen, her subjects could not refrain from testifying their abhorrence of that religion which she professed.

To restore the regular administration of justice, and to reform the internal policy of the country, became the next object of the Queen's care. The laws enacted for preservation of public order, and the security of private property, were nearly the same in Scotland as in every other civilized country. But the nature of the Scottish constitution, the feebleness of regal authority, the exorbitant power of the nobles, the violence of faction, and the fierce manners of the people, rendered the execution of these laws feeble, irregular, and partial. In the counties which border on England, this defect was most apparent; and the consequences of it most sensibly felt.— The inhabitants, strangers to industry, averse from labour, and unacquainted with the arts of peace, subsisted chiefly by spoil and pillage; and, being confederated in septs or clans, committed these excesses not only with impunity, but even with honour. During the unsettled state of the kingdom from the death of James V., this dangerous license had grown to an unusual height; and the inroads and rapine of those freebooters were become no less intolerable to their own countrymen than to the English. To restrain and punish these outrages was an action equally popular in both kingdoms. The Prior of St. Andrews was the person chosen for

G

this important service, and extraordinary powers, together with the title of the Queen's Lieutenant, were vested in him for that purpose

Nothing can be more surprising to men accustomed to regular government, than the preparations made on this occasion. They were such as might be expected in the rudest and most imperfect state of society. The freeholders of eleven several counties, with all their followers completely armed, were summoned to assist the Lieutenant in the discharge of his office. Every thing resembled a military expedition, rather than the progress of a court of justice. The Prior executed his commission with such vigour and prudence as acquired him a great increase of reputation and popularity among his countrymen. Numbers of the banditti suffered the punishment due to their crimes; and, by the impartial and rigorous administration of justice, order and tranquillity were restored to that part of the kingdom.

During the absence of the Prior of St. Andrew's, the leaders of the popish faction seem to have taken some steps towards insinuating themselves into the Queen's favour and confidence. But the Archbishop of St. Andrew's, the most remarkable person in the party for abilities and political address, was received with little favour at court; and, whatever secret partiality the Queen might have towards those who professed the same religion with herself, she discovered no inclination at that time to take the administration of affairs out of the hands to which she had already committed it.

The cold reception of the Archbishop of St. Andrew's was owing to his connexion with the house of Hamilton; from which the Queen was much alienated. The Duke of Guise and the Cardinal could never forgive the zeal with which the Duke of Chatelherault and his son the Earl of Arran had espoused the cause of the Congregation. Princes seldom view their successors without jealousy and distrust. The Prior of St. Andrew's, perhaps, dreaded the Duke as a rival in power. All these causes concurred in infusing into the Queen's mind an aversion for that family. The Duke indulging his love of retirement, lived at a distance from court, without taking pains to insinuate himself into favour; and though the Earl of Arran openly aspired to marry the Queen, he, by a most unpardonable act of imprudence, was the only nobleman of distinction who opposed Mary's enjoying the exercise of her religion; and, by rashly entering a public protestation against it, entirely forfeited her favour. At the same time, the sordid parsimony of his father obliged him either to hide himself in some retirement, or to appear in a manner unbecoming his dignity as first Prince of the blood, or his high pretensions as suitor to the Queen. His love inflamed by disappointment, and his impatience exasperated by neglect, preyed gradually on his reason, and, after many extravagancies, broke out at last in ungovernable frenzy.

Dec. 20.] Towards the end of the year, a convention of estates was held, chiefly on account of ecclesiastical affairs. The assembly of the church, which sat at the same time, presented a petition, containing many demands with respect to the suppression of Popery, the encouraging the Protestant religion, and the providing for the maintenance of the clergy. The last was a matter of great importance, and the steps taken towards it deserve to be traced.

Though the number of Protestant preachers was now considerably increased, many more were still wanted, in every corner of the kingdom. No legal provision having been made for them, they had hitherto drawn a scanty and precarious subsistence from the benevolence of their people. To suffer the ministers of an established church to continue in this state of indigence and dependence was an indecency equally repugnant to the principles of religion and to the maxims of sound policy; and would have justified all the imputations of avarice with which the Reformation was then loaded by its enemies. The revenues of the Popish church were the only fund which could be employed for their relief; but, during the three last years, the state of these was greatly altered. A great majority of abbots, priors, and other heads of religious houses, had, either from a sense of duty, or from views of interest, renounced the errors of Popery; and, notwithstanding this change in their sentiments, they retained their ancient revenues. Almost the whole order of bishops, and several of the other dignitaries, still adhered to the Romish superstition; and, though debarred from every spiritual function, continued to enjoy the temporalities of their benefices. Some laymen, especially those who had been active in promoting the Reformation, had, under various pretences and amidst the licence of civil wars, got into their hands possessions which belonged to the church. Thus, before any part of the ancient ecclesiastical revenues could be applied towards the maintenance of the Protestant ministers, many different interests were to be adjusted; many claims to be examined; and the prejudices and passions of the two contending parties required the application of a delicate hand. After much contention, the following plan was approved by a majority of voices, and acquiesced in even by the Popish clergy themselves. An exact account of the value of ecclesiastical benefices throughout the kingdom was appointed to be taken. The present incumbents, to whatever party they adhered, were allowed to keep possession: two thirds of their whole revenue were reserved for their own use, the remainder was annexed to the crown; and out of that the Queen undertook to assign a sufficient maintenance for the Protestant clergy.

As most of the bishops and several of the other dignitaries were still firmly attached to the Popish religion, the extirpation of the whole order, rather than an act of such extraordinary indulgence, might have been expected from the zeal of the preachers, and from that spirit which had hitherto animated the nation. But, on this occasion, other principles obstructed the operations of such as were purely religious. Zeal for liberty, and the love of wealth, two passions extremely opposite, concurred in determining the Protestant leaders to fall in with this plan, which deviated so manifestly from the maxims by which they had hitherto regulated their conduct.

If the reformers had been allowed to act without control, and to level all distinctions in the church, the great revenues annexed to ecclesiastical dignities could not, with any colour of justice, have been retained by those in whose hands they now were ; but must either have been distributed amongst the Protestant clergy, who performed all religious offices, or must have fallen to the Queen, from the bounty of whose ancestors the greater part of them was originally derived. The former scheme, however suitable to the religious spirit of many among the people was attended with manifold danger. The Popish ecclesiastics had acquired a share in the national property, which far exceed the proportion that was consistent with the happiness of the kingdom ; and the nobles were determined to guard against this evil, by preventing the return of those possessions into the hands of the church. Nor was the latter, which exposed the constitution to more imminent hazard, to be avoided with less care. Even that circumscribed prerogative, which the Scottish Kings possessed, was the object of jealousy to the nobles. If they had allowed the crown to seize the spoils of the church, such an increase of power must have followed that accession of property as would have raised the royal authority above control, and have rendered the most limited Prince in Europe the most absolute and independent. The reign of Henry VIII. presented a recent and alarming example of this nature. The wealth which flowed in upon that Prince, from the suppression of the monasteries, not only changed the maxims of his government, but the temper of his mind ; and he who had formerly submitted to his Parliaments, and courted his people, dictated from that time to the former with intolerable insolence, and tyrannized over the latter with unprecedented authority. And if his policy had not been extremely shortsighted, if he had not squandered what he acquired, with a profusion equal to his rapaciousness, and which defeated his ambition, he might have established despotism in England on a basis so broad and strong as all the efforts of the subjects would never have been able to shake. In Scotland, where the riches of the clergy bore as great a proportion to the wealth of the kingdom, the acquisition of church lands would have been of no less importance to the crown, and no less fatal to the aristocracy. The nobles, for this reason, guarded against such an increase of the royal power, and thereby secured their own independence.

Avarice mingled itself with their concern for the interest of their order. The reuniting the possessions of the church to the crown, or the bestowing them on the Protestant clergy, would have been a fatal blow, both to those nobles who had, by fraud or violence, seized part of these revenues, and to those abbots and priors who had totally renounced their ecclesiastical character. But as the plan which was proposed gave some sanction to their usurpation, they promoted it with their utmost influence. The Popish ecclesiastics, though the lopping off a third of their revenues was by no means agreeable to them, consented, under the present circumstances, to sacrifice a part of their possessions, in order to purchase the secure enjoyment of the remainder ; and, after deeming the whole irrecoverably lost, they considered whatever they could retrieve as so much gain. Many of the ancient dignitaries were men of noble birth ; and, as they no longer entertained hopes of restoring the Popish religion, they wished their own relations, rather than the crown or the Protestant clergy, to be enriched with the spoils of the church. They connived, for this reason, at the encroachments of the nobles; they even aided their avarice and violence; they dealt out the patrimony of the church among their own relations, and, by granting *feus* and perpetual leases of lands and tithes, gave, to the utmost of their power, some colour of legal possession to what was formerly mere usurpation. Many vestiges of such alienation still remain. The nobles, with the concurrence of the incumbents, daily extended their encroachments, and gradually stripped the ecclesiastics of their richest and most valuable possessions. Even that third part, which was given up in order to silence the clamours of the Protestant clergy, and to be some equivalent to the crown for its claims, amounted to no considerable sum. The *thirds* due by the more powerful nobles, especially by such as had embraced the Reformation, were almost universally remitted. Others, by producing fradulent metals; by estimating the corn, and other payments in kind, at an under value; and by the connivance of collectors, greatly diminished the charge against themselves: and the nobles had much reason to be satisfied with a device which, at so small expense, secured to them so valuable possessions.

Nor were the Protestant clergy considerable gainers by this new regulation; they found it to be a more easy matter to kindle zeal than to extinguish avarice. Those very men, whom formerly they had swayed with absolute authority, were now deaf to all their remonstrances. The Prior of St. Andrew's, the Earl of Argyll, the Earl of Morton, and Maitland, all the most zealous leaders of the Congregation, were appointed to assign, or as it was called, to *modify* their stipends. A hundred marks Scottish was the allowance which their liberality afforded to the generality of ministers. To a few three hundred marks were granted. About twenty-four thousand pounds Scottish appears to have been the whole sum allotted for the maintenance of a national church established by law, and esteemed throughout the kingdom the true church of God. Even this sum was paid with little exactness, and the ministers were kept in the same poverty and dependence as formerly.

1562.] The gentleness of the Queen's administration, and the elegance of her court, had mitigated, in some degree, the ferocity of the nobles, and accustomed them to greater mildness and humanity; while, at the same time, her presence and authority were a check to their factious and tumultuary spirit. But, as the state of order and tranquillity was not natural to the feudal aristocracy, it could not be of long continuance; and this year became remarkable for the most violent eruptions of intestine discord and animosity.

Among the great and independent nobility of Scotland, a monarch could possess little authority, and exercise no extensive or rigorous jurisdiction. The interfering of interest, the unsettled state of property, the frequency of public commotions, and the fierceness of their own manners sowed among the great families the seeds of many quarrels and contentions. These, as we have already observed, were frequently decided not by law, but by vio-

lence. The offended baron, without having recourse to the monarch, or acknowledging his superior authority, assembled his own
followers, and invaded the lands of his rival in a hostile manner.
Together with his estate and honours, every nobleman transmitted
some hereditary feud to his posterity, who were bound in honour to
adopt and to prosecute it with unabated rancour.

Such a dissension had subsisted between the house of Hamilton
and the Earl of Bothwell, and was heightened by mutual injuries
during the late commotions. The Earl of Arran and Bothwell,
happening to attend the court at the same time, their followers
quarrelled frequently in the streets of Edinburgh [February], and
excited dangerous tumults in that city. At last, the mediation of
their friends, particularly of Knox, brought about a reconcilement,
but an unfortunate one to both these noblemen.

A few days after, Arran came to Knox, and, with the utmost
terror and confusion, confessed first to him, and then to the Prior
of St. Andrew's, that, in order to obtain the sole direction of affairs,
Bothwell, and his kinsmen the Hamiltons, had conspired to murder
the Prior, Maitland, and the other favourites of the Queen. The
Duke of Chatelherault regarded the Prior as a rival, who had sup-
planted him in the Queen's favour, and who filled that place at the
helm, which he imagined to be due to himself, as first Prince of the
blood. Bothwell, on account of the personal injuries which he had
received from the Prior during the hostile operations of the two
contending parties, was no less exasperated against him. But
whether he and the Hamiltons had agreed to cement their new
alliance with the blood of their common enemy, or whether the
conspiracy existed only in the frantic and disordered imagination
of the Earl of Arran, it is impossible, amidst the contradiction of
historians and the defectiveness of records, positively to determine.
Among men inflamed with resentment and impatient for revenge,
rash expressions might be uttered, and violent and criminal expedients proposed; and on that foundation Arran's distempered
fancy might rear the whole superstructure of conspiracy. All the
persons accused denied their guilt with the utmost confidence.
But the known characters of the men, and the violent spirit of the
age, added greatly to the probability of the accusation, and abundantly justify the conduct of the Queen's ministers, who confined
Bothwell, Arran, and a few of the ringleaders in separate prisons,
and obliged the Duke to surrender the strong castle of Dumbarton,
which he had held ever since the time of his resigning the office
of Regent.

The designs of the Earl of Huntly against the Prior of St.
Andrew's were deeper laid, and produced more memorable and
more tragical events. George Gordon Earl of Huntly, having been
one of the nobles who conspired against James III., and who raised
his son James IV. to the throne, enjoyed a great share in the confidence of that generous Prince. By his bounty, great accessions of
wealth and power were added to a family already opulent and powerful. On the death of that monarch, Alexander the next Earl,
being appointed Lord-lieutenant of all the counties beyond Forth,
left the other nobles to contend for offices at court; and retiring to

the north, where his estate and influence lay, resided there in a
kind of princely independence. The chieftans in that part of the
kingdom dreaded the growing dominion of such a dangerous neighbour, but were unable to prevent his encroachments. Some of his
rivals he secretly undermined, others he subdued by open force.
His estate far exceeded that of any other subject, and his *superiori-
ties* and jurisdictions extended over many of the northern counties.
With power and possessions so extensive, under two long and feeble
minorities, and amidst the shock of civil commotions, the Earls of
Huntly might have indulged the most elevated hopes. But,
happily for the crown, an active and enterprising spirit was not
the characteristic of that family; and, whatever object their ambition might have in view, they chose rather to acquire it by political address than to seize it openly and by force of arms.

The conduct of George the present Earl, during the late commotions, had been perfectly suitable to the character of the family in
that age, dubious, variable, and crafty. While the success of the
Lords of the Congregation was uncertain, he assisted the Queen
Regent in her attempts to crush them. When their affairs put
on a better aspect, he pretended to join them, but never
heartily favoured their cause. He was courted and feared by each
of the contending parties; both connived at his encroachments in
the north; and by artifice and force, which he well knew how to
employ alternately and in their proper places, he added, every day,
to the exorbitant power and wealth which he possessed.

He observed the growing reputation and authority of the Prior
of St. Andrew's with the greatest jealousy and concern, and considered him as a rival who had engrossed that share in the Queen's
confidence, to which his own zeal for the Popish religion seemed to
give him a preferable title. Personal injuries soon increased the
misunderstanding occasioned by rivalship in power. The Queen
determined to reward the services of the Prior of St. Andrew's, by
creating him an Earl, and made choice of Mar, as the place whence
he should take his title; and, that he might be better able to support his new honour, bestowed upon him, at the same time, the
lands of that name. These were part of the royal demesnes, but
the Earls of Huntly had been permitted, for several years, to keep
possession of them. [Feb. 1.] On this occasion the Earl not only
complained, with some reason, of the loss which he sustained, but
had real cause to be alarmed at the intrusion of a formidable
neighbour into the heart of his territories, who might be able to
rival his power, and excite his oppressed vassals to shake off his
yoke.

June 27.] An incident, which happened soon after, increased and
confirmed Huntly's suspicions. Sir John Gordon, his third son,
and Lord Ogilvie, had a dispute about the property of an estate.
This dispute became a deadly quarrel. They happened unfortunately to meet in the streets of Edinburgh; and being both well
attended with armed followers, a scuffle ensued, in which Lord
Ogilvie was dangerously wounded by Sir John. The magistrates
seized both the offenders, and the Queen commanded them to be
strictly confined. Under any regular government, such a breach

of public peace and order would expose the person offending to certain punishment. At this time some severity was necessary, in order to vindicate the Queen's authority from an insult the most heinous which had been offered to it since her return into Scotland. But in an age accustomed to licence and anarchy, even this moderate exercise of her power, in ordering them to be kept in custody, was deemed an act of intolerable rigour; and the friends of each party began to convene their vassals and dependants, in order to overawe or to frustrate the decisions of justice. Meanwhile Gordon made his escape out of prison, and flying into Aberdeenshire, complained loudly of the indignity with which he had been treated; and, as all the Queen's actions were at this juncture imputed to the Earl of Mar, this added not a little to the resentment which Huntly had conceived against that nobleman.

Aug.] At the very time when these passions fermented, with the utmost violence, in the minds of the Earl of Huntly and his family. the Queen happened to set out on a progress into the northern parts of the kingdom. She was attended by the Earls of Mar, and Morton, Maitland, and other leaders of that party. The presence of the Queen in a country where no name greater than the Earl of Huntly's had been heard of, and no power superior to his had been exercised, for many years, was an event abundantly mortifying to that haughty nobleman. But while the Queen was entirely under the direction of Mar, all her actions were more apt to be misrepresented, and construed into injuries; and a thousand circumstances could not but occur to awaken Huntly's jealousy, to offend his pride, and to inflame his resentment. Amidst the agitation of so many violent passions, some eruption was unavoidable.

On Mary's arrival in the north, Huntly employed his wife, a woman capable of executing the commission with abundance of dexterity, to soothe the Queen, and to intercede for pardon to their son. But the Queen peremptorily required that he should again deliver himself into the hands of justice, and rely on her clemency. Gordon was persuaded to do so; and being enjoined by the Queen to enter himself prisoner in the castle of Stirling, he promised likewise to obey that command. Lord Erskine, Mar's uncle, was at that time governor of this fort. The Queen's severity, and the place in which she appointed Gordon to be confined, were interpreted to be new marks of Mar's rancour, and augmented the hatred of the Gordons against him.

Sept. 1.] Meantime, Sir John Gordon set out towards Stirling; but, instead of performing his promise to the Queen, made his escape from his guards, and returned to take the command of his followers, who were rising in arms all over the north. These were destined to second and improve the blow, by which his father proposed, secretly and at once, to cut off, Mar, Morton, and Maitland, his principal adversaries. The time and place for perpetrating this horrid deed were frequently appointed; but the executing of it was wonderfully prevented, by some of those unforeseen accidents which so often occur to disconcert the schemes and to intimidate the hearts of assassins. Huntly's own house, at Strathbogie, was the last and most convenient scene appointed for committing the intended violence. But on her journey thither, the Queen heard of young Gordon's flight and rebellion, and, refusing in the first transports of her indignation to enter under the father's roof, by that fortunate expression of her resentment saved her ministers from unavoidable destruction.

The ill-success of these efforts of private revenge precipitated Huntly into open rebellion. As the Queen was entirely under the direction of his rivals, it was impossible to compass their ruin, without violating the allegiance which he owed his sovereign. On her arrival at Inverness, the commanding officer in the castle, by Huntly's orders, shut the gates against her. Mary was obliged to lodge in the town, which was open and defenceless; but this, too, was quickly surrounded by a multitude of the Earl's followers. The utmost consternation seized the Queen, who was attended by a very slender train. She every moment expected the approach of the rebels, and some ships were already ordered into the river to secure her escape. The loyalty of the Munroes, Frasers, Mackintoshes, and some neighbouring clans, who took arms in her defence, saved her from this danger. By their assistance, she even forced the castle to surrender, and inflicted on the Governor the punishment which his insolence deserved.

This open act of disobedience was the occasion of a measure more galling to Huntly than any the Queen had hitherto taken. Lord Erskine having pretended a right to the Earldom of Mar, Stewart resigned it in his favour; and at the same time Mary conferred upon him the title of Earl of Murray, with the estate annexed to that dignity, which had been in the possession of the Earl of Huntly since the year 1548. From this encroachment upon his domains he concluded that his family was devoted to destruction; and, dreading to be stripped gradually of all those possessions which, in reward of their services, the gratitude of the crown had bestowed on himself, or his ancestors, he no longer disguised his intentions, but, in defiance of the Queen's proclamation, openly took arms. Instead of yielding those places of strength, which Mary required him to surrender, his followers dispersed or cut in pieces the parties which she dispatched to take possession of them; and he himself advancing with a considerable body of men towards Aberdeen, to which place the Queen was now returned, filled her small court with consternation. Murray had only a handful of men in whom he could confide. In order to form the appearance of an army, he was obliged to call in the assistance of the neighbouring barons: but as most of these either favoured Huntly's designs, or stood in awe of his power, from them no cordial or effectual service could be expected.

Oct. 28.] With these troops, however, Murray, who could gain nothing but delay, marched briskly towards the enemy. He found them at Corichie, posted to great advantage; he commanded his northern associates instantly to begin the attack; but on the first motion of the enemy they treacherously turned their back; and Huntly's followers, throwing aside their spears and breaking their ranks, drew their swords and rushed forward to the pursuit. It

G 5

was then that Murray gave proof, both of steady courage and prudent conduct. He stood immoveable on a rising ground with the small but trusty body of his adherents, who, presenting their spears to the enemy, received them with a determined resolution which they little expected. The Highland broad sword is not a weapon fit to encounter the Scottish spear. In every civil commotion, the superiority of the latter has been evident, and has always decided the contest. On this occasion the irregular attack of Huntly's troops was easily repulsed by Murray's firm battalion. Before they recovered from the confusion occasioned by this unforeseen resistance, Murray's northern troops, who had fled so shamefully in the beginning of the action, willing to regain their credit with the victorious party, fell upon them, and completed the rout. Huntly himself, who was extremely corpulent, was trodden to death in the pursuit. His sons, Sir John and Adam, were taken, and Murray returned in triumph to Aberdeen with his prisoners.

The trial of men taken in actual rebellion against their sovereign was extremely short. Three days after the battle, Sir John Gordon was beheaded at Aberdeen. His brother Adam was pardoned on account of his youth. Lord Gordon, who had been privy to his father's designs, was seized in the south, and upon trial found guilty of treason; but, through the Queen's clemency, the punishment was remitted. The first parliament proceeded against this great family with the utmost rigour of law, and reduced their power and fortune to the lowest ebb*.

As the fall of the Earl of Huntly is the most important of this year, it would have been improper to interrupt the narrative by taking notice of lesser transactions, which may now be related with equal propriety.

In the beginning of summer, Mary, who was desirous of entering into a more intimate correspondence and familiarity with Elizabeth, employed Maitland to desire a personal interview with her, somewhere in the north of England. As this proposal could not be rejected with decency, the time, the place, and the circumstances of the meeting were instantly agreed upon. But Elizabeth was prudent enough not to admit into her kingdom a rival who outshone herself so far in beauty and gracefulness of person; and who excelled so eminently in all the arts of insinuation and address. Under pretence of being confined to London, by the attention which she was obliged to give to the civil wars in France, she put off the interview for that season, and prevented her subjects from seeing the Scottish Queen, the charms of whose appearance and behaviour she envied, and had some reason to dread.

* This conspiracy of the Earl of Huntly is one of the most intricate and mysterious passages in Scottish history. As it was a transaction purely domestic, and in which the English were little interested, few original papers concerning it have been found in Cecil's Collection, the great storehouse of evidence and information with regard to the affairs of this period.

Buchanan supposes Mary to have formed a design about this time of destroying Murray, and of employing the power of the Earl of Huntly for this purpose. But his account of this whole transaction appears to be so void of truth, and even of probability, as to deserve no serious examination. At that time Mary wanted power, and seems to have had no inclination to commit any act of violence upon her brother.

During this year the assembly of the church met twice. [June 2, Dec. 25.] In both those meetings were exhibited many complaints of the poverty and dependence of the church; and many murmurs against the negligence or avarice of those who had been appointed to collect and to distribute the small fund appropriated for the maintenance of preachers. A petition, craving redress of their grievances, was presented to the Queen; but without any effect. There was no reason to expect that Mary would discover any forwardness to grant the request of such supplicants. As her ministers, though all most zealous Protestants, were themselves growing rich on the inheritance of the church, they were equally regardless of the indigence and demands of their brethren.

1563.] Mary had now continued above two years in a state of widowhood. Her gentle administration had secured the hearts of her subjects, who were impatient for her marriage, and wished the crown to descend in the right line from their ancient monarchs. She herself was the most amiable woman of the age; and the fame of her accomplishments, together with the favourable circumstance of her having one kingdom already in her possession, and the prospect of mounting the throne of another, prompted many different Princes to solicit an alliance so illustrious. Scotland by its situation, threw so much weight and power into whatever scale it fell that all Europe waited with solicitude for Mary's determination; and no event in that age excited stronger political fears and jealousies; none interested more deeply the passions of several Princes, or gave rise to more contradictory intrigues, than the marriage of the Queen.

The Princes of the house of Austria remembered what vast projects the French had founded on their former alliance with the Queen of Scots; and though the unexpected death, first of Henry and then of Francis, had hindered these from taking effect. yet if Mary should again make choice of a husband among the French Princes, the same designs might be revived and prosecuted with better success.

In order to prevent this, the Emperor entered into a negotiation with the Cardinal of Lorrain, who had proposed to marry the Scottish Queen to the Archduke Charles, Ferdinand's third son. The matter was communicated to Mary; and Melvil, who at that time attended the Elector Palatine, was commanded to inquire into the character and situation of the Archduke.

Philip II., though no less apprehensive of Mary's falling once more into the hands of France, envied his uncle Ferdinand the acquisition of so important a prize; and, as his own insatiable ambition grasped at all the kingdoms of Europe, he employed his ambassador at the French court to solicit the Princes of Lorrain in behalf of his son Don Carlos, at that time the heir of all the extensive dominions which belonged to the Spanish monarchy.

Catherine of Medicis, on the other hand, dreaded the marriage of the Scottish Queen with any of the Austrian Princes, which would have added so much to the power and pretensions of that ambitious race. Her jealousy of the Princes of Lorrain rendered her no less averse from an alliance which, by securing to them the protection of the Emperor or King of Spain, would give new boldness to their enterprising spirit, and enable them to set the power of the crown, which they already rivaled, at open defiance : and as she was afraid that these splendid proposals of the Austrian family would dazzle the young Queen, she instantly dispatched Castelnau into Scotland, to offer her in marriage the Duke of Anjou, the brother of her former husband, who soon after mounted the throne of France.

Mary attentively weighed the pretensions of so many rivals. The Archduke had little to recommend him but his high birth. The example of Henry VIII. was a warning against contracting a marriage with the brother of her former husband ; and she could not bear the thoughts of appearing in France, in a rank inferior to that which she had formerly held in that kingdom. She listened, therefore, with partiality, to the Spanish propositions, and the prospect of such vast power and dominions flattered the ambition of a young and aspiring Princess.

Three several circumstances, however, concurred to divert Mary from any thoughts of a foreign alliance.

The first of these was the murder of her uncle the Duke of Guise. The violence and ambition of that nobleman had involved his country in a civil war ; which was conducted with furious animosity and various success. At last the Duke laid siege to Orleans, the bulwark of the Protestant cause ; and he had reduced that city to the last extremity, when he was assassinated by the frantic zeal of Poltrot. This blow proved fatal to the Queen of Scots. The young Duke was a minor ; and the Cardinal of Lorrain, though subtle and intriguing, wanted that undaunted and enterprising courage, which rendered the ambition of his brother so formidable. Catherine, instead of encouraging the ambition or furthering the pretensions of her daughter-in-law, took pleasure in mortifying the one, and in disappointing the other. In this situation, and without a protector, it became necessary for Mary to contract her views, and to proceed with caution ; and, whatever prospect of advantage might allure her, she would venture upon no dangerous or doubtful measure.

The second circumstance which weighed with Mary was the opinion of the Queen of England. The marriage of the Scottish Queen interested Elizabeth more deeply than any other Prince ; and she observed all her deliberations concerning it with the most anxious attention. She herself seems early to have formed a resolution of living unmarried, and she discovered no small inclination to impose the same law on the Queen of Scots. She had already experienced what use might be made of Mary's power and pretensions to invade her dominions, and to disturb her possession of the crown. The death of Francis II. had happily delivered her from this danger, which she determined to guard against for the future with the utmost care. As the restless ambition of the Austrian Princes, the avowed and bigoted patrons of the Catholic superstition, made her, in a particular manner, dread their neighbourhood, she instructed Randolph to remonstrate, in the strongest terms, against any alliance with them ; and to acquaint Mary, that as she herself would consider such a match to be a breach of the personal friendship in which they were so happily united; so the English nation would regard it as the dissolution of that confederacy which now subsisted between the two kingdoms; that in order to preserve their own religion and liberties, they would, in all probability, take some step prejudical to her right of succession, which, as she well knew, they neither wanted power nor pretences to invalidate and set aside. This threatening was accompanied with a promise, but expressed in very ambiguous terms, that if Mary's choice of a husband should prove agreeable to the English nation, Elizabeth would appoint proper persons to examine her title to the succession, and, if well founded, command it to be publicly recognised. She observed, however, a mysterious silence concerning the person on whom she wished the choice of the Scottish Queen to fall. The revealing of the secret was reserved for some future negotiation. Meanwhile she threw out some obscure hints, that a native of Britain, or one not of princely rank, would be her safest and most inoffensive choice. An advice, offered with such an air of superiority and command, mortified, no doubt, the pride of the Scottish Queen. But, under her present circumstances, she was obliged to bear this indignity. Destitute of all foreign assistance, and intent upon the English succession, the great object of her wishes and ambition, it became necessary to court a rival, whom, without manifest imprudence, she could not venture to offend.

The inclination of her own subjects was another, and not the least considerable circumstance, which called for Mary's attention at this conjuncture. They had been taught, by the fatal experiment of her former marriage, to dread a union with any great Prince, whose power might be employed to oppress their religion and liberties. They trembled at the thoughts of a match with a foreigner; and if the crown should be strengthened by new dominions and alliances, they foresaw that the royal prerogative would would soon be stretched beyond its ancient and legal limits. Their eagerness to prevent this could hardly fail of throwing them once more into the arms of England. Elizabeth would be ready to afford them her aid towards obstructing a measure so disagreeable to herself. It was easy for them to seize the person of the sovereign. By the assistance of the English fleet, they could render it difficult for any foreign Prince to land in Scotland. The Roman Catholics, now an inconsiderable party in the kingdom, and dispirited by the loss of the Earl of Huntly, could give no obstruction to their designs. To what violent extremes the national abhorrence of a foreign yoke might have been carried is manifest from what she had already seen and experienced.

For these reasons Mary laid aside, at that time, all thoughts of foreign alliance, and seemed willing to sacrifice her own ambition, in order to remove the jealousies of Elizabeth, and to quiet the fears of her own subjects.

The Parliament met this year, for the first time since the Queen's return into Scotland. [May 26.] Mary's administration had hitherto been extremely popular. Her ministers possessed the confidence of the nation; and, by consequence, the proceedings of that assembly

were conducted with perfect unanimity. The grant of the Earldom
of Murray to the Prior of St. Andrew's was confirmed ; the Earl of
Huntly, and several of his vassals and dependants, were attainted: the
attainder against Kirkaldy of Grange, and some of his accomplices
in the murder of Cardinal Beatoun, was reversed* : the act of oblivion, mentioned in the treaty of Edinburgh, received the royal
sanction. But Mary, who had determined never to ratify that
treaty, took care that this sanction should not be deemed any ac-
knowledgement of its validity; she granted her consent merely in
condescension to the Lords in Parliament, who on their knees besought her to allay the jealousies and apprehensions of her subjects
by such a gracious law.†

No attempt was made, in this Parliament, to procure the Queen's
assent to the laws establishing the Protestant religion. Her ministers, though zealous Protestants themselves, were aware that this
could not be urged without manifest danger and imprudence. She
had consented, through their influence, to tolerate and protect the
reformed doctrine. They had even prevailed on her to imprison and
prosecute the Archbishop of St. Andrew's, and Prior of Withorn,
for celebrating mass contrary to her proclamation. Mary, however,
was still passionately devoted to the Romish church; and though,
from political motives, she had granted a temporary protection of
opinions which she disapproved, there were no grounds to hope that
she would agree to establish them for perpetuity. The moderation
of those who professed it was the best method for reconciling the
Queen to the Protestant religion. Time might abate her bigotry.
Her prejudices might wear off gradually, and at last she might yield
to the wishes of her people, what their importunity or their violence could never have extorted. Many laws of importance were
to be proposed in Parliament; and to defeat all these, by such a
fruitless and ill timed application to the Queen, would have been
equally injurious to individuals and detrimental to the public.
The zeal of the Protestant clergy was deaf to all these considerations of prudence of policy. Eager and impatient, it brooked no
delay : severe and inflexible, it would condescend to no compliances. The leading men of that order insisted, that this opportunity of establishing religion by law was not to be neglected. They
pronounced the moderation of the courtiers apostasy ; and their endeavours to gain the Queen they reckoned criminal and servile.
Knox solemnly renounced the friendship of the Earl of Murray, as
a man devoted to Mary, and so blindly zealous for her service as to
become regardless of those objects which he had hitherto esteemed
most sacred. This rupture, which is a strong proof of Murray's sincere attachment to the Queen at that period, continued above a year
and a half.

The preachers, being disappointed by the men in whom they
placed the greatest confidence, gave vent to their indignation in
their pulpits. These echoed more loudly than ever with declamations against idolatry ; with dismal presages concerning the Queen's
marriage with a foreigner; and with bitter reproaches against those
who, from interested motives, had deserted that cause which they

* Knox, 330.   † Parl, 9, Q. Mary, c, 67. Spotsw. 188.

once reckoned it their honour to support. The people, inflamed by such vehement declamations, which were dictated by a zeal more sincere than prudent, proceeded to rash and unjustifiable acts of violence. [Aug.] During the Queen's absence, on a progress into the west, mass continued to be celebrated in her chapel at Holy-rood-house. The multitude of those who openly resorted thither gave great offence to the citizens of Edinburgh, who, being free from restraint which the royal presence imposed, assembled in a riotous manner, interrupted the service, and filled such as were present with the utmost consternation. Two of the ringleaders in this tumult were seized, and a day appointed for their trial.

Oct. 8.] Knox, who deemed the zeal of these persons laudable, and their conduct meritorious, considered them as sufferers in a good cause; and in order to screen them from danger, he issued circular letters, requiring all who professed the true religion, or were concerned for the preservation of it, to assemble at Edinburgh, on the day of trial, that by their presence they might comfort and assist their distressed brethren. One of these letters fell into the Queen's hands. To assemble the subjects without the authority of the sovereign was construed to be treason, and a resolution was taken to prosecute Knox for that crime, before the privy council. [Dec. 15.] Happily for him, his judges were not only zealous Protestants, but the very men who, during the late commotions, had openly resisted and set at defiance the Queen's authority. It was under precedents drawn from their own conduct that Knox endeavoured to shelter himself. Nor would it have been an easy matter to these counsellors to have found out a distinction, by which they could censure him without condemning themselves. After a long hearing, to the astonishment of Lethington and the other courtiers, he was unanimously acquitted. Sinclair, Bishop of Ross, and president of the Court of Session, a zealous papist, heartily concurred with the other counsellors in this decision; a remarkable fact, which shows the unsettled state of government in that age; the low condition to which regal authority was then sunk; and the impunity with which subjects might invade those rights of the crown which are now held sacred.

1564.] The marriage of the Scottish Queen continued still to be the object of attention and intrigue. Though Elizabeth, even while she wished to direct Mary, treated her with a disgustful reserve; though she kept her, without necessity, in a state of suspense; and hinted often at the person whom she destined to be her husband, without directly mentioning his name; yet Mary framed all her actions to express such prudent respect for the English Queen, that foreign Princes began to imagine she had given herself up implicitly to her direction. The prospect of this union alarmed Catherine of Medicis. Though Catherine had taken pleasure all along in doing ill offices to the Queen of Scots; though soon after the Duke of Guise's death, she had put upon her a most mortifying indignity, by stopping the payment of her dowry, by depriving her subject the Duke of Chatelherault of his pension, and by bestowing the command of the Scottish guards on a Frenchman; she resolved, however, to prevent this dangerous conjunction of the British

Queens. For this purpose she now employed all her art to appease Mary, to whom she had given so many causes of offence. The arrears of her dowry were instantly paid; more punctual remittances were promised for the future; and offers made, not only to restore but to extend the privileges of the Scottish nation in France. It was easy for Mary to penetrate into the motives of this sudden change; she well knew the character of her mother in-law, and laid little stress upon professions of friendship which came from a Princess of such a false and unfeeling heart.

The negotiation with England, relative to the marriage, suffered no interruption from this application of the French Queen. As Mary, in compliance with the wishes of her subjects, and pressed by the strongest motives of interest, determined speedily to marry, Elizabeth was obliged to break that unaccountable silence which she had hitherto affected. The secret was disclosed, and her favourite Lord Robert Dudley, afterwards Earl of Leicester, was declared to be the happy man whom she had chosen to be the husband of a Queen courted by many Princes. Elizabeth's wisdom and penetration were remarkable in the choice of her ministers; in distinguishing her favourites, those great qualities were less conspicuous. She was influenced in two cases so opposite, by merit of very different kinds. Their capacity for business, their knowledge, their prudence, were the talents to which alone she attended in choosing her ministers; whereas beauty and gracefulness of person, polished manners, and courtly address, were the accomplishments on which she bestowed her favour. She acted in one case with the wisdom of a Queen, in the other she discovered the weakness of a woman. To this Leicester owed his grandeur. Though remarkable neither for eminence in virtue nor superiority of abilities, the Queen's partiality distinguished him on every occasion. She raised him to the highest honours, she bestowed on him the most important employments, and manifested an affection so disproportionate to his merit, that, in the opinion of that age, it could be accounted for only by the power of planetary influence.

The high spirit of the Scottish Queen could not well bear the first overture of a match with a subject. Her own rank, the splendour of her former marriage, and the solicitations at this time of so many powerful Princes, crowded into her thoughts and made her sensibly feel how humbling and disrespectful Elizabeth's proposal was. She dissembled, however, with the English resident; and though she declared, in strong terms, what a degradation she would deem this alliance, which brought along with it no advantage that could justify such neglect of her own dignity, she mentioned the Earl of Leicester, notwithstanding, in terms full of respect.

Elizabeth, we may presume, did not wish that the proposal should be received in any other manner. After the extraordinary marks she had given of her own attachment to Leicester, and while he was still in the very height of favour, it is not probable she could think seriously of bestowing him upon another. It was not her aim to persuade, but only to amuse Mary. Almost three years were elapsed since her return into Scotland; and though solicited by her subjects, and courted by the greatest Princes in Europe, she had hitherto been prevented from marrying, chiefly by the artifices of Elizabeth. If at this time the English Queen could have engaged Mary to listen to her proposal in favour of Leicester, her power over this creature of her own would have enabled her to protract the negotiation at pleasure; and, by keeping her rival unmarried, she would have rendered the prospect of her succession less acceptable to the English.

Leicester's own situation was extremely delicate and embarrassing. To gain possession of the most amiable woman of the age, to carry away this prize from so many contending Princes, to mount the throne of an ancient kingdom, might have flattered the ambition of a subject much more considerable than him. He saw all these advantages, no doubt; and, in secret, they made their full impression on him. But, without offending Elizabeth, he durst not venture on the most distant discovery of his sentiments, or take any steps towards facilitating his acquisition of objects so worthy of desire.

On the other hand, Elizabeth's partiality towards him, which she was at no pains to conceal, might inspire him with hopes of attaining the supreme rank in a kingdom more illustrious than Scotland. Elizabeth had often declared that nothing but her resolution to lead a single life, and his being born her own subject, would have hindered her from choosing the Earl of Leicester for a husband. Such considerations of prudence are however, often surmounted by love; and Leicester might flatter himself, that the violence of her affection would at length triumph both over the maxims of policy and the scruples of pride. These hopes induced him, now and then, to conclude the proposal of his marriage with the Scottish Queen to be a project for his destruction; and he imputed it to the malice of Cecil, who, under the specious pretence of doing him honour, intended to ruin him in the good opinion both of Elizabeth and Mary.

A treaty of marriage, proposed by one Queen, who dreaded its success; listened to by another, who was secretly determined against it; and scarcely desired by the man himself, whose interest and reputation it was calculated, in appearance, to promote; could not, under so many unfavourable circumstances, be brought to a fortunate issue. Both Elizabeth and Mary continued, however, to act with equal dissimulation. The former, notwithstanding her fears of losing Leicester, solicited warmly in his behalf. The latter, though she began about this time to cast her eyes upon another subject of England, did not at once venture finally to reject Elizabeth's favourite.

The person towards whom Mary began to turn her thoughts, was Henry Stewart Lord Darnly, eldest son of the Earl of Lennox. That nobleman, having been driven out of Scotland, under the Duke of Catelherault, had lived in banishment for twenty years. His wife, Lady Margaret Douglas, was Mary's most dangerous rival in her claim upon the English succession. She was the daughter of Margaret, the eldest sister of Henry VIII., by the Earl of Angus, whom that Queen married after the death of her husband James IV. In that age, the right and order of succession was not settled with the same accuracy as at present. Time, and the decision of almost every case that can possibly happen, have at last introduced certainty into a matter, which naturally is subject to all the variety arising from the caprice of lawyers, guided by obscure and often imaginary analogies. The Countess of Lennox, though born of a second marriage, was one degree nearer the royal blood of England than Mary. She was the daughter, Mary only the granddaughter of Margaret. This was not the only advantage over Mary which the Countess of Lennox enjoyed. She was born in England, and, by a maxim of law in that country, with regard to private inheritances, " whoever is not born in England, or at least of parents who, at the time of his birth, were in the obedience of the King of England, cannot enjoy any inheritance in the kingdom." This maxim, Hales, an English lawyer, produced in a treatise which he published at this time, and endeavoured to apply it to the right of succession to the crown. In a private cause these pretexts might have given rise to a long and doubtful litigation; where a crown was at stake, such nice disputes and subtilities were to be avoided with the utmost care. If Darnly should happen to contract an alliance with any of the powerful families in England, or should publicly profess the Protestant religion, these plausible and popular topics might be so urged as to prove fatal to the pretensions of a foreigner and of a Papist.

Mary was aware of all this ; and, in order to prevent any danger from that quarter, had early endeavoured to cultivate a friendly correspondence with the family of Lennox. In the year 1562, both the Earl and the Lady Margaret were taken into custody by Elizabeth's orders, on account of their holding a secret correspondence with the Scottish Queen.

From the time that Mary became sensible of the difficulties which would attend her marrying a foreign Prince, she entered into a still closer connexion with the Earl of Lennox, and invited him to return into Scotland. This she endeavoured to conceal from Elizabeth ; but a transaction of so much importance did not escape the notice of that discerning Princess. She observed but did not interrupt it. Nothing could fall in more perfectly with her views concerning Scottish affairs. She was pleased to see the pride of the Scottish Queen stoop at last to the thoughts of taking a subject to her bed. Darnly was in no situation to excite her jealousy or her fears. His father's estate lay in England, and by means of this pledge she hoped to keep the negociation entirely in her own hands, to play the same game of artifice and delay, which she had planned out, if her recommendation of Leicester had been more favourably received.

As before the union of the two crowns no subject of one kingdom could pass into the other without the permission of both sovereigns ; no sooner did Lennox, under pretence of prosecuting his wife's claim upon the earldom of Angus, apply to Elizabeth for her licence to go into Scotland, than he obtained it. Together with it, she gave him letters, warmly recommending his person and cause to Mary's friendship and protection. But at the same time, as it was her manner to involve all her transactions with regard to Scotland in some degree of perplexity and contradicton, she warned Mary, that this indulgence of Lennox might prove fatal to herself, as his return could not fail of reviving the ancient animosity between him and the house of Hamilton.

This admonition gave umbrage to Mary, and drew from her an angry reply, which occasioned for some time a total interruption of correspondence between the two Queens. Mary was not a little alarmed at this; she both dreaded the effects of Elizabeth's resentment, and felt sensibly the disadvantage of being excluded from a free intercourse with England, where her ambassadors had all along carried on, with some success, secret negotiations, which increased the number of her partisans, and paved her way towards the throne. In order to remove the causes of the present difficulty, Melvil was sent express to the court of England. He found it no difficult matter to bring about a reconcilement; and soon re-established the appearance, but not the confidence, of friendship, which was all that had subsisted for some time between the two Queens.

During this negociation, Elizabeth's professions of love to Mary, and Melvil's replies in the name of his mistress, were made in the language of the warmest and most cordial friendship. But what Melvil truly observes with respect to Elizabeth, may be extended without injustice to both Queens. " There was neither plain dealing nor upright meaning, but great dissimulation, envy, and fear."

Lennox, however, in consequence of the licence which he had obtained, set out for Scotland, and was received by the Queen, not only with the respect due to a nobleman so nearly allied to the royal family, but treated with a distinguished familiarity which could not fail of inspiring him with more elevated hopes. The rumour of his son's marriage to the Queen began to spread over the kingdom; and the eyes of all Scotland were turned upon him as the father of their future master. The Duke of Chatelherault was the first to take the alarm. He considered Lennox as the ancient and hereditary enemy of the house of Hamilton; and, in his grandeur, saw the ruin of himself and his friends. But the Queen interposed her authority to prevent any violent rupture, and employed all her influence to bring about an accomodation of the differences.

The powerful family of Douglas no less dreaded Lennox's return, from an apprehension that he would wrest the earldom of Angus out of their hands. But the Queen, who well knew how dangerous it would be to irritate Morton, and other great men of that name, prevailed on Lennox to purchase their friendship by allowing his Lady's claim upon the earldom of Angus to drop.

After these preliminary steps, Mary ventured to call a meeting of parliament [Dec.] The act of forfeiture passed against Lennox in the year 1545 was repealed, and he was publicly restored to the honours and estate of his ancestors.*

June 25, Dec. 25.] The ecclesiastical transactions of this year were not considerable. In the assemblies of the church, the same complaints of the increase of idolatry, the same representations concerning the poverty of the clergy were renewed. The reply which the Queen made to these, and her promises of redress, were

*See Append. No. IX.

more satisfying to the Protestants than any they had hitherto obtained. But notwithstanding her declarations in their favour, they
could not help harbouring many suspicions concerning Mary's designs against their religion. She had never once consented to hear
any preacher of the reformed doctrine. She had abated nothing of
her bigoted attachment to the Romish faith. The genius of that
superstition, averse at all times from toleration, was in that age
fierce and unrelenting. Mary had given her friends on the continent repeated assurances of her resolution to re-establish the
Catholic church. She had industriously avoided every opportunity
of ratifying the acts of parliament 1560, in favour of the Reformation. Even the protection which, ever since her return, she had
afforded the Protestant religion, was merely temporary, and declared, by her own proclamation, to be of force only "till she
should take some final order in the matter of religion." The vigilant zeal of the preachers was inattentive to none of these circumstances. The coldness of their principal leaders, who were at this
time entirely devoted to the court, added to their jealousies and
fears. These they uttered to the people, in language which they
deemed suitable to the necessity of the times, and which the Queen
reckoned disrespectful and insolent. In a meeting of the General
Assembly, Maitland publicly accused Knox of teaching seditious
doctrine, concerning the right of subjects to resist those sovereigns
who trespass against the duty which they owe to the people. Knox
was not backward to justify what he had taught; and upon this
general doctrine of resistance, so just in its own nature, but so
delicate in its application to particular cases, there ensued a debate
which admirably displays the talents and character of both the dis-
putants; the acuteness of the former, embellished with learning,
but prone to subtilty : the vigorous understanding of the latter, de-
lighting in bold sentiments, and superior to all fear.

1565.] Two years had already been consumed in fruitless negotiations concerning the marriage of the Scottish Queen. Mary had
full leisure and opportunity to discern the fallacy and deceit of all
Elizabeth's proceedings with respect to it. But, in order to set the
real intentions of the English Queen in a clear light, and to bring
her to some explicit declaration of her sentiments, Mary at last
intimated to Randolph [Feb. 5], that, on condition her right of succession to the crown of England were publicly acknowledged, she
was ready to yield to the solicitations of his mistress in behalf of
Leicester. Nothing can be further than this from the mind and
intention of Elizabeth. The right of succession was a mystery,
which, during her whole reign, her jealousy preserved untouched
and unexplained. She had promised, however, when she first began
to interest herself in the marriage of the Scottish Queen, all that
was now demanded. How to retreat with decency, how to elude
her former offer, was on that occount not a little perplexing.

The facility with which Lord Darnly obtained permission to
visit the court of Scotland, was owing, in all probability, to that
embarrassment. From the time of Melvil's embassy, the Countess
of Lennox had warmly solicited this liberty for her son. Elizabeth
was no stranger to the ambitious hopes with which that young

nobleman flattered himself. She had received repeated advices from her ministers, of the sentiments which Mary began to entertain in his favour. It was entirely in her power to prevent his stirring out of London. In the present conjuncture, however, nothing could be of more advantage to her than Darnly's journey into Scotland. She had already brought one actor upon the stage, who under her management had, for a long time amused the Scottish Queen. She hoped, no less absolutely, to direct the motions of Darnly, who was likewise her subject; and again to involve Mary in all the tedious intricacies of negociation. These motives determined Elizabeth and her ministers to yield to the solicitations of the Countess of Lennox.

But this deep laid scheme was in a moment disconcerted. Such unexpected events, as the fancy of poets ascribe to love, are sometimes really produced by that passion. An affair which had been the object of so many political intrigues, and had moved and interested so many princes, was at last decided by the sudden liking of two young persons. Lord Darnly was at this time in the first bloom and vigour of youth. In beauty and gracefulness of person he surpassed all his contemporaries; he excelled eminently in such arts as add case and elegance to external form, and which enabled it not only to dazzle but to please. Mary was of an age, and of a temper, to feel the full power of these accomplishments. The impression which Lord Darnly made upon her was to amuse and entertain this illustrious guest: and in all those scenes of gaiety, Darnly, whose qualifications were altogeter superficial and showy, appeared to great advantage. His conquest of the Queen's heart became complete; and inclination now prompted her to conclude her marriage, the first thoughts of which had been suggested by considerations merely political.

Elizabeth contributed, and perhaps not without design, to increase the violence of this passion. Soon after Darnly's arrival in Scotland, she, in return to that message whereby Mary had signified her willingness to accept of Leicester, gave an answer in such terms as plainly unravelled her original intention in that intrigue. She promised, if the Scottish Queen's marriage with Leicester should take place, to advance him to great honours; but, with regard to Mary's title to the English succession, she would neither suffer any legal inquiry to be made concerning it, nor permit it to be publicly recognised, until she herself should declare her resolution never to marry. Notwithstanding Elizabeth's former promises, Mary had reason to expect every thing contained in this reply; her high spirit, however, could not bear with patience such a cruel discovery of the contempt, the artifice, and mockerv, with which, under the veil of friendship, she had been so long abused. She burst into tears of indignation, and expressed, with the utmost bitterness, her sense of that disingenuous craft which had been employed to deceive her.

The natural effect of this indignation was to add to the impetuosity with which she pursued her own scheme. Blinded by resentment as well as by love, she observed no defects in the man whom she had chosen; and began to take the necessary steps towards accomplishing her design, with all the impatience natural to those passions.

As Darnly was so nearly related to the Queen, the canon law made it necessary to obtain the Pope's dispensation before the celebration of the marriage. For this purpose she early set on foot a negociation with the court of Rome.

She was busy, at the same time, in procuring the consent of the French King and his mother. Having communicated her design, and the motives which determined her choice, to Castelnau, the French ambassador, she employed him, as the most proper person, to bring his court to fall in with her views. Among other arguments to this purpose, Castelnau mentioned Mary's attachment to Darnly, which he represented to be so violent and deep rooted, that it was no longer in her power to break off the match. Nor were the French ministers backward in encouraging Mary's passion. Her pride would never stoop to an alliance with a subject of France. By this choice they were delivered from the apprehension of a match with any of the Austrian Princes, as well as the danger of too close a union with Elizabeth; and as Darnly professed the Roman Catholic religion, this suited the bigoted schemes which that court adopted.

While Mary was endeavouring to reconcile foreign courts to a measure which she had so much at heart, Darnly and his father, by their behaviour, were raising up enemies at home to obstruct it. Lennox had, during the former part of his life, discovered no great compass of abilities or political wisdom; and appears to have been a man of a weak understanding and violent passions. Darnly was not the superior to his father in understanding, and all his passions were still more impetuous. To these he added that insolence, which the advantage of external form, when accompanied with no quality more valauble, is apt to inspire. Intoxicated with the Queen's favour, he began already to assume the haughtiness of a King, and to put on that imperious air, which majesty itself can scarcely render tolerable.

It was by the advice, or at least with the consent of Murray and his party, that Lennox had been invited in Scotland: and yet, no sooner did he acquire a firm footing in that kingdom than he began to enter into secret cabals with those noblemen who were known to be avowed enemies to Murray, and, with regard to religion, to be either neutrals, or favourers of popery. Darnly, still more imprudent, allowed some rash expressions concerning those favours which the Queen's bounty had conferred upon Murray to escape him.

But, above all these, the familiarity which Darnly cultivated with David Rizio, contributed to increase the suspicion and disgust of the nobles.

The low birth and indigent condition of this man placed him in a station in which he ought naturally to have remained unknown to posterity. But what fortune called him to act and suffer in Scotland, obliges history to descend from its dignity, and to record his adventures. He was the son of a musician in Turin, and, having accompanied the Piedmontese ambassador in Scotland, gained admission into the Queen's family, and (her French secretary happening to return at that time into his own country) was preferred by her to that office. He now began to make a figure in court, and to appear as a man of consequence. The whole train of suitors and expectants, who have an extreme sagacity in discovering the paths which lead most directly to success, applied to him. His recommendations were observed to have great influence over the Queen, and he grew to be considered not only as a favourite, but as a minister. Nor was Rizio careful to abate that envy which always attends such an extraordinary and rapid change of fortune. He studied, on the contrary, to display the whole extent of his favour. He affected to talk openly and familiarly with the Queen in public. He equalled the greatest and most opulent subjects, in richness of dress, and in the number of his attendants. He discovered, in all his behaviour, that assuming insolence with which unmerited prosperity inspires an ignoble mind. It was with the utmost indignation that the nobles beheld the power, it was with the utmost difficulty that they tolerated the arrogance, of this unworthy minion. Even in the Queen's presence they could not forbear treating him with marks of contempt. Nor was it his exorbitant power alone which exasperated the Scots. They considered him, and not without reason, as a dangerous enemy to the Protestant religion, and suspected that he held, for this purpose, a secret correspondence with the court of Rome.

It was Darnly's misfortune to fall under the management of this man, who by flattery and assiduity easily gained on his vanity and inexperience. All Rizio's influence with the Queen was employed in his behalf, and contributed without doubt, towards establishing him more firmly in her affections. But whatever benefit Darnly might reap from his patronage, it did not counterbalance the contempt, and even infamy, to which he was exposed on account of his familiarity with such an upstart.

Though Darnly made daily progress in the Queen's affection, she conducted herself, however, with such prudent reserve, as to impose on Randolph, the English resident, a man otherwise shrewd and penetrating. It appears, from his letters at this period, that he entertained not the least suspicion of the intrigue which was carrying on; and gave his court repeated assurances, that the Scottish Queen had no design of marrying Darnly. In the midst of this security, Mary dispatched Maitland to signify her intention to Elizabeth, and to solicit her consent to the marriage with Darnly. This embassy was the first thing which opened the eyes of Randolph.

April 18.] Elizabeth affected the greatest surprise at this sudden resolution of the Scottish Queen, but without reason. The train was laid by herself, and she had no cause to wonder when it took effect. She expressed at the same time her disapprobation of the match in the strongest terms; and pretended to see many dangers and inconveniences arising from it to both kingdoms. But this too was mere affectation. Mary had often and plainly declared her resolution to marry. It was impossible she could make any choice more inoffensive. The danger of introducing a foreign interest into Britain, which Elizabeth had so justly dreaded, was entirely avoided. Darnly, who though allied to both crowns, and possessed of lands in both kingdoms, could be formidable to neither. It is evident, from all these circumtances, that Elizabeth's apprehensions of danger could not possibly be serious; and that in all her violent declarations against Darnly, there was much more of grimace than of reality.

There were not wanting, however, political motives of much weight to induce that artful Princess to put on the appearance of great displeasure. Mary, intimidated by this, might perhaps delay her marriage; which Elizabeth desired to obstruct with a weakness that little suited the dignity of her mind and the elevation of her character. Besides, the tranquillity of her own kingdom was the great object of Elizabeth's policy; and, by declaring her dissatisfaction with Mary's conduct, she hoped to alarm that party in Scotland which was attached to the English interest, and to encourage such of the nobles as secretly disapproved the match, openly to oppose it. The seeds of discord would by this means be scattered through that kingdom. Intestine commotions might arise. Amidst these, Mary could form none of these dangerous schemes to which the union of her people might have prompted her. Elizabeth would become the umpire between the Scottish Queen and her contending subjects; and England might look on with security, while a storm which she had raised, wasted the only kingdom which could possibly disturb its peace.

May 1.] In prosecution of this scheme, she laid before her privy council the message of the Scottish Queen, and consulted them with regard to the answer she should return. Their determination, it is easy to conceive, was perfectly conformable to her secret views. They drew up a remonstrance against the intended match, full of the imaginary dangers with which that event threatened the kingdom. Nor did she think it enough to signify her disapprobation of the measure, either by Maitland, Mary's ambassador, or by Randolph, her own resident in Scotland: in order to add more dignity to the farce which she chose to act, she appointed Sir Nicholas Throgmorton her ambassador extraordinary. She commanded him to declare, in the strongest terms, her dissatisfaction with the step which Mary proposed to take; and at the same time to produce the determination of the privy council as an evidence that the sentiments of the nation were not different from her own. Not long after, she confined the Countess of Lennox as a prisoner, first in her house, and then sent her to the tower.

Intelligence of all this reached Scotland before the arrival of the English ambassador. In the first transports of her indignation, Mary resolved no longer to keep any measures with Elizabeth; and sent orders to Maitland, who accompanied Throgmorton, to return instantly to the English court, and in her name to declare to Elizabeth that, after having been amused so long to so little purpose; after having been fooled and imposed on so grossly by her artifices; she was now resolved to gratify her own inclination, and to ask no other consent but that of her own subjects, in the choice of a husband. Maitland, with his usual sagacity, foresaw all the effects of such a rash and angry message, and ventured rather to incur the displeasure of his mistress, by disobeying her commands, than to be made the instrument of tearing asunder so violently the few remaining ties which still linked together the two Queens.

Mary herself soon became sensible of her error. She received the English ambassador with respect; justified her conduct with decency; and though unalterable in her resolution, she affected a wonderful solicitude to reconcile Elizabeth to the measure; and even pretended, out of complaisance towards her, to put off the consummation of the marriage for some months. It is probable, however, that the want of the Pope's dispensation, and the prospect of gaining the consent of her own subjects, were the real motives of this delay.

This consent Mary laboured with the utmost industry to obtain. The Earl of Murray was the person in the kingdom, whose concurrence was of the greatest importance; but she had reason to fear that it would not be procured without extreme difficulty. From the time of Lennox's return into Scotland, Murray perceived that the Queen's affections began gradually to be estranged from him. Darnly, Athol, Rizio, and all the court favourites, combined against him. His ambitious spirit could not brook this diminution of his power, which his former services had so little merited. He retired into the country, and gave way to rivals with whom he was unable to contend. The return of the Earl of Bothwell, his avowed enemy, who had been accused of a design upon his life, and who had resided for some time in foreign countries, obliged him to attend to his own safety. No entreaty of the Queen could persuade him to a reconcilement with that nobleman. He insisted on having him brought to public trial, and prevailed, by his importunity, to have a day fixed for it. Bothwell durst not appear in opposition to a man, who came to the place of trial attended by five thousand of his followers on horseback. He was once more constrained to leave the kingdom; but, by the Queen's command, the sentence of outlawry, which is incurred by nonappearance, was not pronounced against him.

Mary, sensible, at the same time, of how much importance it was to gain a subject so powerful and so popular as the Earl of Murray, invited him back to court [May 8], and received him with many demonstrations of respect and confidence. At last she desired him to set an example to her other subjects by subscribing a paper containing a formal approbation of her marriage with Darnly. Murray had many reasons to hesitate, and even to withhold his assent. Darnly had not only undermined his credit with the Queen, but discovered, on every occasion, a rooted aversion to his person. By consenting to his elevation to the throne, he would give him such an accession of dignity and power as no man willingly bestows on an enemy. The unhappy consequences which might follow upon a breach with England, were likewise of considerable weight with Murray. He had always openly preferred a confederacy with England, before the ancient alliance with France. By his means, chiefly, this change in the system of national politics

H

had been brought about. A league with England had been established ; and he could not think of sacrificing, to a rash and youthful passion, an alliance of so much utility to the kingdom ; and which he and the other nobles were bound by every obligation to maintain. Nor was the interest of religion forgotten on this occasion. Mary, though surrounded by Protestant counsellors, had found means to hold a dangerous correspondence with foreign Catholics. She had even courted the Pope's protection, who had sent her a subsidy of eight thousand crowns. Though Mary had hitherto endeavoured to bridle the zeal of the reformed clergy, and to set the Queen's conduct in the most favourable light, yet her obstinate adherence to her own religion could not fail of alarming him ; and by her resolution to marry a Papist, the hope of reclaiming her, by a union with a Protestant, was for ever cut off. Each of these considerations had its influence on Murray, and all of them determined him to decline complying at that time with the Queen's request.

The convention of nobles, which was assembled a few days after [May 14], discovered a greater disposition to gratify the Queen. Many of them, without hesitation, expressed their approbation of the intended match ; but as others were startled at the same dangers which had alarmed Murray, or were influenced by his example to refuse their consent, another convention was appointed at Perth, in order to deliberate more fully concerning this matter.

Meanwhile Mary gave a public evidence of her own inclination, by conferring upon Darnly titles of honour peculiar to the royal family. The opposition she had hitherto met with, and the many contrivances employed to thwart and disappoint her inclination, produced their usual effect on her heart ; they confirmed her passion, and increased its violence. The simplicity of that age imputed an affection so excessive to the influence of witchcraft. It was owing, however, to no other charm than the irresistible power of youth and beauty over a young and tender heart. Darnly grew giddy with his prosperity. Flattered by the love of a Queen, and the applause of many among her subjects, his natural haughtiness and insolence became insupportable, and he could no longer bear advice, far less contradiction. Lord Ruthven happening to be the first person who informed him that Mary, in order to soothe Elizabeth, had delayed for some time creating him Duke of Albany, he, in a frenzy of rage, drew his dagger, and attempted to stab him. It required all Mary's attention to prevent his falling under that contempt to which such behaviour deservedly exposed him.

In no scene of her life was ever Mary's own address more remarkably displayed. Love sharpened her invention, and made her study every method of gaining her subjects. Many of the nobles she won by her address, and more by her promises. On some she bestowed lands, to others she gave new titles of honour. She even condescended to court the Protestant clergy ; and having invited three of their superintendants to Stirling, she declared, in strong terms, her resolution to protect their religion, expressed her willingness to be present at a conference upon the points in doctrine which were disputed between the Protestants and Papists, and went so far as to show some desire to hear such of their preachers as were most remarkable for their moderation. By these arts the Queen gained wonderfully upon the people, who, unless their jealousy be raised by repeated injuries, are always ready to view the actions of their sovereign with an indulgent eye.

On the other hand, Murray and his associates were plainly the dupes of Elizabeth's policy. She talked in so high a strain of her displeasure at the intended match; she treated Lady Lennox with so much rigour; she wrote to the Scottish Queen in such high terms; she recalled the Earl of Lennox and his son in such a peremptory manner, and with such severe denunciations of her vengeance if they should presume to disobey; that all these expressions of aversion fully persuaded them of her sincerity. This belief fortified their scruples with respect to the match, and encouraged them to oppose it. They began with forming among themselves bonds of confederacy and mutual defence; they entered into a secret correspondence with the English resident, in order to secure Elizabeth's assistance when it should become needful; they endeavoured to fill the nation with such apprehensions of danger as might counterbalance the influence of those arts which the Queen had employed.

Besides these intrigues, there were secretly carried on, by both parties, dark designs of a more criminal nature, and more suited to the spirit of the age. Darnly, impatient of that opposition, which he imputed wholly to Murray, and resolving at any rate to get rid of such a powerful enemy, formed a plot to assassinate him during the meeting of the convention at Perth. Murray, on his part, despairing of preventing the marriage by any other means, had, together with the Duke of Chatelherault and the Earl of Argyll, concerted measures for seizing Darnly, and carrying him a prisoner into England.

If either of these conspiracies had taken effect, this convention might have been attended with consequences extremely tragical; but both were rendered abortive by the vigilance or good fortune of those against whom they were formed. Murray, being warned of his danger by some retainers to the court who still favoured his interest, avoided the blow by not going to Perth. Mary, receiving intelligence of Murray's enterprise, retired with the utmost expedition, along with Darnly, to the other side of Forth. Conscious, on both sides, of guilt, and inflamed with resentment, it was impossible they could either forget the violence which themselves had meditated, or forgive the injuries intended against them. From that moment all hope of reconcilement was at an end, and their mutual enmity burst out with every symptom of implacable hatred.

On Mary's return to Edinburgh, she summoned her vassals by proclamation, and solicited them by her letters to repair thither in arms, for the protection of her person against her foreign and domestic enemies. She was obeyed with all the promptness and alacrity with which subjects run to defend a mild and popular administration. This popularity, however, she owed in a great measure to Murray, who had directed her administration with great prudence. But the crime of opposing her marriage obliterated the memory of his former services; and Mary, impatient of contradiction, and apt to consider those who disputed her will as enemies to her person, determined to let him feel the whole weight of her vengeance. For this purpose she summoned him to appear before her upon a short warning, to answer to such things as should be laid to his charge. At this very time, Murray and the Lords who adhered to him were assembled at Stirling, to deliberate what course they should hold in such a difficult conjuncture. But the current of popular favour ran so strongly against them, and, notwithstanding some fears and jealousies, there prevailed in the nation such a general disposition to gratify the Queen in a matter which so nearly concerned her, that, without coming to any other conclusion than to implore the Queen of England's protection, they put an end to their ineffectual consultations, and returned every man to his own house.

Together with this discovery of the weakness of her enemies, the confluence of her subjects from all corners of the kingdom afforded Mary an agreeable proof of her own strength. While the Queen was in this prosperous situation, she determined to bring to a period an affair which had so long engrossed her heart and occupied her attention. On the 29th of July she married Lord Darnly. The ceremony was performed in the Queen's chapel, according to the rites of the Romish church; the Pope's bull dispensing with their marriage having been previously obtained. She issued at the same time proclamations, conferring the title of King of the Scots upon her husband, and commanding that henceforth all writs at law should run in the joint names of King and Queen.* Nothing can be a stronger proof of the violence of Mary's love, or the weakness of her councils, than this last step. Whether she had any right to choose a husband without consent of parliament, was, in that age, a matter of some dispute: that she had no right to confer upon him, by her private authority, the title and dignity of King, or by a simple proclamation to raise her husband to be the master of her people, seems to be beyond all doubt. Francis II., indeed bore the same title. It was not, however, the gift of the Queen, but of the nation; and the consent of Parliament was obtained before he ventured to assume it. Darnly's condition, as a subject, rendered it still more necessary to have the concurrence of the supreme council in his favour. Such a violent and unprecedented stretch of prerogative, as the substituting a proclamation in place of an act of parliament, might have justly alarmed the nation. But at that time the Queen possessed so entirely the confidence of her subjects, that, notwithstanding all the clamours of the malecontents, no symptoms of general discontent appeared on that account.

Even amidst that scene of joy which always accompanies successful love, Mary did not suffer the course of her vengeance against the malecontent nobles to be interrupted. Three days after the

* See Appendix No. XI.

marriage, Murray was again summoned to court, under the severest penalties, and upon his nonappearance, the rigour of justice took place, and he was declared an outlaw. At the same time the Queen set at liberty Lord Gordon, who, ever since his father's insurrection in the year 1562, had been detained a prisoner; she recalled the Earl of Sutherland, who, on account of his concern in that conspiracy, had fled into Flanders; and she permitted Bothwell to return again into Scotland. The first and last of these were among the most powerful subjects in the kingdom, and all of them animated with implacable hatred to Murray, whom they deemed the enemy of their families and the author of their own sufferings. This common hatred became the foundation of the strictest union with the Queen, and gained them an ascendant over all her councils. Murray himself considered this confederacy with his avowed enemies, as a more certain indication than any measure she had yet taken of her inexorable resentment.

The malcontents had not yet openly taken up arms.* But the Queen having ordered her subjects to march against them, they were driven to the last extremity. They found themselves unable to make head against the numerous forces which Mary had assembled; and fled into Argyleshire, in expectation of aid from Elizabeth, to whom they had secretly dispatched a messenger, in order to implore her immediate assistance.

Meanwhile Elizabeth endeavoured to embarrass Mary, by a new declaration of disgust at her conduct. She blamed both her choice of Lord Darnly, and the precipitation with which she had concluded the marriage. She required Lennox and Darnly, whom she still called her subjects, to return into England; and at the same time she warmly interceded in behalf of Murray, whose behaviour she represented to be not only innocent but laudable. This message, so mortifying to the pride of the Queen, and so full of contempt for her husband, was rendered still more insupportable by the petulant and saucy demeanour of Tamworth, the person who delivered it. Mary vindicated her own conduct with warmth, but with great strength of reason: and rejected the intercession in behalf of Murray, not without signs of resentment at Elizabeth's pretending to intermeddle in the internal government of her kingdom.

She did not, on that account, intermit in the least the ardour with which she pursued Murray and his adherents.† They now appeared openly in arms, and having received a small supply in money from Elizabeth, were endeavouring to raise their followers in the western counties. But Mary's vigilance hindered them from as-

---

* After their fruitless consultation in Stirling, the Lords retired to their own houses. Keith, 304. Murray was still at St. Andrew's on July 22. Keith, 306. By the places of rendezvous, appointed for the inhabitants of the different counties, August 4, it appears that the Queen's intention was to march into Fife, the county in which Murray, Rhodes, Kirkaldy, and other chiefs of the malcontents resided. Keith, 310. Their flight into the west, Keith, 312, prevented this expedition, and the former rendezvous was altered. Keith, 310.

† The most considerable persons who joined Murray were the Duke of Chatelherault, the Earls of Argyll, Glencairn, Rothes, Lord Boyd and Ochiltree; the Lairds of Grange, Cunninghamhead, Balcomie, Carmylie, Lawers, Bar, Dreghorn, Pitarrow, Comptroller, and the Tutor of Pictur. Knox, 382.

sembling in any considerable body. All her military operations at that time were concerted with wisdom, executed with vigour, and attended with success. In order to encourage her troops, she marched along with them, rode with loaded pistols, and endured all the fatigues of war with admirable fortitude. Her alacrity inspired her forces with an invincible resolution, which, together with their superiority in number, deterred the malcontents from facing them in the field : but, having artfully passed the Queen's army, they marched with great rapidity to Edinburgh, and endeavoured to rouse the inhabitants of that city to arms. [Aug. 31.] The Queen did not suffer them to remain long unmolested ; and on her approach they were forced to abandon that place, and retire in confusion towards the western borders.

As it was uncertain, for some time what route they had taken, Mary employed that interval in providing for the security of the counties in the heart of the kingdom. She seized the places of strength which belonged to the rebels ; and obliged the considerable barons in those shires which she most suspected, to join in associations for her defence. Having thus left all the country behind her in tranquillity, she, with an army eighteen thousand strong, marched towards Dumfries, where the rebels then were. During their retreat, they had sent letters to the Queen from almost every place where they halted, full of submission, and containing various overtures towards an accommodation. But Mary, who determined not to let slip such a favourable opportunity of crushing the mutinous spirit of her subjects, rejected them with disdain. As she advanced, the malecontents retired ; and having received no effectual aid from Elizabeth,* they despaired of any other means of safety, fled into England [Oct. 20], and put themselves under the protection of the Earl of Bedford, warden of the marches.

Nothing which Bedford's personal friendship for Murray could supply was wanting to render their retreat agreeable. But Elizabeth herself treated them with extreme neglect. She had fully gained her end, and, by their means, had excited such discord and jealousies among the Scots, as would, in all probability, long distract and weaken Mary's councils. Her business now was to save appearances, and to justify herself to the ministers of France and Spain, who accused her of fomenting the troubles in Scotland by her intrigues. The expedient she contrived for her vindication strongly displays her own character, and the wretched condition of exiles, who are obliged to depend on a foreign Prince. Murray, and Hamilton, Abbot of Kilwinning, being appointed by the other fugitives to wait on Elizabeth, instead of meeting with that welcome reception which was due to men who, out of confidence in her promises, and in order to forward her designs, had hazarded their lives and fortunes, could not even obtain the favour of an audience, until they had nearly consented to acknowledge, in the presence of the French and Spanish ambassadors, that Elizabeth had given them no encouragement to take arms. No sooner did

* See Append. No. XII. XIII.

they make this declaration, than she astonished them with this reply: " You have declared the truth; I am far from setting an example of rebellion to my own subjects, by countenancing those who rebel against their lawful Prince. The treason of which you have been guilty is detestable; and as traitors I banish you from my presence." Notwithstanding this scene of farce and of falsehood, so dishonourable to all the persons who acted a part in it, Elizabeth permitted the malecontents peaceably to reside in her dominions, supplied them secretly with money, and renewed her intercession with the Scottish Queen in their favour.

The advantage she had gained over them did not satisfy Mary; she resolved to follow the blow, and to prevent a party which she dreaded from ever receiving any footing in the nation. With this view, she called a meeting of parliament; and, in order that a sentence of forfeiture might be legally pronounced against the banished lords, she summoned them, by formal proclamation, to appear before it.

Dec. 1.] The Duke of Chatelherault, on his humble application, obtained a separate pardon; but not without difficulty, as the King violently opposed it. He was obliged, however, to leave the kingdom, and to reside for some time in France.

The numerous forces which Mary brought into the field, the vigour with which she acted, and the length of time she kept them in arms, resemble the efforts of a Prince with revenues much more considerable than those which she possessed. But armies were then levied and maintained by Princes at small charge. The vassal followed his superior, and the superior attended the monarch, at his own expense. Six hundred horsemen, however, and three companies of foot, besides her guards, received regular pay from the Queen. This extraordinary charge, together with the disbursements occasioned by her marriage, exhausted a treasury which was far from being rich. In this exigency, many devices were fallen upon for raising money. Fines were levied on the towns of St. Andrew's, Perth, and Dundee, which were suspected of favouring the malecontents. An unusual tax was imposed on the boroughs throughout the kingdom; and a great sum was demanded of the citizens of Edinburgh, by way of loan. This unprecedented exaction alarmed the citizens. They had recourse to difficulties, and started delays, in order to evade it. These Mary construed to be acts of avowed disobedience, and instantly committed several of them to prison. But this severity did not subdue the undaunted spirit of liberty which prevailed among the inhabitants. The Queen was obliged to mortage to the city the *superiority* of the town of Leith, by which she obtained a considerable sum of money. The thirds of ecclesiastical benefices proved another source whence the Queen derived some supply. About this time we find the Protestant clergy complaining more bitterly than ever of their poverty. The army, it is probable, exhausted a great part of that fund which was appropriated for their maintenance.

The assemblies of the church were not unconcerned spectators of the commotions of this turbulent year. In the meeting held the 24th of June, previous to the Queen's marriage, several of the malecontent nobles were present, and seem to have had great influence on its decisions. The high strain in which the assembly addressed the Queen had been imputed only to those fears and jealousies with regard to religion, which they endeavoured to infuse into the nation. The assembly complained, with some bitterness, of the stop which had been put to the progress of the Reformation by the Queen's arrival in Scotland ; they required not only the total suppression of the popish worship throughout the kingdom, but even in the Queen's own chapel ; and, besides the legal establishment of the Protestant religion, they demanded that Mary herself should publicly embrace it. The Queen, after some deliberation, replied, that neither her conscience nor her interest would permit her to take such a step. The former would for ever reproach her for a change which proceeded from no inward conviction ; the latter would suffer for the offence which her apostacy must give to the King of France, and her other allies on the Continent.

It is remarkable, that the prosperous condition of the Queen's affairs, during this reign, began to work some change in favour of her religion. The Earls of Lennox, Athol, and Cassils, openly attended mass ; she herself afforded the Catholics a more avowed protection than formerly ; and, by her permission, some of the ancient monks ventured to preach publicly to the people.

BOOK IV.

1566.

As the day appointed for the meeting of parliament approached, Mary and her ministers were employed in deliberating concerning the course which it was most proper to hold with regard to the exiled nobles. Many motives prompted her to set no bounds to the rigour of justice. The malecontents had laboured to defeat a scheme, which her interest conspired with her passions in rendering dear to her ; they were the leaders of a party whose friendship she had been obliged to court, while she held their principles in abhorrence ; and they were firmly attached to a rival, whom she had good reason both to fear and to hate.

But, on the other hand, several weighty considerations might be heard. The noblemen whose fate was in suspense were among the most powerful subjects in the kingdom ; their wealth great, their connexions extensive, and their adherents numerous. They were now at her mercy, the objects of compassion, and suing for pardon, with the most humble submission.

In those circumstances, an act of clemency would exalt the Queen's character, and appear no less splendid among foreigners than acceptible to her own subjects. Mary herself, though highly incensed, was not inexorable; but the king's rage was implacable and unrelenting. They were solicited in behalf of the fugitives from various quarters. Morton, Ruthven, Maitland, and all who had been members of the Congregation, were not forgetful of their ancient union with Murray and his fellow-sufferers; nor neglectful of their safety, which they deemed of great importance to the kingdom. Melvil, who at that time possessed the Queen's confidence, seconded their solicitations. And Murray, having stooped so low as to court Rizio, that favourite, who was desirous of securing his protection against the king, whose displeasure he had lately incurred, seconded the intercessions of his other friends with the whole of his influence. The interposition of Sir Nicholas Throgmorton, who had lately been Elizabeth's ambassador in Scotland, in behalf of the exiles, was of more weight than all these, and attended with more success. Throgmorton, out of enmity to Cecil, had embarked deeply in all the intrigues which were carried on at the English court, in order to undermine the power and credit of that minister. He espoused, for this reason, the cause of the Scottish Queen, towards whose title and pretensions the other was known to bear little favour; and ventured, in the present critical juncture, to write a letter to Mary, containing the most salutary advices with regard to her conduct. He recommended the pardoning of the Earl of Murray and his associates, as a measure no less prudent than popular. "An action of this nature," says he, " the pure effect of Your Majesty's generosity, will spread the fame of your lenity and moderation, and engage the English to look towards your accession to the throne, not only without prejudice, but with desire. By the same means, a perfect harmony will be restored among your own subjects, who, if any rupture should happen with England, will serve you with that grateful zeal which your clemency cannot fail of inspiring."

These prudent remonstrances of Throgmorton, to which his reputation for wisdom and known attachment to the Queen added great authority, made a deep impression on her spirit. Her courtiers cultivated this happy disposition, and prevailed on her, notwithstanding the King's inflexible temper, to sacrifice her own private resentment to the intercession of her subjects and the wishes of her friends. With this view the parliament, which had been called to meet on the 4th of February, was prorogued to the 7th of April; and in the mean time she was busy in considering the manner and form in which she should extend her favour to the lords who were under disgrace.

Though Mary discovered on this occasion a mind naturally prone to humanity and capable of forgiving, she wanted firmness, however, to resist the influence which was fatally employed to disappoint the effects of this amiable disposition. About this time, and at no great distance from each other, two envoys arrived from the French King. The former was intrusted with matters of mere ceremony alone; he congratulated the Queen on her marriage, and invested the King with the ensigns of the order of St. Michael.

The instructions of the latter related to matters of more importance, and produced greater effects.

An interview between Charles IX. and his sister the Queen of
Spain had been often proposed: and after many obstacles arising
from the opposition of political interest, was at last appointed at
Bayonne. Catharine of Medicis accompanied her son; the Duke
of Alva attended his mistress. Amidst the scenes of public pomp
and pleasure, which seemed to be the sole occupation of both
courts, a scheme was formed, and measures concerted, for exterminating the Hugonots in France, the Protestants in the Low Countries, and for suppressing the Reformation throughout all Europe.
The active policy of Pope Pius IV., and the zeal of the Cardinal of
Lorrain, confirmed and encouraged dispositions so suitable to the
genius of the Romish religion, and so beneficial to their own order.

It was an account of this holy league which the second French
envoy brought to Mary, conjuring her at the same time, in the
name of the King of France and the Cardinal of Lorrain, not to
restore the leaders of the Protestants in her kingdom to power and
favour, at the very time when the Catholic Princes were combined
to destroy that sect in all the countries of Europe.

Popery is a species of false religion, remarkable for the strong
possession it takes of the heart. Contrived by men of deep insight
in the human character, and improved by the experience and observation of many successive ages, it arrived at last to a degree of
perfection which no former system of superstition had ever attained.
There is no power in the understanding, and no passion in the
heart, to which it does not present objects adapted to rouse and to
interest them. Neither the love of pleasure which at that time
prevailed in the court of France, nor the pursuits of ambition
which occupied the court of Spain, had secured them from the dominion of bigotry. Laymen and courtiers were agitated with that
furious and unmerciful zeal which is commonly considered as peculiar to ecclesiastics; and Kings and ministers thought themselves
bound in conscience to extirpate the Protestant doctrine. Mary
herself was deeply tinctured with all the prejudices of Popery;
a passionate attachment to that superstition is visible in every part
of her character, and runs through all the scenes of her life; she
was devoted too with the utmost submission to the Princes of Lorrain, her uncles; and had been accustomed from her infancy to
listen to all their advices with a filial respect. The prospect of restoring the public exercise of her own religion, the pleasure of
complying with her uncles, and the hopes of gratifying the French
monarch, whom the present situation of her affairs in England
made it necessary to court, counterbalanced all the prudent considerations which had formerly weighed with her. She instantly
joined the confederacy, which had been formed for the destruction
of the Protestants, and altered the whole plan of her conduct with
regard to Murray and his adherents.*

To this fatal resolution may be imputed all the subsequent calamities of Mary's life. Ever since her return into Scotland, fortune

* See Append. No. XIV.

may be said to have been propitious to her rather than adverse; and if her prosperity did not rise to any great height, it had, however, suffered no considerable interruption. A thick and settled cloud of adversity, with few gleams of hope, and none of real enjoyment, covers the remainder of her days.

The effects of the new system which Mary had adopted were soon visible. The time of the prorogation of parliament was shortened; and by a new proclamation the 12th of March was fixed for its meeting. Mary resolved, without any further delay, to proceed to the attainder of the rebel lords, and at the same time determined to take some steps towards the re-establishment of the Romish religion in Scotland.* The lords of the Articles were chosen, as usual, to prepare the business which was to come before the parliament. They were all persons in whom the Queen could confide, and bent to promote her designs. The ruin of Murray and his party seemed now inevitable, and the danger of the reformed church imminent, when an event unexpectedly happened which saved both. If we regard either the barbarity of that age, when such acts of violence were common, or the mean condition of the unhappy person who suffered, the event is little remarkable; but if we reflect upon the circumstances with which it was attended, or upon the consequences which followed it, it appears extremely memorable; and the rise and progress of it deserved to be traced with great care.

Darnly's external accomplishments had excited that sudden and violent passion which raised him to the throne. But the qualities of his mind corresponded ill with the beauty of his person. Of a weak understanding, and without experience; conceited, at the same time, of his own abilities, and ascribing his extraordinary success entirely to his distinguished merit; all the Queen's favour made no impression on such a temper. All her gentleness could not bridle his imperious and ungovernable spirit. All her attention to place about him persons capable of directing his conduct, could not preserve him from rash and imprudent actions. Fond of all the amusements, and even prone to all the vices of youth, he became by degrees careless of her person, and a stranger to her company. To a woman, and a Queen, such behaviour was intolerable. The lower she had stooped in order to raise him, his be-

* It is not on the authority of Knox alone, that we charge the Queen with the design of re-establishing the Roman Catholic religion, or at least of exempting the professors of it from the rigour of those penal laws to which they were subjected. He indeed asserts that the altars, which would have been erected in the church of St. Giles, were already provided, 294. 1. Mary herself, in a letter to the Archbishop of Glasgow, her ambassador in France, acknowledges, "that in that Parliament she intended to have done some good, with respect to restoring the old religion" Keith, 331. 2. The Spiritual Lords. i. e. the Popish Ecclesiastics, had, by her authority, resumed their ancient place in that assembly. Ibid 3. She had joined the confederacy at Bayonne. Keith, Append. 177. 4. She allowed mass to be celebrated in different parts of the kingdom. ibid.; and declared that she would have mass free for all men who would hear it. Good. vol. i. 274. 5. Blackwood, who was furnished by the Archbishop of Glasgow with materials for writing his " Martyre de Marie," affirms, that the Queen intended to have procured, in this Parliament, if not the re-establishment of the Catholic religion, at least something for the ease of Catholics. Jebb, vol. ii. 204.

haviour appeared the more ungenerous and criminal: and in proportion to the strength of her first affection was the violence with
which her disappointed passion now operated. A few months after
the marriage their domestic quarrels began to be observed. The
extravagance of Darnly's ambition gave rise to these. Instead of
being satisfied with a share in the administration of government,
or with the title of King, which Mary, by an unprecedented stretch
of power, had conferred on him, he demanded the Crown Matrimonial with most insolent importunity.* Though Mary alleged that
this gift was beyond her power, and that the authority of Parliament must be interposed to bestow it, he wanted either understanding to comprehend or temper to admit so just a defence; and
often renewed and urged his request.

Rizio, whom the King had at first taken into great confidence,
did not humour him in these follies. By this he incurred Henry's
displeasure; and as it was impossible for Mary to behave towards her husband with the same affection which distinguished
the first and happy days of their union, he imputed this coldness,
not to his own behaviour, which had so well merited it, but to the
insinuations of Rizio. Mary's own conduct confirmed and strengthened these suspicions. She treated this stranger with a familiarity,
and admitted him to a share in her confidence, to which neither
his first condition nor the office she had lately bestowed on him
gave him any title. He was perpetually in her presence, intermed-
dled in every business, and, together with a few favourites, was the
companion of all her private amusements. The haughty spirit of
of Darnly could not bear the intrusion of such an upstart; and
impatient of any delay, and unrestrained by any scruple, he instantly resolved to get rid of him by violence.

At the same time another design, which took its rise from very
different motives, was carrying on against the life of Rizio. Morton, Ruthven, Lindsay, and Maitland were the contrivers of it. In
all former commotions they had been strictly united with Murray,
though in the late insurrection they had deserted him for various
reasons. Morton was nearly allied to the family of Angus; and,
during the minority of the present Earl, acted as chief of the name
of Douglas. Ruthven was married to the King's aunt. Lindsay's
wife was of the same blood. All these had warmly concurred with
the Queen in promoting a marriage which did so much honour to
the house of Douglas, and naturally expected that, under a King of
their own blood, the chief management of affairs would be committed to them. Maitland, with his usual sagacity, foresaw that Murray's opposition to the match would prove dangerous and ineffectual; but whoever ruled at court, he hoped, by his dexterity and
talents, to render himself necessary and of importance. They were
all equally disappointed in their expectations. The King's head-
strong temper rendered him incapable of advice. The Queen could

* Keith. 329. Id. Ap. 165. 166. Knox, 404. The eagerness of the King to obtain the "Crown Matrimonial," is not surprising, when the extent of the powers
which that title conveyed, as explained in the text and note, is taken into consideration.

not help distrusting men who had been so long and so intimately connected with Murray, and gave herself up entirely to such counsellors as complied with all her inclinations. The return of that nobleman and his followers was therefore the only event which would restore Morton, Maitland, and their associates to their former ascendant over the Queen's councils. For this reason, nothing could be more mortifying to them than the resolution which Mary had taken to treat the exiles with rigour. This they imputed to Rizio, who, after he had engaged to aid Murray with all his interest, was now the most active instrument in promoting the measures which were concerted for the ruin of that nobleman. This officious zeal completed the disgust which they had conceived against him, and inspired them with thoughts of vengeance in nowise suitable to justice, to humanity, or to their own dignity.

While they were ruminating upon their scheme, the King communicated his resolution to be avenged of Rizio to Lord Ruthven, and implored his assistance and that of his friends towards the execution of this design. Nothing could be more acceptable to them than this overture. They saw at once all the advantages they would reap by the concurrence of such an associate. Their own private revenge upon Rizio would pass, they hoped, for an act of obedience to the King; and they did not despair of obtaining the restoration of their banished friends and security for the Protestant religion, as the price of their compliance with his will.

But as Henry was no less fickle than rash, they hesitated for some time, and determined to advance no further, without taking every possible precaution for their own safety. They did not, in the mean time, suffer the King's resentment to abate. Morton, who was inferior to no man of that intriguing age in all the arts of insinuation and address, took the young Prince under his management. He wrought upon his ruling passion, ambition to obtain the Matrimonial Crown. He represented Rizio's credit with the Queen to be the chief and only obstacle to his success in that demand. This minion alone, he said, possessed her confidence; and out of complaisance to him, her subjects, her nobility, and even her husband, were excluded from any participation of her secret counsels. Under the appearance of a confidence merely political, he insinuated, and the King perhaps believed that a familiarity of a quite different and very criminal nature might be concealed.* Such vari-

---

* Of all our historians, Buchanan alone avowedly accuses Mary of a criminal love for Rizio, 340. 344. Knox slightly insinuates that such a suspicion was entertained, 391. Melvil. in a conversation with the Queen, intimates that he was afraid her familiarity with Rizio might be liable to misconstruction, 110. The King himself seems, both by Melvil's account, and by his expostulation with the Queen, which Ruthven mentions, to have given credit to these suspicions. Melv. 127. Keith, Append. 123, 124. That the King's suspicions were strong is likewise evident from the paper published, Append. No. XV. But in opposition to these suspicions, and they are nothing more, we may observe that Raulet, the Queen's French secretary, was dismissed from her service, and Rizio advanced to that office, in December, 1564. Keith, 268. It was in consequence of this preferment, that he acquired his great credit with the Queen. Melv. 107, Darnly arrived in Scotland about two months after. Keith, 269. The Queen immediately conceived for him a passion which had all the symptoms of genuine and

ous and complicated passions raged in the King's bosom with the utmost fury. He became more impatient that ever of any delay, and even threatened to strike the intended blow with his own hand. At last, preliminaries were settled on both sides, and articles for their mutual security agreed upon. The King engaged to prevent the attainder of the banished Lords, to consent to their return into Scotland, to obtain for them an ample remission of all their crimes, and to support, to the utmost of his power, the religion which was now established in the kingdom. On their parts, they undertook to procure the Crown Matrimonial for Henry, to secure his right of succession if the Queen should die before him without any issue, and to defend that right to the uttermost against whatever person should presume to dispute it ; and if either Rizio or any other person should happen to be killed in prosecuting the design, the King promised to acknowledge himself to be the author of the enterprise, and to protect those who were embarked in it.

Nothing now remained but to concert the plan of operation, to choose the actors, and to assign them their parts in perpetrating this detestable crime. Every circumstance here paints and characterises the manners and men of that age, and fills us with horror at both. The place chosen for committing such a deed was the Queen's bed-chamber. Though Mary was now in the sixth month of her pregnancy, and though Rizio might have been seized elsewhere without difficulty, the King pitched upon this place, that he might enjoy the malicious pleasure of reproaching Rizio with his crimes before the Queen's face. The Earl of Morton, the Lord High Chancellor of the kingdom, undertook to direct an enterprise, carried on in defiance of all the laws of which he was bound to be the guardian. The Lord Ruthven, who had been confined to his bed for three months by a very dangerous distemper, and who was still so feeble that he could hardly walk, or bear the weight of his own armour, was intrusted with the executive part ; and while he himself needed to be supported by two men, he came abroad to commit a murder in the presence of his sovereign.

On the 9th of March, Morton entered the court of the palace with a hundred and sixty men ; and without noise, or meeting with any resistance, seized all the gates. While the Queen was at supper with the Countess of Argyll, Rizio, and a few other persons, the King suddenly entered the apartment by a private passage. At his back was Ruthven, clad in complete armour, and with that ghastly and horrid look which long sickness had given him. Three or four of his most trusty accomplices followed him. Such an unusual appearance alarmed those who were present. Rizio instantly

violent love. Rizio aided this passion and promoted the marriage with all his interest. Melv. III. During some months after the marriage, the Queen's fondness for Darnly continued. She soon proved with child. From this enumeration of circumstances, it appears almost immpossible that the Queen, unless we suppose her to have been a woman utterly abandoned, could carry on any criminal intrigue with Rizio. But the silence of Randolph, the English resident, a man abundantly ready to mention and to aggravate Mary's faults, and who does not once insinuate that her confidence in Rizio concealed any thing criminal, is in itself a sufficient vindication of her innocence.

apprehended that he was the victim at whom the blow was aimed; and in the utmost consternation retired behind the Queen, of whom he laid hold, hoping that the reverence due to her person might prove some protection to him. The conspirators had proceeded too far to be restained by any consideration of that kind. Numbers of armed men rushed into the chamber. Ruthven drew his dagger, and with a furious mien and voice commanded Rizio to leave a place of which he was unworthy, and which he had occupied too long. Mary employed tears, and entreaties, and threatenings, to save her favourite. But, notwithstanding all these, he was torn from her by violence, and before he could be dragged through the next apartment, the rage of his enemies put an end to his life, piercing his body with fifty-six wounds.*

Athol, Huntly, Bothwell, and other confidants of the Queen, who had apartments, in the palace, were alarmed at the uproar, and filled with the utmost terror on their own account; but either no violence was intended against them, or the conspirators durst not shed the noblest blood in the kingdom in the same illegal manner with which they had ventured to take the life of a stranger. Some of them were dismissed, and others made their escape.

The conspirators, in the mean time, kept possession of the palace, and guarded the Queen with the utmost care. A proclamation was published by the King, prohibiting the parliament to meet on the day appointed; and measures were taken by him for preventing any tumult in the city.† Murray, Rothes, and their followers being informed of every step taken against Rizio, arrived at Edinburgh next evening. Murray was graciously received both by the King and Queen: by the former, on account of the articles which had been agreed upon between them; by the latter, because she hoped to prevail on him, by gentle treatment, not to take part with the murderers of Rizio. Their power she still felt and dreaded; and the insult which they had offered to her authority, and even to her person, so far exceeded any crime she could impute to Murray that, in hopes of wreaking her vengeance on them, she became extremely willing to be reconciled to him. The obligations, however, which Murray lay under to men who had hazarded their lives on his account, engaged him to labour for their safety. The Queen, who scarce had the liberty of choice left, was persuaded to admit Morton and Ruthven into her presence, and to grant them the promise of pardon in whatever terms they should deem necessary for their own security.

The King, meanwhile, stood astonished at the boldness and success of his own enterprise, and uncertain what course to hold. The Queen observed his irresolution, and availed herself of it. She employed all her art to disengage him from his new associates. His consciousness of the insult which he had offered to so illustrious a benefactress inspired him with uncommon facility and complaisance. In spite of all the warnings he received to distrust the Queen's artifices, she prevailed on him [March 11], to dismiss the

* See Appendix, No. XV.   † Keith, Appendix, 126.

guards which the conspirators had placed on her person; and that same night he made his escape along with her, attended by three persons only, and retired to Dunbar. The scheme of their flight had been communicated to Huntly and Bothwell, and they were quickly joined by them and several other of the nobles. Bothwell's estate lay in that corner of the kingdom, and his followers crowded to their chief in such numbers as soon enabled the Queen to set the power of the conspirators at defiance.

This sudden flight filled them with inexpressible consternation. They had obtained a promise of pardon; and it now appeared from the Queen's conduct, that nothing more was intended by this promise than to amuse them and to gain time. They ventured, however, to demand the accomplishment of it; but their messenger was detained a prisoner, and the Queen, advancing towards Edinburgh at the head of eight thousand men, talked in the highest strain of resentment and revenge. She had the address, at the same time, to separate Murray and his associates from the conspirators against Rizio. Sensible that the union of these parties would form a confederacy which might prove formidable to the crown, she expressed great willingness to receive the former into favour; towards the latter she declared herself inexorable. Murray and his followers were no less willing to accept a pardon on her terms. The conspirators against Rizio, deprived of every resource, and incapable of resistance, fled precipitately to Newcastle [March 10], having thus changed situations with Murray and his party, who left that place a few days before.

No man so remarkable for wisdom, and even for cunning, as the Earl of Morton, ever engaged in a more unfortunate enterprise. Deserted basely by the King, who denied his knowledge of the conspiracy by public proclamations, and abandoned ungenerously by Murray and his party, he was obliged to flee from his native country, to resign the highest office, and to part with one of the most opulent fortunes in the kingdom.

On her return to Edinburgh, Mary began to proceed against those concerned in the murder of Rizzio with the utmost rigour of the law. But, in praise of her clemency, it must be observed, that only two persons, and these of no inconsiderable rank, suffered for this crime.

In this conspiracy there is one circumstance which, though somewhat detached, deserves not to be forgotten. In the confederacy between the King and the conspirators, the real intention of which was assassination, the preserving of the reformed church is, nevertheless, one of the most considerable articles; and the same men, who were preparing to violate one of the first duties of morality, affected the highest regard for religion. History relates these extravagances of the human mind, without pretending to justify, or even to account for them; and, regulating her own opinions by the eternal and immutable laws of justice and of virtue, points out such inconsistencies as features of the age which she describes, and records them for the instruction of ages to come.

As this is the second instance of deliberate assassination which has occurred, and as we shall hereafter meet with many other instances of the same crime, the causes which gave rise to a practice so shocking to humanity deserve our particular attention. Resentment is, for obvious and wise reasons, one of the strongest passions of the human mind. The natural demand of this passion is, that the person who feels the injury should himself inflict the vengeance due on that account. The permitting this, however, would have been destructive to society; and punishment would have known no bounds, either in severity or in duration. For this reason, in the very infancy of the social state, the sword was taken out of private hands, and committed to the magistrate. But at first, while laws aimed at restraining, they really strengthened the principle of revenge. The earliest and most simple punishment for crimes was retaliation; the offender forfeited limb for limb, and life for life. The payment of compensation to the person injured succeeded to the rigour of the former institution. In both of these, the gratification of private revenge was the object of law; and he who suffered the wrong was the only person who had a right to pursue, to exact, or to remit the punishment. While laws allowed such full scope to the revenge of one party, the interests of the other were not neglected. If the evidence of his guilt did not amount to a full proof, or if he reckoned himself unjustly accused, the person to whom a crime was imputed had a right to challenge his adversary to single combat, and, on obtaining the victory, vindicated his own honour. In almost every cause, whether civil or criminal, arms were appealed to, in defence, either of the innocence or the property of the parties. Justice had seldom need to use her balance; the sword alone decided every contest. The passion of revenge was nourished by all these means, and grew, by daily indulgence, to be incredibly strong. Mankind became habituated to blood, not only in times of war, but of peace; and from this, as well as other causes, contracted an amazing ferocity of temper and of manners. This ferocity, however, made it necessary to discourage the trial by combat; to abolish the payment of compensations in criminal cases; and to think of some milder method of terminating disputes concerning civil rights. The punishments for crimes became more severe, and the regulations concerning property more fixed; but the Princes, whose province it was to inflict the one and to enforce the other, possessed little power. Great offenders despised their authority; smaller ones sheltered themselves under the jurisdiction of those from whose protection they expected impunity. The administration of justice was extremely feeble and dilatory. An attempt to punish the crimes of a chieftain, or even of his vassals, often excited rebellions and civil wars. To nobles, haughty and independent, among whom the causes of discord were many and unavoidable, who were quick in discerning an injury, and impatient to revenge it; who deemed it infamous to submit to an enemy, and cowardly to forgive him; who considered the right of punishing those who had injured them as a privilege of their order and a mark of independence; such slow proceedings were extremely unsatisfactory. The blood of their adversary was, in their opinion, the only thing which could wash away an affront : where that was not shed, their revenge was disappointed, and their courage became suspected, and a stain was left on their honour. That vengeance, which the impotent hand of the magistrate could not inflict, their own could easily execute. Under governments so feeble, men assumed, as in a state of nature, the right of judging and redressing their own wrongs; and thus assassination, a crime of all others the most destructive to society, came not only to be allowed, but to be reckoned honourable.

The history of Europe, during the fourteenth and fifteenth centuries, abounds with detestable instances of this crime. It prevailed chiefly among the French and Scots, between whom there was a close intercourse at that time, and a surprising resemblance in their national characters. In 1407, the only brother of the King of France was murdered publicly in the streets of Paris; and so far was this horrible action from meeting with proper punishment, that an eminent lawyer was allowed to plead in defence of it before the peers of France, and avowedly to maintain the lawfulness of assassination. In 1417, it required all the eloquence and authority of the famous Gerson, to prevail on the council of Constance to condemn this proposition, "That there are some cases in which assassination is a virtue more meritorious in a knight than in a squire, and more meritorious in a king than in a knight." The number of eminent persons who were murdered in France and Scotland, on account either of private, or political, or religious quarrels, during the fifteenth and sixteenth centuries, is almost incredible. Even after those causes, which first gave rise to this barbarous practice, were removed; after the jurisdiction of magistrates, and the authority of laws, were better established, and become more universal; after the progress of learning and philosophy had polished the manners and humanized the minds of men, this crime continued in some degree. It was towards the close of the seventeenth century before it disappeared in France. The additional vigour, which the Royal authority acquired by the accession of James VI. to the throne of England, seems to have put a stop to it in Scotland.

The influence, however, of any national custom, both on the understanding and on the heart, and how far it may go towards perverting or extinguishing moral principles of the greatest importance, is remarkable. The authors of those ages have perfectly imbibed the sentiments of their contemporaries with regard to assassination; and they who had leisure to reflect and to judge appear to be no more shocked at this crime than the persons who committed it during the heat and impetuosity of passion. Buchanan describes the murder of Cardinal Beatoun of Rizio, without expressing those feelings which are natural to a man, or that indignation which became an historian. Knox, whose mind was fiercer and more unpolished, relates the death of Beatoun and of the Duke of Guise, not only without censure, but with the utmost exultation. On the other hand, the Bishop of Ross mentions the assassination of the Earl of Murray with some degree of applause.

Blackwood dwells upon it with the most indecent triumph, and ascribes it directly to the hand of God. Lord Ruthven, the principal actor in the conspiracy against Rizio, wrote an account of it some short time before his own death, and in all his long narrative there is not one expression of regret, or one symptom of compunction, for a crime no less dishonourable than barbarous. Morton, equally guilty of the same crime, entertained the same sentiments concerning it; and in his last moments, neither he himself nor the ministers who attended him seem to have considered it as an action which called for repentance; even then he talks of *David's slaughter* as coolly as if it had been an innocent or commendable deed. The vices of another age astonish and shock us; the vices of our own become familiar, and excite little horror. I return from this digression to the course of the history.

The charm which had at first attached the Queen to Darnly, and held them for some time in a happy union, was now entirely dissolved; and love no longer covering his follies and vices with its friendly veil,they appeared to Mary in their full dimension and deformity.* Though Henry published a proclamation disclaiming any knowledge of the conspiracy against Rizio, the Queen was fully convinced that he was not only accessary to the contrivance, but to the commission of that odious crime. That very power which, with liberal and unsuspicious fondness, she had conferred upon him, he had employed to insult her authority, to limit her prerogative, and to endanger her person. Such an outrage it was impossible any woman could bear or forgive. Cold civilities, secret distrust, frequent quarrels, succeeded to their former transports of affection and confidence. The Queen's favours were no longer conveyed through his hands. The crowd of expectants ceased to court his patronage, which they found to avail so little. Among the nobles, some dreaded his furious temper, others complained of his perfidiousness; and all of them despised the weakness of his understanding and the inconstancy of his heart. The people themselves observed some parts of his conduct which little suited the dignity of a King. Addicted to drunkenness, beyond what the manners of that age could bear, and indulging irregular passions, which even the licentiousness of youth could not excuse, he, by his indecent behaviour, provoked the Queen to the utmost; and the passions which it occasioned often forced tears from her eyes, both in public and private. Her aversion for him increased every day, and could be no longer concealed. He was often absent from court, appeared there with little splendour, and was trusted with no power. Avoided equally by those who endeavoured to please the Queen, who favoured Morton and his associates, or who adhered to the house of Hamilton, he was left almost alone in a neglected and unpitied solitude.

About this time a new favourite grew into great credit with the Queen, and soon gained an ascendant over her heart, which encouraged his enterprising genius to form designs that proved fatal to

* See Append. No. XVI.

himself, and was the occasion of all Mary's subsequent misfortunes.
This was James Hepburn, Earl of Bothwell, the head of an ancient
family, and, by his extensive possessions and numerous vassals, one
of the most powerful nobles in the kingdom. Even in that turbulent age, when so many vast projects were laid open to an aspiring
mind, and invited it into action, no man's ambition was more daring
than Bothwell's, or had recourse to bolder or more singular expedients for obtaining power.* When almost every person of distinction in the kingdom, whether Papist or Protestant, had joined the
Congregation in opposing the dangerous encroachments of the
French upon the liberties of the nation, he, though an avowed
Protestant, adhered to the Queen Regent, and acted with vigour on
her side. The success which attended the arms of the Congregation
having obliged him to retire into France, he was taken into the
Queen's service, and continued with her until her return into
Scotland. From that period, every step of his conduct towards
Mary was remarkably dutiful; and amidst all the shiftings of faction, we scarcely ever find him holding any course which could be
offensive to her. When Murray's proceedings with regard to her
marriage gave umbrage to the Queen, she recalled Bothwell from
that banishment into which she had been obliged with reluctance
to drive him, and considered his zeal and abilities as the most powerful supports of her authority. When the conspirators against
Rizio seized her person, he became the chief instrument of recovering her liberty, and served her, on that occasion, with so much fidelity and success as made the deepest impression on her mind, and
greatly increased the confidence which she had hitherto placed in
him. Her gratitude loaded him with marks of her bounty; she
raised him to offices of profit and trust, and transacted no matter
of importance without his advice. By complaisance and assiduity
he confirmed and fortified these dispositions of the Queen in his
favour, and insensibly paved the way towards that vast project
which his immoderate ambition had already conceived, and which,
in spite of many difficulties, and at the expense of many crimes, he
at last accomplished.

The hour of the Queen's delivery now approached. As her
palace was only defended by a slender guard, it seemed imprudent
to expose her person, at this time, to the insults she might suffer in
a kingdom torn by factions, and prone to mutiny. For this reason
the privy council advised the Queen to fix her residence in the
castle of Edinburgh, the strongest fortress in the kingdom, and the
most proper place for the security of her person. In order to render
this security more perfect, Mary laboured to extinguish the domestic

* The enterprising spirit of Bothwell was so conspicuous as to procure him
several marks of distinction during his residence in France. Hardwick's State
Papers, i 143. Throgmorton, the English ambassador at Paris, and one of the
most sagacious ministers employed by Elizabeth, points him out as a person who
was to be dreaded and observed. " The Earl of Bothwell," says he in a letter,
Nov. 23, 1560, " is departed to return into Scotland, and hath made boast that he
will do great things, and live in Scotland in despite of all men. He is a glorious,
rash, and hazardous young man; and therefore it were meet that his adversaries
should both have an eye to him, and also keep him short." Ibid. p. 149.

feuds which divided some of the principal nobles. Murray and Argyll were exasperated against Huntly and Bothwell by reciprocal and repeated injuries. The Queen, by her authority and entreaties, effected a reconcilement among them, and drew from them a promise to bury their discords in everlasting oblivion. This reconcilement Mary had so much at heart, that she made it the condition on which she again received Murray into her favour.

On the 19th of June, Mary was delivered of her only son James, a Prince whose birth was happy for the whole island, and unfortunate to her alone. His accession to the throne of England united the two divided kingdoms into one mighty monarchy, and established the power of great Britain on a firm foundation; while she, torn early from her son by the cruelty of her fate, was never allowed to indulge those tender passions, nor to taste those joys which fill the heart of a mother.

Melvil was instantly dispatched to London with an account of this event. It struck Elizabeth, at first, in a sensible manner; and the advantage and superiority which her rival had acquired by the birth of a son forced tears from her eyes. But before Melvil was admitted to audience, she had so far recovered the command of herself, as to receive him not only with decency, but with excessive cheerfulness; and willingly accepted the invitation which Mary gave her, to stand godmother to her son.

As Mary loved splendour and magnificence, she resolved to celebrate the baptism of the young Prince with great pomp; and for that purpose sent invitations of the same kind to the French King, and to the Duke of Savoy, the uncle of her former husband.

The Queen, on her recovery, discovered no change in her sentiments in respect to the King.* The death of Rizio, and the countenance he had given to an action so insolent and unjustifiable, were still fresh in her memory. She was frequently pensive and dejected. Though Henry sometimes attended at court, and accompanied her in her progresses through different parts of the kingdom, he met with little reverence from the nobles, while Mary treated him with the greatest reserve, and did not suffer him to possess any authority. The breach between them became every day day more and more apparent. Attempts were made towards a reconcilement, particularly by Castelnau, the French ambassador; but, after such a violent rupture, it was found no easy matter to bind the knot anew; and, although he prevailed on the King and Queen to pass two nights together, we may, with great probability, pronounce this appearance of union, in which Castelnau trusted, not to have been sincere; we know with certainty that it was not lasting.

Bothwell, all this while, was the Queen's prime confidant. Without his participation no business was concluded, and no favour bestowed. Together with this ascendant over her councils, Bothwell, if we may believe the contemporary historians, acquired no less sway over her heart. But at what precise time this ambitious

* See Append. No. xvii.

Lord first allowed the sentiments of a lover to occupy the place of that duty and respect which a subject owes his sovereign; or when Mary, instead of gratitude for his faithful services, felt a passion of another nature rising in her bosom, it is no easy matter to determine. Such delicate transitions of passion can be discerned only by those who are admitted near the persons of the parties, and who can view the secret workings of the heart with calm and acute observation. Neither Knox nor Buchanan enjoyed these advantages. Their humble station allowed them only a distant access to the Queen and her favourite. And the ardour of their zeal, as well as the violence of their prejudices, rendered their opinions rash, precipitate, and inaccurate. It is by the effects of this reciprocal passion, rather than by their accounts of it, that subsequent historians can judge of its reality.

Adventurous as Bothwell's project to gain the Queen may appear, it was formed and carried on under very favourable circumstances. Mary was young, gay, and affable. She possessed great sensibility of temper, and was capable of the utmost tenderness of affection. She had placed her love on a very unworthy object, who requited it with ingratitude, and treated her with neglect, with insolence, and with brutality. All these she felt and resented. In this situation, the attention and complaisance of a man who had vindicated her authority and protected her person, who entered into all her views, who soothed all her passions, who watched and improved every opportunity of insinuating his design and recommending his passion, could hardly fail of making an impression on a heart of such a frame as Mary's.

The haughty spirit of Darnly, nursed up in flattery and accustomed to command, could not bear the contempt under which he had now fallen, and the state of insignificance to which he saw himself reduced. But, in a country where he was universally hated or despised, he could never hope to form a party, which would second any attempt he might make to recover power. He addressed himself, therefore, to the Pope, and to the Kings of France and Spain, with many professions of his own zeal for the Catholic religion, and with bitter complaints against the Queen, for neglecting to promote that interest: and, soon after, he took a resolution, equally wild and desperate, of embarking on board a ship which he provided, and of flying into foreign parts. It is almost impossible to form any satisfactory conjecture concerning the motives which influence a capricious and irregular mind. He hoped, perhaps, to recommend himself to the Catholic Princes on the continent by his zeal for religion, and that they would employ their interest towards reinstating him in the possession of that power which he had lost. Perhaps he expected nothing more than the comfort of hiding the disgrace, under which he was now fallen, among strangers, who had never been witnesses of his former prosperity.

He communicated the design to the French ambassador, Le Croc, and to his father the Earl of Lennox. They both endeavoured to dissuade him from it, but without success. Lennox, who seems, as well as his son, to have lost the Queen's confidence, and who, about this time, was seldom at court, instantly communicated the matter to her by a letter. Henry, who had refused to accompany the Queen from Stirling to Edinburgh, was likewise absent from court. He arrived there, however, on the same day she received the account of his intended flight. But he was more than usually wayward and peevish; and, scrupling to enter the palace unless certain Lords who attended the Queen were dismissed, Mary was obliged to meet him without the gates. At last he suffered her to conduct him into her own apartment. She endeavoured to draw from him the strange resolution which he had taken, and to divert him from it. In spite, however, of all her arguments and entreaties, he remained silent and inflexible. Next day the privy council, by her direction expostulated with him on the same head. He persisted, notwithstanding, in his sullenness and obstinacy; and neither deigned to explain the motives of his conduct, nor signified any intention of altering it. As he left the apartment, he turned towards the Queen, and told her that she should not see his face again for a long time. A few days after, he wrote to Mary, and mentioned two things as the grounds of his disgust. She herself, he said, no longer admitted him into any confidence, and had deprived him of all power; and the nobles, after her example, treated him with open neglect, so that he appeared in every place without the dignity and splendour of a King.

Nothing could be more mortifying to Mary than this intended flight of the King's, which would have spread the infamy of their domestic quarrel all over Europe. Compassion for a monarch, who would then appear to be forced into exile by her neglect and ill usage, might have disposed mankind to entertain sentiments, concerning the causes of their discord, little to her advantage. In order, therefore, to prepossess the minds of her allies, and to screen her reputation from any censure with which Darnly might endeavour to load it, the privy council transmitted a narrative of this whole transaction both to the King and to the Queen-mother of France. It was drawn with great art, and sets Mary's conduct in the most favourable point of view.

About this time the licence of the borderers called for redress; and Mary resolving to hold a court of justice at Jedburgh, the inhabitants of several adjacent counties were summoned to attend their Sovereign in arms, according to custom. Bothwell was at that time lieutenant or warden of all the marches, an office among the most important in the kingdom; and, though usually divided into three distinct governments, bestowed by the Queen's favour upon him alone. In order to display his own valour and activity in the discharge of this trust, he attempted to sieze a gang of banditti, who, lurking among the marshes of Liddesdale, infested the rest of the country. But while he was laying hold upon one of those desperadoes [Oct. 16], he was wounded by him in several places, so that his followers were obliged to carry him to Hermitage castle. Mary instantly flew thither with an impatience which has been considered as marking the anxiety of a lover, but little suited the

dignity of a Queen*. Finding that Bothwell was threatened with
no dangerous symptom, she returned the same day to Jedburgh.
The fatigue of such a journey, added to the anguish of mind she
had suffered on Bothwell's account, threw her next morning into a
violent fever. Her life was despaired of; but her youth, and the
vigour of her constitution, resisted the malignity of her disease.
During the continuance of the Queen's illness, the King, who resided at Stirling, never came near Jedburgh; and when he afterwards thought fit to make his appearance there [Nov. 5], he met
with such a cold reception as did not encourage him to make any
long stay. Mary soon recovered strength enough to return along the
eastern borders to Dunbar.

While she resided in this place, her attention was turned towards
England. Elizabeth, notwithstanding her promise and even proclamations to the contrary, not only allowed, but encouraged Morton and his associates to remain in England. Mary, on the other
hand, offered her protection to several English fugitives. Each
Queen watched the motions of the other with a jealous attention
and secretly countenanced the practices which were carrying on to
disturb the administration of her rival.

For this purpose Mary's ambassador, Robert Melvil, and her other
emissaries were extremely active and successful. We may ascribe,
in a good degree, to their intrigues, that spirit which appeared in
the parliament of England, and which raised a storm that threatened
Elizabeth's domestic tranquility more than any other event of her
reign, and required all her art and dexterity to allay it.

Elizabeth had now reigned eight years without discovering the
least intention to marry. A violent distemper with which she had
lately been seized, having endangered her life, and alarmed the nation with the prospect of all those calamities which are occasioned
by a disputed and dubious succession, a motion was made, and
eagerly listened to in both houses, for addressing the Queen to provide against any such danger in times to come, either by signifying
her own resolution to marry, or by consenting to an act establishing
the order of succession to the crown. Her love to her subjects, her
duty to the public, her concern for posterity, it was asserted, not
only called upon but obliged her to take one of these steps. The insuperable aversion which she had all along discovered for marriage
made it improbable that she would choose the former; and if she
complied with the latter request, no title to the crown could, with
any colour of justice, be set in opposition to that of the Scottish

* The distance between Jedburgh and Hermitage is eighteen Scottish miles,
through a country almost impassable. The season of the year was far advanced.
Bothwell seems to have been wounded in a scuffle, occasioned by the despair of a
single man, rather than any open insurrection of the borderers. It does not appear that the Queen was attended by any considerable train. Had any military
operation been necessary, as is supposed Good vol. i. 304, it would have been
extremely improper to risque the Queen's person in an expedition against thieves.
As soon as the Queen found Bothwell to be in no danger, she instantly returned;
and after this we hear no more of the insurrection, nor have we any proof that the
rioters took refuge in England. As there is no further evidence with respect to the
motives of this extraordinary journey, the reader must judge what degree of credit
is due to Knox and Buchanan, who ascribe it to the Queen's love of Bothwell.

Queen. Elizabeth was sagacious enough to see the remotest consequences of this motion, and observed them with the greatest anxiety. Mary, by refusing so often to ratify the treaty of Edinburgh, had plainly intimated a design of embracing the first promising opportunity for prosecuting her right to the English crown; and by her secret negociations, she had gained many to favour her title. All the Roman Catholics ardently wished for her succession. Her gentleness and humanity had removed many of those apprehensions which the Protestants entertained on account of her religion. The court faction, which envied the power of Cecil, and endeavoured to wrest the administration out of his hands, advanced the pretensions of the Scottish Queen in opposition to him. The union of the two kingdoms was a desirable object to all wise men in both nations; and the birth of the young Prince was a security for the continuance of this blessing, and gave hopes of its perpetuity.

Under these circumstances, and while the nation was in such a temper, a parliamentary declaration of Mary's title would have been highly detrimental to Elizabeth. The present unsettled state of the succession left much in her power. Her resentment alone might have gone far towards excluding any of the competitors from the crown; and the dread of this had hitherto restrained and overawed the ambition of the Scottish Queen. But if this check should be removed by the legal acknowledgment of her title, Mary would be more at liberty to pursue her dangerous designs, and to act without fear or reserve. Her partisans were already meditating schemes for insurrections in different parts of the kingdom; and an act of parliament, recognising the rights of that Princess, whose pretensions they favoured, would have been nothing less than a signal to arms; and, notwithstanding Elizabeth's just title to the affections of her subjects, might have shaken and endangered her throne.

While this matter remained in suspense in both houses, an account of it was transmitted to Mary by Melvil her ambassador. As she did not want advocates for her right, even among those who were near Elizabeth's person, she endeavoured to cultivate the disposition which appeared towards settling the right of succession in her favour, by a letter to the privy counsellors of England. She expressed in it a grateful sense of Elizabeth's friendship, which she ascribes chiefly to their good offices with their Sovereign in her behalf. She declared her resolution to live in perpetual amity with England, without urging or pursuing her claim upon the crown any further than should be agreeable to the Queen. But, at the same time, as her right of succession was undoubted, she hoped it would be examined with candour, and judged of with impartiality. The nobles who attended her wrote to the English privy council in the same strain. Mary artfully gave these letters the air of being nothing more than the declaration of her own and of her subjects' gratitude towards Elizabeth. But, as she could not be ignorant of the jealousy and fear with which Elizabeth observed the proceedings of Parliament, a step so uncommon as this, of one Prince's entering into public correspondence with the privy counsellors of an-

I

other, could not be otherwise construed than as taken with an intention to encourage the spirit which had already been raised among
the English. In this light it seems to have appeared to Elizabeth
herself. But the disposition of her people rendering it necessary
to treat Mary's person with great decency, and her title with much
regard, she mentioned it to her only in the softest language.

Nothing, however, could be a more cruel mortification to a Princess of Elizabeth's character than the temper which both houses of
Parliament discovered on this occasion. She bent all her policy to
defeat or elude the motion. After allowing the first heat of their
zeal to evaporate, she called into her presence a certain number of
each house. She soothed and caressed them; she threatened and
promised; she remitted subsidies which were due, and refused those
which were ordered; and, in the end, prevailed to have this formidable motion, put off for that session. Happily for her, the conduct of the Scottish Queen, and the misfortunes which befell her,
prevented the revival of such a motion in any future parliament.

Meantime, in order to preseve the reputation of impartiality,
and that she might not drive Mary into any desperate measure, she
committed to the Tower one Thornton, who had published something derogatory to the right of the Scottish line; and signified
her displeasure against a member of the House of Commons, who
seemed, by some words in a speech, to glance at Mary.

Amidst all her other cares, Mary was ever solicitous to promote
the interest of that religion which she professed. The re establishment of the Romish doctrine seems to have been her favourite
passion; and though the design was concealed with care and conducted with caution, she pursued it with a persevering zeal. At
this time she ventured to lay aside somewhat of her usual reserve;
and the aid which she expected from the Popish Princes, who had
engaged in the league of Bayonne, encouraged her to take a step
which, if we consider the temper of the nation, appears to be extremely bold. Having formerly held a secret correspondence with
the court of Rome, she now resolved to allow a nuncio from the
Pope publicly to enter her dominions. Cardinal Laurea, at that
time Bishop of Mondovi, was the person on whom Pius V. conferred this office, and along with him he sent the Queen a present of
twenty thousand crowns. It is not the character of the papal court
to open its treasury upon distant or imaginary hopes. The business of the nuncio into Scotland could be no other than to attempt a reconciliation of that kingdom to the Romish see. Thus
Mary herself understood it; and, in her answer to a letter which
she received from the Pope, after expressing her grateful sense of
his paternal care and liberality, she promises that she would bend
her whole strength towards the re-establishment and propagation of
the Catholic faith; that she would receive the nuncio with every possible demonstration of respect, and concur with the utmost vigour
in all his designs towards the honour of God, and restoring peace
to the kingdom; that she would celebrate the baptism of the
Prince according to the ceremonies which the Romish ritual prescribes, hoping that her subjects would be taught, by this example,
again to reverence the sacraments of the church, which they had

so long treated with contempt; and that she would be careful to instil early into her son the principles of a sincere love and attachment to the Catholic faith. But though the nuncio was already arrived at Paris, and had sent over one of his attendants with part of the money, the Queen did not think the juncture proper for his reception. Elizabeth was preparing to send a magnificent embassy into Scotland, against the time of the Prince's baptism, and as it would have been improper to offend her, she wisely contrived, under various pretences, to detain Laurea at Paris. The convulsions into which the kingdom was thrown soon after made it impossible for him to pursue his journey any further.

At the very time that Mary was secretly carrying on these negotiations for subverting the reformed church, she did not scruple publicly to employ her authority towards obtaining for its ministers a more certain and comfortable subsistence. During this year, she issued several proclamations and acts of council for that purpose, and readily approved of every scheme which was proposed for the more effectual payment of their stipends. This part of her conduct does little honour to Mary's integrity: and though justified by the example of Princes, who often reckon falsehood and deceit among the necessary arts of government, and even authorised by the pernicious casuistry of the Romish church, which transfers breach of faith to heretics from the list of crimes to that of duties; such dissimulation, however, must be numbered among those blemishes which never stain a truly great and generous character.

As neither the French nor Piedmontese ambassadors were yet arrived, the baptism of the Prince was put off from time to time. Meanwhile, Mary fixed her residence at Craigmillar. Such retirement, perhaps, suited the present temper of her mind, and induced her to prefer it before her own palace of Holyrood-house. Her aversion for the King grew every day more confirmed, and was become altogether incurable. A deep melancholy succeeded to that gaiety of spirit which was natural to her. The rashness and levity of her own choice, and the King's ingratitude and obstinacy, filled her with shame and despair. A variety of passions preyed at once on a mind, all whose sensations were exquisite, and all its emotions strong, and often extorted from her the last wish of the unfortunate, that life itself might come to an end.

But as the Earl of Bedford and the Count de Brienne, the English and French ambassadors, whom she had long expected, arrived about this time, Mary was obliged to suppress what passed in her bosom, and to set out for Stirling in order to celebrate the baptism of her son. Bedford was attended by a numerous and splendid train, and brought presents from Elizabeth, suitable to her own dignity, and the respect with which she affected, at that time, to treat the Queen of Scots. Great preparations had been made by Mary, and the magnificence displayed by her on this occasion exceeded whatever had been formerly known in Scotland. The ceremony itself was performed [Dec. 17], according to the rites of the Romish Church. But neither Bedford nor any of the Scottish nobles who professed the Protestant religion, entered within the gates of the chapel. The spirit of that age, firm and uncomplying, would not, upon any inducement, condescend to witness an action which is deemed idolatrous.

Henry's behaviour, at this juncture, perfectly discovers the excess of his caprice, as well as of his folly. He chose to reside at Stirling, but confined himself to his own apartment; and, as the Queen distrusted every nobleman who ventured to converse with him, he was left in absolute solitude. Nothing could be more singular, or was less expected, than his choosing to appear in a manner that both published the contempt under which he had fallen, and, by exposing the Queen's domestic unhappiness to the observation of so many foreigners, looked like a step taken on purpose to mortify and to offend her. Mary felt this insult sensibly; and, notwithstanding all her efforts to assume the gaiety which suited the occasion, and which was necessary for the polite reception of her guests, she was sometimes obliged to retire, in order to be at liberty to indulge her sorrow, and give vent to her tears. The King still persisted in his design of retiring into foreign parts, and daily threatened to put it in execution*.

The ceremony of witnessing the Prince's baptism was not the sole business of Bedford's embassy. His instructions contained an overture which ought to have gone far towards extinguishing those jealousies which had so long subsisted between the two Queens. The treaty of Edinburgh, which had been so often mentioned, was the principal occasion of these. The spirit, however, which had risen to such a height in the late parliament, the power of the party which favoured the Scottish Queen's title, the number and activity of her agents in different parts of the kingdom, alarmed Elizabeth, and induced her to forego any advantage which the ambiguous and artful expressions in that treaty might afford her. Nothing was now demanded of Mary, but to renounce any title to

---

*Camden affirms, 401, that Bedford was commanded by Elizabeth not to give Darnley the title of King. As this was an indignity not to be borne either by Mary or her husband, it has been asserted to be the cause of the King's absence from the ceremony of his son's baptism. Keith, 360. Good. 319. But, 1. No such thing is to be found among Bedford's instructions, the original of which still remains. Keith, 356. 2. Bedford's advice to the Queen by Melvil is utterly inconsistent with Camden's assertion. Melv. 153. Melvil's account is confirmed by Elizabeth's instructions to Sir Henry Norris, where she affirms that she commanded Bedford to employ his best offices towards reconciling Mary to her husband, which she had attempted to no purpose. Digges's Compl. Ambas. p. 13. A paper published, Appendix, No. XVIII., proves the same thing. 3. Le Croc, the French resident mentions the King's absence, but without giving that reason for it, which has been founded on Camden's words, though, if that had been the real one, it is hardly possible to conceive that he should have neglected to mention it. Le Croc's first letter is dated December 2, some time prior to the arrival of the Earl of Bedford in Scotland; and when his instructions, either public or secret, could hardly be known. Le Croc plainly supposes that the discord between the King and Queen was the cause of his absence from the baptism, and his account of this matter is that which I have followed. Keith, Pref. vii. 4. He informs his court, that on account of the difference betwixt the King and the Queen, he had refused to hold any further correspondence with the former, though he appears, in many instances, to have been his great confidant. Ibid. 5. As the King was not present at the baptism, he seems to have been excluded from any share in the ordinary administration of business. Two acts of privy council, one on the 20th, and the other on the 21st of December, are found in Keith, 562. They both run in the Queen's name alone. The King seems not to have been present. This could not be owing to Elizabeth's instructions to Bedford.

the crown of England during Elizabeth's life and the lives of her posterity; who, on the other hand, engaged to take no step which might prove injurious to Mary's claim upon the succession.

Mary could not with decency reject a proposition so equitable: she insisted, however, that Elizabeth should order the right upon which she claimed, to be legally examined, and publicly recognised, and particularly that the testament of Henry VIII., whereby he had excluded the descendants of his eldest sister the Queen of Scotland, from the place due to them in the order of succession, might be produced, and considered by the English nobility. Mary's ministers had credulously embraced an opinion, that this testament which they so justly conceived to be injurious to their mistress was a mere forgery; and on different occasions had urged Elizabeth to produce it. Mary would have suffered considerably by gaining this point. The original testament is still extant, and not the least doubt can be entertained of its genuineness and authenticity. But it was not Elizabeth's intention to weaken or to set aside the title of the house of Stuart. She aimed at nothing more than to keep the question concerning the succession perplexed and undecided; and by industriously eluding this request, she did, in one respect, real service to Mary's cause.

A few days after the baptism of the Prince, Morton and all the other conspirators against Rizio obtained their pardon, and leave to return into Scotland. Mary, who had hitherto continued inexorable to every entreaty in their behalf, yielded at last to the solicitations of Bothwell. He could hope for no success in those bold designs on which his ambition resolved to venture, without drawing aid from every quarter. By procuring a favour for Morton and his associates, of which they had good reason to despair, he expected to secure a band of faithful and determined adherents.

The King still remained at Stirling, in solitude and under contempt. His impatience in this situation, together with the alarm given him by the rumour of the design to seize his person, was the occasion of his leaving that place in an abrupt manner, and retiring to his father at Glasgow.

Two assemblies of the church were held during this year [June 25, Dec.25]. New complaints were made, and upon good grounds, of the poverty and contempt under which the Protestant clergy were suffered to languish. Penurious as the allotment for their subsistence was, they had not received the least part of what was due for the preceding year. Nothing less than a zeal ready to endure and to suffer every thing for a good cause, could have persuaded men to adhere to a church so indigent and so neglected. The extraordinary expenses occasioned by the Prince's baptism had exhausted the Queen's treasury, and the sums appropriated for the subsistence of the clergy were diverted into other channels. The Queen was therefore obliged to prevent the just remonstrances of the assembly, by falling on some new method for the relief of the church. Some symptoms of liberality, some stretch towards munificence, might have been expected in an assignment which was made with an intention of soothing and silencing the clergy. But both the Queen and the nobles held fast the riches of the church which they had seized. A sum which, at the highest computation, can hardly be reckoned equal to nine thousand pounds sterling, was deemed sufficient for the maintenence of a whole national church, by men who had lately seen single monasteries possessed of revenues far superior in value.

The ecclesiastics in that age bore the grievances which affected themselves alone with astonishing patience; but, whenever the reformed religion was threatened, they were extremely apt to be alarmed, and to proclaim, in the loudest manner, their apprehension of danger. A just occasion of this kind was given them a short time before the meeting of the assembly. The usurped and oppressive jurisdiction of the spiritual courts had been abolished by the Parliament in the year 1560, and commissaries were appointed to hear and determine the causes which formerly came under their cognizance. Among the few acts of that Parliament to which Mary had paid any regard, this was one. She had confirmed the authority of the commissaries, and had given them instructions for directing their proceedings, which are still of great authority in that court. From the time of their first appointment, these judges had continued in the uninterrupted exercise of their function, when of a sudden the Queen issued a proclamation, restoring the Archbishop of St. Andrew's to his ancient jurisdiction, and depriving the commissaries of all authority.

A motive, which cannot be justified, rendered the Queen not unwilling to venture upon this rash action. She had been contriving for some time how to re-establish the Popish religion; and the restoring of the ancient ecclesiastics to their former jurisdiction seemed to be a considerable step towards that end. The motives which prompted Bothwell, to whose influence over the Queen this action must be chiefly imputed, was still more criminal. His enterprising ambition had already formed that bold design, which he soon after put in execution; and the use we shall hereafter find him making of that authority which the Popish ecclesiastics regained, discovers the reasons of his present conduct in contributing to revive their power. The Protestant clergy were not unconcerned spectators of an event which threatened their religion with unavoidable destruction; but, as they despaired of obtaining the proper remedy from the Queen herself, they addressed a remonstrance to the whole body of the Protestant nobility, full of that ardent zeal for religion, which the danger to which it was exposed at that time seemed to require. What effects this vehement exhortation might have produced, we have no opportunity of judging, the attention of the nation being quickly turned towards events of another and more tragical nature.

1567.] Immediately upon the King's leaving Stirling, and before he could reach Glasgow, he was seized with a dangerous distemper. The symptoms which attended it were violent and unusual, and in that age it was commonly imputed to the effects of poison. It is impossible, amidst the contradictions of historians, to decide with certainty concerning its nature or its cause. His life was in the utmost danger; but, after lingering for some weeks, the vigour of his constitution surmounted the malignity of his disease.

Mary's neglect of the King on this occasion was equal to that with which he had treated her during her illness at Jedburgh. She no longer felt that warmth of conjugal affection which prompts to sympathy, and delights in all those tender offices which soothe and alleviate sickness and pain. At this juncture, she did not even put on the appearance of this passion. Notwithstanding the King's danger, she amused herself with excursions to different parts of the country, and suffered near a month to elapse before she visited him at Glasgow. By that time the violence of the distemper was over, and the King, though weak and languishing, was out of all danger.

The breach between Mary and her husband was not occasioned by any of those slight disgusts which interrupt the domestic union, without dissolving it altogether. Almost all the passions which operate with greatest violence on a female mind, and drive it to the most dangerous extremes, concurred in raising and fomenting this unhappy quarrel. Ingratitude for the favours she had bestowed, contempt of her person, violations of the marriage-vow, encroachments on her power, conspiracies against her favourites, jealousy, insolence, and obstinacy, were the injuries of which Mary had great reason to complain. She felt them with the utmost sensibility; and, added to the anguish of disappointed love, they produced those symptoms of despair which we have already described. Her resentment against the King seems not to have abated from the time of his leaving Stirling. In a letter written with her own hand to her ambassador in France, on the day before she set out for Glasgow, no tokens of sudden reconcilement appear. On the contrary [Jan. 20], she mentions, with some bitterness, the King's ingratitude, the jealousy with which he observed her actions, and the inclination she discovered to disturb her government; and at the same time talks of all his attempts with the utmost scorn.

After this discovery of Mary's sentiments, at the time of her departure from Edinburgh to Glasgow, a visit to the King, which had been neglected when his situation rendered it most necessary, appears singular; and it could hardly be expected that any thing but marks of jealousy and distrust should appear in such an interview. This, however, was far from being the case: she not only visited Henry, but, by all her words and actions, endeavoured to express an uncommon affection for him: and though this made impression on the credulous spirit of her husband, no less flexible on some occasions than obstinate on others; yet to those who are acquainted with the human heart, and who know how seldom and how slowly such wounds in domestic happiness are healed, this sudden transition will appear with a very suspicious air, and will be considered by them as the effect of artifice.

But it is not on suspicion alone that Mary is charged with dissimulation in this part of her conduct. Two of her famous letters to Bothwell were written during her stay at Glasgow, and fully lay open this scene of iniquity. He had so far succeeded in his ambitious and criminal design, as to gain an absolute ascendant over the Queen; and, in a situation such as Mary's, merit not so conspicuous, services of far inferior importance, and address much less insinuating than Bothwell's, may be supposed to steal imperceptibly on a female heart, and entirely to overcome it. Unhappily, among those in the higher ranks of life, scruples with regard to conjugal fidelity are, often, neither many nor strong: nor did the manners of that court in which Mary had been educated contribute to increase or to fortify them. The amorous turn of Francis I. and Henry II., the licentiousness of the military character in that age, and the liberty of appearing in all companies, which began to be allowed to women, who had not yet acquired that delicacy of sentiment and those polished manners which alone can render this liberty innocent, had introduced among the French an astonishing relaxation in domestic morals. Such examples, which were familiar to Mary from her infancy, could hardly fail of diminishing that horror of vice which is natural to a virtuous mind. The King's behaviour would render the first approach of forbidden sentiments less shocking; resentment and disappointed love would be apt to represent whatever soothed her revenge as justifiable on that account; and so many concurring causes might, almost imperceptibly, kindle a new passion in her heart.

But, whatever opinion we may form with regard to the rise and progress of this passion, the letters themselves breathe all the ardour and tenderness of love. The affection which Mary there expresses for Bothwell, fully accounts for every subsequent part of her conduct; which, without admitting this circumstance, appears altogether mysterious, inconsistent, and inexplicable. That reconcilement with her husband, of which, if we allow it to be genuine, it is impossible to give any plausible account, is discovered, by the Queen's own confession, to have been mere artifice and deceit. As her aversion for her husband, and the suspicious attention with which she observed his conduct, became universally known, her ears were officiously filled, as is usual in such cases, with groundless or aggravated accounts of his actions. By some she was told, that the King intended to seize the person of the Prince his son, and in his name to usurp the government; by others she was assured that he resolved instantly to leave the kingdom; that a vessel was hired for this purpose, and lay in the river Clyde ready to receive him. The last was what Mary chiefly dreaded. Henry's retiring into a foreign country must have been highly dishonourable to the Queen, and would have entirely disconcerted Bothwell's measures. While he resided at Glasgow, at a distance from her, and in that part of the kingdom where the interest of his family was greatest, he might with more facility accomplish his designs. In order, therefore, to prevent his executing any such wild scheme, it was necessary to bring him to some place where he would be more immediately under her own eye. For this purpose, she first employed all her art to regain his confidence, and then proposed to remove him to the neighbourhood of Edinburgh, under pretence that there he would have easier access to the advice of physicians, and that she herself could attend him without being absent from her son. The King was weak enough to suffer himself to be persuaded; and, being still feeble and incapable of bearing fatigue, was carried in a litter to Edinburgh.

The place prepared for his reception was a house belonging to the provost of a collegiate church, called Kirk of Field. It stood almost upon the same spot where the house belonging to the principal of the university now stands. Such a situation, on a rising ground, and at that time in an open field, had all the advantages of healthful air to recommend it; but, on the other hand, the solitude of the place rendered it extremely proper for the commission of that crime, with a view to which it seems manifestly to have been chosen.

Mary continued to attend the King with the most assiduous care. She seldom was absent from him through the day; she slept two nights in the chamber under his apartment. She heaped on him so many marks of tenderness and confidence, as in a great measure quieted those suspicions which had so long disturbed him. But while he was fondly indulging in dreams of the return of his former happiness, he stood on the very brink of destruction. On Sunday, the 9th of February, about eleven at night, the Queen left the Kirk of Field, in order to be present at a masque in the palace. At two next morning, the house in which the King lay was blown up with gunpowder. The noise and shock which this sudden explosion occasioned alarmed the whole city. The inhabitants ran to the place whence it came. The dead body of the King, with that of a servant who slept in the same room, was found lying in an adjacent garden without the city wall, untouched by fire, and with no bruise or mark of violence.

Such was the unhappy fate of Henry Stuart Lord Darnly, in the twenty-first year of his age. The indulgence of fortune, and his own external accomplishments, without any other merit, had raised him to a height of dignity of which he was altogether unworthy. By his folly and ingratitude, he lost the heart of a woman who doted on him to distraction. His insolence and inconstancy alienated from him such of the nobles as had contributed most zealously towards his elevation. His levity and caprice exposed him to the scorn of the people, who once revered him as the descendant of their ancient Kings and heroes. Had he died a natural death, his end would have been unlamented, and his memory have been forgotten; but the cruel circumstances of his murder, and the shameful remissness in neglecting to avenge it, have made his name to be remembered with regret, and have rendered him the object of pity, to which he had otherwise no title.

Every one's imagination was at work to guess who had contrived and executed this execrable deed. The suspicion fell, with almost general consent, on Bothwell; and some reflections were thrown out, as if the Queen herself were no stranger to the crime. Of Bothwell's guilt there remains the fullest evidence that the nature of the action will admit. The Queen's known sentiments with regard to her husband gave a great appearance of probability to the imputation with which she was loaded*.

* See Dissertation concerning the murder of Henry Darnly, and the genuineness of Mary's letters to Bothwell, Appendix.

Two days after the murder, a proclamation was issued by the Queen, offering a considerable reward to any person who should discover those who had been guilty of such a horrid and detestable crime; and though Bothwell was now one of the greatest subjects in the kingdom, formidable on account of his own power, and protected by the Queen's favour, it was impossible to suppress the sentiments and indignation of the people. Papers were affixed to the most public places of the city, accusing him of the murder, and naming his accomplices; pictures appeared to the same purpose; and voices were heard in the middle of the night, charging him with that barbarous action. But the authors of these rumours did not confine their accusations to Bothwell alone; they insinuated that the Queen herself was accessary to the crime. This bold accusation, which so directly attacked Mary's reputation, drew the attention of her council; and, by engaging them in an inquiry after the authors of these libels, diverted them from searching for the murderers of the King. It could scarce be expected that Mary herself would be extremely solicitous to discover those who had rid her of a husband whom she had so violently hated. It was Bothwell's interest, who had the supreme direction of this, as well as of all other affairs, to stifle and suppress whatever evidence should be offered, and to cover, if possible, the whole transaction under the veil of darkness and of silence. Some inquiry, however, was made, and some persons called before the council; but the examination was conducted with the most indecent remissness, and in such a manner as to let in no light upon that scene of guilt.

It was not her own subjects alone who suspected Mary of having been accessary to this unnatural crime; nor did an opinion so dishonourable to her character owe its rise and progress to the jealousy and malice of her factious nobles. The report of the manner and circumstances of the King's murder spread quickly over all Europe; and even in that age, which was accustomed to deeds of violence, it excited universal horror. As her unhappy breach with her husband had long been matter of public discourse, the first conjectures which were formed with regard to his death, were extremely to her disadvantage. Her friends, at a loss what apology to offer for her conduct, called on her to prosecute the murderers with the utmost diligence, and expected that the rigour of her proceedings would prove the best and fullest vindication of her innocence.

Lennox at the same time incited Mary to vengeance with incessant importunity. This nobleman had shared in his son's disgrace, and being treated by Mary with neglect, usually resided at a distance from court. Roused, however, by an event no less shocking to the heart of a father, than fatal to all his schemes of ambition, he ventured to write to the Queen [Feb. 21], and to offer his advice with respect to the most effectual method for discovering and convicting those who had so cruelly deprived him of a son, and her of a husband. He urged her to prosecute those who were guilty with vigour, and to bring them to a speedy trial; he declared his own suspicion of Bothwell, and of those who were named as his accomplices; he required that, out of regard to decency, and in order to encourage evidence to appear against them, the persons accused of such an atrocious crime should be committed to custody, or at least excluded from her court and presence.

Mary was then at Seaton whither she had retired after the burial of the King, whose body was deposited among the monarchs of Scotland in a private but decent manner. The former part of the Earl's demand could not on any pretence be eluded; and it was resolved to bring Bothwell immediately to trial. But, instead of confining him to any prison, Mary admitted him into all her councils, and allowed a person, universally reputed the murderer of her husband, to enjoy all the security, the dignity, and the power of a favourite. The offices which Bothwell already possessed, gave him the command of all the south of Scotland. The castle of Edinburgh, however, was a place of so much consequence that he wished earnestly to have it in his own power. The Queen, in order to prevail on the Earl of Mar to surrender it, consented to put the person of the young Prince in his hands [March 19], and immediately bestowed the government of that important fortress upon Bothwell. So many steps in her conduct inconsistent with all the rules of prudence and of decency, must be imputed to an excess either of folly or of love. Mary's known character fully vindicates her from the former; of the latter, many and striking proofs soon appeared.

No direct evidence had yet appeared against Bothwell; but as time might bring to light the circumstances of a crime in which so many accomplices were concerned, it was of great importance to hurry over the trial, while nothing more than general suspicions, and uncertain surmises, could be produced by his accusers. For this reason, in a meeting of privy council held on the 28th of March, the 12th of April was appointed for the day of trial. Though the law allowed, and the manner in which criminal causes were carried on in that age required, a much longer interval, it appears from several circumstances that this short space was considerably contracted, and that Lennox had only eleven day's warning to prepare for accusing a person so far superior to himself both in power and in favour.* No man could be less in a condition to contend with an antagonist who was thus supported. Though Lennox's paternal estate had been restored to him when he was recalled into Scotland, it seems to have been considerably impaired during his banishment. His vassals, while he resided in England,

* The act of privy council, appointing the day of Bothwell's trial. bears date March the 28th, which happened on a Thursday Anders. vol. i. 50 The Queen's warrant to the messengers, empowering them to summon Lennox to be present, is dated on the 29th. Anders. vol. ii. 97. He was summoned by public proclamation at the cross of Edinburgh on the same day. Ibid. 100 He was summoned at his dwelling houses in Glasgow and Dumbarton on the 30th of March, the 1st and 2d days of April. Ibid 101. He was summoned at Perth, April 1st. Ibid. 102. Though Lennox resided at that time forty miles from Edinburgh, the citation might have been given him sooner. Such an unnecessary delay affords some cause for suspicion. It is true. Mary, in her letter, March 24th, invited Lennox to come to Edinburgh the ensuing week : this gave him warning some day- sooner, that she intended to bring on the trial without delay But the precise time could not be legally or certainly known to Lennox sooner than ten to twelve days before the day on which he was required to appear. By the law and practice of Scotland, at that time, parties were summoned, in cases of treason, forty days previous to the trial.

had been accustomed to some degree of independence, and he had not recovered that ascendant over them which a feudal chief usually possessed. He had no reason to expect the concurrence of any of those factions into which the nobles were divided. During the short period of his son's prosperity, he had taken such steps as gave rise to an open breach with Murray and all his adherents. The partisans of the house of Hamilton were his hereditary and mortal enemies. Huntly was linked in the closest confederacy with Bothwell; and thus, to the disgrace of the nation, Lennox stood alone in a cause where both honour and humanity called so loudly on his countrymen to second him.

It is remarkable too, that Bothwell himself was present, and sat as a member in that meeting of privy council which gave directions with regard to the time and manner of his own trial; and he still enjoyed not only full liberty, but was received into the Queen's presence with the same distinguished familiarity as formerly.

Nothing could be a more cruel disappointment to the wishes and resentment of a father than such a premature trial; every step towards which seemed to be taken by directions from the person who was himself accused of the crime, and calculated on purpose to conceal rather than to detect his guilt. Lennox foresaw what would be the issue of this mock inquiry, and with how little safety to himself, or success to his cause, he could venture to appear on the day prefixed. In his former letters, though under expressions the most respectful, some symptoms of his distrusting the Queen may be discovered. He spoke out now in plain language. He complained of the injury done him, by hurrying on the trial with such illegal precipitation. He represented once more the indecency of allowing Bothwell not only to enjoy personal liberty, but to retain his former influence over her councils. He again required her, as she regarded her own honour, to give some evidence of her sincerity in prosecuting the murderer, by confining the person who was on good grounds suspected to be the author of it; and, till that were done, he signified his own resolution not to be present at a trial, the manner and circumstances of which were so irregular and unsatisfactory.

He seems, however, to have expected little success from this application to Mary; and therefore at the same time besought Elizabeth to interpose, in order to obtain such a delay as he demanded. Nothing can be a stronger proof how violently he suspected the one Queen than his submitting to implore the aid of the other, who had treated his son with the utmost contempt, and himself and family with the greatest rigour. Elizabeth, who was never unwilling to interpose in the affairs of Scotland, wrote instantly to Mary, advised her to delay the trial for some time, and urged in such strong terms the same arguments which Lennox had used, as might have convinced her to what an unfavourable construction her conduct would be liable, if she persisted in her present method of proceeding.*

Neither her entreaties, however, nor those of Lennox could pre-

* See Appendix, No. XIX.

vail to have the trial put off. On the day appointed Bothwell appeared. but with such a formidable retinue, that it would have been dangerous to condemn, and impossible to punish him. Besides a numerous body of his friends and vassals, assembled, according to custom, from different parts of the kingdom, he was attended by a band of hired soldiers, who marched with flying colours along the streets of Edinburgh. A court of justice was held with the accustomed formalities. An indictment was presented against Bothwell, and Lennox was called upon to make good accusation. In his name appeared Robert Cunningham, one of his dependants. He excused his master's absence, on account of the shortness of the time, which prevented his assembling his friends and vassals, without whose assistance he could not with safety venture to set himself in opposition to such a powerful antagonist. For this reason. he desired the court to stop proceeding, and protested, that any sentence which should be passed at that time ought to be deemed illegal and void. Bothwell, on the other hand, insisted that the court should instantly proceed to trial. One of Lennox's own letters, in which he craved of the Queen to prosecute the murders without delay, was produced. Cunningham's objections were overruled ; and the jury, consisting of peers and barons of the first rank, found Bothwell not guilty of the crime.

No person appeared as an accuser, not a single witness was examined, nor any evidence produced against him. The jury, under these circumstances, could do nothing else but acquit him. Their verdict, however, was far from gratifying the wishes or silencing the murmurs of the people. Every circumstance in the trial gave grounds for suspicion, and excited indignation ; and the judgment pronounced, instead of being a proof of Bothwell's innocence, was esteemed an argument of his guilt. Pasquinades and libels were affixed to different places, expressing the sentiments of the public with the utmost virulence of language.

The jury themselves seem to have been aware of the censure to which their proceedings would be exposed ; and, at the same time that they returned their verdict acquitting Bothwell, the Earl of Caithness protested, in their name, that no crime should be imputed to them on that account, because no accuser had appeared, and no proof was brought of the indictment. He took notice likewise, that the 9th instead of the 10th of February was mentioned in the indictment, as the day on which the murder had been committed : a circumstance which discovers the extreme inaccuracy of those who prepared the indictment ; and at a time when men were disposed, and not without reason, to be suspicious of every thing, this small matter contributed to confirm and to increase their suspicions.

Even Bothwell himself did not rely on the judgment which he had obtained in his favour as a full vindication of his innocence. Immediately after his acquittal, he, in compliance with a custom which was not then obsolete, published a writing, in which he offered to fight in a single combat any gentleman of good fame, who should presume to accuse him of being accessary to the murder of the King.

Mary, however, continued to treat him as if he had been cleared by the most unexceptionable and satisfactory evidence. The ascendant he had gained over her heart, as well as over her councils, was more visible than ever; and Lennox, who could not expect that his own person could be safe in a country where the murderer of his son had been absolved without regard to justice, and loaded with honours in contempt of decency, fled with precipitation towards England.

Two days after the trial [April 14], a parliament was held, at the opening of which the Queen distinguished Bothwell, by appointing him to carry the sceptre before her. Most of the acts passed in this assembly were calculated on purpose to strengthen his party, and to promote his designs. He obtained the ratification of all the possessions and honours which the partiality of the Queen had conferred upon him ; and the act to that effect contained the strongest declarations of his faithful services to the crown in all times past. The surrender of the castle of Edinburgh by Mar was confirmed. The law of attainder against Huntly was repealed, and he and his adherents were restored to the estates and honours of their ancestors. Several of those who had been on the jury which acquitted Bothwell obtained ratifications of the grants made in their favour; and, as pasquinades daily multiplied, a law was passed whereby those into whose hands any paper of that kind fell, were commanded instantly to destroy it ; and if, through their neglect, it should be allowed to spread, they were subjected to a capital punishment, in the same manner as if they had been the original authors.

But the absolute dominion which Bothwell had acquired over Mary's mind, appeared in the clearest manner, by an act in favour of the Protestant religion, to which at this time she gave her assent. Mary's attachment to the Romish faith was uniform and superstitious ; she had never laid aside the design, nor lost the hopes, of restoring it. She had of late come under new engagements to that purpose, and in consequence of these had ventured upon some steps more public and vigorous than any she had formerly taken. But though none of these circumstances were unknown to Bothwell, there were powerful motives which prompted him at this juncture to conciliate the good will of the Protestants, by exerting himself in order to procure for them some additional security in the exercise of their religion. That which they enjoyed at present was very precarious, being founded entirely on the royal proclamation issued soon after the arrival of the Queen in Scotland, which in express terms was declared to be only a temporary regulation. From that period, neither the solicitations of the general assemblies of the church, nor the entreaties of her people, could extort from Mary any concession in favour of the Protestant religion, on which the professors might rest with greater confidence. This, howcr, by the more powerful influence of Bothwell, they now obtained. An act was passed in this Parliament, repealing all the laws, canon, civil, and municipal, adverse to the reformed religion, and exempting such as had embraced it from the penalties to which they might have been subjected by these laws, either on account of their past conduct or present profession : declaring at the same time that their persons, estates, honours, and benefices, were taken under public protection against every court, civil or ecclesiastical, that might attempt to molest them on account of their religious sentiments. Thus the Protestants, instead of holding their sacred rights by no better tenure than a declaration of royal indulgence, which might be revoked at pleasure, obtained legal and parliamentary protection in the exercise of their religion. By prevailing on the Queen to assent to this law, Bothwell seems to have flattered himself that he would acquire such merit, both with the clergy and with the people, as might induce them to favour his ambitious schemes, and to connive at what he had done, or might do, in order to accomplish them. The Protestants accordingly, though this act was far from amounting to a legal establishment of the reformed faith, seem to have considered it as an additional security of such importance that it was published among the laws enacted in a Parliament held towards the close of this year, under very different leaders.

Every step taken by Bothwell had hitherto been attended with all the success which his most sanguine wishes could expect. He had entirely gained the Queen's heart; the murder of the King had excited no public commotion ; he had been acquitted by his peers of any share in that crime ; and the decision had been in some sort ratified in parliament. But in a kingdom where the regal authority was so extremely limited, and the power of the nobles so formidable, he durst not venture on the last action, towards which all his ambitious projects tended, without their approbation. In order to secure this, he immediately after the dissolution of parliament [April 19], invited all the nobles who were present to an entertainment. Having filled the house with his friends and dependants, and surrounded it with armed men, he opened to the company his intention of marrying the Queen, whose consent, he told them, he had already obtained ; and demanded their approbation of this match, which, he said, was no less acceptable to their sovereign than honourable to himself. Huntly and Seaton, who were privy to all Bothwell's schemes, promoted them with the utmost zeal ; and the popish ecclesiastics, who were absolutely devoted to the Queen, and ready to soothe her passions, instantly declared their satisfaction with what he had proposed. The rest, who dreaded the exorbitant power which Bothwell had acquired, and observed the Queen's growing affection towards him in all her actions, were willing to make a merit of yielding to a measure which they could neither oppose nor defeat. Some few were confounded and enraged. But in the end Bothwell, partly by promises and flattery, partly by terror and force, prevailed on all who were present to subscribe a paper which leaves a deeper stain than any occurrence in that age on the honour and character of the nation.

This paper contained the strongest declarations of Bothwell's innocence, and the most ample acknowledgment of his good services to the kingdom. If any future accusation should be brought against him on account of the King's murder, the subscribers promised to stand by him as one man, and to hazard their lives and fortunes in his defence. They recommended him to the Queen as the most proper person she could choose for her husband : and if she should condescend to bestow on him that mark of her regard, they undertook to promote the marriage, and to join him with all their forces in opposing any person who endeavoured to obstruct it. Among the subscribers of this paper we find some who were the Queen's chief confidants, others who were strangers to her counsels, and obnoxious to her displeasure ; some who faithfully adhered to her through all the vicissitudes of her fortune, and others who became the principal authors of her sufferings ; some passionately attached to the Romish superstition, and others zealous advocates for the Protestant faith. No common interest can be supposed to have united men of such opposite principles and parties, in recommending to their sovereign a step so injurious to her honour, and so fatal to her peace. This strange coalition was the effect of much artifice, and must be considered as the boldest and most masterly stroke of Bothwell's address. It is observable, that amidst all the altercations and mutual reproaches of the two parties which arose in the kingdom, this unworthy transaction is seldom mentioned. Conscious on both sides, that in this particular their conduct could ill bear examination, and would redound little to their fame, they always touch upon it unwillingly, and with a tender hand, seeming desirous that it should remain in darkness, or be buried in oblivion. But as so many persons who, both at that time and ever after, possessed the Queen's favour, subscribed this paper, the suspicion becomes strong, that Bothwell's ambitious hopes were neither unknown to Mary, nor disapproved by her.

These suspicions are confirmed by the most direct proof. Melvil at that time enjoyed a considerable share in her favour. He, as well as his brother, kept a secret correspondence in England with those who favoured her pretensions to that crown. The rumour of her intended marriage with Bothwell, having spread early in that kingdom, excited universal indignation ; and Melvil received a letter from thence, which represented, in the strongest terms, what would be the fatal effects of such an imprudent step. He put this letter into the Queen's hands, and enforced it with the utmost warmth. She not only disregarded those remonstrances, but communicated the matter to Bothwell ; and Melvil, in order to save his life, was obliged to fly from court, whither he durst not return till the Earl's rage began to abate. At the same time Elizabeth warned Mary of the danger and infamy to which she would expose herself by such an indecent choice : but an advice from her met with still less regard.

Three days after the rising of Parliament, Mary went from Edinburgh to Stirling, in order to visit the Prince her son. Bothwell had now brought his schemes to full maturity ; and every precaution being taken which could render it safe to enter on the last and decisive step, the natural impetuosity of his spirit did not suffer him to deliberate any longer. Under pretence of an expedition against the freebooters, on the borders, he assembled his followers ; and marching out of Edinburgh with a thousand horse [April 24], turned suddenly toward Linlithgow, met the Queen on her return near that place, dispersed her slender train without resistance, seized on her person, and conducted her, together with a few of her courtiers, as a prisoner to his castle at Dunbar. She expressed neither surprise, nor terror, nor indignation, at such an outrage committed on her person, and such an insult offered to her authority, but seemed to yield without struggle or regret. Melvil was at that time one of her attendants; and the officer by whom he was seized informed him that nothing was done without the Queen's own consent. If we may rely on the letters published in Mary's name, the scheme had been communicated to her, and every step towards it was taken with her participation and advice.

Both the Queen and Bothwell thought it of advantage to employ this appearance of violence. It afforded her a decent excuse for her conduct; and while she could plead that it was owing to force rather than choice, she hoped that her reputation, among foreigners at least, would escape without censure, or be exposed to less reproach. Bothwell could not help distrusting all the methods which had hitherto been used for vindicating him from any concern in the murder of the King. Something was still wanting for his security, and for quieting his guilty fears. This was a pardon under the great seal. By the laws of Scotland the most henious crime must be mentioned by name in a pardon, and then all lesser offences are deemed to be included under the general clause, *and all other crimes whatsoever.* To seize the person of the Prince, is high treason; and Bothwell hoped that a pardon obtained for this would extend to every thing of which he had been accused.

Bothwell having now got the Queen's person into his hands, it would have been unbecoming either a politician or a man of gallantry to have delayed consummating his schemes. The first step towards this was to have his marriage with Lady Jane Gordon, the Earl of Huntly's sister, dissolved. In order to accomplish that, in a manner consistent with the ideas of the Queen on the one hand, and with the sentiments of his countrymen on the other, two different processes became necessary; one founded on the maxims of the canon law, the other accommodated to the tenets of the reformed church. Bothwell accordingly commenced a suit, in his own name, in the spiritual court of the Archbishop of St. Andrew's [April 27], the jurisdiction of which the Queen had restored, by a special commission granted for this purpose, and pleaded that Lady Jane and himself, being cousins within the prohibited degrees, and having married without a papal dispensation, their union was null from the beginning. At the same time he prevailed with Lady Jane to apply to the Protestant Court of Commissaries for a divorce, on account of his having been guilty of adultery. The influence of Bothwell was of equal weight in both courts. In the course of four days, with the same indecent and suspicious precipitancy, the one declared the marriage illegal and null, the other pronounced a sentence of divorce.

While this infamous transaction was carrying on, the Queen resided at Dunbar, detained as a prisoner, but treated with the greatest respect. Soon after [May 3], Bothwell, with a numerous train of his dependants, conducted her to Edinburgh; but, instead of lodging her in the palace of Holyrood-house, he conveyed her to the castle, of which he was governor. The discontent of the nation rendered this precaution necessary. In a house unfortified, and of easy access, the Queen might have been rescued without difficulty out of his hands. In a place of strength she was secured from all the attempts of his enemies.

One small difficulty still remained to be surmounted. As the Queen was kept in a sort of captivity by Bothwell, a marriage concluded in that condition might be imputed to force, and be held invalid. In order to obviate this, Mary appeared in the court of session, and in the presence of the chancellor and other judges, and several of the nobility, declared that she was now at full liberty; and though Bothwell's violence in seizing her person had at first excited her indignation, yet his respectful behaviour since that time had not only appeased her resentment, but determined her to raise him to higher honours.

What these were, soon became public. The title of Duke of Orkney was conferred upon Bothwell: and on the 15th of May his marriage with the Queen, which had so long been the object of his wishes, and the motives of his crimes, was solemnized. The ceremony was performed in public, according to the rites of the Protestant church, by Adam Bothwell, Bishop of Orkney, one of the few prelates who had embraced the Reformation, and on the same day was celebrated in private according to the forms prescribed by the Popish religion. The boldness with which Craig, the minister who was commanded to publish the banns, testified against the design; the small number of the nobles who were present at the marriage, and the sullen and disrespectful silence of the people when the Queen appered in public, were manifest symptoms of the violent and general dissatisfaction of her own subjects. The refusal of Le Croc, the French ambassador, to be present at the nuptial ceremony or entertainment, discovers the sentiments of her allies with regard to this part of her conduct; and although every other action in Mary's life could be justified by the rules of prudence, or reconciled to the principles of virtue, this fatal marriage would remain an incontestable proof of her rashness, if not of her guilt.

Mary's first care was to offer some apology for her conduct to the courts of France or England. The instructions to her ambassadors still remain, and are drawn by a masterly hand. But, under all the artificial and false colouring she employs, it is easy to discover, not only that many of the steps she had taken were unjustifiable, but that she herself was conscious that they could not be justified.

The title of King was the only thing which was not bestowed upon Bothwell. Notwithstanding her attachment to him, Mary remembered the inconveniences which had arisen from the rash advancement of her former husband to that honour. She agreed, however, that he should sign, in token of consent, all the public writs issued in her name. But, though the Queen withheld from him the title of King, he possessed, nevertheless, regal power in its full extent. The Queen's person was in his hands; she was surrounded more closely than ever by his creatures; none of her subjects could obtain audience without his permission; and, unless in his own presence, none but his confidants were permitted to converse with her. The Scottish monarchs were accustomed to live among their subjects as fathers or as equals, without distrust, and with little state; armed guards standing at the doors of the royal apartment, difficulty of access, distance and retirement, were things unknown and unpopular.

These precautions were necessary for securing to Bothwell the power which he had acquired. But, without being master of the person of the young Prince, he esteemed all that he had gained to be precarious and uncertain. The Queen had committed her son to the care of the Earl of Mar. The fidelity and loyalty of that nobleman were too well known to expect that he would be willing to put the Prince into the hands of the man who was so violently suspected of having murdered his father. Bothwell, however, laboured to get the Prince into his power, with an anxiety which gave rise to the blackest suspicions. All his address as well' as authority, were employed to persuade or to force Mar into a compliance with his demands. And it is no slight proof, both of the firmness and dexterity of that nobleman, that he preserved a life of so much importance to the nation, from being in the power of a man, whom fear or ambition might have prompted to violent attempts against it.

The eyes of the neighbouring nations were fixed, at that time, upon the great events which had happened in Scotland during three months; a King murdered with the utmost cruelty, in the prime of his days, and in his capital city; the person suspected of that odious crime suffered not only to appear publicly in every place, but admitted into the presence of the Queen, distinguished by her favour, and intrusted with the chief direction of her affairs; subjected to a trial which was carried on with most shameless partiality, and acquitted by a sentence which served only to confirm the suspicions of his guilt; divorced from his wife, on pretences frivolous or indecent; and, after all this, instead of meeting with the ignominy due to his actions, or the punishment merited by his crimes, permitted openly, and without opposition, to marry a Queen, the wife of the Prince whom he had assassinated, and the guardian of those laws which he had been guilty of violating. Such a quick succession of incidents, so singular and so detestable, in the space of three months, is not to be found in any other history. They left, in the opinions of foreigners, a mark of infamy on the character of the nation. The Scots were held in abhorrence all over Europe; they durst hardly appear any where in public; and after suffering so many atrocious deeds to pass with impunity, they were universally reproached as men void of courage or of humanity, as equally regardless of the reputation of the Queen and the honour of their country.*

These reproaches roused the nobles, who had been hitherto amused by Bothwell's artifices, or intimidated by his power. The manner in which he exercised the authority which he acquired, his repeated attempts to become master of the Prince's person, together with some rash threatenings against him, which he let fall,

* See Appendix, No. XXI.

added to the violence and promptitude of their resolutions. A
considerable body of them assembled at Stirling, and entered into
an association for the defence of the Prince's person.   Argyll,
Athol, Mar, Morton, Glencairn, Home, Lindsay, Boyd, Murray of
Tullybardin, Kirkaldy of Grange, and Maitland the Secretary,
were the heads of this confederacy. Stewart, Earl of Athol, was
remarkable for a uniform and bigoted attachment to popery; but
his indignation on account of the murder of the King, to whom he
was nearly allied, and his zeal for the safety of the Prince, overcame,
on this occasion, all considerations of religion, and united him with
the most zealous Protestants. Several of the other nobles acted,
without question, from a laudable concern for the safety of the
Prince and the honour of their country. But the spirit which
some of them discovered during the subsequent revolutions leaves
little room to doubt, that ambition or resentment were the real
motives of their conduct; and that, on many occasions, while they
were pursuing ends just and necessary, they were actuated by principles and passions altogether unjustifiable.

The first accounts of this league filled the Queen and Bothwell
with great consternation. They were no strangers to the sentiments of the nation with respect to their conduct; and though
their marriage had not met with public opposition, they knew that
it had not been carried on without the secret disgust and murmurings
of all ranks of men. They foresaw the violence with which this
indignation would burst out, after having been so long suppressed ;
and, in order to prepare for the storm, Mary issued a proclamation
[May 28,] requiring her subjects to take arms, and to attend her husband by a day appointed. At the same time she published a sort
of manifesto, in which she laboured to vindicate her government
from those imputations with which it had been loaded, and employed the strongest terms to express her concern for the safety and
welfare of the Prince her son. Neither of these produced any considerable effect. Her proclamation was ill obeyed, and her manifesto
met with little credit.

The confederate Lords carried on their preparations with no less
activity, and with much more success. Among a warlike people,
men of so much power and popularity found it an easy matter to
raise an army. They were ready to march before the Queen and
Bothwell were in a condition to resist them. The castle of Edinburgh was the place whither the Queen ought naturally to have retired, and there her person might have been perfectly safe. But
the confederates had fallen on means to shake or corrupt the fidelity
of Sir James Balfour, the deputy governor, and Bothwell durst not
commit to him such an important trust. He conducted the Queen
[June 6] to the castle of Borthwick ; and on the appearance of Lord
Home, with a body of his followers, before that place, he fled with
precipitation to Dunbar, and was followed by the Queen disguised
in men's clothes. The confederates advanced towards Edinburgh
where Huntly endeavoured, in vain, to animate the inhabitants to
defend the town against them. They entered without opposition,
and were instantly joined by many of the citizens, whose zeal became the firmest support of their cause.

In order to set their own conduct in the most favourable light, and to rouse the public indignation against Bothwell, the nobles published a declaration of the motives which had induced them to take arms. All Bothwell's past crimes were enumerated, all his wicked intentions displayed and aggravated, and every true Scotchman was called upon to join them in avenging the one and preventing the other.

Meanwhile Bothwell assembled his forces at Dunbar; and as he had many dependants in that corner, he soon gathered such strength that he ventured to advance towards the confederates. Their troops were not numerous; the suddenness and secrecy of their enterprise gave their friends at a distance no time to join them; and, as it does not appear that they were supported either with money or fed with hopes by the Queen of England, they could not have kept long in a body. But, on the other hand, Bothwell durst not risk a delay. His army followed him with reluctance in this quarrel, and served him with no cordial affection; so that his only hope of success was in surprising the enemy, or in striking the blow before his troops had leisure to recollect themselves, or to imbibe the same unfavourable opinion of his actions which had spread over the rest of the nation. These motives determined the Queen to march forward with an inconsiderate and fatal speed.

On the first intelligence of her approach, the confederates advanced to meet her. They found her forces drawn up almost on the same ground which the English had occupied before the battle of Pinkie [July 15]. The numbers on both sides were nearly equal; but there was no equality in point of discipline. The Queen's army consisted chiefly of a multitude, hastily assembled, without courage or experience in war. The troops of the confederates were composed of gentlemen of rank and reputation, followed by their most trusty dependants, who were no less brave than zealous.

Le Croc, the French ambassador, who was in the field, laboured by negotiating both with the Queen and the nobles, to put an end to the quarrel without the effusion of blood. He represented to the confederates the Queen's inclinations towards peace, and her willingness to pardon the offences which they had committed. Morton replied with warmth, that they had taken arms not against the Queen, but against the murderer of her husband; and if he were given up to justice, or banished from her presence, she should find them ready to yield the obedience which is due from subjects to their sovereign. Glencairn added, that they did not come to ask pardon for any offence, but to punish those who had offended. Such haughty answers convinced the ambassador that his mediation would be ineffectual, and that their passions were too high to allow them to listen to any pacific propositions, or to think of retreating after having proceeded so far.

The Queen's army was posted to advantage on a rising ground. The confederates advanced to the attack resolutely, but slowly, and with the caution which was natural on that unhappy field. Her troops were alarmed at their approach, and discovered no inclination to fight. Mary endeavoured to animate them; she wept, she threatened, she reproached them with cowardice, but all in vain.

A few of Bothwell's immediate attendants were eager for the encounter; the rest stood wavering and irresolute, and some began to
steal out of the field. Bothwell attempted to inspirit them, by
offering to decide the quarrel, and to vindicate his own inocence, in
single combat with any of his adversaries. Kirkaldy of Grange,
Murray of Tullibardin, and Lord Lindsay, contended for the honour
of entering the lists against him. But this challenge proved to be a
mere bravado. Either the consciousness of guilt deprived Bothwell
of his courage, or the Queen, by her authority, forbade the combat.

After the symptoms of fear discovered by her followers, Mary
would have been inexcusable had she hazarded a battle. To have
retreated in the face of an enemy who had already surrounded the
hill on which she stood with part of their cavalry, was utterly impracticable. In this situation, she was under the cruel necessity of
putting herself into the hands of those subjects who had taken
arms against her. She demanded an interview with Kirkaldy, a
brave and generous man, who commanded an advanced body of the
enemy. He, with the consent and in the name of the leaders of the
party, promised that, on condition she would dismiss Bothwell
from her presence, and govern the kingdom by the advice of her
nobles, they would honour and obey her as their sovereign.

During this parley, Bothwell took his last farewell of the Queen
and rode off the field with a few followers. This dismal reverse
happened exactly one month after that marriage which had cost him
so many crimes to accomplish, and which leaves so foul a stain on
Mary's memory.

As soon as Bothwell retired, Mary surrendered to Kirkaldy, who
conducted her toward the confederate army, the leaders of which
received her with much respect; and Morton, in their name, made
ample professions of their future loyalty and obedience. But she
was treated by the common soldiers with the utmost insolence and
indignity. As she marched along, they poured upon her all the
opprobrious names which are bestowed only on the lowest and most
infamous criminals. Wherever she turned her eyes, they held up
before her a standard, on which was painted the dead body of the
late King, stretched on the ground, and the young Prince kneeling
before it, and uttering these words, "Judge and revenge my cause
O Lord!" Mary turned with horror from such a shocking sight.
She began already to feel the wretched condition to which a captive
Prince is reduced. She uttered the most bitter complaints, she
melted into tears, and could hardly be kept from sinking to the
ground. The confederates conducted her towards Edinburgh;
and, in spite of many delays, and after looking, with the fondness
and credulity natural to the unfortunate, for some extraordinary
relief, she arrived there. The streets were covered with multitudes, whom zeal or curiosity had drawn together, to behold such
an unusual scene. The Queen, worn out with fatigue, covered with
dust, and bedewed with tears, was exposed as a spectacle to her
own subjects, and led to the provost's house. Notwithstanding all
her arguments and entreaties, the same standard was carried before
her, and the same insults and reproaches repeated. A woman,
young, beautiful, and in distress, is naturally the object of com-

passion. The comparison of their present misery with their former splendour, usually softens us in favour of illustrious sufferers. But the people beheld the deplorable situation of their sovereign with insensibility; and so strong was their persuasion of her guilt, and so great the violence of their indignation, that the sufferings of their Queen did not, in any degree, mitigate their resentment, or procure her that sympathy which is seldom denied to unfortunate Princes.

BOOK V.

1567.

THE confederate Lords had proceeded to such extremities against their Sovereign that it now became almost impossible for them either to stop short or to pursue a course less violent. Many of the nobles had refused to concur with them in their enterprise; others openly condemned it. A small circumstance might abate that indignation with which the multitude were at present animated against the Queen, and deprive them of that popular applause which was the chief foundation of their power. These considerations inclined some of them to treat the Queen with great lenity.

But, on the other hand, Mary's affection for Bothwell continued as violent as ever; she obstinately refused to hearken to any proposal for dissolving their marriage, and determined not to abandon a man, for whose love she had already sacrificed so much*. If they should allow her to recover the supreme power, the first exertion of it would be to recall Bothwell; and they had reason, both from his resentment, from her conduct, and from their own, to expect the severest effects of her vengeance. These considerations surmounted every other motive; and, reckoning themselves absolved by Mary's incurable attachment to Bothwell, from the engagements which they had come under when she yielded herself a prisoner, they, without regarding the duty which they owed her as their Queen, and without consulting the rest of the nobles, carried her next evening, under a strong guard, to the castle of Lochlevin, and signed a warrant to William Douglas, the owner of it, to detain her as a prisoner. This castle is situated in a small island in the middle of a lake. Douglas, to whom it belonged, was a near relation of Morton's, and had married the Earl of Murray's mother. In this place under strict custody, with a few attendants, and subjected to the insults of a haughty woman, who boasted daily of being the lawful wife of James V., Mary suffered all the rigour and miseries of captivity.

Immediately after the Queen's imprisonment the confederates were at the utmost pains to strengthen their party; they entered

* See Appendix, No. XXII.

into new bonds of association; they assumed the title of *Lords of the Secret Council*, and without any other right arrogated to themselves the whole regal authority. One of their first acts of power was to search the city of Edinburgh for such as had been concerned in the murder of the King. This show of zeal gained reputation to themselves, and threw an oblique reflection on the Queen for her remissness. Several suspected persons were seized. Captain Blackadder and three others were condemned and executed. But no discovery of importance was made. If we believe some historians, they were convicted by sufficient evidence; if we give credit to others, their sentence was unjust, and they denied, with their last breath, any knowledge of the crime for which they suffered.

An unexpected accident, however, put into the hands of Mary's enemies, what they deemed the fullest evidence of her guilt. Bothwell having left in the castle of Edinburgh a casket containing several sonnets and letters written with the Queen's own hand, he now sent one of his confidants to bring to him this precious deposite. But as his messenger returned, he was intercepted, and the casket seized by Morton. The contents of it were always produced by the party as the most ample justification of their own conduct; and to these they continually appealed as the most unanswerable proof of their not having loaded their sovereign with the imputation of imaginary crimes*.

But the confederates, notwithstanding their extraordinary success, were still far from being perfectly at ease. That so small a part of the nobles should pretend to dispose of the person of their sovereign, or to assume the authority which belonged to her, without the concurrence of the rest, was deemed by many of that body, to be unprecedented and presumptuous. Several of these were now assembled at Hamilton, in order to deliberate what course they should hold in this difficult conjuncture. The confederates made some attempts towards a coalition with them, but without effect. They employed the mediation of the assembly of the church, to draw them to a personal interview at Edinburgh, but with no better success. That party, however, though its numbers were formidable, and the power of its leaders great, soon lost reputation by the want of unanimity and vigour; all its consultations evaporated in murmurs and complaints, and no scheme was concerted for obstructing the progress of the confederates.

There appeared some prospect of danger from another quarter. This great revolution in Scotland had been carried on without any aid from Elizabeth, and even without her knowledge. Though she was far from being displeased at seeing the affairs of that kingdom embroiled, or a rival whom she hated reduced to distress; she neither wished that it should be in the power of the one faction entirely to suppress the other, nor could she view the steps taken by the confederates without great offence. Notwithstanding the popular maxims by which she governed her own subjects, her notions of royal prerogative were very exalted. The confederates had, in her opinion, encroached on the authority of their sovereign,

* See Dissertation at the end of the History.

which they had no right to control, and had offered violence to her person, which it was their duty to esteem sacred. They had set a dangerous example to other subjects, and Mary's cause became the common cause of Princes. If ever Elizabeth was influenced with regard to the affairs of Scotland by the feelings of her heart, rather than by considerations of interest, it was on this occasion. Mary, in her present condition, degraded from her throne, and covered with the infamy attending an accusation of such atrocious crimes, could be no longer the object of Elizabeth's jealousy, either as a woman or as a Queen. Sympathy with a sovereign in distress seems, for a moment to have touched a heart not very susceptible of tender sentiments; and while these were yet warm, she dispatched Throkmorton into Scotland [June 30], with power to negociate both with the Queen and with the confederates. In his instructions there appears a remarkable solicitude for Mary's liberty, and even for her reputation; and the terms upon which she proposed to re-establish the concord between the Queen and her subjects, appear to be so reasonable and well digested, as might have ensured the safety and happiness of both. Zealous as Throkmorton was to accomplish this, all his endeavours and address proved ineffectual. He found not only the confederate nobles, but the nation in general, so far alienated from the Queen, and so much offended with the indecent precipitancy of her marriage with the reputed murderer of her former husband, as to be incapable of listening to any proposition in her favour.

During the state of anarchy occasioned by the imprisonment of the Queen, and the dissolution of the established government, which afforded such ample scope for political speculation, four different schemes had been proposed for the settlement of the nation. One, that Mary should be replaced upon the throne, but under various and strict limitations. The second, that she should resign the crown to her son, and, retiring out of the kingdom, should reside, during the remainder of her days, either in England or in France. The third, that Mary should be brought to public trial for her crimes, and, after conviction, of which no doubt was entertained, should be kept in perpetual imprisonment. The fourth, that after trial and condemnation, capital punishment should be inflicted upon her. Throkmorton, though disposed, as well by his own inclination as in comformity to the spirit of his instructions, to view matters in the light most favourable to Mary, informed his court, that the milder schemes, recommended by Maitland alone, would undoubtedly be reprobated, and one of the more rigorous carried into execution.

In justification of this rigour, the confederates maintained that Mary's affection for Bothwell was still unabated, and openly avowed by her; that she rejected with disdain every proposal for dissolving their marriage; and declared, that she would forego every comfort, and endure any extremity, rather than give her consent to that measure. While these were her sentiments, they contended, that concern for the public welfare, as well as attention to their own safety, rendered it necessary to put it out of the Queen's power to restore a daring man, exasperated by recent injuries, to his former station, which must needs prove fatal to both. Notwithstanding their solicitude to conciliate the good will of Elizabeth, they fore-saw clearly what would be the effect, at this juncture, of Throk-morton's interposition in behalf of the Queen; and that she, elated with the prospect of protection, would refuse to listen to the over-tures which they were about to make to her. For this reason they peremptorily denied Throkmorton's access to their prisoner; and what propositions he made to them in her behalf they either re-fused or eluded.

Meanwhile they deliberated with the utmost anxiety concerning the settlement of the nation, and the future disposal of the Queen's person. Elizabeth, observing that Throkmorton made no progress in his negotiations with them, and that they would listen to none of his demands in Mary's favour, turned towards that party of the nobles who were assembled at Hamilton, incited them to take arms in order to restore their Queen to liberty, and pro-mised to assist them in such an attempt to the utmost of her power.* But they discovered no greater union and vigour than formerly, and, behaving like men who had given up all concern either for their Queen or their country, tamely allowed an incon-siderable part of their body, whether we consider it with respect to numbers or to power, to settle the government of the kingdom, and to dispose of the Queen's person at pleasure. Many consultations were held, and various opinions arose with regard to each of these. Some seemed desirous of adhering to the plan on which the con-federacy was at first formed; and after punishing the murderers of the King, and dissolving the marriage with Bothwell; after pro-viding for the safety of the young Prince, and the security of the Protestant religion; they proposed to re-establish the Queen in the possession of her legal authority. The success with which their arms had been accompanied inspired others with bolder and more des-perate thoughts, and nothing less would satisfy them than the trial, the condemnation, and punishment of the Queen herself, as the principal conspirator against the life of her husband and the safety of her son: the former was Maitland's system, and breathed too much of a pacific and moderate spirit, to be agreeable to the tem-per or wishes of the party. The latter was recommended by the clergy, and warmly adopted by many laics; but the nobles durst not, or would not, venture on such an unprecedented and audacious deed.†

Both parties agreed at last upon a scheme, neither so moderate as the one nor so daring as the other. Mary was to be persuaded or forced to resign the crown; the young Prince was to be proclaimed King, and the Earl of Murray was to be appointed to govern the kingdom, during his minority, with the name and authority of Re-gent. With regard to the Queen's own person, nothing was deter-mined. It seems to have been the intention of the confederates to

---

* See Append. No. XXIII.

† The intention of putting the Queen to death seems to have been carried on by some of her subjects: at this time we often find Elizabeth boasting that Mary owed her life to her interposition. Digges's Compl. Amb. 14, &c. See Append. No. XVIII.

keep her in perpetual imprisonment; but in order to intimidate herself, and to overawe her partisans, they still reserved to themselves the power of prooceeding to more violent extremes.

It was obvious to foresee difficulties in the execution of this plan. Mary was young, ambitious, high spirited, and accustomed to command. To induce her to acknowledge her own incapacity for governing, to renounce the dignity and power which she was born to enjoy, to become dependent on her own subjects, to consent to her own bondage, and to invest those persons whom she considered as the authors of all her calamities with that honour and authority of which she herself was stripped, were points hard to be gained. These, however, the confederates attempted, and they did not want means to ensure success. Mary had endured, for several weeks, all the hardships and terror of a prison; no prospect of liberty appeared; none of her subjects had either taken arms, or so much as solicited her relief; no person, in whom she could confide, was admitted into her presence; even the ambassadors of the French King, and Queen of England, were refused access to her. In this solitary state, without a counsellor or a friend, under the pressure of distress and the apprehension of danger, it was natural for a woman to hearken almost to any overtures. The confederates took advantage of her condition and of her fears. They employed Lord Lindsay, the fiercest zealot in the party, to communicate their scheme to the Queen, and to obtain her subscription to those papers which were necessary for rendering it effectual. He executed his commission with harshness and brutality. Certain death was before Mary's eyes if she refused to comply with his demands. At the same time she was informed by Sir Robert Melvil, in the name of Athol, Maitland, and Kirkaldy, the persons among the confederates who were most attentive to her interest, that a resignation, extorted by fear, and granted during her imprisonment, was void in law, and might be revoked as soon as she recovered liberty. Throkmorton, by a note which he found means of conveying to her, suggested the same thing. Deference to their opinion, as well as concern for her own safety, obliged her to yield to every thing which was required, and to sign all the papers which Lindsay presented to her. By one of these she resigned the crown, renounced all share in the government of the kingdom, and consented to the coronation of the young King. By another [July 24], she appointed the Earl of Murray Regent, and conferred upon him all the powers and privileges of that high office. By a third, she substituted some other noblemen in Murray's place. if he should refuse the honour which was designed for him. Mary, when she subscribed these deeds, was bathed in tears; and while she gave away, as it were with her own hands, the sceptre which she had swayed so long, she felt a pang of grief and indignation, one of the severest, perhaps, which can touch the human heart.

The confederates endeavoured to give this resignation all the weight and validity in their power, by proceeding without delay to crown the young Prince. The ceremony was performed at Stirling [July 29], with much solemnity, in the presence of all the nobles of the party, a considerable number of lesser barons, and a great assembly of the people. From that time all public writs were issued, and the government carried on, in the name of James VI.

. No revolution so great was ever effected with more ease, or by means so unequal to the end. In a warlike age, and in less time than two months, a part of the nobles, who neither possessed the chief power nor the greatest wealth in the nation, and who never brought three thousand men into the field, seized, imprisoned, and dethroned their Queen, and, without shedding a single drop of blood, set her son, an infant of a year old, on the throne.

During this rapid progress of the confederates, the eyes of all the nation were turned on them with astonishment; and various and contradictory opinions were formed concerning the extraordinary steps which they had taken.

Even under the aristocratical form of government which prevails in Scotland, said the favourers of the Queen, and notwithstanding the exorbitant privileges of the nobles, the Prince possesses considerable power, and his person is treated with great veneration. No encroachments should be made on the former, and no injury offered to the latter, but in cases where the liberty and happiness of the nation cannot be secured by any other means. Such cases seldom exist, and it belongs not to any part, but to the whole, or at least to a majority of the society, to judge of their existence. By what action could it be pretended that Mary had invaded the rights or property of her subjects, or what scheme had she formed against the liberty and constitution of the kingdom? Were fears, and suspicions, and surmises, enough to justify the imprisoning and the deposing a Queen, to whom the crown descended from so long a race of monarchs? The principal author of whatever was reckoned culpable in her conduct was now driven from her presence. The murderers of the King might have been brought to condign punishment, the safety of the Prince have been secured, and the Protestant religion have been established, without wresting the sceptre out of her hands, or condemning her to perpetual imprisonment. Whatever right a free Parliament might have had to proceed to such a rigorous conclusion, or whatever name its determination might have merited, a sentence of this nature, passed by a small party of the nobility, without acknowledging or consulting the rest of the nation, must be deemed a rebellion against the government, and a conspiracy against the person of their sovereign.

The partisans of the confederates reasoned very differently. It is evident, said they, that Mary either previously gave consent to the King's murder, or did afterwards approve of that horrid action. Her attachment to Bothwell, the power and honours which she has conferred upon him, the manner in which she suffered his trial to be carried on, and the indecent speed with which she married a man stained with so many crimes, raise strong suspicions of the former, and put the latter beyond all doubt. To have suffered the supreme power to continue in the hands of an ambitious man, capable of the most atrocious and desperate actions, would have been disgraceful to the nation, dishonourable to the Queen, and dangerous to the Prince. Recourse was therefore had to arms. The Queen had been compelled to abandon a husband so unworthy of herself. But her affection toward him still continuing unabated; her indignation against the authors of this separation being visible, and often expressed in the strongest terms; they, by restoring her to her ancient authority, would have armed her with power to destroy themselves, have enabled her to recall Bothwell, and have afforded her an opportunity of pursuing schemes fatal to the nation with greater eagerness, and with more success. Nothing therefore remained, but one bold action to deliver themselves and their country from all future fears. The expedient they had chosen was no less respectful to the royal blood, than necessary for the public safety. While one Prince was set aside as incapable of governing, the crown was placed on his head who was the undoubted representative of their ancient Kings.

Whatever opinion posterity may form on comparing the arguments of two contending parties, whatever sentiments we may entertain concerning the justice or necessity of that course which the confederates held, it cannot be denied that their conduct, so far as regarded themselves, was extremely prudent. Other expedients, less rigorous towards Mary, might have been found for settling the nation; but, after the injuries which they had already offered the Queen, there was none so effectual for securing their own safety, or perpetuating their own power.

To a great part of the nation, the conduct of the confederates appeared not only wise, but just. The King's accession to the throne was every where proclaimed, and his authority submitted to without opposition. Though several of the nobles were still assembled at Hamilton, and seemed to be entering into combination against his government, an association for supporting it was formed and signed by so many persons of power and influence throughout the nation, as entirely discouraged the attempt.

The return of the Earl of Murray, about this time, added strength to the party, and gave it a regular and finished form. Soonafter the murder of the King, this nobleman had retired into France, upon what pretence historians do not mention. During his residence there, he had held a close correspondence with the chiefs of the confederacy, and, at their desire, he now returned. He seemed, at first, unwilling to accept the office of Regent. This hesitation cannot be ascribed to the scruples either of diffidence or of duty. Murray wanted neither the abilities nor the ambition which might incite him to aspire to this high dignity. He had received the first accounts of his promotion with the utmost satisfaction; but, by appearing to continue for some days in suspense, he gained time to view with attention the ground on which he was to act; to balance the strength and resources of the two contending factions; and to examine whether the foundation on which his future fame and success must rest, were sound and firm.

Before he declared his final resolution, he waited on Mary at Lochlevin. This visit, to a sister, and a Queen, in a prison, from which he had neither any intention to relieve her, nor to mitigate the rigour of her confinement, may be mentioned among the circumstances which discover the great want of delicacy and refinement in that age. Murray, naturally rough and uncourtly in his manner, expostulated so warmly with the Queen concerning her past conduct, and charged her faults so home upon her, that Mary, who had flattered herself with more gentle and brotherly treatment from him, melted into tears, and abandoned herself entirely to despair. This interview, from which Murray could reap no political advantage, and wherein he discovered a spirit so unrelenting, may be reckoned among the most bitter circumstances in Mary's life, and is certainly one of the most unjustifiable steps in his conduct.

Soon after his return from Lochlevin, Murray accepted the office of Regent, and began to act in that character without opposition. [Aug. 22.]

Amidst so many great and unexpected events, the fate of Bothwell, the chief cause of them all, had almost been forgotten. After his flight from his confederates, he lurked for some time among his vassals in the neighbourhood of Dunbar. But finding it impossible for him to make head, in that country, against his enemies, or even to secure himself from their pursuit, he fled for shelter to his kinsman the Bishop of Murray; and when he, overawed by the confederates, was obliged to abandon him, he retired to the Orkney Isles. Hunted from place to place, deserted by his friends, and accompanied by a few retainers as desperate as himself, he suffered at once the miseries of infamy and of want. His indigence forced him upon a course of life which added to his infamy. He armed a few small vessels which followed him from Dunbar, and, attacking every vessel which fell in his way, endeavoured to procure subsistence for himself and his followers by piracy. Kirkaldy and Murray of Tullibardin were sent against him by the confederates: and, surprising him while he rode at anchor, scattered his small fleet, took a part of it, and obliged him to fly with a single ship towards Norway. On that coast he fell in with a vessel richly laden, and immediately attacked it; the Norwegians sailed with armed boats to its assistance, and, after a desperate fight, Bothwell and all his crew were taken prisoners. His name and quality were both unknown, and he was treated at first with all the indignity and rigour which the odious crime of piracy merited. His real character was soon discovered; and, though it saved him from the infamous death to which his associates were condemned, it could neither procure his liberty, nor mitigate the hardships of his imprisonment. He languished two years in this unhappy condition; melancholy and despair deprived him of reason, and at last he ended his days unpitied by his countrymen, and unassisted by strangers. Few men ever accomplished their ambitious projects by worse means, or reaped from them less satisfaction. The early part of his life was restless and enterprising, full of dangers and vicissitudes. His enjoyment of the grandeur, which he attained by so many crimes, was extremely short; embittered by much anxiety, and disquieted by many fears. In his latter years, he suffered the most intolerable calamities to which the wretched are subject, and from which persons who moved in so high a sphere are commonly exempted.

The good effects of Murray's accession to the regency were quickly felt. The party forming for the Queen was weak, irresolute, and disunited; and no sooner was the government of the kingdom in the hands of a man so remarkable both for his abilities and popularity, than the nobles, of whom it was composed, lost all hopes of gaining ground, and began to treat separately with the Regent.— So many of them were brought to acknowledge the King's authority, that scarce any appearance of opposition to the established government was left in the kingdom. Had they adhered to the Queen with any firmness, it is probable, from her disposition at that time, that she would have afforded them such assistance as might have enabled them to face their enemies in the field. But there appeared so little vigour or harmony in their councils, that she was discouraged from espousing their cause; and the Regent, taking advantage of their situation, obliged them to submit to his government, without granting any terms either to themselves or the Queen.

The Regent was no less successful in his attempt to get into his hands the places of strength in the kingdom. Balfour, the deputy governor, surrendered the castle of Edinburgh; and as the reward of his treachery, in deserting Bothwell his patron, obtained terms of great advantage to himself. The governor of Dunbar, who discovered greater fidelity, was soon forced to capitulate: some other small forts surrendered without resistance.

This face of tranquillity in the nation encouraged the Regent to call a meeting of parliament [Dec. 15]. Nothing was wanting to confirm the King's authority, and the proceedings of the confederates, except the approbation of the supreme court; and, after the success which had attended all their measures, there could be little doubt of obtaining it. The numbers that resorted to an assembly which was called to deliberate on matters of so much importance, were great. The meeting was opened with the utmost solemnity, and all its acts passed with much unanimity. Many, however, of the lords who had discovered the warmest attachment to the Queen, were present. But they had made their peace with the Regent.— Argyll, Huntly, and Herries, acknowledged, openly in parliament, that their behaviour towards the King had been undutiful and criminal.[*] Their compliance, in this manner, with the measures of the Regent's party, was either the condition on which they were admitted into favour, or intended as a proof of the sincerity of their reconcilement.

The Parliament granted every thing the confederates could demand, either for the safety of their own persons, or the security of that form of government which they had established in the kingdom. Mary's resignation of the crown was accepted, and declared to be valid. The King's authority, and Murray's election, were recognised and confirmed. The imprisoning the Queen, and all the other proceedings of the confederates, were pronounced lawful.— The letters which Mary had written to Bothwell were produced, and she was declared to be accessary to the murder of the King.— At the same time, all the acts of parliament of 1560, in favour of the Protestant religion, were publicly ratified. New statutes to

* See Appendix, No. XXIV.

the same purpose were enacted; and nothing that could contribute
to root out the remains of Popery, or to encourage the growth of
the Reformation, was neglected.

It is observable, however, that the same parsimonious spirit
prevailed in this parliament as in that of the year 1560.—
The Protestant clergy, notwithstanding many discouragements,
and their extreme poverty, had for seven years performed their
religious offices in the kingdom. The expedients fallen upon
for their subsistence had hitherto proved ineffectual, or were intended to be so. But notwithstanding their known indigence, and
the warm remonstrances of the assembly of the church, which met
this year, the Parliament did nothing more for their relief than
prescribe some new regulations concerning the payment of the
thirds of benefices, which did not produce any considerable change
in the situation of the clergy.

1568.] A few days after the dissolution of parliament [Jan. 3],
four of Bothwell's dependants were convicted of being guilty of
the King's murder, and suffered death as traitors. Their confessions
brought to light many circumstances relative to the manner of
committing that barbarous crime; but they were persons of low
rank, and seem not to have been admitted into the secrets of the
conspiracy.

Notwithstanding their universal submission to the Regent's authority, there still abounded in the kingdom many secret murmurs
and cabals. The partisans of the house of Hamilton reckoned
Murray's promotion an injury to the Duke of Chatelherault, who,
as first Prince of the blood, had, in their opinion, an undoubted
right to be Regent. The length and rigour of Mary's sufferings
began to move many to commiserate her case. All who leaned to
the ancient opinions in religion dreaded the effects of Murray's
zeal. And he, though his abilities were great, did not possess the
talents requisite for soothing the rage and removing the jealousies
of the different factions. By insinuation, or address, he might
have gained or softened many who had opposed him; but he was a
stranger to these gentle arts. His virtues were severe; and his deportment towards his equals, especially after his elevation to the
Regency, distant and haughty. This behaviour offended some of
the nobles, and alarmed others. The Queen's faction, which had
been so easily dispersed, began again to gather and unite, and was
secretly favoured by some who had hitherto zealously concurred
with the confederates.

Such was the favourable disposition of the nation towards the
Queen, when she recovered her liberty, in a manner no less surprising to her friends, than unexpected by her enemies. Several
attempts had been made to procure her an opportunity of escaping,
which some unforeseen accident, or the vigilance of her keepers,
had hitherto disappointed. At last, Mary employed all her art to
gain George Douglas, her brother's keeper, a youth of eighteen.—
As her manners were naturally affable and insinuating, she treated
him with the most flattering distinction. She even allowed him to
entertain the most ambitious hopes, by letting fall some expressions, as if she would chosen him for her husband. At his age, and

in such circumstances, it was impossible to resist such a temptation. He yielded, and drew others into the plot. On Sunday, the 2d of May, while his brother sat at supper, and the rest of the family were retired to their devotions, one of his accomplices found means to steal the keys out of his brother's chamber, and, opening the gates to the Queen and one of her maids, locked them behind her, and then threw the keys into the lake. Mary ran with precipitation to the boat which was prepared for her, and, on reaching the shore, was received with the utmost joy by Douglas, Lord Seaton, and Sir James Hamilton, who with a few attendants waited for her. She instantly mounted on horseback, and rode at full speed towards Niddrie, Lord Seaton's seat in West Lothian. She arrived there that night, without being pursued or interrupted. After halting three hours, she set out for Hamilton; and travelling at the same pace, she reached it next morning.

On the first news of Mary's escape, her friends, whom, in their present disposition, a much smaller accident would have roused, ran to arms. In a few days, her court was filled with a great and splendid train of nobles, accompained by such numbers of followers as formed an army above six thousand strong. In their presence she declared that the resignation of the crown, and the other deeds which she had signed during her imprisonment, were extorted from her by fear. Sir Robert Melvil confirmed her declaration; and on that, as well as on other accounts, a council of the nobles and chief men of her party pronounced all these transactions void and illegal. At the same time [May 8], an association was formed for the defence of her person and authority, and subscribed by nine earls, nine bishops, eighteen lords, and many gentlemen of distinction. Among them were several who had been present in the last parliament, and who had signed the counter-association in defence of the King's government; but such sudden changes were then so common as to be no matter of reproach.

At the time when the Queen made her escape, the Regent was at Glasgow, holding a court of justice. An event so contrary to their expectations, and so fatal to their schemes, gave a great shock to his adherents. Many of them appeared wavering and irresolute; others began to carry on private negociations with the Queen; and some openly revolted to her side. In so difficult a juncture, where his own fame and the being of the party depended on his choice, the Regent's most faithful associates were divided in opinion. Some advised him to retire, without loss of time, to Stirling. The Queen's army was already strong, and only eight miles distant; the adjacent country was full of friends and dependants of the house of Hamilton, and other lords of the Queen's faction; Glasgow was a large and unfortified town; his own train consisted of no greater number than was usual in time of peace; all these reasons pleaded for a retreat. But, on the other hand, arguments were urged of no inconsiderable weight. The citizens of Glasgow were well affected to the cause; the vassals of Glencairn, Lennox, and Semple, lay near at hand, and were both numerous and full of zeal: succours might arrive from other parts of the kingdom in a few

K 5

days; in war, success depends upon reputation, as much as upon numbers; reputation is gained, or lost, by the first step one takes: on all these considerations, a retreat would be attended with all the ignominy of a flight, and would at once dispirit his friends, and inspire his enemies with boldness. In such dangerous exigencies as this, the superiority of Murray's genius appeared, and enabled him both to choose with wisdom and to act with vigour. He declared against retreating, and fixed his head-quarters at Glasgow. And while he amused the Queen for some days, by pretending to hearken to some overtures which she made for accommodating their differences, he was employed with the utmost industry, in drawing together his adherents from different parts of the kingdom. He was soon in a condition to take the field; and, though far inferior to the enemy in number, he confided so much in the valour of his troops and the experience of his officers, that he broke off the negociation, and determined to hazard a battle.

At the same time [May 13], the Queen's generals had commanded her army to move. Their intention was, to conduct her to Dumbarton-castle, a place of great strength, which the Regent had not been able to wrest from the hands of Lord Fleming the governor; but if the enemy should endeavour to interrupt their march, they resolved not to decline an engagement. In Mary's situation, no resolution could be more imprudent. A part only of her forces were assembled. Huntly, Ogilvie, and the northern clans, were soon expected; her sufferings had removed or diminished the prejudices of many among her subjects; the address with which she surmounted the dangers that obstructed her escape, dazzled and interested the people; the sudden confluence of so many nobles added lustre to her cause; she might assuredly depend on the friendship and countenance of France; she had reason to expect the protection of England; her enemies could not possible look for support from that quarter. She had much to hope from pursuing slow and cautious measures; they had every thing to fear.

But Mary, whose hopes were naturally sanguine, and her passions impetuous, was so elevated, by her sudden transition from the depth of distress to such an unusual appearance of prosperity, that she never doubted of success. Her army, which was almost double to the enemy in number, consisted chiefly of the Hamiltons and their dependants. Of these the Archbishop of St. Andrew's had the chief direction, and hoped, by a victory, not only to crush Murray, the ancient enemy of his house, but to get the person of the Queen into his hands, and to oblige her either to marry one of the Duke's sons, or at least to commit the chief direction of her affairs to himself. His ambition proved fatal to the Queen, to himself, and to his family.

Mary's imprudence in resolving to fight was not greater than the ill conduct of her generals in the battle. Between the two armies, and on the road towards Dumbarton, there was an eminence called Langside Hill. This the Regent had the precaution to seize, and posted his troops in a small village, and among some gardens and enclosures adjacent. In this advantageous situation he waited the approach of the enemy, whose superiority in cavalry could be of no benefit to them on such broken ground. The Hamiltons, who composed the vanguard, ran so eagerly to the attack, that they put themselves out of breath, and left the main battle far behind. The encounter of the spearmen was fierce and desperate; but as the forces of the Hamiltons were exposed, on the one flank, to a continued fire from a body of musqueteers, attacked on the other by the Regent's most choice troops, and not supported by the rest of the Queen's army, they were soon obliged to give ground, and the rout immediately became universal. Few victories in a civil war, and among a fierce people, have been pursued with less violence, or attended with less bloodshed. Three hundred fell in the field: in the flight almost none were killed. The Regent and his principal officers rode about, beseeching the soldiers to spare their countrymen. The number of prisoners was great, and among them many persons of distinction. The Regent marched back to Glasgow, and returned thanks to God for this great, and, on his side, almost bloodless victory.

During the engagement, Mary stood on a hill at no great distance, and beheld all that passed in the field, with such emotions of mind as are not easily described. When she saw the army, which was her last hope, thrown into irretrievable confusion, her spirit, which all her past misfortunes had not been able entirely to subdue, sunk altogether. In the utmost consternation, she began her flight; and so lively were her impressions of fear that she never closed her eyes till she reached the abbey of Drundrenan in Galloway, full sixty Scottish miles from the place of battle.

These revolutions in Mary's fortune had been no less rapid than singular. In the short space of eleven days she had been a prisoner at the mercy of her most inveterate enemies; she had seen a powerful army under her command, and a numerous train of nobles at her devotion: and now she was obliged to fly, in the utmost danger of her life, and to lurk, with a few attendants, in a corner of her kingdom. Not thinking herself safe even in that retreat, her fears impelled her to an action, the most unadvised, as well as the most unfortunate, in her whole life. This was her retiring into England; a step, which, on many accounts, ought to have appeared to her rash and dangerous.

Before Mary's arrival in Scotland, mutual distrust and jealousies had arisen between her and Elizabeth. All their subsequent transactions had contributed to exasperate and inflame these passions. She had endeavoured, by secret negociations and intrigues, to disturb the tranquility of Elizabeth's government, and to advance her own pretensions to the English crown. Elizabeth, who possessed great power, and acted with less reserve, had openly supported Mary's rebellious subjects, and fomented all the dissensions and troubles in which her reign had been involved. The maxims of policy still authorized that Queen to pursue the same course; as, by keeping Scotland in confusion, she effectually secured the peace of own kingdom. The Regent, after his victory, had marched to Edinburgh, and, not knowing what course the Queen had taken, it was several days before he thought of pursuing her. She might have been concealed in that retired corner, among subjects devoted to her interest, until her party, which was dispersed rather than broken by the late defeat, should gather such strength that she could again appear with safety at their head. There was not any danger which she ought not to have run, rather than throw herself into the hands of an enemy, from whom she had already suffered so many injuries, and who was prompted, both by inclination and by interest, to renew them.

But, on the other hand, during Mary's confinement, Elizabeth had declared against the proceedings of her subjects, and solicited for her liberty, with a warmth which had all the appearance of sincerity. She had invited her to take refuge in England, and had promised to meet her in person, and to give her such a reception as was due to a Queen, a kinswoman, and an ally. Whatever apprehension Elizabeth might entertain of Mary's designs while she had power in her hands, she was at present the object, not of fear, but of pity; and to take advantage of her situation would be both ungenerous and inhuman. The horrors of a prison were fresh in Mary's memory; and if she should fall a second time into the hands of her subjects, there was no injury to which the presumption of success might not embolden them to proceed. To attempt escaping into France was dangerous, and, in her situation, almost impossible; nor could she bear the thoughts of appearing as an exile and a fugitive in that kingdom where she had once enjoyed all the splendour of a Queen. England remained her only asylum; and in spite of the entreaties of Lord Herries, Fleming, and her other attendants, who conjured her, even on their knees, not to confide in Elizabeth's promises of generosity, her infatuation was invincible, and she resolved to fly thither. Herries, by her command, wrote to Lowther the deputy governor of Carlisle, to know what reception he would give her; and, before his answer could return, her fear and impatience were so great that she got into a fisher-boat [May 16], and, with about twenty attendants, landed at Workington, in Cumberland, and thence she was conducted with many marks of respect to Carlisle.

As soon as Mary arrived in England, she wrote a long letter to the Queen, representing, in the strongest terms, the injuries which she had suffered from her own subjects, and imploring that pity and assistance which her present situation demanded. An event so extraordinary, and the conduct which might be proper in consequence of it, drew the attention and employed the thoughts of Elizabeth and her council. If their deliberations had been influenced by considerations of justice or generosity alone, they would not have found them long or intricate. A Queen, vanquished by her own subjects, and threatened by them with the loss of her liberty or of her life, had fled from their violence, and thrown herself into the arms of her nearest neighbour and ally, from whom she had received repeated assurances of friendship and protection. These circumstances entitled her to respect and to compassion, and required that she should either be restored to her own kingdom, or at least be left at full liberty to seek aid from any other quarter. But with Elizabeth and her counsellors the question was not, what was most just or generous, but what was most beneficial to herself and to the English nation. Three different resolutions might have been taken, with regard to the Queen of Scots. To reinstate her in her throne was one; to allow her to retire into France was another; to detain her in England was a third. Each of these drew consequences after it, of the utmost importance, which were examined, as appears from papers still extant, with that minute accuracy which Elizabeth's ministers employed in all their consultations upon affairs of moment.

To restore Mary to the full exercise of the royal authority in Scotland, they observed, would render her more powerful than ever. The nobles who were most firmly attached to the English interest would quickly feel the utmost weight of her resentment. As the gratitude of Princes is seldom strong or lasting, regard to her own interest might soon efface the memory of her obligations to Elizabeth, and prompt her to renew the alliance of the Scottish nation with France, and revive her own pretensions to the English crown. Nor was it possible to fetter and circumscribe the Scottish Queen, by any conditions that would prevent these dangers. Her party in Scotland was numerous and powerful. Her return, even without any support from England, would inspire her friends with new zeal and courage; a single victory might give them the superiority, which they had lost by a single defeat, and render Mary a more formidable rival than ever to Elizabeth.

The dangers arising from suffering Mary to return into France were no less obvious. The French King could not refuse his assistance towards restoring his sister and ally to her throne. Elizabeth would, once more, see a foreign army in the island, overawing the Scots, and ready to enter her kingdom; and, if the commotions in France, on account of religion, were settled, the Princes of Lorrain might resume their ambitious projects, and the united forces of France and Scotland might invade England where it is weakest and most defenceless.

Nothing therefore remained but to detain her in England; and to permit her either to live at liberty there, or to confine her in a prison. The former was a dangerous experiment. Her court would become a place of resort to all the Roman Catholics, to the disaffected, and to the lovers of innovation. Though Elizabeth affected to represent Mary's pretensions to the English crown as ill founded, she was not ignorant that they did not appear in that light to the nation, and that many thought them preferable even to her own title. If the activity of her emissaries had gained her so many abettors, her own personal influence was much more to be dreaded: her beauty, her address, her sufferings, by the admiration and pity which they would excite, could not fail of making many converts to her party.

It was indeed to be apprehended, that the treating Mary as a prisoner would excite universal indignation against Elizabeth; and that by this unexampled severity towards a Queen, who implored, and to whom she had promised her protection, she would forfeit the praise of justice and humanity, which was hitherto due to her administration. But the English monarchs were often so solicitous to secure their kingdom against the Scots as to be little scrupulous about the means which they employed for that purpose. Henry IV. had seized the heir of the crown of Scotland, who was forced by the violence of a storm to take refuge in one of the ports of his kingdom; and, in contempt of the rights of hospitality, without regarding his tender age, or the tears and entreaties of his father, detained him a prisoner for many years. This action, though detested by posterity, Elizabeth resolved now to imitate. Her virtue was not more proof than that of Henry had been, against the temptations of interest; and the possession of a present advantage was preferred to the prospect of future fame. The satisfaction which she felt in mortifying a rival, whose beauty and accomplishments she envied, had, perhaps, no less influence than political considerations in bringing her to this resolution. But at the same time, in order to screen herself from the censure which this conduct merited, and to make her treatment of the Scottish Queen look like the effect of necessity rather than of choice, she determined to assume the appearance of concern for her interest, and of deep sympathy with her sufferings.

With this view [May 20], she instantly dispatched Lord Scrope, warden of the west marches, and Sir Francis Knollys, her vicechamberlain, to the Queen of Scots, with letters full of expressions of kindness and condolence. But, at the same time, they had private instructions to watch all her motions, and to take care that she should not escape into her own kingdom. On their arrival, Mary demanded a personal interview with the Queen, that she might lay before her the injuries which she had suffered, and receive from her those friendly offices which she had been encourged to expect. They answered, that it was with reluctance admission into the presence of their sovereign was at present denied her; that while she lay under the imputation of a crime so horrid as the murder of her husband, their mistress, to whom he was so nearly allied, could not, without bringing a stain upon her own reputation, admit her into her presence; but, as soon as she had cleared herself from that aspersion, they promised her a reception suitable to her dignity, and aid proportioned to her distress.

Nothing could be more artful than this pretence: and it was the occasion of leading the Queen of Scots into the snare in which Elizabeth and her ministers wished to entangle her. Mary expressed the utmost surprise at this unexpected manner of evading her request; but, as she could not believe so many professions of friendship to be void of sincerity, she frankly offered to submit her cause to the cognizance of Elizabeth, and undertook to produce such proofs of her own innocence, and of the falsehood of the accusations brought against her, as should fully remove the scruples and satisfy the delicacy of the English Queen. This was the very point to which Elizabeth laboured to bring the matter. In consequence of this appeal of the Scottish Queen, she now considered herself as the umpire between her and her subjects, and foresaw that she would have it entirely in her own power to protract the inquiry to any length, and to perplex and involve it in endless difficulties. In the mean time, she was furnished with a plausible reason for keeping her at a distance from court, and for refusing to contribute towards replacing her on the throne. As Mary's conduct had been extremely incautious, and the presumptions of her guilt were many and strong, it was not impossible her subjects might make good their charge against her; and if this should be the result of the inquiry, she would thenceforth cease to be the object of regard or of compassion, and the treating her with coldness and neglect would merit little censure. In a matter so dark and mysterious, there was no probability that Mary could bring proofs of her innocence so incontested as to render the conduct of the English Queen altogether culpable; and, perhaps, impatience under restraint, suspicion of Elizabeth's partiality, or the discovery of her artifices, might engage Mary in such cabals as would justify the using her with greater rigour.

Elizabeth early perceived many advantages which would arise from an inquiry into the conduct of the Scottish Queen, carried on under her direction. There was some danger, however, that Mary might discover her secret intentions too soon, and, by receding from the offer which she had made, endeavour to disappoint them. But, even in that event, she determined not to drop the inquiry, and had thought of several different expedients for carrying it on. The Countess of Lennox, convinced that Mary was accessary to the murder of her son, and thirsting for that vengeance which it was natural for a mother to demand, had implored Elizabeth's justice, and solicited her, with many tears, in her own name and in her husband's, to bring the Scottish Queen to a trial for that crime. The parent of that unhappy Prince had a just right to prefer this accusation; nor could she, who was their nearest kinswoman, be condemned for listening to so equitable a demand. Besides, as the Scottish nobles openly accused Mary of the same crime, and pretended to be able to confirm their charge by sufficient proof, it would be no difficult matter to prevail on them to petition the Queen of England to take cognizance of their proceedings against their sovereign; and it was the opinion of the English council, that it would be reasonable to comply with the request. At the same time, the obsolete claim of the superiority of England over Scotland began to be talked of; and, on that account, it was pretended that the decision of the contest between Mary and her subjects belonged of right to Elizabeth. But, though Elizabeth revolved all these expedients in her mind, and kept them in reserve to be made use of as occasion might require, she wished that the inquiry into Mary's conduct should appear to be undertaken purely in compliance with her own demand, and in order to vindicate her innocence; and so long as that appearance could be preserved, none of the other expedients were to be employed.

When Mary consented to submit her cause to Elizabeth, she was far from suspecting that any bad consequences could follow, or that any dangerous pretensions could be founded on her offer. She expected that Elizabeth herself would receive and examine her defences. She meant to consider her as an equal, for whose satisfaction she was willing to explain any part of her conduct that was liable to censure, not to acknowledge her as a superior, before whom she was bound to plead her cause. But Elizabeth put a very different sense on Mary's offer. She considered herself as chosen to be judge in the controversy between the Scottish Queen and her subjects, and began to act in that capacity. She proposed to appoint commissioners to hear the pleadings of both parties, and wrote to the Regent of Scotland to empower proper persons to appear before them in his name, and to produce what he could alledge in vindication of his proceedings against his sovereign.

Mary had hitherto relied with unaccountable credulity on Elizabeth's professions of regard, and expected that so many kind speeches would at last be accompanied with some suitable actions. But this proposal entirely undeceived her. She plainly perceived the artifice of Elizabeth's conduct, and saw what a diminution it would be to her own honour to appear on a level with her rebellious subjects, and to stand together with them at the bar of a superior and a judge. She retracted the offer which she had made, and which had been perverted to a purpose so contrary to her intention. She demanded, with more earnestness than ever, to be admitted into Elizabeth's presence; and wrote to her [July 13], in a strain very different from what she had formerly used, and which fully discovers the grief and indignation that preyed on her heart. "In my present situation," says she, "I neither will nor can reply to the accusations of my subjects. I am ready, of my own accord, and out of friendship to you, to satisfy your scruples, and to vindicate my own conduct. My subjects are not my equals; nor will I, by submitting my cause to a judicial trial, acknowledge them to be so. I fled into your arms, as into those of my nearest relation and most perfect friend. I did you honour, as I imagined, in choosing you, preferably to any other Prince, to be the restorer of an injured Queen. Was it ever known that a Prince was blamed for hearing, in person, the complaints of those who appealed to his justice, against the false accusations of their enemies? You admitted into your presence my bastard brother, who had been guilty of rebellion; and you deny me that honour! God forbid that I should be the occasion of bringing any stain upon your reputation! I expected that your manner of treating me would have added lustre to it. Suffer me either to implore the aid of other Princes, whose delicacy on this head will be less, and their resentment of my wrongs greater; or let me receive from your hands that assistance which it becomes you, more than any other Prince, to grant; and, by that benefit, bind me to yourself in the indissoluble ties of gratitude."

This letter somewhat disconcerted Elizabeth's plan, but did not divert her from the prosecution of it. She laid the matter before the privy council [June 20], and it was there determined, notwithstanding the entreaties and remonstrances of the Scottish Queen, to go on with the inquiry into her conduct; and, until that were finished, it was agreed that Elizabeth could not, consistently with her own honour, or with the safety of her government, either give her the assistance which she demanded, or permit her to retire out of the kingdom. Lest she should have an opportunity of escaping, while she resided so near Scotland, it was thought advisable to remove her to some place at a greater distance from the borders.

While the English court was occupied in these deliberations, the Regent did not neglect to improve the victory at Langside. That event was of the utmost importance to him. It not only drove the Queen herself out of the kingdom, but left her adherents dispersed, and without a leader, at his mercy. He seemed resolved, at first, to proceed against them with the utmost rigour. Six persons of some distinction, who had been taken prisoners in the battle, were tried, and condemned to death, as rebels against the King's government. They were led to the place of execution, but, by the powerful intercession of Knox, they obtained a pardon. Hamilton of Bothwelhaugh was one of the number, who lived to give both the Regent and Knox reason to repent of this commendable act of lenity.

Soon after the Regent marched with an army, consisting of four thousand horse and one thousand foot, towards the west borders. The nobles in this part of the kingdom were all the Queen's adherents; but, as they had no force sufficient to obstruct his progress, he must either have obliged them to submit to the King, or would have laid waste their lands with fire and sword. But Elizabeth, whose interest it was to keep Scotland in confusion, by preserving the balance between the two parties, and who was endeavouring to soothe the Scottish Queen by gentle treatment, interposed at her desire. After keeping the field two weeks, the Regent, in compliance to the English ambassador, dismissed his forces; and an expedition, which might have proved fatal to his opponents, ended with a few acts of severity.

The resolution of the English privy council, with regard to Mary's person, was soon carried into execution; and, without regarding her remonstrances or complaints, she was conducted to Bolton, a castle of Lord Scrope's, on the borders of Yorkshire* [July 13]. In this place her correspondence with her friends in Scotland became more difficult, and any prospect of making her escape was entirely cut off. She now felt herself to be completely in Elizabeth's power, and though treated as yet with the respect due to a Queen, her real condition was that of a prisoner. Mary knew what it was to be deprived of liberty, and dreaded it as the worst of all evils. While the remembrance of her late imprisonment was still lively, and the terror of a new one filled her mind, Elizabeth thought it a proper juncture to renew her former proposition [July 28], that she would suffer the Regent and his adherents to be called into England, and consent to their being heard in defence of their own conduct. She declared it to be far from her intention to claim any right of judging between Mary and her subjects, or of degrading her so far as to require that she should answer to their accusations. On the contrary, Murray and his associates were summoned to appear, in order to justify their conduct in treating their sovereign so harshly, and to vindicate themselves from those crimes with which she had charged them. On her part, Elizabeth promised, whatever should

* See Appendix, No. XXV.

be the issue of this inquiry, to employ all her power and influence towards replacing Mary on her throne, under a few limitations by no means unreasonable. Mary, deceived by this seeming attention to her dignity as a Queen, soothed, on one hand, by a promise more flattering than any which she had hitherto received from Elizabeth, and urged, on the other, by the feelings which were natural on being conducted into a more interior part of England, and kept there in more rigorous confinement, complied at length with what Elizabeth required, and promised to send commissioners to the conferences appointed to be held at York.

In order to persuade Elizabeth that she desired nothing so much as to render the union between them as close as possible, she showed a disposition to relax somewhat in one point; with regard to which, during all her past and subsequent misfortunes, she was uniformly inflexible. She expressed a great veneration for the liturgy of the the church of England; she was often present at religious worship, according to the rites of the reformed church: made choice of a Protestant clergyman to be her chaplain; heard him preach against the errors of popery with attention and seeming pleasure; and discovered all the symptoms of an approaching conversion.* Such was Mary's known and bigoted attachment to the popish religion that it is impossible to believe her sincere in this part of her conduct; nor can any thing mark more strongly the wretchedness of her condition, and the excess of her fears, than that they betrayed her into dissimulation, in a matter concerning which her sentiments were, at all other times, scrupulously delicate.

At this time the Regent called a parliament [Aug. 18], in order to proceed to the forfeiture of those who refused to acknowledge the King's authority. The Queen's adherents were alarmed, and Argyll and Huntly, whom Mary had appointed her lieutenants, the one in the south and the other in the north of Scotland, began to assemble forces to obstruct this meeting. Compassion for the Queen, and envy at those who governed in the King's name, had added so much strength to the party that the Regent would have found it difficult to withstand its efforts. But as Mary had submitted her cause to Elizabeth, she could not refuse, at her desire, to command her friends to lay down their arms and wait patiently until matters were brought to a decision in England. By procuring this cessation of arms, Elizabeth afforded as seasonable relief to the Regent's faction, as she had formerly given to the Queen's.

The Regent, however, would not consent, even at Elizabeth's request, to put off the meeting of parliament.† But we may ascribe to her influence, as well as to the eloquence of Maitland, who laboured to prevent the one half of his countrymen from exterminating the other, any appearances of moderation which this Parliament discovered in its proceedings. The most violent opponents of the King's government were forfeited; the rest were allowed still to hope for favour.

No sooner did the Queen of Scots submit her cause to her rival, than Elizabeth required the Regent to send to York deputies pre-

* See Appendix, No XXVI.   † See Appendix, No XXVII.

perly instructed for vindicating his conduct, in presence of her commissioners. It was not without hesitation and anxiety that the Regent consented to this measure. His authority was already established in Scotland, and confirmed by Parliament. To suffer its validity now to be called in question, and subjected to a foreign jurisdiction, was extremely mortifying. To accuse his sovereign before strangers, the ancient enemies of the Scottish name, was an odious task. To fail in this accusation was dangerous; to succeed in it was disgraceful. But the strength of the adverse faction daily increased. He dreaded the interposition of the French King in its behalf. In his situation, and in a matter which Elizabeth had so much at heart, her commands were neither to be disputed nor disobeyed.*

The necessity of repairing in person to York added to the ignominy of the step which he was obliged to take. All his associates declined the office; they were unwilling to expose themselves to the odium and danger with which it was easy to foresee that the discharge of it would be attended, unless he himself consented to share these in common with them. [Sept. 18.] The Earl of Morton, Bothwell Bishop of Orkney, Pitcairn Commendator of Dumfermline, and Lord Lindsay, were joined with him in commission. Macgill of Rankeilor, and Balnaves of Hallhill, two eminent civilians, George Buchanan, Murray's faithful adherent, a man whose genius did honour to the age, Maitland, and several others, were appointed to attend them as assistants. Maitland owed this distinction to the Regent's fear, rather than to his affection. He had warmly remonstrated against this measure. He wished his country to continue in friendship with England, but not to become dependent on that nation. He was desirous of re-establishing the Queen in some degree of power, not inconsistent with that which the King possessed; and the Regent could not, with safety, leave behind him a man, whose views were so contrary to his own, and who, by his superior abilities, had acquired an influence in the nation, equal to that which others derived from the antiquity and power of their families.

Mary empowered Lesley Bishop of Ross, Lord Livingston, Lord Boyd, Lord Herries, Gavin Hamilton Commendator of Kilwilnning, Sir John Gordon of Lochnivar, and Sir James Cockburn of Stirling, to appear in her name.

Elizabeth nominated Thomas Howard Duke of Norfolk, Thomas Radcliff Earl of Sussex, and Sir Ralph Sadler, her commissioners to hear both parties.

The 4th of October was the day fixed for opening the *conference.* The great abilities of the deputies on both sides, the dignity of the judges before whom they were to appear, the high rank of the persons whose cause was to be heard, and the importance of the points in dispute, rendered the whole transaction no less illustrious than it was singular. The situation in which Elizabeth appeared on this occasion, strikes us with an air of magnificence. Her rival, an independent Queen, and the heir of an ancient race of monarchs,

* See Appendix, No. XXVIII.

was a prisoner in her hands, and appeared by her ambassadors, before her tribunal. The Regent of Scotland, who represented the majesty and possessed the authority of a King, stood in person at the bar. And the fate of a kingdom, whose power her ancestors had often dreaded, but could never subdue, was now at her disposal.

The views, however, with which the several parties consented to this conference, and the issue to which they expected to bring it, were extremely different.

Mary's chief object was the recovering her former authority.—This induced her to consent to a measure against which she had long struggled. Elizabeth's promises gave her ground for entertaining hopes of being restored to her kingdom ; in order to which she would willingly have made any concessions to the King's party; and the influence of the English Queen, under her present situation, might have led her to many more. The Regent aimed at nothing but securing Elizabeth's protection to his party, and seems not to have had the most distant thoughts of coming to any composition with Mary. Elizabeth's views were more various, and her schemes more intricate. She seemed to be full of concern for Mary's honour, and solicitous that she should wipe off the aspersions which blemished her character. This she pretended to be the intention of the conference ; amusing Mary, and eluding the solicitations of the French and Spanish ambassadors in her behalf, by repeated promises of assisting her, as soon as she could venture to do so without bringing disgrace upon herself. But under this veil of friendship and generosity, Elizabeth concealed sentiments of a different nature. She expected that the Regent would accuse Mary of being accessary to the murder of her husband. She encouraged him, as far as decency would permit, to take this desperate step.—And as this accusation might terminate in two different ways, she had concerted measures for her future conduct suitable to each of these. If the charge against Mary should appear to be well founded, she resolved to pronounce her unworthy of wearing a crown, and to declare that she would never burden her own conscience with the guilt of an action so detestable as the restoring her to her kingdom. If it should happen, that what her accusers alleged did not amount to a proof of guilt, but only of mal-administration, she determined to set on foot a treaty for restoring her, but on such conditions as would render her hereafter dependent, not only upon England, but upon her own subjects. As every step in the progress of the conference, as well as the final result of it, was in Elizabeth's own power, she would still be at liberty to choose which of these courses she should hold; or, if there appeared to be any danger or inconvenience in pursuing either of them, she might protract the whole cause by endless delays, and involve it in inextricable perplexity.

The conference, however, was opened with much solemnity. But the very first step discovered it to be Elizabeth's intention to inflame, rather than to extinguish, the dissensions and animosities among the Scots. No endeavours were used to reconcile the contending parties, or to mollify the fierceness of their hatred, by bringing the Queen to offer pardon for what was past, or her subjects to promise more dutiful obedience for the future. On the contrary, Mary's commissioners were permitted to prefer a complaint against the Regent and his party, containing an enumeration of their treasonable actions, of their seizing her person by force of arms, committing her to prison. compelling her to resign the crown, and making use of her son's name to colour their usurpation of the whole royal authority; and of all these enormities they required such speedy and effectual address as the injuries of one Queen demanded from the justice of another.

It was then expected that the Regent would have disclosed all the circumstances of that unnatural crime to which he pretended the Queen had been accessary, and would have produced evidence in support of his charge. But, far, from accusing Mary, the Regent did not even answer the complaints brought against himself. He discovered a reluctance at undertaking that office, and started many doubts and scruples, with regard to which he demanded to be resolved by Elizabeth herself. His reserve and hesitation were no less surprising to the greater part of the English commissioners than to his own associates. They knew that he could not vindicate his own conduct without charging the murder upon the Queen, and he had not hitherto shown any extraordinary delicacy on that head. An intrigue, however, had been secretly carried on, since his arrival at York, which explains this mystery.

The Duke of Norfolk was, at that time, the most powerful and most popular man in England. His wife was lately dead; and he began already to form a project, which he afterwards more openly avowed, of mounting the throne of Scotland by a marriage with the Queen of Scots. He saw the infamy which would be the consequence of a public accusation against Mary, and how prejudicial it might be to her pretensions to the English succession. In order to save her from this cruel mortification, he applied to Maitland, and expressed his astonishment at seeing a man of so much reputation for wisdom, concurring with the Regent in a measure so dishonourable to themselves, to their Queen, and to their country; submitting the public transactions of the nation to the judgment of foreigners; and publishing the ignominy and exposing the faults of their sovereign, which they were bound, in good policy, as well as in duty, to conceal and to cover. It was easy for Maitland, whose sentiments were the same with the Duke's, to vindicate his own conduct. He assured him he had employed all his credit to dissuade his countrymen from this measure; and would still contribute, to the utmost of his power, to divert them from it. This encouraged Norfolk to communicate the matter to the Regent. He repeated and enforced the same arguments which he had used with Maitland. He warned him of the danger to which he must expose himself by such a violent action as the public accusation of his sovereign. Mary would never forgive a man who had endeavoured to fix such a brand of infamy on her character. If she ever recovered any degree of power, his destruction would be inevitable, and he would justly merit it at her hands. Nor would Elizabeth screen him from this, by a public approbation of his conduct. For,

whatever evidence of Mary's guilt he might produce, she was resolved to give no definitive sentence in the cause. Let him only
demand that the matter should be brought to a decision immediately after hearing the proof, and he would be fully convinced how
false and insidious her intentions were and, by consequence, how
improper it would be for him to appear as the accuser of his own
sovereign.   The candour which Norfolk seemed to discover in
these remonstrances, as well as the truth which they contained,
made a deep impression on the Regent.   He daily received the
strongest assurances of Mary's willingness to be reconciled to him,
if he abstained from accusing her of such an odious crime, together
with the denunciation of her irreconcilable hatred, if he acted a
contrary part.   All these considerations concurred in determining
him to alter his purpose, and to make trial of the expedient which
the Duke had suggested.

He demanded, therefore [Oct. 9], to be informed, before he proceeded further, whether the English commissioners were empowered
to declare the Queen guilty, by a judicial act ; whether they would
promise to pass sentence, without delay : whether the Queen should
be kept under such restraint, as to prevent her from disturbing
the government now established in Scotland ; and whether Elizabeth, if she approved of the proceedings of the King's party, would,
engage to protect it for the future?   The paper containing these
demands was signed by himself alone, without communicating it to
any of his attendants, except Maitland and Melvil.   But, lest so
many precautions should excite any suspicion of their proceedings,
from some consciousness of defect in the evidence which he had to
produce against his sovereign, Murray empowered Lethington,
Macgill, and Buchanan, to wait upon the Duke of Norfolk, the
Earl of Sussex, and Sir Ralph Sadler, and to lay before them, not
in their public characters as commissioners, but as private persons,
Mary's letters to Bothwell, her sonnets, and all the other papers
upon which was founded the charge of her being accessary to the
murder of the King, and to declare that this confidential communication was made to them, with a view to learn whether the
Queen of England would consider this evidence as sufficient to establish the truth of the accusation.   Nothing could be more natural than the Regent's solicitude to know on what footing he
stood.   To have ventured on a step so uncommon and dangerous,
as the accusing his sovereign, without previously ascertaining that
he might take it with safety, would have been unpardonable imprudence.   But Elizabeth, who did not expect that he would have
moved any such difficulty, had not empowered her commissioners
to give him that satisfaction which he demanded.   It became necessary to transmit the articles to herself, and by the light in which
Norfolk placed them, it is easy to see that he wished that they
should make no slight impression on Elizabeth and her ministers.
"Think not the Scots," said he, "over-scrupulous or precise.   Let
us view their conduct as we would wish our own to be viewed in a
like situation.   The game they play is deep ; their estates, their
lives, their honour, are at stake.   It is now in their own power to

be reconciled to their Queen, or to offend her irrecoverably; and, in a matter of so much importance, the utmost degree of caution is not excessive."

While the English commissioners waited for fuller instructions with regard to the Regent's demands, he gave an answer to the complaint which had been offered in the name of the Scottish Queen. It was expressed in terms perfectly conformable to the system which he had at that time adopted. It contained no insinuation of the Queen's being accessary to the murder of her husband; the bitterness of style peculiar to the age was considerably abated; and though he pleaded, that the infamy of the marriage with Bothwell made it necessary to take arms in order to dissolve it; though Mary's attachment to a man so odious justified the keeping her for some time under restraint; yet nothing more was said on these subjects than was barely requisite in his own defence. The Queen's commissioners did not fail to reply. But while the article with respect to the murder remained untouched, these were only skirmishes at a distance, of no consequeunce towards ending the contest, and were little regarded by Elizabeth or her commissioners.

The conference had, hitherto, been conducted in a manner which disappointed Elizabeth's views, and produced none of those discoveries which she had expected. The distance between York and London, and the necessity of consulting her upon every difficulty which occurred, consumed much time. Norfolk's negociation with the Scottish Regent, however secretly carried on, was not, in all probability, unknown to a Princess so remarkable for her sagacity in penetrating the designs of her enemies, and seeing through their deepest schemes. Instead, therefore, of returning any answer to the Regent's demands, she resolved to remove the conference to Westminster, and to appoint new commissioners, in whom she could more absolutely confide. Both the Queen of Scots and the Regent were brought, without difficulty to approve of this resolution.

We often find Mary boasting of the superiority in argument obtained by her commissioners during the conference at York, and how, by the strength of their reasons, they confounded her adversaries, and silenced all their cavils. The dispute stood, at that time, on a footing which rendered her victory not only apparent, but easy. Her participation of the guilt of the King's murder was the circumstance upon which her subjects must have rested, as a justification of their violent proceedings against her; and, while they industriously avoided mentioning that, her cause gained as much as that of her adversaries lost by suppressing this capital argument.

Elizabeth resolved that Mary should not enjoy the same advantage in the conference to be held at Westminster. She deliberated with the utmost anxiety, how she might overcome the Regent's scruples, and persuade him to accuse the Queen. She considered of the most proper method for bringing Mary's commissioners to answer such an accusation; and as she foresaw that the promises with which it was necessary to allure the Regent, and which it was impossible to conceal from the Scottish Queen, would naturally exasperate her to a great degree, she determined to guard her more narrowly than ever; and, though Lord Scrope had given her no reason to distrust his vigilance or fidelity, yet, because he was the Duke of Norfolk's brother-in-law, she thought it proper to remove the Queen as soon as possible to Tuthbury in Staffordshire, and commit her to the keeping of the Earl of Shrewsbury, to whom that castle belonged.

Mary began to suspect the design of this second conference; and notwithstanding the satisfaction she expressed at seeing her cause taken more immediately under the Queen's own eye, she framed her instructions to her commissioners in such a manner as to avoid being brought under the necessity of answering the accusation of her subjects, if they should be so desperate as to exhibit one against her. These suspicions were soon confirmed by a circumstance extremely mortifying. The Regent having arrived at London, in order to be present at the conference, was immediately admitted into Elizabeth's presence, and received by her, not only with respect, but with affection. This Mary justly considered as an open declaration of the Queen's partiality towards her adversaries. In the first emotions of her resentment [Nov. 22], she wrote to her commissioners, and commanded them to complain, in the presence of the English nobles, and before the ambassadors of foreign Princes, of the usuage she had hitherto met with, and the additional injuries which she had reason to apprehend. Her rebellious subjects were allowed access to the Queen, she was excluded from her presence; they enjoyed full liberty, she languished under a long imprisonment; they were encouraged to accuse her, in defending herself, she laboured under every disadvantage. For these reasons she once more renewed her demand, of being admitted into the Queen's presence; and, if that were denied, she instructed them to declare, that she recalled the consent which she had given to the conference at Westminster, and protested, that whatever was done there should be held to be null and invalid.

This, perhaps, was the most prudent resolution Mary could have taken. The pretences on which she declined the conference were plausible, and the juncture for offering them well chosen. But either the Queen's letter did not reach her commissioners in due time, or they suffered themselves to be deceived by Elizabeth's professions of regard for their mistress, and consented to the opening of the conference.

To the commissioners who had appeared in her name at York [Nov. 25], Elizabeth now added Sir Nicholas Bacon, keeper of the great seal, the Earls of Arundel and Leicester, Lord Clinton, and Sir William Cecil. The difficulties which obstructed the proceedings at York were quickly removed. A satisfying answer was given to the Regent's demands; nor was he so much disposed to hesitate, and raise objections, as formerly. His negociation with Norfolk had been discovered to Morton by some of Mary's attendants, and he had communicated it to Cecil. His personal safety, as well as the continuance of his power, depended on Elizabeth. By favouring Mary, she might at any time ruin him; and by a question which she artfully started, concerning the person who had a right, by the law of Scotland, to govern the kingdom during a minority, she let him see, that even without restoring the Queen, it was an easy matter for her to deprive him of the supreme direction of affairs. These considerations, which were powerfully seconded by most of his attendants, at length determined the Regent to produce his accusation against the Queen.

He endeavoured to lessen the obloquy with which he was sensible this action would be attended, by protesting that it was with the utmost reluctance he undertook this disagreeable task; that his party had long suffered their conduct to be misconstrued, and had borne the worst imputations in silence, rather than expose the crimes of their sovereign to the eyes of strangers; but that now the insolence and importunity of the adverse faction forced them to publish what they had hitherto, though with loss to themselves endeavoured to conceal. These pretexts are decent; and the considerations which he mentions had, during some time, a real influence upon the conduct of the party; but, since the meeting of Parliament held in December, they had discovered so little delicacy and reserve with respect to the Queen's actions, as renders it impossible to give credit to those studied professions. The Regent and his associates were drawn, it is plain, partly by the necessity of their affairs, and partly by Elizabeth's artifices, into a situation where no liberty of choice was left to them; and they were obliged either to acknowledge themselves to be guilty of rebellion, or to charge Mary with having been accessary to the commission of the murder.

The accusation itself was conceived in the strongest terms. Mary was charged, not only with having consented to the murder, but with being accessary to the contrivance and execution of it. Bothwell, it was pretended, had been screened from the pursuits of justice by her favour; and she had formed designs no less dangerous to the life of the young Prince, than subversive of the liberties and constitution of the kingdom. If any of these crimes should be denied, an offer was made to produce the most ample and undoubted evidence in confirmation of the charge.

At the next meeting of the commissioners [Nov. 29], the Earl of Lennox appeared before them; and after bewailing the tragical and unnatural murder of his son, he implored Elizabeth's justice against the Queen of Scots, whom he accused, upon oath, of being the author of that crime, and produced papers, which, as he pretended, would make good what he alleged. The entrance of a new actor on the stage so opportunely, and at a juncture so critical, can scarcely be imputed to chance. This contrivance was manifestly Elizabeth's, in order to increase, by this additional accusation, the infamy of the Scottish Queen.

Mary's commissioners expressed the utmost surprise and indignation at the Regent's presumption in loading the Queen with calumnies [Dec. 4], which, as they affirmed, she had so little merited. But, instead of attempting to vindicate her honour, by a reply to the charge, they had recourse to an article in their instructions, which they had formerly neglected to mention in its proper place. They demanded an audience of Elizabeth; and having renewed

L

their mistress's request of a personal interview, they protested, if that were denied her, against all the future proceedings of the commissioners. A protestation of this nature, offered just at the critical time when such a bold accusation had been preferred against Mary, and when the proofs in support of it were ready to be examined, gave reason to suspect that she dreaded the event of that examination. This suspicion received the strongest confirmation from another circumstance; Ross and Herries, before they were introduced to Elizabeth, in order to make this protestation, privately acquainted Leicester and Cecil, that as their mistress had from the beginning, discovered an inclination towards bringing the differences between herself and her subjects to an amicable accommodation, so she was still desirous, notwithstanding the Regent's audacious accusation, that they should be terminated in that manner.

Such moderation seems hardly to be compatible with the strong resentment which calumniated innocence naturally feels; or with that eagerness to vindicate itself which it always discovers. In Mary's situation, an offer so ill-timed must be considered as a confession of the weakness of her cause. The known character of her commissioners exempts them from the imputation of folly, or the ...., that the conduct of their mistress could not bear so strict a scrutiny as must be made into it, if they should reply to the accusation preferred by Murray against her, seems to be the most probable motive of this imprudent proposal, by which they endeavoured to avoid it.

It appeared in this light to Elizabeth [Dec. 4], and afforded her a pretence for rejecting it. She represented to Mary's commissioners, that in the present juncture, nothing could be so dishonourable to their mistress as an accommodation; and that the matter would seem to be huddled up in this manner, merely to suppress discoveries, and to hide her shame; nor was it possible that Mary could be admitted, with any decency, into her presence, while she lay under the infamy of such a public accusation.

Upon this repulse Mary's commissioners withdrew; and as they had declined answering, there seemed now to be no further reason for the Regent's producing the proofs in support of his charge. But without getting these into her hands, Elizabeth's schemes were incomplete; and her artifice for this purpose was as mean, but as successful, as any she had hitherto employed. She commanded her commissioners to testify her indignation and displeasure at the Regent's presumption in forgetting so far the duty of a subject, as to accuse his sovereign of such atrocious crimes. He, in order to regain the good opinion of such a powerful protectress, offered to show that his accusations were not malicious or ill-grounded. Then were produced and submitted to the inspection of the English commissioners, the acts of the Scottish Parliament in confirmation of the Regent's authority, and of the Queen's resignation ; the confession of the persons executed for the King's murder; and the fatal casket which contained the letters, sonnets, and contracts that have been so often mentioned.

As soon as Elizabeth got these into her possession, she laid them before the privy council [Dec. 14], to which she joined on this occasion several noblemen of the greatest eminence in her kingdom; in order that they might have an opportunity of considering the mode in which an inquiry of such public importance had been hitherto conducted, as well as the amount of the evidence now brought against a person who claimed a preferable right of succession to the English crown. In this respectable assembly all the proceedings in the conferences at York and Westminster were reviewed, and the evidence produced by the Regent of Scotland against his sovereign was examined with attention. In particular, the letters and other papers said to be written by the Queen of Scots, were completely compared, "for the manner of writing and orthography," with a variety of letters which Elizabeth had received at different times from the Scottish Queen; and, as the result of a most accurate collation, the members of the privy council, and noblemen conjoined with them, declared that no difference between these could be discovered. Elizabeth having established a fact so unfavourable to her rival, began to lay aside the expressions of friendship and respect which she had hitherto used in all her letters to the Scottish Queen. She wrote to her now in such terms, as if the presumptions of her guilt had amounted almost to certainty; she blamed her for refusing to vindicate herself from an accusation which could not be left unanswered, without a manifest injury to her character, and plainly intimated, that unless that were done, no change would be made in her present situation. She hoped that such a discovery of her sentiments would intimidate Mary, who was hardly recovered from the shock of the Regent's attack on her reputation, and force her to confirm her resignation of the crown, to ratify Murray's authority as Regent, and to consent that both herself and her son should reside in England, under English protection. This scheme Elizabeth had much at heart; she proposed it both to Mary and to her commissioners, and neglected no argument or artifice that could possibly recommend it. Mary saw how fatal this would prove to her reputation, to her pretensions, and even to her personal safety. She rejected it without hesitation. "Death," said she, "is less dreadful than such an ignominious step. Rather than give away, with my own hands, the crown which descended to me from my ancestor, I will part with my life; but the last words that I utter, shall be those of a Queen of Scotland."[*]

At the same time she seems to have been sensible how open her reputation lay to censure, while she suffered such a public accusation to remain unanswered; and though the conference was now dissolved, she empowered her commissioners to present a reply to the allegations of her enemies, in which she denied in the strongest terms the crimes imputed to her; and recriminated upon the Regent and his party, by accusing them of having devised and executed the murder of the king. [Dec. 24.] The Regent and his associates asserted their innocence with great warmth. Mary continued to insist on a personal interview, a condition which she knew

* See Appendix, No. XXX.

would never be granted. Elizabeth urged her to vindicate her own honour. But it is evident from the delays, the evasions, and subterfuges, to which both Queens had recourse by turns, that Mary avoided, and Elizabeth did not desire to make, any further progress in the inquiry.

1569.] The Regent was now impatient to return into Scotland, where his adversaries were endeavouring, in his absence, to raise some commotions. Before he set out, [Feb. 2.] he was called into the privy council, to receive a final declaration of Elizabeth's sentiments. Cecil acquainted him, in her name, that, on one hand, nothing had been objected to his conduct, which she could reckon detrimental to his honour, or inconsistent with his duty; nor had he, on the other hand, produced any thing against his sovereign, on which she could found an unfavourable opinion of her actions; and, for this reason, she resolved to leave all the affairs of Scotland precisely in the same situation in which she had found them at the beginning of the conference. The Queen's commissioners were dismissed much in the same manner.

After the attention of both nations had been fixed so earnestly on this conference upwards of four months, such a conclusion of the whole appears, at first sight, trifling and ridiculous. Nothing, however, could be more favourable to Elizabeth's future schemes. Notwithstanding her seeming impartiality, she had no thoughts of continuing neuter; nor was she at any loss on whom to bestow her protection. Before the Regent left London, she supplied him with a considerable sum of money, and engaged to support the King's authority to the utmost of her power. Mary, by her own conduct, fortified this resolution. Enraged at the repeated instances of Elizabeth's artifice and deceit, which she had discovered during the progress of the conference, and despairing of ever obtaining any succour from her, she endeavoured to rouse her own adherents in Scotland to arms, by imputing such designs to Elizabeth and Murray, as could not fail to inspire every Scotchman with indignation. Murray, she pretended, had agreed to convey the Prince her son to England; to surrender to Elizabeth the places of greatest strength in the kingdom; and to acknowledge the dependence of the Scottish upon the English nation. In return for this, Murray was to be declared the lawful heir to the crown of Scotland; and, at the same time, the question with regard to the English succession was to be decided in favour of the Earl of Hartford, who had promised to marry one of Cecil's daughters. An account of these wild and chimerical projects was spread industriously among the Scots. Elizabeth, perceiving it was calculated of purpose to bring her government into disreputation, laboured to destroy its effects, by a counter proclamation, and became more disgusted than ever with the Scottish Queen.*

The Regent on his return, found the kingdom in the utmost tranquillity. But the rage of the Queen's adherents, which had been suspended in expectation that the conference in England would terminate to her advantage, was now ready to break out

* See Appendix, No. XXXI.

with all the violence of civil war. They were encouraged too by the appearance of a leader, whose high quality and pretensions entitled him to great authority in the nation. This was the Duke of Chatelherault, who had resided for some years in France, and was now sent over by that court with a small supply of money, in hopes that the presence of the first nobleman in the kingdom would strengthen the Queen's party. Elizabeth had detained him in England for some months, under various pretences, but was obliged at last to suffer him to proceed on his journey. Before his departure [Feb. 29], Mary invested him with the high dignity of her lieutenant-general in Scotland, together with the fantastic title of her adopted father.

The Regent did not give him time to form his party into any regular body. He assembled an army with his usual expedition, and marched to Glasgow. The followers of Argyll and Huntly, who composed the chief part of the Queen's faction, being seated in corners of the kingdom very distant from each other, and many of the Duke's dependants having been killed or taken in the battle of Langside, the spirit and strength of his adherents were totally broken, and an accommodation with the Regent was the only thing which could prevent the ruin of his estate and vassals. This was effected without difficulty, and on no unreasonable terms. The Duke promised to acknowledge the authority both of the King and of the Regent; and to claim no jurisdiction in consequence of the commission which he had received from the Queen. The Regent bound himself to repeal the act which had passed for attainting several of the Queen's adherents; to restore all who would submit to the King's government to the possession of their estates and honours; and to hold a convention, wherein all the differences between the two parties should be settled by mutual consent. The Duke gave hostages for his faithful performance of the treaty; and, in token of their sincerity, he and Lord Herries accompanied the Regent to Stirling, and visited the young King.

Argyll and Huntly refused to be included in this treaty. A secret negotiation was carrying on in England, in favour of the captive Queen, with so much success that her affairs began to wear a better aspect, and her return into her own kingdom seemed to be an event not very distant. The French King had lately obtained such advantages over the Hugonots, that the extinction of that party appeared to be inevitable; and France, by recovering domestic tranquillity, would be no longer prevented from protecting her friends in Britain. These circumstances not only influenced Argyll and Huntly, but made so deep an impression on the Duke, that he appeared to be wavering and irresolute, and plainly discovered that he wished to evade the accomplishment of the treaty. The Regent saw the danger of allowing the Duke to shake himself loose, in this manner, from his engagements; and instantly formed a resolution equally bold and politic. He commanded his guards to sieze Chatelherault in his own house in Edinburgh, whither he had come in order to attend the convention agreed upon; and, regardless either of his dignity as the first nobleman in the kingdom and next heir to the crown, or of the promises of personal security, on which he had relied, committed him and Lord Herries prisoners to the castle of Edinburgh. A blow so fatal and unexpected dispirited the party. Argyll submitted to the King's government, and made his peace with the Regent on very easy terms; and Huntly being left alone, was at last obliged to lay down his arms.

Soon after, Lord Boyd returned into Scotland, and brought letters to the Regent, both from the English and Scottish Queens. A convention was held at Perth, in order to consider them. Elizabeth's letter contained three different proposals with regard to Mary: that she should either be restored to the full possession of her former authority; or be admitted to reign jointly with the King her son; or at least be allowed to reside in Scotland in some decent retirement, without any share in the administration of government. These overtures were extorted by the importunity of Fenelon the French ambassador, and have some appearance of being favourable to the captive Queen. They were, however, perfectly suitable to Elizabeth's general system with regard to Scottish affairs. Among propositions so unequal and disproportionate, she easily saw where the choice would fall. The two former were rejected; and long delays must necessarily have intervened, and many difficulties have arisen, before every circumstance relative to the last could be finally adjusted.

Mary, in her letter, demanded that her marriage with Bothwell should be reviewed by the proper judges, and, if found invalid, should be dissolved by a legal sentence of divorce. This fatal marriage was the principal source of all the calamities she had endured for two years; a divorce was the only thing which could repair the injuries her reputation had suffered by that step. It was her interest to have proposed it early; and it is not easy to account for her long silence with respect to this point. Her particular motive for proposing it at this time began to be so well known, that the demand was rejected by the convention of estates. They imputed it not so much to any abhorrence of Bothwell, as to her eagerness to conclude a marriage with the Duke of Norfolk.

This marriage was the object of that secret negotiation in England which I have already mentioned. The fertile and projecting genius of Maitland first conceived this scheme. During the conference at York, he communicated it to the Duke himself, and to the Bishop of Ross. The former readily closed with a scheme so flattering to his ambition. The latter considered it as a probable device for restoring his mistress to liberty, and replacing her on her throne. Nor was Mary, with whom Norfolk held a correspondence by means of his sister Lady Scrope, averse from a measure, which would have restored her to her kingdom with so much splendour. The sudden removal of the conference from York to Westminster suspended, but did not break off, this intrigue. Maitland and Ross were still the Duke's prompters and his agents; and many letters and love-tokens were exchanged between him and the Queen of Scots.

But as he could not hope, that under an administration so vigilant as Elizabeth's such an intrigue could be kept long concealed, he attempted to deceive her by the appearance of openness and candour, an artifice which seldom fails of success. He mentioned to her the rumour that was spread of his marriage with the Scottish Queen; he complained of it as a groundless calumny; and disclaimed all thoughts of that kind, with many expressions full of contempt both for Mary's character and dominions. Jealous as Elizabeth was of every thing relative to the Queen of Scots, she seemed to have credited these professions. But, instead of discontinuing the negotiation, he renewed it with greater vigour, and admitted into it new associates. Among these was the Regent of Scotland. He had given great offence to Norfolk, by his public accusation of the Queen, in breach of the contract into which he had entered at York. He was then ready to return into Scotland. The influence of the Duke in the north of England was great. The Earls of Northumberland and Westmorland, the most powerful noblemen in that part of the kingdom, threatened to revenge upon the Regent the injuries which he had done his sovereign. Murray, in order to secure a safe return into Scotland, addressed himself to Norfolk; and after some apology for his past conduct, he insinuated that the Duke's scheme of marrying the Queen his sister was no less acceptable to him than beneficial to both kingdoms, and that he would concur with the utmost ardour in promoting so desirable an event. Norfolk heard him with the credulity natural to those who are passionately bent upon any design. He wrote to the two Earls to desist from any hostile attempt against Murray, and to that he owed his passage through the northern counties without disturbance.

Encouraged by his success in gaining the Regent, he next attempted to draw the English nobles to approve his design. The nation began to despair of Elizabeth's marrying. Her jealousy kept the question with regard to the right of succession undecided. The memory of the civil wars which had desolated England for more than a century, on account of the disputed titles of the houses of York and Lancaster, was still recent. Almost all the ancient nobility had perished, and the nation itself had been brought to the brink of destruction in that unhappy contest. The Scottish Queen, though her right of succession was generally held to be undoubted, might meet with formidable competitors. She might marry a foreign and a Popish Prince, and bring both liberty and religion into danger. But, by marrying her to an Englishman, a zealous Protestant, the most powerful and the most universally beloved of all the nobility, an effectual remedy seemed to be provided against all these evils. The greater part of the Peers, either directly or tacitly, approved of it, as a salutary project. The Earls of Arundel, Pembroke, Leicester, and Lord Lumley, subscribed a letter to the Scottish Queen, written with Leicester's hand, in which they warmly recommended the match, but insisted, by way of preliminary, on Mary's promise, that she should attempt nothing, in consequence of her pretensions to the English crown, prejudical to Elizabeth, or to her posterity: that she should consent to a league, offensive and defensive, between the two kingdoms; that she should confirm the present establishment of religion in Scotland, and receive into favour such of her subjects as had appeared in arms against her. Upon her agreeing to the marriage and ratifying these articles, they engaged that the English nobles would not only concur in restoring her immediately to her own throne, but in securing to her that of England in reversion. Mary readily consented to all these proposals, except the second, with regard to which she demanded some time for consulting her ancient ally the French King.

The whole of this negotiation was industriously concealed from Elizabeth. Her jealousy of the Scottish Queen was well known, nor could it be expected that she would willingly come into a measure which tended so visibly to save the reputation and to increase the power of her rival. But, in a matter of so much consequence to the nation, the taking a few steps without her knowledge could hardly be reckoned criminal; and while every person concerned, even Mary and Norfolk themselves, declared, that nothing should be concluded without obtaining her consent, the duty and allegiance of subjects seemed to be fully preserved. The greater part of the nobles regarded the matter in this light. Those who conducted the intrigue had further and more dangerous views. They saw the advantage which Mary would obtain by this treaty, to be present and certain; and the execution of the promises which she came under, to be distant and uncertain. They had early communicated their scheme to the Kings of France and Spain, and obtained their approbation. A treaty concerning which they consulted foreign Princes, while they concealed it from their own sovereign, could not be deemed innocent. They hoped, however, that the union of such a number of the chief persons in the kingom would render it necessary for Elizabeth to comply; they flattered themselves that a combination so strong would be altogether irresistible; and such was their confidence of success, that when a plan was concerted in the north of England for rescuing Mary out of the hands of her keepers, Norfolk, who was afraid that if she recovered her liberty her sentiments in his favour might change, used all his interest to dissuade the conspirators from attempting it.

In this situation did the affair remain, when Lord Boyd arrived from England; and besides the letters which he produced publicly, brought others in ciphers from Norfolk and Throkmorton, to the Regent, and to Maitland. These were full of the most sanguine hopes. All the nobles of England concurred, said they, in favouring the design.—Every preliminary was adjusted; nor was it possible that a scheme so deeply laid, conducted with so much art, and supported both by power and by numbers, could miscarry, or be defeated in the execution. Nothing now was wanting but the concluding ceremony. It depended on the Regent to hasten that, by procuring a sentence of divorce, which would remove the only obstacle that stood in the way. This was expected of him, in consequence of his promise to Norfolk; and if he regarded either his interest or his fame, or even his safety, he would not fail to fulfil these engagements*.

See Appendix, No. XXXII.

But the Regent was now in very different circumstances from those which had formerly induced him to affect an approbation of Norfolk's schemes. He saw that the downfall of his own power must be the first consequence of the Duke's success; and if the Queen, who considered him as the chief author of all her misfortunes, should recover her ancient authority, he could never expect favour, nor scarce hope for impunity. No wonder he declined a step so fatal to himself, and which would have established the grandeur of another on the ruins of his own. This refusal occasioned a delay. But, as every other circumstance was settled, the Bishop of Ross, in the name of his mistress, and the Duke, in person, declared, in presence of the French ambassador, their mutual consent to the marriage, and a contract to this purpose was signed, and intrusted to the keeping of the ambassador.

The intrigue was now in so many hands, that it could not long remain a secret. It began to be whispered at court; and Elizabeth calling the Duke into her presence [Aug. 13], expressed the utmost indignation at his conduct, and charged him to lay aside all thoughts of prosecuting such a dangerous design. Soon after Leicester, who perhaps had countenanced the project with no other intention, revealed all the circumstances of it to the Queen. Pembroke, Arundel, Lumley, and Throkmorton were confined and examined. Mary was watched more narrowly than ever; and Hastings, Earl of Huntingdon, who pretended to dispute with the Scottish Queen her right to the succession, being joined in commission with Shrewsbury, rendered her imprisonment more intolerable by the excess of his vigilance and rigour. The Scottish Regent, threatened with Elizabeth's displeasure, meanly betrayed the Duke; put his letters into her hands, and furnished all the intelligence in his power*. The Duke himself retired first to Howard House, and then, in contempt of the summons to appear before the privy council, fled to his seat in Norfolk. Intimidated by the imprisonment of his associates; coldly received by his friends in that county; unprepared for a rebellion; and unwilling perhaps to rebel; he hesitated for some days, and at last obeyed a second call, and repaired to Windsor [Oct. 3]. He was first kept as a prisoner in a private house, and then sent to the Tower. After being confined there upwards of nine months, he was released upon his humble submission to Elizabeth, giving her a promise, on his allegiance, to hold no further correspondence with the Queen of Scots. During the progress of Norfolk's negotiations, the Queen's partisans in Scotland, who made no doubt of their issuing in her restoration to the throne, with an increase of authority, were wonderfully elevated. Maitland was the soul of that party, and the person whose activity and ability the Regent chiefly dreaded. He had laid the plan of that intrigue which had kindled such combustion in England. He continued to foment the spirit of disaffection in Scotland, and had seduced from the Regent Lord Home, Kirkaldy, and several of his former associates. While he enjoyed liberty, the Regent could not reckon

* See Appendix, No. XXXIII.

his own power secure. For this reason, having by an artificeallured Maitland to Stirling, he employed Captain Crawford, one of his creatures, to accuse him of being accessary to the murder of the King; and under that pretence he was arrested, and carried as a prisoner to Edinburgh. He would soon have been brought to trial, but was saved by the friendship of Kirkaldy, governor of the castle, who, by pretending a warrant for that purpose from the Regent, got him out of the hands of the person to whose care he was committed, and conducted him into the castle, which from that time was entirely under Maitland's command. The loss of a place of so much importance, and the defection of a man so eminent for military skill as Kirkaldy, brought the Regent into some disreputation, for which, however, the success of his ally Elizabeth, about this time, abundantly compensated.

The intrigue carried on for restoring the Scottish Queen to liberty having been discovered and disappointed, an attempt was made to the same purpose by force of arms but the issue of it was not more fortunate. The Earls of Northumberland and Westmorland, though little distinguished by their personal abilities, were two of the most ancient and powerful of the English peers. Their estates in the northern counties were great, and they possessed that influence over the inhabitants, which was hereditary in the popular and martial families of Percy and of Nevil. They were both attached to the Popish religion, and discontented with the court, where new men and a new system prevailed. Ever since Mary's arrival in England, they had warmly espoused her interest; and zeal for Popery, opposition to the court, and commiseration of her sufferings, had engaged them in different plots for her relief. Notwithstanding the vigilance of her keeper, they held a close correspondence with her, and communicated to her all their designs. They were privy to Norfolk's schemes; but the caution with which he preceeded did not suit their ardour and impetuosity. The liberty of the Scottish Queen was not their sole object. They aimed at bringing about a change in the religion, and a revolution in the government, of the kingdom. For this reason they solicited the aid of the King of Spain, the avowed and zealous patron of Popery in that age. Nothing could be more delightful to the restless spirit of Philip, or more necessary towards facilitating his schemes in the Netherlands than the involving England in the confusion and miseries of a civil war. The Duke of Alva, by his direction, encouraged the two Earls, and promised, as soon as they either took the field with their forces, or surprised any place of strength, or rescued the Queen of Scots, that he would supply them both with money and a strong body of troops. La Mothe, the governor of Dunkirk, in the disguise of a sailor, sounded the ports where it would be most proper to land. And Chiapini Vitelli, one of Alva's ablest officers, was dispatched into England, on pretence of settling some commercial difference between the two nations: but in reality that the rebels might be sure of a leader of experience as soon as they ventured to take arms.

The conduct of this negotiation occasioned many meetings and messages between the two Earls. Elizabeth was informed of these;

and though she suspected nothing of their real design, she concluded that they were among the number of Norfolk's confidants.
They were summoned, for this reason, to repair to court. Conscious
of guilt, and afraid of discovery, they delayed giving obedience. A
second and more peremptory order was issued [Nov. 9]. This they
could not decline, without shaking off their allegiance; and, as no
time was left for deliberation, they instantly erected their standard
against their sovereign. The re-establishing the Catholic religion,
the settling the order of succession to the crown, the defence of the
ancient nobility, were the motives which they alleged to justify
their rebellion. Many of the lower people flocked to them with
such arms as they could procure; and, had the capacity of their
leaders been in any degree equal to the enterprise, it must have
soon grown to be extremely formidable. Elizabeth acted with prudence and vigour, and was served by her subjects with fidelity and
ardour. On the first rumour of an insurrection, Mary was removed
to Coventry, a place of strength, which could not be taken without
a regular siege; a detachment of the rebels, which was sent to rescue her, returned without success. Troops were assembled in different parts of the kingdom; as they advanced the malcontents retired. In their retreat their numbers dwindled away, and their
spirits sank. Despair and uncertainty whither to direct their flight,
kept together for some time a small body of them among the mountains of Northumberland; but they were at length obliged to disperse, and the chiefs took refuge among the Scottish borderers
[Dec. 21]. The two Earls, together with the Countess of Northumberland, wandering for some days in the wastes of Liddisdale, were
plundered by the banditti, exposed to the rigour of the season, and
left destitute of the necessaries of life. Westmorland was concealed
by Scott of Buccleugh and Ker of Ferniherst, and afterwards conveyed into the Netherlands. Northumberland was seized by the
Regent, who had marched with some troops towards the borders,
to prevent any impression the rebels might make on those mutinous provinces.

Amidst so many surprising events, the affairs of the church, for
two years, have almost escaped our notice. Its general assemblies
were held regularly; but no business of much importance employed
their attention. As the number of the Protestant clergy daily increased, the deficiency of the funds set apart for their subsistence
became greater, and was more sensibly felt. Many efforts were
made towards recovering the ancient patrimony of the church, or
at least as much of it as was possessed by the Popish incumbents, a
a race of men who were now not only useless but burdensome to the
nation. But though the manner in which the Regent received the
addresses and complaints of the general assemblies, was very different from that to which they had been accustomed, no effectual
remedy was provided; and while they suffered intolerable oppression, and groaned under extreme poverty, fair words and liberal
promises were all they were able to obtain.

1570]. Elizabeth now began to be weary of keeping such a prisoner as the Queen of Scots. During the former year, the tranquillity of her government had been disturbed, first by a secret combi-

nation of some of her nobles, then by the rebellion of others; and she often declared, not without reason, that Mary was the *hidden cause* of both. Many of her own subjects favoured or pitied the captive Queen ; the Roman Catholic Princes on the Continent were warmly interested in her cause. The detaining her any longer in England, she foresaw, would be made the pretext or occasion of perpetual cabals and insurrections among the former; and might expose her to the hostile attempts of the latter. She resolved, therefore to give up Mary into the hands of the Regent, after stipulating with him, not only that her days should not be cut short, either by a judical sentence or by secret violence, but that she should be treated in a manner suited to her rank ; and, in order to secure his observance of this, she required that six of the chief noblemen in the kingdom should be sent into England as hostages. With respect to the safe custody of the Queen, she relied on Murray's vigilance, whose security, no less than her own, depended on preventing Mary from re-ascending the throne. The negotiation for this purpose was carried some length, when it was discovered by the vigilance of the Bishop of Ross, who, together with the French and Spanish ambassadors, remonstrated against the infamy of such an action, and represented the surrendering the Queen to her rebellious subjects to be the same thing as if Elizabeth should, by her own authority, condemn her to instant death. This procured a delay; and the murder of the Regent prevented the revival of that design.

Hamilton of Bothwellbaugh was the person who committed this barbarous action. He had been condemned to death soon after the battle of Langside, as I have already related, and owed his life to the Regent's clemency. But part of his estate had been bestowed upon one of the Regent's favourites, who seized his house, and turned out his wife naked, in a cold night, into the open fields, where, before next morning, she became furiously mad. This injury made a deeper impression upon him than the benefit which he had received, and from that moment he vowed to be revenged upon the Regent. Party-rage strengthened and inflamed his private resentment. His kinsmen, the Hamiltons, applauded the enterprise. The maxims of that age justified the most desperate course which he could take to obtain vengeance. He followed the Regent for some time, and watched for an opportunity to strike the blow. He resolved at last to wait till his enemy should arrive at Linlithgow, through which he was to pass in his way from Stirling to Edinburgh. He took his stand in a wooden gallery, which had a window towards the street; spread a feather bed on the floor, to hinder the noise of his feet from being heard : hung up a black cloth behind him, that his shadow might not be observed from without ; and after all this preparation calmly expected the Regent's approach, who had lodged during the night in a part of the town not far distant. Some indistinct information of the danger which threatened him had been conveyed to the Regent, and he paid so much regard to it that he resolved to return by the same gate through which he had entered, and to fetch a compass round the town. But as the crowd about the gate was great, and he himself unacquainted with fear, he proceeded directly along the street ; and, the throng of the people obliging him to move very slowly, gave the assassin time to take so true an aim, that he shot him with a single bullet through the lower part of his belly, and killed the horse of a gentleman who rode on his other side. His followers instantly endeavoured to break into the house whence the blow had come, but they found the door strongly barricaded ; and before it could be forced open, Hamilton had mounted a fleet horse, which stood ready for him at a back passage, and was got far beyond their reach. The Regent died the same night of his wound.

There is no person in that age about whom historians have been more divided, or whose character has been drawn in such opposite colours. Personal intrepidity, military skill, sagacity, and vigour in the administration of civil affairs, are virtues which even his enemies allow him to have possessed in an eminent degree. His moral qualities are more dubious, and ought neither to be praised nor censured without great reserve, and many distinctions. In a fierce age he was capable of using victory with humanity, and of treating the vanquished with moderation. A patron of learning, which among martial nobles, was either unknown or despised. Zealous for religion, to a degree which distinguished him even at a time when professions of that kind were not uncommon. His confidence in his friends was extreme, and inferior only to his liberality towards them, which knew no bounds. A disinterested passion for the liberty of his country prompted him to oppose the pernicious system which the Princes of Lorrain had obliged the Queen-mother to pursue. On Mary's return into Scotland, he served her with a zeal and affection, to which he sacrificed the friendship of those who were most attached to his person. But, on the other hand, his ambition was immoderate ; and events happened that opened to him vast projects, which allured his enterprising genius, and led him to actions inconsistent with the duty of a subject. His treatment of the Queen, to whose bounty he was so much indebted, was unbrotherly and ungrateful. The dependence on Elizabeth, under which he brought Scotland, was disgraceful to the nation. He deceived and betrayed Norfolk with a baseness unworthy of a man of honour. His elevation to such unexpected dignity inspired him with new passions, with haughtiness and reserve ; and instead of his natural manner, which was blunt and open, he affected the arts of dissimulation and refinement. Fond, towards the end of his life, of flattery, and impatient of advice, his creatures, by soothing his vanity, led him astray, while his ancient friends stood at a distance, and predicted his approaching fall. But, amidst the turbulence and confusion of that factious period, he dispensed justice with so much impartiality, he repressed the licentious borderers with so much courage, and established such uncommon order and tranquillity in the country, that his administration was extremely popular, and he was long and affectionately remembered among the commons, by the name of the *Good Regent.*

BOOK VI.

1570.

THE unexpected blow, by which the Regent was cut off, struck the King's party with the utmost consternation. Elizabeth bewailed his death as the most fatal disaster which could have befallen her kingdom; and was inconsolable to a degree that little suited her dignity. Mary's adherents exulted, as if now her restoration were not only certain, but near at hand. The infamy of the crime naturally fell on those who expressed such indecent joy at the commission of it; and, as the assassin made his escape on a horse which belonged to Lord Claud Hamilton, and fled directly to Hamilton, where he was received in triumph, it was concluded that the Regent had fallen a sacrifice to the resentment of the Queen's party, rather than to the revenge of a private man. On the day after the murder, Scott of Buccleugh, and Ker of Ferniherst, both zealous abettors of the Queen's cause, entered England in a hostile manner, and plundered and burned the country, the inhabitants of which expected no such outrage. If the Regent had been alive, they would scarce have ventured on such an irregular incursion, nor could it well have happened so soon after his death, unless they had been privy to the crime.

This was not the only irregularity to which the anarchy that followed the Regent's death gave occasion. During such general confusion, men hoped for universal impunity, and broke out into excesses of every kind. As it was impossible to restrain these without a settled form of government, a convention of the nobles was held, in order to deliberate concerning the election of a Regent [Feb. 12]. The Queen's adherents refused to be present at the meeting, and protested against its proceedings.—The King's own party was irresolute, and divided in opinion.—Maitland, whom Kirkaldy had set at liberty, and who obtained from the nobles then assembled a declaration acquitting him of the crime which had been laid to his charge, endeavoured to bring about a coalition of the two parties, by proposing to admit the Queen to the joint administration of government with her son. Elizabeth, adhering to her ancient system with regard to Scottish affairs, laboured, notwithstanding the solicitations of Mary's friends*, to multiply and to penetrate the factions which tore in pieces the kingdom. Randolph, whom she dispatched into Scotland on the first news of the Regent's death, and who was her usual agent for such services, found all parties so exasperated by mutual injuries, and so full of irreconcilable rancour, that it cost him little trouble to inflame their animosity. The convention broke up without coming to any

* See Appendix, No. XXXIV.

agreement; and a new meeting, to which the nobles of all parties were invited, was appointed on the 1st of May.

Meantime, Maitland, and Kirkaldy, who still continued to acknowledge the King's authority, were at the utmost pains to restore some degree of harmony among their countrymen. They procured for this purpose an amicable conference among the leaders of the two factions. But while the one demanded the restoration of the Queen, as the only thing which could re-establish the public tranquillity; while the other esteemed the King's authority to be so sacred that it was on no account to be called in question or impaired; and neither of them would recede in the least point from their opinions, they separated without any prospect of concord. Both were rendered more averse from reconcilement, by the hope of foreign aid. An envoy arrived from France with promises of powerful succour to the Queen's adherents; and, as the civil wars in that kingdom seemed to be on the point of terminating in peace, it was expected that Charles would soon be at liberty to fulfil what he promised. On the other hand, the Earl of Sussex was assembling a powerful army on the borders, and its operations could not fail of adding spirit and strength to the King's party.

Though the attempt towards a coalition of the factions proved ineffectual, it contributed somewhat to moderate or suspend their rage; but they soon began to act with their usual violence. Morton, the most vigilant and able leader on the King's side, solicited Elizabeth to interpose, without delay, for the safety of a party so devoted to her interest, and which stood so much in need of her assistance. The chiefs of the Queen's faction, assembling at Linlithgow [April 10], marched thence to Edinburgh; and Kirkaldy, who was both governor of the castle and provost of the town, prevailed on the citizens, though with some difficulty, to admit them within the gates. Together with Kirkaldy, the Earl of Athol and Maitland acceded almost openly to their party; and the Duke and Lord Herries, having recovered liberty by Kirkaldy's favour, resumed the places which they had formerly held in their councils. Encouraged by the acquisition of persons so illustrious by their birth, or so eminent for their abilities, they published a proclamation, declaring their intention to support the Queen's authority, and seemed resolved not to leave the city before the meeting of the approaching Convention, in which, by their numbers and influence, they did not doubt of securing a majority of voices on their side.

At the same time they had formed a design of kindling war between the two kindoms. If they could engage them in hostilities, and revive their ancient emulation and antipathy, they hoped not only to dissolve a confederacy of great advantage to the King's cause, but to reconcile their countrymen to the Queen, Elizabeth's natural and most dangerous rival. With this view they had immediately after the murder of the Regent, prompted Scott and Ker to commence hostilities, and had since instigated them to continue and extend their depredations. As Elizabeth foresaw, on the one hand, the dangerous consequences of rendering this a national quarrel; and resolved, on the other, not to suffer such an insult on her government to pass with impunity; she issued a proclamation, declaring that she imputed the outrages which had been committed on the borders not to the Scottish nation, but to a few desperate and ill-designing persons; that with the former she was resolved to maintain an inviolable friendship, whereas the duty which she owed to her own subjects obliged her to chastise the licentiousness of the latter. Sussex and Scrope accordingly entered Scotland, the one on the east, the other on the west borders, and laid waste the adjacent countries with fire and sword. Fame magnified the number and progress of their troops; and Mary's adherents, not thinking themselves safe in Edinburgh, the inhabitants whereof were ill-affected to their cause, retired to Linlithgow [April 28]. There, by a public proclamation, they asserted the Queen's authority, and forbad giving obedience to any but the Duke, or the Earls of Argyll and Huntly, whom she had constituted her lieutenants in the kingdom.

The nobles who continued faithful to the King, though considerably weakened by the defection of so many of their friends, assembled at Edinburgh on the day appointed. They issued a counter proclamation, declaring such as appeared for the Queen enemies of their country; and charging them with the murder both of the late King and of the Regent [May 1]. They could not, however, presume so much on their own strength as to venture either to elect a Regent, or to take the field against the Queen's party; but the assistance which they received from Elizabeth enabled them to do both. By her order Sir William Drury marched into Scotland with a thousand foot and three hundred horse; the King's adherents joined him with a considerable body of troops; and advanced towards Glasgow, where the adverse party had already begun hostilities by attacking the castle, they forced them to retire, plundering the neighbouring country, which belonged to the Hamiltons, and, after seizing some of their castles, and razing others, returned to Edinburgh.

Under Drury's protection the Earl of Lennox returned into Scotland. It was natural to commit the government of the kingdom to him during the minority of his grandson.

His illustrious birth, and alliance with the royal family of England as well as of Scotland, rendered him worthy of that honour. His resentment against Mary being implacable, and his estate lying in England, and his family residing there, Elizabeth considered him as a man who, both from inclination and from interest, would act in concert with her, and ardently wished that he might succeed Murray in the office of Regent. But, on many accounts, she did not think it prudent to discover her own sentiments, or to favour his pretensions too openly. The civil wars in France, which had been excited partly by real and partly by pretended zeal for religion, and carried on with a fierceness that did it real dishonour, appeared now to be on the point of coming to an issue; and after shedding the best blood and wasting the richest provinces in the kingdom, both parties desired peace with an ardour that facilitated the negotiations which were carrying on for that purpose. Charles IX. was known to be a passionate admirer of Mary's beauty. Nor could he in honour suffer a Queen of France, and the most ancient ally of his crown, to languish in her present cruel situation without attempting to procure her relief. He had hitherto been obliged to satisfy himself with remonstrating, by his ambassadors, against the indignity with which she had been treated. But if he were once at full liberty to pursue his inclinations, Elizabeth would have every thing to dread from the impetuosity of his temper and the power of his arms. It therefore became necessary for her to act with some reserve, and not to appear avowedly to countenance the choice of a Regent, in contempt of Mary's authority. The jealousy and prejudices of the Scots required no less management. Had she openly supported Lennox's claim; had she recommended him to the Convention, as the candidate of whom she approved; this might have roused the independent spirit of the nobles, and by too plain a discovery of her intention she might have defeated its success. For these reasons she hesitated long, and returned ambiguous answers to all the messages which she received from the King's party. A more explicit declaration of her sentiments was at last obtained, and an event of an extraordinary nature seems to have been the occasion of it. Pope Pius V. having issued a bull, whereby he excommunicated Elizabeth, deprived of her kingdom, and absolved her subjects from their oath of allegiance; Felton, an Englishman, had the boldness to affix it on the gates of the Bishop of London's palace. In former ages a Pope, moved by his own ambition, or pride, or bigotry, denounced this fatal sentence against the most powerful monarchs; but as the authority of the court of Rome was now less regarded, its proceedings were more cautious; and it was only when roused by some powerful Prince that the thunders of the church were ever heard. Elizabeth, therefore, imputed this step which the Pope had taken, to a combination of the Roman Catholic Princes against her, and suspected that some plot was formed in favour of the Scottish Queen. In that event she knew that the safety of her own kingdom depended on preserving her influence in Scotland; and in order to strengthen this she renewed her promises of protecting the King's adherents, encouraging them to proceed to the election of a Regent, and even ventured to point out the Earl of Lennox as the person who had the best title. That honour was accordingly conferred upon him in a Convention of the whole party held on the 12th of July[*].

The Regent's first care was to prevent the meeting of the Parliament, which the Queen's party had summoned to convene at Linlithgow. Having effected that, he marched against the Earl of Huntly, Mary's lieutenant in the north, and forced the garrison which he had placed in Brechin to surrender at discretion. Soon after, he made himself master of some other castles. Emboldened by this successful beginning of his administration, as well as by the appearance of a considerable army, with which the Earl of Sussex hovered on the borders, he deprived Maitland of his office of secretary, and proclaimed him, the Duke, Huntly, and other leaders of the Queen's party, traitors and enemies of their country.

In this desperate situation of their affairs, the Queen's adherents had recourse to the King of Spain,* with whom Mary had held a close correspondence ever since her confinement in England. They prevailed on the Duke of Alva to send two of his officers to take a view of the country, and to examine its coasts and harbours; and obtained from them a small supply of money and arms, which were sent to the Earl of Huntly. But this aid, so disproportionate to their exigencies, would have availed them little. They were indebted for their safety to a treaty which Elizabeth was carrying on, under colour of restoring the captive Queen to her throne. The first step in this negociation had been taken in the month of May; but hitherto little progress was made in it. The peace concluded between the Roman Catholics and Hugonots in France, and her apprehensions that Charles would interpose with vigour in behalf of his sister-in-law, quickened Elizabeth's motions. She affected to treat her prisoner with more indulgence, she listened more graciously to the solicitations of foreign ambassadors in her favour, and seemed fully determined to replace her on the throne of her ancestors. As a proof of her sincerity, she laboured to procure a cessation of arms between the two contending factions in Scotland. Lennox, elated with the good fortune which had hitherto attended his administration, and flattering himself with an easy triumph over enemies whose estates were wasted, and their forces dispirited, refused for some time to come into this measure. It was not safe for him, however, to dispute the will of his protectress. A cessation of hostilities during two months, to commence on the third of September, was agreed upon; and, being renewed from time to time, it continued till the first of April next year.

Soon after, Elizabeth dispatched Cecil and Sir Walter Mildmay to the Queen of Scots. The dignity of these ambassadors, the former her prime minister, the latter chancellor of the exchequer and one of her ablest counsellors, convinced all parties that the negotiation was serious, and the hour of Mary's liberty was now approaching. The propositions which they made to her were advantageous to Elizabeth, but such as a prince in Mary's situation had reason to expect. The ratification of the treaty of Edinburgh; the renouncing any pretensions to the English crown, during Elizabeth's own life, or that of her posterity; the adhering to the alliance between the two kingdoms; the pardoning her subjects who had taken arms against her; and her promising to hold no correspondence, and to countenance no enterprise, that might disturb Elizabeth's government; were among the chief articles. By way of security for the accomplishment of these, they demanded that some persons of rank should be given as hostages, that the Prince her son should reside in England, and that a few castles on the border should be put into Elizabeth's hands. To some of these propositions Mary consented; some she endeavoured to mitigate; and others she attempted to evade. In the mean time, she transmitted copies of them to the Pope, to the Kings of France and Spain, and to the Duke of Alva. She insinuated, that without some timely and vigorous interposition in her behalf, she would be obliged to accept

* See Appendix, No. XXXVI.

of these hard conditions, and to purchase liberty at any price. But the Pope was a distant and feeble ally, and by his great efforts at this time against the Turks, his treasury was entirely exhausted. Charles had already begun to meditate that conspiracy against the Hugonots, which marks his reign with such infamy; and it required much leisure and perfect tranquillity, to bring that execrable plan to maturity. Philip was employed in fitting out that fleet which acquired so much renown to the Christian arms, by the victory over the infidels at Lepanto; the Moors in Spain threatened an insurrection; and his subjects in the Netherlands, provoked by much oppression and many indignities, were breaking out into open rebellion. All of them, for these different reasons, advised Mary, without depending on their aid, to conclude the treaty on the best terms she could procure.

Mary accordingly consented to many of Elizabeth's demands, and discovered a facility of disposition which promised still further concessions. But no concession she could have made would have satisfied Elizabeth, who, in spite of her repeated professions of sincerity to foreign ambassadors, and notwithstanding the solemnity with which she carried on the treaty, had no other object in it than to amuse Mary's allies, and to gain time. After having so long treated a Queen, who fled to her for refuge, in so ungenerous a manner, she could not now dismiss her with safety. Under all the disadvantages of a rigorous confinement, Mary had found means to excite commotions in England which were extremely formidable. What desperate effects of her just resentment might be expected, if she were set at liberty, and recovered her former power? What engagements could bind her not to revenge the wrongs which she had suffered, nor to take advantage of the favourable conjunctures that might present themselves? Was it possible for her to give such security for her behaviour, in times to come, as might remove all suspicions and fears? And was there not good cause to conclude, that no future benefits could ever obliterate the memory of past injuries? It was thus Elizabeth reasoned; though she continued to act as if her views had been entirely different. She appointed seven of her privy counsellors to be commissioners for settling the articles of the treaty; and as Mary had already named the Bishops of Ross and Galloway, and Lord Livingston, for her ambassadors, she required the Regent to empower proper persons to appear in behalf of the King. The Earl of Morton, Pitcairn abbot of Dunfermling, and Sir James Macgil, were the persons chosen by the Regent. They prepared for their journey as slowly as Elizabeth herself could have wished [Feb. 19, 1571]. At length they arrived at London, and met the commissioners of the two Queens. Mary's ambassadors discovered the strongest inclination to comply with every thing that would remove the obstacles which stood in the way of their mistress's liberty. But when Morton and his associates were called upon to vindicate their conduct, and to explain the sentiments of their party, they began, in justification of their treatment of the Queen, to advance such maxims concerning the limited powers of Princes, and the natural right of subjects to resist and to control them, as were extremely shocking to Elizabeth, whose notions of regal prerogative, as has been formerly observed, were very exalted. With regard to the authority which the King now possessed, they declared they neither had, nor could possibly receive, instructions to consent to any treaty that tended to subvert or even to impair it in the least degree. Nothing could be more trifling and ridiculous than such a reply from the commissioners of the King of Scots to the Queen of England. His party depended absolutely on her protection; it was by persons devoted to her he had been seated on the throne, and to her power he owed the continuance of his reign. With the utmost ease she could have brought them to hold very different language; and whatever conditions she might have thought fit to subscribe, they would have had no other choice but to submit. This declaration, however, she affected to consider as an insuperable difficulty; and finding that there was no reason to dread any danger from the French King, who had not discovered that eagerness in support of Mary which was expected, the reply made by Morton [March 24], furnished her with a pretence for putting a stop to the negotiation, until the Regent should send ambassadors with more ample powers. Thus, after being amused for ten months with the hopes of liberty, the unhappy Queen of Scots remained under stricter custody than ever, and without any prospect of escaping from it; while those subjects who still adhered to her were exposed, without ally or protector, to the rage of enemies, whom their success in this negotiation rendered still more insolent.

On the day after the expiration of the truce, which had been observed with little exactness on either side, Captain Crawford of Jordan Hill, a gallant and enterprising officer, performed a service of great importance to the Regent, by surprising the castle of Dumbarton. This was the only fortified place in the kingdom of which the Queen had kept possession ever since the commencement of the civil wars. Its situation, on the top of a high and almost inaccessible rock which rises in the middle of a plain, rendered it extremely strong, and, in the opinion of that age, impregnable: as it commanded the river Clyde, it was of great consequence, and was deemed the most proper place in the kingdom for landing any foreign troops that might come to Mary's aid. The strength of the place rendered Lord Fleming, the governor, more secure than he ought to have been, considering its importance. A soldier who had served in the garrison, and had been disgusted by some ill usage, proposed the scheme to the Regent, endeavoured to demonstrate that it was practicable, and offered himself to go the foremost man on the enterprise. It was thought prudent to risk any danger for so great a prize. Scaling ladders, and whatever else might be necessary, were prepared with the utmost secrecy and dispatch. All the avenues to the castle were seized, that no intelligence of the design might reach the governor. Towards evening Crawford marched from Glasgow with a small but determined band. By midnight they arrived at the bottom of the rock. The moon was set, and the sky, which had hitherto been extremely clear, was covered with a thick fog. It was where the rock was highest that the assailants made their attempt, because in that place there were few sentinels and they hoped to find them least alert. The first ladder was scarcely fixed, when the weight and eagerness of those who mounted brought it to the ground. None of the assailants were hurt by the fall, and none of the garrison alarmed at the noise. Their guide and Crawford scrambled up the rock, and fastened the ladder to the roots of a tree which grew in a cleft. This place they all reached with the utmost difficulty, but were still at a great distance from the foot of the wall. Their ladder was made fast a second time; but in the middle of the ascent they met with an unforeseen difficulty. One of their companions was seized with some sudden fit, and clung, seemingly without life, to the ladder. All were at a stand. It was impossible to pass him. To tumble him headlong was cruel; and might occasion a discovery. But Crawford's presence of mind did not forsake him. He ordered the soldier to be bound fast to the ladder, that he might not fall when the fit was over; and turning the other side of the ladder, they mounted with ease over his belly. Day now began to break, and there still remained a high wall to scale; but after surmounting so many great difficulties, this was soon accomplished. A sentry observed the first man who appeared on the parapet, and had just time to give the alarm, before he was knocked on the head. The officers and soldiers of the garrison ran out naked, unarmed, and more solicitous about their own safety than capable of making resistance. The assailants rushed forwards, with repeated shouts and with the utmost fury; took possession of the magazine; seized the cannon, and turned them against their enemies. Lord Fleming got into a small boat, and fled all alone into Argyleshire. Crawford, in reward of his valour and good conduct, remained master of the castle; and as he did not lose a single man in the enterprise, he enjoyed his success with unmixed pleasure. Lady Fleming, Verac, the French envoy, and Hamilton, Archbishop of St. Andrew's, were the prisoners of greatest distinction.

Verac's character protected him from the usage which he merited by his activity in stirring up enemies against the King. The Regent treated the lady with great politeness and humanity. But a very different fate awaited the Archbishop; he was carried under a strong guard to Stirling; and as he had formerly been attainted by act of parliament, he was, without any formal trial, condemned to be hanged; and on the fourth day after he was taken, the sentence was executed. An attempt was made to convict him of being accessary to the murder both of the King and Regent, but these accusations were supported by no proof. Our historians observe, that he was the first Bishop in Scotland who died by the hands of the executioner. The high offices he had enjoyed, both in church and state, ought to have exempted him from a punishment inflicted only on the lowest criminals. But his zeal for the Queen, his abilities, and his profession, rendered him odious and formidable to the King's adherents. Lennox hated him as the person by whose councils the reputation and power of the house of Hamilton were supported. Party rage and personal enmity dictated that indecent sentence, for which some colour was sought by imputing to him such odious crimes.

The loss of Dumbarton, and the severe treatment of the Archbishop, perplexed no less than they enraged the Queen's party; and
hostilities were renewed with all the fierceness which disappointment and indignation can inspire. Kirkaldy, who, during the
truce, had taken care to increase the number of his garrison, and
to provide every thing necessary for his defence, issued a proclamation declaring Lennox's authority unlawful and usurped; commanded all who favoured his cause to leave the town within six
hours; seized the arms belonging to the citizens; planted a bat-
tery on the steeple of St. Giles's, repaired the walls, and fortified
the gates of the city; and, though the affections of the inhabitants
leaned a different way, held out the metropolis against the Regent.
The Duke, Huntly, Home, Herries, and other chiefs of that faction,
repaired to Edinburgh with their followers; and, having received a
small sum of money and some ammunition from France, formed no
contemptible army within the walls. On the other side, Morton
seized Leith and fortified it: and the Regent joined him with a
considerable body of men. While the armies lay so near each
other, daily skirmishes happened, and with various success. The
Queen's party was not strong enough to take the field against the
Regent, nor was his superiority so great as to undertake the siege
of the castle or of the town.

Some time before Edinburgh fell into the hands of his enemies,
the Regent had summoned a parliament to meet in that place. In
order to prevent any objection against the lawfulness of the meeting, the members obeyed the proclamation as exactly as possible
[May 14], and assembled in a house at the head of the Cannongate,
which, though without the walls, lies within the liberties of the
city. Kirkaldy exerted himself to the utmost to interrupt their
meeting; but they were so strongly guarded that all efforts were
vain. They passed an act attainting Maitland and a few others,
and then adjourned to the 28th of August.

The other party, in order that their proceedings might be countenanced by the same show of legal authority, held a meeting of parliament soon after. There was produced in this assembly a declaration by the Queen of the invalidity of that deed whereby she had
resigned the crown, and consented to the coronation of her son.
Conformable to this declaration, an act was passed pronouncing the
resignation to have been extorted by fear; to be null in itself, and
in all its consequences; and enjoining all good subjects to acknowledge the Queen alone to be their lawful sovereign, and to support
those who acted in her name. The present establishment of the
Protestant religion was confirmed by another statute; and, in imitation of the adverse party, a new meeting was appointed on the
26th of August.

Meanwhile all the miseries of civil war desolated the kingdom.
Fellow-citizens, friends, brothers took different sides, and ranged
themselves, under the standards of the contending factions. In every
county, and almost in every town and village, *King's men* and *Queen's
men* were names of distinction. Political hatred dissolved all natural
ties, and extinguished the reciprocal good will and confidence which
holds mankind together in society. Religious zeal mingled itself

with these civil distinctions, and contributed not a little to heighten and to inflame them.

The factions which divided the kingdom were, in appearance, only two; but in both these there were persons with views and principles so different from each other that they ought to be distinguished. With some, considerations of religion were predominant, and they either adhered to the Queen, because they hoped by her means to re-establish Popery, or they defended the King's authority, as the best support of the Protestant faith. Among these the opposition was violent and irreconcileable. Others were influenced by political motives only, or allured by views of interest: the Regent aimed at uniting these, and did not despair of gaining, by gentle arts, many of Mary's adherents to acknowledge the King's authority. Maitland and Kirkaldy had formed the same design of a coalition, but on such terms that the Queen might be restored to some share in the government, and the kingdom shake off its dependence upon England. Morton, the ablest, the most ambitious, and the most powerful man of the King's party, held a particular course; and, moving only as he was prompted by the court of England, thwarted every measure that tended towards a reconcilement of the factions; and as he served Elizabeth with much fidelity, he derived both power and credit from her avowed protection.

The time appointed by both parties for the meeting of their parliaments now approached. Only three peers and two bishops appeared in that which was held in the Queen's name at Edinburgh. But, contemptible as their numbers were, they passed an act for attainting upwards of two hundred of the adverse faction. The meeting in Stirling was numerous and splendid. The Regent had prevailed on the Earls of Argyll, Eglington, Cassils, and Lord Boyd, to acknowledge the King's authority. The three Earls were among the most powerful nobles in the kingdom, and had hitherto been zealous in the Queen's cause. Lord Boyd had been one of Mary's commissioners at York and Westminster, and since that time had been admitted into all her most secret councils. But, during that turbulent period, the conduct of individuals, as well as the principles of faction, varied so often, that the sense of honour, a chief preservative of consistence in character, was entirely lost; and, without any regard to decorum, men suddenly abandoned one party, and adopted all the violent passions of the other. The defection, however, of so many persons of distinction, not only weakened the Queen's party, but added reputation to her adversaries.

After the example of the parliament of Edinburgh, that at Stirling began with framing acts against the opposite faction. But in the midst of all the security, which confidence in their own number or distance from danger could inspire, they were awakened early in the morning of September the third by the shouts of the enemy in the heart of the town. In a moment the houses of every person of distinction were surrounded, and before they knew what to think of so strange an event, the Regent, the Earls of Argyll, Morton, Glencairn, Cassils, Eglington, Montrose, Buchan, the Lords Sempil, Cathcart, and Ogilvie, were all made prisoners, and mounted behind troopers, who were ready to carry them to Edinburgh.—

Kirkaldy was the author of this daring enterprise; and if he had not been induced, by the ill-timed solicitude of his friends about his safety, not to hazard his own person in conducting it, that day might have terminated the contest between the two factions, and have restored peace to this country. By his direction four hundred men, under the command of Huntly, Lord Claude Hamilton, and Scott of Buccleugh, set out for Edinburgh, and the better to conceal their design, marched towards the south. But they soon wheeled to the right, and, horses having been provided for the infantry, rode straight to Stirling. By four in the morning they arrived there ; not one sentry was posted on the walls, not a single man was awake about the place. They met with no resistance from any person whom they attempted to seize, except Morton. He, defending his house with obstinate valour, they were obliged to set it on fire, and he did not surrender till forced out of it by the flames. In performing this, some time was consumed ; and the private men, unaccustomed to regular discipline, left their colours, and began to rifle the houses and shops of the citizens. The noise and uproar in the town reached the castle. The Earl of Mar sallied out with thirty soldiers, and fired briskly upon the enemy, of whom almost none but the officers kept together in a body. The townsmen took arms to assist their governor ; a sudden panic struck the assailants ; some fled ; some surrendered themselves to their own prisoners ; and had not the borderers, who followed Scott, prevented a pursuit, by carrying off all the horses within the place, not a man would have escaped. If the Regent had not unfortunately been killed, the loss on the King's side would have been as inconsiderable as the alarm was great. *Think on the Archbishop of St. Andrew's.* was the word among the Queen's soldiers ; and Lennox fell a sacrifice to his memory. The officer to whom he surrendered, endeavouring to protect him, lost his own life in his defence. He was slain, according to the general opinion, by command of Lord Claude Hamilton. Kirkaldy had the glory of concerting this plan with great secrecy and prudence ; but Morton's fortunate obstinacy, and the want of discipline among his troops, deprived him of success, the only thing wanting to render this equal to the most applauded military enterprises of the kind.

As so many of the nobles were assembled, they proceeded without delay to the election of a Regent [Sept. 6]. Argyll, Morton, and Mar were candidates for the office. Mar was chosen by a majority of voices. Amidst all the fierce dissensions which had prevailed so long in Scotland, he had distinguished himself by his moderation, his humanity, and his disinterestedness. As his power was far inferior to Argyll's, and his abilities not so great as Morton's, he was, for these reasons, less formidable to the other nobles. His merit, too, in having so lately rescued the leaders of the party from imminent destruction, contributed not a little to his preferment.

While these things were carrying on in Scotland, the transactions in England were no less interesting to Mary, and still more fatal to her cause. The parliament of that kingdom, which met in April, passed an act, by which it was declared to be high treason to claim any right to the crown during the life of the Queen; to affirm that the title of any other person was better than hers, or to maintain that the parliament had not power to limit the order of succession. This remarkable statute was intended not only for the security of their own sovereign, but to curb the restless and intriguing spirit of the Scottish Queen and her adherents.

At this time a treaty of marriage between the Queen and the Duke of Anjou, the French King's brother, was well advanced.— Both courts seemed to desire it with equal ardour, and gave out, with the utmost confidence, that it could not fail of taking place. Neither of them, however, wished it success; and they encouraged it for no other end, but because it served to cover or to promote their particular designs.

The whole policy of Catherine of Medicis was bent towards the accomplishment of her detestable project for the destruction of the Hugouot chiefs; and by carrying on a negociation for the marriage of her son with a Princess who was justly esteemed the protectress of that party, by yielding some things in point of religion, and by discovering an indifference with regard to others, she hoped to amuse all the Protestants in Europe, and to lull asleep the jealousy even of the Hugonots themselves. Elizabeth flattered herself with reaping advantages of another kind. During the pendancy of the negociation, the French could not with decency give any open assistance to the Scottish Queen; if they conceived any hopes of success in the treaty of marriage, they would of course interest themselves but coldly in her concerns; Mary herself must be dejected at loosing an ally, whom she had hitherto reckoned her most powerful protector; and, by interrupting her correspondence with France, one source, at least, of the cabals and intrigues which disturbed the kingdom would be stopped. Both Queens succeeded in their schemes. Catherine's artifices imposed ,upon Elizabeth, and blinded the Hugonots. The French discovered the utmost indifference about the interest of the Scottish Queen; and Mary, considering that court as already united with her rival, turned for protection with more eagerness than ever towards the King of Spain. Philip, whose dark and thoughtful mind delighted in the mystery of intrigue, had held a secret correspondence with Mary for some time, by means of the Bishop of Ross, and had supplied both herself and her adherents in Scotland with small sums of money. Ridolphi, a Florentine gentleman, who resided at London under the character of a banker, and who acted privately as an agent for the Pope, was the person whom the bishop intrusted with his negotiation. Mary thought it necessary likewise to communicate the secret to the Duke of Norfolk, whom Elizabeth had lately restored to liberty, upon his solemn promise to have no further intercourse with the Queen of Scots. This promise, however, he regarded so little that he continued to keep a constant correspondence with the captive Queen; while she laboured to nourish his ambitious hopes, and to strengthen his amorous attachment by letters written in the fondest carressing strain. Some of these he must have received at the very time when he made that solemn promise of holding no further intercourse with her, in consequence of which

M

Elizabeth restored him to liberty. Mary, still considering him as her future husband, took no step in any matter of moment without his advice.

Ridolphi, in conference with Norfolk, omitted none of those arguments, and spared none of those promises, which are the usual incentives to rebellion. The Pope, he told him, had a great sum in readiness to bestow in so good a cause. The Duke of Alva had undertaken to land ten thousand men not far from London. The Catholics, to a man, would rise in arms. Many of the nobles were ripe for a revolt, and wanted only a leader. Half their nation had turned their eyes towards him, and called on him to revenge the unmerited injuries which he himself had suffered; and to rescue an unfortunate Queen, who offered him her hand and her crown as the reward of his success. Norfolk approved of the design, and though he refused to give Ridolphi any letter of credit, allowed him to use his name in negotiating with the Pope and Alva. The Bishop of Ross, who, from the violence of his temper, and impatience to procure relief for his mistress, was apt to run into rash and desperate designs, advised the Duke to assemble secretly a few of his followers, and at once to seize Elizabeth's person. But this the Duke rejected as a scheme equally wild and hazardous. Meanwhile, the English court had received some imperfect information of the plot, by intercepting one of Ridolphi's agents; and an accident happened, which brought to light all the circumstances of it. The Duke had employed Hickford to transmit to Lord Herries some money, which was to be distributed among Mary's friends in Scotland. A person not in the secret was intrusted with conveying it to the borders; and he, suspecting it from the weight to be gold, whereas he had been told that it was silver, carried it directly to the privy council. The Duke, his domestics, all and who were privy or could be suspected of being privy to the design, were taken into custody. Never did the accomplices in a conspiracy discover less firmness, or servants betray an indulgent master with greater baseness [Sep. 7]. Every one confessed the whole of what he knew. Hickford gave directions how to find the papers which he had hidden. The Duke himself, relying at first on the fidelity of his associates, and believing all dangerous papers to have been destroyed, confidently asserted his own innocence; but when their depositions and papers themselves were produced, astonished at their treachery, he acknowledged his guilt and implored the Queen's mercy. His offence was too heinous, and too often repeated, to obtain pardon; and Elizabeth thought it necessary to deter her subjects, by his punishment, from holding correspondence with the Queen of Scots or her emissaries. Being tried by his peers, he was found guilty of high treason, and, after several delays, suffered death for the crime.

The discovery of this conspiracy produced many effects extremely detrimental to Mary's interest. The Bishop of Ross, who appeared, by the confession of all concerned, to be the prime mover in every cabal against Elizabeth, was taken into custody, his papers searched, himself committed to the Tower, treated with the utmost rigour, threatened with capital punishment, and, after a long confinement, set at liberty on condition that he should leave the kingdom. Mary was not only deprived of a servant equally eminent for his zeal and his abilities, but was denied from that time the privilege of having an ambassador at the English court. The Spanish ambassador, whom the power and dignity of the Prince he represented exempted from such insults as Ross had suffered, was commanded to leave England. As there was now the clearest evidence that Mary, from resentment of the wrongs she had suffered, and impatience of the captivity in which she was held, would not scruple to engage in the most hostile and desperate enterprises against the established government and religion, she began to be regarded as a public enemy, and was kept under a stricter guard than formerly; the number of her domestics was abridged, and no person permitted to see her but in presence of her keepers.

At the same time, Elizabeth, foreseeing the storm which was gathering on the Continent against her kingdom, began to wish that tranquillity were restored in Scotland; and, irritated by Mary's late attempt against her government, she determined to act without disguise or ambiguity in favour of the King's party. This resolution she intimated to the leaders of both factions [Oct 23]. Mary, she told them, had held such a criminal correspondence with her avowed enemies, and had excited such dangerous conspiracies both against her crown and her life, that she would henceforth consider her as unworthy of protection, and would never consent to restore her to liberty, far less to replace her on her throne. She exhorted them, therefore, to unite in acknowledging the King's authority. She promised to procure, by her mediation, equitable terms for those who had hitherto opposed it. But if they still continued refractory, she threatened to employ her utmost power to compel them to submit*. Though this declaration did not produce an immediate effect; though hostilities continued in the neighbourhood of Edinburgh; though Huntly's brother, Sir Adam Gordon, by his bravery and good conduct, had routed the King's adherents in the North in many encounters; yet, such an explicit discovery of Elizabeth's sentiments contributed not a little to animate one party, and to depress the spirit and hopes of the other.

1572.] As Morton, who commanded the Regent's forces, lay at Leith, and Kirkaldy still held out the town and castle of Edinburgh, scarce a day passed without a skirmish; and while both avoided any decisive action, they harassed each other by attacking small parties, beating up quarters, and intercepting convoys. These operations, though little memorable in themselves, kept the passions of both factions in perpetual exercise and agitation, and wrought them up, at last, to a degree of fury which rendered them regardless not only of the laws of war, but of the principles of humanity. Nor was it in the field alone, and during the heat of combat, that this implacable rage appeared; both parties hanged the prisoners which they took, of whatever rank or quality, without mercy and without trial. Great numbers suffered in this shocking manner; the unhappy victims were led by fifties at a time to execution; and it was not till both sides had smarted severely that they discon-

* See Appendix, No. XXXVII.

tinued this barbarous practice, so reproachful to the character of the nation. Meanwhile, those in the town and castle, though they had received a supply of money from the duke of Alva, began to suffer for want of provisions. As Morton had destroyed all the mills in the neighbourhood of the city, and had planted small garrisons in all the houses of strength around it, scarcity daily increased. At last all the miseries of famine were felt, and they must have been soon reduced to such extremities as would have forced them to capitulate, if the English and French ambassador had not procured a suspension of hostilities between the two parties.

Though the negociations for a marriage between Elizabeth and the Duke of Anjou had been fruitless, both Charles and she were desirous of concluding a defensive alliance between the two crowns. He considered such a treaty not only as the best advice for blinding the Protestants, against whom the conspiracy was now almost ripe for execution ; but as a good precaution, likewise, against the dangerous consequences to which that atrocious measure might expose him. Elizabeth, who had hitherto reigned without a single ally, now saw her kingdom so threatened with intestine commotions, or exposed to invasions from abroad, that she was extremely solicitous to secure the aid of so powerful a neighbour. The difficulties arising from the situation of the Scottish Queen were the chief occasions of any delay. Charles demanded some terms of advantage for Mary and her party. Elizabeth refused to listen to any proposition of that kind. Her obstinacy overcame the faint efforts of the French Monarch. Mary's name was not so much as mentioned in the treaty ; and with regard to Scottish affairs, a short article was inserted, in general and ambiguous terms [April 11,] to this purpose : "That the parties contracting shall make no innovations in Scotland ; nor suffer any stranger to enter and foment the factions there ; but it shall be lawful for the Queen of England to chastise, by force of arms, those Scots who shall continue to harbour the English rebels now in Scotland." In consequence of this treaty, France and England affected to act in concert with regard to Scotland, and Le Croc and Sir William Drury appeared there in the name of their respective sovereigns. By their mediations, a truce for two months was agreed upon, and during that time conferences were to be held between the leaders of the opposite factions, in order to accommodate their differences, and restore peace to the kingdom. This truce afforded a seasonable interval of tranquillity to the Queen's adherents in the South; but in the North it proved fatal to her interest. Sir Adam Gordon had still maintained his reputation and superiority there. Several parties, under different officers, were sent against him. Some of them he attacked in the field ; against others he employed stratagem ; and as his courage and conduct were equal, none of his enterprises failed of success. He made war too with the humanity which became so gallant a man, and gained ground by that, no less than by the terror of his arms. If he had not been obliged by the truce to suspend his operations, he would in all probability have brought that part of the kingdom to submit entirely to the Queen's authority.

Notwithstanding Gordon's bravery and success, Mary's interest was on the decline, not only in her own kingdom, but among the English. Nothing could be more offensive to that nation, jealous of foreigners, and terrified at the prospect of the Spanish yoke, than her negotiations with the Duke of Alva. The parliament, which met in May, proceeded against her as the most dangerous enemy of the kingdom ; and, after a solemn conference between the Lords and Commons, both houses agreed in bringing in a bill to declare her guilty of high treason, and to deprive her of all right of succession to the crown. This *great cause*, as it was then called, occupied them during the whole session, and was carried on with much unanimity. Elizabeth, though she applauded their zeal and approved greatly of the course they were taking, was satisfied with showing Mary what she might expect from the resentment of the nation ; but as she did not yet think it time to proceed to the most violent extremity against her, she prorogued the parliament.

These severe proceedings of the English parliament were not more mortifying to Mary than the coldness and neglect of her allies the French. The Duke of Montmorency, indeed, who came over to ratify the league with Elizabeth, made a show of interesting himself in favour of the Scottish Queen ; but, instead of soliciting for her liberty, or her restoration to her throne, all that he demanded was a slight mitigation of the rigour of her imprisonment. Even this small request he urged with so little warmth or importunity that no regard was paid to it.

The alliance with France afforded Elizabeth much satisfaction, and she expected from it a great increase of security. She now turned her whole attention towards Scotland, where the animosities of the two factions were still so high, and so many interfering interests to be adjusted, than a general pacification seemed to be at a great distance. But while she laboured to bring them to some agreement, an event happened which filled a great part of Europe with astonishment and with horror. This was the massacre of Paris ; an attempt, to which there is no parallel in the history of mankind, either for the long train of craft and dissimulation with which it was contrived, or for the cruelty and barbarity with which it was carried into execution. By the most solemn promises of safety and of favour, the leaders of the Protestants were drawn to court ; and though doomed to destruction, they were received with caresses, loaded with honours, and treated, for seven months, with every possible mark of familiarity and of confidence. In the midst of their security [Aug. 24], the warrant for their destruction was issued by their sovereign, on whose word they had relied ; and, in obedience to it, their countrymen, their fellow citizens, and companions imbrued their hands in their blood. Ten thousand Protestants, without distinction of age, or sex, or condition, were murdered in Paris alone. The same barbarous orders were sent to other parts of the kingdom, and a like carnage ensued. This deed, which no Popish writer in the present age mentions without detestation, was at that time applauded in Spain ; and at Rome solemn thanksgivings were offered to God for its success. But among the Protestants it excited incredible horror ; a striking picture of which is drawn by the French ambassador at the court of England, in his account of his first audience after the massacre. " A gloomy sorrow," says he, " sat on every face; silence, as in the dead of night, reigned through all the chambers of the royal apartment ; the ladies and courtiers were ranged on each side, all clad in deep mourning, and as I passed through them, not one bestowed on me a civil look, or made the least return to my salutes."

But horror was not the only passion with which this event inspired the Protestants ; it filled them with fear. They considered it as the prelude to some greater blow, and believed, not without much probability, that all the Popish Princes had conspired the destruction of their sect. This opinion was of no small disservice to Mary's affairs in Scotland. Many of her adherents were Protestants ; and, though they wished her restoration, were not willing on that account, to sacrifice the faith which they professed. They dreaded her attachment to a religion which allowed its votaries to violate the most solemn engagements, and prompted them to perpetrate the most barbarous crimes. A general confederacy of the Protestants seemed to them the only thing that could uphold the Reformation against the league which was formed to overturn it. Nor could the present establishment of religion be long maintained in Britain, but by a strict union with Elizabeth, and by the concurrence of both nations in espousing the defence of it as a common cause.

Encouraged by this general disposition to place confidence in her, Elizabeth resumed a scheme which she had formed during the regency of the Earl of Murray, of sending Mary as a prisoner into Scotland. But her sentiments and situation were now very different from what they had been during her negotiation with Murray. Her animosity against the Queen of Scots was greatly augmented by recent experience, which taught her that she had inclination, as well as power, not only to disturb the tranquillity of her reign, but to wrest from her the crown ; the party in Scotland favourable to Mary was almost entirely broken; and there was no reason to dread any danger from France, which still continued to court her friendship. She aimed, accordingly, at something very different from that which she had in view three years before. Then she discovered a laudable solicitude, not only for the safety of Mary's life, but for securing to her treatment suited to her rank. Now she required, as an express condition, that immediately after Mary's arrival in in Scotland, she should be brought to public trial; and, having no doubt that sentence would be passed according to her deserts, she insisted that, for the good of both kingdoms, it should be executed without delay. No transaction, perhaps, in Elizabeth's reign, merits more severe censure. Eager to cut short the days of a rival, the object both of her hatred and dread, and no less anxious to avoid the blame to which such a deed of violence might expose her, she laboured, with timid and ungenerous artifice, to transfer the odium of it from herself to Mary's own subjects. The Earl of Mar, happily for the honour of his country, had more virtue than to listen to such an ignominious proposal ; and Elizabeth did not venture to renew it.

While she was engaged in pursing this insidious measure, the Regent was more honourably employed in endeavouring to negotiate a general peace among his countrymen. As he laboured for this purpose with the utmost zeal, and the adverse faction placed entire confidence in his integrity, his endeavours could hardly have failed of being successful. Maitland and Kirkaldy came so near to an agreement with him that scarce any thing remained, except the formality of signing the treaty. But Morton had not forgotten the disappointment he met with in his pretensions to the regency; his abilities, his wealth, and the patronage of the court of England, gave him greater sway with the party than even the Regent himself; and he took pleasure in thwarting every measure pursued by him. He was afraid that, if Maitland and his associates recovered any share in the administration, his own influence would be considerably diminished; and the Regent, by their means, would acquire that ascendant which belonged to his station. With him concurred all those who were in possession of the lands which belonged to any of the Queen's party. His ambition, and their avarice, frustrated the Regents's pious intentions, and retarded a blessing so necessary to the kingdom as the establishment of peace.

Such a discovery of the selfishness and ambition which reigned among his party, made a deep impression on the Regent, who loved his country, and wished for peace with much ardour. This inward grief broke his spirit, and by degrees brought on a settled melancholy, that ended in a distemper, of which he died on the 29th of October. He was, perhaps, the only person in the kingdom who could have enjoyed the office of Regent without envy, and have left it without loss of reputation. Notwithstanding their mutual animosities, both factions acknowledged his views to be honourable, and his integrity to be uncorrupted.

No competitor now appeared against Morton. The Queen of England powerfully supported his claim, and, notwithstanding the fears of the people, and the jealousy of the nobles, he was elected Regent [Nov. 24]; the fourth who, in the space of five years, had held that dangerous office.

As the truce had been prolonged to the 1st of January, this gave him an opportunity of continuing the negotiations with the opposite party, which had been set on foot by his predecessors. They produced no effects, however, till the beginning of the next year.

Before we proceed to these, some events, hitherto untouched, deserve our notice.

The Earl of Northumberland, who had been kept prisoner in Lochlevin ever since his flight into Scotland, in the year 1569, was given up to Lord Hunsdon, Governor of Berwick; and, being carried to York, suffered there the punishment of his rebellion. The King's party were so sensible of their dependence on Elizabeth's protection that it was scarcely possible for them to refuse putting into her hands a person who had taken up arms against her; but, as a sum of money was paid on that account, and shared between Morton and Douglas of Lochlevin, the former of whom, during his exile in England, had been much indebted to Northumberland's friendship, the abandoning this unhappy nobleman, in such a manner, to certain destruction, was universally condemned as a most ungrateful and mercenary action.

This year was remarkable for a considerable innovation in the government of the church. Soon after the Reformation, the popish bishops had been confirmed by law in possession of part of their benefices ; but the spiritual jurisdiction, which belonged to their order, was exercised by superintendants, though with more moderate authority. On the death of the Archbishop of St. Andrew's, Morton obtained from the crown a grant of the temporalities of that see. But as it was thought indecent for a layman to hold a benefice to which the cure of souls was annexed, he procured Douglas, rector of the university of St. Andrew's, to be chosen Archbishop ; and, allotting him a small pension out of the revenues of the see, retained the remainder in his own hands. The nobles, who saw the advantages which they might reap from such a practice supported him in the execution of his plan. It gave great offence, however, to the clergy, who, instead of perpetuating an order whose name and power were odious to them, wished that the revenues which had belonged to it might be employed in supplying such parishes as were still unprovided with settled pastors. But, on the one hand, it would have been rash in the clergy to have irritated too many noblemen, on whom the very existence of the Protestant church in Scotland depended ; and Morton, on the other , conducted his scheme with such dexterity, and managed them with so much art, that it was at last agreed, in a convention composed of the leading men among the clergy, together with a committee of privy council, " That the name and office of Archbishop and Bishop should be continued during the King's minority, and these dignities be conferred upon the best qualified among the Protestant ministers; but that, with regard to their spiritual jurisdictions, they should be subject to the General Assembly of the church." The rules to be observed in their election, and the persons who were to supply the place and enjoy the privileges which belonged to the dean and chapter in times of Popery, were likewise particularly specified. The whole being laid before the General Assembly, after some exceptions to the name of *Archbishop, Dean, Chapter,* &c., and a protestation that it should be considered only as a temporary constitution, until one more perfect could be introduced, it obtained the approbation of that court. Even Knox, who was prevented from attending the assembly by the ill state of his health, though he declaimed loudly against the simonical paction to which Douglas owed his preferment, and blamed the nomination of a person worn out with age and infirmities, to an office which required unimpaired vigour both of body and mind, seems not to have condemned the proceedings of the convention ; and, in a letter to the assembly, approved of some of the regulations with respect to the election of bishops, as worthy of being carefully observed*. In consequence of the Assembly's consent to the plan agreed upon in the convention, Douglas was installed in his office, and at the same time an Arch-

*See Appendix, No. XXXVIII.

bishop of Glasgow and a Bishop of Dunkeld were chosen from among the Protestant clergy. They were all admitted to the place in parliament which belonged to the ecclesiastical order. But in imitation of the example set by Morton, such bargains were made with them by different noblemen, as gave them possession only of a very small part of the revenues which belonged to their sees.

Soon after the dissolution of this assembly [Nov. 27], Knox, the prime instrument of spreading and establishing the reformed religion in Scotland, ended his life in the sixty-seventh year of his age. Zeal, intrepidity, disinterestedness, were virtues which he possessed in an eminent degree. He was acquainted too with the learning cultivated among divines in that age; and excelled in that species of eloquence which is calculated to rouse and to inflame. His maxims, however, were often too severe, and the impetuosity of his temper excessive. Rigid and uncomplying himself, he showed no indulgence to the infirmities of others. Regardless of the distinctions of rank and charcter, he uttered his admonitions with an acrimony and vehemence more apt to irritate than to reclaim. This often betrayed him into indecent and undutiful expressions with respect to the Queen's person and conduct. Those very qualities, however, which now render his character less amiable, fitted him to be the instrument of Providence for advancing the Reformation among a fierce people, and enabling him to face dangers, and to surmount opposition, from which a person of a more gentle spirit would have been apt to shrink back. By an unwearied application to study and business, as well as by the frequency and fervour of his public discourses, he had worn out a constitution naturally robust. During a lingering illness he discovered the utmost fortitude; and met the approaches of death with a magnanimity inseparable for his character. He was constantly employed in acts of devotion, and comforted himself with those prospects of immortality which not only preserve good men from desponding, but fill them with exultation in their last moments. The Earl of Morton, who was present at his funeral, pronounced his eulogium in a few words, the more honourable for Knox, as they came from one whom he had often censured with peculiar severity: "There lies He, who never feared the face of man."

[1573.] Though Morton did not desire peace from such generous motives as the former Regent, he laboured, however, in good earnest, to establish it. The public confusions and calamities, to which he owed his power and importance when he was only the second person in the nation, were extremely detrimental to him now that he was raised to be the first. While so many of the nobles continued in arms against him, his authority as Regent was partial, feeble, and precarious. Elizabeth was no less desirous of extinguishing the flame which she had kindled and kept so long alive in Scotland. She had discovered the alliance with France, from which she had expected such advantages, to be no foundation of security. Though appearances of friendship still subsisted between her and that court, and Charles daily renewed his protestations of inviolable adherence

x 5

to the treaty, she was convinced, by a fatal example, how little she ought to rely on the promises or oaths of that perfidious monarch. Her ambassador warned her that the French held secret correspondence with Mary's adherents in Scotland, and encouraged them in their obstinacy. The Duke of Alva carried on his intrigues in that kingdom with less disguise. She was persuaded that they would embrace the first serene interval, which the commotions in France and in the Netherlands would allow them, and openly attempt to land a body of men in Scotland. She resolved, therefore, to prevent their getting any footing in the island, and to cut off all their hopes of finding any assistance there, by uniting the two parties.

The situation of Mary's adherents enabled the Regent to carry on his negotiations with them to great advantage. They were now divided into two factions. At the head of the one were Chatelherault and Huntly. Maitland and Kirkaldy were the leaders of the other. Their high rank, their extensive property, and the numbers of their followers, rendered the former considerable. The latter were indebted for their importance to their personal abilities, and to the strength of the castle of Edinburgh, which was in their possession. The Regent had no intention to comprehend both in the same treaty; but as he dreaded that the Queen's party, if it remained entire, would be able to thwart and embarrass his administration, he resolved to divide and weaken it by a separate negotiation. He made the first overture to Kirkaldy and his associates, and endeavoured to renew the negotiation with them, which, during the life of his predecessor, had been broken off by his own artifices. But Kirkaldy knew Morton's views, and system of government, to be very different from those of the former Regent. Maitland considered him as a personal and implacable enemy. They received repeated assurances of protection from France; and though the siege of Rochelle employed the French arms at that time, the same hopes, which had so often deceived the party, still amused them, and they expected that the obstinacy of the Hugonots would soon be subdued, and that Charles would then be at liberty to act with vigour in Scotland. Meanwhile a supply of money was sent, and if the castle could be held out till Whitsunday, effectual aid was promised. Maitland's genius delighted in forming schemes that were dangerous; and Kirkaldy possessed the intrepidity necessary for putting them in execution. The castle, they knew, was so situated that it might defy all the Regent's power. Elizabeth, they hoped, would not violate the treaty with France, by sending forces to his assistance; and if the French should be able to land any considerable body of men, it might be possible to deliver the Queen from captivity, or at least to balance the influence of France and England in such a manner as to rescue Scotland from the dishonourable dependence upon the latter, under which it had fallen. This splendid but chimerical project they preferred to the friendship of Morton. They encouraged the negotiation, however, because it served to gain time; they proposed for the same purpose, that the whole of the Queen's party should be comprehended in it, and that Kirkaldy should retain the command of the castle six months after the treaty was signed. His interest prompted the Regent to reject the former; his penetration discovered the danger of complying with the latter; and all hopes of accommodation vanished.

As soon as the truce expired, Kirkaldy began to fire on the city of Edinburgh, which, by the return of the inhabitants whom he had expelled, was devoted as zealously as ever to the King's cause. But, as the Regent had now set on foot a treaty with Chatelherault and Huntly, the cessation of arms still continued with them.

They were less scrupulous than the other party, and listened eagerly to his overtures. The Duke was naturally unsteady, and the approach of old age increased his irresolution, and aversion to action. The miseries of civil discord had afflicted Scotland almost five years, a length of time far beyond the duration of any former contest. The war, instead of doing service, had been detrimental to the Queen; and more ruinous than any foreign invasion to the kingdom. In prosecuting it, neither party had gained much honour; both had suffered great losses and had exhausted their own estates in wasting those of their adversaries. The commons were in the utmost misery, and longed ardently for a peace, which might terminate this fruitless but destructive quarrel.

A great step was taken towards this desirable event, by the treaty concluded at Perth [Feb. 23], between the Regent on one hand, and Chatelherault and Huntly on the other, under the mediation of of Killegrew, Elizabeth's ambassador*. The chief articles in it were these : That all the parties comprehended in the treaty should declare their approbation of the reformed religion now established in the kingdom ; that they should submit to the King's government, and own Morton's authority as Regent ; that they should acknowledge every thing done in opposition to the King, since his coronation, to be illegal ; that on both sides the prisoners who had been taken should be set at liberty, and the estates which had been forfeited should be restored to their proper owners; that the act of attainder passed against the Queen's adherents should be repealed, and indemnity granted for all the crimes of which they had been guilty since the 15th of June, 1567 ; and that the treaty should be ratified by the common consent of both parties in parliament.

Kirkaldy, though abandoned by his associates, who neither discovered solicitude nor made provision for his safety, did not lose courage, nor entertain any thoughts of accommodation. Though all Scotland had now submitted to the King, he still resolved to defend the castle in the Queen's name, and to wait the arrival of the promised succours. The Regent was in want of every thing necessary for carrying on a siege. But Elizabeth, who, determined at any rate to bring the dissensions in Scotland to a period before the French could find leisure to take part in the quarrel, soon afforded him sufficient supplies. Sir William Drury marched into Scotland with fifteen hundred foot, and a considerable train of artillery. The Regent joined him with all his forces; and trenches were opened and approaches regularly carried on against the castle.

† See Appendix, No. XXXIX.

[April 25.] Kirkaldy, though discouraged by the loss of a great sum of money remitted to him from France, and which fell into the Regent's hands through the treachery of Sir James Balfour, the most corrupt man of that age, defended himself with bravery augmented by despair. Three-and-thirty days he resisted all the efforts of the Scotch and English, who pushed on their attacks with courage and with emulation. Nor did he demand a parley, till the fortifications were battered down, and one of the wells in the castle dried up, and the other choked with rubbish. Even then, his spirit was unsubdued, and he determined rather to fall gloriously behind the last intrenchment than to yield to his inveterate enemies. But his garrison was not animated with the same heroic or desperate resolution, and, rising in a mutiny, forced him to capitulate. He surrendered himself to Drury [May 29,] who promised, in the name of his mistress, that he should be favourably treated. Together with him James Kirkaldy, his brother, Lord Home, Maitland, Sir Robert Melvil, a few citizens of Edinburgh, and about one hundred and sixty soldiers, were made prisoners.

Several of the officers, who had been kept in pay during the war, prevailed on their men to accompany them into the Low Countries, and entering into the service of the States, added, by their gallant behaviour, to the reputation for military virtue which has always been the characteristic of the Scottish nation.

Thus by the treaty with Chatelherault and Huntly, and the surrender of the castle, the civil wars in Scotland were brought to a period. When we review the state of the nation, and compare the strength of the two factions, Mary's partisans among the nobles appear, manifestly, to have been superior both in numbers and in power. But these advantages were more than counterbalanced by others, which their antagonists enjoyed. Political abilities, military skill, and all the talents which times of action form, or call forth, appeared chiefly on the King's side. Nor could their enemies boast of any man, who equalled the intrepidity of Murray, tempered with wisdom ; the profound sagacity of Morton ; the subtle genius and insinuating address of Maitland ; or the successful valour of Kirkaldy ; all of which were at first employed in laying the foundation of the King's authority. On the one side, measures were concerted with prudence, and executed with vigour ; on the other, their resolutions were rash, and their conduct feeble. The people, animated with zeal for religion, and prompted by indignation against the Queen, warmly supported the King's cause. The clergy threw the whole weight of their popularity into the same scale. By means of these, as well as by the powerful interposition of England, the King's government was finally established. Mary lost even that shadow of sovereignty which, amidst all her sufferings, she had hitherto retained among part of her own subjects. As she was no longer permitted to have an ambassador at the court of England, the only mark of dignity which she had for some time enjoyed there, she must henceforth be considered as an exile stripped of all the ensigns of royalty ; guarded with anxiety in the one kingdom, and totally deserted or forgotten in the other.

Kirkaldy and his associates remained in Drury's custody, and were treated by him with great humanity, until the Queen of England, whose prisoners they were, should determine their fate. Morton insisted that they should suffer the punishment due to their rebellion and obstinacy; and declared that, so long as they were allowed to live, he did not reckon his own person or authority secure; and Elizabeth, without regarding Drury's honour, or his promises in her name, gave them up to the Regent's disposal. He first confined them to separate prisons [Aug. 3]; and soon after, with Elizabeth's consent, condemned Kirkaldy and his brother to be hanged at the cross of Edinburgh. Maitland, who did not expect to be treated more favourably, prevented the ignominy of a public execution by a voluntary death, and " ended his days," says Melvil, " after the old Roman fashion."

While the Regent was wreaking his vengeance on the remains of her party in Scotland, Mary, incapable of affording them any relief, bewailed their misfortunes in the solitude of her prison. At the same time her health began to be much impaired by confinement and want of exercise. At the entreaty of the French ambassador, Lord Shrewsbury, her keeper, was permitted to conduct her to Buxton Wells, not far from Tuthbury, the place of her imprisonment. Cecil, who had lately been created Baron of Burleigh, and Lord High Treasurer of England, happened to be there at the same time. Though no minister ever entered more warmly into the views of a sovereign, or gave stronger proofs of his fidelity and attachment than this great man, yet such was Elizabeth's distrust of every person who approached the Queen of Scots, that her suspicions, in consequence of this interview, seem to have extended even to him; and while Mary justly reckoned him her most dangerous enemy, he found some difficulty in persuading his own mistress that he was not partial to that unhappy Queen.

The Duke of Alva was this year recalled from the government of the Netherlands, where his haughty and oppressive administration roused a spirit, in attempting to subdue which Spain exhausted its treasures, ruined its armies, and lost its glory. Requesens, who succeeded him, was of a milder temper, and of a less enterprising genius. This event delivered Elizabeth from the perpetual disquietude occasioned by Alva's negociations with the Scottish Queen, and his zeal for her interest.

1570]. Though Scotland was now settled in profound peace, many of the evils which accompany civil war were still felt. The restraints of law, which in times of public confusion are little regarded even by civilized nations, were totally despised by a fierce people unaccustomed to a regular administration of justice. The disorders in every corner of the kingdom were become intolerable, and, under the protection of the one or the other faction, crimes of every kind were committed with impunity. The Regent set himself to redress these, and by his industry and vigour, order and security were re-established in the kingdom. But he lost there reputation due to this important service, by the avarice which he discovered in performing it; and his own exactions became more pernicious to the nation than all the irregularities which he restrained.[*]

* See Append. No. XL.

Spies and informers were every where employed; the remembrance of old offences was revived; imaginary crimes were invented; petty trespasses were aggravated; and delinquents were forced to compound for their lives by the payment of exorbitant fines. At the same time the current coin was debased; licenses were sold for carrying on prohibited branches of commerce; unusual taxes were imposed on commodities; and all the refinements in oppression, from which nations so imperfectly polished as the Scots are usually exempted, were put in practice. None of these were complained of more loudly, or with greater reason, than his injustice towards the church. The thirds of benefices, out of which the clergy received their subsistence, had always been slowly and irregularly paid to collectors appointed by the general assembly; and during the civil wars, no payment could be obtained in several parts of the kingdom. Under colour of redressing this grievance, and upon a promise of assigning every minister a stipend within his own parish, the Regent extorted from the church the thirds to which they had a right by law. But the clergy, instead of reaping any advantage from this alteration, found that payments became more irregular and dilatory than ever. One minister was commonly burthened with the care of four or five parishes, a pitiful salary was allotted him, and the Regent's insatiable avarice seized on the rest of the fund.

The death of Charles IX., which happened this year, was a new misfortune to the Scottish Queen. Henry III., who succeeded him, had not the same attachment to her person; and his jealousy of the house of Guise, and obsequiousness to the Queen mother, greatly alienated him from her interest.

1575.] The death of the Duke of Chatelherault, [Jan. 22,] must likewise be considered as some loss to Mary. As the parliament had frequently declared him next heir to the crown, this entitled him to great respect among his countrymen, and enabled him, more than any other person in the kingdom, to counterbalance the Regent's power.

Soon after, at one of the usual interviews between the wardens of the Scottish and English marches, a scuffle happened, in which the English were worsted: a few killed on the spot; and Sir James Forrester, the warden, with several gentlemen who attended him taken prisoners. But both Elizabeth and the Regent were too sensible of the advantage which resulted from the good understanding that subsisted between the two kingdoms, to allow this slight accident to interrupt it.

The domestic tranquillity of the kingdom was in some danger of being disturbed by another cause. Though the persons raised to the dignity of bishops possessed very small revenues and a very moderate degree of power, the clergy, to whom the Regent and all his measures were become extremely odious, began to be jealous of that order. Knowing that corruptions steal into the church gradually, under honourable names and upon decent pretences, they were afraid that from small beginnings, the hierarchy might grow in time to be as powerful and oppressive as ever. The chief author of these suspicions was Mr. Andrew Melvil, a man distinguished by his uncommon erudition, by the severity of his manners, and the intrepidity of his mind. But, bred up in the retirement of a college, he was unacquainted with the arts of life; and being more attentive to the ends which he pursued than to the means which he employed for promoting them, he often defeated laudable designs by the impetuosity and imprudence with which he carried them on. A question was moved by him in the assembly, "Whether the office of Bishop, as now exercised in the kingdom, were agreeable to the word of God?" In the ecclesiastical judicatories continual complaints were made of the bishops for neglect of duty, many of which their known remissness too well justified. The Bishop of Dunkeld, being accused of dilapidating his benefice, was found guilty by the assembly. The Regent, instead of checking, connived at these disputes about ecclesiastical government, as they diverted the zeal of the clergy from attending to his daily encroachments on the patrimony of the church.

1576.] The weight of the Regent's oppressive administration had hitherto fallen chiefly on those in the lower and middle rank; but he began now to take such steps as convinced the nobles that their dignity would not long exempt them from feeling the effect of his power. An accident, which was a frequent cause of dissension among the Scottish nobles, occasioned a difference between the Earls of Argyll and Athol. A vassal of the former had made some depredations on the lands of the latter, Athol took arms to punish the offender—Argyll to protect him; and this ignoble quarrel they were ready to decide in the field, when the Regent, by interposing his authority, obliged them to disband their forces. Both of them had been guilty of irregularities, which, though common, were contrary to the letter of the law. Of these the Regent took advantage, and resolved to found on them a charge of treason. This design was revealed to the two Earls by one of Morton's retainers. The common danger to which they were exposed compelled them to forget old quarrels, and unite in a close confederacy for their mutual defence. Their junction rendered them formidable; they despised the summons which the Regent gave them to appear before a court of justice; and he was obliged to desist from any further prosecution. But the injury he intended made a deep impression on their minds, and drew upon him severe vengeance.

Nor was he more successful in an attempt which he made to load Lord Claud Hamilton with the guilt of having formed a conspiracy against his life. Though those who were supposed to be his accomplices were seized and tortured, no evidence of any thing criminal appeared; but, on the contrary, many circumstances discovered his innocence, as well as the Regent's secret views in imputing to him, such an odious design.

1577.] The Scottish nobles, who were almost equal to their monarchs in power, and treated by them with much distinction, observed these arbitrary proceedings of a Regent with the utmost indignation. The people who, under a form of government extremely simple, had been little accustomed to the burden of taxes, complained loudly of the Regent's rapacity; and all began to turn their eyes towards the young King, from whom they expected the

redress of all their grievances, and the return of a more gentle and
more equal administration.

James was now in the twelfth year of his age. The Queen soon
after his birth had committed him to the care of the Earl of Mar,
and during the civil wars he had resided securely in the castle of
Stirling. Alexander Erskine, that nobleman's brother, had the
chief direction of his education. Under him the famous Buchanan
acted as preceptor, together with three other masters, the most
eminent the nation afforded for skill in those sciences which were
deemed necessary for a prince. As the young King showed an uncommon passion for learning, and made great progress in it, the
Scots fancied that they already discovered in him all those virtues
which the fondness or credulity of subjects usually ascribes to
princes during their minority. But as James was still far from that
age at which the law permitted him to assume the reins of government, the Regent did not sufficiently attend to the sentiments of
the people, nor reflect how naturally these prejudices in his favour
might encourage the King to anticipate that period. He not only
neglected to secure the friendship of those who were about the
King's person, and who possessed his ear, but had even exasperated
some of them by personal injuries. Their resentment concurred
with the ambition of others, in infusing into the King early suspicions of Morton's power and designs. A King, they told him, had
often reason to fear, seldom to love a Regent. Prompted by ambition and by interest, he would endeavour to keep the Prince in
perpetual infancy, at a distance from his subjects, and unacquainted
with business. A small degree of vigour, however, was sufficient to
break the yoke. Subjects naturally reverence their sovereign, and
become impatient of the temporary and delegated jurisdiction of a
Regent. Morton had governed with rigour unknown to the
ancient Monarchs of Scotland. The nation groaned under his oppressions, and would welcome the first prospect of a milder administration. At present the King's name was hardly mentioned in
Scotland, his friends were without influence, and his favourites
without honour. But one effort would discover Morton's power to
be as feeble as it was arbitrary. The same attempt would put himself in possession of his just authority, and rescue the nation from
intolerable tyranny. If he did not regard his own rights as a King,
let him listen at least to the cries of his people.

These suggestions made a deep impression on the young King,
who was trained up in an opinion that he was born to command.
His approbation of the design, however, was of small consequence
without the concurrence of the nobles. The Earls of Argyll and
Athol, two of the most powerful of that body, were animated with
implacable resentment against the Regent. To them the cabal in
Stirling Castle communicated the plot which was on foot; and they
entering warmly into it, Alexander Erskine, who, since the death
of his brother, and during the minority of his nephew, had the
command of that fort and the custody of the King's person, admitted them secretly into the King's presence. They gave him the
same account of the misery of his subjects, under the Regent's
arbitrary administration; they complained loudly of the injustice

with which themselves had been treated, and besought the King, as the only means for redressing the grievances of the nation, to call a council of all the nobles. James consented, and letters were issued in his name for that purpose; but the two Earls took care that they should be sent only to such as were known to bear no good will to Morton.

The number of these was, however, so considerable, that on the day appointed, by far the greater part of the nobles assembled at Stirling; and so highly were they incensed against Morton, that, although, on receiving intelligence of Argyll and Athol's interview with the King [March 24, 1578], he had made a feint as if he would resign the Regency, they advised the King, without regarding this offer, to deprive him of his office, and to take the administration of government into his own hands. Lord Glamis, the chancellor, and Herries, were appointed to signify this resolution to Morton, who was at that time in Dalkeith, which was his usual place of residence. Nothing could equal the joy with which this unexpected resolution filled the nation, but the surprise which was occasioned by the seeming alacrity with which the Regent descended from so high a station. He neither wanted sagacity to foresee the danger of resigning, nor inclination to keep possession of an office, for the expiration of which, the law had fixed so distant a term. But all the sources whence the faction, of which he was the head derived their strength had either failed, or now supplied his adversaries with the means of humbling him. The commons, the city of Edinburgh, and the clergy, were all totally alienated from him by his repeated oppressions. Elizabeth, having but lately bound herself by treaty to send a considerable body of troops to the assistance of the inhabitants of the Netherlands, who were struggling for liberty, had little leisure to attend to the affairs of Scotland; and as she had nothing to dread from France, in whose councils the Princes of Lorrain, had not, at that time, much influence, she was not displeased, perhaps, at the birth of new factions in the kingdom. Even those nobles who had long been joined with Morton in faction, or whom he had attached to his person by benefits, Glamis, Lindsay, Ruthven, Pitcairn the secretary, Murray of Tullibardin, comptroller, all deserted his falling fortunes, and appeared in the council at Stirling. So many concurring circumstances convinced Morton of his weakness, and determined him to give way to a torrent which was too impetuous to be resisted. He attended the Chancellor and Herries to Edinburgh [March 12]; was present when the king's acceptance of the government was proclaimed; and, in the presence of the people, surrendered to the King all the authority to which he had any claim in virtue of his office. This ceremony was accompanied with such excessive joy and acclamations of the multitude, as added, no doubt, to the anguish which an ambitious spirit must feel, when compelled to renounce supreme power; and convinced Morton how entirely he had lost the affections of his countrymen. He obtained, however, from the King, an act, containing the approbation of everything done by him in the exercise of his office, and a pardon, in the most ample form that his fear or caution could devise, of all past offences, crimes, and treasons. The nobles, who adhered to the King, bound themselves under a great penalty, to procure the ratification of this act in the first parliament.

A council of twelve peers was appointed to assist the King in the administration of affairs. Morton, deserted by his own party, and unable to struggle with the faction which governed absolutely at court, retired to one of his seats, and seemed to enjoy the tranquillity, and to be occupied only in the amusements of a country life. His mind, however, was deeply disquieted with all the uneasy reflections which accompany disappointed ambition, and intent on schemes for recovering his former grandeur. Even in this retreat, which the people called the *Lion's Den*, his wealth and abilities rendered him formidable ; and the new counsellors were so imprudent as to rouse him, by the precipitancy with which they hastened to strip him of all the remains of power. They required him to surrender the Castle of Edinburgh, which was still in his possession. He refused at first to do so, and began to prepare for its defence ; but the citizens of Edinburgh having taken arms, and repulsed part of the garrison, which was sent out to guard a convoy of provisions, he was obliged to give up that important fortress without resistance. This encouraged his adversaries to call a Parliament, to meet at Edinburgh, and to multiply their demands upon him in such a manner, as convinced him that nothing less than his utter ruin would satisfy their inveterate hatred.

Their power and popularity, however, began already to decline. The Chancellor, the ablest and most moderate man in the party, having been killed at Stirling in an accidental rencounter between his followers and those of the Earl of Crawford ; Athol, who was appointed his successor in that high office, the Earls of Eglington, Caithness, and Lord Ogilvie, all the prime favourites at court, were either avowed Papists, or suspecting of leaning to the opinions of that sect. In an age when the return of Popery was so much and so justly dreaded, this gave universal alarm. As Morton had always treated the Papists with rigour, this unseasonable favour to persons of that religion made all zealous Protestants remember that circumstance in his administration with great praise.

Morton, to whom none of these particulars were unknown, thought this the proper juncture for sitting to work the instruments which he had been preparing. Having gained the confidence of the Earl of Mar, and of the Countess his mother, he insinuated to them, that Alexander Erskine had formed a plot to deprive his nephew of the government of Stirling Castle, and the custody of the King's person ; and easily induced an ambitious woman, and a youth of twenty, to employ force to prevent this supposed injury. The Earl repairing suddenly to Stirling [April 26], and being admitted as usual into the castle with his attendants, seized the gates early in the morning, and turned out his uncle, who dreaded no danger from his hands. The soldiers of the garrison submitted to him as their governor, and, with little danger and no effusion of blood, he became master both of the King's person and of the fortress.

An event so unexpected occasioned great consternation. Though

Morton's hand did not appear in the execution, he was universally believed to be the author of the attempt. The new counsellors saw it to be necessary, for their own safety, to change their measures, and, instead of pursuing him with such implacable resentment, to enter into terms of accommodation with an adversary still so capable of creating them trouble. Four were named on each side to adjust their differences. They met not far from Dalkeith; and when they had brought matters near to a conclusion, Morton, who was too sagacious not to improve the advantage which their security and their attention to the treaty afforded him, set out in the night-time for Stirling, and, having gained Murray of Tullibardin, Mar's uncle, was admitted by him into the castle [May 24]; and managing matters there with the usual dexterity, he soon had more entirely the command of the fort than the Earl himself. He was likewise admitted to a seat in the privy council, and acquired as complete an ascendant in it.

As the time appointed for the meeting of Parliament at Edinburgh now approached, this gave him some anxiety. He was afraid of conducting the young King to a city whose inhabitants were so much at the devotion of the adverse faction. He was no less unwilling to leave James behind at Stirling. In order to avoid this dilemma he issued a proclamation in the King's name, changing the place of meeting from Edinburgh to Stirling Castle. This Athol and his party represented as a step altogether unconstitutional. The King, said they, is Morton's prisoner: the pretended counsellors are his slaves; a parliament, to which all the nobles may repair without fear, and where they may deliberate with freedom, is absolutely necessary for settling the nation after disorders of such long continuance. But an assembly called contrary to all form, held within the walls of a garrison, and overawed by armed men, what safety could members expect? what liberty could prevail in debate? or what benefit result to the public? The parliament met, however, on the day appointed [July 25], and, notwithstanding the protestation of the Earl of Montrose and Lord Lindsay, in the name of their party, proceeded to business. The King's acceptance of the government was confirmed; the act granted to Morton, for his security, ratified; some regulations with regard to the numbers and authority of the privy council were agreed upon; and a pension for life granted to the Countess of Mar, who had been so instrumental in bringing about the late revolution.

Meanwhile Argyll, Athol, and their followers took arms, upon the specious pretence of rescuing the King from captivity, and the kingdom from oppression. James himself, impatient of the servitude in which he was held by a man whom he had long been taught to hate, secretly encouraged their enterprise; though at the same time he was obliged not only to disavow them in public, but to levy forces against them, and even to declare, by proclamation, that he was perfectly free from any constraint, either upon his person or his will [Aug. 11]. Both sides quickly took the field. Argyll and Athol were at the head of seven thousand men; the Earl of Angus, Morton's nephew, met them with an army five thousand strong; neither party, however, was eager to engage. Morton distrusted the fidelity of his own troops. The two Earls were sensible that a single victory, however complete, would not be decisive; and, as they were in no condition to undertake the siege of Stirling Castle, where the King was kept, their strength would soon be exhausted, while Morton's own wealth, and the patronage of the Queen of England might furnish him with endless resources. By the mediation of Bowes, whom Elizabeth had sent into Scotland to negotiate an accommodation between the two factions, a treaty was concluded, in consequence of which Argyll and Athol were admitted into the king's presence; some of their party were added to the privy council; and a convention of nobles called, in order to bring all remaining differences to an amicable issue.

As soon as James assumed the government into his own hands, he dispatched the abbot of Dunfermling to inform Elizabeth of that event; to offer to renew the alliance between the two kingdoms; and to demand possession of the estate which had lately fallen to him by the death of his grandmother the Countess of Lennox. The lady's second son had left one daughter, Arabella Stewart, who was born in England. And as the chief objection against the pretensions of the Scottish line to the crown of England was that maxim of English law which excludes aliens from any right of inheritance within the kingdom, Elizabeth by granting this demand, would have established a precedent in James's favour, that might have been deemed decisive with regard to a point which it had been her constant care to keep undecided. Without suffering this delicate question to be tried, or allowing any new light to be thrown on that which she considered as the great mystery of her reign, she commanded Lord Burleigh, master of the wards, to sequester the rents of the estate; and, by this method of proceeding, gave the Scottish King early warning how necessary it would be to court her favour, if ever he hoped for success in claims of greater importance, but equally liable to be controverted.

1579.] After many delays, and with much difficulty, the contending nobles were at last brought to some agreement. But it was followed by a tragical event. Morton, in token of reconcilement, having invited the leaders of the opposite party to a great entertainment, Athol the chancellor was soon taken ill, and died within a few days [April 24]. The symptoms and violence of the disease gave rise to strong suspicions of his being poisoned; and though the physicians who opened his body differed in opinion as to the cause of the distemper, the Chancellor's relations publicly accused Morton of that odious crime. The advantage which visibly accrued to him by the removal of a man of great abilities, and averse from all his measures, was deemed a sufficient proof of his guilt by the people, who are ever fond of imputing the death of eminent persons to extraordinary causes.

The office of chancellor was bestowed upon Argyll, whom this preferment reconciled, in a great measure, to Morton's administration. He had now recovered all the authority which he possessed during his regency, and had entirely broken or baffled the power and cabals of his enemies. None of the great families remained to be the objects of his jealousy, or to obstruct his designs, but that of Hamilton. The Earl of Arran, the eldest brother, had never recovered the shock which he received from the ill success of his passion for the Queen, and had now altogether lost his reason. Lord John, the second brother, was in the possession of the family estate; Lord Claud was commendator of Paisley; both of them young men, ambitious and enterprising. Morton dreaded their influence in the kingdom; the courtiers hoped to share their spoils among them; and as all princes naturally view their successors with jealousy and hatred, it was easy to infuse these passions into the mind of the young King. A pretence was at hand to justify the most violent proceedings. The pardon, stipulated in the treaty of Perth, did not extend to such as were accessary to the murder of the Regents Murray and Lennox. Lord John and his brother were suspected of being the authors of both these crimes, and had been included in a general act of attainder on that account. Without summoning them to trial, or examining a single witness to prove the charge, this attainder was now thought sufficient to subject them to all the penalties which they would have incurred by being formally convicted. The Earls of Morton, Mar, and Eglinton, together with the Lords Ruthven, Boyd, and Cathcart, received a commission to seize their persons and estates. On a few hours warning a considerable body of troops was ready, and marched towards Hamilton in hostile array. Happily the two brothers made their escape, though with great difficulty. But their lands were confiscated; the castles of Hamilton and Draffan besieged; those who defended them punished. The Earl of Arran, though incapable from his situation of committing any crime, was involved, by a shameful abuse of law, in the common ruin of his family; and, as if he too could have been guilty of rebellion, he was confined a close prisoner. These proceedings, so contrary to the fundamental principles of justice, were all ratified in the subsequent parliament.

About this time Mary sent, by Naue her secretary, a letter to her son, together with some jewels of value, and a vest embroidered with her own hand. But, as she gave him only the title of Prince of Scotland, the messenger was dismissed without being admitted into his presence.

Though Elizabeth had at this time no particula easohrn to fear any attempt of the Popish Princes in Mary's favour, se stll continued to guard her with the same anxious care. The acquisition of Portugal on the one hand, and the defence of the Netherlands on the other, fully employed the councils and arms of Spain. France, torn in pieces by intestine commotions, and under a weak and capricious Prince, despised and distrusted by his own subjects, was in no condition to disturb its neighbours. Elizabeth had long amused that court by carrying on a treaty of marriage with the Duke of Alencon, the King's brother. But whether, at the age of forty-five, she really intended to marry a Prince of twenty; whether the pleasure of being flattered and courted made her listen to the addresses of so young a lover, whom she allowed to visit her at two different times, and treated with the most distinguishing respect; or whether considerations of interest predominated in this as well as in every other transaction of her reign, are problems in history which we are not concerned to resolve. During the progress of this negotiation, which was drawn out to an extraordinary length, Mary could expect no assistance from the French court, and seems to have held little correspondence with it; and there was no period in her reign, wherein Elizabeth enjoyed more perfect security.

Morton seems at this time to have been equally secure; but his security was not so well founded. He had weathered out one storm, had crushed his adversaries, and was again in possession of the sole direction of affairs. But as the King was now of an age when the character and dispositions of the mind begin to unfold themselves, and become visible, the smallest attention to these might have convinced him, that there was reason to expect new and more dangerous attacks on his power. James early discovered that excessive attachment to favourites, which accompanied him through his whole life. This passion, which naturally arises from inexperience and youthful warmth of heart, was, at his age, far from being culpable; nor could it be well expected that the choice of the objects on whom he placed his affections should be made with great skill. The most considerable of them was Esme Stewart, a native of France, and son of a second brother of the Earl of Lennox. He was distinguished by the title of Lord D'Aubigne, an estate in France, which descended to him from his ancestors, on whom it had been conferred in reward of their valour and services to the French crown. He arrived in Scotland about this time [Sept. 8], on purpose to demand the estate and title of Lennox, to which he pretended a legal right. He was received at first by the King with the respect due to so near a relation. The gracefulness of his person, the elegance of his dress, and courtly behaviour, made a great impression on James, who, even in his more mature years, was little able to resist these frivolous charms; and his affection flowed with its usual rapidity and profusion. Within a few days after Stewart's appearance at court, he was created Lord Aberbrothock, soon after Earl and then Duke of Lennox, Governor of Dumbarton Castle, Captain of the Guard, First Lord of the Bedchamber, and Lord High Chamberlain. At the same time, and without any of the envy or emulation which is usual among candidates for favour, Captain James Stewart, the second son of Lord Ochiltree, grew into great confidence. But, notwithstanding this union, Lennox and Captain Stewart were persons of very opposite characters. The former was naturally gentle, humane, candid; but unacquainted with the state of the country, and misled or misinformed by those whom he trusted; not unworthy to be the companion of the young King in his amusements, but utterly disqualified for acting as a minister in directing his affairs. The latter was remarkable for all the vices which render a man formidable to his country, and a pernicious counsellor to his Prince; nor did he possess any one virtue to counterbalance these vices, unless dexterity in conducting his own designs, and an enterprising courage superior to the sense of danger, may pass by that name. Unrestrained by religion, regardless of decency, and undismayed by opposition, he aimed at objects seemingly unattainable; but, under a

Prince void of experience, and blind to all the defects of those who had gained his favour, his audacity was successful; and honours, wealth, and power, were the reward of his crimes.

Both his favourites concurred in employing their whole address to undermine Morton's credit, which alone obstructed their full possession of power. As James had been bred up with an aversion for that nobleman, who endeavoured rather to maintain the authority of a tutor, than to act with the obsequiousness of a minister, they found it no difficult matter to accomplish their design. Morton, who could no longer keep the King shut up within the walls of Stirling Castle, having called a parliament [Oct 17] to meet at Edinburgh, brought him thither. James made his entry into the capital with great solemnity; the citizens received him with the loudest acclamations of joy, and with many expensive pageants, according to the mode of that age. After a long period of thirty-seven years, during which Scotland had been subjected to the delegated power of Regents, or to the feeble government of a woman; after having suffered all the miseries of civil war, and felt the insolence of foreign armies, the nation rejoiced to see the sceptre once more in the hands of a King. Fond even of that shadow of authority, which a Prince of fifteen could possess, the Scots flattered themselves, that union, order, and tranquillity, would now be restored to the kingdom. James opened the parliament with extraordinary pomp, but nothing remarkable passed in it.

[1580.] These demonstrations, however, of the people's love and attachment to their sovereign, encouraged the favourites to continue their insinuations against Morton; and as the King now resided in the palace of Holyrood House, to which all his subjects had access, the cabal against the Earl grew daily stronger, and the intrigue which occasioned his fall ripened gradually.

Morton began to be sensible of his danger, and endeavoured to put a stop to the career of Lennox's preferment, by representing him as a formidable enemy to the reformed religion, a secret agent in favour of Popery, and a known emissary of the house of Guise. The clergy, apt to believe every rumour of this kind, spread the alarm among the people. But Lennox, either out of complaisance to his master, or convinced by the arguments of some learned divines whom the King appointed to instruct him in the principles of the Protestant religion, publicly renounced the errors of Popery, in the Church of St. Giles, and declared himself a member of the church of Scotland, by signing her Confession of Faith. This, though it did not remove all suspicions, nor silence some zealous preachers, abated, in some degree, the force of the accusation.

On the other hand, a rumour prevailed that Morton was preparing to seize the King's person, and to carry him into England. Whether despair of maintaining his power by any other means, had driven him to make any overture of that kind to the English court, or whether it was a calumny invented by his adversaries to render him odious, cannot now be determined with certainty. As he declared at his death that such a design had never entered into his thoughts, the latter seems to be most probable. It afforded a pretence, however, for reviving the office of lord chamberlain, which had been for some time disused. That honour was conferred on Lennox. Alexander Erskine, Morton's capital enemy, was his deputy; they had under them a band of gentleman, who were appointed constantly to attend the King, and to guard his person.

Morton was not ignorant of what his enemies intended to insinuate by such unusual precautions for the King's safety; and, as his last resource, applied to Elizabeth, whose protection had often stood him in stead in his greatest difficulties. In consequence of this application, Bowes, her envoy, accused Lennox of practices against the peace of the two kingdoms, and insisted in her name, that he should instantly be removed from the privy council. Such an unprecedented demand was considered by the counsellors as an affront to the King, and an encroachment on the independence of the kingdom. They affected to call in question the envoy's powers, and upon that pretence refused him further audience; and he retiring in disgust, and without taking leave, Sir Alexander Home was sent to expostulate with Elizabeth on the subject. After the treatment which her envoy had received, Elizabeth thought it below her dignity to admit Home into her presence. Burleigh, to whom he was commanded to impart his commission, reproached him with his master's ingratitude towards a benefactress who had placed the crown on his head, and required him to advise the King to beware of sacrificing the friendship of so necessary an alley to the giddy humours of a young man without experience, and strongly suspected of principles and attachments incompatible with the happiness of the Scottish nation.

This accusation of Lennox hastened, in all probability, Morton's fall. The act of indemnity, which he had obtained when he resigned the regency, was worded with such scrupulous exactness, as almost screened him from any legal prosecution. The murder of the late King was the only crime which could not, with decency, be inserted in a pardon granted by his son. Here Morton still lay open to the penalties of the law, and Captain Stewart, who shunned no action, however desperate, if it led to power or to favour, entered the council-chamber while the King and nobles were assembled, and [Dec. 30], falling on his knees, accused Morton of being accessary, or, according to the language of the Scottish law, *art and part*, in the conspiracy against the life of His Majesty's father, and offered, under the usual penalties, to verify this charge by legal evidence. Morton, who was present, heard this accusation with firmness; and replied with a disdainful smile, proceeding either from contempt of the infamous character of his accuser, or from consciousness of his innocence, "that his own zeal in punishing those who were suspected of that detestable crime, might well exempt himself from any suspicion of being accessary to it; nevertheless, he would cheerfully submit to a trial, either in that place or in any other court; and doubted not but his own innocence and the malice of his enemies would then appear in the clearest light." Stewart, who was still on his knees, began to inquire how he would reconcile his bestowing so many honours on Archibald Douglas, whom he certainly knew to be one of the murderers, with his pretended zeal against that crime. Morton was ready to answer. But the King commanded both to be removed [1581]. The Earl was confined, first of all to his own house, and then committed to the castle of Edinburgh, of which Alexander Erskine was governor; and, as if it had not been a sufficient indignity to subject him to the power of one of his enemies, he was soon after carried to Dumbarton, of which Lennox had the command. A warrant was likewise issued for apprehending Archibald Douglas; but he, having received timely intelligence of the approaching danger, fled into England.

The Earl of Angus, who imputed these violent proceedings not to hatred against Morton alone, but to the ancient enmity between the houses of Stewart and of Douglas, and who believed that a conspiracy was now formed for the destruction of all who bore that name, was ready to take arms in order to rescue his kinsman. But Morton absolutely forbade any such attempt, and declared that he would rather suffer ten thousand deaths than bring an imputation upon his own character by seeming to decline a trial.

Elizabeth did not fail to interpose, with warmth, in behalf of a man who had contributed so much to preserve her influence over Scotland. The late transactions in that kingdom had given her great uneasiness. The power which Lennox had acquired independent of her was dangerous; the treatment her ambassadors had met with differed greatly from the respect with which the Scots were in use to receive her ministers; and the attack now made on Morton, fully convinced her that there was an intention to sow the seeds of discord between the two nations, and to seduce James into a new alliance with France, or into a marrirge with some Popish Princess. Full of these apprehensions, she ordered a considerable body of troops to be assembled on the borders of Scotland, and dispatched Randolph as her ambassador into that kingdom. He addressed himself not only to James, and to his council, but to a convention of estates met at that time. He began with enumerating the extraordinary benefits which Elizabeth had conferred on the Scottish nation : that without demanding a single foot of land for herself, without encroaching on the liberties of the kingdom in the smallest article, she had, at the expense of the blood of her subjects and the treasures of her crown, rescued the Scots from the dominion of France, established among them true religion, and put them in possession of their ancient rights : that from the beginning of civil dissensions in the kingdom, she had protected those who espoused the King's cause, and by her assistance alone, the crown had been preserved on his head, and all the attempts of the adverse faction baffled : that a union, unknown to their ancestors, but equally beneficial to both kingdoms, had subsisted for a long period of years, and though so many Popish Princes had combined to disturb this happy state of things, her care, and their constancy, had hitherto defeated all these efforts : that she had observed of late an unusual coldness, distrust, and estrangement in the Scottish council, which she could impute to none but to Lennox, a subject of France, a retainer to the house of Guise, bred up in the errors of popery, and still suspected of favouring that superstition. Not

x

satisfied with having mounted so fast to an uncommon height of power, which he exercised with all the rashness of youth, and all the ignorance of a stranger; nor thinking it enough to have deprived the Earl of Morton of the authority due to his abilities and experience, he had conspired the ruin of that nobleman, who had often exposed his life in the King's cause, who had contributed more than any other subject to place him on the throne, to resist the encroachments of Popery, and to preserve the union between the two kingdoms. If any zeal for religion remained among the nobles in Scotland, if they wished for the continuance of amity with England, if they valued the privileges of their own order, he called upon them, in the name of his mistress, to remove such a pernicious counsellor as Lennox from the presence of the young King, to rescue Morton out of the hands of his avowed enemy, and secure to him the benefit of a fair and impartial trial : and if force was necessary towards accomplishing a design so salutary to the King and kingdom, he promised them the protection of his mistress in the enterprise, and whatever assistance they should demand, either of men or money.

But these extraordinary remonstrances, accompanied with such an unusual appeal from the King to his subjects. were not the only means employed by Elizabeth in favour of Morton, and against Lennox. She persuaded the Prince of Orange to send an agent into Scotland, and, under colour of complimenting James on account of the valour which many of his subjects had displayed in the service of the States, to enter into a long detail of the restless enterprises of the Popish Princes against the Protestant religion ; to beseech him to adhere inviolably to the alliance with England, the only barrier which secured his kingdom against their dangerous cabals ; and, above all things, to distrust the insinuations of those who endeavoured to weaken or to dissolve that union between the British nations, which all the Protestants in Europe beheld with so much pleasure.*

James's counsellors were too intent upon the destruction of their enemy to listen to these remonstrances. The officious interposition of the Prince of Orange, the haughty tone of Elizabeth's message, and her avowed attempt to excite subjects to rebel against their sovereign, were considered as unexampled insults on the majesty and independence of a crowned head. A general and evasive answer was given to Randolph. James prepared to assert his own dignity with spirit. All those suspected of favouring Morton were turned out of office, some of them were required to surrender themselves prisoners; the men capable of bearing arms, throughout the kingdom were commanded to be in readiness to take the field ; and troops were levied and posted on the borders. The English ambassador, finding that neither the public manifesto which he had delivered to the convention, nor his private cabals with the nobles, could excite them to arms, fled in the night time out of Scotland, where libels against him had been daily published, and even attempts made upon his life. In both kingdoms every thing wore a

* See Append. No. XLI.

hostile aspect. But Elizabeth, though she wished to have intimidated the Scottish King by her preparations, had no inclination to enter into a war with him; and the troops on the borders, which had given such umbrage, were soon dispersed.

The greater solicitude Elizabeth discovered for Morton's safety, the more eagerly did his enemies drive on their schemes for his destruction. Captain Stewart, his accuser, was first appointed *tutor* to the Earl of Arran, and soon after both the title and estate of his unhappy ward, to which he advanced some frivolous claim, were conferred upon him. The new-made peer was commanded to conduct Morton from Dumbarton to Edinburgh; and by that choice the Earl was not only warned what fate he might expect, but had the cruel mortification of seeing his deadly enemy already loaded with honours, in reward of the malice with which he had contributed to his ruin.

The records of the court of *justiciary* at this period are lost. The account which our historians give of Morton's trial is inaccurate and unsatisfactory. The proceedings against him seem to have been carried on with violence. During the trial, great bodies of armed men were drawn up in different parts of the city. The jury was composed of the Earl's known enemies; and though he challenged several of them, his objections were overruled. After a short consultation, his peers found him guilty of concealing, and of being *art and part* in the conspiracy against the life of the late King. The first part of the verdict did not surprise him, but he twice repeated the words *art and part* with some vehemence, and added, "God knows it is not so." The doom which the law decrees against a traitor was pronounced. The King, however, remitted the cruel and ignominious part of the sentence, and appointed that he should suffer death next day, by being beheaded.

During that awful interval, Morton possessed the utmost composure of mind. He supped cheerfully; slept a part of the night in his usual manner, and employed the rest of his time in religious conferences, and in acts of devotion with some ministers of the city. The clergymen who attended him, dealt freely with his conscience, and pressed his crimes home upon him. What he confessed with regard to the crime for which he suffered was remarkable, and supplies in some measure the imperfection of our records. He acknowledged, that on his return from England, after the death of Rizio, Bothwell had informed him of the conspiracy against the King, which the Queen, as he told him, knew of and approved: that he solicited him to concur in the execution of it, which at that time he absolutely declined; that soon after Bothwell himself and Archibald Douglas, in his name, renewing their solicitations to the same purpose, he had required a warrant under the Queen's hand, authorizing the attempt, and as that had never been produced, he had refused to be any further concerned in the matter. "But" continued he, "as I neither consented to this treasonable act, nor assisted in the committing of it, so it was impossible for me to reveal, or to prevent it. To whom could I make the discovery? The Queen was author of the enterprise. Darnly was such a changeling, that no secret could be safely communicated to him. Huntly and Bothwell, who bore the chief sway in the kingdom, were themselves the perpetrators of the crime. These circumstances, it must be confessed, go some length towards extenuating Morton's guilt; and though his apology for the favour he had shown to Archibald Douglas, whom he knew to be one of the conspirators, be far less satisfactory, no uneasy reflections seems to have disquieted his own mind on that account. When his keepers told him that the guards were attending, and all things in readiness, "I praise my God," said he, "I am ready likewise." Arran commanded these guards; and even in those moments when the most implacable hatred is apt to relent, the malice of his enemies could not forbear this insult. On the scaffold, his behaviour was calm; his countenance and voice much unaltered; and, after some time spent in devotion, he suffered death with the intrepidity which became the name of Douglas. His head was placed on the public gaol of Edinburgh: and his body after lying till sunset on the scaffold covered with a beggarly cloak, was carried by common porters to the usual burial-place for criminals. None of his friends durst accompany it to the grave, or discover their gratitude and respect by any symptoms of sorrow.

Arran, no less profligate in private life than audacious in his public conduct, soon after drew the attention of his countrymen by his infamous marriage with the Countess of March. Before he grew into favour at court, he had been often entertained in her husband's house, and without regarding the laws of hospitality or of gratitude, carried on a criminal intrigue with the wife of his benefactor, a woman young and beautiful, but, according to the description of a cotemporary historian, "intolerable in all the imperfections incident to her sex." Impatient of any restraint upon their mutual desires, they, with equal ardour, wished to avow their union publicly, and to legitmate, by a marriage, the offspring of their unlawful passion. The Countess petitioned to be divorced from her husband, for a reason which no modest woman will ever plead. The judges, overawed by Arran, passed sentence without delay [July 6]. This infamous scene was concluded by a marriage, solemnized with great pomp, and beheld by all ranks of men with horror.

A parliament was held this year [Oct. 24], at the opening of which some disputes arose between Arran and the new created Duke of Lennox. Arran, haughty by nature, and pushed on by his wife's ambition, began to affect an equality with the Duke, under whose protection he had hitherto been contented to place himself. After various attempts to form a party in the council against Lennox, he found him fixed so firmly in the King's affections that it was impossible to shake him; and, rather than lose all interest at court, from which he was banished, he made the most humble submissions to the favourite, and again recovered his former credit. This rupture contributed, however, to render the Duke still more odious to the nation. During the continuance of it, Arran affected to court the clergy, pretended an extraordinary zeal for the Protestant religion, and laboured to confirm the suspicions which were entertained of his rival, as an emissary of the house of Guise, and a favourer of Popery. As he was supposed to be acquainted with the Duke's most secret designs, his calumnies were listened to with greater credit than was due to his character. To this rivalship between Lennox and Arran, during the continuance of which each endeavoured to conciliate the good will of the clergy, we must ascribe several acts of this parliament uncommonly favourable to the church, particularly one which abolished the practice introduced by Morton, of appointing but one minister to several parishes.

No notice had been taken for several years of ecclesiastical affairs. While the civil government underwent so many extraordinary revolutions. Two objects chiefly engrossed the attention of the clergy. The one was, the forming a system of discipline, or ecclesiastical polity. After long labour, and many difficulties, this system was at last brought to some degree of perfection. The assembly solemnly approved of it, and appointed it to be laid before the privy council in order to obtain the ratification of it in parliament. But Morton, during his administration, and those who, after his fall, governed the King, were equally unwilling to see it carried into execution; and, by starting difficulties and throwing in objections, prevented it from receiving a legal sanction. The other point in view was the abolition of the episcopal order. The bishops were so devoted to the King, to whom they owed their promotion, that the function itself was by some reckoned dangerous to civil liberty. Being allowed a seat in parliament, and distinguished by titles of honour, these not only occasioned many avocations from their spiritual functions, but soon rendered their character and manners extremely different from those of the clergy in that age. The nobles viewed their power with jealousy; the populace considered their lives as profane; and both wished their downfall with equal ardour. The personal emulation between Melvil and Adamson, a man of learning and eminent for his popular eloquence, who was promoted, on the death of Douglas to be Archbishop of St. Andrew's mingled itself with the passions on each side, and heightened them. Attacks were made in every assembly on the order of bishops; their privileges were gradually circumscribed; and at last an act was passed, declaring the office of bishop, as it was then exercised within the realm, to have neither foundation nor warrant in the word of God; and requiring, under pain of excommunication, all who now possessed that office, instantly to resign it, and to abstain from preaching or administering the sacraments until they should receive permission from the General Assembly. The court did not acquiesce in this decree. A vacancy happening soon after in the see of Glasgow, Montgomery minister at Stirling, a man vain, fickle, presumptuous, and more apt, by the blemishes in his character, to have alienated the people from the order already beloved, than to reconcile them to one which was the object of their hatred, made an infamous simonical bargain with Lennox, and on his recommendation was chosen archbishop. The presbytery of Stirling, of which he was a member, the presbytery of Glasgow, whither he was to be translated, the General Assembly, vied with each other in prosecuting him on that account. In order to screen Montgomery, James made trial both of gentle and of rigorous measures, and both were equally ineffectual. The General Assembly was just ready to pronounce against him the sentence of excommunication, when a herald entered, and commanded them in the King's name, and under pain of rebellion, to stop further proceedings. Even this injunction they despised; and though Montgomery, by his tears and seeming penitence, procured a short respite, the sentence was at last issued by their appointment, and published in all the churches throughout the kingdom.

The firmness of the clergy in a collective body was not greater than the boldness of some individuals, particularly of the ministers of Edinburgh. They inveighed daily against the corruptions in the administration ; and, with the freedom of speech admitted into the pulpit in that age, named Lennox and Arran the chief authors of the grievances under which the church and kingdom groaned. The courtiers, in their turn, complained to the King of the insolent and seditious spirit of the clergy. In order to check the boldness of their discourses, James issued a proclamation, commanding Dury, one of the most popular ministers, not only to leave the town, but to abstain from preaching in any other place. Dury complained to the judicatories of this encroachment upon the immunities of his office. They approved of the doctrine which he had delivered ; and he determined to disregard the royal proclamation. But the magistrates being determined to compel him to leave the city, according to the King's orders, he was obliged to abandon his charge, after protesting publicly at the cross of Edinburgh against the violence which was put upon him. The people accompanied him to the gates with tears and lamentations; and the clergy denounced the vengeance of heaven against the authors of this outrage.

In this perilous situation stood the church, the authority of its judicators called in question, and the liberty of the pulpit restrained, when a sudden revolution of the civil government procured them unexpected relief.

The two favourites, by their ascendancy over the King, possessed uncontrolled power in the kingdom, and exercised it with the utmost wantonness. James usually resided at Dalkeith or Kinneil, the seats of Lennox and of Arran, and was attended by such company, and employed in such amusements, as were not suitable to his dignity. The services of those who had contributed most to place the crown on his head were but little remembered. Many who had opposed him with the greatest virulence, enjoyed the rewards and honours to which the others were entitled. Exalted notions of regal prerogative, utterly inconsistent with the constitution of Scotland, being instilled by his favourites into the mind of the young monarch, unfortunately made, at that early age, a deep impression there, and became the source of almost all his subsequent errors in the government of both kingdoms. Courts of justice were held in almost every county, the proprietors of land were called before them, and upon the slightest neglect of any of the numerous forms which are peculiar to the feudal holdings they were fined with unusual and intolerable rigour. The lord chamberlain revived the obsolete jurisdiction of his office over the boroughs, and they were subjected to actions no less grievous. A design seemed likewise to have been formed to exasperate Elizabeth, and to dissolve the alliance with her, which all good Protestants esteemed the chief security of their religion in Scotland. A close correspondence was carried on between the King and his mother, and considerable progress made towards uniting their titles to the crown by such a treaty of association as Maitland had projected ; which could not fail of endangering or diminishing his authority, and must have proved fatal to those who had acted against her with the greatest vigour.

All these circumstances irritated the impatient spirit of the Scottish nobles, who resolved to tolerate no longer the insolence of the two minions, or to stand by while their presumption and inexperience ruined both the king and the kingdom. Elizabeth, who during the administration of the four Regents, had the entire direction of the affairs of Scotland, felt herself deprived of all influence in that kingdom ever since the death of Morton, and was ready to countenance any attempt to rescue the King out of the hands of favourites who were leading him into measures so repugnant to all her views. The Earls of Mar and Glencairn, Lord Ruthven, lately created Earl of Gowrie, Lord Lindsay, Lord Boyd, the tutor of Glamis, the eldest son of Lord Oliphant, with several barons and gentlemen of distinction, entered into a combination for that purpose; and as changes in administration, which among polished nations are brought about slowly and silently by artifice and intrigue, were in that rude age effected suddenly and by violence, the King's situation, and the security of the favourites, encouraged the conspirators to have immediate recourse to force.

James, after having resided for some time in Athol, where he enjoyed his favourite amusement of hunting, was now returning towards Edinburgh with a small train. He was invited to Ruthven Castle, which lay in his way ; and as he suspected no danger, he went thither in hopes of further sport [Aug. 13]. The multitude of strangers whom he found there gave him some uneasiness; and as those who were in the secret arrived every moment from different parts, the appearance of so many new faces increased his fears. He concealed his uneasiness, however, with the utmost care; and next morning prepared for the field, expecting to find there some opportunity of making his escape. But just as he was ready to depart, the nobles entered his bedchamber in a body, and presented a memorial against the illegal and oppressive actions of his two favourites, whom they represented as most dangerous enemies to the religion and liberties of the nation. James, though he received this remonstrance with the complaisance which was necessary in his present situation, was extremely impatient to be gone; but as he approached the door of his apartment, the tutor Glamis rudely stopped him. The King complained, expostulated, threatened, and, finding all these without effect, burst into tears: "No matter," said Glamis fiercely, "better children weep than bearded men." These words made a deep impression on the King's mind, and were never forgotten. The conspirators, without regarding his tears or indignation, dismissed such of his followers as they suspected; allowed none but persons of their own party to have access to him; and, though they treated him with great respect, guarded his person with the utmost care. This enterprise is usually called, by our historians, *The Raid of Ruthven.*

Lennox and Arran were astonished to the last degree at an event so unexpected, and so fatal to their power. The former endeavoured, but without success, to excite the inhabitants of Edinburgh to take arms in order to rescue their sovereign from captivity. The latter with his usual impetuosity mounted on horseback the moment he heard what had befallen the King, and with a few followers rode towards Ruthven Castle; and as a considerable body of the conspirators, under the command of the Earl of Mar, lay in his way ready to oppose him, he separated himself from his companions, and with two attendants arrived at the gate of the castle. At the sight of a man so odious to his country, the indignation of the conspirators rose, and instant death must have been the punishment of his rashness, if the friendship of Gowrie, or some other cause not explained by our historians, had not saved a life so pernicious to the kingdom. He was confined, however to the castle of Stirling, without being admitted into the King's presence.

The King, though really the prisoner of his own subjects, with whose conduct he could not help discovering many symptoms of disgust, was obliged to publish a proclamation, signifying his approbation of their enterprise, declaring that he was at full liberty, without any restraint or violence offered to his person; and forbidding any attempt against those concerned in the *Raid of Ruthven,* under pretence of rescuing him out of their hands [Aug. 28]. At the same time he commanded Lennox to leave Scotland before the 20th of September.

Soon after Sir George Carey and Robert Bowes arrived as embassadors from Elizabeth. The pretext of their embassy was to enquire after the King's safety; to encourage and countenance the conspirators was the real motive of it. By their intercession the Earl of Angus, who, ever since the death of his uncle Morton, had lived in exile, obtained leave to return. And the accession of a nobleman so powerful and so popular strengthened the faction.

Lennox whose amiable and gentle qualities had procured him many friends and who received private assurances that the King's favour towards him was in no degree abated, seemed resolved at first to pay no regard to a command extorted by violence, and no less disagreeable to James than it was rigorous with regard to himself. But the power of his enemies, who were masters of the King's person, who were secretly supported by Elizabeth, and openly applauded by the clergy, deterred him from any enterprise the success of which was dubious, and the danger certain both to himself and to his sovereign. He put off the time of his departure, however, by various artifices in expectation either that James might make his escape from the conspirators, or fortune might present some more favourable opportunity of taking arms for his relief.

On the other hand, the conspirators were extremely solicitous not only to secure the approbation of their countrymen, but to obtain some legal sanction of their enterprise. For this purpose they published a long declaration, containing the motives which had induced them to venture on such an irregular step, and endeavoured to heighten the public indignation against the favourites, by representing in the strongest colours their inexperience and insolence, their contempt of the nobles, their violation of the privileges of the church, and their oppression of the people. They obliged the King, who could not with safety refuse any of their demands, to grant them a remission in the most ample form; and, not satisfied with that, they applied to the assembly of the church, and easily procured an act [Oct. 3], declaring, "that they had done good and acceptable service to God, to their sovereign, and to their native country;" and requiring all sincere Protestants to concur with them in carrying forward such a laudable enterprise. In order to add the greater weight to this act, every minister was enjoined to read it in his own pulpit, and to inflict the censures of the church on those who set themselves in opposition to so good a cause. A convention of estates assembled a few days after, passed an act to the same effect, and granted full indemnity to the conspirators for every thing they had done.

James was conducted by them first to Stirling, and afterwards to the palace of Holyrood house; and though he was received every where with the external marks of respect due to his dignity, his motions were carefully observed, and he was under a restraint no less strict than at the first moment when he was seized by the conspirators. Lennox, after eluding many commands to depart out of the kingdom, was at last obliged to begin his journey, He lingered, however, for some time in the neighbourhood of Edinburgh, as if he had still intended to make some effort towards restoring the King to liberty. But either from the gentleness of his own disposition, averse to bloodshed and the disorders of civil war, or from some other cause unknown to us, he abandoned the design and set out for France by the way of England. The King issued the order for his departure [Dec. 30], with no less reluctance than the Duke obeyed it : and both mourned a separation which neither of them had power to prevent. Soon after his arrival in France, the fatigue of the journey, or the anguish of his mind, threw him into a fever. In his last moments he discovered such a firm adherence to the Protestant faith as fully vindicates his memory from the imputation of an attachment to Popery, with which he had been uncharitably loaded in Scotland. As he was the earliest and best beloved, he was, perhaps, the most deserving, though not the most able, of all James's favourites. The warmth and tenderness of his master's affection for him were not abated by death itself. By many acts of kindness and generosity towards his posterity, the King not only did great honour to the memory of Lennox, but set his own character in one of its most favourable points of view.

The success of the conspiracy which deprived King James of liberty made a great noise over all Europe, and at last reached the ears of Mary in the prison to which she was confined. As her own experience had taught her what injuries a captive Prince is exposed

N 5

to suffer; and as many of those who were now concerned in the
enterprise against her son were the same persons whom she considered as the chief authors of her own misfortunes, it was natural
for the tenderness of a mother to apprehend that the same calamities were ready to fall on his head; and such a prospect did not
fail of adding to the distress and horror of her own situation. In
the anguish of her heart she wrote to Elizabeth, complaining in
the bitterest terms of the unprecedented rigour with which she
herself had been treated, and beseeching her not to abandon her
son to the mercy of his rebellious subjects; nor permit him to be
involved in the same misfortunes under which she had so long
groaned. The peculiar vigour and acrimony of style, for which
this letter is remarkable, discovered both the high spirit of the
Scottish Queen, unsubdued by her sufferings, and the violence of
her indignation at Elizabeth's artifices and severity. But it was ill
adapted to gain the end which she had in view, and accordingly it
neither procured any mitigation of the rigour of her own confinement, nor any interposition in favour of the King.

1583.] Henry III., who, though he feared and hated the Princes
of Guise, was often obliged to court their favour, interposed with
warmth, in order to extricate James out of the hands of a party so
entirely devoted to the English interest. He commanded M. de
la Motte Fenelon, his ambassador at the court of England, to repair to Edinburgh, and to contribute his utmost endeavours towards placing James in a situation more suitable to his dignity.
As Elizabeth could not with decency refuse him liberty to execute
his commission, she appointed Davison to attend him into Scotland as her envoy, under colour of concurring with him in the
negotiation, but in reality to be a spy upon his motions and to obstruct his success. James, whose title to the crown had not hitherto been recognised by any of the Princes on the continent, was
extremely fond of such an honourable embassy from the French
Monarch, and on that account, as well as for the sake of the errand
on which he came, received Fenelon with great respect [Jan. 7].
The nobles, in whose power the King was, did not relish this interposition of the French court, which had long lost its ancient influence over the affairs of Scotland. The clergy were alarmed at the
danger to which religion would be exposed, if the Princes of Guise
should recover any ascendant over the public councils. Though
the King tried every method for restraining them within the
bounds of decency, they declared against the court of France,
against the Princes of Guise, against the ambassador, against entering into any alliance with such notorious persecutors of the church
of God, with a vehemence which no regular government would now
tolerate, but which was then extremely common. The ambassador,
watched by Davison, distrusted by the nobles, and exposed to the
insults of the clergy and of the people, returned into England
without procuring any change in the King's situation, or receiving
any answer to a proposal which he made, that the government
should be carried on in the joint name of James and the Queen his
mother.*

* See Append. No. XLII.

Meanwhile James, though he dissembled with great art, became every day more uneasy under his confinement; his uneasiness rendered him continually attentive to find out a proper opportunity for making his escape; and to this attention he at last owed his liberty, which the King of France was not able, nor the Queen of England willing, to procure for him. As the conspirators had forced Lennox out of the kingdom, and kept Arran at a distance from court, they grew secure; and imagining that time had reconciled the King to his situation they watched him with little care. Some occasions of discord had arisen among themselves; and the French ambassador, by fomenting these during the time of his residence of Scotland, had weakened the union, in which alone their safety consisted. Colonel William Stewart, the commander of the band of gentlemen who guarded the King's person, being gained by James, had the principal merit in the scheme for restoring his master to liberty. Under pretence of paying a visit to the Earl of March, his grand-uncle, James was permitted to go from Falkland to St. Andrew's [June 27th]. That he might not create any suspicion, he lodged at first in an open defenceless house in the town, but pretending a curiosity to see the castle, no sooner was he entered with some of his attendants whom he could trust, than Colonel Stewart commanded the gates to be shut, and excluded all the rest of his train. Next morning the Earls of Argyll, Huntly, Crawford, Montrose, Rothes, with others to whom the secret had been communicated, entered the town with their followers; and though Mar, with several of the leaders of the faction, appeared in arms, they found themselves so far outnumbered that it was in vain to think of recovering possession of the King's person, which had been in their power somewhat longer than ten months. James was naturally of so soft and ductile a temper that those who were near his person commonly made a deep impression on his heart, which was formed to be under the sway of favourites. As he remained implacable and unreconciled to the conspirators during so long a time, and at a period of life when resentments are rather violent than lasting, they must either have improved the opportunities of insinuating themselves into favour with little dexterity, or the indignation, with which this first insult to his person and authority filled him, must have been very great.

His joy at his escape was youthful and excessive. He resolved, however, by the advice of Sir James Melvil, and his wisest counsellors, to act with the utmost moderation. Having called into his presence the leaders of both factions, the neighbouring gentry, the deputies of the adjacent boroughs, the ministers and the heads of colleges, he declared, that although he had been held under restraint for some time by violence, he would not impute that as a crime to any man, but, without remembering the irregularities which had been so frequent during his minority, would pass a general act of oblivion, and govern all his subjects with undistinguishing and equal affection. As an evidence of his sincerity he visited the Earl of Gowrie at Ruthven Castle, and granted him a full pardon of any guilt he had contracted by the crime committed in that very place.

But James did not adhere long to this prudent and moderate plan. His former favourite, the Earl of Arran, had been permitted for some time to reside at Kinneil, one of his country seats. As soon as the King felt himself at liberty, his love for him began to revive, and he expressed a strong desire to see him. The courtiers violently opposed the return of a minion, whose insolent and over-bearing temper they dreaded as much as the nation detested his crimes. James, however, continued his importunity, and promising that he should continue with him no longer than one day, they were obliged to yield. This interview rekindled ancient affection ; the King forgot his promise ; Arran regained his ascendant over him ; and within a few days resumed the exercise of power, with all the arrogance of an undeserving favourite, and all the rashness peculiar to himself.

The first effect of his influence was a proclamation with regard to those concerned in the *Raid of Ruthven.* They were required to acknowledge their crime in the humblest manner ; and the King promised to grant them a full pardon, provided their future conduct were such as did not oblige him to remember past mis-carriages. The tenor of this proclamation was extremely different from the act of oblivion which the conspirators had been en-couraged to expect. Nor did any of them reckon it safe to rely on a promise clogged with such an equivocal condition, and granted by a young Prince under the dominion of a minister void of faith, regardless of decency, and transported by the desire of revenge even beyond the usual ferocity of his temper. Many of the leaders, who had at first appeared openly at court, retired to their own houses ; and, foreseeing the dangerous storm which was gathering, began to look for a retreat in foreign countries.

Elizabeth, who had all along protected the conspirators, was ex-tremely disgusted with measures which tended so visibly to their destruction, and wrote to the King [Aug 7], a harsh and haughty letter reproaching him, in a style very uncommon among Princes, with a breach of faith in recalling Arran to court, and with im-prudence in proceeding so rigorously against his best and most faithful subjects. James, with a becoming dignity, replied, that promises extorted by violence , and conditions yielded out of fear, were no longer binding when these were removed ; that it belonged to him alone to choose what ministers he would employ in his ser-vice ; and that though he resolved to treat the conspirators at Ruthven with the utmost clemency, it was necessary, for the suport of his authority, that such an insult on his person should not pass altogether uncensured.

Elizabeth's letter was quickly followed [Sep. 1] by Walsingham her secretary, whom she appointed her ambassador to James, and who appeared at the Scottish court with a splendour and magnifi-cence well calculated to please and dazzle a young Prince. Wal-singham was admitted to several conferences with James himself, in which he insisted on the same topics contained in the letter, and the King repeated his former answers.

After suffering several indignities from the arrogance of Arran and his creatures, he returned to England without concluding any new treaty with the King. Walsingham was, next to Burleigh, the minister on whom the chief weight of the English administration rested ; and when a person of his rank stepped so far out of the ordinary road of business as to undertake a long journey in his old age, and under a declining state of health, some affair of consequence was supposed to be the cause, or some important event was expected to be the effect of this measure. But as nothing conspicuous either occasioned or followed this embassy, it is probable that Elizabeth had no other intention in employing this sagacious minister than to discover with exactness the capacity and disposition of the Scottish King, who was now arrived at a time of life when with some degree of certainty, conjectures might be formed concerning his character and future conduct. As James possed talents of that kind which make a better figure in conversation than in action, he gained a great deal by this interview with the English secretary, who, notwithstanding the cold reception which he met with, gave such an advantageous representation of his abilities, as determined Elizabeth to treat him, henceforward, with greater decency and respect.

Elizabeth's eagerness to protect the conspirators rendered James more violent in his proceedings against them. As they had all refused to accept of pardon upon the terms which he had offered, they were required, by a new proclamation, to surrender themselves prisoners. The Earl of Angus alone complied ; the rest either fled into England, or obtained the King's licence to retire into foreign parts. A convention of estates was held [Dec. 17], the members of which, deceived by an unworthy artifice of Arran's, declared those concerned in the *Raid of Ruthven* to have been guilty of high treason ; appointed the act passed last year approving of their conduct to be expunged out of the records ; and engaged to support the King in prosecuting the fugitives with the utmost rigour of law.

The conspirators, though far from having done any thing that was uncommon in that age, among mutinous nobles, and under an unsettled state of government, must be acknowledged to have been guilty of an act of treason against their sovereign ; and James, who considered their conduct in this light, had good reason to boast of his clemency, when he offered to pardon them upon their confessing their crime. But, on the other hand, it must be allowed that, after the King's voluntary promise of a general oblivion, they had some reason to complain of a breach of faith, and, without the most unpardonable imprudence, they could not have put their lives in Arran's power.

1584.] The interest of the church was considerably affected by these contrary revolutions. While the conspirators kept possession of power, the clergy not only recovered, but they extended their privileges. As they had formerly declared the hierarchy to be unlawful, they took some bold measures towards exterminating the episcopal order out of the church ; and it was owing more to Adamson's dexterity in perplexing and lengthening out the process for that purpose, than to their own want of zeal, that they did not deprive, and perhaps excommunicate, all the bishops in Scotland.

When the King recovered his liberty, things put on a very different aspect. The favour bestowed upon Arran, the enemy of every
thing decent and sacred, and the rigorous prosecution of those
nobles who had been the most zealous defenders of the Protestant
cause, were considered as sure presages of the approaching ruin of
the church. The clergy could not conceal their apprehensions, nor
view his impending danger in silence. Dury, who had been restored to his office as one of the ministers of Edinburgh, openly applauded the *Raid of Ruthven* in the pulpit; at which the King was
so enraged that, notwithstanding some symptoms of his submission,
he commanded him to resign his charges in the city. Mr. Andrew
Melvil, being summoned before the privy council to answer for the
doctrine which he had uttered in a sermon at St. Andrew's and
accused of comparing the present grievances of the nation with
those under James III., and of intimating obliquely that they
ought to be redressed in the same manner, thought it incumbent
on him to behave with great firmness. He declined the jurisdiction of a civil court in a cause which he maintained to be purely
ecclesiastical; the presbytery, of which he was a member, had, as
he contended, the sole right to call him to account, for words spoken
in the pulpit; and neither the King nor council could judge, of the
doctrine delivered by preachers without violating the immunities of
the church. This exemption from civil jurisdiction was a privilege which the Popish ecclesiastics, who were most admirable
judges of whatever contributed to increase the lustre or power of
their body, had long struggled for, and at last obtained. If the same
plea had now been admitted, the Protestant clergy would have become independent on the civil magistrate; and an order of men
extremely useful to society, while they inculcate those duties which
tend to promote its happiness and tranquillity, might have become
no less pernicious, by teaching without fear or control the most
dangerous principles, or by exciting their hearers to the most desperate and lawless actions. The King, jealous to excess of his prerogative, was alarmed at this daring encroachment on it; and as Melvil, by his learning and zeal, had acquired the reputation and
authority of head of the party, he resolved to punish him with the
rigour which that pre-eminence rendered necessary, and to discourage, by a timely severity, the revival of such a dangerous claim.
Melvil, however, avoided his rage by flying into England; and the
pulpits resounded with complaints that the King had extinguished
the light of learning in the kingdom, and deprived the church of
the ablest and most faithful guardian of its liberties and discipline.

These violent declamations of the clergy against the measures of
the court were extremely acceptable to the people. The conspirators, though driven out of the kingdom, still possessed great influence there; and as they had every thing to fear from the resentment of a young Prince, irritated by the furious counsels of Arran,
they never ceased soliciting their adherents to take arms in their
defence. Gowrie, the only person among them who had submitted
to the King, and accepted of a pardon, soon repented of a step
which lost him the esteem of the one party, without gaining the
confidence of the other; and, after suffering many mortifications

from the King's neglect and the haughtiness of Arran, he was at last commanded to leave Scotland, and to reside in France. While he waited at Dundee for an opportunity to embark, he was informed that the Earls of Angus, Mar, and the tutor of Glamis, had concerted a scheme for surprising the castle of Stirling. In his situation, little persuasion was necessary to draw him to engage in it. Under various pretexts he put off his voyage, and lay ready to take arms on the day fixed by the conspirators for the execution of their enterprise. His lingering so long at Dundee, without any apparent reason, awakened the suspicion of the court, proved fatal to himself, and disappointed the success of the conspiracy. Colonel William Stewart surrounded the house where he lodged with a body of soldiers, and, in spite of his resistance, took him prisoner. Two days after, Angus, Mar, and Glamis seized the castle of Stirling, and, erecting their standard there, published a manifesto, declaring that they took arms for no other reason but to remove from the King's presence a minion who had acquired power by the most unworthy actions, and who exercised it with the most intolerable insolence. The account of Gowrie's imprisonment struck a damp upon their spirits. They imputed it to treachery on his part, and suspected, that as he had formerly deserted, he had now betrayed them. At the same time Elizabeth having neglected to supply them in good time with a sum of money, which she had promised to them, and their friends and vassals coming in slowly, they appeared irresolute and disheartened; and as the King, who acted with great vigour, advanced towards them at the head of twenty thousand men, they fled precipitately towards England, and with difficulty made their escape. This rash and feeble attempt produced such effects as usually follow disappointed conspiracies. It not only hurt the cause for which it was undertaken, but added strength and reputation to the King; confirmed Arran's power; and enabled them to pursue their measures with more boldness and greater success. Gowrie was the first victim of their resentment. After a very informal trial, a jury of peers found him guilty of treason, and he was publicly beheaded at Stirling.

To humble the church was the King's next step. But as it became necessary, for this purpose, to call in the aid of the legislative authority, a parliament was hastily summoned [May 22]: and while so many of the nobles were banished out of the kingdom, or forbidden to appear in the King's presence; while Arran's haughtiness kept some at a distance, and intimidated others; the meeting consisted only of such as were absolutely at the devotion of the court. In order to conceal the laws which were framing from the knowledge of the clergy, the lords of the articles were sworn to secrecy; and when some of the ministers, who either suspected or were informed of the danger, deputed one of their number to declare their apprehensions to the King, he was seized at the palace gate, and carried to a distant prison. Others, attempting to enter the parliament house, were refused admittance; and such laws were passed as totally overturned the constitution and discipline of the church. The refusing to acknowledge the jurisdiction of the privy council; the pretending an exemption from the authority of

the civil courts; the attempting to diminish the rights and privileges of any of the three estates in parliament, were declared to be
high treason. The holding assemblies, whether civil or ecclesiastical, without the King's permission or appointment; the uttering,
either privately or publicly, in sermons or in declamations, any
false and scandalous reports against the King, his ancestors, or
ministers, were pronounced capital crimes.

When these laws were published at the cross of Edinburgh, according to the ancient custom, Mr. Robert Pont, minister of St.
Cuthbert's and one of the lords of session, solemnly protested against
them, in the name of his brethren, because they had been passed
without the knowledge or consent of the church. Ever since the
Reformation, the pulpits and ecclesiastical judicatories had both
been esteemed sacred. In the former, the clergy had been accustomed to censure and admonish with unbounded liberty. In the
latter, they exercised an uncontroled and independent jurisdiction.
The blow was now aimed at both these privileges. These new
statutes were calculated to render churchmen as inconsiderable as
they were indigent; and as the avarice of the nobles had stripped
them of the wealth, the King's ambition was about to deprive them
of the power which once belonged to their order. No wonder the
alarm was universal, and the complaints loud. All the ministers
of Edinburgh forsook their charge, and fled into England. The
most eminent clergymen throughout the kingdom imitated their
example. Desolation and astonishment appeared in every part of
the Scottish church; the people bewailed the loss of pastors whom
they esteemed; and, full of consternation at an event so unexpected,
openly expressed their rage against Arran, and began to suspect the
King himself to be an enemy to the reformed religion.

BOOK VII.

1584.

WHILE Scotland was torn by intestine factions, Elizabeth was
alarmed with the rumour of a project in agitation for setting Mary
at liberty. Francis Throkmorton, a Chesire gentleman, was suspected of being deeply concerned in the design, and on that suspicion he was taken into custody. Among his papers were found
two lists, one of the principal harbours in the kingdom, with an
account of their situation, and of the depth of water in each; the
other, of all the eminent Roman Catholics in England. This circumstance confirmed the suspicion against him, and some dark and
desperate conspiracy was supposed ready to break out. At first he
boldly avowed his innocence, and declared that the two papers
were forged by the Queen's ministers, in order to intimidate or
ensnare him; and he even endured the rack with the utmost forti-

tude. But being brought a second time to the place of torture, his resolution failed him, and he not only acknowledged that he had held a secret correspondence with the Queen of Scots, but discovered a design that was formed to invade England. The Duke of Guise, he said, undertook to furnish troops, and to conduct the enterprise. The Pope and King of Spain were to supply the money necessary for carrying it on; all the English exiles were ready to take arms; many of the Catholics at home would be ready to join them at their landing; Mendoza, the Spanish ambassador, who was the life of the conspiracy, spared no pains in fomenting the spirit of disaffection among the English, or in hastening the preparations on the continent; and by his command, he made the two lists, the copies whereof had been found in his possession. This confession he retraced at his trial; returned to it again after sentence was passed on him; and retracted it once more at the place of execution.

To us in the present age who are assisted in forming our opinion of this matter by the light which time and history have thrown upon the designs and characters of the Princes of Guise, many circumstances of Throkmorton's confession appears to be extremely remote from truth, or even from probability. The Duke of Guise was, at that juncture, far from being in a situation to undertake foreign conquests. Without either power or office at court; hated by the King, and persecuted by the favourites; he had no leisure for any thoughts of disturbing the quiet of neighbouring states; his vast and ambitious mind was wholly occupied in laying the foundation of that famous league which shook the throne of France. But at the time when Elizabeth detected this conspiracy, the close union between the house of Guise and Philip was remarkable to all Europe; and as their great enterprise against Henry III. was not yet disclosed, as they endeavoured to conceal that under their threatenings to invade England, Throkmorton's discovery appeared to be extremely probable; and Elizabeth, who knew how ardently all the parties mentioned by him wished her downfal, thought that she could not guard her kingdom with too much care. The indiscreet zeal of the English exiles increased her fears. Not satisfied with incessant outcries against her severity towards the Scottish Queen, and her cruel persecution of her Catholic subjects, not thinking it enough that one Pope had threatened her with the sentence of excommunication, and another had actually pronounced it, they now began to disperse books and writings, in which they endeavoured to persuade their disciples, that it would be a meritorious action to take away her life; they openly exhorted the maids of honour to treat her as Judith did Holofernes, and, by such an illustrious deed, to render their own names honourable and sacred in the church throughout all future ages. For all these reasons, Elizabeth not only inflicted the punishment of a traitor on Throkmorton, but commanded the Spanish ambassador instantly to leave England; and that she might be in no danger of being attacked within the island, she determined to use her utmost efforts in order to recover that influence over the Scottish councils, which she had for some time entirely lost.

There was three different methods by which Elizabeth might hope to accomplish this; either by furnishing such effectual aid to the banished nobles as would enable them to resume the chief direction of affairs; or by entering into such a treaty with Mary, as might intimidate her son, who, being now accustomed to govern, would not be averse from agreeing to any terms rather than resign the sceptre, or admit an associate in the throne; or, by gaining the Earl of Arran, to secure the direction of the King his master. The last was not only the easiest and speediest, but most likely to be successful. This Elizabeth resolved to pursue, but without laying the other two altogther aside. With this view she sent Davidson, one of her principal secretaries, a man of abilities and address, into Scotland. A minister so venal as Arran, hated by his own countrymen, and holding his power by the most precarious of all tenures, the favour of a young Prince, accepted Elizabeth's offers without hesitation, and deemed the acquisition of her protection to be the most solid foundation of his own greatness [Aug. 13]. Soon after he consented to an interview with Lord Hunsdon, the governor of Berwick, and being honoured with the pompous title of Lieutenant General for the King, he appeared at the place appointed with a splendid train. In Hunsdon's presence he renewed his promises of an inviolable and faithful attachment to the English interest, and assured him that James should enter into a negotiation which might tend to interrupt the peace between the two kingdoms; and as Elizabeth began to entertain the same fears and jealousies concerning the King's marriage, which had formerly disquieted her with regard to his mother's, he undertook to prevent James from listening to any overture of that kind, until he had previously obtained the Queen of England's consent.*

The banished lords and their adherents soon selt the effects of Arran's friendship with England. As Elizabeth had permitted them to take refuge in her dominions, and several of her ministers were of opinion that she ought to employ her arms in defence of their cause, the fear of this was the only thing which restrained James and his favourite from proceeding to such extremities against them as might have excited the pity or indignation of the English, and have prompted them to exert themselves with vigour in their behalf. But every apprehension of this kind being now removed [Aug. 22], they ventured to call a parliament, in which an act was passed, attainting Angus, Mar, Glamis, and a great number of their followers. Their estates devolved to the crown; and, according to the practice of the Scottish monarchs who were obliged to reward the faction which adhered to them, by dividing with it the spoils of the vanquished, James dealt out the greater part of these to Arran and his associates.

Nor was the treatment of the clergy less rigorous. All ministers, readers, and professors in colleges were enjoined to subscribe, within forty days, a paper testifying their approbation of the laws concerning the church enacted in the last parliament. Many, overawed or corrupted by the court, yielded obedience; others stood out. The stipends of the latter were sequestered, some of the more active committed to prison, and numbers compelled to fly

*See Append. No. XLIII.

the kingdom. Such as complied fell under the suspicion of acting from mercenary or ambitious motives. Such as adhered to their principles, and suffered in consequence of it, acquired a high reputation, by giving this convincing evidence of their firmness and sincerity. The judicatories of the church were almost entirely suppressed. In some places scarce as many ministers remained as to perform the duties of religious worship; they sunk in reputation among the people; and being prohibited not only from discoursing of public affairs, but obliged by the jealousy of the administration to frame every sentiment and expression in such a manner as to give the court no offence, their sermons were deemed languid, insipid, and contemptible; and it became the general opinion, that together with the most virtuous of the nobles and the most faithful of the clergy, the power and vigour of religion were now banished out of the kingdom.

Meanwhile, Elizabeth was carrying on one of those fruitless negotiations with the Queen of Scots, which it had become almost matter of form to renew every year. They served not only to amuse that unhappy Princess with some prospect of liberty, but furnished an apology for eluding the solicitations of foreign powers on her behalf; and were of use to overawe James, by shewing him that she could at any time set free a dangerous rival to dispute his authority. These treaties she suffered to proceed to what length she pleased, and never wanted a pretence for breaking them off when they became no longer necessary. The treaty now on foot was not, perhaps, more sincere than many which preceded it; the reasons, however, which rendered it ineffectual were far from being frivolous.

As Crichton, a Jesuit, was sailing from Flanders towards Scotland, the ship on board of which he was a passenger happened to be chased by pirates, who, in that age, often infested the narrow seas. Crichton, in great confusion, tore in pieces some papers in his custody, and threw them away; but, by a very extraordinary accident, the wind blew them into the ship, and they were immediately taken up by some of the passengers, who carried them to Wade, the clerk of the privy council. He, with great industry and patience, joined them together, and they were found to contain the account of a plot, said to have been formed by the King of Spain and the Duke of Guise, for invading England. The people were not yet recovered from the fear and anxiety occasioned by the conspiracy in which Throkmorton had been engaged; and as his discoveries appeared now to be confirmed by additional evidence, not only all their former apprehensions recurred, but the consternation become general and excessive. As all the dangers, with which England had been threatened for some years, flowed either immediately from Mary herself, or from such as made use of her name to justify their insurrections and conspiracies, this gradually diminished the compassion due to her situation, and the English, instead of pitying, began to fear and to hate her. Elizabeth, under whose wise and pacific reign the English enjoyed tranquillity, and had opened sources of wealth unknown to their ancestors, was extremely beloved by all her people; and regard to her safety, not less than to their own interest, animated them against the Scottish Queen. In order to discourage her adherents, it was thought necessary to convince them, by some public deed, of the attachment of the English to their own sovereign, and that any attempt against her life would prove fatal to her rival. With this view an *association* was framed [Oct 19], the subscribers of which bound themselves by the most solemn oaths, " to defend the Queen against all her enemies, foreign and domestic ; and if violence should be offered to her life, in order to favour the title of any pretender to the crown, they not only engaged never to allow or acknowledge the person or persons by whom, or for whom, such a detestable act should be committed, but vowed, in the presence of the eternal God, to prosecute such person or persons to the death, and to pursue them, with their utmost vengeance, to their utter overthrow and extirpation." Persons of all ranks subscribed this combination with the greatest eagerness and unanimity.

Mary considered this association, not only as an avowed design to exclude her from all right of succession, but as the certain and immediate forerunner of her destruction. In order to avert this, she made such feeble efforts as were still in her power, and sent Naue, her secretary, to court, with offers of more entire resignation to the will of Elizabeth, in every point which had been the occasion of their long enmity, than all her sufferings hitherto had been able to extort. But whether Mary adhered inflexibly to her privileges as an independent sovereign, or, yielding to the necessity of her situation, endeavoured by concession to sooth her rival, she was equally unsuccessful. Her firmness was imputed to obstinacy, or to the secret hope of foreign assistance ; her concessions were either believed to be sincere, or to flow from the fear of some imminent danger. Her present willingness, however, to comply with any terms was so great that Walsingham warmly urged his mistress to come to a final agreement with her*. But Elizabeth was persuaded, that it was the spirit raised by the association which had rendered her so passive and complaint. She always imagined that there was something mysterious and deceitful in all Mary's actions, and suspected her of carrying on a dangerous correspondence with the English Catholics, both within and without the kingdom. Nor were her suspicions altogether void of foundation. Mary had, about this time, written a letter to Sir Francis Inglefield, urging him to hasten the execution of what she calls the *Great Plot or designment*, without hesitating on account of any danger in which it might involve her life, which she would most willingly part with, if by that sacrifice she could procure relief for so great a number of the oppressed children of the church. Instead, therefore, of hearkening to the overtures which the Scottish Queen made, or granting any mitigation of the hardships of which she complained, Elizabeth resolved to take her out of the hands of the Earl of Shrewsbury, and to appoint Sir Amias Paulet and Sir Drue Drury to be her keepers. Shrewsbury had discharged his trust with great fidelity, during fifteen years, but,

* See Appendix, No. XLIV.

at the same time, had treated Mary with gentleness and respect, and had always sweetened harsh commands by the humanity with which he put them in execution. The same politeness was not to be expected from men of an inferior rank, whose severe vigilance perhaps was their chief recommendation to that employment, and the only merit by which they could pretend to gain favour or preferment.

As James was no less eager than ever to deprive the banished nobles of Elizabeth's protection, he appointed the Master of Gray his ambassador to the court of England, and intrusted him with the conduct of a negotiation for that purpose. For this honour he was indebted to the envy and jealousy of the Earl of Arran. Gray possessed all the talents of a courtier; a graceful person, an insinuating address, boundless ambition, and a restless and intriguing spirit. During his residence in France, he had been admitted into the most intimate familiarity with the Duke of Guise, and, in order to gain his favour, had renounced the Protestant religion, and professed the utmost zeal for the captive Queen, who carried on a secret correspondence with him, from which she expected great advantages. On his return into Scotland, he paid court to James with extraordinary assiduity, and his accomplishments did not fail to make their usual impression on the King's heart. Arran, who had introduced him, began quickly to dread his growing favour; and, flattering himself that absence would efface any sentiments of tenderness which were forming in the mind of a young Prince, pointed him out by his malicious praises as the most proper person in the kingdom for an embassy of such importance; and contributed to raise him to that high dignity, in order to hasten his fall. Elizabeth, who had an admirable dexterity in discovering the proper instruments for carrying on her designs, endeavoured by caresses, and by presents, to secure Gray to her interest. The former flattered his vanity, which was great; the latter supplied his profuseness, which was still greater. He abandoned himself without reserve to Elizabeth's direction, and not only undertook to retain the King under the influence of England, but acted as a spy upon the Scottish Queen, and betrayed to her rival every secret that he could draw from her by his high pretensions of zeal in her service.

Gray's credit with the English court was extremely galling to the banished nobles. Elizabeth no longer thought of employing her power to restore them; she found it easier to govern Scotland by corrupting the King's favourites; and, in compliance with Gray's solicitations [Dec. 31], she commanded the exiles to leave the north of England, and to remove into the heart of the kingdom. This rendered it difficult for them to hold any correspondence with their partisans in Scotland, and almost impossible to return thither without her permission. Gray, by gaining a point which James had so much at heart, riveted himself more firmly than ever in his favour; and, by acquiring greater reputation, became capable of serving Elizabeth with greater success.

1585.] Arran had now possessed for some time all the power, the riches, and the honours, that his immoderate ambition could desire,

or the fondness of a Prince, who set no limits to his liberality towards his favourites, could bestow. The office of lord chancellor,
the highest and most important in the kingdom, was conferred
upon him, even during the life of the Earl of Argyll, who succeded
Athol in that dignity; and the public beheld with astonishment
and indignation, a man educated as a soldier of fortune, ignorant of
law, and a contemner of justice, appointed to preside in parliament,
in the privy council, in the court of session, and intrusted with the
supreme disposal of the property of his fellow subjects. He was, at
the same time, governor of the castles of Stirling and Edinburgh,
the two principal forts in Scotland; provost of the city of Edinburgh; and, as if by all these accumulated dignities his merits were
not sufficiently recompensed, he had been created lieutenant-general over the whole kingdom. No person was admitted into the
King's presence without his permission; no favour could be obtained but by his mediation.   James, occupied with youthful
amusements, devolved upon him the whole regal authority. Such
unmerited elevation increased his natural arrogance, and rendered
it intolerable. He was no longer content with the condition of a
subject, but pretended to derive his pedigree from Murdo Duke of
Albany: and boasted openly, that his title to the crown was preferable to that of the King himself. But, together with these
thoughts of royalty, he retained the meanness suitable to his primitive indigence.   His venality as a judge was scandalous, and was
exceeded only by that of his wife, who, in defiance of decency, made
herself a party in almost every suit that came to be decided, employed her influence to corrupt or overawe the judges, and almost
openly dictated their decisions. His rapaciousness as a minister
was insatiable. Not satisfied with the revenues of so many offices;
with the estate and honours which belonged to the family of Hamilton; or with the greater part of Gowrie's lands, which had fallen
to his share; he grasped at the possessions of several of the nobles.
He required Lord Maxwell to exchange part of his estate for the
forfeited lands of Kinneil; and because he was unwilling to quit an
ancient inheritance for a possession so precarious, he stirred up
against him his hereditary rival, the laird of Johnson, and involved
that corner of the kingdom in a civil war. He committed to
prison the Earl of Athol, Lord Home, and the Master of Cassils; the
first, because he would not divorce his wife, the daughter of the
Earl of Gowrie, and entail his estate on him; the second, because
he was unwilling to part with some lands adjacent to Arran's
estates; and the third, for refusing to lend him money. His spies
and informers filled the whole country, and intruded themselves
into every company. The nearest neighbours distrusted and feared
each other. All familiar society was at an end. Even the common
intercourses of humanity were interrupted, no man knowing in
whom to confide or where to utter his complaints. There is not
perhaps in history an example of a minister so universally detestable to a nation, or who more justly deserved its detestation.

Arran, notwithstanding, regardless of the sentiments and despising the murmurs of the people, gave a loose to his natural temper,
and proceeded to acts still more violent. David Home of Argaty,

and Patrick his brother, having received letters from one of the banished lords about private business, were condemned and put to death, for holding correspondence with rebels. Cunninghame of Drumwhasel, and Douglas of Mains, two gentlemen of honour and reputation, were accused of having conspired with the exiled nobles to seize the King's person : a single witness only appeared; the evidence they produced of their innocence was unanswerable; their accuser himself not long after acknowledged that he had been suborned by Arran; and all men believed the charge against them to be groundless : they were found guilty, notwithstanding, and suffered the death of traitors.

About the same time that these gentlemen were punished for a pretended conspiracy, Elizabeth's life was endangered by a real one. Parry, a doctor of laws, and a member of the house of commons, a man vain and fantastic, but of a resolute spirit, had lately been reconciled to the church of Rome; and fraught with the zeal of a new convert, he offered to demonstrate the sincerity of his attachment to the religion which he had embraced by killing Elizabeth. Cardinal Allan had published a book, to prove the murder of an excommunicated Prince to be not only lawful, but a meritorious action. The Pope's nuncio at Venice, the Jesuits both there and at Paris, the English exiles, all approved of the design. The Pope himself exhorted him to persevere; and granted him for his encouragement a plenary indulgence, and remission of his sins. Cardinal di Como wrote to him a letter to the same purpose; but though he often got access to the Queen, fear, or some remaining sense of duty, restrained him from perpetrating the crime. Happily his intention was at last discovered by Nevil, the only person in England to whom he had communicated it; and having himself voluntarily confessed his guilt, he suffered the punishment which it deserved.

These repeated conspiracies against their sovereign awakened the indignation of the English Parliament, and produced a very extraordinary statute, which, in the end, proved fatal to the Queen of Scots. By this law, the association in defence of Elizabeth's life was ratified; and it was further enacted, "That if any rebellion shall be excited in the kingdom, or any thing attempted to the hurt of Her Majesty's person, *by or for* any person pretending a title to the crown, the Queen shall empower twenty-four persons, by a commission under the great seal, to examine into, and pass sentence upon such offences; and after judgment given, a proclamation shall be issued, declaring the persons whom they find guilty excluded from any right to the crown; and Her Majesty's subjects may lawfully pursue every one of them to the death, with all their aiders and abetters; and if any design against the life of the Queen take effect, the persons *by or for* whom such a detestable act is executed, and *their issues*, being in anywise assenting or privy to the same, shall be disabled for ever from pretending to the crown, and be pursued to the death in the like manner." This act was plainly levelled at the Queen of Scots; and, whether we consider it as a voluntary expression of the zeal and concern of the nation for the safety of Elizabeth, or whether we impute it to the influence which that artful Princess preserved over her parliaments, it is no easy matter to reconcile it with the general principles of justice or humanity. Mary was thereby rendered accountable not only for her own actions, but for those of others; in consequence of which she might forfeit her right of succession, and even her life itself.

Mary justly considered this act as a warning to prepare for the worst extremities. Elizabeth's ministers, it is probable, had resolved by this time to take away her life; and suffered books to be published, in order to persuade the nation that this cruel and unprecedented measure was not only necessary but just. Even that short period of her days which remained they rendered uncomfortable, by every hardship and indignity which it was in their power to inflict. Almost all her servants were dismissed, she was treated no longer with the respect due to a Queen; and, though the rigour of seventeen years' imprisonment had broken her constitution, she was confined to two ruinous chambers, scarcely habitable, even in the middle of summer, by reason of cold. Notwithstanding the scantiness of her revenue, she had been accustomed to distribute regularly some alms among the poor in the village adjoining to the castle. Paulet now refused her liberty to perform this pious and humane office, which had afforded her great consolation amidst her own sufferings. The castle in which she resided was converted into a common prison; and a young man, suspected of Popery, was confined there, and treated under her eye with such rigour that he died of the ill usage. She often complained to Elizabeth of these multiplied injuries, and expostulated as became a woman and a Queen; but as no political reason now obliged that Princess to amuse her any longer with fallacious hopes, far from granting her any redress, she did not even deign to give her any answer. The King of France, closely allied to Elizabeth, on whom he depended for assistance against his rebellious subjects, was afraid of espousing Mary's cause with any warmth; and all his solicitations in her behalf were feeble, formal, and inefficacious. But Castelnau, the French ambassador, whose compassion and zeal for the unhappy Queen supplied the defects in his instructions, remonstrated with such vigour against the indignities to which she was exposed, that, by his importunity, he prevailed at length to have her removed to Tuthbury; though she was confined the greater part of another winter in her present wretched habitation.

Neither the insults of her enemies nor the neglect of her friends made such an impression on Mary as the ingratitude of her son. James had hitherto treated his mother with filial respect, and had even entered into negotiations with her, which gave umbrage to Elizabeth. But as it was not the interest of the English Queen that his good correspondence should continue, Gray, who, on his return to Scotland, found his favour with the King greatly increased by the success of his embassy, persuaded him to write a harsh and undutiful letter to his mother, in which he expressly refused to acknowledge her to be Queen of Scotland, or to consider his affairs as connected, in any wise, with hers. This cruel requital of her maternal tenderness overwhelmed Mary with sorrow and despair. "Was it for this," said she, in a letter to the French ambassador [March 24], "that I have endured so much, in order to preserve for him the inheritance to which I have a just right? I am far from envying his authority in Scotland. I desire no power there; nor wish to set my foot in that kingdom, if it were not for the pleasure of once embracing a son, whom I have hitherto loved with too tender affection. Whatever he either enjoys or expects, he derived it from me. From him I never received assistance, supply, or benefit of any kind. Let not my allies treat him any longer as a King: he holds that dignity by my consent; and if a speedy repentance do not appease my just resentment, I will load him with a parent's curse, and surrender my crown, with all my pretensions, to one who will receive them with gratitude, and defend them with vigour.* The love which James bore to his mother, whom he had never known, and whom he had been early taught to consider as one of the most abandoned persons of her sex, cannot be supposed ever to have been ardent; and he did not now take any pains to regain her favour. But whether her indignation at his undutiful behaviour, added to her bigoted attachment to Popery, prompted Mary at any time to think seriously of disinheriting her son; or whether these threatenings were uttered in a sudden sally of disappointed affection, it is now no easy matter to determine. Some papers which are still extant seem to render the former not improbable†.

Cares of another kind, and no less disquieting, occupied Elizabeth's thoughts. The calm which she had long enjoyed seemed now to be at an end; and such storms were gathering in every quarter as filled her with just alarm. All the neighbouring nations had undergone revolutions extremely to her disadvantage. The great qualities which Henry III. had displayed in his youth, and which raised the expectations of his subjects so high, vanished on his ascending the throne; and his acquiring supreme power seems not only to have corrupted his heart, but to have impaired his understanding. He soon lost the esteem and affection of the nation; and a life divided between the austerities of a superstitious devotion, and the extravagancies of the most dissolute debauchery, rendered him as contemptible as he was odious on account of his rapaciousness, his profusion, and the fondness with which he doted on many unworthy minions. On the death of his only brother, those sentiments of the people burst out with violence. Henry had no children, and though but thirty-two years of age, the succession of the crown was already considered as open. The King of Navarre, a distant descendant of the royal family, but the undoubted heir to the crown, was a zealous Protestant. The prospect of an event so fatal to their religion, as his ascending the throne of France, alarmed all the Catholics in Europe; and induced the Duke of Guise, countenanced by the Pope and aided by the King of Spain, to appear as the defender of the Romish faith, and the asserter of the Cardinal of Bourbon's right to the crown. In order to unite the party, a bond of confederacy was formed, distinguished by the name of the *Holy League*. All ranks of men joined in it with emulation. The spirit spread with the irresistible rapidity which

* See Append. No. XLV. † See Append. No. XLVI.

was natural to religious passions in that age. The destruction of
the Reformation, not only in France, but all over Europe, seemed
to be the object and wish of the whole party; and the Duke of
Guise, the head of this mighty and zealous body, acquired authority
in the kingdom far superior to that which the King himself possessed. Philip 11. by the conquest of Portugal, had greatly increased
the naval power of Spain, and had at last reduced under his dominion all that portion of the continent which lies beyond the
Pyrenean mountains, and which nature seems to have destined to
form one great monarchy. William Prince of Orange, who first
encouraged the inhabitants of the Netherlands to assert their
liberties, and whose wisdom and valour formed and protected the
rising commonwealth, had fallen by the hands of an assassin. The
superior genius of the Prince of Parma had given an entire turn to
the fate of war in the Low Countries; all his enterprises, concerted
with consummate skill, and executed with equal bravery, had been
attended with success; and the Dutch, reduced to the last extremity, were on the point of falling under the dominion of their ancient
master.

None of those circumstances to which Elizabeth had hitherto
owed her security existed any longer. She could derive no advantage from the jealousy which had subsisted between France and
Spain; Philip, by means of his confederacy with the Duke of
Guise, had an equal sway in the councils of both kingdoms. The
Hugonots were unable to contend with the power of the League;
and little could be expected from any diversion which they might
create. Nor was it probable that the Netherlands could long employ the arms or divide the strength of Spain. In this situation of
the affairs of Europe, it became necessary for Elizabeth to form a
new plan of conduct; and her wisdom in forming it was not greater
than the vigour with which she carried it on. The measures most
suitable to her natural temper, and which she had hitherto pursued, were cautious and safe: those which she now adopted were
enterprising and hazardous. She preferred peace, but was not
afraid of war; and was capable, when compelled by necessity, not
only of defending herself with spirit, but of attacking her enemies
with a boldness which averted danger from her own dominions.
She immediately furnished the Hugonots with a considerable
supply in money. She carried on a private negotiation with
Henry III., who, though compelled to join the League, hated the
leaders of it, and wished for their destruction. She openly undertook the protection of the Dutch commonwealth, and sent a powerful army to its assistance. She endeavoured to form a general confederacy of the Protestant Princes, in opposition to the Popish
league. She determined to proceed with the utmost rigour against
the Queen of Scots, whose sufferings and rights afforded her enemies a specious pretence for invading her dominions. She resolved
to redouble her endeavours, in order to effect a closer union with
Scotland, and to extend and perpetuate her influence over the
councils of that nation.

She found it no difficult matter to induce most of the Scottish
courtiers to promote all her designs. Gray, Sir John Maitland,

who had been advanced to the office of secretary, which his brother formerly held, Sir Lewis Bellenden, the justice clerk, who had succeeded Gray as the King's resident at London, were the persons in whom she chiefly confided. In order to direct and quicken their motions, she dispatched [May 29] Sir Edward Wotton, along with Bellenden, into Scotland. This man was gay, well bred, and entertaining; he excelled in all the exercises for which James had a passion, and amused the young king by relating the adventures which he had met with, and the observations he had made during a long residence in foreign countries; but, under the veil of these superficial qualities, he concealed a dangerous and intriguing spirit. He soon grew into high favour with James; and while he was seemingly attentive only to pleasure and diversions, he acquired influence over the public councils to a degree which was indecent for a stranger to possess.

Nothing, however, could be more acceptable to the nation, than the proposal which he made of a strict alliance between the two kingdoms, in defence of the reformed religion. The rapid and alarming progress of the Popish league seemed to call on all Protestant Princes to unite for the preservation of their common faith. James embraced the overture with warmth [July 29], and a convention of estates empowered him to conclude such a treaty, and engaged to ratify it in parliament. The alacrity with which James concurred in this measure must not be wholly ascribed either to his own zeal, or to Wotton's address; it was owing in part to Elizabeth's liberality. As a mark of her motherly affection for the young King, she settled on him an annual pension of five thousand pounds; the same sum which her father had allotted her before she ascended the throne. This circumstance, which she took care to mention, rendered a sum, which in that age was far from being inconsiderable, a very acceptable present to the King, whose revenues, during a long minority, had been almost totally dissipated.

But the chief object of Wotton's intrigues was to ruin Arran. While a minion so odious to the nation continued to govern the King, his assistance could be of little advantage to Elizabeth. And though Arran, ever since his interview with Hunsdon, had appeared extremely for her interest, she could place no great confidence in a man whose conduct was so capricious and irregular, and who, notwithstanding his protestations to the contrary, still continued a secret correspondence both with Mary and with the Duke of Guise. The banished lords were attached to England from affection as well as principle, and were the only persons among the Scots whom, in any dangerous exigency, she could thoroughly trust. Before Bellenden left London, they had been summoned thither, under colour of vindicating themselves from his accusations, but, in reality, to concert with him the most proper measures for restoring them to their country. Wotton pursued this plan, and endeavoured to ripen it for execution ; and it was greatly facilitated by an event neither uncommon nor considerable. Sir John Forster, and Ker of Ferniherst, the English and Scottish wardens of the middle marches, having met, according to the custom of the bor-

ders, about midsummer, a fray arose, and Lord Russel, the Earl of
Bedford's eldest son, happened to be killed. This scuffle was purely
accidental; but Elizabeth chose to consider it as a design formed
by Ker, at the instigation of Arran, to involve the two kingdoms in
war. She insisted that both should be delivered up to her; and,
though James eluded that demand, he was obliged to confine Arran
in St. Andrew's, and Ker in Aberdeen. During his absence from
court, Wotton and his associates carried on their intrigues without
interruption. By their advice [Oct. 16], the banished nobles endeavoured to accommodate their differences with Lord John and
Lord Claud, the Duke of Chatelherault's two sons, whom Morton's
violence had driven out of the kingdom. Their common sufferings
and common interest induced both parties to bury in oblivion the
ancient discord which had subsisted between the houses of Hamilton and Douglas. By Elizabeth's permission, they returned in a
body to the borders of Scotland. Arran, who had again recovered
favour, insisted on putting the kingdom in a posture of defence;
but Gray, Bellenden, and Maitland, secretly thwarted all his measures. Some necessary orders they prevented from being issued:
others they rendered ineffectual by the manner of execution; and
all of them were obeyed slowly, and with reluctance.

Wotton's fertile brain was, at the same time, big with another and
more dangerous plot. He had contrived to seize the King, and to
carry him by force into England. But the design was happily
discovered; and, in order to avoid the punishment which his
treachery merited, he departed without taking leave.

Meanwhile the banished lords hastened the execution of their enterprise; and, as their friends and vassals were now ready to join
them, they entered Scotland. Wherever they came, they were wel-
comed as the deliverers of their country, and the most fervent
prayers were addressed to Heaven for the success of their arms.
They advanced, without losing a moment, towards Stirling, at the
head of ten thousand men. The King, though he had assembled an
army superior in number, could not venture to meet them in the
field with troops whose loyalty was extremely dubious, and who at
best were far from being hearty in the cause; nor was either the
town or castle provided for siege. The gates, however, of both were
shut, and the nobles encamped at St. Ninian's [Nov. 2]. That
same night they surprised the town, or, more probably, it was betrayed into their hands; and Arran, who had undertaken to defend
it, was obliged to save himself by a precipitate flight. Next morning they invested the castle, in which there were not provisions for
twenty-four hours; and James was necessitated immediately to
hearken to terms of accommodation. They were not so elated with
success as to urge extravagant demands, nor was the King unwilling
to make every reasonable concession. They obtained a pardon, in
the most ample form, of all the offences which they had committed; the principal forts in the kingdom were, by way of security
put into their hands; Crawford, Montrose, and Colonel Stewart
were removed from the King's presence; and a parliament was
called in order to establish tranquillity in the nation.

Dec. 10.] Though a great majority in this parliament consisted of the confederate nobles and their adherents, they were far from discovering a vindictive spirit. Satisfied with procuring an act, restoring them to their ancient honours and estates, and ratifying the pardon granted by the King, they seemed to forget all past errors in the administration, and spared James the mortification of seeing his ministers branded with any public note of infamy. Arran alone, deprived of all his honours, stripped of his borrowed spoils, and declared an enemy to his country by public proclamation, sunk back into obscurity, and must henceforth be mentioned by his primitive title of Captain James Stewart. As he had been, during his unmerited prosperity, the object of the hatred and indignation of his countrymen, they beheld his fall without pity, nor did all his sufferings mitigate their resentment in the least degree.

The clergy were the only body of men who obtained no redress of their grievances by this revolution. The confederate nobles had all along affected to be considered as guardians of the privileges and discipline of the church. In all their manifestos they had declared their resolution to restore these, and by that popular pretence had gained many friends. It was now natural to expect some fruit of these promises, and some returns of gratitude towards many of the most eminent preachers who had suffered in their cause, and who demanded the repeal of the laws passed the preceding year. The King, however, was resolute to maintain these laws in full authority; and as the nobles were extremely solicitous not to disgust him by insisting on any disagreeable request, the claims of the church in this as well as in many other instances were sacrificed to the interest of the laity. The ministers gave vent to their indignation in the pulpit, and their impatience under the disappointment broke out in some expressions extremely disrespectful even towards the King himself.

1586.] The Archbishop of St. Andrew's, too, felt the effects of their anger. The provincial synod of Fife summoned him to appear, and to answer for his contempt of the decrees of former assemblies, in presuming to exercise the functions of a bishop. Though he refused to acknowledge the jurisdiction of the court, and appealed from it to the King, a sentence of excommunication, equally indecent and irregular, was pronounced against him. Adamson, with no less indecency, thundered his archiepiscopal excommunication against Melvil, and some other of his opponents.

Soon after [April 13,] a general assembly was held, in which the King, with some difficulty, obtained an act, permitting the name and office of bishop still to continue in the church. The power of the order, however, was considerably retrenched. The exercise of discipline, and the inspection of the life and doctrine of the clergy, were committed to presbyteries, in which bishops should be allowed no other pre-eminence but that of presiding as perpetual moderators. They themselves were declared to be subject, in the same manner as other pastors, to the jurisdiction of the general assembly. As the discussion of the Archbishop's appeal might have kindled unusual heats in the assembly, that affair was terminated by compromise. He renounced any claim of supremacy over the church, and promised to demean himself suitably to the character of a bishop, as described by St. Paul. The assembly, without examining the foundations of the sentence of excommunication, declared that it should be held of no effect, and restored him to all the privileges which he enjoyed before it was pronounced. Notwithstanding the extraordinary tenderness shown for the honour of the synod, and the delicacy and respect with which its jurisdiction was treated, several members were so zealous as to protest against this decision.

The Court of Scotland was now filled with persons so warmly attached to Elizabeth, that the league between the two kingdoms, which had been proposed last year, met with no interruption, but from D'Esneval, the French envoy. James himself first offered to renew the negotiations. Elizabeth did not suffer such a favourable opportunity to slip, and instantly dispatched Randolph [July 5], to conclude a treaty, which she so much desired. The danger to which the Protestant religion was exposed, by the late combination of the Popish powers for its destruction, and the necessity of a strict confederacy among those who had embraced the Reformation, in order to obstruct their pernicious designs, were mentioned as the foundation of the league. The chief articles in it were, that both parties should bind themselves to defend the Evangelical religion; that the league should be offensive and defensive against all who shall endeavour to disturb the exercise of religion in either kingdom; that if any one of the two parties be invaded, the other, notwithstanding any former alliance, should not, directly, or indirectly, assist the invader; that if England be invaded in any part remote from Scotland, James should assist the Queen with two thousand horse and five thousand foot; that if the enemy landed or approached within sixty miles of Scotland, the King should take the field with his whole forces, in the same manner as he would do in defence of his whole kingdom. Elizabeth, in return, undertook to act in defence of Scotland, if it should be invaded. At the same time she assured the King that no step should be taken, which might derogate in any degree from his pretensions to the English crown. Elizabeth expressed great satisfaction with a treaty, which rendered Scotland a useful ally, instead of a dangerous neighbour, and afforded her a degree of security on that side, which all her ancestors aimed at, but none of them had ever obtained. Zeal for religion, together with the blessings of peace which both kingdoms had enjoyed during a considerable period, had so far abated the violence of national antipathy, that the King's conduct was universally acceptable to his own people.

The acquittal of Archibald Douglas, at this time, exposed James to much and deserved censure. This man was deeply engaged in the conspiracy against the life of the King his father. Both Morton and Binny, one of his own servants, who suffered for that crime, had accused him of being present at the murder.[*] He had escaped punishment by flying into England, and James had often required Elizabeth to deliver up a person so unworthy of her protection. He now obtained a license, from the King himself, to return into Scotland; and after undergoing a mock trial, calculated to conceal

* See Appendix, No. XLVII.

rather than to detect his guilt, he was not only taken into favour by the King, but sent back to the court of England with the honourable character of his ambassador. James was now of such an age that his youth and inexperience cannot be pleaded in excuse for this indecent transaction. It must be imputed to the excessive facility of his temper, which often led him to gratify his courtiers at the expense of his own dignity and reputation.

Not long after, the inconsiderate affection of the English Catholics towards Mary, and their implacable resentment against Elizabeth, gave rise to a conspiracy which proved fatal to the one Queen, left an indelible stain on the reputation of the other, and presented a spectacle to Europe, of which there had hitherto been no example in the history of mankind.

Doctor Gifford, Gilbert Gifford, and Hodgson, priests educated in the seminary at Rheims, had adopted an extravagant and enthusiastic notion, that the bull of Pius V. against Elizabeth was dictated immediately by the Holy Ghost. This wild opinion they instilled into Savage, an officer in the Spanish army, noted for his furious zeal and daring courage; and persuaded him that no service could be so acceptable to heaven, as to take away the life of an excommunicated heretic. Savage, eager to obtain the crown of martyrdom, bound himself by a solemn vow to kill Elizabeth. Ballard, a pragmatical priest of that seminary, had at that time come over to Paris [April 26], and solicited Mendoza, the Spanish ambassador there, to procure an invasion of England, while the affairs of the League were so prosperous, and the kingdom left naked by sending so many of the Queen's best troops into the Netherlands. Paget and the English exiles demonstrated the fruitlessness of such an attempt, unless Elizabeth were first cut off, or the invaders secured of a powerful concurrence on their landing. If it could be hoped that either of these events would happen, effectual aid was promised; and in the mean time Ballard was sent back to renew his intrigues.

May 15.] He communicated his designs to Anthony Babington, a young gentleman in Derbyshire, of a large fortune and many amiable qualities, who having contracted, during his residence in France, a familiarity with the Archbishop of Glasgow, had been recommended by him to the Queen of Scots. He concurred with Paget in considering the death of Elizabeth as a necessary preliminary to any invasion. Ballard gave him hopes than an end would soon be put to her days, and imparted to him Savage's vow, who was now in London waiting for an opportunity to strike the blow. But Babington thought the attempt of too much importance to rely on a single hand for the execution of it, and proposed that five resolute gentlemen should be joined with Savage in an enterprise, the success of which was the foundation of all their hopes. He offered to find out persons willing to undertake the service, whose honour, secrecy, and courage, they might safely trust. He accordingly opened the matter to Edward Windsor, Thomas Salisbury, Charles Tinley, Chidioc Tichbourne, Robert Gage, John Travers, Robert Barnwell, John Charnock, Henry Dun, John Jones, and Robert Polly; all of them, except Polly, whose bustling forward zeal introduced him into their society, gentlemen of good families, united together in the bonds of private friendship, strengthened by the more powerful tie of religious zeal. Many consultations were held; their plan of operations was at last settled; and their different parts assigned [June]. Babington himself was appointed to rescue the Queen of Scots; Salisbury, with some others, undertook to excite several counties to take arms; the murder of the Queen, the most dangerous and important service of all, fell to Tichbourne and Savage, with four associates. So totally had their bigoted prejudices extinguished the principles of honour, and the sentiments of humanity suitable to their rank, that, without scruple or compunction, they undertook an action which is viewed with horror, even when committed by the meanest and most profligate of mankind. This attempt, on the contrary, appeared to them no less honourable than it was desperate; and in order to perpetrate the memory of it, they had a picture drawn, containing the portraits of the six assassins, with that of Babington in the middle, and a motto intimating that they were jointly embarked in some hazardous design.

The conspirators, as appears by this wanton and imprudent instance of vanity, seem to have thought a discovery hardly possible, and neither distrusted the fidelity of their companions nor doubted the success of their undertaking. But while they believed that their machinations were carried on with the most profound and impenetrable secrecy, every step they took was fully known to Walsingham. Polly was one of his spies, and had entered into the conspiracy with no other design than to betray his associates. Gilbert Gifford too, having been sent over to England to quicken the motions of the conspirators, had been gained by Walsingham, and gave him sure intelligence of all their projects. That vigilant minister immediately imparted the discoveries which he had made to Elizabeth; and, without communicating the matter to any other of the counsellors, they agreed, in order to understand the plot more perfectly, to wait until it was ripened into some form, and brought near the point of execution.

At last, Elizabeth thought it dangerous and criminal to expose her own life, and to tempt Providence any further. Ballard, the prime mover in the whole conspiracy, was arrested [Aug. 4]. His associates, disconcerted and struck with astonishment, endeavoured to save themselves by flight. But within a few days, all of them, except Windsor, were seized in different places of the kingdom, and committed to the Tower. Though they had undertaken the part, they wanted the firm and determined spirit of assassins; and, influenced by fear or by hope, at once confessed all that they knew. The indignation of the people, and their impatience to revenge such an execrable combination against the life of their sovereign, hastened their trial, and all of them suffered the death of traitors.

Thus far Elizabeth's conduct may be pronounced both prudent and laudable, nor can she be accused of violating any law of humanity, or of taking any precautions beyond what were necessary for her own safety. But a tragical scene followed, with regard to which posterity will pass a very different judgment.

The frantic zeal of a few rash young men accounts sufficiently for all the wild and wicked designs which they had formed. But this was not the light in which Elizabeth and her ministers chose to place the conspiracy. They wished to persuade the nation, that Babington and his associates should be considered merely as instruments employed by the Queen of Scots, the real though secret author of so many attempts against the life of Elizabeth, and the peace of her kingdoms. They produced letters, which they ascribed to her, in support of this charge. These, as they gave out, had come into their hands by the following singular and mysterious method of conveyance. Gifford, on his return into England, had been trusted by some of the exiles with letters to Mary; but, in order to make a trial of his fidelity and address, they were only blank papers made up in that form. These being safely delivered by him, he was afterwards employed without further scruple. Walsingham having found means to gain this man, he, by the permission of that minister, and the connivance of Paulet, bribed a tradesman in the neighbourhood of Chartley, whither Mary had been conveyed, who deposited the letters in a hole in the wall of the castle, covered with a loose stone. Thence they were taken by the Queen, and in the same manner her answers returned. All these were carried to Walsingham, opened by him, deciphered, sealed again so dexterously that the fraud could not be perceived, and then transmitted to the persons to whom they were directed. Two letters to Babington, with several to Mendoza, Paget, Englefield, and the English fugitives, were procured by this artifice. It was given out, that in these letters Mary approved of the conspiracy, and even of the assassination; that she directed them to proceed with the utmost circumspection, and not to take arms until foreign auxiliaries were ready to join them; that she recommended the Earl of Arundel, his brothers, and the young Earl of Northumberland, as proper persons to conduct and to add reputation to their enterprise; that she advised them, if possible, to excite at the same time some commotion in Ireland: and, above all, besought them to concert with care the means of her own escape, suggesting to them several expedients for that purpose.

All these circumstances were opened at the trial of the conspirators; and while the nation was under the influence of those terrors which the association had raised, and the late danger had augmented, they were believed without hesitation or inquiry, and spread a general alarm. Mary's zeal for her religion was well known; and in that age, examples of the violent and sanguinary spirit which it inspired were numerous. All the cabals against the peace of the kingdom for many years had been carried on in her name; and it now appears evidently, said the English, that the safety of the one Queen is incompatible with that of the other. Why then, added they, should the tranquillity of England be sacrificed for the sake of a stranger? Why is a life so dear to the nation exposed to the repeated assaults of an exasperated rival? The case supposed in the association has now happened, the sacred person of our sovereign has been threatened, and why should not an injured people execute that just vengeance which they had vowed?

No sentiments could be more agreeable than these to Elizabeth

o 5

and her ministers. They themselves had at first propagated them
among the people, and they now served both as an apology and a
motive for their proceeding to such extremities against the Scottish Queen as they had long meditated. The more numerous the
injuries were which Elizabeth had heaped on Mary, the more she
feared and hated that unhappy Queen, and came at last to be persuaded that there could be no other security for her own life, but
the death of her rival. Burleigh and Walsingham had promoted
so zealously all Elizabeth's measures with regard to Scottish affairs,
and had acted with so little reserve in opposition to Mary, that
they had reason to dread the most violent effects of her resentment
if ever she should mount the throne of England. From this additional consideration they endeavoured, with the utmost earnestness,
to hinder an event so fatal to themselves, by confirming their mistress's fear and hatred of the Scottish Queen.

Meanwhile Mary was guarded with unusual vigilance, and great
care was taken to keep her ignorant of the discovery of the conspiracy. Sir Thomas George was at last sent from court to acquaint her both of it, and of the imputation with which she was
loaded as accessary to that crime, and he surprised her with the
account just as she had got on horseback to ride out along with
her keepers. She was struck with astonishment, and would have
returned to her apartment, but she was not permitted; and, in her
absence, her private closet was broke open, her cabinet and papers
were seized, sealed and sent up to court. Her principal domestics
too were arrested, and committed to different keepers. Nau and
Curle, her two secretaries, the one a native of France, the other of
Scotland, were carried prisoners to London. All the money in her
custody, amounting to little more than two thousand pounds, was
secured*. And after leading her about for some days, from one
gentleman's house to another, she was conveyed to Fotheringay, a
strong castle in Northamptonshire.

No further evidence could now be expected against Mary, and
nothing remained but to decide what should be her fate. With
regard to this, Elizabeth and those ministers in whom she chiefly
confided seem to have taken their resolution; but there was still
great variety of sentiments among her other counsellors. Some
thought it sufficient to dismiss all Mary's attendants, and to keep her
under such close restraint, as would cut off all possibility of corres-
ponding with the enemies of the kingdom; and as her constitution,
broken by long confinement, and her spirit dejected with so many
sorrows, could not long support such an additional load, the Queen
and nation would soon be delivered from all their fears. But
though it might be easy to secure Mary's own person, it was impossible to diminish the reverence which the Roman Catholics had
for her name, or to extinguish the compassion with which they
viewed her sufferings; while such sentiments continued, insurrections and invasions would never be wanting for her relief, and the
only effect of any new rigour would be to render these attempts
more frequent and more dangerous. For this reason the expedient
was rejected.

* See Appendix, No. XLVIII.

A public and legal trial, though the most unexampled, was judged the most unexceptionable method of proceeding; and it had at the same time an appearance of justice, accompanied with an air of dignity. It was in vain to search the ancient records for any statute or precedent to justify such an uncommon step as the trial of a foreign Prince, who had not entered the kingdom in arms, but who had fled thither for refuge. The proceedings against her were founded on the act of last parliament, and by applying it in this manner, the intention of those who had framed that severe statute became more apparent.

Elizabeth resolved that no circumstance of pomp or solemnity should be wanting, which could render this transaction such as became the dignity of the person to be tried. She appointed, by a commission under the great seal, forty persons, the most illustrious in the kingdom by their birth or offices, together with five of the judges, to hear and decide this great cause. Many difficulties were started by the lawyers about the name and title by which Mary should be arraigned; and while the essentials of justice were so grossly violated, the empty forms of it were the objects of their care. They at length agreed that she should be styled "Mary, daughter and heir of James V., late King of Scots, commonly called Queen of Scots, and Dowager of France."

After the many indignities which she had lately suffered, Mary could no longer doubt but that her destruction was determined on. She expected every moment to end her days by poison, or by some of those secret means usually employed against captive Princes. Lest the malice of her enemies, at the same time that it deprived her of life, should endeavour likewise to blast her reputation, she wrote to the Duke of Guise, and vindicated herself, in the strongest terms, from the imputation of encouraging or of being accessary to the conspiracy for assassinating Elizabeth. In the solitude of her prison, the strange resolution of bringing her to a public trial had not reached her ears, nor did the idea of anything so unprecedented and so repugnant to regal majesty, once enter into her thoughts.

On the 11th of October, the commissioners appointed by Elizabeth arrived at Fotheringay. Next morning, they delivered a letter from their sovereign to Mary, in which, after the bitterest reproaches and accusations, she informed her, that regard for the happiness of the nation had at last rendered it necessary to make a public inquiry into her conduct, and therefore required her, as she had lived so long under the protection of the laws of England, to submit now to the trial which they ordained to be taken of her crimes. Mary, though surprised at this message, was neither appalled at the danger, nor unmindful of her own dignity. She protested, in the most solemn manner, that she was innocent of the crime laid to her charge, and had never countenanced any attempt against the life of the Queen of England; but, at the same time, refused to acknowledge the jurisdiction of her commissioners. "I came into the kingdom," said she, "an independent sovereign, to implore the Queen's assistance, not to subject myself to her authority. Nor is my spirit so broken by its past misfortunes, or so intimidated by present dangers, as to stoop to anything which is

unbecoming the majesty of a crowned head, or that will disgrace
the ancestors from whom I am descended, and the son to whom I
shall leave my throne. If I must be tried, Princes alone can be my
peers. The Queen of England's subjects, however noble their birth
may be, are of a rank inferior to mine. Ever since my arrival in
this kingdom I have been confined as a prisoner. Its laws never
afforded me any protection. Let them not now be perverted in
order to take away my life."

The commissioners employed arguments and entreaties to overcome Mary's resolution. They even threatened to proceed according to the forms of law, and to pass sentence against her on account
of her contumacy in refusing to plead; she persisted, however, for
two days, to decline their jurisdiction. An argument, used by
Hatton, the vice-chamberlain, at last prevailed. He told her that,
by avoiding a trial, she injured her own reputation, and deprived
herself of the only opportunity of setting her innocence in a clear
light; and that nothing would be more agreeable to them, or more
acceptable to the Queen, their mistress, than to be convinced, by
undoubted evidence, that she had been unjustly loaded with foul
aspersions.

No wonder that pretexts so plausible should impose on the un-
wary Queen, or that she, unassisted at that time by any friend or
counsellor, should not be able to detect and elude all the artifices
of Elizabeth's ablest ministers. In a situation equally melancholy
and under circumstances nearly similar, her grandson Charles I.
refused with the utmost firmness, to acknowledge the usurped jurisdiction of the high court of justice; and posterity has approved
his conduct, as suitable to the dignity of a King. If Mary was less
constant in her resolution, it must be imputed solely to her anxious
desire of vindicating her own honour.

At her appearance before the judges [Oct. 14], who were seated
in the great hall of the castle, where they received her with much
ceremony, she took care to protest, that by condescending to hear
and to give an answer to the accusations which should be brought
against her, she neither acknowledged the jurisdiction of the court
nor admitted the validity and justice of those acts by which they
pretended to try her.

The chancellor, by a counter protestation, endeavoured to vindicate the authority of the court.

Then Elizabeth's attorney and solicitor opened the charge against
her, with all the circumstances of the late conspiracy. Copies of
Mary's letters to Mendoza, Babington, Englefield, and Paget, were
produced. Babington's confession, those of Ballard, Savage, and
the other conspirators, together with the declarations of Nau and
Curle, her secretaries, were read, and the whole ranged in the most
specious order which the art of the lawyers could devise, and
heightened by every colour their eloquence could add.

Mary listened to their harangues attentively, and without the
least emotion. But at the mention of the Earl of Arundel's name,
who was then confined in the Tower, she broke out into this tender
and generous exclamation; "Alas, how much has the noble house
of Howard suffered for my sake!"

When the Queen's counsel had finished, Mary stood up, and with great magnanimity, and equal presence of mind, began her defence. She bewailed the unhappiness of her own situation, that after a captivity of nineteen years, during which she had suffered treatment no less cruel than unmerited, she was at last loaded with an accusation, which tended not only to rob her of her right of succession, and to deprive her of life itself, but to transmit her name with infamy to future ages ; that, without regarding the sacred rights of sovereignty, she was now subjected to laws framed against private persons : though an anointed Queen, commanded to appear before the tribunal of subjects ; and, like a common criminal, her honour exposed to the petulant tongues of lawyers, capable of wresting her words, and of misrepresenting her actions ; that even in this dishonourable situation, she was denied the privileges usually granted to criminals, and obliged to undertake her own defence, without the presence of any friend with whom to advise, without the aid of counsel, and without the use of her own papers.

She then proceeded to the particular articles in the accusation. She absolutely denied any correspondence with Babington or Ballard ; copies only of her pretended letters to them were produced ; though nothing less than her hand-writing or subscription was sufficient to convict her of such an odious crime ; no proof could be brought that their letters were delivered into her hands, or that any answer was returned by her direction : the confessions of wretches condemned and executed for such a detestable action were of little weight ; fear or hope might extort from them many things inconsistent with truth, nor ought the honour of a Queen to be stained by such vile testimony. The declaration of her secretaries was not more conclusive ; promises and threats might easily overcome the resolution of two strangers ; in order to screen themselves, they might throw the blame on her : but they could discover nothing to her prejudice without violating, in the first place, the oath of fidelity which they had sworn to her ; and their perjury in one instance rendered them unworthy of credit in another : the letters to the Spanish ambassador were either nothing more than copies, or contained only what was perfectly innocent : "I have often," continued she, "made such efforts for the recovery of my liberty as are natural to a human creature. Convinced, by the sad experience of so many years, that it was in vain to expect it from the justice or generosity of the Queen of England, I have frequently solicited foreign Princes, and called upon all my friends to employ their whole interest for my relief. I have likewise endeavoured to procure for the English Catholics some mitigation of the rigour with which they are now treated ; and if I could hope, by my death, to deliver them from oppression, am willing to die for their sake. I wish, however, to imitate the example of Esther and Judith, and would rather make intercession for my people than shed the blood of the meanest creature in order to save them. I have often checked the intemperate zeal of my adherents, when either the severity of their own persecutions, or indignation at the unheard-of injuries which I have endured, were apt to precipitate them into violent councils. I have even warned the Queen of dangers to which these harsh proceedings exposed herself. And worn out, as I now am, with cares and sufferings, the prospect of a crown is not so inviting that I should ruin my soul in order to obtain it. I am no stranger to the feelings of humanity, nor unacquainted with the duties of religion, and abhor the detestable crime of assassination, as equally repugnant to both. And, if ever I have given consent by my words, or even by my thoughts, to any attempt against the life of the Queen of England, far from declining the judgment of men, I shall not even pray for the mercy of God."

Two different days did Mary appear before the judges, and in every part of her behaviour maintained the magnanimity of a Queen, tempered with the gentleness and modesty of a woman.

The commissioners, by Elizabeth's express command, adjourned without pronouncing any sentence, to the Star Chamber, in Westminster, [Oct. 25]. When assembled in that place, Nau and Curle were brought into court, and confirmed their former declaration upon oath; and after reviewing all their proceedings, the commissioners unanimously declared Mary "to be accessary to Babington's conspiracy, and to have imagined divers matters tending to the hurt, death, and destruction of Elizabeth, contrary to the express words of the statute made for the security of the Queen's life.

It is no easy matter to determine whether the injustice in appointing this trial, or the irregularity in conducting it, were greatest and most flagrant. By what right did Elizabeth claim authority over an independent Queen? Was Mary bound to comply with the laws of a foreign kingdom? How could the subjects of another Prince become her judges? Or, if such an insult on royalty were allowed,, ought not the common forms of justice to have been observed? If the testimony of Babington and his associates was so explicit, why did not Elizabeth spare them for a few weeks, and, by confronting them with Mary, overwhelm her with the full conviction of her crimes? Nau and Curle were both alive, wherefore did not they appear at Fotheringay? and for what reason were they produced in the Star Chamber, where Mary was not present to hear what they deposed? Was this suspicious evidence enough to condemn a Queen? Ought the meanest criminal to have been found guilty upon such feeble and inconclusive proofs?

It was not, however, on the evidence produced at her trial, that the sentence against Mary was founded. That served as a pretence to justify, but was not the cause of the violent steps taken by Elizabeth and her ministers towards her destruction; and was employed to give some appearance of justice to what was the offspring of jealousy and fear. The nation, blinded with resentment against Mary, and solicitous to secure the life of its own sovereign from every danger, observed no irregularities in the proceedings, and attended to no defects in the proof, but grasped at the suspicions and probabilities, as if they had been irrefragable demonstrations.

The parliament met a few days after sentence was pronounced against Mary. In that illustrious assembly more temper and discernment than are to be found among the people might have been expected. Both lords and commons, however, were equally under the dominion of popular prejudices and passions, and the same excess of zeal, or of fear, which prevailed in the nation, is apparent in all their proceedings. They entered with impatience upon an inquiry into the conspiracy, and the danger which threatened the Queen's life as well as the peace of the kingdom. All the papers which had been produced at Fotheringhay were laid before them; and, after many violent invectives against the Queen of Scots, both houses unanimously ratified the proceedings of the commissioners by whom she had been tried, and declared the sentence against her to be just and well founded. Not satisfied with this, they presented a joint address to the Queen, beseeching her, as she regarded her own safety, the preservation of the Protestant religion, the welfare and wishes of her people, to publish the sentence; and without further delay to inflict on a rival, no less irreclaimable than dangerous, the punishment which she had merited by so many crimes. This request, dictated by fears unworthy of that great assembly, was enforced by reasons still more unworthy. They were drawn not from justice, but from conveniency. The most rigorous confinement, it was pretended, could not curb Mary's intriguing spirit; her address was found, by long experience, to be an overmatch for the vigilance and jealousy of all her keepers; the severest penal laws could not restrain her adherents, who, while they believed her person to be sacred, would despise any danger to which themselves alone were exposed; several foreign Princes were ready to second their attempts, and waited only a proper opportunity for invading the kingdom, and asserting the Scottish Queen's title to the crown. Her life, they contended, was, for these reasons incompatable with Elizabeth's safety; and if she were spared out of a false clemency, the Queen's person, the religion and liberties of the kingdom, could not be one moment secure. Necessity required that she should be sacrificed in order to preserve these; and to prove this sacrifice to be no less just than necessary, several examples in history were produced, and many texts of scripture quoted: but both the one and the other were misapplied, and distorted from their true meaning.

Nothing, however, could be more acceptable to Elizabeth than an address in this strain. It extricated her out of a situation extremely embarrassing; and without depriving her of the power of sparing, it enabled her to punish her rival with less appearance of blame. If she chose the former, the whole honour would rebound to her own clemency. If she determined on the latter, whatever was rigorous might now seem to be extorted by the solicitations of her people rather than to flow from her own inclination. Her answer, however, was in a style which she often used, ambiguous and evasive, under the appearance of openness and candour; full of such professions of regard for her people as served to heighten their loyalty; of such complaints of Mary's ingratitude as were calculated to excite their indignation; and of such insinuation that her own life was in danger as could not fail to keep alive their fears. In the end, she besought them to save her the infamy and the pain of delivering up a Queen, her nearest kinswoman, to punishment; and to consider whether it might not still be possible to provide for the public security, without forcing her to imbrue her hands in royal blood.

The true meaning of this reply was easily understood. The lords and commons renewed their former request with additional importunity, which was far from being either unexpected, or offensive. Elizabeth did not return any answer more explicit; and, having obtained such a public sanction of her proceedings, there was no longer any reason for protracting this scene of dissimulation; there was even some danger that her feigned difficulties might at last be be treated as real ones; she therefore prorogued the parliament, and reserved in her own hands the sole disposal of her rival's fate.

All the princes in Europe observed the proceedings against Mary with astonishment and horror; and even Henry III., notwithstanding his known aversion to the house of Guise, was obliged to interpose on her behalf, and to prepare in defence of the common rights of royalty. Aubespine, his resident ambassador, and Bellievre, who was sent with an entraordinary commission to the same purpose, interceeded for Mary with great appearance of warmth. They employed all the arguments which the cause naturally suggested; they pleaded from justice, from generosity, and humanity: they intermingled reproaches and threats; but to all these Elizabeth continued deaf and inexorable: and having received some intimation of Henry's real unconcern about the fate of the Scottish Queen and knowing his antipathy to all the race of Guise, she trusted that these loud remonstrances would be followed by no violent resentment.

She paid no greater regard to the solicitations of the Scottish King, which, as they were urged with greater sincerity, merited more attention. Though her commissioners had been extremely careful to soothe James, by publishing a declaration that their sentence against Mary did, in no degree, derogate from his honour, or invalidate any title which he formerly possessed; he beheld the indignities to which his mother had been exposed with filial concern, and with the sentiments which became a King. The pride of the Scottish nation was roused by the insult offered to the blood of their monarchs, and called upon him to employ the most vigorous efforts, in order to prevent or to revenge the Queen's death. At first he could hardly believe that Elizabeth would venture upon an action so unprecedented, which tended so visibly to render the persons of Princes less sacred in the eyes of the people, and which degraded the regal dignity, of which, at other times, she was so remarkable jealous. But as soon as the extraordinary steps which she took discovered her intention, he dispatched Sir William Keith to London; who, together with Douglas, his ambassador in ordinary, remonstrated, in the strongest terms, against the injury done to an independent Queen, in subjecting her to be tried like a private person, and by laws to which she owed no obedience; and besought Elizabeth not to add to this injury by suffering a sentence unjust in itself, as well as dishonourable to the King of Scots, to be put into execution.*

Elizabeth returning no answer to these remonstrances of his

* See Append. No. XLIX.

ambassador, James wrote to her with his own hand, complaining in the bitterest terms of her conduct, not without threats that both his duty and his honour would oblige him to renounce her friendship, and to act as became a son when called to revenge his mother's wrongs. At the same time he assembled the nobles, who promised to stand by him in so good a cause. He appointed ambassadors to France, Spain, and Denmark, in order to implore the aid of these courts; and took other steps towards executing his threats with vigour. The high strain of his letter enraged Elizabeth to such a degree that she was ready to dismiss his ambassadors without any reply. But his preparations alarmed and embarrassed her ministers, and at their entreaty she returned a soft and evasive answer, promising to listen to any overture from the King, that tended to his mother's safety; and to suspend the execution of the sentence until the arrival of new ambassadors from Scotland.

Meanwhile she commanded the sentence against Mary to be published [Dec. 6], and forgot not to inform the people that this was extorted from her by the repeated entreaty of both houses of parliament. At the same time she dispatched Lord Buckhurst and Beale to acquaint Mary with the sentence, and how importunately the nation demanded the execution of it; and though she had not hitherto yielded to these solicitations, she advised her to prepare for an event which might become necessary for securing the Protestant religion, as well as quieting the minds of the people. Mary received the message not only without symptoms of fear, but with expressions of triumph. "No wonder," said she, "the English should now thirst for the blood of a foreign Prince; they have often offered violence to their own monarchs. But after so many sufferings, death comes to me as a welcome deliverer. I am proud to think that my life is deemed of importance to the Catholic religion, and as a martyr for it I am now willing to die."

After the publication of the sentence, Mary was stripped of every remaining mark of royalty. The canopy of state in her apartment was pulled down; Paulet entered her chamber, and approached her person without any ceremony; and even appeared covered in her presence [Dec. 19]. Shocked with these indignities, and offended at this gross familiarity, to which she had never been accustomed, Mary once more complained to Elizabeth; and at the same time, as her last request, entreated that she would permit her servants to carry her dead body into France, to be laid among her ancestors in hallowed ground; that some of her domestics might be present at her death, to bear witness of her innocence, and firm adherence to the Catholic faith; that all her servants might be suffered to leave the kingdom, and to enjoy those small legacies which she should bestow on them, as testimonies of her affection; and that, in the meantime, her almoner, or some other Catholic priest, might be allowed to attend her, and to assist her in preparing for an eternal world. She besought her, in the name of Jesus, by the soul and memory of Henry VII., their common progenitor, by their near consanguinity, and the royal dignity with which they were both invested, to gratify her in these particulars, and to indulge her so far as to signify her compliance by a letter under her own hand. Whether Mary's letter was ever delivered to Elizabeth is uncertain.

No answer was returned, and no regard paid to her requests. She was offered a Protestant bishop or dean to attend her. Them she rejected, and, without any clergyman to direct her devotions, she prepared, in great tranquillity, for the approach of death, which she now believed to be at no great distance.

1587.] James, without losing a moment, sent new ambassadors to London [Jan. 1]. These were the Master of Gray, and Sir Robert Melvil. In order to remove Elizabeth's fears, they offered that their master would become bound that no conspiracy should be undertaken against her person, or the peace of the kingdom, with Mary's consent; and, for the faithful performance of this, would deliver some of the most considerable Scottish nobles as hostages. If this were not thought sufficient, they proposed that Mary should resign all her rights and pretensions to her son, from whom nothing injurious to the Protestant religion, or inconsistent with Elizabeth's safety, could be feared. The former proposal Elizabeth rejected as insecure; the latter, as dangerous. The ambassadors were then instructed to talk in a higher tone; and Melvil executed the commission with fidelity and zeal. But Gray, with his usual perfidy, deceived his master, who trusted him with a negotiation of so much importance, and betrayed the Queen whom he was employed to save. He encouraged and urged Elizabeth to execute the sentence against her rival. He often repeated the old proverbial sentence, "The dead cannot bite." And whatever should happen, he undertook to pacify the King's rage, or at least to prevent any violent effects of his resentment.

Elizabeth, meanwhile, discovered all the symptoms of the most violent agitation and disquietude of mind. She shunned society, she was often found in a melancholy and musing posture, and repeating with much emphasis these sentences, which she borrowed from some of the devices then in vogue; *Aut fer aut feri; ne feriare, feri.* Much, no doubt, of this apparent uneasiness must be imputed to dissimulation; it was impossible, however that a Princess naturally so cautious as Elizabeth, should venture on an action, which might expose her memory to infamy, and her life and kingdom to danger, without reflecting deeply, and hesitating long. The people waited her determination in suspense and anxiety; and, lest their fear or their zeal should subside, rumours of danger were artfully invented and propagated with the utmost industry. Aubespine, the French ambassador, was accused of having suborned an assassin to murder the Queen. The Spanish fleet was said by some to be already arrived at Milford-haven. Others affirmed that the Duke of Guise had landed with a strong army in Sussex. Now it was reported that the northern counties were up in arms; next day, that the Scots had entered England with all their forces; and a conspiracy, it was whispered, was on foot for seizing the Queen and burning the city. The panic grew every day more violent; and the people, astonished and enraged, called for the execution of the sentence against Mary, as the only thing which could restore tranquillity to the kingdom.

While these sentiments prevailed among her subjects, Elizabeth

See Appendix, No. L.

thought she might safely venture to strike the blow which she had so long meditated. She commanded Davison, one of the secretaries of state, to bring to her the fatal warrant [Feb. 1]; and her behaviour on that occasion plainly showed, that it is not to humanity that we must ascribe her forbearance hitherto. At the very moment she was signing the writ which gave up a woman, a Queen, and her own nearest relation, into the hands of the executioner, she was capable of jesting. "Go," says she to Davison, "and tell Walsingham what I have now done, though I am afraid he will die for grief when he hears it." Her chief anxiety was how to secure the advantages which would arise from Mary's death, without appearing to have given her consent to a deed so odious. She often hinted to Paulet and Drury, as well as to some other courtiers, that now was the time to discover the sincerity of their concern for her safety, and that she expected their zeal would extricate her out of her present perplexity. But they were wise enough to seem not to understand her meaning. Even after the warrant was signed, she commanded a letter to be written to Paulet in less ambiguous terms, complaining of his remissness in sparing so long the life of her capital enemy, and begging him to remember at last what was incumbent on him as an affectionate subject, as well as what he was bound to do by the oath of association, and to deliver his sovereign from continual fear and danger, by shortening the days of his prisoner. Paulet, though rigorous and harsh, and often brutal in the discharge of what he thought his duty, as Mary's keeper, was nevertheless a man of honour and integrity. He rejected the proposal with disdain; and lamenting that he should ever have been deemed capable of acting the part of an assassin, he declared that the Queen might dispose of his life at her pleasure, but that he would never stain his own honour, nor leave an everlasting mark of infamy on his posterity, by lending his hand to perpetrate so foul a crime. On the receipt of this answer, Elizabeth became extremely peevish; and calling him a *dainty* and *precise fellow*, who would promise much but perform nothing, she proposed to employ one Wingfield, who had both courage and inclination to strike the blow. But Davison remonstrating against this, as a deed dishonourable in itself, and of dangerous example, she again declared her intention that the sentence pronounced by the commissioners should be executed according to law; and as she had already signed the warrant, she begged that no further application might be made to her on that head. By this, the privy counsellers thought themselves sufficiently authorized to proceed; and prompted, as they pretended, by zeal for the Queen's safety, or instigated, as is more probable, by the apprehension of the danger to which they would themselves be exposed, if the life of the Queen of Scots were spared, they assembled in the council-chamber; and by a letter under all their hands, empowered the Earls of Shrewsbury and Kent together with the high sheriff of the county, to see the sentence put into execution.

On Tuesday the 7th of February, the two Earls arrived at Fotheringay, and demanded access to the Queen, read in her presence the warrant for execution, and required her to prepare to die next morning. Mary heard them to the end without emotion, and crossing herself in the name of the Father. and of the Son, and of the Holy Ghost, "That soul," said she, "is not worthy the joys of Heaven, which repines because the body must endure the stroke of the executioner; and though I did not expect that the Queen of England would set the first example of violating the sacred person of a sovereign Prince, I willingly submit to that which Providence has decreed to be my lot;" and laying her hand on a Bible, which happened to be near her, she solemnly protested that she was innocent of the conspiracy which Babington had carried on against Elizabeth's life. She then mentioned the requests contained in her letter to Elizabeth, but obtained no satisfactory answer. She entreated with particular earnestness, that now in her last moments her almoner might be suffered to attend her, and that she might enjoy the consolation of those pious institutions prescribed by her religion. Even this favour, which is usually granted to the vilest criminal, was absolutely denied.

Her attendants, during this conversation, were bathed in tears, and, though overawed by the presence of the two Earls, with difficulty suppressed their anguish; but no sooner did Kent and Shrewsbury withdraw, than they ran to their mistress, and burst out into the most passionate expressions of tenderness and sorrow. Mary, however, not only retained perfect composure of mind herself, but endeavoured to moderate their excessive grief; and falling on her knees with all her domestics round her, she thanked Heaven that her sufferings were now so near an end, and prayed that she might be enabled to endure what still remained with decency and with fortitude. The greater part of the evening she employed in settling her worldly affairs. She wrote her testament with her own hand. Her money, her jewels, and her clothes, she distributed among her servants, according to their rank or merit. She wrote a short letter to the king of France, and another to the Duke of Guise, full of tender but magnanimous sentiments, and recommended her soul to their prayers, and her afflicted servants to their protection. At supper she ate temperately, as usual, and conversed not only with ease, but with cheerfulness; she drank to every one of her servants, and asked their forgiveness, if ever she had failed in any part of her duty towards them. At her wonted time she went to bed, and slept calmly a few hours. Early in the morning she retired into her closet, and employed a considerable time in devotion. At eight o'clock the high sheriff and his officers entered her chamber, and found her still kneeling at the altar. She immediately started up, and with a majestic mein, and a countenance undismayed, and even cheerful, advanced towards the place of execution, leaning on two of Paulet's attendants. She was dressed in a mourning habit, but with an elegance and splendour which she had laid aside except on a few festival days. An *Agnus Dei* hung by a pomander chain at her neck; her beads at her girdle; and in her hand she carried a crucifix of ivory. At the bottom of the stairs, the two Earls, attended by several gentlemen from the neighbouring counties, received her; and there Sir Andrew Melvil, the Master of her household, who had been secluded for some weeks from her presence, was permitted to take his last farewell. At the sight of a mistress whom he tenderly loved, in such a situation, he melted into tears; and as he was bewailing her conditon, and complaining of his hard fate, in being appointed to carry the account of such a mournful event into Scotland, Mary replied, "Weep not, good Melvil, there is at present great cause for rejoicing. Thou shalt this day see Mary Stuart delivered from all her cares, and such an end put to her tedious sufferings as she has long expected. Bear witness that I die constant in my religon; firm in my fidelity towards Scotland; and unchanged in my affection to France. Commend me to my son. Tell him I have done nothing injurious to his kingdom, to his honour, or to his rights; and God forgive all those who have thirsted, without cause, for my blood!"

With much difficulty, and after many entreaties, she prevailed on the two Earls to allow Melvil, together with three of her men servants and two of her maids, to attend her to the scaffold. It was erected in the same hall where she had been tried, raised a little above the floor, and covered, as well as a chair, the cushion, and block, with black cloth. Mary mounted the steps with alacrity beheld all this apparatus of death with an unaltered countenance, and signing herself with the cross, she sat down in the chair. Beale read the warrant for execution with a loud voice, to which she listened with a careless air, and like one occupied in other thoughts. Then the Dean of Peterborough began a devout discourse, suitable to her present condition, and offered up prayers to Heaven in her behalf; but she declared that she could not in conscience hearken to the one, nor join with the other; and kneeling down, repeated a Latin prayer. When the dean had finished his devotions she, with an audible voice, and in the English tongue, recommended unto God the afflicted state of the church, and prayed for prosperity to her son, and for a long life and peaceable reign to Elizabeth. She declared that she hoped for mercy only through the death of Christ, at the foot of whose image she now willingly shed her blood; and lifting up and kissing the crucifix, she thus addressed it : "As thy arms, O Jesus, were extended on the cross; so with the outstretched arms of thy mercy receive me, and forgive my sins."

She then prepared for the block, by taking off her veil and upper garments; and one of the executioners rudely endeavouring to assist, she gently checked him, and said with a smile, that she had not been accustomed to undress before so many spectators, nor to be served by such valets. With calm but undaunted fortitude she laid her neck on the block; and while one executioner held her hands, the other, at the second stroke, cut off her head, which falling out of its attire, discovered her hair already grown quite gray with cares and sorrows. The excutioner held it up still streaming with blood, and the Dean crying out, "So perish all Queen Elizabeth's enemies!" the Earl of Kent alone answered Amen. The rest of the spectators continued silent, and drowned in tears; being incapable, at that moment, of any other sentiments but those of pity or admiration*.

See Appendix, No. LI.

Such was the tragical death of Mary, Queen of Scots, after a life of forty-four years and two months, almost nineteen years of which she passed in captivity. The political parties which were formed in the kingdom during her reign have subsisted under various denominations ever since that time. The rancour with which they were at first animated hath descended to succeeding ages, and their prejudices, as well as their rage, have been perpetuated, aud even augmented. Among historians, who were under the dominion of all these passions, and who have either ascribed to her every virtuous and amiable quality, or have imputed to her all the vices of which the human heart is susceptible, we search in vain for Mary's real character. She neither merited the exaggerated praises of the one, nor the distinguished censure of the other.

To all the charms of beauty, and the utmost elegance of external form, she added those accomplishments which render their impression irresistible. Polite, affable, insinuating, sprightly, and capable of speaking and of writing with equal ease and dignity. Sudden, however, and violent in all her attachments; because her heart was warm and unsuspicious. Impatient of contradiction : because she had been accustomed from her infancy to be treated as a Queen. No stranger, on some occasions, to dissimulation ; which, in that perfidious court where she received her education, was reckoned among the necessary arts of government. Not insensible of flattery, or unconscious of that pleasure with which almost every woman beholds the influence of her own beauty. Formed with the qualities which we love, not with the talents that we admire, she was an agreeable woman rather than an illustrious Queen. The vivacity of her spirit, not sufficiently tempered with sound judgment, and the warmth of her heart, which was not at all times under the restraint of discretion, betrayed her both into errors and into crimes. To say that she was always unfortunate will not account for that long and almost uninterrupted succession of calamities which befell her; we must likewise add, that she was often imprudent. Her passion for Darnly was rash, youthful, and excessive ; and though the sudden transition to the opposite extreme was the natural effect of her ill requited love, and of his ingratitude, insolence, and brutality ; yet neither these, nor Bothwell's artful address and important services, can justify her attachment to that nobleman. Even the manners of the age, licentious as they were, are no apology for this unhappy passion ; nor can they induce us to look on that tragical and infamous scene which followed upon it, with less abhorrence. Humanity will draw a veil over this part of her character which it cannot approve, and may, perhaps. prompt some to impute some of her actions to her situation, more than to her disposition ; and to lament the unhappiness of the former, rather than excuse the perverseness of the latter. Mary's sufferings exceed, both in degree and in duration, those tragical distresses which fancy has feigned to excite sorrow and commiseration ; and while we survey them, we are apt altogether to forget her frailties, we think of her faults with less indignation, and approve of our tears, as if they were shed for a person who had attained much nearer to pure virtue.

With regard to the Queen's person, a circumstance not to be omitted in writing the history of female reign, all contemporary author agree in ascribing to Mary the utmost beauty of countenance, and elegance of shape, of which the human form is capable. Her hair was black, though, according to the fashion of that age, she frequently wore borrowed locks, and of different colours. Her eyes were a dark gray; her complexion was exquisitely fine; and her hands and arms remarkably delicate, both as to shape and colour. Her statute was of a height that rose to the majestic. She danced, she walked, and rode with equal grace. Her taste for music was just, and she both sung and played upon the lute with uncommon skill. Towards the end of her life, long confinement, and the coldness of the houses in which she had been imprisoned, brought on a rheumatism, which often deprived her of the use of her limbs. No man, says Brantome, ever beheld her person without admiration and love, or will read her history without sorrow.

None of her women were suffered to come near her dead body, which was carried into a room adjoining to the place of execution, where it lay for some days, covered with a coarse cloth torn from a billiard table. The block, the scaffold, the aprons of the executioners, and every thing stained with her blood, were reduced to ashes. Not long after, Elizabeth appointed her body to be buried in the cathedral of Peterborough with royal magnificence. But this vulgar artifice was employed in vain; the pageantry of a pompous funeral did not efface the memory of those injuries which laid Mary in her grave. James, soon after his accession to the English throne, ordered her body to be removed to Westminister Abbey, and to be deposited among the monarchs of England.

Elizabeth affected to receive the accounts of Mary's death with the most violent emotions of surprise and concern. Sighs, tears, lamentations, and mourning, were all employed to display the reality and greatness of her sorrow. Evident marks of dissimulation and artifice may be traced through every period of Elizabeth's proceedings against the life of the Scottish Queen. The commission for bringing Mary to a public trial was seemingly extorted from her by the entreaties of her privy counsellors. She delayed publishing the sentence against her till she was twice solicited by both houses of parliament. Nor did she sign the warrant for execution without the utmost apparent reluctance. One scene more of the boldest and most solemn deceit remained to be exhibited, She undertook to make the world believe that Mary had been put to death without her knowledge and against her will, Davison, who neither suspected her intention nor his own danger, was her instrument in carrying on this artifice, and fell a victim to it.

It was his duty, as secretary of state to lay before her the warrant for execution, in order to be signed; and by her command he carried it to the great seal. She pretended, however, that she had charged him not to communicate what she had done to any person, nor to suffer the warrant to go out of his hands, without her express permission; that, in contempt of this order, he had not only revealed

the matter to several of her ministers, but had, in concert with them
assembled her privy counsellors, by whom, without her consent or
knowledge, the warrant was issued, and the Earls of Shrewsbury
and Kent empowered to put it in execution. Though Davison denied all this, and with circumstances which bear the strongest marks
of truth and credibility ; though it can scarcely be conceived that
her privy council, composed of the persons in whom she most confided, of her ministers and favourites, would assemble within the
walls of her palace, and venture to transact a matter of so much importance without her privity, and contrary to her inclination ; yet
so far did she carry her dissimulation that, with all the signs of displeasure and of rage, she banished most of her counsellors out of
her presence ; and treated Burleigh in particular, so harshly, and
with such marks of disgust, that he gave himself up for lost, and in
the deepest affliction wrote to the Queen, begging leave to resign all
his places, that he might retire to his own estate. Davison she instantly deprived of his office, and committed him a close prisoner to
the Tower [March]. He was soon after brought to a solemn trial
in the Star Chamber, condemned to pay a fine of ten thousand
pounds, and to imprisoned during the Queen's pleasure. He languished several years in confinement, and never recovered any degree of favour or of power. As her jealousy and fear had bereaved
the Queen of Scots of life, in order to palliate this part of her conduct, Elizabeth made no scruple of sacrificing the reputation and
happiness of one of the most virtuous and able men in her kingdom.*

This solemn farce, for it deserves no better name, furnished
Elizabeth, however, with an apology to the King of Scots. As the
prospect of his mother's danger had excited the King's filial care
and concern, the account of her death filled him with grief and
resentment. His subjects felt the dishonour done to him and to
the nation. In order to sooth both, Elizabeth instantly dispatched
Robert Cary, one of Lord Hunsdon's sons, with a letter expressing
her extreme affliction on account of that miserable accident, which
as she pretended, had happened far contrary to her appointment
or intention. James would not permit her messenger to enter
Scotland, and with some difficulty received a memorial which he
sent from Berwick.   It contained the tale concerning Davison
dressed up with all the circumstances which tended to exculpate
Elizabeth, and to throw the whole blame on his rashness or
treachery. Such a defence gave little satisfaction, and was considered as mockery added to insult ; and many of the nobles, as
well as the King, breathed nothing but revenge. Elizabeth was extremely solicitous to pacify them, and she wanted neither able
instruments nor plausible reasons, in order to accomplish this.
Leicester wrote to the King, and Walsingham to Secretary Maitland.
They represented the certain destruction to which James would expose himself, if, with the forces of Scotland alone, he should
venture to attack a kingdom so far superior in power ; that the
history of past ages, as well as his mother's sad experience, might
convince him, that nothing could be more dangerous or deceitful
than dependance on foreign aid ; that the King of France would

See Appendix, No. LII.

never wish to see the British kingdoms united under one monarch, nor contribute to invest a Prince so nearly allied to the house of Guise with such formidable power; that Philip might be a more active ally, but would certainly prove a more dangerous one; and under pretence of assisting him would assert his own right to the English crown, which he already began openly to claim; that the same statute, on which the sentence of death against his mother had been founded, would justify the excluding him from the succession to the crown; that the English, naturally averse from the dominion of strangers, would not fail, if exasperated by his hostilities, to apply it in that manner; that Elizabeth was disposed to repair the wrong which the mother had suffered, by her tenderness and affection towards the son; and that, by engaging in a fruitless war, he would deprive himself of a noble inheritance, which, by cultivating her friendship, he must infallibly obtain. These representations, added to the, consciousness of his own weakness, to the smallness of his revenues to the mutinous spirit of some of the nobles, to the dubious fidelity of others, and to the influence of that faction which was entirely at Elizabeth's devotion, convinced James that a war with England, however just, would in the present juncture be altogether impolitical. All these considerations induced him to stifle his resentment; to appear satisfied with the punishment inflicted on Davison; and to preserve all the semblances of friendship with the English court. In this manner did the cloud which threatened such a storm pass away. Mary's death, like that of a common criminal, remained unavenged by any Prince; and, whatever infamy Elizabeth might incur, she was exposed to no new danger on that account.

Mary's death, however, proved fatal to the Master of Gray, and lost him the King's favour, which he had for some time possessed. He was become as odious to the nation as favourites who acquire power without merit, and exercise it without discretion, usually are. The treacherous part which he had acted during his late embassy was no secret, and filled James, who at length came to the knowledge of it, with astonishment. The courtiers observed the symptoms of disgust arising in the King's mind, his enemies seized the opportunity, and Sir William Stewart, in revenge of the perfidy with which Gray had betrayed his brother Captain James [May 10], publicly accused him before a convention of nobles, not only of having contributed, by his advice and suggestions, to take away the life of the Queen, but of holding correspondence with Popish Princes, in order to subvert the religion established in the kingdom. Gray, unsupported by the King, deserted by all, and conscious of his own guilt, made a feeble defence. He was condemned to perpetual banishment, a punishment very unequal to his crimes. But the King was unwilling to abandon one whom he had once favoured so highly to the rigour of justice; and Lord Hamilton, his near relation, and the other nobles who had lately returned from exile, in gratitude for the zeal with which he had served them, interceded warmly in his behalf.

Having thus accomplished the destruction of one of his enemies,

Captain James Stewart thought the juncture favourable for prosecuting his revenge on them all. He singled out Secretary Maitland, the most eminent both for abilities and enmity to him; and offered to prove that he was no less accessary than Gray to the Queen's death, and had even formed a design of delivering up the King himself into the hands of the English. But time and absence had, in a great measure, extinguished the King's affection for a minion who so little deserved it. All the courtiers combined against him as a common enemy; and, instead of gaining his point, he had the mortification to see the office of Chancellor conferred upon Maitland, who, together with that dignity, enjoyed all the power and influence of a prime minister.

In the assembly of the church, which met this year, the same hatred to the order of Bishops, and the same jealousy and fear of their encroachments, appeared. But as the King was now of full age, and a parliament was summoned on that occasion, the clergy remained satisfied with appointing some of their number to represent their grievances to that court, from which great things were expected.

Previous to this meeting of parliament, James attempted a work worthy of a King. The deadly feuds which subsisted between many of the great families, and which weretransmitted from one generation to another, weakened the strength of the kingdom; contributed, more than any other circumstance, to preserve a fierce and barbarous spirit among the nobles; and proved the occasion of many disasters to themselves and to their country. After many preparatory negotiations he invited the contending parties to a royal entertainment in the palace of Holyrood House; and partly by his authority, partly by his entreaties, obtained their promise to bury their dissensions in perpetual oblivion. From thence he conducted them, in solemn procession, through the streets of Edinburgh, marching by pairs, each hand in hand with his enemy. A collation of wine and sweetmeats was prepared at the public cross, and there they drank to each other with all the signs of reciprocal forgiveness and of future friendship. The people, who were present at a spectacle so unusual, conceived the most sanguine hopes of seeing concord and tranquillity established in every part of the kingdom, and testified their satisfaction by repeated acclamations. Unhappily, the effects of this reconciliation were not correspondent either to the pious endeavours of the King, or to the fond wishes of the people.

The first care of the parliament was the security of the Protestant religion. All the laws passed in its favour since the Reformation were ratified; and a new and severe one was enacted against seminary priests and jesuits, whose restless industry in making proselytes brought many of them into Scotland about this time. Two acts of this parliament deserve more particular notice on account of the consequences with which they were followed.

The one respected the lands of the church. As the public revenues were not sufficient for defraying the King's ordinary charges; as the administration of the government became more complicated and more expensive; as James was naturally profuse, and a stranger to economy, it was necessary on all these accounts to provide some fund proportioned to his exigencies. But no considerable sum could be levied on the commons, who did not enjoy the benefit of an extensive commerce. The nobles were unaccustomed to bear the burden of heavy taxes. The revenues of the church were the only source whence a proper supply could be drawn. Notwithstanding all the depredations of the laity since the Reformation, and the various devices which they had employed to seize the church lands, some considerable portion of them remained still unalienated, and were held either by the bishops who possessed the benefices, or were granted to laymen during pleasure. All these lands were in this parliament annexed, by one general law, to the crown, and the King was empowered to apply the rents of them to his own use. The tithes alone were reserved for the maintenance of the persons who served the cure, and the principal mansion-house, with a few acres of land by way of glebe, allotted for their residence. By this great accession of property, it is natural to conclude that the King must· have acquired a vast increase of power, and the influence of the nobles have suffered a proportional diminution. The very reverse of this seems, however, to have been the case. Almost all grants of church-lands, prior to this act, were thereby confirmed ; and titles, which were formerly reckoned precarious, derived thence the sanction of parliamentary authority. James was likewise authorized, during a limited time, to make new alienations ; and such was the facility of his temper, ever ready to yield to the solicitations of his servants, and to gratify their most extravagant demands, that not only during the time limited, but throughout his whole reign, he was continually employed in bestowing, and his parliament in ratifying grants of this kind to his nobles ; hence little advantage accrued to the crown from that which might have been so valuable an addition to its revenues. The bishops, however, were great sufferers by the law. But at this juncture neither the King nor his ministers were solicitous about the interests of an order of men, odious to the people, and persecuted by the clergy. Their enemies promoted the law with the utmost zeal. The prospect of sharing in their spoils induced all parties to consent to it ; and after a step so fatal to the wealth and power of the dignified clergy, it was no difficult matter to introduce that change in the government of the church which soon after took place.

The change which the other statute produced in the civil constitution was no less remarkable. Under the feudal system, every freeholder, or immediate vassal of the crown, had a right to be present in parliament. These freeholders were originally few in number, but possessed of great and extensive property. By degrees these vast possessions were divided by the proprietors themselves, or parceled out by the Prince, or split by other accidents. The number of freeholders became greater, and their condition more unequal ; besides the ancient barons, who preserved their estates and their power unimpaired, there arose another order whose rights were the same, though their wealth and influence were far inferior. But, in rude ages, when the art of government was ex-

tremely imperfect, when parliaments were seldom assembled, and
deliberated on matters little interesting to a martial people, few of
the *lesser barons* took their seats, and the whole parliamentary
jurisdiction was exercised by the *greater barons*, in conjunction
with the ecclesiastical order.   James 1., fond of imitating the
forms of the English constitution, to which he had been long accustomed, and desirous of providing a counterpoise to the power of
the great nobles, procured an act in the year 1427, dispensing with
the personal attendance of the lesser barons, and empowering those
in each county to choose two commissioners to represent them in
parliament. This law, like many other regulations of that wise
Prince, produced little effect. All the King's vassals continued, as
formerly, possessed of a right to be present in parliament; but,
unless in some extraordinary conjunctures, the greater barons
alone attended. But by means of the Reformation the constitution had undergone a great change. The aristocratical power of
the nobles had been much increased, and the influence of the
ecclesiastical order, which the crown usually employed to check
their usurpation and to balance their authority, had diminished in
proportion. Many of the abbeys and priories had been erected
into temporal peerages; and the Protestant bishops, an indigent
race of men and odious to the nation, were far from possessing the
weight and credit which their predecessors derived from their own
exorbitant wealth and the superstitious reverence of the people.
In this situation the King had recourse to the expedient employed
by James I., and obtained a law reviving the statute of 1427; and
from that time the commons of Scotland have sent their representatives to parliament. An act which tended so visibly to abridge
their authority did not pass without opposition from many of the
nobles. But as the King had a right to summon the lesser barons
to attend in person, others were apprehensive of seeing the house
filled with a multitude of his dependents, and consented the more
willingly to a law which laid them under the restriction of appearing only by their representatives.

The year 1588 began with a universal expectation throughout all
Europe that it was to be distinguished by wonderful events and revolutions. Several astrologers, according to the accounts of contemporary historians, had predicted this; and the situation of affairs in the two principal kingdoms of Europe was such that a sagacious observer, without any supernatural intelligence, might have
hazarded the prediction and have foreseen the approach of some
grand crisis. In France it was evident from the astonishing progress of the League conducted by a leader whose ambition was restrained by no scruples, and whose genius had hitherto surmounted
all difficulties; as well as from the timid, variable, and impolitic
councils of Henry III., that either that monarch must submit to
abandon the throne of which he was unworthy, or by some sudden
and daring blow cut off this formidable rival. Accordingly, in the
beginning of the year, the Duke of Guise drove his master out of
his capital city, and forced him to conclude a peace which left him
only the shadow of royalty; and before the year expired he himself
fell a victim to the resentment and fear of Henry and to his own

security. In Spain the operations were such as promised something still more uncommon. During three years Philip had employed all the power of his European domininions, and exhausted the treasures of the Indies, in vast preparations for war. A fleet, the greatest that had ever appeared on the ocean, was ready to sail from Lisbon, and a numerous land army was assembled to embark on board of it. Its destination was still unknown, though many circumstances made it probable that the blow was aimed, in the first place, against England. Elizabeth had long given secret aid to the revolted provinces in the Low Countries, and now openly afforded them her protection. A numerous body of her troops was in their service; the Earl of Leicester commanded their armies; she had great sway in the civil government of the republic; and some of its most considerable towns were in her possession. Her fleets had insulted the coasts of Spain, intercepted the galleons from the West Indies, and threatened the colonies there. Roused by so many injuries, allured by views of ambition, and animated by a superstitious zeal for propagating the Romish religion, Philip resolved not only to invade but to conquer England, to which his descent from the house of Lancaster and the donation of Pope Sixtus V. gave him in his own opinion a double title.

Elizabeth saw the danger approach, and prepared to encounter it. The measures for the defence of her kingdom were concerted and carried on with the wisdom and vigour which distinguished her reign. Her chief care was to secure the friendship of the King of Scots. She had treated the Queen his mother with a rigour unknown among Princes; she had often used himself harshly, and with contempt; and though he had hitherto prudently suppressed his resentment of these injuries, she did not believe it to be altogether extinguished, and was afraid that in her present situation it might burst out with fatal violence. Philip, sensible how much an alliance with Scotland would facilitate his enterprise, courted James with the utmost assiduity. He excited him to revenge his mother's wrongs; he flattered him with the hopes of sharing his conquests; and offered him in marriage his daughter the Infanta Isabella. At the same time Scotland swarmed with priests, his emissaries, who seduced some of the nobles to Popery and corrupted others with bribes and promises. Huntly, Arrol, Crawford, were heads of a faction which openly espoused the interest of Spain. Lord Maxwell, arriving from that court, began to assemble his followers, and to take arms, that he might be ready to join the Spaniards. In order to counterbalance all these, Elizabeth made the warmest professions of friendship to the King; and Ashby, her ambassador, entertained him with magnificent hopes and promises. He assured him that his right of succession to the crown should be publicly acknowledged in England: that he should be created a duke in that kingdom; and he should be admitted to some share in the government; and receive a considerable pension annually. James, it is probable, was too well acquainted with Elizabeth's arts to rely entirely on these promises. But he understood his own interest in the present juncture and pursued it with much steadiness. He rejected an alliance with Spain as dangerous. He refused to admit into his presence an ambassador from the Pope. He seized Colonel Semple, an agent of the Prince of Parma. He drove many of the seminary priests out of the kingdom. He marched suddenly to Dumfries, dispersed Maxwell's followers, and took him prisoner. In a convention of the nobles he declared his resolution to adhere inviolably to the league with England; and, without listening to the suggestions of revenge, determined to act in concert with Elizabeth against the common enemy of the Protestant faith. He put the kingdom in a posture of defence, and levied troops to obstruct the landing of the Spaniards. He offered to send an army to Elizabeth's assistance, and told her ambassador that he expected no other favour from the King of Spain but that which Polyphemus had promised to Ulysses, that when he had devoured all his companions he would make him his last morsel.

The zeal of the people on this occasion was not inferior to that of the King; and the extraordinary danger with which they were threatened suggested to them an extraordinary expedient for their security. A bond was framed for the maintenance of true religion, as well as the defence of the King's person and government, in opposition to all enemies foreign and domestic. This contained a confession of the Protestant faith, a particular renunciation of the errors of Popery, and the most solemn promises, in the name and through the strength of God, of adhering to each other in supporting the former and contending against the latter to the utmost of their power. The King, the nobles, the clergy, and the people subscribed with equal alacrity. Strange or uncommon as such a combination may now appear, many circumstances contributed at that time to recommend it, and to render the idea familiar to the Scots. When roused by an extraordinary event or alarmed by any public danger, the people of Israel were accustomed to bind themselves by a solemn covenant to adhere to that religion which the Almighty had established among them; this the Scots considered as a sacred precedent which it became them to imitate. In that age no considerable enterprise was undertaken in Scotland without a bond of mutual defence, which all concerned reckoned necessary for their security. The form of this religious confederacy is plainly borrowed from those political ones of which so many instances have occurred; the articles, stipulations, and peculiar mode of expression are exactly the same in both. Almost all the considerable Popish Princes were then joined in a league for extirpating the reformed religion, and nothing could be more natural, or seemed more efficacious, than to enter into a counter association in order to oppose the progress of that formidable conspiracy. To these causes did the *covenant*, which is so famous in history, owe its origin. It was renewed at different times during the reign of James. It was revived with great solemnity, though with considerable alterations, in the year 1638. It was adopted by the English in the year 1643, and enforced by the civil and ecclesiastical authority of both kingdoms. The political purposes to which it was then made subservient, and the violent and unconstitutional measures which it was then employed to promote, it is not our province to explain. But at the juncture in which it was first introduced, we may pronounce it to have been a prudent and laudable device for the defence of the religion and liberties of the nation; nor were the terms in which it was conceived other than might have been expected from men alarmed with the impending danger of Popery, and threatened with an invasion by the most bigoted and most powerful Prince in Europe.

Philip's eagerness to conquer England did not inspire him either with the vigour or dispatch necessary to insure the success of so mighty an enterprise. His fleet, which ought to have sailed in April, did not enter the English channel till the middle of July. It hovered many days on the coast in expectation of being joined by the Prince of Parma, who was blocked up in the ports of Flanders by a Dutch squadron. Continual disasters pursued the Spaniards during that time; successive storms and battles, which were well known, conspired with their own ill conduct to disappoint their enterprise. And by the blessing of Providence which watched with remarkable care over the Protestant religion and the liberties of Britain, the English valour scattered and destroyed the Armada on which Philip had arrogantly bestowed the name of Invincible. After being driven out of the English seas, their shattered ships were forced to steer their course toward Spain round Scotland and Ireland. Many of them suffered shipwreck on these dangerous and unknown coasts. Though James kept his subjects under arms to watch the motions of the Spaniards and to prevent their landing in an hostile manner, he received with great humanity seven hundred who were forced ashore by a tempest, and after supplying them with necessaries permitted them to return into their own country.

On the retreat of the Spaniards Elizabeth sent an ambassador to congratulate with James, and to compliment him on the firmness and generosity he had discovered during a conjuncture so dangerous. But none of Ashby's promises were any longer remembered, that minister was even accused of having exceeded his powers by his too liberal offers; and conscious of his own falsehood, or ashamed of being disowned by his court he withdrew secretly out of Scotland.

1589]. Philip, convinced by fatal experience of his own rashness in attempting the conquest of England by a naval armament, equipped at so great a distance, and subjected in all its operations to the delays and uncertainties arising from sea and wind, resolved to make his attack in another form, and to adopt the plan which the Princes of Lorrain had long meditated, of invading England through Scotland. A body of his troops he imagined might be easily wafted over from the Low Countries to that kingdom; and if they could once obtain footing or procure assistance there, the frontier of England was open and defenceless, and the northern counties full of Roman Catholics, who would receive them with open arms. Meanwhile a descent might be threatened on the southern coast, which would divide the English army, distract their councils, and throw the whole kingdom into terrible convulsions. In order to prepare the way for the execution of this design, he remitted a considerable sum of money to Bruce, a seminary priest in Scotland, and employed him, together with Hay, Crighton, and Tyrie, Scottish Jesuits, to gain over as many persons of distinction as possible to his interest.

Zeal for Popery, and the artful insinuations of these emissaries, induced several noblemen to favour a measure which tended so manifestly to the destruction of their country. Huntly, though the King had lately given him in marriage the daughter of his favourite the Duke of Lennox, continued warmly attached to the Romish Church. Crawford and Errol were animated with the zeal of new converts. They all engaged in a correspondence with the Prince of Parma, and, in their letters to him, offered their service to the King of Spain, and undertook with the aid of six thousand men, to render him master of Scotland, and to bring so many of their vassals into the field, that he should be able to enter England with a numerous army. Francis Stewart, gandson of James V.* whom the King created Earl of Bothwell, though influenced by no motive of religion, for he still adhered to the Protestant faith, was prompted merely by caprice, and the restlessness of his nature, to join in this treasonable correspondence.

All these letters were intercepted in England [Feb. 17]. Elizabeth, alarmed at the danger which threatened her own kingdom, sent them immediately to the King, and, reproaching him with his former lenity towards the Popish party, called upon him to check this formidable conspiracy by a proper severity. But James, though firmly attached to the Protestant religion, though profoundly versed in the theological controversies between the Reformers and the Church of Rome, though he had employed himself at that early period of life, in writing a commentary on the Revelations, in which he laboured to prove the Pope to be Antichrist, had, nevertheless, already adopted those maxims concerning the treatment of the Roman Catholics, to which he adhered through the rest of his life. The Roman Catholics were at this time a very powerful and active party in England; they were far from being an inconsiderable faction in his own kingdom. The Pope and the King of Spain were ready to take part in all their machinations, and to second every effort of their bigotry. The opposition of such a body to his succession to the crown of England, added to the averseness of the English from the government of strangers, might create him many difficulties. In order to avoid these, he thought it necessary to soothe rather than to irritate the Roman Catholics, and to reconcile them to his succcession, by the hopes of gentler treatment, and some mitigation of the rigour of those laws which were now in force against them. This attempt to gain one party by promises of indulgence and acts of clemency, while he adhered with all the obstinacy of a disputant to the doctrines and tenets of the other, has given an air of mystery, and even of contradiction, to this part of the King's character. The Papists, with the credulity of a sect struggling to obtain power, believed his heart to be wholly theirs; and the Protestants, with the jealousy inseparable from those who are already in possession of power, viewed every act of lenity as a mark of indifference, or a symptom of apostacy. In order to please both, James often aimed at an excessive refinement, mingled with dissimulation, in which he imagined the perfection of government and of king craft to consist.

*He was the son of John Prior of Coldingham, one of James's natural children.

His behaviour on this occasion was agreeable to these general maxims. Notwithstanding the solicitations of the Queen of England, enforced by the zealous remonstrances of his own clergy, a short imprisonment was the only punishment he inflicted upon Huntly and his associates. But he soon had reason to repent an act of clemency so inconsistent with the dignity of government. The first use which the conspirators made of their liberty was, to assemble their followers; and, under pretence of removing Chancellor Maitland, an able minister, but warmly devoted to the English interest, from the King's council and presence they attempted to seize James himself. This attempt being defeated, partly by Maitland's vigilance and partly by their own ill-conduct, they were forced to retire to the North, where they openly erected the standard of rebellion. But as the King's government was not generally unpopular, or his ministers odious, their own vassals joined them slowly, and discovered no zeal in the cause. The King, in person, advancing against them with such forces as he could suddenly levy, they durst not rely so much on the fidelity of the troops, which, though superior in numbers, followed them with reluctance, as to hazard a battle; but suffering them to disperse, they surrendered to the King, and threw themselves on his mercy. Huntly, Errol, Crawford, and Bothwell, were all brought to public trial. Repeated acts of treason were easily proved against them. The King, however, did not permit any sentence to be pronounced, and after keeping them a few months in confinement, he took occasion, amidst the public festivity and rejoicings at the approach of his marriage, to set them at liberty.

As James was the only descendant of the ancient monarchs of Scotland in the direct line; as all hopes of uniting the crowns of the two kingdoms would have expired with him; as the Earl of Arran, the presumptive heir to the throne, was lunatic; the King's marriage was, on all these accounts, an event which the nation wished for with the utmost ardour. He himself was no less desirous of accomplishing it; and had made overtures for that purpose to the eldest daughter of Frederick II. King of Denmark. But Elizabeth, jealous of every thing that would render the accession of the house of Stewart more acceptable to the English, endeavoured to perplex James in the same manner she had done Mary, and employed as many artifices to defeat or to retard his marriage. His ministers, gained by bribes and promises, seconded her intention; and though several different ambassadors were sent from Scotland to Denmark, they produced powers so limited, or insisted on conditions so extravagant, that Frederick could not believe the King to be in earnest; and, suspecting that there was some design to deceive or amuse him, gave his daughter in marriage to the Duke of Brunswick. Not discouraged by this disappointment, which he imputed entirely to the conduct of his own ministers, James made addresses to the Princess Anne, Frederick's second daughter. Though Elizabeth endeavoured to divert him from this by recommending Catherine, the king of Navarre's sister, as a more advantageous match; though she prevailed on the privy coun-

cil of Scotland to declare against the alliance with Denmark, he
persisted in his choice ; and despairing of overcoming the obstinacy
of his own ministers in any other manner, he secretly encouraged
the citizens of Edinburgh to take arms. They threatened to tear
in pieces the chancellor, whom they accused as the person whose
artifices had hitherto disappointed the wishes of the King and
the expectations of his people. In consequence of this, the
Earl Marischal was sent into Denmark at the head of a splendid embassy. He received ample powers and instructions,
drawn with the King's own hand. The marriage articles were
quickly agreed upon, and the young Queen set sail towards Scotland. James made great preparations for her reception, and waited
her landing with all the impatience of a lover ; when the unwel-
come account arrived, that a violent tempest had risen, which
drove back her fleet to Norway, in a condition so shattered that
there was little hope of its putting again to sea before the spring.
This unexpected disappointment he felt with the utmost sensibility.
He instantly fitted out some ships, and, without communicating his
intention to any of his council, sailed in person, attended by the
chancellor, several noblemen, and a train of three hundred persons,
in quest of his bride [Oct 22]. He arrived safely in a small harbour near Upslo, where the Queen then resided. There the marriage was solemnized [Nov. 24] ; and as it would have been rash to
trust those boisterous seas in the winter season, James accepted the
invitation of the court of Denmark, and, repairing to Copenhagen,
passed several months there, amidst continual feasting and amusements, in which both the Queen and himself had great delight.

No event in the King's life appears to be a wider deviation from
his general character than this sudden sally. His son Charles I.
was capable of that excessive admiration of the other sex, which
arises from great sensibility of heart, heightened by elegance of
taste; and the romantic air of his journey into Spain suited such a
disposition. But James was not susceptible of any refined gallantry, and always expressed that contempt for the female character
which a pedantic erudition, unacquainted with politeness, is apt to
inspire. He was exasperated, however, and rendered impatient by
the many obstacles which had been laid in his way. He was anxious to secure the political advantages which he expected from
marriage; and fearing that a delay might afford Elizabeth and his
own ministers an opportunity of thwarting him by new intrigues,
he suddenly took the resolution of preventing them, by a voyage
from which he expected to return in a few weeks. The nation
seemed to applaud his conduct, and to be pleased with this appearance of amorous ardour in a young Prince. Notwithstanding his
absence so long beyond the time he expected, the nobles, the clergy
and the people, vied with one another in loyalty and obedience ;
and no period of the King's reign was more remarkable for tranquillity, or more free from any eruption of those factions which so
often disturbed the kingdom.

BOOK VI.

1590.

On the 1st of May the King and Queen arrived at Leith, and were received by their subjects with every possible expression of joy. The solemnity of the Queen's coronation was conducted with great magnificence: but so low had the order of bishops fallen in the opinion of the public, that none of them were present on that occasion; and Mr. Robert Bruce, a Presbyterian minister of great reputation, set the crown on her head, administered the sacred unction, and performed the other customary ceremonies.

The zeal and success with which many of the clergy had contributed towards preserving peace and order in the kingdom, during his absence, reconciled James, in a great degree, to their persons, and even to the Presbyterian form of government. In presence of an assembly which met this year [Aug. 4.] he made high encomiums on the discipline as well as the doctrine of the church, promised to adhere inviolably to both, and permitted the assembly to frame such acts as gradually abolished all the remains of episcopal jurisdiction, and paved the way for a full and legal establishment of the Presbyterian model.

1591.] An event happened soon after, which afforded the clergy no small triumph. Archbishop Adamson, their ancient opponent, having fallen under the King's displeasure, having been deprived of the revenues of his see in consequence of the act of annexation, and being oppressed with age, with poverty, and diseases, made the meanest submission to the clergy, and delivered to the assembly a formal recantation of all his opinions concerning church government, which had been matter of offence to the Presbyterians. Such a confession, from the most learned person of the episcopal order, was considered as a testimony which the force of truth had extorted from an adversary.

Meanwhile, the King's excessive clemency towards offenders multiplied crimes of all kinds, and encouraged such acts of violence as brought his government under contempt, and proved fatal to many of his subjects. The history of several years, about this time, is filled with accounts of the deadly quarrels between the great families, and of murders and assassinations perpetrated in the most audacious manner, and with circumstances of the utmost barbarity. All the defects in the feudal aristocracy were now felt more keenly, perhaps, than at any other period in the history of Scotland, and universal licence and anarchy prevailed to a degree scarce consistent with the preservation of society: while the King, too gentle to punish, or too feeble to act with vigour, suffered all these enormities to pass with impunity.

But though James connived at real crimes, witchcraft, which is commonly an imaginary one, engrossed his attention, and those suspected of it felt the whole weight of his authority. Many persons, neither extremely old nor wretchedly poor, which were usually held to be certain indications of this crime, but masters of families, and matrons of a decent rank, and in the middle age of life, were seized and tortured. Though their confessions contained the most absurd and incredible circumstances, the King's prejudices, those of the clergy and of the people, conspired in believing their extravagancies without hesitation, and in punishing their persons without mercy. Some of these unhappy sufferers accused Bothwell of having consulted them, in order to know the time of the King's death, and of having employed their art to raise the storms which had endangered the Queen's life, and had detained James so long in Denmark. Upon this evidence that nobleman was committed to prison. His turbulent and haughty spirit could neither submit to the restraint, nor brook such an indignity. Having gained his keepers, he made his escape: and imputing the accusation to the artifices of his enemy the chancellor, he assembled his followers, under pretence of driving him from the King's councils. Being favoured by some of the King's attendants, he was admitted by a secret passage, under cloud of night, into the court of the palace of Holyrood House. He advanced directly towards the royal apartment; but happily before he entered, the alarm was taken, and the doors shut. While he attempted to burst open some of them [Dec. 27,] and set fire to others, the citizens of Edinburgh had time to run to their arms, and he escaped with the utmost difficulty; owing his safety to the darkness of the night, and the precipitancy with which he fled.

1592.] He retired towards the north; and the King having unadvisedly given a commission to the Earl of Huntly to pursue him and his followers with fire and sword, he, under colour of executing that commission, gratified his private revenge, and surrounded the house of the Earl of Murray, burned it to the ground, and slew Murray himself [Feb. 8]. The murder of a young nobleman of such promising virtues, and the heir of the Regent Murray, the darling of the people, excited universal indignation. The citizens of Edinburgh rose in a tumultuous manner; and, though they were restrained, by the care of the magistrates, from any acts of violence, they threw aside all respect for the King and his ministers, and openly insulted and threatened both. While this mutinous spirit continued, James thought it prudent to withdraw from the city, and fix his residence for some time at Glasgow. There Huntly surrendered himself to justice; and, notwithstanding the atrociousness of the crime, and the clamours of the people, the power of the chancellor, with whom he was now closely confederated and the King's regard for the memory of the Duke of Lennox, whose daughter he had married, not only protected him from the sentence which such an odious action merited, but exempted him from the formality of a public trial.

A step of much importance was taken soon after with regard to the government of the church. The clergy had long complained of the encroachments made upon their privileges and jurisdiction by the acts of parliament 1684; and though these laws had lost much of their force, they resolved to petition the parliament which was approaching to repeal them in form. The juncture for pushing such a measure was well chosen. The King had lost much of the public favour by his lenity towards the Popish faction, and still more by his remissness in pursuing the murderers of the Earl of Murray. The chancellor had not only a powerful party of the courtiers combined against him, but was become odious to the people, who imputed to him every false step in the King's conduct. Bothwell still lurked in the kingdom, and, being secretly supported by all the enemies of Maitland's administration, was ready every moment to renew his audacious enterprise. James, for all these reasons, was extremely willing to indulge the clergy in their request, and not only consented to a law, whereby the acts of 1584 were rescinded or explained, but he carried his complaisance still further, and permitted the parliament to establish the presbyterian government, in its general assemblies, provincial synods, presbyteries, and kirk sessions, with all the different branches of their discipline and jurisdiction, in the most ample manner. All the zeal and authority of the clergy, even under the administration of Regents, from whom they might have expected the most partial favour, could not obtain the sanction of law, in conformation of their mode of ecclesiastical government. No Prince was ever less disposed than James to approve a system, the republican genius of which inspired a passion for liberty extremely repugnant to his exalted notions of royal prerogative. Nor could any aversion be more inveterate than his to the austere and uncomplying character of the presbyterian clergy in that age; who, more eminent for zeal than for policy, often contradicted his opinions, and censured his conduct, with a freedom equally offensive to his dogmatism as a theologian, and to his pride as a King. His situation, however, obliged him frequently to conceal or to dissemble his sentiments; and, as he often disgusted his subjects by indulging the Popish faction more than they approved, he endeavoured to atone for this by his concessions to the presbyterian clergy, more liberal than he himself would otherwise have chosen to grant.

In this parliament, Bothwell and all his adherents were attainted. But he soon made a new attempt to seize the King at Falkland; and James, betrayed by some of his courtiers, and feebly defended by others, who wished well to Bothwell as the chancellor's avowed enemy, owed his safety to the fidelity and vigilance of Sir Robert Melvil, and to the irresolution of Bothwell's associates.

Scarcely was this danger over, when the nation was alarmed with the discovery of a new and more formidable conspiracy. George Ker, the Lord Newbattle's brother, being seized as he was ready to set sail for Spain, many suspicious papers were found in his custody; and among these several blanks signed by the Earls of Angus, Huntly, and Errol. By this extraordinary precaution they hoped to escape any danger of discovery. But Ker's resolution shrinking when torture was threatened, he confessed that he was employed by these noblemen to carry on a negotiation with the King of Spain; that the blanks subscribed with their names were to be filled up by Crichton and Tyrie; that they were instructed to offer the faithful service of the three Earls to that monarch; and to solicit him to land a body of his troops, either in Galloway or at the mouth of Clyde, with which they undertook, in the first place, to establish the Roman Catholic religion in Scotland, and then to invade England with the whole forces of the kingdom. David Graham of Fintry, and Barclay of Ladyland, whom he accused of being privy to the conspiracy, were taken into custody, and confirmed all the circumstances of his confessions.

1593.] The nation having been kept for some time in continual terror and agitation by so many successive conspiracies, the discovery of this new danger completed the panic. All ranks of men, as if the enemy had already been at their gates, thought themselves called upon to stand forth in defence of their country. The ministers of Edinburgh, without waiting for any warrant from the King, who happened at that time to be absent from the capital, and without having received any legal commission, assembled a considerable number of peers and barons, in order to provide an instant security against the impending danger. They seized the Earl of Angus, and committed him to the castle; they examined Ker; and prepared a remonstrance to be laid before the King, concerning the state of the nation, and the necessity of prosecuting the conspirators with becoming vigour. James, though jealous of every encroachment on his prerogative, and offended with his subjects, who, instead of petitioning, seemed to prescribe to him, found it necessary, during the violence of the ferment, not only to adopt their plan, but even to declare that no consideration should ever induce him to pardon such as had been guilty of so odious a treason. He summoned the Earls of Huntly and Arrol to surrender themselves to justice. Graham of Fintry, whom his peers pronounced to be guilty of treason, he commanded to be publicly beheaded [Jan. 8]; and marching into the north at the head of an army, the two earls, together with Angus, who had escaped out of prison, retired to the mountains. He placed garrisons in the castles which belonged to them; compelled their vassals, and the barons in the adjacent counties, to subscribe a bond containing professions of their loyalty towards him, and of their firm adherence to the Protestant faith; and, the better to secure the tranquillity of that part of the kingdom, constituted the Earls of Athol and Marischal his lieutenants there.

Having finished this expedition, James returned to Edinburgh [March 18], where he found Lord Borrough, an extraordinary ambassador from the court of England. Elizabeth, alarmed at the discovery of a conspiracy which she considered as no less formidable to her own kingdom than to Scotland, reproached James with his former remissness, and urged him, as he regarded the preservation of the Protestant religion, or the dignity of his own crown, to punish this repeated treason with rigour; and if he could not apprehend the persons, at least to confiscate the estates of such audacious rebels. She weakened, however, the force of these requests, by interceding at the same time in behalf of Bothwell, whom, according to her usual policy, in nourishing a factious spirit among the Scottish nobles, she had taken under her protection. James absolutely refused to listen to any intercession in favour of one who had so often, and with so much outrage, insulted both his government and his person. With regard to the Popish conspirators, he declared his resolution to prosecute them with vigour; but that he might be the better able to do so, he demanded a small sum of money from Elizabeth, which she, distrustful perhaps of the manner in which he might apply it, showed no inclination to grant. The zeal, however, and importunity of his own subjects obliged him to call a parliament, in order to pass an act of attainder against the three earls. But before it met, Ker made his escape out of prison, and on pretence that legal evidence of their guilt could not be produced, nothing was concluded against them. The King himself was universally suspected of having contrived this artifice, on purpose to elude the requests of the Queen of England, and to disappoint the wishes of his own people; and therefore, in order to soothe the clergy, who exclaimed loudly against his conduct, he gave way to the passing of an act, which ordained such as obstinately contemned the censures of the church to be declared outlaws.

While the terror excited by the Popish conspiracy possessed the nation, the court had been divided by two rival factions, which contended for the chief direction of affairs. At the head of one was the chancellor, in whom the King reposed entire confidence. For that very reason, perhaps, he had fallen early under the Queen's displeasure. The Duke of Lennox, the Earl of Athol, Lord Ochiltree, and all the name of Stewart espoused her quarrel, and widened the breach. James, fond no less of domestic tranquillity than of public peace, advised his favourite to retire, for some time, in hopes that the Queen's resentment would subside. But as he stood in need, in the present juncture, of the assistance of an able minister, he had recalled him to court. In order to prevent him from recovering his former power, the Stewarts had recourse to an expedient no less illegal than desperate. Having combined with Bothwell, who was of the same name, they brought him back secretly into Scotland [July 24]; and, seizing the gates of the palace, introduced him into the royal apartment with a numerous train of armed followers. James, though deserted by all his courtiers, and incapable of resistance, discovered more indignation than fear, and, reproaching them for their treachery, called on the Earl to finish his treasons by piercing his sovereign to the heart. But Bothwell fell on his knees, and implored pardon. The King was not in a condition to refuse his demands. A few days after he signed a capitulation with this successful traitor, to whom he was really a prisoner, whereby he bound himself to grant him a remission for all past offences, and to procure the ratification of it in parliament; and in the mean time to dismiss the chancellor, the Master of Glamis, Lord Home, and Sir George Home, from his councils and presence. Bothwell, on his part consented to remove from court, though he left there as many of his associates as he thought sufficient to prevent the return of the adverse faction.

But it was now no easy matter to keep the King under the same kind of bondage to which he had been often subject during his minority. He discovered so much impatience to shake off his fetters that those who had imposed durst not continue the restraint. They permitted him to call a convention of the nobles at Stirling, and to repair thither himself [Sept. 7]. All Bothwell's enemies, and all who were desirous of gaining the King's favour by appearing to be so, obeyed the summons. They pronounced the insult offered to the King's person and authority to be high treason, and declared him absolved from any obligation to observe conditions extorted by force, and which violated so essentially his royal prerogative. James, however, still proffered him a pardon, provided he would sue for it as an act of mercy, and promise to retire out of the kingdom. These conditions Bothwell rejected with disdain, and, betaking himself once more to arms, attempted to surprise the King ; but finding him on his guard fled to the borders.

The King's ardour against Bothwell, compared with his slow and evasive proceedings against the Popish lords, occasioned a general disgust among his subjects : and was imputed either to an excessive attachment to the persons of those conspirators, or to a secret partiality towards their opinions ; both which gave rise to no unreasonable fears [Sept. 25]. The clergy, as the immediate guardians of the Protestant religion, thought themselves bound, in such a juncture, to take extraordinary steps for its preservation. The provincial synod of Fife happening to meet at that time, a motion was made to excommunicate all concerned in the late conspiracy, as obstinate and irreclaimable Papists ; and though none of the conspirators resided within the bounds of the synod, or were subject to its jurisdiction, such was the zeal of the members, that, overlooking this irregularity, they pronounced against them the sentence of excommunication, to which the act of the last parliament added new terrors. Lest this should be imputed to a few men, and accounted the act of a small part of the church, deputies were appointed to attend the adjacent synods, and to desire their approbation and concurrence.

An event happened a few weeks after, which increased the people's suspicions of the King. As he was marching on an expedition against the borderers [Oct. 17], the three Popish earls, coming suddenly into his presence, offered to submit themselves to a legal trial ; and James, without committing them to custody, appointed a day for that purpose. They prepared to appear with a formidable train of their friends and vassals. But in the mean time the clergy, together with many peers and barons, assembled at Edinburgh, remonstrated against the King's extreme indulgence with great boldness, and demanded of him, according to the regular course of justice, to commit to sure custody persons charged with the highest acts of treason, who could not be brought to a legal trial until they were absolved from the censures of the church ; and to call a convention of estates, to deliberate concerning the method of proceeding against them. At the same time they offered to accompany him in arms to the place of trial, lest such audacious and powerful criminals should overawe justice, and dictate to the judges, to whom they pretended to submit. James, though extremely offended, both with the irregularity of their proceedings, and the presumption of their demands, found it expedient to put off the day of trial, and to call a convention of estates, in order to quiet the fears and jealousies of the people. By being humoured in this point, their suspicions began gradually to abate, and the chancellor managed the convention so artfully, that he himself, together with a few other members, were empowered to pronounce a final sentence upon the conspirators [Nov. 26]. After much deliberation they ordained, that the three earls and their associates should be exempted from all further inquiry or prosecution, on account of their correspondence with Spain; that before the 1st day of February, they should either submit to the church, and publicly renounce the errors of Popery, or remove out of the kingdom; that, before the 1st of January, they should declare which of these alternatives they would embrace; that they should find surety for their peaceable demeanour for the future; and that if if they failed to signify their choice in due time, they should lose the benefit of this act of *abolition*, and remain exposed to all the pains of law.

1594.] By this lenity towards the conspirators, James incurred much reproach, and gained no advantage. Devoted to the Popish superstition, submissive to all the dictates of their priests, and buoyed up with hopes and promises of foreign aid, the three earls refused to accept of the conditions, and continued their treasonable correspondence with the court of Spain. A convention of estates [Jan. 18] pronounced them to have forfeited the benefit of the articles which were offered; and the King required them, by proclamation, to surrender themselves to justice. The presence of the English ambassador contributed, perhaps, to the vigour of these proceedings. Elizabeth, ever attentive to James's motions, and imputing his reluctance to punish the Popish lords to a secret approbation of their designs, had sent Lord Zouche to represent once more, the danger to which he exposed himself by this false moderation; and to require him to exercise that rigour which their crimes, as well as the posture of affairs rendered necessary. Though the steps now taken by the King silenced all complaints on that head, yet Zouche, forgetful of his character as an ambassador, entered into private negociations with such of the Scottish nobles as disapproved of the King's measures, and held almost an open correspondence with Bothwell, who, according to the usual artifice of malecontents, pretended much solicitude for reforming the disorders of the commonwealth; and covered his own ambition with the specious veil of zeal against those counsellors who restrained the King from pursuing the avowed enemies of the Protestant faith. Zouche encouraged him, in the name of his mistress, to take arms against his sovereign.

Meanwhile the King and the clergy were filled with mutual distrust of each other. They were jealous, perhaps, to excess, that James's affections leaned too much towards the Popish faction. He suspected them, without good reason, of prompting Bothwell to rebellion, and even of supplying him with money for that purpose. Little instigation, indeed, was wanting to rouse such a

turbulent spirit as Bothwell's to any daring enterprise. He appear
ed suddenly within a mile of Edinburgh, at the head of four
hundred horse- The pretences by which he endeavoured to justify
this insurrection, were extremly popular ; zeal for religion, enmity
to Popery, concern for the King's honour, and for the liberties of
the nation. James was totally unprovided for his own defence ; ho
had no infantry, and was accompanied only with a few horsemen of
Lord Home's train. In this extremity; he implored the aid of the
citizens of Edinburgh ; and in order to encourage them to act with
zeal, he promised to proceed against the Popish lords with the utmost rigour of law. Animated by their ministers, the citizens ran
cheerfully to their arms, and advanced, with the King at their head
against Bothwell : but he notwithstanding his success in putting
to flight Lord Home, who had rashly charged him with a far inferior number of cavalry, retired to Dalkeith without daring to
attack the King. His followers abandoned him soon after, and discouraged by so many successive disappointments, could never afterwards be brought to venture into the field. He betook himself to
his usual lurking places in the north of England ; but Elizabeth
in compliance with the King's remonstrances, obliged him to quit
his retreat.

No sooner was the King delivered from one danger, than he was
called to attend to another. The Popish lords, in consequence of
their negociations with Spain [April 3], received, in the spring, a
supply of money from Philip. What bold designs this might inspire,
it was no easy matter to conjecture. From men under the dominion
of bigotry, and whom indulgence could not reclaim, the most
desperate actions were to be dreaded. The Assembly of the church
immediately took the alarm ; remonstrated against them with
more bitterness than ever ; and unanimously ratified the sentence
of excommunication pronounced by the synod of Fife. James
himself provoked by their obstinacy and ingratitude, and afraid
that his long forbearance would not only be generally displeasing,
to his own subjects, but give rise to unfavourable suspicions among
the English, exerted himself with unusual vigour. He called a
parliament [June 8]; laid before it all the circumstances and
aggravations of the conspiracy ; and though there were but few members present, and several of these connected with the conspirators by
blood or friendship, he prevailed on them, by his influence and importunity, to pronounce the most rigorous sentence which the law
can inflict. They were declared to be guilty of high treason, and
their estates and honours forfeited. At the same time, statutes
more severe than ever, were enacted against the professors of the
Popish religion.

How to put this sentence in execution was a matter of great
difficulty. Three powerful barons, cantoned in a part of the
country of difficult access, surrounded with numerous vassals,
and supported by aid from a foreign Prince, were more than an
overmatch for a Scottish monarch. No entreaty could prevail on
Elizabeth to advance the money necessary for defraying the expenses of an expedition against them. To attack them in person,
with his own forces alone, might have exposed James both to dis-

grace and to danger. He had recourse to the only expedient which remained in such a situation, for aiding the impotence of sovereign authority; he delegated his authority to the Earl of Argyll and Lord Forbes, the leaders of two clans at enmity with the conspirators; and gave them a commission to invade their lands, and to seize the castles which belonged to them. Bothwell, notwithstanding all his high pretensions of zeal for the Protestant relligion, having now entered into close confederacy with them, the danger became every day more urgent. Argyll, solicited by the King, and roused by the clergy, took the field at the head of seven thousand men. Huntly and Errol met him at Glenlivat, with an army far inferior in number, but composed chiefly of gentlemen of the low countries, mounted on horseback, and who brought along with them a train of field pieces. They encountered each other [Oct. 3] with all the fury which hereditary and ancient rivalship add to undisciplined courage. [1595.] But the Highlanders, disconcerted by the first discharge of the cannon, to which they were little accustomed, and unable to resist the impression of cavalry, were soon put to flight; and Argyll, a gallant young man of eighteen, was carried by his friends out of the field, weeping with indignation at their disgrace, and calling on them to stand, and to vindicate the honour of their name.

On the first intelligence of this defeat, James, though obliged to pawn his jewels in order to raise money, assembled a small body of troops, and marched towards the north. He was joined by the Irvines, Keiths, Leslys, Forbeses, and other clans at enmity with Huntly and Errol, who having lost several of their principal followers at Glenlivat, and others refusing to bear arms against the King in person, were obliged to retire to the mountains. James wasted their lands; put garrisons in some of their castles; burned others; and left the Duke of Lennox as his lieutenant in that part of the kingdom, with a body of men sufficient to restrain them from gathering to any head there, or from infesting the low country. Reduced at last to extreme distress by the rigour of the season, and the desertion of their followers, they obtained the King's permission to go beyond the seas, and gave security that they should neither return without his licence, nor engage in any new intrigues against the Protestant religion, or the peace of the kingdom.

By their exile tranquillity was re-established in the north of Scotland; and the firmness and vigour which James had displayed, in his last proceedings against them, regained him, in a great degree, the confidence of his Protestant subjects. But he sunk in the same proportion, and for the same reason, in the esteem of the Roman Catholics. They had asserted his mother's right to the crown of England with so much warmth, that they could not, with any decency, reject his; and the indulgence, with which he affected to treat the professors of the Popish religion, inspired them with such hopes, that they viewed his accession to the throne as no undesirable event. But the rigour with which the King had lately pursued the conspirators, and the severe statutes against Popery to which he had given his consent, convinced them now that these hopes were visionary; and they began to look about in quest of some new

successor, whose rights they might oppose to his. The Papists who
resided in England turned their eyes towards the Earl of Essex,
whose generous mind, though firmly established in the Protestant
faith, abhorred the severities inflicted in that age on account of religious opinions. Those of the same sect, who were in exile, formed
a bolder scheme, and one more suitable to their situation. They
advanced the claim of the Infanta of Spain ; and Parsons the Jesuit
published a Book, in which, by false quotations from history, by
fabulous genealogies, and absurd arguments, intermingled with
bitter invectives against the King of Scots, he endeavoured to prove
the Infanta's title to the English crown to be preferable to his.
Philip, though involved already in a war both with France and
England, and scarce able to defend the remains of the Burgundian
provinces against the Dutch commonwealth, eagerly grasped at this
airy project. The dread of a Spanish pretender to the crown, and
the opposition which the Papists began to form against the King's
succession, contributed not a little to remove the prejudices of the
Protestants, and to prepare the way for that event.

Bothwell, whose name has been so often mentioned as the dis-
turber of the King's tranquility, and of the peace of the kingdom,
was now in a wretched condition. Abandoned by the Queen of
England on account of his confederacy with the Popish lords ; excommunicated by the church for the same reason ; and deserted, in
his distress, by his own followers ; he was obliged to fly for safety
to France, and thence to Spain and Italy, where, after renouncing
the Protestant faith, he led many years an obscure and indigent
life, remarkable only for a low and infamous debauchery. The
King, though extremely ready to sacrifice the strongest resentment
to the slightest acknowledgments, could never be softened by his
submission, nor be induced to listen to any intercession in his
behalf.

This year the King lost Chancellor Maitland, an able minister,
on whom he had long devolved the whole weight of public affairs.
As James loved him while alive, he wrote, in honour of his memory, a copy of verses which, when compared with the compositions
of that age, are far from being elegant.

Soon after his death a considerable change was made in the administration. At that time, the annual charges of government far
exceeded the King's revenues. The Queen was fond of expensive
amusements. James himself was a stranger to economy. It became necessary, for all these reasons, to levy the public revenues
with greater order and rigour, and to husband them with more
care. This important trust was committed to eight gentlemen
of the law, who, from their number, were called *Octavians*. The
powers vested in them were ample, and almost unlimited. The
King bound himself neither to add to their number, nor to supply
any vacancy that might happen without their consent : and, knowing the facility of his own temper, agreed that no alienation of
his revenue, no grant of a pension, or order on the treasury should
be held valid, unless it was ratified by the subscription of five
of the commissioners; all their acts and decisions were declared
to be of equal force with the sentence of judges in civil courts;

and in consequence of them, and without any other warrant, any person might be arrested, or their goods seized. Such extensive jurisdiction, together with the absolute disposal of the public money, drew the whole executive part of government into their hands. United among themselves, they gradually undermined the rest of the King's ministers, and seized on every lucrative or honourable office. The ancient servants of the crown repined at being obliged to quit their stations to new men. [1596.] The favourites and young courtiers murmured at seeing the King's liberality stinted by their prescriptions. And the clergy exclaimed against some of them as known apostates to Popery, and suspected others of secretly favouring it. They retained their power, however, notwithstanding this general combination against them; and they owed it entirely to the order and economy which they introduced into the administration of the finances, by which the necessary expenses of government were more easily defrayed than in any other period of the King's reign.

The rumour of vast preparations which Philip was said to be carrying on at this time, filled both England and Scotland with the dread of a new invasion. James took proper measures for the defence of his kingdom. But these did not satisfy the zeal of the clergy, whose suspicions of the King's sincerity began to revive; and as he had permitted the wives of the banished peers to levy the rents of their estates, and to live in their houses, they charged him with rendering the act of forfeiture ineffectual, by supporting the avowed enemies of the Protestant faith. The assembly of the church [March 24] took under consideration the state of the kingdom, and having appointed a day of public fasting, they solemnly renewed the covenant by which the nation was bound to adhere to the Protestant faith, and to defend it against all aggressors. A committee, consisting of the most eminent clergymen, and of many barons and gentlemen of distinction, waited on the King, and laid before him a plan for the security of the kingdom, and the preservation of religion. They urged him to appropriate the estates of the banished lords as a fund for the maintenance of soldiers; to take the strictest precautions for preventing the return of such turbulent subjects into the country; and to pursue all who were suspected of being their adherents with the utmost rigour.

Nothing could be more repugnant to the King's schemes, or more disagreeable to his inclination, than these propositions. Averse, through his whole life, to any course where he expected opposition or danger; and fond of attaining his ends with the character of moderation, and by the arts of policy, he observed with concern the prejudices against him which were growing among the Roman Catholics, and resolved to make some atonement for that part of his conduct which had drawn upon him their indignation. Elizabeth was now well advanced in years; her life had lately been in danger; if any Popish competitor should arise to dispute his right of succession, a faction so powerful as that of the banished lords might be extremely formidable; and any division among his own subjects might prove fatal at a junction which would require their united and most vigorous efforts. Instead, therefore, of the addi-

tional severities which the assembly proposed, James had thoughts
of mitigating the punishment which they already suffered. And
as they were surrounded, during their residence in foreign parts,
by Philip's emissaries; as resentment might dispose them to listen
more favourably than ever to their suggestions; as despair might
drive them to still more atrocious actions; he resolved to recall
them, under certain conditions, into their native country. Encouraged by these sentiments of the King in their favour, of which
they did not want intelligence, and wearied already of the depend-
ant and anxious life of exiles, they ventured to return secretly into
Scotland. Soon after, they presented a petition to the King, begging his permission to reside at their own houses, and offering to
give security for their peaceable and dutiful behaviour. James
called a convention of estates to deliberate on a matter of such importance, and by their advice he granted the petition.

The members of a committee appointed by the last general assembly, as soon as they were informed of this, met at Edinburgh, and,
with all the precipitancy of fear and of zeal, took such resolutions
as they thought necessary for the safety of the kingdom. They
wrote circular letters to all the presbyteries in Scotland; they
warned them of the approaching danger; they exhorted them to
stir up their people to the defence of their just rights; they commanded them to publish in all their pulpits the act excommunicat-
ing the Popish lords; and enjoined them to lay all those who were
suspected of favouring Popery under the same censure by a summary sentence, and without observing the usual formalites of a trial.
As the danger seemed too pressing to wait for the stated meetings
of the judicatories of the church, they made choice of the most
eminent clergymen in different corners of the kingdom, appointed
them to reside constantly at Edinburgh, and to meet every day
with the ministers of that city, under the name of the *Standing
Council of the Church*, and vested in this body the supreme authority, by enjoining it, in imitation of the ancient Roman form, to
take care that the church should receive no detriment.

These proceedings, no less unconstitutional than unprecedented,
were manifest encroachments on the royal prerogative, and bold steps
towards open rebellion. The King's conduct, however, justified in
some degree such excesses. His lenity towards the Papists, so repug
nant to the principles of that age; his pardoning the conspirators,
notwithstanding repeated promises to the contrary; the respect he
paid to lady Huntly, who was attached to the Romish religion no less
than her husband, his committing the care of his daughter, the Princess Elizabeth, to Lady Levingston, who was infected with the same
superstition; the contempt with which he talked on all occasions,
both of the characters of ministers and of their function, were circumstances which might have filled minds, not prone by nature to
jealousy, with some suspicious; and might have precipitated into
rash counsels those who were far removed from intemperate zeal. But,
however powerful the motives might be which influenced the clergy,
or however laudable the end they had in view, they conducted their
measures with no address, and even with little prudence. James discovered a strong inclination to avoid a rupture with the church, and,

jealous as he was of his prerogative, would willingly have made many accessions for the sake of peace. By his command, some of the privy counsellers had an interview with the more moderate among the clergy, and inquired whether Huntly and his associates might not, upon making proper acknowledgments, be again received into the bosom of the church, and be exempted from any further punishments on account of his past apostasy and treasons. They replied, that though the gate of mercy stood always open for those who repented and returned, yet as those noblemen had been guilty of idolatry, a crime deserving death both by the law of God and of man, the civil magistrate could not legally grant them a pardon; and even though the church should absolve them, it was his duty to inflict punishment upon them. This inflexibility in those who were reckoned the most compliant of the order filled the King with indignation, which the imprudence and obstinacy of a private clergyman heightened into rage.

Mr. David Black, minister of St. Andrew's, discoursing in one of his sermons, according to custom, concerning the state of the nation, affirmed that the King had permitted the Popish lords to return into Scotland, and by that action had discovered the treachery of his own heart; that all Kings were the devil's children; that Satan had now the guidance of the court; that the Queen of England was an atheist; that the judges were miscreants and bribers; the nobility godless and degenerate; the privy counsellors cormorants and men of no religion; and in his prayer for the Queen he used these words, We must pray for her for fashion sake, but we have no cause, she will never do us good. James commanded him to be summoned before the privy council [Nov. 10], to answer for such seditious expressions; and the clergy, instead of abandoning him to the punishment which such a petulant and criminal attack upon his superiors deserved, were so imprudent as to espouse his cause, as if it had been the common one of the whole order. The controversy concerning the immunities of the pulpit, and the rights of the clergy to testify against vices of every kind, which had been agitated in 1584, was now revived. It was pretended that, with regard to their sacred function, ministers were subject to the church alone; that it belonged only to their ecclesiastical superiors to judge of the truth or falsehood of doctrines delivered in the pulpit; that if, upon any pretence whatever, the King usurped this jurisdiction, the church would, from that moment, sink under servitude to the civil magistrate; that, instead of reproving vice with that honest boldness which had often been of great advantage to individuals, and the most wholesome to the kingdom, the clergy would learn to flatter the passions of the Prince, and to connive at the vices of others; that the King's eagerness to punish the indiscretion of a Protestant minister, while he was so ready to pardon the crimes of Popish conspirators, called on them to stand upon their guard, and that now was the time to contend for their privileges, and to prevent any encroachment on those rights, of which the church had been in possession ever since the Reformation. Influenced by these considerations, the council of the church enjoined Black to decline the jurisdiction of the privy council. Proud of such an opportunity to display his zeal, he presented a paper to that purpose, and with the utmost firmness refused to plead, or to answer the questions which were put to him. In order to add greater weight to these proceedings, the council of the church transmitted the *declinature* to all the presbyteries throughout the kingdom, and enjoined every minister to subscribe it in testimony of his approbation.

James defended his rights with no less vigour than they were attacked. Sensible of the contempt under which his authority must fall, if the clergy should be permitted publicly, and with impunity, to calumniate his ministers, and even to censure himself; and knowing, by former examples, what unequal reparation for such offences he might expect from the judicatories of the church, he urged on the inquiry into Black's conduct, and issued a proclamation, commanding the members of the council of the church to leave Edinburgh, and to return to their own parishes. Black, instead of submitting, renewed his *declinature;* and the members of the council, in defiance of the proclamation, declared, that as they met by the authority of the church, obedience to it was a duty still more sacred than that which they owed to the King himself. The privy council, notwithstanding Black's refusing to plead, proceeded in the trial; and, after a solemn inquiry, pronounced him guilty of the crimes of which he had been accused; but referred it to the King to appoint what punishment he should suffer.

Meanwhile, many endeavours were used to bring matters to an accommodation. Almost every day produced some new scheme of reconcilement ; but, through the King's fickleness, the obstinacy of the clergy, or the intrigues of the courtiers, they all proved ineffectual. Both parties appealed to the people, and by reciprocal and exaggerated accusations endeavoured to render each other odious. Insolence, sedition, treason, were the crimes with which James charged the clergy ; while they made the pulpits resound with complaints of his excessive lenity towards Papists, and of the no less excessive rigour with which he oppressed the established church. Exasperated by their bold invectives, he, at last, sentenced Black to retire beyond the river Spey, and to reside there during his pleasure ; and once more commanding the members of the standing council to depart from Edinburgh, he required all the ministers in the kingdom to subscribe a bond, obliging themselves to submit, in the same manner as other subjects, to the jurisdiction of the civil courts in matters of a civil nature.

This decisive measure excited all the violent passions which possess disappointed factions; and deeds no less violent immediately followed. These must be imputed in part to the artifices of some courtiers who expected to reap advantage from the calamities of their country, or who hoped to lessen the authority of the Octavians, by engaging them in hostilities with the church. On one hand, they informed the King that the citizens of Edinburgh were under arms every night, and had planted a strong guard round the house of their ministers. James, in order to put a stop to this imaginary insult on his government, issued a proclamation, commanding twenty-four of the principal citizens to leave the town within six hours. On the other hand, they wrote to the ministers, advising them to look to their own safety, as Huntly had been secretly admitted to an interview with the King, and had been the author of the severe proclamation against the citizens of Edinburgh. They doubted no more of the truth of this intelligence, than the King had done of that which he received, and fell as blindly into the snare. The letter came to their hands just as one of their number was going to mount the pulpit. They resolved that he should acquaint the people of their danger [Dec. 17]; and he painted it with all the strong colours which men naturally employ in describing any dreadful and instant calamity. When the sermon was over, he desired the nobles and gentlemen to assemble in the *Little Church*. The whole multitude, terrified at what they had heard, crowded thither; they promised and vowed to stand by the clergy, they drew up a petition to the King, craving the redress of those grievances of which the church complained, and beseeching him to deliver them from all future apprehensions of danger, by removing such of his counsellors as were known to be enemies of the Protestant religion. Two peers, and two gentlemen, two burgesses and two ministers, were appointed to present it. The King happened to be in the great hall of the Tolbooth, where the court of session was sitting. The manner in which the petition was delivered as well as its contents, offended him. He gave a haughty reply; the petitioners insisted with warmth; and a promiscuous multitude pressing into the room, James retired abruptly into another apartment, and commanded the gates to be shut behind him. The deputies returned to the multitude, who were still assembled, and to whom a minister had been reading, in their absence, the story of Haman. When they reported that the King had refused to listen to their petitions, the church was filled in a moment with noise, threatenings, execrations, and all the outrage and confusion of a popular tumult. Some called for their arms, some to bring out the wicked Haman: others cried ' The sword of the Lord and of Gideon;' and rushing out with the most furious impetuosity, surrounded the Tolbooth, threatening the King himself, and demanding some of his counsellors, whom they named, that they might tear them in pieces. The magistrates of the city, partly by authority, partly by force, endeavoured to quell the tumult; the King attempted to soothe the malecontents, by promising to receive their petitions, when presented in a regular manner; the ministers, sensible of their own rashness in kindling such a flame, seconded both; and the rage of the populace subsiding as suddenly as it had arisen, they all dispersed, and the King returned to the palace; happy in having escaped from an insurrection, which, through the instantaneous and unconcerted effect of popular fury, had exposed his life to imminent danger, and was considered by him as an unpardonable affront to his authority.

As soon as he retired, the leaders of the malecontents assembled, in order to prepare their petition. The punishment of the Popish lords; the removal of those counsellors who were suspected of favouring their persons or opinions; the repeal of all the late acts of council, subversive of the authority of the church; together with an act approving the proceeding of the standing council, were the chief of their demands. But the King's indignation was still so high, that the deputies, chosen for this purpose, durst not venture that night to present requests which could not fail of kindling his rage anew. Before next morning, James, with all his attendants, withdrew to Linlithgow: the session, and other courts of justice, were required to leave a city where it was no longer consistent either with their safety or their dignity to remain; and the noblemen and barons were commanded to return to their own houses, and not to reassemble without the King's permission. The vigour with which the King acted struck a damp upon the spirits of his adversaries. The citizens, sensible how much they would suffer by his absence, and the removal of the courts of justice, repented already of their conduct. The ministers alone resolved to maintain the contest. They endeavoured to prevent the nobles from dispersing; they inflamed the people by violent invectives against the King; they laboured to procure subscriptions to an association for their mutual defence; and, conscious what lustre and power the junction of some of the greater nobles would add to their cause, the ministers of Endinburgh wrote to Lord Hamilton, that the people, moved by the word of God, and provoked by the injuries offered to the church, had taken arms; that many of the nobles had determined to protect the Protestant religion, which owed its establishment to the piety and valour of their ancestors; that they wanted only a leader to unite them, and to inspire them with vigour; that his zeal for the good cause, no less than his noble birth, entitled him to that honour: they conjured him, therefore, not to disappoint their hopes and wishes, nor to refuse the suffering church that aid which she so much needed. Lord Hamilton, instead of complying with their desire, carried the letter directly to the King, whom this new insult irritated to such a degree, that he commanded the magistrates of Edinburgh instantly to seize their ministers, as manifest incendiaries and encouragers of rebellion. The magistrates, in order to regain the King's favour, were preparing to obey; and the ministers, who saw no other hope of safety, fled towards England.

1597.] This unsuccessful insurrection, instead of overturning, established the King's authority. Those concerned in it were confounded and dispersed. [Jan. 3]. The rest of James's subjects, in order to avoid suspicion, or to gain his favour, contended who should be most forward to execute his vengeance. A convention of estates being called, pronounced the late insurrection to be high treason; ordained every minister to subscribe a declaration of his submission to the King's jurisdiction, in all matters civil and criminal; empowered magistrates to commit instantly to prison any minister, who, in his sermons, should utter any indecent reflections on the King's conduct; prohibited any ecclesiastical judicatory to meet without the King's licence; commanded that no person should be elected a magistrate of Edinburgh, for the future, without the King's approbation; and that, in the mean time, the present magistrates should either discover and inflict condign punishment on the authors of the late tumult, or the city itself should be subjected to all the penalties of that treasonable action.

Armed with the authority of these decrees, James resolved to crush entirely the mutinous spirit of his subjects. As the clergy had hitherto derived their chief credit and strength from the favour and zeal of the citizens of Edinburgh, his first care was to humble them. Though the magistrates submitted to him in the most abject terms; though they vindicated themselves and their fellow citizens from the most distant intention of violating his royal person or authority; though, after the strictest scrutiny, no circumstances that could fix on them the suspicion of premeditated rebellion had been discovered; though many of the nobles, and such of the clergy as still retained any degree of favour, interceded in their behalf; neither acknowledgments nor intercessions were of the least avail. The King continued inexorable; [Feb. 28] the city was declared to have forfeited its privileges as a corporation, and to be liable to all the penalties of treason. The capital of the kingdom, deprived of magistrates, deserted by its ministers, abandoned by the courts of justice, and proscribed by the King, remained in desolation and despair. The courtiers even threatened to raze the city to the foundation, and to erect a pillar where it stood, as an everlasting monument of the King's vengeance, and of the guilt of its inhabitants. At last, in compliance with Elizabeth, who interposed in their favour, and moved by the continual solicitations of the nobles, James absolved the citizens from the penalties of law, but at the same time he stripped them of their most important privileges; [March 21] they were neither allowed to elect their own magistrates nor their own ministers: many new burdens were imposed on them: and a considerable sum of money was exacted by way of peace-offering.

James was, meanwhile, equally assiduous, and no less successful in circumscribing the jurisdiction of the church. Experience had discovered that to attempt this by acts of parliament, and sentences of privy council, was both ineffectual and odious. He had recourse now to an expedient more artful, and better calculated for obtaining his end. The ecclesiastical judicatories were composed of many members; the majority of the clergy were extremely indigent, and unprovided of legal stipends; the ministers in the neighbourhood of Edinburgh, notwithstanding the party established by the presbyterian government, had assumed a leading in the church, which filled their brethren with envy; every numerous body of men is susceptible of sudden and strong impressions, and liable to be influenced, corrupted, or overawed. Induced by these considerations, James thought it possible to gain the clergy, whom he had in vain attempted to subdue. Proper agents were set to work all over the kingdom; promises, flattery, and threats were employed; the usurpations of the brethren near the capital were aggravated; the jealousy of their power, which was growing in the distant provinces, was augmented; and two different general assemblies were held, in both which, notwithstanding the zeal and boldness wherewith a few leading clergymen defended the privileges of the church, a majority declared in favour of those measures which were agreeable to the King. Many practices, which had continued since the Reformation, were condemned; many points of discipline, which had hitherto been reckoned sacred and uncontroverted, were given up; the licence with which ministers discoursed of political matters was restrained; the freedom with which they inveighed against particular persons was censured; sentences of summary excommunication were declared unlawful; the convoking a general assembly, without the King's permission, was prohibited; and the right of nominating ministers to the principal towns was vested in the crown. Thus, the clergy themselves surrendered privileges which it would have been dangerous to invade, and voluntarily submitted to a yoke more intolerable than any James would have ventured to impose by force; while such as continued to oppose his measures, instead of their former popular topic of the King's violent encroachments on a jurisdiction which did not belong to him, were obliged to turn their outcries against the corruptions of their own order.

By the authority of these general assemblies, the Popish earls were allowed to make a public recantation of their errors; were absolved from the sentence of excommunication; and received into the bosom of the church. But, not many years after, they relapsed into their former errors, were again reconciled to the church of Rome, and by their apostasy justified, in some degree, the fears and the scruples of the clergy with regard to their absolution.

The ministers of Edinburgh owed to the intercession of these assemblies the liberty of returning to their charges in the city. But this liberty was clogged in such a manner as greatly abridged their power. The city was divided into distinct parishes; the number of ministers doubled; persons on whose fidelity the King could rely were fixed in the new parishes; and these circumstances, added to the authority of the late decrees of the church, contributed to confirm that absolute dominion in the ecclesiastical affairs, which James possessed during the remainder of his reign.

The King was so intent on new modelling the church, that the other transactions of this period scarce deserve to be remembered. The Octavians, envied by the other courtiers, and splitting into factions among themselves, resigned their commission; and the administration of the revenue returning into its former channel, both the King and the nation were deprived of the benefit of their regular and frugal economy.

Dec. 19.] Towards the end of the year a parliament was held in order to restore Huntly and his associates to their estates and honours, by repealing the act of forfeiture passed against them. The authority of this supreme court was likewise employed to introduce a further innovation into the church; but, conformable to the system which the King had now adopted, the motion for this purpose took its rise from the clergy themselves. As the act of general annexation, and that establishing the Presbyterian government, had reduced the few bishops, who still survived, to poverty and contempt; as those who possessed the abbeys and priories were mere laymen, and many of them temporal peers, few or none of the ecclesiastical order remained to vote in parliament; and by means of that, the influence of the crown was considerably diminished there, and a proper balance to the power and number of the nobles was wanting. But the prejudice which the nation had conceived against the name and character of bishops were so violent that James was obliged, with the utmost care, to avoid the appearance of a design to revive that order. [1598.] He prevailed, therefore, on the commission appointed by the last general assembly to complain to the parliament, that the church was the only body in the kingdom destitute of its representatives in that supreme court, where it so nearly concerned every order to have some, who were bound to defend its rights; and to crave that a competent number of the clergy should be admitted, according to ancient custom, to a seat there. In compliance with this request, an act was passed, by which those ministers, on whom the King should confer the vacant bishoprics and abbeys, were entitled to a vote in parliament; and, that the clergy might conceive no jealousy of any encroachment upon their privileges, it was remitted to the general assembly, to determine what spiritual jurisdiction or authority in the government of the church these persons should possess.

The King, however, found it no easy matter to obtain the concurrence of the ecclesiastical judicatories, in which the act of parliament met with a fierce opposition. Though the clergy perceived how much lustre this new privilege would reflect upon their order; though they were not insensible of the great accession of personal power and dignity, which many of them would acquire, by being admitted into the supreme council of the nation, their abhorrence of the episcopacy was extreme; and to that they sacrificed every consideration of interest or ambition. All the King's professions of regard for the present constitution of the church did not convince them of his sincerity; all the devices that could be invented for restraining and circumscribing the jurisdiction of such as were to be raised to this new honour, did not diminish their jealousy and fear. Their own experience had taught them with what insinuating progress the hierarchy advances, and though admitted at first with moderate authority, and under specious pretences, how rapidly it extends its dominion. "Varnish over this scheme," said one of the leading clergymen, "with what colours you please; deck the intruder with the utmost art; under all this disguise I see the horns of his mitre." The same sentiments prevailed among many of his brethren, and induced them to reject power and honours, with as much zeal as ever those of their order courted them. Many, however, were allured by the hopes of preferment; the King himself, and his ministers, employed the same arts, which they had tried so successfully last year; and, after long debates, and much opposition, the general assembly declared that it was lawful for ministers to accept of a seat in parliament [March 7]; that it would be highly beneficial to the church to have its representatives in that supreme court; and that fifty-one persons, a number nearly equal to that of the ecclesiastics who were anciently called to parliament, should be chosen from among the clergy for

that purpose. The manner of their election, together with the
powers to be vested in them, were left undecided for the present,
and furnished matter of future deliberation.

1599.] As the prospect of succeeding to the crown of England
drew nearer, James multiplied precautions in order to render it
certain. As he was allied to many of the Princes of Germany by
his marriage, he sent ambassadors extraordinary to their several
courts, in order to explain the justness of his title to the English
throne, and to desire their assistance, if any competitor should
arise to dispute his undoubted rights. These Princes readily acknowledged the equity of his claim; but the aid which they could
afford him was distant and feeble. At the same time, Edward
Bruce, Abbot of Kinloss, his ambassador at the English court, soli-
citated Elizabeth, with the utmost warmth, to recognise his title by
some public deed, and to deliver her own subjects from the calamities which are occasioned by an uncertain or disputed succession.
But age had strengthened all the passions which had hitherto induced Elizabeth to keep this great question obscure and undecided;
and a general and evasive answer was all that James could obtain.
As no impression could be made on the Queen, the ambassador was
commanded to sound the disposition of her subjects, and to try
what progress he could make in gaining them. Bruce possessed all
the talents of secrecy, judgment, and address, requisite for conducting a negotiation no less delicate than important. A minister of
this character was entitled to the confidence of the English. Many
of the highest rank unbosomed themselves to him without reserve,
and gave him repeated assurances of their resolution to assert his
master's right in opposition to every pretender. As several
pamphlets were dispersed at this time in England, containing objections to his title, James employed some learned men in his
kingdom to answer these cavillers, and to explain the advantages
which would result to both kingdoms by the union of the crowns.
These books were eagerly read, and contributed not a little to reconcile the English to that event. A book published this year by
the King himself, produced an effect still more favourable. It was
entitled *Basilicon Doron*, and contained precepts concerning the
art of government, addressed to Prince Henry his son. Notwithstanding the great alterations and refinements in national taste
since that time, we must allow this to be no contemptible performance, and not to be inferior to the works of most contemporary
writers, either in purity of style or justness of composition. Even
the vain parade of erudition with which it abounds, and which
now disgusts us, raised the admiration of that age; and as it was
filled with all those general rules which speculative authors deliver for rendering a nation happy, and of which James could discourse with great plausibility, though often incapable of putting
them in practice, the English conceived a high opinion of his
abilities, and expected an increase of national honour and prosperity under a Prince so profoundly skilled in politics, and who
gave such a specimen both of his wisdom and of his love to his
people.

The Queen of England's sentiments concerning James were different from those of her subjects. His excessive indulgence towards the Popish lords; the facility with which he pardoned their repeated treasons; his restoring Beatoun, the Popish Archbishop of Glasgow, who had fled out of Scotland at the time of the Reformation, to the possession of the temporalities of that benefice; the appointing him his ambassador at the court of France; the applause he bestowed, in the Basilicon Doron, on those who adhered to the Queen his mother; Elizabeth considered as so many indications of a mind alienated from the Protestant religion; and suspected that he would soon revolt from the profession of it. These suspicions seemed to be fully confirmed by a discovery which came from the Master of Gray, who resided at that time in Italy, and who, rather than suffer his intriguing spirit to be idle, demeaned himself so far as to act as a spy for the English court. He conveyed to Elizabeth the copy of a letter, written by James to Pope Clement VIII., in which the King, after many expressions of regard for that Pontiff, and of gratitude for his favours, declared his firm resolution to treat the Roman Catholics with indulgence; and, in order to render the intercourse between the court of Rome and Scotland more frequent and familiar, he solicited the Pope to promote Drummond, Bishop of Vaison, a Scotsman, to the dignity of a Cardinal. Elizabeth, who had received by another channel some imperfect intelligence of this correspondence, was filled with just surprise, and immediately dispatched Bowes into Scotland, to inquire more fully into the truth of the matter, and to reproach James for an action so unbecoming a Protestant Prince. He was astonished at the accusation, and with a confidence which nothing but the consciousness of innocence could inspire, affirmed the whole to be a mere calumny, and the letter itself to be forged by his enemies, on purpose to bring his sincerity in religion to be suspected. Elphingston, the secretary of state, denied the matter with equal solemnity. It came, however, to be known by a very singular accident, which happened some years after, that the information which Elizabeth had received was well founded, though, at the same time, the King's declarations of his own innocence were perfectly consistent with truth. Cardinal Bellarmine, in a reply which he published to a controversial treatise, of which the King was the author, accused him of having abandoned the favourable sentiments which he had once entertained of the Roman Catholic religion, and as a proof of this, quoted his letter to Clement VIII. It was impossible any longer to believe this to be a fiction; and it was a matter too delicate to be passed over without strict inquiry. James immediately examined Elphingston, and his confession unravelled the whole mystery. He acknowledged that he had shuffled in this letter among other papers, which he laid before the King to be signed, who suspecting no such deceit, subscribed it together with the rest, and without knowing what it contained; that he had no other motive, however, to this action, but zeal for his Majesty's service; and by flattering the Roman Catholics with hopes of indulgence under the King's government, he imagined that he was paving the way for his more easy accession to the English throne. The privy council of England entertained very different sentiments of the secretary's conduct. In their opinion, not only the King's reputation had been exposed to reproach, but his life to danger, by this rash imposture; they even imparted the gunpowder treason to the rage and disappointment of the Papists, upon finding that the hopes which this letter inspired, were frustrated. The secretary was sent a prisoner into Scotland, to be tried for high treason. His peers found him guilty, but, by the Queen's intercession, he obtained a pardon.

According to the account of other historians, James himself was no stranger to this correspondence with the Pope; and, if we believe them, Elphingston being intimidated by the threats of the English council, and deceived by the artifices of the Earl of Dunbar, concealed some circumstances in his narrative of this transaction, and falsified others; and, at the expense of his own fame, and with the danger of his own life, endeavoured to draw a veil over this part of his master conduct.

But whether we impute the writing of this letter to the secretary's officious zeal or to the King's command, it is certain that about this time James was at the utmost pains to gain the friendship of the Roman Catholic Princes, as a necessary precaution towards facilitating his accession to the English throne. Lord Hotham, who was himself a Papist, was intrusted with a secret commission to the Pope; the Archbishop of Glasgow was an active instrument with those of his own religion. The Pope expressed such favourable sentiments both of the King and of his rights to the crown of England, that James thought himself bound, some years after, to acknowledge the obligation in a public manner. Sir James Lindsay made great progress in gaining the English Papists to acknowledge his Majesty's title. Of all these intrigues Elizabeth received obscure hints from different quarters. The more imperfectly she knew, the more violently she suspected the King's designs; and, the natural jealousy of her temper increasing with age, she observed his conduct with greater solicitude than ever.

1600.] The questions with regard to the election and power of the representatives of the church, were finally decided this year by the General Assembly, which met at Montrose [March 28]. That place was chosen as most convenient for the ministers of the north, among whom the King's influence chiefly lay. Although great numbers resorted from the northern provinces, and the King employed his whole interest, and the authority of his own presence to gain a majority, the following regulations were with difficulty agreed on. That the general assembly shall recommend six persons to every vacant benefice which gave a title to a seat in parliament, out of whom the King shall nominate one; that the person so elected, after obtaining his seat in parliament, shall neither propose nor consent to any thing there that may effect the interest of the church, without special instructions to that purpose; that he shall be answerable for his conduct to every general assembly; and submit to its censure, without appeal, upon pain of infamy and excommunication; that he shall discharge the duties of a pastor in a particular congregation; that he shall not usurp any ecclesiastical jurisdiction superior to that of his other brethren; that if the church inflict on him the censure of deprivation, he shall thereby

forfeit his seat in parliament; and he shall annually resign his
commission to the General Assembly, which may be restored to
him, or not, as the assembly, with the King's approbation, shall
judge most expedient for the good of the church. Nothing could
be more repugnant to the idea of episcopal government, than these
regulations. It was not in consequence of rights derived from
their office, but of powers conferred by a commission, that the ecclesiastical persons were to be admitted to a seat in parliament; they
were the representatives, not the superiors of the clergy. Destitute of all spiritual authority, even their jurisdiction was temporary. James, however, flattered himself that they would soon be
able to shake off these fetters, and gradually acquire all the privileges which belonged to the episcopal order. The clergy dreaded
the same thing; and of course he contended for the nomination of
these commissioners, and they opposed it, not so much on account
of the powers then vested in them, as of those to which it was believed they would soon attain.

BOOK VIII.

CONTINUED.

1600.

DURING this summer the kingdom enjoyed an unusual tranquillity.
The clergy after many struggles were brought under great subjection; the Popish earls were restored to their estates and honours by
the authority of Parliament, and with the consent of the church;
the rest of the nobles were at peace among themselves, and obedient to the royal authority; when, in the midst of this security,
the King's life was exposed to the utmost danger by a conspiracy
altogether unexpected and almost inexplicable. The authors of it
were John Ruthven, Earl of Gowrie, and his brother Alexander,
the sons of that Earl who was beheaded in the year 1584. Nature
had adorned both these young men, especially the elder brother,
with many accomplishments, to which education had added its
most elegant improvements. More learned than is usual among
persons of their rank; more religious than is common at their age
of life; generous, brave, popular; their countrymen, far from
thinking them capable of any atrocious crime, conceived the most
sanguine hopes of their early virtues. Notwithstanding all these
noble qualities, some unknown motive engaged them in a conspiracy, which, if we adhere to the account commonly received, must
be transmitted to posterity as one of the most wicked, as well as
one of the worst concerted, of which history makes any mention.

On the 5th of August, as the King, who resided during the hunt-

q 5

ing season in his palace of Falkland, was going out to his sport
early in the morning he was accosted by Mr. Alexander Ruthven,
who, with an air of great importance, told the King that the evening before he had met an unknown man of a suspicious aspect
walking alone in a by-path near his brother's house at Perth; and,
on searching him, had found under his cloak a pot filled with a
great quantity of foreign gold; that he had immediately seized
both him and his treasure, and, without communicating the matter
to any person, had kept him confined and bound in a solitary
house; and that he thought it his duty to impart such a singular
event first of all to his Majesty.   James immediately suspected
this unknown person to be a seminary priest supplied with foreign
coin in order to excite new commotions in the kingdom; and resolved to empower the magistrates of Perth to call the person before them, and to inquire into all the circumstances of the story.
Ruthven violently opposed this resolution, and with many arguments urged the King to ride directly to Perth and examine the
matter in person.   Meanwhile the chase began; and James, notwithstanding his passion for that amusement, could not help ruminating upon the strangeness of the tale, and on Ruthven's importunity.   At last he called him, and promised when the sport was
over to set out for Perth.   The chase, however, continued long;
and Ruthven, who all the while kept close by the King, was still
urging him to make haste.   At the death of the buck he would not
allow James to stay till a fresh horse was brought him; and observing the Duke of Lennox and the Earl of Mar preparing to accompany the King, he entreated him to countermand them.   This
James refused; and though Ruthven's impatience and anxiety, as
well as the apparent perturbation in his whole behaviour, raised
some suspicions in his mind; yet his own curiosity, and Ruthven's
solicitations, prevailed on him to set out for Perth.   When within
a mile of the town, Ruthven rode forward to inform his brother of
the King's arrival, though he had already dispatched two messengers for that purpose.   At a little distance from the town, the Earl,
attended by several of the citizens, met the King, who had only
twenty persons in his train.   No preparations were made for the
King's entertainment; the Earl appeared pensive and embarrassed,
and was at no pains to atone, by his courtesy or hospitality, for the
bad fare with which he treated his guests.   When the King's re-
past was over, his attendants were led to dine in another room,
and he being left almost alone, Ruthven whispered him that now
was the time to go to the chamber where the unknown person was
kept.   James commanded him to bring Sir Thomas Erskine along
with them; but instead of that, Ruthven ordered him not to follow:
and conducting the King up a staircase, and then through several
apartments, the doors of which he locked behind him, led him at
last into a small study in which there stood a man clad in armour,
with a sword and dagger by his side.   The King, who expected to
have found one disarmed and bound, started at the sight, and inquired if this was the person; but Ruthven, snatching the dagger
from the girdle of the man in armour, and holding it to the King's
breast, "Remember," said he, "how unjustly my father suffered

by your command; you are now my prisoner; submit to my disposal without resistance or outcry; or this dagger shall instantly avenge his blood." James expostulated with Ruthven, entreated, and flattered him. The man whom he found in the study stood all the while trembling and dismayed, without courage to aid the King or to second his aggressor. Ruthven protested that if the King raised no outcry his life should be safe; and moved by some unknown reason, retired in order to call his brother, leaving to the man in armour the care of the King, whom he bound by oath not to make any noise during his absence.

While the King was in this dangerous situation, his attendants growing impatient to know whither he had retired, one of Gowrie's domestics entered the room hastily and told them that the King had just rode away towards Falkland. All of them rushed out into the street; and the Earl, in the utmost hurry, called for their horses. But by this time his brother had returned to the King, and swearing that now that there was no remedy he must die, offered to bind his hands. Unarmed as James was, he scorned to submit to that indignity; and closing with the assassin, a fierce struggle ensued. The man in armour stood, as formerly, amazed and motionless; and the King, dragging Ruthven towards a window which during his absence he had persuaded the person with whom he was left to open, cried with a wild and affrighted voice, "Treason! treason! Help! I am murdered!" His attendants heard and knew the voice, and saw at the window a hand which grasped the King's neck with violence. They flew with precipitation to his assistance. Lennox and Mar, with the greater number, ran up the principal staircase, where they found all the doors shut, which they battered with the utmost fury, endeavouring to burst them open. But Sir John Ramsey, entering by a back stair which led to the apartment, found the door open; and rushing on Ruthven, who was still struggling with the King, struck him twice with his dagger, and thrust him towards the staircase, where Sir Thomas Erskine and Sir Hugh Herries met and killed him; he crying with his last breath, "Alas! I am not to blame for this action." During this scuffle the man who had been concealed in the study escaped unobserved. Together with Ramsay, Erskine, and Herries, one Wilson, a footman, entered the room where the King was, and before they had time to shut the door Gowrie rushed in with a drawn sword in each hand, followed by seven of his attendants well armed, and with a loud voice threatened them all with instant death. They immediately thrust the King into the little study, and shutting the door upon him, encountered the Earl. Notwithstanding the inequality of numbers, Sir John Ramsey pierced Gowrie through the heart, and he fell down dead without uttering a word; his followers, having received several wounds, immediately fled. Three of the King's defenders were likewise hurt in the conflict. A dreadful noise continued still at the opposite door, where many persons laboured in vain to force a passage; and the King being assured that they were Lennox, Mar, and his other friends, it was opened on the outside. They ran to the King, whom they unexpectedly found safe, with transports of congratulation: and he, falling on his knees, with all his attendants around him, offered solemn thanks to God for such a wonderful deliverance. The danger, however, was not yet over. The inhabitants of the town, whose provost Gowrie was, and by whom he was extremely beloved, hearing the fate of the two brothers, ran to their arms, and surrounded the house, threatening revenge, with many insolent and opprobrious speeches against the King. James endeavoured to pacify the enraged multitude by speaking to them from the window; he admitted their magistrates into the house; related to them all the circumstances of the fact; and their fury subsiding by degrees they dispersed. On searching the Earl's pockets for papers that might discover his designs and accomplices, nothing was found but a small parchment bag, full of magical characters and words of enchantment; and if we may believe the account of the conspiracy published by the King, " while these were about him the wound of which he died bled not ; but as soon as they were taken away the blood gushed out in great abundance." After all the dangerous adventures of this busy day, the King returned in the evening to Falkland, having committed the dead bodies of the two brothers to the custody of the magistrates of Perth.

Notwithstanding the minute detail which the King gave of all the circumstances of this conspiracy against his life, the motives which induced the two brothers to attempt an action so detestable, the end they had in view, and the accomplices on whose aid they depended, were altogether unknown. The words of Ruthven to the King gave some grounds to think that the desire of revenging their father's death had instigated them to this attempt. But whatever injuries their father had suffered, it is scarcely probable that they could impute them to the King, whose youth, as well as his subjection at that time to the violence of a faction, exempted him from being the object of resentment, on account of actions which were not done by his command. James had even endeavoured to repair the wrongs which the father had suffered by benefits to his children; and Gowrie himself, sensible of his favour, had acknowledged it with the warmest expressions of gratitude. Three of the Earl's attendants, being convicted of assisting him in this assault on the King's servants, were executed at Perth; but they could give no light into the motives which had prompted their master to an action so repugnant to these acknowledgments. Diligent search was made for the person concealed in the study, and from him great discoveries were expected. But Andrew Henderson, the Earl's steward, who upon a promise of pardon confessed himself to be the man, was as much a stranger to his master's design as the rest; and though placed in the study by Gowrie's command, he did not even know for what end that station had been assigned him. The whole transaction remained as impenetrably dark as ever; and the two brothers, it was concluded, had concerted their scheme without either confidant or accomplice, with unexampled secrecy as well as wickedness.

An accident no less strange than the other circumstances of the story, and which happened nine years after, discovered that this opinion, however plausible, was ill founded; and that the two brothers had not carried on their machinations all alone. One Sprot, a notary, having whispered among several persons that he knew some secrets relating to Gowrie's conspiracy, the privy counsel thought the matter worthy of their attention, and ordered him to be seized. His confessions was partly voluntary and partly forced from him by torture. According to his account, Logan of Restalrig, a gentleman of an opulent fortune, but of dissolute morals, was privy to all Gowrie's intentions, and an accomplice in his crimes. Mr. Ruthven, he said, had frequent interviews with Logan in order to concert the plan of their operations; the Earl had corresponded with him to the same purpose; and one Bour, Logan's confidant, was trusted with the secret, and carried letters between them. Both Logan and Bour were now dead. But Sprot affirmed that he had read letters written both by Gowrie and Logan on that occasion; and in confirmation of his testimony, several of Logan's letters, which a curiosity fatal to himself had prompted Sprot to steal from among Bour's papers, were produced. These were compared by the privy council with papers of Logan's handwriting, and the resemblance was manifest. Persons of undoubted credit, and well qualified to judge of the matter, examined them and swore to their authenticity. Death itself did not exempt Logan from prosecution; his bones were dug up and tried for high treason, and, by a sentence equally odious and illegal, his lands were forfeited and his posterity declared infamous. Sprot was condemned to be hanged for misprison of treason. He adhered to his confession to the last, and having promised on the scaffold to give the spectators a sign in confirmation of the truth of what he had deposed, he thrice clapped his hands after he was thrown off the ladder by the executioner.

But though it be thus unexpectedly discovered that Gowrie did did not act without associates, little additional light is thrown by this discovery on the motives and intention of his conduct. It appears almost incredible that two young men of such distinguished virtue should revolt all at once from their duty and attempt a crime so attrocious as the murder of their sovereign. It appears still more improbable that they should have concerted their undertaking with so little foresight and prudence. If they intended that the deed should have remained concealed, they could not have chosen a more improper scene for executing it than their own house. If they intended that Henderson should have struck the blow, they could not have pitched on a man more destitute of the courage that must direct the hand of an assassin; nor could they expect that he, unsolicited and unacquainted with their purpose, would venture on such a desperate action. If Ruthven meant to stab the King with his own hand, why did he withdraw the dagger after it was pointed at his breast? How could he leave the King after such a plain declaration of his intention? Was it not preposterous to commit him to the keeping of such a timid associate as Henderson? For what purpose did he waste time in binding the hands of an unarmed man, whom he might easily have dispatched with his sword? Had Providence permitted them to imbrue their hands in the blood of their sovereign, what advantage could have accrued to them by his death? And what claims or pretensions could they have opposed to the rights of his children? Inevitable and instant vengeance, together with perpetual infamy, were the only consequences they could expect to follow such a crime.

On the other hand, it is impossible to believe that the King had formed any design against the life of the two brothers. They had not incurred his indignation by any crime; and were in no degree the objects of his jealousy or hatred; nor was he of a spirit so sanguinary, or so noted for rash and desperate valour, as to have attempted to murder them in their own house, where they were surrounded with many domestics, he only with a slender and unarmed train; where they could call to their assistance the inhabitants of a city at the devotion of their family, while he was at a distance from all aid; and least of all would he have chosen for his associates in such an enterprise the Earl of Mar and the Duke of Lennox, the former connected in close friendship with the House of Gowrie, and the latter married to one of the Earl's sisters.

Whichsoever of these opposite systems we embrace, whether we impute the intention of murder to Gowrie or to the King, insuperperable difficulties arise, and we are involved in darkness, mystery, and contradictions. Perhaps the source of the whole conspiracy ought to be searched for deeper, and by deriving it from a more remote cause we may discover it to be less criminal.

To keep the King of Scots in continual dependance was one great object of Elizabeth's policy. In order to this she sometimes soothed him, and sometimes bribed his ministers and favourites; and when she failed of attaining her end by these means, she encouraged the clergy to render any administration which she distrusted unpopular, by decrying it, or stirred up some faction of the nobles to oppose and to overturn it. In that fierce age men little acquainted with the arts of undermining a ministry by intrigue, had recourse to the ruder practice of rendering themselves masters of the King's person, that they might thereby obtain the direction of his councils. Those nobles who seized the King at the *Raid of Ruthven*, were instigated and supported by Elizabeth. Bothwell in all his wild attempts enjoyed her protection, and when they miscarried he was secure of a retreat in her dominions. The connexion which James had been forming of late with the Roman Catholic Princes, his secret negotiations in England with her subjects, and the maxims by which he governed his own kingdom, all contributed to excite her jealousy. She dreaded some great revolution in Scotland to be approaching, and it was her interest to prevent it. The Earl of Gowrie was one of the most powerful of the Scottish nobles, and descended from ancestors warmly attached to the English interest. He had adopted the same system, and believed the welfare of his country to be inseparably connected with the subsistence of the alliance between the two kingdoms. During his residence at Paris he had contracted an intimate friendship with Sir Henry Neville, the Queen's ambassador there, and was recommended by him to his court as a person of whom great use might be made. Elizabeth received him as he passed through England with distinguished marks of respect and favour. From all these circumstances a suspicion may arise that the plan of the conspiracy against the King was formed at that time in concert with her. Such a suspicion prevailed in that age, and from the letters of Nicholson Elizabeth's agent in Scotland, it appears not to be destitute of foundation. An English ship was observed hovering for some time in the mouth of the Frith of Forth. The Earl's two younger brothers fled into England after the ill success of the conspiracy, and were protected by Elizabeth. James himself, though he prudently concealed it, took great umbrage at her behaviour. None, however, of Elizabeth's intrigues in Scotland tended to hurt the King's person, but only to circumscribe his authority and to thwart his schemes. His life was the surest safeguard of her own, and restrained the Popish pretenders to her crown, and their abettors, from desperate attempts, to which their impatience and bigotry might otherwise have urged them on. To have encouraged Gowrie to murder his sovereign would, on her part, have been an act of the utmost imprudence. Nor does this seem to have been the intention of the two brothers. Mr. Ruthven, first of all, endeavoured to decoy the King to Perth without any attendants. When these proved more numerous than was expected, the Earl employed a stratagem in order to separate them from the King, by pretending that he had rode away towards Falkland, and by calling hastily for their horses that they might follow him. By their shutting James up meanwhile in a distant corner of the house, and by attempting to bind his hands, their design seeems to have been rather to seize than to assasinate him. Though Gowrie had not collected his followers in such numbers as to have been able to detain him long a prisoner in that part of the kingdom by open force, he might soon have been conveyed aboard the English ship, which waited perhaps to receive him; and he might have been landed at Fastcastle, a house of Logan's, in which, according to many obscure hints in his letters, some rendezvous of the conspirators was to be held. Amidst the surprise and terror into which the King must have been thrown by the violence offered to him, it was extremely natural for him to conclude that his life was sought. It was the interest of all his followers to confirm him in this belief, and to magnify his danger, in order to add to the importance and merit of their own services. Thus his fear and their vanity, aided by the credulity and wonder which the contemplation of any great and tragical event, when not fully understood, is apt to inspire, augmented the whole transaction. On the other hand, the extravagance and improbability of the circumstances which were added, detracted from the credit of those which really happened: and even furnished pretences for calling in question the truth of the whole conspiracy.

The account of what had happened at Perth reached Edinburgh next morning. The privy council commanded the ministers of that city instantly to assemble their people; and after relating to them the circumstances of the conspiracy formed against the King's life, to return public thanks to God for the protection which he had so visibly afforded him. But as the first accounts transmitted to Edinburgh, written in a hurry, and while the circumstances of the conspiracy were but imperfectly known, and the passions which it

excited strongly felt, were indistinct, exaggerated, and contradictory, the ministers laid hold of this; and though they offered to give
public thanks to God for the King's safety, they refused to enter
into any detail of the particulars, or to utter from the chair of truth
what appeared to be still dubious and uncertain.

A few days after the King returned to Edinburgh; and though
Galloway, the minister of his own chapel, made an harangue to the
people at the public cross, in which he recited all the circumstances of the conspiracy; though James himself, in their hearing,
confirmed his account; though he commanded a narrative of the
whole transaction to be published; the ministers of that city, as
well as many of their brethren, still continued incredulous and un-
convinced. Their high esteem of Gowrie, their jealousy of every
part of the King's conduct, added to some false and many improbable circumstances in the narrative, not only led them to suspect the
whole, but gave their suspicions an air of credibility. But at length
the King, partly by arguments, partly by threats, prevailed on all
of them, except Mr. Robert Bruce, to own that they were convinced
of the truth of the conspiracy. He could be brought no farther
than to declare that he reverenced the King's account of the transaction, but could not say that he himself was persuaded of the
truth of it. The scruples or obstinacy of a single man would
have been little regarded; but as the same spirit of incredulity began to spread among the people, the example of one in so high reputation for integrity and abilities was extremely dangerous. The
King was at the utmost pains to convince and to gain Bruce; but
finding it impossible to remove his doubts, he deprived him of his
benefice, and after repeated delays, and many attempts towards a
reconcilement, banished him the kingdom.

The proceedings of parliament were not retarded by any scruples
of this sort. The dead bodies of the two brothers were produced
there according to law; an indictment for high treason was preferred against them; witnesses were examined; and by an unanimous sentence their estates and honours were forfeited; the punishment due to traitors was inflicted on their dead bodies; and as if
the punishment hitherto in use did not express sufficient detestation of their crimes, the parliament enacted that the surname of
Ruthven should be abolished; and in order to preserve the memory
of the King's miraculous escape, and to declare the sense which the
nation had of the Divine Goodness to all future ages, appointed the
5th of August to be observed annually as a day of public thanks-
giving.

1601]. Though Gowrie's conspiracy occasioned a sudden and a
great alarm, it was followed by no consequences of importance:
and having been concerted by the two brothers either without any
associates or with such as were unknown, the danger was over as
soon as discovered. But not long after a conspiracy broke out in
England against Elizabeth, which, though the first danger was instantly dispelled, produced tragical effects, that rendered the close
of that Queen's reign dismal and unhappy. As James was deeply
interested in that event, it merits our particular notice.

The court of England was at this time divided between two pow-

erful factions, which contended for the supreme direction of affairs.
The leader of the one was Robert D'Evreux, Earl of Sussex; Sir
Robert Cecil, the son of Lord Treasurer Burleigh, was at the head
of the other. The former was the most accomplished and the most
popular of all the English nobles; brave, generous, affable; though
impetuous, yet willing to listen to the councils of those whom he
loved; an avowed, but not an implacable enemy; incapable of disguising his own sentiments, or of misrepresenting those of others;
better fitted for a camp than for a court; and of a genius that qualified him for the first place in the administration, with a spirit
which scorned the second as below his merit. He was soon distinguished by the Queen, who, with a profusion uncommon to her,
conferred on him, even in his earliest youth, the highest honours.
Nor did this diminish the esteem and affection of his countrymen;
but by a rare felicity he was at once the favourite of his sovereign
and the darling of the people. Cecil, on the other hand, educated
in a court, and trained under a father deeply skilled in all its arts,
was crafty, insinuating, industrious; and though possessed of talents which fitted him for the highest offices, he did not rely on his
merit alone for attaining them, but availed himself of every advantage which his own address or the mistakes of others afforded him.
Two such men were formed to be rivals and enemies. Essex despised the arts of Cecil as low and base. To Cecil the Earl's magnanimity appeared to be presumption and folly. All the military
men, except Raleigh, favoured Essex. Most of the courtiers adhered to Cecil, whose manners more nearly resembled their own.

As Elizabeth advanced in years the struggle between these factions became more violent. Essex, in order to strengthen himself,
had early courted the friendship of the King of Scots, for whose
right of succession he was a zealous advocate, and held a close correspondence both with him and with his principal ministers. Cecil, devoted to the Queen alone, rose daily to new honours by the
assiduity of his services and the patience with which he expected the reward of them; while the Earl's high spirit and impetuosity sometimes exposed him to checks from a mistress, who, although partial in her affection towards him, could not easily bear
contradiction, and who conferred favours often unwillingly, and
always slowly. His own solicitations, however, seconded maliciously
by his enemies, who wished to remove him to a distance from the
court, advanced him to the command of the army employed in Ireland against Tyrone, and to the office of Lord Lieutenant of that
kingdom, with a commission almost unlimited. His success in that
expedition did not equal either his own promises or the expectations of Elizabeth. The Queen, peevish from her disappointment, and exasperated against Essex by the artifices of his enemies,
wrote him a harsh letter, full of accusations and reproaches. These
his impatient spirit could not bear, and, in the first transports of
his resentment, he proposed to carry over a part of his army into
England, and by driving his enemies from the Queen's presence, to
reinstate himself in favour and in power. But upon more mature
thoughts he abandoned this rash design, and setting sail with a few
officers devoted to his person landed in England, and posted di-

rectly to court. Elizabeth received him without any symptom, either of affection or of displeasure. By proper compliances and acknowledgments, he might have regained his former ascendancy over the Queen. But he thought himself too deeply injured to submit to these. Elizabeth, on the other hand, determined to subdue his haughty temper; and, though her severity drew from him the most humble letters, she confined him to the lord keeper's house, and appointed commissioners to try him, both for his conduct during his government of Ireland, and for leaving that kingdom without her permission. By their sentence, he was suspended from all his offices, except that of master of the horse, and continued a prisoner during the Queen's pleasure. Satisfied with having mortified his pride thus far, Elizabeth did not suffer the sentence to be recorded, and soon after allowed him to retire to his own house. During these transactionss which occupied several months, Essex fluctuated between the allegiance he owed to his sovereign, and the desire of revenge; and sometimes leaned to the one and sometimes to the other. In one of the intervals when the latter prevailed, he sent a messenger into Scotland to encourage the King to assert his own right to the succession by force of arms, and to promise, that, besides the assistance of the Earl, all his friends in England, Lord Mountjoy, now Lord Lieutenant of Ireland, would join him with five thousand men from that kingdom. But James did not choose to hazard the losing of a kingdom, of which he was just about to obtain possession, by a premature attempt to seize it. Mountjoy, too, declined the enterprise, and Essex adopted more dutiful schemes; all thoughts of ambition appearing to be totally effaced out of his mind.

This moderation, which was merely the effect of disgust and disappointment, was not of long continuance; and the Queen, having not only refused to renew a lucrative grant which she had formerly bestowed, but even to admit him into her presence, that new injury drove a temper naturally impatient, and now much fretted, to absolute despair. His friends, instead of soothing his rage or restraining his impetuosity, added to both by their imprudent and interested zeal. After many anxious consultations he determined to attempt to redress his wrongs by violence. But being conscious how unpopular such an enterprise would be if it appeared to proceed from motives of private revenge alone, he endeavoured to give it the semblance of public utility by mingling the King of Scotland's interest with his own. He wrote to James, that the faction which now predominated in the English court had resolved to support the pretensions of the Infanta of Spain to the crown; tnat the places of the greatest importance in the kingdom were put into the hands of his avowed enemies; and that unless he sent ambassadors without delay to insist on the immediate declaration of his right of succession, their measures were so well concerted that all his hopes would be desperate. James, who knew how disagreeable such a proposal would be to the Queen of England, was not willing rashly to expose himself to her displeasure. Essex, nevertheless, blinded by resentment and impatient for revenge, abandoned himself to these passions, and acted like a man guided by frenzy or despair. With two or three hundred followers incompletely armed, he attempted to assault a throne the best established in Europe. Sallying at their head out of his own house, he called on the citizens of London, if they either valued his life or wished to preserve the kingdom from the dominion of the Spaniards, to take arms and to follow his standard. He advanced towards the palace with an intention to drive Cecil and his faction out of the Queen's presence, and to obtain a declaration of the Scottish King's right of succession. But though almost adored by the citizens, not a man would join him in this wild enterprise. Dispirited by their indifference, deserted by some of his own attendants, and almost surrounded by the troops which marched against him under different leaders into the city, he retreated to his own house; and without any bold effort suitable to his present condition, or worthy of his former reputation for courage, he surrendered to his enemies.

As soon as James heard of Essex's ill success, he appointed the Earl of Mar, and Bruce, Abbot of Kinloss, to repair as his ambassadors to the court of England. The former of these was the person by whose means Essex had carried on his correspondence with the King. He was a passionate admirer of the Earl's character, and disposed to attempt every thing that could contribute to his safety. Bruce, united in a close friendship with Mar, was ready to second him with equal zeal. Nor was the purpose of the embassy less friendly to Essex than the choice of his ambassadors: they were commanded to solicit in the warmest manner for the Earl's life; and if they found that the King, by avowing his friends, could either promote their designs or contribute to their safety, they were empowered to lay aside all disguise, and to promise that he would put himself at their head and claim what was due to him by force of arms. But before the ambassadors could reach London, Essex had suffered the punishment which he merited by his treason. Perhaps the fear of their interposing in order to obtain his pardon hastened his death. Elizabeth continued for some time irresolute concerning his fate, and could not bring herself to consign into the hands of the executioner a man who had once possessed her favour so entirely, without a painful struggle between her resentment against his late misconduct and her ancient affection towards him. The distress to which she was now reduced tended naturally to soften the former, while it revived the latter with new tenderness; and the intercession of one faithful friend who had interest with the Queen might perhaps have saved his life, and have procured him a remission which of herself, she was ashamed to grant. But this generous nobleman had at that time no such friend. Elizabeth, solicited incessantly by her ministers and offended with the haughtiness of Essex, who, as she imagined, scorned to sue for pardon, at last commanded the sentence to be put in execution. No sooner was the blow struck than she repented of her own rashness, and bewailed his death with the deepest sorrow. James always considered him as one who had fallen a martyr to his service, and after his accession to the English throne restored his son to his honours, as well as all his associates in the conspiracy, and distinguished them with his favour.

The Scottish ambassadors, finding that they had arrived too late to execute the chief busines committed to their charge, not only concealed that part of their instructions with the utmost care, but congratulated the Queen, in their master's name, on her happy escape from such an audacious conspiracy. Elizabeth, though no stranger to the King's correspondence with Essex, or to that nobleman's intentions of asserting James's right to the crown, was not willing that these should be known to the people, and for that reason received the congratulations of the Scottish ambassadors with all possible marks of credit and good will; and in order to soothe James, and to preserve the appearances of union between the two courts, increased the subsidy which she paid him annually. The ambassadors resided for some time in England, and were employed with great success in renewing and extending the intrigues which Bruce had formerly entered into with the English nobles. As Elizabeth advanced in years the English turned their eyes more and more towards Scotland, and were eager to prevent each other in courting the favour of their future monarch. Assurances of attachment, professions of regard, and promises of support were offered to James from every corner of the kingdom. Cecil himself, perceiving what hopes Essex had founded on the friendship of the Scottish King, and what advantages he might have derived from it, thought it prudent to stand no longer at a distance from a Prince who might so soon become his master. But being sensible at the same time how dangerous such an intercourse might prove under a mistress naturally jealous, and whose jealousy grew stronger with old age; though he entered into a correspondence with him, he carried it on with all the secrecy and caution necessary in his situation and peculiar to his character*. James, having gained the man whose opposition and influence he had hitherto chiefly dreaded, waited, in perfect security, till that event should happen which would open his way to the throne of England. It was with some difficulty that he restrained within proper bounds his adherents in that kingdom, who, labouring to distinguish themselves by that officious zeal with which a Prince who has a near prospect of mounting the throne is always served, urged him to allow a motion to be made in parliament for declaring his right of succession to the crown. James prudently discouraged that design; but it was with no small satisfaction that he observed the ascendent he was acquiring in a court the dictates of which he had been so long obliged to obey; and which had either prescribed or thwarted every step he had taken during the whole course of his reign.

1602.] Notwithstanding the violent struggles of the political factions which divided the court, and the frequent revolutions which had happened there since the King first took the reins of government into his own hands, Scotland had enjoyed unusual tranquillity, being undisturbed by any foreign enemy, and free from any intestine commotion of long continuance. During this period James endeavoured to civilize the Highlands and the Isles, a part

* See Appendix, No. LIII.

of his dominions too much neglected by former monarchs, though the reformation of it was an object highly worthy of their care. The long peace with England had afforded an opportunity of subduing the licentious spirit of the borderers, and of restraining their depredations, often no less ruinous to their countrymen than to their enemies. The inhabitants of the Low Country began, gradually, to forget the use of arms, and to become attentive to the arts of peace. But the Highlanders, retaining their natural fierceness, averse from labour, and inured to rapine, infested their more industrious neighbours by their continual incursions. James, being solicitous not only to repress their inroads, but to render them useful subjects, had at different times enacted many wise laws extremely conductive to these ends. All landlords, or chiefs of clans, were enjoined to permit no persons to reside on their estates who could not find sufficient surety for their good behaviour; they were required to make a list of all suspicious persons under their jurisdiction, to bind themselves to deliver them to justice, and to idemnify those who should suffer by their robberies; and, in order to ascertain the faithful performance of these articles, the chiefs themselves were obliged to give hostages to the King, or to put pledges in his hands. Three towns, which might serve as a retreat for the industrious, and a nursery for arts and commerce, were appointed to be built in different parts of the Highlands; one in Cantire, another in Lochaber, and a third in the Isle of Lewis; and, in order to draw inhabitants thither, all the privileges of royal boroughs were to be conferred upon them. Finding it however, to be no easy matter to inspire the natives of those countries with the love of industry, a resolution was taken to plant among them colonies of people from the more industrious counties. The first experiment was made on the Isle of Lewis; and as it was advantageously situated for the fishing trade, a source from which Scotland ought naturally to derive great wealth, the colony transported thither was drawn out of Fife, the inhabitants of which were well skilled in that branch of commerce. But, before they had remained there long enough to manifest the good effects of this institution, the islanders, enraged at seeing their country occupied by those intruders, took arms, and, surprising them in the night time, murdered some of them, and compelled the rest to abandon the settlement. The King's attention being soon after turned to other subjects, we hear no more of this salutary project. Though James did not pursue the design with that steady application and perseverance without which it is impossible to change the manners of a whole people, he had the glory, however, not only of having first conceived the thought, but of having first pointed out the proper method of introducing the civil arts of life into that part of the island.

1603.] After having long enjoyed a good state of health, the effect of a sound constitution, and the reward of uncommon regularity and temperance, Elizabeth began this winter to feel her vigour decrease, and to be sensible of the infirmities of old age. Having removed on a very stormy day from Westminster to Richmond [Jan. 31], whither she was impatient to retire, her complaints increased. She had no formed fever: her pulse was good; but she ate little, and could not sleep. Her distemper seemed to proceed from a deep melancholy, which appeared both in her countenance and behaviour. She delighted in solitude; she sat constantly in the dark; and was often drowned in tears.

No sooner was the Queen's indisposition known than persons of all ranks, and of all different sects and parties, redoubled their applications to the King of Scots, and vied with each other in professions of attachment to his person, and in promises of submission to his government. Even some of Elizabeth's own servants, weary of the length of her reign, fond of novelty, impatient to get rid of the burden of gratitude for past benefits, and expecting to share in the liberality of a new Prince, began to desert her : and crowds of people hurried towards Scotland, eager to preoccupy the favour of the successor, or afraid of being too late in paying homage to him.

Meanwhile the Queen's disease increased, and her melancholy appeared to be settled and incurable. Various conjectures were formed concerning the causes of a disorder from which she seemed to be exempted by the natural cheerfulness of her temper. Some imputed it to her being forced, contrary to her inclination, to pardon the Earl of Tyrone, whose rebellion had for many years created her much trouble. Others imagined that it arose from observing the ingratitude of her courtiers and the levity of her people, who beheld her health declining with most indecent indifference, and looked forward to the accession of the Scottish King with an impatience which they could not conceal. The most common opinion at that time, and perhaps the most probable was, that it flowed from grief for the Earl of Essex. She retained an extraordinary regard for the memory of that unfortunate nobleman ; and though she often complained of his obstinacy, seldom mentioned his name without tears. An accident happened soon after her retiring to Richmond which revived her affection with new tenderness, and embittered her sorrows. The Countess of Nottingham, being on her deathbed, desired to see the Queen in order to reveal something to her, without discovering which she could not die in peace. When the Queen came into her chamber, she told her, that while Essex lay under sentence of death he was desirous of imploring pardon in the manner which the Queen herself had prescribed, by returning a ring which during the height of his favour she had given him, with a promise that if, in any future distress, he sent that back to her as a token, it should entitle him to her protection; that Lady Scrope was the person he intended to employ in order to present it; that, by a mistake, it was put into her hands instead of Lady Scrope's ; and that she having communicated the matter to her husband, one of Essex's most implacable enemies, he had forbid her either to carry the ring to the Queen or to return it to the Earl. The countess having thus disclosed her secret, begged the Queen's forgiveness ; but Elizabeth, who now saw both the malice of the Earl's enemies, and how unjustly she had suspected him of inflexible obstinacy, replied, "God may forgive you, but I never can;" and left the room in great emotion. From that moment her spirit sunk entirely; she could scarce taste food; she refused all the medicnes prescribed by her physicians; declaring that she wished to die, and would live no longer. No entreaty could prevail on her to go to bed; she sat on cushions during ten days and nights, pensive and silent, holding her finger almost continually in her mouth, with her eyes open, and fixed on the ground. The only thing to which she seemed to give any attention, was the acts of devotion performed in her apartment by the bishop of Canterbury; and in these she joined with great appearance of fervour. Wasted, at last, as well by anguish of mind as by long abstinence, she expired without a struggle, on Thursday the twenty-fourth day of March, in the seventieth year of her age, and in the forty-fifth of her reign.

Foreigners often accuse the English of indifference and disrespect towards their Princes; but without reason. No people are more grateful than they to those monarchs who merit their gratitude. The names of Edward III. and Henry V. are mentioned by the English of this age with the same warmth as they were by those who shared in the blessings and splendour of their reigns. The memory of Elizabeth is still adored in England. The historians of that kingdom, after celebrating her love of her people; her sagacity in discerning their true interest: her steadiness in pursuing it; her wisdom in the choice of ministers; the glory she acquired by arms; the tranquillity she secured to her subjects; and the increase of fame, of riches, and of commerce, which were the fruits of all these; justly rank her among the most illustrious Princes. Even the defects in her character, they observe, were not of a kind pernicious to her people. Her excessive frugality was not accompanied with the love of hoarding; and though it prevented some great undertakings, and rendered the success of others incomplete, it introduced economy into her administration, and exempted the nation from many burdens, which a monarch more profuse or more enterprising must have imposed. Her slowness in rewarding her servants sometimes discouraged useful merit; but it prevented the undeserving from acquiring power and wealth to which they had no title. Her extreme jealousy of those Princes who pretended to dispute her right to the crown led her to take such precautions as tended no less to the public safety than to her own; and to court the affections of her people as the firmest support of her throne. Such is the picture which the English draw of this great Queen.

Whoever undertakes to write the history of Scotland finds himself obliged, frequently, to view her in a very different and in a less amiable light. Her authority in that kingdom, during the greater part of her reign, was little inferior to that which she possessed in her own. But this authority, acquired at first by a service of great importance to the nation, she exercised in a manner extremely pernicious to its happiness. By her industry in fomenting the rage of the two contending factions; by supplying the one with partial aid; by feeding the other with false hopes; by balancing their power so artfully that each of them was able to distress, and neither of them to subdue the other; she rendered Scotland long the seat of discord, confusion, and bloodshed; and her craft and intrigues, effecting what the valour of her ancestors could not accomplish, reduced that kingdom to a state of dependance on England. The maxims of policy, often little consonant to those of morality, may, perhaps, justify this conduct. But no apology can be offered for her behaviour to Queen Mary; a scene of dissimulation without necessity, and of severity beyond example. In almost all her other actions Elizabeth is the object of our highest admiration; in this we must allow that she not only laid aside the magnanimity which became a Queen, but the feelings natural to a woman.

Though Elizabeth would never permit the question concerning the right of succession to the crown to be determined in parliament; nor declare her own sentiments concerning a point which she wished to remain an impenetrable mystery; she had, however, formed, no design of excluding the Scottish King from an inheritance to which his title was undoubted. A short time before her death she broke the silence which she had so long preserved on that subject and told Cecil and the Lord Admiral, "That her throne was the throne of Kings; that she would have no mean person to ascend it, and that her cousin the King of Scots should be her successor." This she confirmed on her deathbed. As soon as she breathed her last, the Lords of the privy council proclaimed James King of England. All the intrigues carried on by foreigners in favour of the titles of the Infanta, all the cabals formed within the kingdom to support the titles of Lady Arabella and the Earl of Hartford, disappeared in a moment; the nobles and people, forgetting their ancient hostilities with Scotland and their aversion for the dominion of strangers, testified their satisfaction with louder acclamations than were usual at the accession of their native Princes. Amidst this tumult of joy, a motion made by a few patriots, who proposed to prescribe some conditions to the successor, and to exact from him the redress of some grievances, before they called him to the throne, was scarcely heard; and Cecil, by stifling it, added to his stock of merit with his new master. Sir Charles Percy, brother of the Earl of Northumberland, and Thomas Somerset, the Earl of Worcester's son, were dispatched to Scotland with a letter to the King, signed by all the peers and privy counsellors then in London; informing him of the Queen's death, of his accession to the throne, of their care to recognise his title, and of the universal applause with which the public proclamation of it had been attended. They made the utmost haste to deliver this welcome message; but were prevented by the zeal of Sir Robert Carey, Lord Hundson's youngest son, who, setting out a few hours after Elizabeth's death, arrived at Edinburgh on Saturday night, just as the King had gone to bed. He was immediately admitted into the royal apartment, and kneeling by the King's bed, acquainted him with the death of Elizabeth, saluted him King of England, Scotland, France, and Ireland; and as a token of the truth of the intelligence which he brought, presented him a ring, which his sister Lady Scrope had taken from the Queen's finger after her death. James heard him with a decent composure. But as Carey was only a private messenger the information which he brought was not made public, and the King kept his apartment till the arrival of Percy and Somerset. Then his titles were solemnly proclaimed; and his own subjects expressed no less joy than the English, at this increase of his dignity. As his presence was absolutely necessary in England, where the people were extremely impatient to see their new sovereign, he prepared to set out for that kingdom without delay. He appointed his Queen to follow him within a few weeks. He committed the government of Scotland to his privy council. He entrusted the care of his children to different noblemen. On the Sunday before his departure he repaired to the church of St. Giles, and after hearing a sermon, in which the preacher displayed the greatness of the Divine goodness in raising him to the throne of such a powerful kingdom without opposition or bloodshed, and exhorted him to express his gratitude, by promoting to the utmost the happiness and prosperity of his subjects; the King rose up, and addressing himself to the people, made many professions of unalterable affection towards them; promised to visit Scotland frequently; assured them that his Scottish subjects, notwithstanding his absence, should feel that he was their native Prince, no less than when he resided among them; and might still trust that his ears should be always open to their petitions, which he would answer with the alacrity and love of a parent. His words were often interrupted by the tears of the whole audience; who, though they exulted at the King's prosperity, were melted into sorrow by these tender declarations.

On the fifth of April he began his journey, with a splendid but not a numerous train; and next day he entered Berwick. Whereever he came immense multitudes were assembled to welcome him; and the principal persons in the different counties through which he passed displayed all their wealth and magnificence in entertainments prepared for him at their houses. Elizabeth had reigned so long in England that most of her subjects remembered no other court but hers, and their notions of the manners and decorums suitable to a Prince were formed upon what they had observed there. It was natural to apply this standard to the behaviour and actions of their new monarch, and to compare him, at first sight, with the Queen on whose throne he was to be placed. James, whose manners were extremely different from hers, suffered by the comparison. He had not that flowing affability by which Elizabeth captivated the hearts of her people; and though easy among a few whom he loved, his indolence could not bear the fatigue of rendering himself agreeable to a mixed multitude. He was no less a stranger to that dignity with which Elizabeth tempered her familiarity. And instead of that well judged frugality with which she conferred titles of honour, he bestowed them with an undistinguishing profusion, that rendered them no longer marks of distinction or rewards of merit. But these were the reflections of the few alone; the multitude continued their acclamations; and amidst these James entered London on the seventh of May, and took peaceable possession of the throne of England.

Thus were united two kingdoms, divided from the earliest accounts of time, but destined by their situation to form one great monarchy. By this junction of its whole native force, Great

Britain had risen to an eminence and authority in Europe which England and Scotland, while separate, could never have attained.

The Scots had so long considered their monarchs as next heirs to the English throne that they had full leisure to reflect on all the consequences of their being advanced to that dignity. But dazzled with the glory of giving a sovereign to their powerful enemy, relying on the partiality of their native Prince, and in full expectation of sharing liberally in the wealth and honours which he would now be able to bestow, they attended little to the most obvious consequences of that great event, and rejoiced at his accession to the throne of England, as if it had been no less beneficial to the kingdom than honourable to the King. They soon had reason, however, to adopt very different sentiments; and from that period we may date a total alteration in the political constitution of Scotland.

The feudal aristocracy, which had been subverted in most nations of Europe by the policy of their princes, or had been undermined by the progress of commerce, still subsisted with full force in Scotland. Many causes had contributed gradually to augment the power of the Scottish nobles ; and even the Reformation which, in every other country where it prevailed added to the authority of the monarch, had increased their wealth and influence. A King possessed of a small revenue, with a prerogative extremely limited and unsupported by a standing army, could not exercise much authority over such potent subjects. He was obliged to govern by expedients ; and the laws derived their force not from his power to execute them, but from the voluntary submission of the nobles. But though this produced a species of government extremely feeble and irregular ; though Scotland, under the name, and with all the outward ensigns of a monarchy, was really subject to an aristocracy the people were not altogether unhappy ; and even in this wild form of a constitution there were principles which tended to their security and advantage. The King, checked and overawed by the nobles, durst venture upon no act of arbitrary power. The nobles, jealous of the King, whose claims and pretensions were many, though his power was small, were afraid of irritating their dependants by unreasonable exactions, and tempered the rigour of aristocratical tyranny with a mildness and equality to which it is naturally a stranger. As long as the military genius of the feudal government remained in vigour, the vassals both of the crown and of the barons were generally not only free from oppression, but were courted by their superiors, whose power and importance were founded on their attachment and love.

But by his accession to the throne of England James acquired such an immense accession of wealth, of power, and of splendour, that the nobles, astonished and intimidated, thought it vain to struggle for privileges which they were now unable to defend. Nor was it from fear alone that they submitted to the yoke : James, partial to his countrymen, and willing that they should partake in his good fortune, loaded them with riches and honours ; and the hope of his favour concurred with the dread of his power, in taming their fierce and independent spirits. The will of the Prince became the supreme law in Scotland; and the nobles strove, with emulation, who should most implicitly obey commands which they had formerly been accustomed to contemn. Satisfied with having subjected the nobles to the crown, the King left them in full possession of their ancient jurisdiction over their own vassals. The extensive rights vested in a feudal chief became in their hands dreadful instruments of oppression ; and the military ideas, on which these rights were founded, being gradually lost or disregarded, nothing, remained to correct or to mitigate the rigour with which they were exercised. The nobles, exhausting their fortunes by the expense of frequent attendance upon the English court, and by attempts to imitate the manners and luxury of their more wealthy neighbours multiplied exactions upon the people, who durst hardly utter complaints which they knew would never reach the ear of their sovereign, nor move him to grant them any redress. From the union of the crowns to the revolution in 1688, Scotland was placed in a political situation of all others the most singular and the most unhappy ; subjected at once to the absolute will of a monarch, and to the oppressive jurisdiction of an aristocracy, it suffered all the miseries peculiar to both these forms of government. Its Kings were despotic ; its nobles were slaves and tyrants ; and the people groaned under the rigorous domination of both.

During this period the nobles, it is true, made one effort to shake off the yoke, and to regain their ancient independency. After the death of James, the Scottish nation was no longer viewed by our monarchs with any partial affection. Charles I, educated among the English, discovered no peculiar attachment to the kingdom of which he was a native. The nobles, perceiving the sceptre to be now in hands less friendly, and swayed by a Prince with whom they had little connection, and over whose councils they had little influence, no longer submitted with the same implicit obedience. Provoked by some encroachments of the King on their order, and apprehensive of others. the remains of their ancient spirit began to appear. They complained and remonstrated. The people, being at the same time, violently disgusted at the innovations in religion, the nobles secretly heightened this disgust ; and their artifices, together with the ill conduct of the court, raised such a spirit that the whole nation took arms against their sovereign with a union and animosity of which there had formerly been no example. Charles brought against them the forces of England, and notwithstanding their own union, and the zeal of the people, the nobles must have sunk in the struggle. But the disaffection which was growing among his English subjects prevented the King from acting with vigour. A civil war broke out in both kingdoms ; and after many battles and revolutions, which are well known, the Scottish nobles, who first began the war, were involved in the same ruin with the throne. At the Restoration, Charles II. regained full possession of the royal prerogative in Scotland ; and the nobles, whose estates were wasted, or their spirit broken by the calamities to which they had been exposed,were less able and less willing than ever to resist the power of the crown. During his reign, and that of James II., the dictates of the monarch were received in Scotland with most abject submission. The poverty to which many of the nobles were reduced rendered them meaner slaves and more intolerable tyrants than ever. The people, always neglected, were now odious, and loaded with every injury on account of their attachment to religious and political principles extremely repugnant to those adopted by their Princes.

The revolution introduced other maxims into the government of Scotland. To increase the authority of the Prince, or to secure the privileges of the nobles, had hitherto been almost the sole object of our laws. The rights of the people were hardly ever mentioned, were disregarded, or unknown. Attention began, henceforward, to be paid to the welfare of the people. By the *Claim of Right*, their liberties were secured ; and the number of their representatives being increased, they gradually acquired new weight and consideration in parliament. As they came to enjoy more security and greater power, their minds began to open and to form more extensive plans of commerce, of industry, and of police. But the aristocratical spirit, which still predominated, together with many other accidents, retarded the improvement and happiness of the nation.

Another great event completed what the revolution had begun. The political power of the nobles, already broken by the union of the two crowns, was almost annihilated by the union of the two kingdoms. Instead of making a part, as formerly, of the supreme assembly of the nation; instead of bearing the most considerable sway there, the peers of Scotland are admitted into the British parliament by their representatives only, and form but an inconsiderable part of one of those bodies in which the legislative authority is vested. They themselves are excluded absolutely from the House of Commons, and even their eldest sons are not permitted to represent their countrymen in that august assembly. Nor have their feudal privileges remained to compensate for this extinction of their political authority. As commerce advanced in its progress, and government attained nearer to perfection, these were insensibly circumscribed, and at last, by laws no less arbitrary to the public than fatal to the nobles, they have been almost totally abolished. As the nobles were deprived of power the people acquired liberty. Exempted from burdens to which they were formerly subject, screened from oppression to which they had been long exposed, and adopted into a constitution whose genius and laws were more liberal than their own, they have extended their commerce, refined their manners, made improvements in the elegancies of life, and cultivated the arts and sciences.

This survey of the political state of Scotland, in which events and their causes have been mentioned rather than developed, enables us to point out three eras, from each of which we may date some great alteration in one or other of the three different members of which the supreme legislative assembly is composed. At their accession to the throne of England, the Kings of Scotland, once the most limited, became in an instant the most absolute Princes in Europe, and exercised a despotic authority, which their parliaments were unable to control or their nobles to resist. At the *union* of the two kingdoms, the feudal aristocracy, which had subsisted so many ages, and with power so exorbitant, was overturned, and the Scottish nobles, having surrendered rights and pre-eminences peculiar to their order, reduced themselves to a condition which is no longer the terror and envy of other subjects. *Since the union,* the commons, anciently neglected by their King, and seldom courted by the nobles, have emerged into dignity ; and, being admitted to a participation of all the privileges which the English had purchased at the expense of so much blood, must now be deemed a body not less considerable in the one kingdom than they have long been in the other.

The church felt the effects of the absolute power which the King acquired by his accession : and its revolutions, too, are worthy of notice. James, during the latter years of his administration in Scotland, had revived the name and office of bishops. But they possessed no ecclesiastical jurisdiction or pre-eminence ; their revenues were inconsiderable, and they were scarcely distinguished by any thing but by their seat in parliament, and by being the object of the clergy's jealousy and the people's hatred. The King, delighted with the splendour and authority which the English bishops enjoyed, and eager to effect a union in the ecclesiastical policy, which he had in vain attempted in the civil government of the two kingdoms, resolved to bring both churches to an exact conformity with each other. Three Scotsmen were consecrated bishops at London. From them their brethren were commanded to receive orders. Ceremonies unknown in Scotland were imposed ; and though the clergy, less obsequious than the nobles, boldly opposed these innovations, James, long practised and well skilled in the arts of managing them, obtained at length their compliance. But Charles I., a superstitious Prince, unacquainted with the genius of the Scots, imprudent and precipitant in all the measures he pursued in that kingdom, pressing too eagerly the reception of the English liturgy, and indiscreetly attempting a resumption of church lands, kindled the flames of civil war ; and the people being left at liberty to indulge their own wishes, the episcopal church was overturned, and the Presbyterian government and discipline were re established with new vigour. Together with monarchy, episcopacy was restored in Scotland. A form of government so odious to the people required force to uphold it ; and though not only the whole rigour of authority, but all the barbarity of persecution, were employed in its support, the aversion of the nation was insurmountable, and it subsisted with difficulty. At the Revolution, the inclinations of the people were thought worthy the attention of the legislature, the Presbyterian government was again established, and being ratified by the union, is still maintained in that kingdom.

Nor did the influence of the accession extend to the civil and ecclesiastical constitutions alone ; the genius of the nation, its taste and spirit, things of a nature still more delicate, were sensibly affected by that event. When learning revived in the fifteenth and sixteenth centuries, all the modern languages were in a state extremely barbarous, devoid of elegance, of vigour, and even of perspicuity. No author thought of writing in language so ill adapted

to express and embellish his sentiments, or of erecting a work for
immortality with such rude and perishable materials. As the spirit
which prevailed at that time did not owe its rise to any original
effort of the human mind, but was excited chiefly by admiration of
the ancients, which began then to be studied with attention in
every part of Europe, their compositions were deemed not only the
standards of taste and of sentiment, but of style; and even the languages in which they wrote were thought to be peculiar, and almost
consecrated to learning and the muses. Not only the manner of
the ancients was imitated, but their language was adopted; and extravagant as the attempt may appear to write in a dead tongue, in
which men were not accustomed to think, and which they could
not speak or even pronounce, the success of it was astonishing. As
they formed their style upon the purest models; as they were un-
infected with those barbarisms which the inaccuracy of familiar
conversation, the affectation of courts, intercourse with strangers,
and a thousand other causes, introduce into living languages; many
moderns having attained to a degree of elegance in their Latin compositions which the Romans themselves scarce possessed beyond the
limits of the Augustin age. While this was almost the only species
of composition, and all authors, by using one common language,
could be brought to a nearer comparison, the Scottish writers were
not inferior to those of any other nation. The happy genius of
Buchanan, equally formed to excel in prose and in verse, more
various, more original, and more elegant than that of almost any
other modern who writes in Latin, reflects, with regard to this particular, the greatest lustre on his country.

But the labour attending the study of a dead tongue was irksome; the unequal return for their industry which authors met
with, who could be read and admired only within the narrow circle
of the learned, was mortifying; and men, instead of wasting half
their lives in learning the language of the Romans, began to refine
and to polish their own. The modern tongues were found to be
susceptible of beauties and graces, which, if not equal to those of
the ancient ones, were at least more attainable. The Italians having first set the example, Latin was no longer used in works of
taste; it was confined to books of science; and the politer nations
have banished it even from these. The Scots, we may presume,
would have had no cause to regret this change in the public taste,
and would still have been able to maintain some equality with
other nations, in their pursuit of literary honour. The English and
Scottish languages, derived from the same sources, were at the end
of the sixteenth century in a state nearly similar, differing from
one another somewhat in orthography, though not only the words
but the idioms were much the same. The letters of several Scottish statesman of that age are not inferior in elegance or in purity
to those of the English ministers with whom they corresponded.
James himself was master of a style far from contemptible; and by
his example and encouragement the Scottish language might have
kept pace with the English in refinement. Scotland might have had
a series of authors in its own, as well as in the Latin language to
boast of; and the improvements in taste, in the arts, and in the

sciences, which spread over the polished nations of Europe, would not have been unknown there.

But, at the very time when other nations were beginning to drop the use of Latin in works of taste, and to make trial of the strength and compass of their own languages, Scotland ceased to be a kingdom. The transports of joy, which the accession at first occasioned, were soon over: and the Scots, being at once deprived of all the objects that refine or animate a people; of the presence of their Prince, of the concourse of nobles, of the splendour and elegance of a court, a universal dejection of spirit seems to have seized the nation. The court being withdrawn, no domestic standard of propriety and correctness of speech remained; the few compositions that Scotland produced were tried by the English standard, and every word or phrase that varied in the least from that was condemned as barbarous; whereas, if the two nations had continued distinct, each might have retained idioms and forms of speech peculiar to itself; and these rendered fashionable by the example of a court, and supported by the authority of writers of reputation, might have been viewed in the same light with the varieties occasioned by the different dialects in the Greek tongue; they even might have been considered as beauties; and in many cases might have been used promiscuously by the authors of both nations. But, by the accession, the English naturally became the sole judges and lawgivers in language, and rejected as solecisms every form of speech to which their ear was not accustomed. Nor did the Scots, while the intercourse between the two nations was inconsiderable*, and ancient prejudices were still so violent as to prevent imitation, possess the means of refining their own tongue according to the purity of the English standard. On the contrary, new corruptions flowed into it from every different source. The clergy of Scotland, in that age, were more eminent for piety than for learning; and though there did not arise many authors among them, yet being in possession of the privilege of discoursing publicly to the people, and their sermons being too long, and perhaps too frequent, such hasty productions could not be elegant, and many slovenly and incorrect modes of expression may be traced back to that original. The pleadings of lawyers were equally loose and inaccurate; and that profession having furnished more authors, and the matters of which they treat mingling daily in common discourse and business, many of those vicious forms of speech, which they denominated *Scotticisms*, have been introduced by them into the language. Nor did either the language or public taste receive any improvement in parliament, where a more liberal and more correct

* A remarkable proof of the little intercourse between the English and Scots before the union of the crowns, is to be found in two curious papers, one published by Haynes, the other by Strype. In the year 1567, Elizabeth commanded the Bishop of London to take a survey of all the strangers within the cities of London and Westminster. By this report, which is very minute. it appears that the whole number of Scots at that time was fifty-eight. Haynes, 455. A survey of the same kind was made by Sir Thomas Row, Lord Mayor, A. D. 1568. The number of Scots had then increased to eighty-eight. Strype, iv. Supplement. No. 1. On the accession of James. a considerable number of Scots. especially of the higher rank, resorted to England: but it was not till the union that the intercourse between the two kingdoms became great.

eloquence might have been expected. All business was transacted there by the lords of articles; and they were so servilely devoted to the court, that few debates arose, and, prior to the Revolution, none were conducted with the spirt and vigour natural to a popular assembly.

Thus, during the whole seventeenth century, the English were gradually refining their language and their taste: in Scotland the former was much debased, and the latter almost entirely lost. In the beginning of that period, both nations were emerging out of barbarity; but the distance between them, which was then inconsiderable, became before the end of it immense. Even after science had once dawned upon them, the Scots seemed to be sinking back into ignorance and obscurity; and active and intelligent as they naturally are, they continued, while other nations were eager in the pursuit of fame and knowledge, in a state of languor. This, however, must be imputed to the unhappiness of their political situation, not to any defect of genius; for no sooner was the one removed in any degree than the other began to display itself. The act abolishing the power of the lords of articles, and other salutary laws passed at the Revolution, having introduced freedom of debate into the Scottish parliament, eloquence, with all the arts that accompany or perfect it, became immediate objects of attention; and the example of Fletcher of Salton alone is sufficient to show that the Scots were still capable of generous sentiments, and, notwithstanding some peculiar idioms, were able to express themselves with energy and with elegance.

At length the union having incorporated the two nations, and rendered them one people, the distinctions which had subsisted for many ages gradually wear away; peculiarities disappear; the same manners prevail in both parts of the island; the same authors are read and admired; the same entertainments are frequented by the elegant and polite; and the same standard of taste and of purity in language is established. The Scots, after being placed, during a whole century, in a situation no less fatal to the liberty than to the taste and genius of the nation, were at once put in possession of privileges more valuable than those which their ancestors had formerly enjoyed; and every obstruction that had retarded their pursuit, or prevented their acquisition of literary fame, was totally removed.

A

CRITICAL DISSERTATION

CONCERNING

THE MURDER OF KING HENRY, AND THE GENUINENESS OF THE QUEEN'S LETTERS TO BOTHWELL.

It is not my intention to engage in all the controversies to which the murder of King Henry, or the letters from Queen Mary to Bothwell, have given rise; far less to appear as an adversary to any particular author who hath treated of them. To repeat and expose all the ill founded assertions, with regard to these points, which have flowed from inattention, from prejudice, from partiality, from malevolence, and from dishonesty, would be no less irksome to myself than unacceptable to most of my readers. All I propose is to assist others in forming some judgment concerning the facts in dispute, by stating the proofs produced on each side, with as much brevity as the case will admit, and with the same attention and impartiality which I have endeavoured to exercise in examining other controverted points in the Scottish history.

In order to account for the King's murder, two different systems have been formed. The one supposes Bothwell to have contrived and executed this crime; the other imputes it to the Earls of Murray, Morton, and their party.

The decision of many controverted facts in history is a matter more of curiosity than of use. They stand detached; and whatever we determine with regard to them, the fabric of the story remains untouched. But the fact under dispute in this place is a fundamental and essential one, and according to the opinion which an historian adopts with regard to it, he must vary and dispose the whole of his subsequent narration. An historical system may be tried in two different ways; whether it be consistent with probability, and whether it be supported by evidence.

Those who charge the King's murder upon Bothwell argue in the following manner; and though their reasonings have been mentioned already in different parts of the narrative, it is necessary to repeat them here. Mary's love for Darnley, say they, was a sudden and youthful passion. The beauty of his person, set off by some external frivolous accomplishments, was his chief merit, and gained her affections. His capricious temper soon raised in the Queen a disgust, which broke out on different occasions. His engaging in the conspiracy against Rizio converted this disgust into an antipathy, which she was at no pains to conceal. This breach was, perhaps, in its own nature, irreparable; the King certainly wanted that art and condescension which alone could have repaired it. It

widened every day, and a deep and settled hatred effaced all remains of affection. Bothwell observed this, and was prompted by
ambition, and perhaps by love, to found upon it a scheme which
proved fatal both to the Queen and to himself. He had served
Mary at different times with fidelity and success. He insinuated
himself into her favour, by address and by flattery. By degrees he
gained her heart. In order to gratify his love, or at least his ambition, it was necessary to get rid of the King. Mary had rejected
the proposal which, it is said, had been made to her for obtaining
a divorce. The King was equally hated by the partisans of the
house of Hamilton, a considerable party in the kingdom; by Murray, one of the most powerful and popular persons in his country;
by Morton and his associates, whom he had deceived, and whom
Bothwell had bound to his interest by a recent favour. Among
the people Darnly was fallen under extreme contempt. Bothwell,
might expect, for all these reasons, that the murder of the King
would pass without any inquiry, and might trust to Mary's love,
and to his own address and good fortune, for the accomplishment of
the rest of his wishes. What Bothwell expected really came to
pass. Mary, if not privy herself to the design, connived at an action which rid her of a man whom she had such good reason to detest. A few months after the murder of her husband, she married
the person who was both suspected and accused of having perpetrated that odious crime.

Those who charge the guilt upon Murray and his party, reason
in this manner: Murray, they say, was a man of boundless ambition. Notwithstanding the illegitimacy of his birth, he had
early formed a design of usurping the crown. On the Queen's return into Scotland, he insinuated himself into her favour, and engrossed the whole power into his own hands. He set himself
against every proposal of marriage which was made to her, lest his
chance of succeeding to the crown should be destroyed. He hated
Darnly, and was no less hated by him. In order to be revenged on
him, he entered into a sudden friendship with Bothwell, his ancient
and mortal enemy. He encouraged him to assassinate Henry, by
giving him hopes of marrying the Queen. All this was done with
a design to throw upon the Queen herself the imputation of being
accessary to the murder, and, under that pretext, to destroy Bothwell, to depose and imprison her, and to seize the sceptre which he
had wrested out of her hands.

The former of these systems has an air of probability, is consistent with itself, and solves appearances. In the latter, some assertions are false, some links are wanting in the chain, and effects
appear of which no sufficient cause is produced. Murray, on the
Queen's return into Scotland, served her with great fidelity, and
by his prudent administration rendered her so popular, and so
powerful, as enabled her with ease to quash a formidable insurrection raised by the party of which he was the leader in the year
1565. What motive could induce Murray to murder a Prince
without capacity, without followers, without influence over the
nobles, whom the Queen, by her neglect, had reduced to the lowest
state of contempt, and who, after a long disgrace, had regained (ac-

cording to the most favourable supposition) the precarious possession of her favour only a few days before his death? It is difficult to conceive what Murray had to fear from the King's life. It is still a more difficult matter to guess what he could gain by his death. If we suppose that the Queen had no previous attachment to Bothwell, nothing can appear more chimerical than a scheme to persuade her to marry a man whose wife was still alive, and who was not only suspected, but accused of murdering her former husband. But that such a scheme should really succeed is still more extraordinary.—If Murray had instigated Bothwell to commit the crime, or had himself been accessary to the commission of it, what hopes were there that Bothwell would silently bear from a fellow-criminal all the prosecutions which he suffered, without ever retorting upon him the accusation, or revealing the whole scene of iniquity? An ancient and deadly feud had subsisted between Murray and Bothwell; the Queen with difficulty had brought them to some terms of agreement. But is it probable that Murray would an enemy, to whom he had been so lately reconciled, for his confident in the commission of such an atrocious crime? Or, on the other hand, would it ever enter into the imagination of a wise man, first to raise his rival to supreme power, in hopes that afterwards he might render him odious, by accusing him of crimes which he had not committed, and, in consequence of this unjust charge, should be enabled to deprive him of that power? The most adventurous politician never hazarded such a dangerous experiment. The most credulous folly never trusted such an uncertain chance.

How strong soever these general reasonings may appear to be, it is not upon them alone that we must decide, but according to the particular evidence that is produced. This we now proceed to examine.

That Bothwell was guilty of the King's murder, appears, 1. From the concurring testimony of all the contemporary historians. 2. From the confession of those persons who suffered for assisting at the commission of the crime, and who entered into a minute detail of all its circumstances. Anders, ii 165. 3. From the acknowledgment of Mary's own commissioners, who allow Bothwell to have been one of those who were guilty of this crime. Good. ii. 213. 4. From the express testimony of Lesly, Bishop of Ross, to the same effect with the former. Def. of Q. Mary's Hon. And. i. 76. Id. iii, p. 31. 5. Morton, at his death, declared that Bothwell had solicited him, at different times, to concur in the conspiracy formed against the life of the King; and that he was informed by Archibald Douglas, one of the conspirators, that Bothwell was present at the murder. Crawf. Mem. App. 4. The letter from Douglas to the Queen, which I have published in the Appendix, No. XLVII., confirms Morton's testimony. 6. Lord Herries promises, in his own name, and in the name of the nobles who adhered to the Queen, that they would concur in punishing Bothwell as the murderer of the King. Append. No. XXIV.

The most direct charge ever brought against Murray is in these words of Bishop Lesley: "Is it unknown," addressing himself to the Earl of Murray, "what the Lord Herries said to your face openly, even at your own table, a few days after the murder was committed? Did he not charge you with the foreknowledge of the same murder? Did he not, *nulla circuitione usus*, flatly and plainly burden you, that riding in Fife, and coming with one of your most assured and trusty servants the same day whereon you departed from Edinburgh, you said to him, among other talk, This night, ere morning, Lord Darnly shall lose his life?" Defence of Q. Mary, Anders. ii. 75. But the assertion of a man so heated with faction as Lesly, unless it were supported by proper evidence, is of little weight. The servant, to whom Murray is said to have spoken these words, is not named; nor the manner in which this secret conversation was brought to light mentioned. Lord Herries was one of the most zealous advocates for Mary, and it is remarkable that, in all his negotiation at the court of England, he never once repeated this accusation of Murray. In answering the challenge given him by Lord Lindsay, Herries had a fair opportunity of mentioning Murray's knowledge of the murder; but, though he openly accuses of that crime some of those who adhered to Murray, he industriously avoids any insinuation against Murray himself. Keith, Pref. ii. Mary herself, in conversation with Sir Francis Knolles, accused Morton and Maitland of being privy to the murder, but does not mention Murray. And. iv. 55. When the Bishop of Ross and Lord Herries appeared before the English Council, January 11, 1569, they declared themselves ready, in obedience to the Queen's command, to accuse Murray and his associates of being accessary to the murder; but "they being also required, whether they, or any of them, as of themselves, would accuse the said Earl in special, or any of his adherents, or thought them guilty thereof," they answered, "that they took God to witness that none of them did ever know any thing of the conspiracy of that murder, or were in council and foreknowledge thereof; neither who were devisors, inventors, and executors, of the same, till it was publicly discovered long thereafter by some of the assassins, who suffered death on that account." Good. ii. 308. These words are taken out of a register kept by Ross and and Herries themselves, and seem to be a direct confutation of the Bishop's assertion.

The Earls of Huntley and Argyll, in their *Protestation touching the Murder of the King of Scots*, after mentioning the conference at Craigmillar concerning a divorce, add, "So after these premises, the murder of the King following, we judge in our consciences, and hold for certain and truth, that the Earl of Murray and secretary Lethington were authors, inventors, counsellors and causers of the same murder, in what manner, or by whatsoever persons the same was executed." And. iv. 188. But, 1. This is nothing more than the private opinion or personal affirmation of these two noblemen. 2. The conclusion which they make has no connexion with the premises on which they found it. Because Murray proposed to obtain for the Queen a divorce from her husband with her own consent, it does not follow that therefore he committed the murder without her knowledge. 3. Huntly and Argyll were at that time the leaders of that party opposite to Murray, and animated with all the rage of faction. 4. Both of them were Murray's personal enemies.

Huntly, on account of the treatment which his family and clan had received from that nobleman. Argyll was desirous of being divorced from his wife, with whom he lived on no good terms, Knox, 328, and by whom he had no children. Crawf. Peer. 19. She was Murray's sister, and by his interest Argyll's design was obstructed. Keith 551. These circumstances would go far towards invalidating a positive testimony; they more than counterbalance an indeterminate suspicion. 5. It is altogether uncertain whether Huntly and Argyll ever subscribed this protestation. A copy of such a protestation as the Queen thought would be of advantage to her cause was transmitted to them by her. Anders. iv. b. ii. 186. The protestation itself, published by Anderson, is taken from an unsubscribed copy with blanks for the date and place of subscribing. On the back of this copy, there is pasted, indeed, a paper, which Cecil has marked, "Answer of the Earl of Murray to a writing of the Earls of Huntly and Argyll." Anders. 194, 195. But it can hardly be deemed a reply to the above mentioned protestation. Murray's answer bears date at London, Jan. 19, 1568. The Queen's letter, in which she enclosed a copy of the protestation, bears date at Bowton, Jan. 5, 1568. Now it is scarce to be supposed that the copy could be sent into Scotland, be subscribed by the two Earls, and be seen and answered by Murray in so short a time. Murray's reply seems intended only to prevent the impression which the vague and uncertain accusations of his enemies might make in his absence. Cecil had got the original of the Queen's letter into his custody. Anders. iv. 185. This naturally leads us to conjecture that the letter itself, together with the enclosed protestation, were intercepted before they came to the hands of Huntly and Argyll. Nor is this mere conjecture alone. The letter to Huntly, in which the protestation was enclosed, is to be found, Cott. Lib. Cal. C. 1 fol. 280, and is an original subscribed by Mary, though not written by her own hand, because she seldom chose to write in the English language. The protestation is in the same volume, fol. 282, and is manifestly written by the same person who wrote the Queen's letter. This seems to render it highly probable that both were intercepted. So that much has been founded on a paper not subscribed by the two Earls, and probably never seen by them. Besides, this method which the Queen took of sending a copy to the two Earls, of what was proper for them to declare with regard to a conference held in their own presence, appears somewhat suspicious. It would have been more natural, and not so liable to any misrepresentation, to have desired them to write the most exact account, which they could recollect, of what had passed at the conversation at Craigmillar. 6. But even if all this reasoning should be set aside, and the authenticity of the *protestation* should be admitted in its fullest extent, it may still be a question, what degree of credit should be given to the assertion of the two Earls, who were not only present at the first parliament held by Murray as Regent, in December, 1567, in which the one carried the sceptre, and the other the sword of state, Spotsw. 241, but were both members of the committee of lords of articles, and in that capacity assisted in framing all the acts by which the Queen was deprived of the crown, and her son seated on the throne ; and in particular concurred in the act by which it was declared, that whatever had befallen the Queen "was in her awin default, in sa far as, be divers hir previe letters written halelie with hir awin hand, and send by hir to James sometymo Earle of Bothwell, chief executour of the said horribill murthour, as weill befoir the committing thairof as thairaftir : And be hir ungodlie and dishonourabill proceeding to ane pretendit marriage with him, suddainlie and unprovifitlie thaireftir, it is maist certane that sche was previe, airt and pairt, of the actual devise and deid of the foirnamit murthour of the King her lauchful husband, and thairfoir justlie desirvis quhatsumever hes bene done to hir in ony tyme bygaine, or that sal be usit towards hir, for the said cause." Anders. ii. 251.

The Queen's commissioners at the conference in England accused Murray and his associates of having murderd the King. Good. ii. 281. But this charge is to be considered as a recrimination, exhorted by the accusation preferred against the Queen, and contains nothing more than loose and general affirmations, without descending to such particular circumstances as either ascertain their truth, or discover their falsehood. The same accusation is repeated by the nobles assembled at Dumbarton, Sept. 1568. Good. ii. 359. And the same observation may be made concerning it.

All the Queen's advocates have endeavoured to account for Murray's murdering of the King, by supposing that it was done on purpose that he might have the pretence of disturbing the Queen's administration, and thereby rendering ineffectual her general revocation of crown lands, which would have deprived him and his associates of the best part of their estates. Lesly, Def. of Mary's Hon. p. 73. Anders. iv. part ii. 130. But whoever considers the limited powers of a Scottish monarch will see that such a revocation could not be very formidable to the nobles. Every King of Scotland began his reign with such a revocation ; and as often as it was renewed, the power of the nobles rendered it ineffectual. The best vindication of Murray and his party from this accusation is that which they presented to the Queen of England, and which hath never hitherto been published.

Answer to the Objections and Alledgance of the Queen, alledging the Earl of Murray, Lord Regent, the Earls of Morton, Marr Glencairn, Hume, Ruthvin, &c. to have been moved to ormour, for that they abhorred and might not abide her Revocation of the Alienation made of her Property.

It is answered, that is, alledged but [i. e. without] all appearance, and it appears God has bereft the alledgance of all wit and good remembrance, for thir reasons following.

Imprimis, as to My Lord Regent, he never had occasion to grudge thereat, in respect the Queen made him privy to the same, and took resolution with him for the execution thereof, letting His Lordship know she would assuredly in the samine expect all things she had given to him, and ratefy them in the next parliament as she did indeed : and for that cause wished My Lord to leave behind him Master John Wood, to attend upon the same, to whom she declared, that als well in that as in all other her grants it should be provided, yea of free will did promise and offer before ever he demanded, as it came to pass without any let or impediment; for all was ratified by her command, and hand write, at the parliament, but [i. e. without] any difficulty.

Item as to My Lord of Morton, he could not grudge thereat quba never had of her property worth twenty dollars that ever I knew of.

Item the same, I may say of My Lord Glencairn.

Item the same, I may say of My Lord Hume.

Item the same, I may say of My Lord Ruthven.

Item the same, I may say of My Lord Lindsay.

Only My Lord of Marr, had ane little thing of the property quilk alsua was gladly and liberally confirmed to him, in the said parliament preceding a year; was never ane had any cause of miscontent of that revocation, far less to have put their lives and heritage to so open and manifest ane danger as they did for sic ane frivole cause.

Gyf ever any did make evill countenance, and show any miscontentment of the said revocation, it was My Lord of Argyll in special, quha spak largely in the time of parliament thairanents to the Queen herself, and did complain of the manifest corruption of ane act of parliament past upon Her Majesty's return, and sa did lett any revocation at that time; but the armour for revenge of the King's deid was not till twa months after, at quhat time there was no occasion given thereof, nor never a man had mind thereof.

Having thus examined the evidence which has been produced against the Earls of Murray and Bothwell; we shall next proceed to inquire whether the Queen herself was accessary to the murder of her husband.

No sooner was the violent death of Darnly known, than strong suspicion arose, among some of her subjects, that Mary had given her consent to the commission of that crime. Anders. ii. 156. We are informed, by her own ambassador in France, the Archbishop of Glasgow, that the sentiments of foreigners, on this head, were no less unfavourable to her. Keith, Pref. ix. Many of her nobles loudly accused her of that crime, and a great part of the nation, by supporting them, seem to have allowed the accusation to be well founded.

Some crimes, however, are of such a nature that they hardly admit of a positive or direct proof. Deeds of darkness can seldom be brought perfectly to light. Where persons are accused not of being *principals*, but only of being *accessaries* in the commission of a crime; not of having perpetrated it themselves, but only of giving consent to the commission of it by others; the proof becomes still more difficult: and unless when some accomplice betrays the secret, a proof by circumstances, or presumptive evidence, is all that can be attained. Even in judicial trials, such evidence is sometimes held to be sufficient for condemning criminals. The degree of conviction which such evidence carries along with it is often not inferior to that which arises from positive testimony; and a concurring series of circumstances satisfies the understanding no less than the express declaration of witnesses.

Evidence of both these kinds has been produced against Mary. We shall first consider that which is founded upon circumstances alone.

Some of these suspicious circumstances preceded the King's death ; others were subsequent to it. With regard to the former, we may observe that the Queen's violent love of Darnly was soon converted into an aversion to him no less violent ; and that his own ill conduct and excesses of every kind were such that, if they did not justify, at least they account for this sudden change of her disposition towards him. The rise and progress of this domestic rupture I have traced with great care in the History, and to the proofs of it which may be found in papers published by other authors, I have added those contained in App. XVI. and XVII. Le Croc, the French ambassador, who was an eye witness of what he describes, not only represents her aversion to Darnly to be extreme, but declares that there could be no hopes of a reconcilement between them. [Dec. 12, 1566.] "The Queen is in the hands of physicians, and I do assure you is not at all well : and do believe the principal part of her disease to consist in deep grief and sorrow ; nor does it seem possible to make her forget the same. Still she repeats these words, *I could wish to be dead.* You know very well that the injury she has received is exceeding great, and Her Majesty will never forget it.—To speak my mind freely to you, I do not expect, upon several accounts, any good understanding between them [i, e. the King and Queen], unless God effectually put to his hand.—[Dec. 23.] His bad deportment is incurable ; nor can there ever be any good expected from him, for several reasons, which I might tell you was I present with you. I cannot pretend to foretell how all may turn ; but I will say, that matters cannot subsist long as they are, without being accompanied with sundry bad consequences." Keith, Pref. vii. Had Henry died a natural death at this juncture, it must have been considered as a very fortunate event to the Queen, and as a seasonable deliverance from a husband who had become altogether odious to her. Now, as Henry was murdered a few weeks afterwards, and as nothing had happened to render the Queen's aversion to him less violent, the opinion of those who consider Mary as the author of an event which was manifestly so agreeable to her, will appear perhaps to some of our readers to be neither unnatural nor over refined. If we add to this, what has been observed in the History, that in proportion to the increase of Mary's hatred of her husband, Bothwell seems to have made progress in her favour, and that he became the object not only of her confidence but her attachment, that opinion acquires new strength. It is easy to observe many advantages which might redound to Mary as well as to Bothwell from the King's death ; but excepting them, no person, and no party in the kingdom, could derive the least benefit from that event. Bothwell, accordingly, murdered the King, and it was in that age thought no unwarranted imputation on Mary's character, to suppose that she had consented to the deed.

The steps which the Queen took after her husband's death add strength to that supposition. 1. Melvil, who was in Edinburgh at the time of the King's death, asserts that "every body suspected the Earl of Bothwell; and those who durst speak freely to others, said plainly that it was he." p. 155. 2. Mary having issued a proclamation, on the 12th of February, offering a reward to any person who should discover those who had murdered her husband; And. i. 36; a paper in consequence of this was affixed to the gates of the Talbooth, February 16, in which Bothwell was named as the chief person guilty of that crime, and the Queen herself was accused of having given her consent to it. And. ii. 156. 3. Soon after, February 20, the Earl of Lennox, the King's father, wrote to Mary, conjuring her, by every motive, to prosecute the murderers with the utmost rigour. He plainly declared his own suspicions of Bothwell, and pointed out a method of proceeding against him, and for discovering the authors of that crime, no less obvious than equitable. He advised her to seize, and to commit to sure custody, Bothwell himself, and such as were already named as his accomplices; to call an assembly of the nobles; to issue a proclamation, inviting Bothwell's accusers to appear; and if, on that encouragement, no person appeared to accuse them, to hold them innocent, and to dismiss them without further trial. And. i. 40. 4. Archbishop Beatoun, her ambassador in France, in a letter to Mary, March 9th, employs arguments of the utmost weight to persuade her to prosecute the murderers with the greatest severity. "I can conclude nathing (says he) by quhat Zour Majesty writes to me zourself, that sen it has plesit God to conserve zow to make a rigorous vengeance thereof, that rather than it be not actually taine, it appears to me better in this warld that ze had lost life and all. I ask Your Majestie pardon, that I writ sa far, for I can hear nathing to zour prejudise, but I *man* [must] constraindly writ the samin, that all may come to zour knawledge; for the better remede may be put therto. Heir it is needfull that ze forth shaw now rather than ever of before, the greite vertue, magnanimitie, and constance that God has grantit zow, be quhais grace, I hope ze sall overcome this most heavy envie and displesir of the committing thereof, and conserve that reputation in all godliness, ze have conquist of lang, quhich can appear na wayis mair clearie, than that zou do *sick* [such] justice that the *haill* [whole] world may declare zour innocence, and give testimony for-ever of thair treason that has committed (*but* [withont] fear of God or man) so cruel and ungodlie a murther, quhairof there is sa *meikle* [much] ill spoken, that I am constrainit to ask zow mercy, that neither can I or will I make the rehearsal thereof, which is *owr* [too] odious. But alas! Madame, all over Europe this day, there is na purpose in head sa frequent as of Zour Majestie, and of the present state of zour realm, quhilk is in the most part interpretit sinisterly." Keith, Pref. ix. 5. Elizabeth, as appears from Append. No. XIX. urged the same thing in strong terms. 6. The circumstances of the case itself, no less than these solicitations and remonstrances, called for the utmost vigour in her proceedings. Her husband had been murdered in a cruel manner, almost in her own presence. Her subjects were filled with the utmost horror at the crime. Bothwell, one of her principal favourites, had been publicly accused as the author of it. Reflections, extremely dishonourable to herself, had been thrown out. If indignation, and the love of justice, did not prompt her to pursue the murderers with ardour; decency, at least, and concern for vindicating her own character, should have induced her to avoid any appearance of remissness or want of zeal.

But instead of this, Mary continued to discover in all her actions the utmost partiality towards Bothwell. On the 15th of February. five days after the murder she bestowed on him the reversion of the superiority of the town of Leith, which in the year 1565 she had mortgaged to the citizens of Edinburgh. This grant was of much importance, as it gave him not only the command of the principal port in the kingdom, but a great ascendant over the citizens of Edinburgh, who wished much to keep possession of it. 2. Bothwell being extremely desirous to obtain the command of the castle of Edinburgh, the Queen, in order to prevail on the Earl of Mar to surrender the government of it, offered to commit the young Prince to his custody. Mar consented ; and she instantly appointed Bothwell governor of the castle. And. i. Pref. 64. Keith. 379, note (d). 3. The inquiry into the murder, previous to Bothwell's trial, seems to have been conducted with the utmost remissness. Buchanan exclaims loudly against this. And. ii. 24. Nor was it without reason that he did so, as is evident from a circumstance in the affidavit of Thomas Nelson, one of the king's servants, who was in the house when his master was murdered, and was dug up alive out of the rubbish. Being examined on the Monday after the King's death, " This deponar schew that Bonkle had the key of the sellare, and the Queenis servandis the keyis of her shalmir. Quhilk the laird of Tillibardin hearing, said Hald thair, here is ane ground. Efter quhilk words spokin, thai left of, and procedit na farther in the inquisition." And. iv. part. 167. Had there been any intention to search into the bottom of the matter, a circumstance of so much importance merited the most careful inquiry. 4. Notwithstanding Lennox's repeated solicitations, notwithstanding the reasonableness of his demands, and the necessity of complying with them, in order to encourage any accuser to appear against Bothwell, she not only refused to commit him to custody, or even to remove him from her presence and counsels ; And. i. 42. 48 ; but by the grants which we have mentioned, and by other circumstances, discovered an increase of attachment to him. 5. She could not avoid bringing Bothwell to a public trial; but she permitted him to sit as a member in that meeting of the privy council which directed his own trial ; and the trial itself was carried on with such unnecessary precipitancy, and with so many other suspicious circumstances, as to render his acquittal rather an argument of his guilt than a proof of his innocence. These circumstances have all been mentioned at length in Book IV., and therefore are not repeated in this place. 6. Two days after the trial, Mary gave a public proof of her regard for Bothwell, by appointing him to carry the sceptre before her at the meeting of parliament. Keith, 378. 7. In that parliament, she granted him a ratification of all the great possessions and honours which she had conferred upon him, in which was contained an ample enumeration of all the services he had performed. And. i. 117. 8. Though Melvil, who forsaw that her attachment to Bothwell would at length induce her to marry him, warned her of the infamy and danger which would attend that action, she not only disregarded this salutary admonition, but discovered what had passed between them to Bothwell, which exposed Melvil to his resentment. Melv. 156. 9. Bothwell seized Mary as she returned from Stirling, April 24. If he had done this without her knowledge and consent, such an insult could not have failed to have filled her with the most violent indignation. But according to the account of an old MS. "The friendly love was so highly contracted between this great Princess and her enormous subject that there was no end thereof (for it was constantly esteemed by all men, that either of them loved other carnally), so that she suffered patiently to be led where the lover list, and all the way neither made obstacle, impediment, clamour or resistance, as in such accidents used to be, or that she might have done by her princely authority, being accompanied with the noble Earl of Huntly and Secretary Maitland of Lethington." Keith, 383. Melvil, who was present, confirms this account, and tells us that the officer by whom he was seized informed him that nothing was done without the Queen's consent. Melv. 158. 10. On the 12th day of May, a few days before her marriage, Mary declared that she was then at full liberty, and that though Bothwell had offended her by seizing her person, she was too much satisfied with his dutiful behaviour since that time, and so indebted to him for his past services, that she not only forgave that offence, but resolved to promote him to higher honours. And. i. 87. 11. Even after the confederate nobles had driven Bothwell from the Queen's presence, and though she saw that he was considered as the murderer of her former husband by so great a part of her subjects, her affection did not in the least abate, and she continued to express the most unalterable attachment to him. "I can perceive (says Sir N. Throkmorton) that the rigour with which the Queen is kept proceedeth by order from these men, because that the Queen will not by any means be induced to lend her authority to prosecute the murderer; nor will not consent by any persuasion to abandon the Lord Bothwell for her husband, but avoweth that she will live and die with him; and saith, that if it were put to her choice to relinquish her crown and kingdom, or the Lord Bothwell, she would leave her kingdom and dignity to go a simple damsel with him, and she will never consent that he shall fare worse, or have more harm than herself." Appendix No. XXII. In all their negotiations with Throkmorton, the confederates mention this unalterable attachment of the Queen to Bothwell as a sufficient reason for rejecting his proposals of an accommodation with their sovereign. Keith, 419. 449. This assertion they renewed in the conferences at York. Anders. iv. part ii. p. 66. Murray, in his interview with Mary in Lochleven, charged her with persisting in her inordinate affection to Bothwell. Keith, 446. All these, however, may be considered merely as accusations brought by the confederates, in order to vindicate their rigour towards the Queen. But Throkmorton, who, by his residence in Edinburgh, and by his intercourse with the Queen's partisans, as

well as with her enemies, had many opportunities of discovering
whether or not Mary had expressed herself in such terms, and who
was disposed to view her actions in the most favourable light, appears, by the passage which I have quoted from his letter of the
14th of July, to be persuaded that the confederates had not misrepresented her sentiments. He had soon an opportunity of being
confirmed with greater certainty in this opinion. Although the
confederates had refused him access to the captive Queen, he found
means of holding a secret correspondence with her, and endeavoured
to persuade her to give her consent to have her marriage with
Bothwell dissolved by a sentence of divorce, as the most probable
means of regaining her liberty. " She hath sent me word that she
will in no wise consent unto that, but rather die." Appendix,
No. XXII. There is evidence of the continuance of Mary's
attachment still more explicit. Lord Herries, in the parliament
held the 15th of December, 1567, acknowledged the Queen's inordinate affection to that wicked man, and that she could not be induced by persuasion to leave him ; and that in sequestering her
within Lochlevin, the confederates had done the duty of noblemen. Appendix, No. XXIV. In the year 1571, a conference
was held by some deputies from a convention of clergy, with the
Duke of Chatelherault, Secretary Maitland, Sir James Balfour, and
Kirkaldy ; and an account of it written by Mr. Craig, one of the
ministers of Edinburgh, is extant in Calderwood MSS. Hist. ii.
244. In presence of all these persons, most of whom were in Edinburgh when the Queen was taken at Carberry, Maitland, who was
now an avowed partisan of Mary, declares, that on the same night
she was brought to Edinburgh, he himself had offered, that if she
would abandon Bothwell, she should have as thankful obedience as
ever she had since she came to Scotland. But in no wise would
she consent to leave Bothwell. According to Sir James Melvil, the
Queen found means of writing a letter to Bothwell on the evening
of that day when she was conducted as a prisoner to Edinburgh, in
which she declared her affection to him in the most tender expressions, and her resolution never to abandon him. This letter, he
says, was intercepted by the confederates, and determined them to
confine Mary in the castle of Lochlevin. But as neither Buchanan
nor Knox, both abundantly disposed to avail themselves of every
fact and report that could be employed in order to represent Mary's
conduct as improper and criminal, mentions this letter ; and as the
confederates themselves in their negotiation with Throkmorton, as
well as in their accusations of the Queen before the English commissioners at York and Westminster, maintain the same silence
with regard to it, I am satisfied that Melvil, who wrote his memoirs for the information of his son in his old age, and long after
the events which he records happened, has been mistaken with regard to this particular. From this long enumeration of circumstances, we may, without violence, draw the following conclusion :
Had Mary really been accessary to the murder of her husband ; had
Bothwell perpetrated the crime with her consent, or at her command ; and had she intended to stifle the evidence against him, and
to prevent the discovery of his guilt, she could scarcely have taken

any other steps than those which she took, nor could her conduct have been more repugnant to all the maxims of prudence and of decency.

The positive evidence produced against Mary may be classed under two heads.

1. The depositions of some persons who were employed in committing the murder, particularly of Nicholas Hubert, who in the writing of that age is called *French Paris*. This person, who was Bothwell's servant, and much trusted by him, was twice examined and the original of one of his depositions, and a copy of the other, are still extant. It is pretended that both these are notorious forgeries. But they are remarkable for a simplicity and *naivete* which it is almost impossible to imitate; they abound with a number of minute facts and particularities, which the most dexterous forger could not have easily assembled and connected together with any appearance of probability; and they are filled with circumstances which can scarcely be supposed to have entered the imagination of any man but one of Paris's rank and character. But, at the same time, it must be acknowledged that his depositions contain some improbable circumstances. He seems to have been a foolish talkative fellow; the fear of death, the violence of torture, and the desire of pleasing those in whose power he was, tempted him, perhaps, to feign some circumstances and to exaggerate others. To say that some circumstances in an affidavit are improbable or false is very different from saying that the whole is forged. I suspect the former to be the case here; but I see no appearance of the latter. Be that as it will, some of the most material facts in Paris's affidavits rest upon his single testimony; and for that reason I have not in the History, nor shall I in this place, lay any stress upon them.

2. The letters said to be written by Mary to Bothwell. These have been frequently published. The accident by which the Queen's enemies got them into their possession is related in Book V. When the authenticity of any ancient paper is dubious or contested, it may be ascertained either by external or internal evidence. Both these have been produced in the present case.

I. External proofs of the genuineness of Mary's letters. 1. Murray and the nobles who adhered to him affirm upon their word and honour, that the letters were written with the Queen's own hand, with which they were well acquainted. Good. ii. 64. 92. 2. The letters were publicly produced in the parliament of Scotland, December 1567; and were so far considered as genuine that they are mentioned in the act against Mary, as one chief argument of her guilt. Good. ii. 66, 67. 3. They were shown privately to the Duke of Norfolk, the Earl of Sussex, and Sir Ralph Sadler, Elizabeth's commissioners at York. In the account which they gave of this matter to their mistress, they seem to consider the letters as genuine, and express no suspicion of any forgery; they particularly observe, "that the matter contained in them is such, that it could hardly be invented and devised by any other than herself; for that they discourse of some things which were unknown to any other than to herself and Bothwell; and as it is hard to counterfeit so many, so the matter of them, and the man-

ner how these men came by them is such, as it seemeth that God,
in whose sight murder and bloodshed of the innocent is abominable,
would not permit the same to be hid or concealed." Good ii. 142.
They seem to have made such an impression on the Duke of Norfolk that, in a subsequent letter to Pembroke, Leicester, and Cecil,
he has these words : "If the matter shall be thought as detestable
and manifest to you as, for ought we can perceive, it seemeth here
to us." Good. ii. 154. Nor did Norfolk declare these to be his
sentiments only in public official letters; he expressed himself in
the same manner to his most confidential friends. In a secret conference with the Bishop of Ross at York, the Duke informed him
that he had seen the letters, &c. which the Regent had to produce
against the Queen, whereby there would be such matter proved
against her as would dishonour her for ever. State Trials, edition of
Hargrave, i. 91. Murdin, 52. The Bishop of Ross, if he had known
the letters to be a notorious forgery, must have been naturally led,
in consequence of this declaration. to undeceive the Duke, and to
expose the imposture. But instead of this, the Duke, and he, and
Lethington, after consulting together, agreed, that the Bishop
should write to Mary, then at Bolton, and instruct her to make
such a proposal to Elizabeth as might prevent the public production of the letters and other evidence. State Trials, i. 94. Murdin, 45. Indeed, the whole of this secret conference seems to imply that Lethington, Ross, and Norfolk were conscious of some defect in Mary's cause, and therefore exerted all their ingenuity in
order to avoid a public accusation. Murdin, 52, 53. To Banister,
whom the Duke seems to have trusted more entirely than any
other of his servants, he expressed himself in much the same sort
of terms with regard to the Queen of Scots. State Trials, i. 98.
The words of Banister's evidence are remarkable : "I confess that
I, waiting of my lord and master, when the Earl of Sussex and Mr.
Chancellor of the Duchy that now is, were in commission at York,
did hear his Grace say, that upon examination of the matter of the
murder, it did appear that the Queen of Scots was guilty and privy
to the murder of Lord Darnly, whereby I verily thought that his
Grace would never join in marriage with her." Murdin, 134.
Elizabeth, in her instructions to the Earl of Shrewsbury and Beale,
in 1583, asserts, that both the Duke and Earl of Arundel did declare to herself, that the proof by the view of her letters, did fall
out sufficient against the Queen of Scots; however they were after
drawn to cover her faults and pronounce her innocency. MS. Advoc.
Library. A. iii. 28. p. 314, from Cot. Lib Calig. 9. 4. A similar impression was made upon other contemporaries of Mary by the
production of the letters, which implies a full belief of their being
genuine. Cecil, in his correspondence with Sir Henry Norris, the
English ambassador in France, relates this transaction in terms
which leave no room to doubt with respect to his own private
opinion. In his letter, December 14th, 1568, the very day on
which the letters, &c. were laid before the meeting of privy
counsellors and peers, he informs him, "That the Regent was driven
from his defence, to disclose a full fardel of the naughty matter,
tending to convince the Queen as adviser of the murther, and the

Earl of Bothwell as her executour; and now the Queen's party, so great, refuse to make any answer, and press that their mistress may come in person to answer the matter herself before the Queen's Majesty; which is thought not fit to be granted until the great blot of the marriage with her husband's murtherer, and the evident charges, by letters of her own, to be deviser of the murther, be either razed out or recovered; for that, as the matters are exhibited against her, it is far unseemly for any Prince, or for chaste ears, to be annoyed with the filthy noise thereof; and yet, as being a commissioner, I must and will forbear to pronounce any thing herein certainly, though as a private person I cannot but with horror and trembling think thereof." Cabala, 156. 5. From the correspondence of Bowes, the English resident in Scotland, with Walsingham, in the year 1582, published towards the close of this dissertation, it is manifest that both in England and Scotland, both by Elizabeth and James, both by the Duke of Lennox and Earl of Gowrie, the letters were deemed to be genuine. The eagerness on one side to obtain, and on the other to keep possession of the casket and letters implies that this was the belief of both. These sentiments of contemporaries, who were in a situation to be thoroughly informed and who had abilities to judge with discernment, will, in the opinion of many of my readers, far outweigh theories, suppositions and conjectures, formed at the distance of two centuries. 6. The letters were subjected to a solemn and judicial examination with respect to their authenticity, as far as that can be ascertained by resemblance of character and fashion of writing; for, after the conferences at York and Westminster were finished, Elizabeth, as I have related, assembled her privy counsellors, and joining to them several to the most eminent noblemen in her kingdom, laid before them all the proceedings against the Scottish Queen, and particularly ordered, that "the letters and writing exhibited by the Regent, as the Queen of Scots' letters and writings, should also be shewed, and conference [i. e. comparison] thereof made in their sight, with the letters of the said Queen's, being extant, and heretofore written with her own hand, and sent to the Queen's Majesty; whereby may be searched and examined what difference is betwixt them. Good. ii. 252. They assembled, accordingly at Hampton Court, December 14 and 15, 1568; and. "The originals of the letters supposed to be wrritten with the Queen of Scots' own hand were then also presently produced and perused; and, being read, were duly conferred and compared, for the manner of writing, and fashion of orthography, with sundry other letters long since heretofore written, and sent by the said Queen of Scots to the Queen's Majesty. In collation whereof no difference was found." Good. ii. 256. 7. Mary having written an apological letter for her conduct to the Countess of Lennox, July 10, 1570, she transmitted it to her husband then in Scotland; and he returned to the Countess the following answer: "seeing you have remittit to me, to answer the Queen the King's mother's letters sent to you, what can I say but that I do not marvell to see hir writ the best can for hirself, to seame to purge her of that, quhairof many besydes me are certainly persuadit of the contrary, and I not only assurit by my awin knawledge, but by her handwrit, the confessionis of men gone to the death, and uther infallibil experience. It wull be lang tyme that is hable to put a mattir so notorious in oblivioun, to mak black quhyte, or innocency to appear quhair the contrary is sa weill knawin. The maist indifferent, I trust, doubtis not of the equitie of zoure and my cause, and of the just occasioun of our mislyking. Hir richt dewtie to zow and me, being the parteis interest, were hir trew confessioun and unfeyned repentance of that lamentable fact, odious for hir to be reportit, and sorrowfull for us to think of. God is just, and will not in the end be abused; but as he has manifested the trewth, so will he puneise the iniquity." *Lennox's Orig. Regist. of Letters.* In their public papers, the Queen's enemies may be suspected of advancing what would be most subservient to their cause, not what was agreeable to truth, or what flowed from their own inward conviction. But in a private letter to his own wife, Lennox had no occasion to dissemble; and it is plain, that he not only thought the Queen guilty, but believed the authenticity of her letters to Bothwell. 8. In opposition to all these reasons for the believing the letters, &c. to be authentic, the conduct of the nobles confederated against Mary, in not producing them directly as evidences against her, has been always represented as an irrefragable proof of their being forged. According to the account of the confederates themselves the casket containing the letters was seized by them on the 20th of June, 1567; but the first time that they were judicially stated as evidence against the Queen was in a meeting of the Regent's privy council, December 4th, and they afterwards served as the foundation of the acts made against her in parliament held on the 15th day of the same month. If the letters had been genuine, it is contended, that the obtaining possession of them must have afforded such matter of triumph to the confederates that they would instantly have proclaimed it to the whole world; and in their negotiations with English and French ministers, or with such of their fellow subjects as condemned their proceedings, they would have silenced, at once, every advocate for the Queen, by exhibiting this convincing proof of her guilt. But in this reasoning sufficient attention is not paid to the delicate and perilous situation of the confederates at that juncture. They had taken arms against their sovereign, had seized her person at Carberry Hill, and confined her a prisoner at Lochlevin. A considerable number, however of their fellow subjects, headed by some of the most powerful noblemen in the kingdom, was combined against them. This combination, they soon perceived, they could not hope to break or to vanquish without aid either from France or England. In the former kingdom, Mary's uncles, the Duke of Guise and Cardinal of Lorrain, were at that period all-powerful, and the King himself was devotedly attached to her. If the confederates confined their views to the dissolution of the marriage of the Queen with Bothwell, and to the exclusion of him for ever from her presence, they might hope, perhaps, to be countenanced by Charles IX. and his ministers, who had sent an envoy into Scotland of purpose to dissuade Mary from that ill-fated match; Append. No. XXII.; whereas the loading her publicly with the imputation of being accessary to the murder of her husband would be deemed such an inexpiable crime by the court of France as must cut off every hope of countenance or aid from that quarter. From England, with which the principal confederates had been long and intimately connected, they had many reasons to expect more effectual support ; but, to their astonishment, Elizabeth condemned their proceedings with asperity, warmly espoused the cause of the captive Queen, and was extremely solicitous to obtain her release and restoration. Nor was this merely only one of the artifices which Elizabeth often employed in her transactions with Scotland. Though her most sagacious ministers considered it as the wisest policy to support the confederate lords rather than the Queen of Scots, Elizabeth disregarded their counsel. Her high notions of royal authority, and of the submission due by subjects, induced her, on this occasion, to exert herself in behalf of Mary, not only with sincerity but with zeal; she negociated, she solicited, she threatened. Finding the confederates inflexible, she endeavoured to procure Mary's release by means of that party in Scotland which continued faithful to her, and instructed Throkmorton to correspond with the leaders of it, and to make overtures to that effect. Keith, 451. App. No. XXIII. She even went so far as to direct her ambassador at Paris to concert measures with the French King how they, by their joint efforts, might persuade or compel the Scots to " acknowledge the Queen her good sister to be their sovereign lady and Queen, and renounce their obedience to her son." Keith, 462, 3, 4. From all these circumstances, the confederates had every reason to apprehend that Mary would soon obtain liberty, and by some accommodation be restored to the whole, or at least to a considerable portion of her authority as sovereign. In that event they forsaw, that if they should venture to accuse her publicly of a crime so atrocious as the murder of her husband, they must not only be excluded for ever from power and favour, but from any hope of personal safety. On this account they long confined themselves to that which was originally declared to be the reason of their taking arms; the avenging the King's death, the dissolving the marriage with Bothwell, the inflicting on him condign punishment, or banishing him for ever from the Queen's presence. It appears from the letters of Throkmorton, published by Bishop Keith, and in my Appendix, that his sagacity early discovered that this would be the tenor of their conduct. In his letter from Edinburgh, dated July 14th, he observes, that " They do not forget their own peril conjoined with the danger of the Prince, but, as far as I perceive, they intend not to touch the Queen either in surety or in honour; for they speak of her with respect and reverence, and do affirm, as I do learn, that, the condition aforesaid accomplished [i. e. the separation from Bothwell], they will both put her to liberty, and restore her to her estate." Append. No. XXII. His letter of August 22d contains a declaration made to him by Lethington, in name and in presence of his associates, " That they never meant harm neither to the Queen's person nor to her honour—that they have been contented hitherto to be condemned, as it were, of all princes, strangers, and, namely, of

the Queen of England, being charged of grievous and infamous
titles, as to be noted rebels, traitors, seditious, ingrate, and cruel,
all which they suffer and bear upon their backs, because they will
not justify themselves, nor proceed in any thing that may touch
their sovereign's honour. But in case they be with these defamations continually oppressed, or with the force, aid and practices of
other princes, and namely of the Queen of England, put in danger,
or to an extremity, they shall be compelled to deal otherwise with
the Queen than they intend, or than they desire; for, added he,
you may be sure we will not lose our lives, have our lands forfeited,
and be reputed rebels through the world, seeing we have the means
to justify ourselves." Keith, 448. From this view of the slippery
ground on which they stood at that time, their conduct, in not
producing the letters for several months, appears not only to have
been prudent, but essential to their own safety.

But, at a subsequent period, when the confederates found it necessary to have the form of government which they had established
confirmed by authority of parliament, a different mode of proceeding became requisite. All that had hitherto been done with respect
to the Queen's dismission, the seating the young King upon the
throne, and the appointment of a Regent, was in reality nothing
more than the deed of private men. It required the exhibition of
some legal evidence to procure a constitutional act giving the sanction of its approbation to such violent measures, and to obtain "a
perfect law and security for all them that either by deed, counsel,
or subscription, had entered into that cause since the beginning."
Haynes, 453. This prevailed with the Regent and his secret council, after long deliberation, to agree to produce all the evidence of
which they were possessed ; and upon that production parliament
passed the acts which were required. Such a change had happened
in the state of the kingdom as induced the confederates to venture
upon this change in their conduct. In June, a powerful combination was forming against them, under the leading of the Hamiltons.
In December that combination was broken ; most of the members
of it had acknowledged the King as their lawful sovereign, and had
submitted to the Regent's government. Huntly, Argyll, Herries,
the most powerful noblemen of that party, were present in the parliament, and concurred in all its acts. Edinburgh, Dunbar, Dun-
barton, and all the chief strong holds in the kingdom were now in
the hands of the Regent ; the arms of France had full occupation
in its civil war with the Hugonots. The ardour of Elizabeth's zeal
in behalf of the captive Queen seems to have abated. A step that
would have been followed with ruin to the confederates in June
was attended with little danger in December. From this long de-
duction it appears, that no proof of the letters being forged can be
drawn from the circumstances of their not having been produced
immediately after the 20th of June; but though no public accusation was brought instantly against the Queen, in consequence of
seizing the casket, hints were given by the confederates, that they
possessed evidence sufficient to convict her. This is plainly implied
in a letter of Throkmorton, July 21st, Keith, Pref. p. xii. and more
clearly in the passage which I have quoted from his letter of August 22. In his letter of July 25 the papers contained in the casket

are still more plainly pointed out. "They [i. e. the confederates] say, that they have as apparent proof against her as may be, as well by the testimony of her own handwriting, which they have recovered, as also by sufficient witnesses." Keith, 426.

II. With regard to the internal proofs of the genuineness of the Queen's letters to Bothwell, we may observe, 1. That whenever a paper is forged a with particular intention, the eagerness of the former to establish the point in view, his solicitude to cut off all doubts and cavils, and to avoid any appearance of uncertainty, seldom fail of prompting him to use expressions the most explicit and full to his purpose. The passages foisted into ancient authors by heretics in different ages; the legendary miracles of the Romish saints; the supposititous deeds in their own favour produced by monasteries; are so many proofs of this assertion. No maxim seems to be more certain than this, That a forger is often apt to prove too much, but seldom falls into the error of proving too little. The point which the Queen's enemies had to establish was, "that as the Earl of Bothwell was chief executor of the horrible and unworthy murder perpetrated, &c. so was she of the foreknowledge, counsel, devise, persuader, and commander of the said murder to be done." Good. ii. 207. But of this there are only imperfect hints, obscure intimations, and dark expressions in the letters, which, however convincing evidence they might furnish if found in real letters, bear no resemblance to that glare and superfluity of evidence which forgeries commonly contain. All the advocates for Mary's innocence in her own age, contend that there is nothing in the letters which can serve as a proof of her guilt. Lesley, Blackwood, Turner, &c. abound with passages to this purpose; nor are the sentiments of those in the present age different. "Yet still it might have been expected (says one of her ablest defenders) that some one or other of the points or articles of the accusation should be made out clearly by the proof. But nothing of that is to be seen in the present case. There is nothing in the letters that could plainly show the writer to have been in the foreknowledge, counsel, or device of any murder, far less to have persuaded or commanded it; and as little is there about maintaining or justifying any murders," Good. i. 76. How ill advised were Mary's adversaries, to contract so much guilt, and to practise so many aritices, in order to forge letters, which are so ill contrived for establishing the conclusion they had in view! Had they been so base as to have recourse to forgery, is it not natural to think that they would have produced something more explicit and decisive? 2. It is almost impossible to invent a long narration of fictitious events, consisting of various minute particulars, and to connect these in such a manner with real facts that no mark of fraud shall appear. For this reason, skilful forgers avoid any long detail of circumstances, especially of foreign and superfluous ones, well knowing that the more these are multiplied, the more are the chances of detection increased. Now Mary's letters, especially the first, are filled with a multiplicity of circumstances, extremely natural in a real correspondence, but altogether foreign to the purpose of the Queen's enemies, and which it would have been extreme folly to have inserted, if they had been altogether imaginary, and without foundation. 3. The truth and reality of several circumstances in the letters, and these too of no very public nature, are confirmed by undoubted collateral evidence. Lett. i. Good. ii. p. 4. The Queen is said to have met one of Lennox's gentlemen, and to have had some conversation with him. Thomas Crawford, who was the person, appeared before Elizabeth's commissioners, and confirmed, upon oath, the truth of this circumstance. He likewise declared, that during the Queen's stay at Glasgow, the King repeated to him, every night, whatever had passed through the day between her Majesty and him; and that the account given of these conversations in the first letter, is nearly the same with what the king communicated to him. Good. ii. 245. According to the same letter there was much discourse between the King and Queen concerning Mynto, Heigait, and Walcar. Good. ii. 8. 10, 11. What this might be, was altogether unknown, until a letter of Mary's preserved in the Scottish college at Paris, and published, Keith, Pref. vii. discovered it to be an affair of so much importance as merited all the attention she paid to it at that time. It appears by a letter from the French ambassador, that Mary was subject to a violent pain in her side. Keith. ibid. This circumstance is mentioned, Lett. i. p. 30. in a manner so natural as can scarcely belong to any but a genuine production. 4. If we shall still think it probable to suppose that so many real circumstances were artfully introduced into the letters by the forgers, in order to give an air of authenticity to their production; it will hardly be possible to hold the same opinion concerning the following particular. Before the Queen began her first letter to Bothwell, she, as usual among those who write long letters concerning a variety of subjects, made *notes* or *memorandums* of the particulars she wished to remember; but as she sat up writing during a great part of the night, and after her attendants were asleep, her paper failed her, and she continued her letter upon the same sheet on which she had formerly made her memorandums. This she herself takes notice of, and makes an apology for it: "It is late; I desire never to cease from writing unto you, yet now, after the kissing of your hands, I will end my letter. Excuse my evil writing, and read it twice over. Excuse that thing that is scriblit, for I had na paper zesterday, quhen I wraite that of the memorial." Good. ii. 28. These memorandums still appear in the middle of the letter; and what we have said seems naturally to account for the manner how they might find their way into a real letter. It is scarce to be supposed, however, that any forger would think of placing memorandums in the middle of a letter, where at first sight, they make so absurd and so unnatural an appearance. But if any shall still carry their refinement to such a length, as to suppose that the forgers were so artful as to throw in this circumstance, in order to preserve the appearance of genuineness, they must at least allow that the Queen's enemies, who employed these forgers, could not be ignorant of the design and meaning of these short notes and memorandums; but we find them mistaking them so far as to imagine that they were the *credit of the bearer*, i. e. points concerning which the Queen had given him verbal instructions. Good. ii. 152. This they cannot possibly be; for the Queen herself writes with so much exactness concerning the different points in the memorandums that there was no need of giving any credit or instructions to the bearer concerning them. The memorandums are indeed the *contents* of the letter. 5. Mary, mentioning her conversation with the King, about the affair of Mynto, Heigait, &c. says, "The morne [i. e. to-morrow], I will speik to him upon that point ;" and then adds, "As to the rest of Willie Heigait's, he confessit it ; but it was the morne [i. e. the morning,] after my coming or he did it." Good. ii. 9. This addition, which could not have been made till after the conversation happened, seems either to have been inserted by the Queen into the body of the letter, or, perhaps, she having written it on the margin, it was taken thence into the text. If we suppose the letter to be a real one, and written at different times, as it plainly bears, this circumstance appears to be very natural : but no reason could have induced a forger to have ventured upon such an anachronism, for which there was no necessity. An addition perfectly similar to this, made to a genuine paper, may be found, Good. ii. 282.

But, on the other hand, Mary herself and the advocates for her innocence have contended, that these letters were forged by her enemies, on purpose to blast her reputation, and to justify their own rebellion. It is not necessary to take notice of the arguments which were produced, in her own age, in support of this opinion ; the observations which we have already made, contain a full reply to them. An author, who has inquired into the affairs of that period with great industry, and who has acquired much knowledge of them, has published (as he affirms) a demonstration of the forgery of Mary's letters. This demonstration he founds upon evidence both internal and external. With regard to the former, he observes that the French copy of the Queen's letters is plainly a translation of Buchanan's Latin copy ; which Latin copy is only a translation of the Scottish copy ; and, by consequence, the assertion of the Queen's enemies, that she wrote them originally in French, is altogether groundless, and the whole letters are gross forgeries. He accounts for this strange succession of translations, by supposing that when the forgery was projected, no person could be found capable of writing originally in the French language letters which would pass for the Queen's ; for that reason they were first composed in Scottish ; but unluckily the French interpreter, as he conjectures, did not understand that language : and therefore Buchanan translated them into Latin, and from his Latin they were rendered into French. Good. i. 79, 80.

It is hardly necessary to observe, that no proof whatever is produced of any of these suppositions. The manner of the Scots in that age, when almost every man of rank spent a part of his youth in France, and the intercourse between the two nations was great, renders it altogether improbable that so many complicated operations should be necessary in order to procure a few letters to be written in the French language.

But without insisting further on this, we may observe, that all this author's premises may be granted, and yet his conclusion will not follow, unless he likewise prove that the French letters, as we now have them, are a true copy of those which were produced by Murray and his party in the Scottish parliament, and at York and

Westminister. But this he has not attempted ; and if we attend to
the history of the letters, such an attempt, it is obvious, must have
been unsuccessful. The letters were first published at the end of
Buchanan's *Detection.* The first edition of this treatise was in
Latin, in which language three of the Queen's letters were subjoined
to it ; this Latin edition was printed A.D. 1571. Soon after, a
Scottish translation of it was published, and at the end of it were
printed, likewise in Scottish, the three letters which had formerly
appeared in Latin, and five other letters in Scottish, which were
not in the Latin edition. Next appeared a French translation of
the Detection, and of seven of the letters ; this bears to have been
printed at Edinburgh by Thomas Waltem, 1572. The name of the
place, as well as the printer, is allowed by all parties to be a manifest imposture. Our author, from observing the day of the month
from which the printing is said to have been finished, has asserted
that this edition was printed at London ; but no stress can be laid
upon a date found in a book, where every other circumstance with
regard to the printing is allowed to be false. Blackwood, who
(next to Lesly) was the best informed of all Mary's advocates in
that age, affirms, that the French edition of the Detection was
published in France; "Il [Buchanan] a depuis adjousté a ceste de-
clamation un petit libelle du pretendu marriage du Duc de Norfolk, et de la facon de son proces, et la tout envoyé aux freres a la
Rochelle, lesquels voyants qu'il pouvoit servir a la cause, l'ont
traduit en Fraucois et iceluy fut imprimée a Edinbourg, c'est a
dire a la Rochelle, par Thomas Waltem, nom aposté et fait a plaisir."
Martyre de Marie. Jebb, ii. 256. The author of the *Innocence de
Marie* goes further, and names the French translator of the Detection. "Et icelui premierement composè (comme il semble) par
George Buchanan Escossoys, et depuis traduit en langue Francoise
par un Hugonot, Poitevin (advocat de vocation) Camuz, soy disant
gentilhomme, et un de plus remarquez sediteuz de France." Jebb, i.
425. 443. The concurring testimony of the two contemporary authors, whose residence in France afforded them sufficient means of
information, must outweigh a slight conjecture. The French translator does not pretend to publish the original French letters as
written by the Queen herself; he expressly declares that he translated them from the Latin. Good. i. 103. Had our author attended
to all these cirumstances, he might have saved himself the labour
of so many criticisms to prove that the present French copy of the
letters is a translation from the Latin. The French editor himself
acknowledges it, and, so far as I know, no person ever denied it.

We may observe that the French translator was so ignorant as to
affirm that Mary had written these letters, partly in French, partly
in Scottish. Good. i. 103. Had this translation been published at
London by Cecil, or had it been made by his direction, so gross an
error would not have been admitted into it. This error, however,
was owing to an odd circumstance. In the Scottish translation of
the Detection, two or three sentences of the original French were
prefixed to each letter, which breaking off with an &c. the Scottish
translation of the whole letter followed. This method of printing
translations was not uncommon in that age. The French editor,

observing this, foolishly concluded that the letters had been written partly in French, partly in Scottish.

If we carefully consider those few French sentences of each letter, which still remain, and apply to them that species of criticism by which our author has examined the whole, a clear proof will arise, that there was a French copy not translated from the Latin, but which was itself the original from which both the Latin and Scottish have been translated. This minute criticism must necessarily be disagreeable to many readers; but luckily a few sentences only will be examined, which will render it extremely short.

In the first letter, the French sentence prefixed to it ends with these words, *y faisoit bon*. It is plain this expression, *veu ce que peut un corps saus cœur*, is by no means a translation of *cum plane perinde assem atque corpus sine corde*. The whole sentence has a spirit and elegance in the French, which neither the Latin nor Scottish has retained. *Jusques a la dinee* is not a translation of *toto prandii tempore;* the Scottish translation, *quhile denner time*, expresses the sense of the French more properly; for anciently *quhile* signified *until* as well as *during*. *Je n'ay pas tenu grand propos* is not justly rendered *neque contulerim sermonem cum quoquam;* the phrase used in the French copy is one peculiar to that language, and gives a more probable account of her behaviour than the other. *Jugeant bien qu'il n'y faisoit bon* is not a translation of *ut qui judicarent id non esse ex usu*. The French sentence prefixed to lett. 2. ends with *apprendre*. It is evident that both the Latin and Scottish translations have omitted altogether these words, *et toutefois je ne puis apprendre*. The French sentence prefixed to lett. 3, ends with *presenter*. *J'aye vielle plus tard la haut* is plainly no translation of *diutius illic morata sum;* the sense of the French is better expressed by the Scottish, *I have walkit later there up*. Again, *Pour excuser vostre affaire* is very different from *ad excusandam nostra negotia*. The five remaining letters never appeared in Latin; nor is there any proof of their being ever translated into that language. Four of them, however, are published in French. This entirely overturns our author's hypothesis concerning the necessity of a translation into Latin.

In the Scottish edition of the Detection, the whole *sonnet* is printed in French as well as in Scottish. It is not possible to believe that this Scottish copy could be the original from which the French was translated. The French consists of verses which have both measure and rhyme, and which, in many cases, are far from being inelegant. The Scottish consist of an equal number of lines, but without measure or rhyme. Now, no man could ever think of a thing so absurd and impracticable as to require one to translate a certain number of lines in prose, into an equal number of verses where both measure and rhyme were to be observed. The Scottish, on the contrary, appears manifestly to be a translation of the French; the phrases, the idioms, and many of the words are French and not Scottish. Besides, the Scottish translator has, in several instances, mistaken the sense of the French, and in many more, expresses the sense imperfectly. Had the sonnet been forged, this could not have happened. The directors of the fraud would have understood their own work. I shall satisfy myself with one ex-

ample, in which there is a proof of both of my assertions. Stanza
viii. ver. 9.

> Pour luy j'attendz toute bonne fortune,
> Pour luy je veux garder santè et vie,
> Pour luy tout vertu de suivre j'ay envie.

> For him I attend all good fortune,
> For him I will conserve helthe and life,
> For him I desire to ensue courage.

Attend in the first line is not a Scottish, but a French phrase;
the two other lines do not express the sense of the French, and the
last is absolute nonsense.

The eighth letter was never translated into French. It contains
much refined mysticism about *devices*, a folly of that age, of which
Mary was very fond, as appears from several other circumstances,
particularly from a letter concerning *impresas*, by Drummond of
Hawthornden. If Mary's adversaries forged her letters, they were
certainly employed very idly when they produced this.

From these observations it seems to be evident that there was a
French copy of Mary's letters, of which the Latin and Scottish were
only translations. Nothing now remains of this copy but these few
sentences, which are prefixed to the Scottish translations. The
French editor laid hold of these sentences, and tacked his own
translation to them, which, so far as it is his work, is a servile and
a very wretched translation of Buchanan's Latin; whereas, in those
introductory sentences, we have discovered strong marks of their
being originals, and certain proofs that they are not translated
from the Latin.

It is apparent, too, from comparing the Latin and Scottish translations with these sentences, that the Scottish translator has more
perfectly attained the sense and spirit of the French than that of
the Latin. And as it appears that the letters were very early
translated into Scottish, Good ii. 76, it is probable that Buchanan
made his translation, not from the French, but from the Scottish
copy. Were it necessary, several critical proofs of this might be
produced. One that has been already mentioned seems decisive.
Diutius illic morata sum bears not the least resemblance to *j'ay
veille plus tard la haut;* but if instead of *I walkit* [i. e. watched]
later there up, we suppose that Buchanan read *I waitit, &c.,* this
mistake, into which he might so easily have fallen, accounts for the
error in his translation.

These criticisms, however minute, appear to be well founded.—
But whatever opinion may be formed concerning them, the other
arguments, with regard to the internal evidence, remain in full
force.

The external proofs of the forgery of the Queen's letters, which
our author has produced, appear at first sight to be specious, but
are not more solid than that which we have already examined.—
These proofs may be classed under two heads, I. The erroneous
and contradictory accounts which are said to be given of the letters, upon the first judicial production of them. In the secret
council held Dec. 8, 1597, they are described " as her privie letters

written and subscrivit with her awin hand." Haynes, 454. Good. ii. 64. In the act of parliament, passed on the 15th of the same month, they are described as "her privie letters written halelie with her awin hand." Good. ib. 67. This diversity of description has been considered as a strong presumption of forgery. The manner in which Mr. Hume accounts for this is natural and plausible, vol. v. p. 498. And several ingenious remarks, tending to confirm his observations, are made in a pamphlet lately published, entitled, "Miscellaneous Remarks on the Inquiry into the Evidence against Mary Queen of Scots." To what they have observed it may be added, that the original act of secret council does not now exist; we have only a copy of it found among Cecil's papers, and the transcriber of it has been manifestly so ignorant, or so careless, that an argument founded entirely upon the supposition of his accuracy is of little force. Several errors into which he has fallen, we are enabled to point out, by comparing his copy of the act of secret council with the act of parliament passed in consequence of it.— The former contains a petition to parliament; in the latter the real petition is resumed *verbatim*, and converted into a law. In the copy, the Queen's marriage with Bothwell is called "a priveit marriage," which it certainly was not; for it was celebrated, after proclamation of banns, in St. Giles's church three several days, and with public solemnity; but the act is denominated, "ane pretendit marriage," which is the proper description of it, according to the ideas of the party. In the copy, the Queen is said to be "so thrall and *bludy* affectionat to the privat appetite of the tyran," which is nonsense, but in the act it is "blindly affectionat." In the copy it is said "all nobill and virtuous men abhorring their *traine* and company." In the act, "their tyrannie and companie," which is evidently the true reading, as the other has either no meaning, or is a mere tautology. 2. The other proof of the forgery of the letters is founded upon the impossibility of reconciling the account, given of the time when, and the places from which, the letters are supposed to have been written, with what is certainly known concerning the Queen's motions. According to the paper published, Anders. ii. 269, which has been called Murray's Diary, and which is formed upon the authority of the letters, Mary set out from Edinburgh to Glasgow, January 21, 1567; she arrived there on the 23d; left that place on the 27th; she, together with the King, reached Linlithgow on the 28th, staid in that town only one night, and returned to Edinburgh before the end of the month. But, according to Mr. Goodall, the Queen did not leave Edinburgh until Friday, January 24th; as she staid a night at Callendar, she could not reach Glasgow sooner than the evening of Saturday the 25th; and she returned to Linlithgow on Tuesday the 28th. By consequence, the first letter, which supposes the Queen to have been at least four days in Glasgow, as well as the second letter, which bears date at Glasgow, *Saturday morning*, whereas she did not arrive there until the evening, must be forgeries. That the Queen did not set out for Edinburgh until the 24th of January, it is evident (as he contends) from the public records, which contain a *Precept of a confirmation of a life-rent* by James Boyd to Margaret Chalmers, granted by the

E 5

Queen, on the 24th of January, at Edinburgh ; and likewise a letter of the Queen's, dated at Edinburgh on the same day, appointing James Inglis tailor to the Prince her son. That the King and Queen had returned to Linlithgow on the 28th, appears from a deed, in which they appoint Andrew Ferrier keeper of their palace there, dated at Linlithgow, Jan. 28. Good i. 118.

This has been represented to be not only a convincing, but a legal proof of the forgery of the letters said to have been written by Mary ; but how far it falls short of this will appear from the following considerations :

1. It is evident, from a declaration or confession made by the Bishop of Ross, that before the conferences at York, which were opened in the beginning of October, 1568, Mary had, by an artifice of Maitland's, got into her hands a copy of those letters which her subjects accused her of having written to Bothwell.   Brown's Trial of the Duke of Norfolk, 31, 36.   It is highly probable that the Bishop of Ross had seen the letters before he wrote the defence of Queen Mary's honour in the year 1570.   They were published to all the world, together with Buchanan's Detection, A. D. 1571.   Now, if they had contained an error so gross, and at that time so obvious to discovery, as the supposing the Queen to have passed several days at Glasgow, while she was really at Edinburgh ; had they contained a letter dated at Glasgow, Saturday morning, though she did not arrive there till the evening ; is it possible that she herself, who knew her own motions, or the able and zealous advocates who appeared for her in that age, should not have published and exposed this contradiction, and, by so doing, have blasted at once the credit of such an imposture ?   In disquisitions which are naturally abstruse and intricate, the ingenuity of the latest author may discover many things which have escaped the attention, or baffled the sagacity, of those who have formerly considered the same subject.   But when a matter of fact lay so obvious to view, the circumstance of its being unobserved by the Queen herself, or by any of her adherents, is almost a demonstration that there is some mistake or fallacy in our author's arguments.   So far are any either of our historians or of Mary's defenders from calling in question the common account concerning the time of the Queen's setting out to Glasgow, and her returning from it, that there is not the least appearance of any difference among them with regard to this point.   But farther,

2. Those papers in the public records, on which our author rests the proof of his assertion concerning the Queen's motions, are not the originals subscribed by the Queen, but copies only, or translations of copies of those originals.   It is not necessary, nor would it be very easy, to render this intelligible to persons unacquainted with the forms of law in Scotland ; but every Scotsman conversant in business will understand me when I say that the precept of confirmation of the life rent to Boyd is only a Latin copy or note of a precept, which was sealed with the privy seal, on a warrant from the signet office, proceeding on a signature which bore date at Edinburgh on the 24th of January ; and that the deed in favour of James Inglis is the copy of a letter, sealed with the privy seal, proceeding on a signature which bore date at Edinburgh, January 24.   From all this we may argue, with some degree of reason, that a proof

founded on papers which are so many removes distant from the originals, cannot but be very lame and uncertain.

3. At that time all public papers were issued in the name both of the King and the Queen; by law, the King's subscription was no less requisite to any paper than the Queen's; and therefore, unless the original signatures be produced, in order to ascertain the particular day when each of them signed, or to prove that it was signed only by one of them, the legal proof arising from these papers would be, that both the King and Queen signed them at Edinburgh on the 24th of January.

4. The dates of the warrants or precepts issued by the sovereign in that age seem to have been in a great measure arbitrary, and affixed at the pleasure of the writer; and of consequence, these dates were seldom accurate, are often false, and can never be relied upon. This abuse became so frequent, and was found to be so pernicious, that an act of parliament, A.D. 1592, declared the fixing a false date to a signature to be high treason.

5. There still remain, in the public records, a great number of papers, which prove the necessity of this law, as well as the fallacy of our author's arguments. And though it be no easy matter, at the distance of two centuries, to prove any particular date to be false, yet surprising instances of this kind shall be produced. Nothing is more certain from history, than that the King was at Glasgow 24th January, 1567; and yet the record of signatures from 1565 to 1582, fol. 16th, contains the copy of a signature to Archibald Edmonston, said to have been subscribed by *our sovereign*, i. e. the King and Queen, at Edinburgh, January 24th, 1597; so that if we were to rely implicitly upon the dates in the records of that age, or to hold our author's argument to be good, it would prove that not only the Queen, but the King too was at Edinburgh on the 24th of January.

It appears, from an original letter of the Bishop of Ross, that on the 25th of October, 1566, Mary lay at the point of death; Keith, App. 134; and yet a deed is to be found in the public records, which bears that it was signed by the Queen that day. Privy seal, lib. 35. fol. 89. *Ouchterlony.*

Bothwell seized the Queen as she returned from Stirling, April 24, 1567, and (according to her own account) conducted her to Dunbar with all diligence. And. i. 95. But our author, relying on the dates of some papers which he found in the records, supposes that Bothwell allowed her to stop at Edinburgh, and to transact business there. Nothing can be more improbable than this supposition. We may, therefore, rank the date of the deed to *Wright*, Privy seal, lib. 36. fol. 43, and which is mentioned by our author, vol. i. 124, among the instances of the false dates of papers which were issued in the ordinary course of business in that age. Our author has mistaken the date of the other papers to Forbes, ibid. it is signed April 14th, not April 24th.

If there be any point agreed upon in Mary's history, it is, that she remained at Dunbar from the time that Bothwell carried her thither, till she returned to Edinburgh along with him in the beginning of May. Our author himself allows that she resided twelve days there, vol. i. 367. Now, though there are deeds in the records which bear that they were signed by the Queen at Dunbar during that time, yet there are others which bear that they were signed at Edinburgh, *c. g.* there is one at Edinburgh, April 27th, Privy seal, lib. 36. fol. 97. There are others said to be signed at Dunbar on that day. Lib. 31. Chart. No. 524. 526. Ib. lib. 32. No. 154. 157. There are some signed at Dunbar, April 28th. Others at Edinburgh, April 30th, lib. 32. Chart. No. 492. Others at Dunbar, May 1st. Id. ibid. No. 158. These different charters suppose the Queen to have made so many, unknown, improbable, and inconsistent journies, that they afford the clearest demonstration that the dates in these records ought not to to be depended on.

This becomes more evident from the date of the charter said to be signed April 27th, which happened that year to be on a Sunday, which was not, at that time, a day of business in Scotland, as appears from the books of *sederunt*, then kept by the lords of session.

From this short review of our author's proof of the forgery of the letters to Bothwell, it is evident, that his arguments are far from amounting to demonstration.

Another argument against the genuineness of these letters is founded on the style and composition, which are said to be altogether unworthy of the Queen, and unlike her real productions. It is plain, both from the great accuracy of composition in most of Mary's letters, and even from her solicitude to write them in a fair hand, that she valued herself on those accomplishments, and was desirous of being esteemed an elegant writer. But when she wrote at any time in a hurry, then many marks of inaccuracy appear. A remarkable instance of this may be found in a paper published, Good. ii. 301. Mary's letters to Bothwell were written in the utmost hurry; and yet under all the disadvantages of a translation, they are not destitute either of spirit or of energy. The manner in which she expresses her love to Bothwell has been pronounced indecent and even shocking. But Mary's temper led her to warm expressions of her regard; those refinements of delicacy, which now appear in all the commerce between the sexes, were in that age but little known, even among persons of the highest rank. Among the Earl of Hardwicke's papers, there is a series of letters, from Mary to the Duke of Norfolk, copied from the Harleian library, p. 37. b. 9. fol. 88, in which Mary declares her love to that nobleman in language which would now be reckoned extremely indelicate. Hard. State Papers, i. 189. &c.

Some of Mary's letters to Bothwell were written before the murder of her husband; some of them after that event, and before her marriage to Bothwell. Those which are prior to the death of her husband abound with the fondest expressions of her love to Bothwell, and excite something more than a suspicion that their familiarity had been extremely criminal. We find in them, too, some dark expressions, which her enemies employed to prove that she was no stranger to the schemes which were formed against her husband's life. Of this kind are the following passages: "Alace! I never dissavit ony body; but I remit me altogidder to zour will. Send me advertisement quhat I sall do, and quhatsaever thing come thereof, I sall obey zow. Advise to with zourself, gif ze can find out ony mair secret inventioun by medicine, for he suld tak medicine and the bath at Craigmillar." Good ii. 22. "See not hir quhais fenzeit teiris suld not be sa meikle praisit and estemit, as the trew and faithfull travellis quhilk I sustene for to merit hir place. For obtaining of the quhilk, againis my natural, I betrayis thame that may impesche me. God forgive me," &c. Ibid. 27. "I have walkit later thairup, than I wald have done, gif it had not been to draw something out of him, quhilk this berer will schaw zow, quhilk is the fairest commodity that can be offerit to zour affairs." Ibid. 32. From the letters posterior to the death of her husband, it is evident that the scheme of Bothwell's seizing Mary by force, and carrying her along with him, was contrived in concert with herself, and with her approbation.

With respect to the sonnets, Sir David Dalrymple has proved clearly that they must have been written after the murder of the King and prior to Mary's marriage with Bothwell. But as hardly any part of my narrative is founded upon what is contained in the sonnets, and as in this Dissertation I have been constrained to dwell longer upon minute and verbal criticisms than may be interesting or agreeable to many of my readers, I shall rest satisfied with referring, for information concerning every particular relative to the sonnets, to *Remarks on the History of Scotland*, Chap. XI.

Having thus stated the proof on both sides; having examined at so great a length the different systems with regard to the facts in controversy; it may be expected that I should now pronounce sentence. In my opinion, there are only two conclusions, which can be drawn from the facts which have been enumerated.

One, that Bothwell, prompted by his ambition or love, encouraged by the Queen's known aversion to her husband, and presuming on her attachment to himself, struck the blow without having concerted with her the manner or circumstances of perpetrating that crime. That Mary, instead of testifying much indignation at the deed, or discovering any resentment against Bothwell, who was accused of having committed it, continued to load him with marks of her regard, conducted his trial in such a manner as rendered it impossible to discover his guilt, and soon after, in opposition to all the maxims of decency or of prudence, voluntarily agreed to a marriage with him, which every consideration should have induced her to detest. By this verdict, Mary is not pronounced guilty of having contrived the murder of her husband, or even of having previously given her consent to his death ; but she is not acquitted of having discovered her approbation of the deed, by her behaviour towards him who was the author of it.

The other conclusion is that which Murray and his adherents laboured to establish, " That James, sometymme Earl of Bothwile, was the chiefe executor of the horribill and unworthy murder, perpetrat in the person of umquhile King Henry of gude memory, fader to our soveraine lord, and the Queenis lauchfull husband ; sa was she of the foreknowledge, counsall, devise, perswadar and command of the said murder to be done." Good. ii. 207.

Which of these conclusions is most agreeable to the evidence that has been produced, I leave my readers to determine.

APPENDIX.

No. I. (p. 116.)

A MEMORIAL *of certain Points meet for the restoring the Realm of* SCOTLAND *to the antient Weale.*

[5th August, 1559.   Cotton Lib. Cal. B. x. fol. 17.   From a copy in Secretary Cecil's hand.]

IMPRIMIS, it is to be noted that the best worldly felicity that Scotland can have is either to continue in a perpetual peace with the kingdom of England, or to be made one monarchy with England, as they both make but one island, divided from the rest of the world.

If the first is sought, that is, to be in perpetual peace with England, then must it necessarily be provided that Scotland be not so subject to the appointments of France as is presently, which, being an antient enemy to England, seeketh always to make Scotland an instrument to exercise thereby their malice upon England, and to make a footstool thereof to look over England as they may.

Therefore, when Scotland shall come into the hands of a mere Scottish man in blood, then may there be hope of such accord; but as long as it is at the commandment of the French, there is no hope to have accord long betwixt these two realms.

Therefore, seeing it is at the French King's commandment by reason of his wife, it is to be considered for the weale of Scotland, that until she have children, and during her absence out of the realm, the next heirs to the crown, being the house of the Hamiltons, should have regard hereto, and to see that neither the crown he imposed nor wasted; and, on the other side, the nobility and commonalty ought to force that the laws and the old customs of the realm be not altered, neither that the country be not impoverished by taxes, imprest, or new imposts, after the manner of France; for provision wherein, both by the law of God and man, the French King and his wife may be moved to reform their misgovernance of the land.

And for this purpose it were good that the nobility and commons joined with the next heir of the crown, do seek due reformation of such great abuses as tend to the ruin of their country, which must be done before the French grow too strong and insolent.

First, That it may be provided by the consent of the three estates of the land, that the land may be free from all idolatry like as England is; for justification whereof, if any free general council may be had where the Pope of Rome have not the seat of judgment, they may offer to show their cause to be most agreeable to Christ's religion.

Next, To provide that Scotland might be governed, in all rules and offices, by the ancient blood of the realm, without either captains, lieutenants, or soldiers, as all other Princes govern their countries, and especially that the forts might be in the hands of mere Scottish men.

Thirdly, That they might never be occasioned to enter into wars against England, except England should give the first cause to Scotland.

Fourthly, That no nobleman of Scotland should receive pension of France, except it were whilst he did serve in France, for otherwise thereby the French would shortly corrupt many to betray their own country.

Fiftly, That no office, abbey, living, or commodity, be given to any but mere Scottish men, by the assent of the three estates of the realm.

Sixthly, That there be a council in Scotland appointed in the Queen's absence, to govern the whole realm, and in those cases not to be directed by the French.

Seventhly, That it be by the said three estates appointed how the Queen's revenue of the realm shall be expended, how much the Queen shall have for her portion and estate during her absence, how much shall be limited to the governance and defence of the realm, how much yearly appointed to be kept in treasure.

In these and such like points, if the French King and the Queen be found unwilling, and will withstand these provisions for the weale of the land, then hath the three estates of the realm authority, forwith, to intimte to the said King and Queen their humble requests; and if the same be not effectly granted, then humbly they may commit the governance thereof to the next heir of the crown, binding the same also to observe the laws and ancient rights of the realm.

Finally, If the Queen shall be unwilling to this, as it is likely she will, in respect of the greedy and tyrannous affection of France, then it is apparent that Almighty God is pleased to transfer from her the rule of the kingdom for the weal of it, and this time must be used with great circumspection to avoid the decepts and tromperies of the French.

And then may the realm of Scotland consider, being once made free, what means may be devised by God's goodness to accord the two realms to endure for time to come at the pleasure of Almighty God, in whose hands the hearts of all Princes be.

No. II.   (p. 120.)

A Letter of Maitland of Lethington's, thus directed:

To my loving friend James. Be this delivered at London.

[20th January, 1559-60. Cott. Lib. Cal. B. ix. From the original in his own hand.]

I understand by the last letter I received from yow, that discoursing

with zour oountrymen upon the matter of Scotland, and comoditeys
may ensew to that realm hereafter, giff ze presently assist ws with
zour forces, ze find a nombre of the contrary advise, doubting that
we sall not at length be found trusty friends, nor mean to contynew
iu constant ametye, albeit we promise, but only for avoyding the
present danger make zow to serve our turne, and after being delivered, becum enemies as of before. For profe quhareof, they
alledge things that have past betwixt ws heretofore, and a few pre-
sumptiones tending to the sam end, all grounded upon mistrusts;
quhilks, at the first sicht, have some shewe of apparence; gif men
wey not the circumstances of the matter; but gif they will confer
the tyme past with the present, consider the nature of this caus,
and estate of our contrey, I doubt not but jugment sal be able to
banish mistrust. And first, I wad wish ze should examyne the
cause off the old inmitye betwixt the realms of England and Scotland, and quhat moved our ancestours to enter into ligue with the
Frenche; quhilks by our storeys and registres of antiquiteys appear
to be these. The princes of England, some tyme, alledging a certain
kynde of soverauntye over this realm; some tyme upon hye courage,
or incited by incursions off our bordourares, and semblable occasions, mony tymes enterprised the conquest of ws, and sa far furth
preist it by force of arms, that we wer dryven to great extramiteys,
by loss of our Princes, our noblemen, and a good part of our contrey, sa that experience taught ws that our owne strength was
scarse sufficient to withstand the force of England. The Frenche
zour auncient enemyes, considering well how nature had sa placed
ws in a iland with zow, that na nation was able sa to annoye England as we being enemyes, soucht to joine ws to theym in ligue,
tending by that meane to detourne zour armyes from the invasion
of France, and occupy zow in the defence off zour country at hame,
offering for that effect to bestowe some charges upon ws, and for
compassing off theyr purpos, choysed a tyme to propone the matter, quhen the fresche memory off injuris lately receaved at zour
hands, was sa depely prented on our hartes, that all our myndes
were occupied how to be revenged, and arme ourselfes with the
powar off a forayne Prince against zour enterprises thereafter.

This wes the beginning off our confederacy with France. At
quhilk time, our cronicles maks mention, that some off the wysest
foresaw the perril, and small frute should redound to ws thereof at
lenth: zit had affection sa blinded jugement, that the advise of
the maist part owercame the best. The maist part of all querells
betwixt ws since that tyme, at least quhen the provocation came on
our syde, hes ever fallen out by theyr procurement rather than any
one caus off our selfes: and quhensaever we brack the peace, it come
partly by theyr intysements, partly to eschew the conquest intended
by that realm. But now hes God's providence sa altered the case,
zea changed it to the plat contrary, that now hes the Frenche taken
zour place, and we off very jugement, becum desyrous to have
zow in theyr rowme. Our eyes are opened, we espy how uncareful
they have been of our weile at all tymes, how they made ws ever to
serve theyr turne, drew us in maist dangerous weys for theyr commodite, and nevertheless wad not styck, oft tymes, against the natour of the ligue, to contrak peace, leaving ws in weyr. We see

that their support, off late zeres, wes not grantit for any affection they bare to ws, for pytie they had off our estate, for recompense off the lyke friendship schawin to them in tyme off theyr afflictiones, but for ambition, and insaciable cupidite to reygne, and to mak Scotland ane accessory to the crown of France. This was na friendly office, but mercenary, craving hyre farre exceeding the proportion of theyr deserving: a hale realm for the defence of a part. We see theym manifestly attempt the thing we suspected off zow; we feared ze ment the conquest off Scotland, and they are planely fallen to that work; we hated zow for doubt we had ze ment evill towards ws, and sall we love theym, quhilks bearing the name off frends, go about to bring ws in maist vile servitude? Gif by zour frendly support at this tyme, ze sall declare that not only sute ze not the ruyne off our country, but will preserve the libertie thereof from conquest by strangeares, sall not the occasion off all inimitie with zow, and ligne with theym, be taken away? The causes being removed, how sall the effectes remane? The fear of conquest made ws to hate zow and love theym, the cais changed, quhen we see them planely attempt conquest, and zow schaw us friendship, sall we not hate them, and favour zow? Gif we have schawne sa great constance, continuing sa mony zeares in amity with theym, off quhome we had sa small commodite, quhat sall move us to breake with zow, that off all nationes may do ws greatest plesour?

But ze will say, this mater may be reconcyled and then frends as off before. I think weill peace is the end of all weyr, but off this ze may be assured, we will never sa far trust that reconciliation, that we wil be content to forgo the ametye of England, nor do any thing may bring ws in suspicion with zow. Giff we wold at any tyme to please theym, break with zow, should we not, besydes the losse off estimation and discrediting of ourselfes, perpetually expone our common weill to a maist manifest danger, and becum a pray to theyr tyranny? Quhais aid could we implore, being destitute of zour friendship, giff they off new wald attempt theyr formar enter-prise? Quhat nation myght help ws giff they wald, or wald giff they might? and it is lyke eneuch, they will not stick hereafter to tak theyr time off ws, quhen displesour and grudge hes taken depe rute on baith sydes, seeing ambition has sa impyrit ower theyr reason, that before we had ever done any thing myght offend theym, but by the contrary pleased theym by right and wrang, they did not stick to attempte the subversion of our hale state. I wald ze should not esteeme ws sa barayne of jugement, that we cannot forese our awne perril; or sa foolische, that we will not study by all gode means to entertayne that thing may be our safetye; quhilk consistes all in the relaying of zour friendships. I pray zow con-sider in lyke case, when, in the days of zour Princes off maist noble memory King Henry the VIII and King Edward the VI. meanes wer opened off amytye betwixt baith realms; was not at all tymes the difference of religion the onley stay they were not embraced? Did not the craft of our clergy and power of theyr adherents subvert the devises of the better sort? But now has God off his mercy re-moved that block furth of the way; now is not theyr practise lyke to tak place any mare, when we ar comme to a conformity off doc-trine, and profes the same religion with zow, quhilk I take to be the straytest knot off amitye can be devised. Giff it may be alledged that some off our countrymen, at ony tyme violated theyr promis? giff ze liff to way the circumstances, ze sall fynd the promis is rather brought on by necessite, after a great owerthraw off our men, then comme off fre will, and tending ever to our great incommodite and decay off our haill state, at leist sa taken. But in this case, sall the preservation off our libertie be inseperably joined with the keping off promesse, and the violation off our fayth cast ws in maist miserable servitude. Sa that giff neyther the feare off God, reverence of man, religion, othe, promise, nor warldly honestye wes sufficient to bynd ws, yet sall the zeale off our native countrey, the maintenance off our owne state, the safety of our wyffes and childrene from slavery, compell ws to kepe promisse. I am assured, it is trewly and sincerely ment on our part to continew in perpetual ametye with zow, it sall be uttered by our proceedings. Giff ze be as desirous of it as we ar, assurances may be devysed, quharby all partyes will be out of doubte. There be gode meanes to do it, fit instruments for the purpos, tyme serves weill, the inhabitants of baith realms wish it, God hes wrought in the people's hartes on bayth parties a certaine still agreement upon it, never did, at any tyme, so mony things concurre at ones to knyt it up, the disposition off a few, quahis harts are in Godis hands, may mak up the hale. I hope he quha hes begun this work, and mainteyned it quhile now, by the expectation of man, sale perfyte it.

I pray zow, let not zour men dryve time in consultation, quhether ze sall support ws or no. Seying the matter speaketh for itself, that ze mon take upon zow the defence off our caus, giff ze have any respect for zour awne weill. Their preparatives in France, and levying of men in Germany (quheyroff I am lately advertised). ar not altogyder ordeyned for us, ze at the mark they shote at; they seke our realme, but for ane entrey to zours. Giff they should directly schaw hostilite to zow, they knaw zo wald mak redy for theyme, therefor they do, by indirect meanes, to blind zow, the thing they dare not as zit planely attempte. They seme to invade us to th' end, that having assembled theyr hale forces sa nere zour bordours, they may unlok it to attack zow: It is ane of their ald fetches, making a schew to one place, to lyght on ane other. Remember how covertly zour places about Boulougne were assaizeit, and carried away, ze being in peace as now. How the enterprise of Calais was fynely dissembled, I think ze have not sa sone forgotten. Beware of the third, prevent theyr policy by prudence. Giff ze se not the lyke disposition presently in theym, ze se nathing. It is a gross ignorance to misknaw, what all nations planely speks off. Tak heed ze say not hereafter, "Had I wist;" ane uncomely sentence to procede off a wyse man's mouth. That is onwares chanced on to zow, quhilk zow commonly wissed, that this countrey might be divorsed from the Frensche, and is sa comme to pass as was maist expedient for zow. For giff by your intysement we had taken the mater in hand, ze myght have suspected we would have been ontrusty frends, and na langer continued stedfaste, then perril had appeared. But now, quhen off our self, we have conceyved the hatred, provoked by private injuries, and that theyr evil dealing with ws hes deserved our inimitye, let no man doubt but they sall fynd ws ennemyes in ernest, that sa ungently hes demeyned our countrey, and at quhais hands we look for nathing but all extremitye, giff ever they may get the upper hand. Let not this occasion, sa happely offered, escape zow: giff ze do, neglecting the present opportunite, and hoping to have ever gode luke, comme sleaping upon zow, it is to be feared zour enemye waxe so great, and sa strang, that afterwards quhen ze wald, ze sall not be able to put him down; and then, to zour smart, after the tyme ze will acknowledge zour error. Ze have felt, by experience, quhat harme cometh off oversight, and trusting to zour enemyes promesse. We offer zow the occasion, quheyrby zour former losses may be repayred. Quhilk gif ze let over slyde, suffering ws to be owerrun, quha then, I pray zow, sall stay the Frensche, that they sal not invade zow in zour own boundes, sic is their lust to reygne, that they can neyther be content with theyr fortune present, nor rest and be satisfied when they have gode luck, but will still follow on having in theyr awne brayne conceaved the image of sa great a conquest, quhat think ye sal be the end? Is ther any of sa small jugement, that he doth not foresee already, that theyr hail force sall then be bent against zow?

It sal not be amis, to consider in quhat case the Frensche be presently. Theyr estate is not always sa calme at hame as every man thinketh. And trewly it wes not theyr great redines for weyr made theym to tak this mater on hand, at this tyme, but rather a vayne trust in their awne policy, thinking to have found na resistance, theyr opinion hes deceaved theym, and that makes them now amased. The estates off the empire (as I heare) has suted restitution off th' imperial towns Metz, Toull, and Verdun, quhilk may grow to some besynes; and all thing is not a calme within theyr awne countrey, the les fit they be presently for weyr, the mare oportune esteme ye the tyme for zow. Giff the lyke occasion wer offered to the Frensche against zow, wey, how gladly would they embrace it. Are ze not eschamed of zour sleuth, to spare theym that hes already compassed zour destruction, giff they wer able? Consider with zour self quhilk is to be choysed? To weyr against them out with zour realme or within? Giff quhill ze sleape, we sal be overthrowne, then sall they not fayle to fute zow in zour owne countrey, and use ws as a fote stole to overloke zow. But some will say, perhaps, they meane it not. It is foly to think they wald not giff they wer able, quhen before hand they stick not to giff zour armes, and usurpe the style of zour crown. Then quhat difference there is to camp within zowr awne bounds or without, it is manifest. Giff twa armyes should camp in your countrey, but a moneth; albeit ye receaved na other harme, zit should zowr losse be greatar, nor all the charge ze will nede to bestow on our support will draw to, besydes the dishonour.

Let not men, that eyther lack gode advise, or ar not for particular respects weill affected to the caus, move zow to subtract zour helping hand, by alleging things not apparent, for that they be possible.

It is not, I grant, unpossible that we may receave conditiones of peace; but I see little likelyhode that our ennemyes will offer ws sik as will remove all mistrust, and giff we wald have accepted others, the mater had bene lang or now compounded. Let zow nat

be moved for that they terme ws rebelles and diffames our just
querell with the name of conspiracy against our soverayne. It is
Hir Hyenes ryght we manctayne. It is the liberty off hir realme
we study to preserve with the hazard of our lyves. We are not
(God knaweth) come to this poynt for wantones, as men impacient
of rewll, or willing to schake off the zoke off government, but ar
drawne to it by necessite, to avoyde the tyranny of strangeares,
seaking to defraude ws off lawful government. Giff we should
suffer strangeares to plant themselffes peaceably in all the strenthes
of our realme, fortify the sey-portes, and maist important places,
as ane entre to a plain conquest, now in the minorite of our
soverane, beyng furth of the realme, should we not be thought
oncareful off the common weill, betrayares of our native countrey,
and evill subjects to Her Majeste? Quhat other opinion could
sche have off ws? Might she not justly hereafter call ws to ac-
compt, as negligent ministeres? Giff strangeres should be thus
suffered to broke the chefe offices, beare the hail rewll, alter and
pervert our lawes and liberty at theyr plesour? myght not the
people esteem our noblemen unworthy the place of counsalours?
We mean na wyse to subtrak our obedience from our soverane, to
defraud Hir Hyenes off her dew reverence, rent and revenues off
hir crown. We seke nathing but that Scotland may remane, as of
before, a fre realme, rewlit by Hir Hyenes and hir ministeres, borne
men of the sam; and that the succession of the crown may remane
with the lawful blode.

I wald not ze sould not sa lyttill esteme the friendship of Scotland, that ze juged it not worthy to be embraced. It sall be na
small commodite for zow to be delivered off the annoyance of so
neir a nyghbour, quhais inimitye may more trouble zow, then off
any other nation albeit twyss as puissant, not lyeng dry marche
with zow. Besydes that ze sall not nede to feare the invasion of
any prince lackyng the commodite to invade zow by land, on our
hand. Consider quhat superfluous charges ze bestowe on the
fortification and keping of Barwick : quhilk ze many reduce to a
mean sowme, having ws to frendes. The reamle of Ireland being
of natour a gode and fertill countrey, by reason of the continewalld
unquietnes and lak of policy, ze knaw to be rather a burthen unto
zow than great advantage; and giff it were peaceable may be very
commodious. For pacification quhayroff, it is not onknowne to
zow quhat service we are abill do do. Refuse not theyr com-
moditeys, besides mony ma quhen they are offred. Quhilks albeit
I study not to amplify and dilate, yet is na other countrey able to
zow the lyke, and are the rather to be embraced, for that zour
auncestors, by all meanes, maist carnestly suted our amity, and yet
it was not theyr hap to come by it. The mater hes almaist carryed
me beyond the boundes off a lettre, quharfor, I will leave to trouble
zow after I have geven you this note. I wald wiss that ze, and
they that ar learned, sould rede the twa former orations of
Demosthenes, called Olynthiacæ, and considere quhat counsall that
wyse oratour gave to the Athenians, his countrymen, in a lyke
case ; quhilk hes so great affinite with this cause of ours, that every
word thereoff myght be applyed to our purpos. There may ze
learne of him quhat advise is to be followed, when your nyghbours

hous is on fyre. Thus I bid zow hartely farewell. From Sant Andrews, the 20th of January, 1559.

No. III. (p. 124.)

Part of a Letter from Thomas Randolph to Sir William Cecil, from the Camp before Leith, 29th of April, 1560.

[An original in the Paper Office.]

I WILL only, for this time, discharge myself of my promise to the Earl of Huntly, who so desyreth to be recommended to you, as one who, with all his heart, favoureth this cause, to the uttermost of his power. Half the words that come out of his mouth were able to persuade an unexperienced man to speak farther in his behalf, than I dare be bold to write. I leave it to Your Honour to judge of him, as of a man not unknown to you, and will myself always measure my thoughts as he shall deserve to be spoken of. With much difficulty, and great persuasion, he hath subscribed with the rest of the lords to join with them in this action: whatsomever he can invent to the furtherance of this cause; he hath promised to do with solemn protestation and many words; he trusteth to adjoin many to this cause; and saith, surely that no man shall lie where he taketh part. He hath this day subscribed a bond between England and this nation; he saith, that there was never thing that liked him better.

No. IV. (p. 131.)

Randolph to Cecil, 10th August, 1560. From Edinburgh.

[An original in the Paper Office.]

SINCE the 29th of July, at what time I wrote last to Your Honour, I have heard of nothing worth the reporting. At this present it may please you to know, that the most part of the nobles are here arrived, as Your Honour shall receive their names in writing. The Earl of Huntly excuseth himself by an infirmity in his leg. His lieutenant for this time is the Lord of Lidington, chosen speaker of the parliament, or harangue-maker as these men term it. The first day of their sitting in parliament will be on Thursday next. Hitherto as many as have been present of the lords have communed and devised of certain heads then to be propounded, as, who shall be sent into France, who into England. It is much easier to find them than the other. It seemeth almost to be resolved upon that for England the Master of Maxwell and Laird of Lidington. For France, Pittarow and the justice clerk. Also they have consulted whom they think meetest to name for the XXIV.; of the which the XII. counsellors must be chosen. They intend very shortly to send away Dingwall the herald into France, with the names of those they shall chuse; and also to require the King and Queen's consent unto this parliament. They have devised how to have the contract with England confirmed by authority of parliament; how also to have the articles of the agreement between them and their King and Queen ratified. These things yet have only been had in

communication. For the confirmation of the contract with England, I have no doubt; for that I hear many men very well like
the same, as the Earl of Athol, the Earl of Sutherland, the L.
Glamis, who dined yesterday with the L. James. The Lord James
requested me this present day to bring the contract unto him. I
intend, also, this day, to speak unto the L. Gray, in our L. Gray's
name, for that he promised in my hearing to subscribe, and then
presently would have done it, if the contract could have been had.
For the more assurance against all convenients, I would, besides
that, that I trust it shall be ratified in parliament, that every nobleman in Scotland had put his hand and set his seal, which may
always remain as a notable monument, tho' the act of parliament
be hereafter disannulled. If it might, therefore, stand with your
advice, that the lords might be written unto, now that they are
here present, to that effect, or that I might receive from Your
Honr, some earnest charge to travel herein, I doubt not but it
would serve to good purpose. If it might be also known with what
substantial and efficacious words or charge you desire to have it
confirmed, I think no great difficulty would he made. The Earl
Marshal has often been moved to subscribe, he useth mo delays than
men judged he would. His son told me yesterday, that he would
speak with me at leisure, so did also Drumlanrick; 1 know not to
what purpose: I have caused L. James to be the earnester with the
L. Marshal, for his authority's sake, when of late it was in consultation by what means it might be wrought, that the amity between
these two realms might be perpetual; and among diverse men's
opinion, one said that he knew of no other, but by making them
both one, and that in hope of that mo things were done than
would otherwise have ever been granted : the Earl of Argyll advised him earnestly to stick unto that, that he had promised that it
should pass his power and all the crafty knaves of his counsel (I am
bold to use unto Your H. his own words) to break so godly a purpose. This talk liked well the assisters, howsomever it pleased him
to whom it was spoken unto. The barons, who in time past have
been of the parliament, had yesterday a convention among themselves in the church, in very honest and quiet sort ; they thought
it good to require to be restored unto their ancient liberty, to have
voice in the parliament. They presented that day a bill unto the
lords to that effect, a copy whereof shall be sent as soon as it can
be had. It was answered unto gently, and taken in good part. It
was referred unto the Lords of the Articles, when they are chosen,
to resolve thereupon.—— *Here follows a long paragraph concerning
the fortifications of Dunbar, &c.*—— This present morning, *viz.* the
9th, I understood that the lords intended to be at the Parliament,
which caused me somewhat to stay my letter, to see what I could
hear or learn worth the reporting unto Your Honr. The lords, at
ten of the clock, assembled themselves at the palace, where the
Duke lieth; from whence they departed towards the Tolbooth, as
they were in dignity. Each one being set in his seat, in such order
as Your H. shall receive them in this scroll. The crown, the mace,
the sword, were laid in the Queen's seat. Silence being commanded,
the L. of Lidington began his oration. He excused his insuffici-
ency to occupy that place. He made a brief discourse of things

past, and of what necessity men were forced unto for the defence of their country, what remedy and support it pleased God to send them in the time of their necessity, how much they were bound heartily to acknowledge it, and to require it. He took away the persuasion that was in many men's mind that lay back, that misdeemed other things to be meant than was attempted. He advised all estates to lay all particulars apart, and to bend themselves wholly to the true service of God and of their country. He willed them to remember in what state it had been of long time for lack of government and exercise of justice. In the end, he exhorted them to mutual amity and hearty friendship, and to live with one another as members all of one body.——He prayed God long to maintain his peace and amity with all Princes, especially betwixt the realms of England and Scotland, in the fear of God, and so ended. The clerk of register immediately stood up, and asked them to what matter they would proceed: it was thought necessary that the articles of the peace should be confirmed with the common consent, for that it was thought necessary to send them away with speed into France, and to receive the ratification of them as soon as might be. The articles being read, were immediately agreed unto: a day was appointed to have certain of the nobles subscribe unto them, and to put to their seals, to be sent away by a herald, who shall also bring the ratification again with him. The barons, of whom I have above written, required an answer to their request; somewhat was said unto the contrary. The barons alleged for them custom and authority. It was in the end resolved, that there should be chosen six to join with the Lords of the Articles, and that if they, after good advisement, should find it right and necessary for the commonwealth, it should be ratified at this parliament for a perpetual law. The lords proceeded immediately hereupon to the chusing of the Lords of the Articles. The order is, that the lords spiritual chuse the temporal, and the temporal the spiritual, and the burgesses their own. There was chosen as in this other paper I have written. This being done, the lords departed and accompanied the Duke, all as far as the Bow (which is the gate going out of the high street), and many down into the palace where he lieth. The town all in armour, the trumpets sounding, and other music such as they have. Thus much I report unto Your Honour of that I did both hear and see. Other solemnities have not been used, saving in times long past the lords have had parliament robes, which are now with them wholly out of use.

The names of as many Earls and Lords spiritual and temporal as are assembled at this parliament:

The Duke of Chatelherault.

Earls.	Lords.	Lords Spiritual.
Arran.	Erskine.	St. Andrew's.
Argyll.	Ruthven.	Dunkell.
Athole.	Lindsey.	Athens.
Crawford.	Somerville.	The Bishop of the Isles.
Cassils.	Cathcart.	Abbots and Priors, I know
Marshall.	Hume.	not how many.

Morton.	Livingstone.
Glencairn.	Innermeth.
Sutherland.	Boyd.
Caithness.	Ogilvy.
Rothes.	Fleming.
Mouteith.	Glamis.
	Gray.
	Ochiltree.
	Gordon.

The Lords of the Articles.

Spiritual.	*Temporal.*	*Barons elected to be of the Articles.*
Athens.	The Duke.	Maxwell.
Isles.	Argyll.	Tillibardine.
Lord James.	Marshall.	Cunninghamhead.
Arbroath.	Athole.	Lochenvar.
Newbottle,	Morton.	Pittarrow.
Lindoris.	Glencairn.	Lundy.
Cowpar.	Ruthven.	Ten Provosts of the chief
Kinross.	Erskine.	towns, which also are
Kilwinning.	Boyd.	of the Articles.
	Lindsay.	

So that with the Subprior of St. Andrews, the whole is 36.

It were two long for me to rehearse particularly the disposition, and chiefly the affections of these men, that are at this time chosen Lords of the Articles. May it satisfy your Honour for this time to know that, by the common opinion of men, there was not a substantialler or more sufficient number of all sorts of men chosen in Scotland these many years, nor of whom men had greater hope of good to ensue. This present morning, viz. the 10th, the L. of Lidington made me privy unto your letter; he intendeth, as much as may be, to follow your advice. Some hard points there are. He himself is determined not to go into France. He allegeth many reasons, but speaketh least of that that moveth him most, which is the example of the last, that went on a more grateful message than he shall carry, and stood on other terms with their Prince than he doth, and yet Your Honour knoweth what the whole world judgeth.

Petition of the Lesser Barons to the Parliament held August, 1560.

(Inclosed in Randolph's letter to Cecil, 15th August, 1560.)

MY Lords, unto Your Lordships, humbly means and shows, we the Barons and Freeholders of this realm, your brethren in Christ. That, whereas the causes of true religion and common well of this realm, are, in this present parliament to be treated, ordered, and established to the glory of God, and maintenance of the commonwealth; and we being the greatest number in proportion where the said causes concern, and has been, and yet are ready to bear the greatest part of the charge thereuntil, as well in peace as in war, both with our bodies and with our goods; and seeing there is no place where we may do better service now than in general councils and parliaments, in giving our best advice and reason, vote and councill for the furtherance thereof, for the maintenance of virtue and punishment of vice, as use and custom had been of old by ancient acts of parliament observed in this realm; and whereby we understand that we ought to be heard to reason and vote in all causes concerning the commonwealth, as well in councils as in parliament; otherwise we think that whatsomever ordinances and statutes be made concerning us and our estate, we not being required and suffered to reason and vote at the making thereof, that the same should not oblige us to stand thereto. Thereof it will please Your Lordships to take consideration thereof, and of the charge born and to be born by us, since we are willing to serve truly to the common well of this realm, after our estate, that ye will, in this present parliament, and all consells where the common well of the realm is to be treated, take our advice, counsell and vote, so that, without the same, Your Lordships will suffer nothing to be passed and concluded in parliament or councils aforsaid; and that all acts of parliament, made in times past, concerning us, for our place and estate, and in our favour, be at this present parliament confirmed, approved, and ratified, and act of parliament made thereupon. And Your Lordship's answer humbly beseeches.

Of the success of this petition, the following account is given by Randolph ; Lett. to Cecil, 19 Aug. 1560. The matters concluded and past by common consent on Saturday last, in such solemn sort as the first day that they assembled, are these : First, that the barons, according to an old act of parliament, made in the time of James I. in the year of God, 1427, shall have free voice in parliament, this act passed without any contradiction.

No. V. (p. 135.)

A Letter of Thomas Randolph, the English Resident, to the Right Worshipful Sir William Cecil, Knt. Principal Secretary to the Queen's Majesty.

[9 Aug. 1561. Cott. Lib. B. 10. fo. 32.]

I HAVE received Your Honour's letters of the first of this month, written at Osyes in Essex : and also a letter unto the Lord James, from his kinsman St. Come out of France : in this they agree both that the Queen of Scotland is nothing changed of her purpose in home coming. I assure Your Honour that will be a stout adventure for a sick crased woman, that may be doubted as well what may happen unto her upon the seas, as also how heartily she may be received when she cometh to land of a great number, who are utterly persuaded that she intendeth their utter ruin, come when she will; the preparance is very small whensoever that she arrive, scarcely any man can be persuaded that she hath any such thought in her head. I have shown Your Honour's letter unto the Lord James, Lord Morton, Lord Lidington ; they wish as your Honour doth, that she might be stayed yet for a space, and if it were not for their obedience sake, some of them care not tho' they never saw her face. They travel what they can to prevent the wicked devices of these mischievous purposes of her ministers, but I fear

that that will always be found that *filij hujus seculi*, they do what
they can to stand with the religion, and to maintain amity with
their neighbours; they have also need to look unto themselves, for
their hazard is great, and that they see there is no remedy nor safety
for themselves, but to repose themselves upon the Queen's Majesty our
sovereign's favour and support.   Friends abroad they have none, nor
many in whom they may trust at home.   There are in mind shortly to
try what they may be assured at of the Queen's Majesty, and what they
may assuredly perform of that they intend to offer for their parties.
This the Queen of Scotland above all other things doubteth; this
she seeketh by all means to prevent; and hath caused St. Come, in
her name, earnestly to write to charge him that no such things be
attempted before her coming home: for that it is said that they
too already arrived here out of England for the purpose, what semblance somever the noblemen do make that they are grieved with
their Queen's refusal, that cometh far from their hearts.   They intend to expostulate with me hereupon.   I have my answer ready
enough for them.   If she thrust Englishmen all out of this country,
I doubt not but there will be some of her own that will bear us
some kindness.   Of me she shall be quit, so soon as it pleaseth the
Queen's Majesty, my mistress, no longer to use my service in this
place.   By such talk as I have of late had with the Lord James
and Lord of Lidington, I perceive that they are of mind that immediately of the next convention, I shall repair towards you with
their determinations and resolutions, in all purposes, wherein Your
Honour's advice is earnestly required, and shortly looked for.
Whatsomever I desire myself, I know my will ought to be subject
unto the Queen my sovereign's pleasure, but to content myself,
would God I were so happy as to serve Her Majesty in as mean a
state as ever poor gentleman did to be quit of this place; not that
I do in my heart wax weary of Her Majesty's service, but because
my time and years require some place of more repose and quietness
than I find in this country.   I doubt also my insufficience when
other troubles in this country arise, or ought shall be required of
me to the advancement of Her Majesty's service, that either my
will is not able to compass or my credit sufficient to work to that
effect, as perchance shall be looked for at my hands.   As Your
Honour hath been a means of my continuance in this room, so I
trust that I shall find that continual favour at your hands, that so
soon as it shall stand with the Queen's Majesty's pleasure, I may
give this place unto some far worthier than I am myself, and in the
mean season have my course directed by your good advice how I
may by my contrivance do some such service as may be agreeable
to Her Majesty's will and pleasure.

These few words I am bold to write unto Your Honour of myself.   For the rest, where that is wished that the lords will stoutly
continue yet for one month, I assure Your Honour that there is
yet nothing omitted of their old and accustomed manner of doing,
and seeing that they have brought that unto this point, and should
now prevail, they were unworthy of their lives.

I find not that they are purposed so to leave the matter.   I doubt
more her money than I do her fair words; and yet can I not conceive what great things can be wrought with forty thousand crowns,

and treasure of her own here I know there is no sure or ready means to get it. The Lord of Lidington leaveth nothing at this time unwritten, that he thinketh may be able to satisfye your desire, in knowledge of the present state of things here. Whatsomever cometh of that, he findeth it ever best that she come not ; but if she do come to let her know, at first, what she shall find, which is due obedience and willing service, if she embrace Christ, and desire to live in peace with her neighbours. By such letters as you have last received, Your Honour somewhat understandeth of Mr. Knox himself, and also of others, what is determined, he himself to abide the uttermost, and other never to leave him until God have taken his life, and thus together with what comfort somever it will please you to give him by your letters, that the Queen's Majesty doth not utterly condemn him, or at the least in that point, that he is so sore charged with by his own Queen, that Her Majesty will not allow her doing. I doubt not but it will be a great comfort unto him, and will content many others : his daily prayer is for the maintenance of unity with England, and that God will never suffer men to be so ungrate, as by any persuasion to run headlong unto the destruction of them that have saved their lives and restored their country to liberty. I leave farther, at this time, to trouble Your Honour, desiring God to send such an amity between these two realms that God may be glorified to them of this world.—At Edenborough, the 9th of August, 1561.

No. VI. (p. 140.)

A Letter of Queen Elizabeth to Queen Mary.[*]

[16th of Aug. 1561. Paper Office, from a copy.]

To the right excellent, right high, and mighty Princesse, our right dear and well-beloved sister and cousin the Queen of Scotland.

RIGHT excellent, right high, and mighty Princesse, our right dear and right well-beloved sister and cousin, we greet you well. The Lord of St. Cosme brought to us your letters, dated the 8th of this present at Abbeville, whereby ye signify that although by the answer brought to you by Monsieur Doyzell, ye might have had occasion to have entered into some doubt of our amity, yet after certain purposes passed betwixt you and our ambassador, you would assure us of your good meaning to live with us in amity, and for your purpose therein ye require us to give credit to the said St. Cosme. We have thereunto thought good to answer as followeth : The same St. Cosme hath made like declaration unto us on your part, for your excuse in not ratifying the treaty, as yourself made to our ambassador, and we have briefly answered to every the same points, as he can show you : and if he shall not so do, yet least in the mean season you might be induced to think that your reasons had satisfied us, somerally we assure you, that to our requests your answer cannot be reputed for a satisfaction. For we require no benefit of you, but that you will perform your promise

---

[*] This is the complete paper of which that industrious and impartial collector, Bishop Keith, has published a fragment, from what he calls his shattered MS. 154. note (a) 181.

whereunto you are bound by your seal and your hand, for the refusal whereof we see no reason alledged can serve. Neither covet we any thing, but that which is in your own power as Queen of Scotland, that which yourself in words and speech doth confess, that which your late husband's our good brother's ambassadors and you concluded, that which your own nobility and people were made privy unto, that which indeed made peace and quietness betwixt us, yea that without which no perfect amity can continue betwixt us, as, if it be indifferently weighed, we doubt not but ye will perceive, allow, and accomplish. Nevertheless, perceiving, by the report of the bringer, that you mean furthwith upon your coming home, to follow herein the advice of your council in Scotland, we are content to suspend our conceipt of all unkindness, and do assure you that we be fully resolved, upon this being performed, to unite a sure band of amity, and to live in neighbourhood with you as quietly, friendly, yea as assuredly in the knot of friendship, as we be in the knot of nature and blood. And herein we be so earnestly determined, that the world should see if the contrary should follow (which God forbid) the very occasion to be in you and not in us; as the story witnesseth like of the King your father, our uncle, with whom our father sought to have knitt a perpetual bond by inviting to come in this realm to York, of which matter we know there remain with us, and we think with you, sundry witnesses of our father's earnest good meaning, and of the error whereunto divers evil councillors induced your father; or, finally, where it seemeth that report hath been made unto you, that we had sent our admiral to the seas with our navy to empeache your passage, both your servants do well understand how false that is, knowing for a truth that we have not any more than two or three small barks upon the seas, to apprehend certain pirates, being thereto entreated, and almost compelled by the earnest complaint of the ambassador of our good brother the King of Spain, made of certaine Scottishmen haunting our seas as pirates, under pretence of letters of marque, of which matter also we earnestly require you, at your coming to your realme, to have some good consideration, and the rather for respect that ought to be betwixt your realme and the countries of us, of France, of Spain, and of the house of Burgundy. And so, right excellent, right high, and mighty Princess, we recommend us to you with most earnest request, not to neglect these our friendly and sisterly offers of friendship, which, before God, we mean and intend to accomplish. Given under our signet at Henyngham the 16th of August, in the third year of our reign.

No. VII. (p. 155.)

A Letter of Randolph to the Right Honourable Sir William Cecil, Knight, Principal Secretary to the Queen's Majesty.

[15th of May, 1563. Paper Office, from the original.]

Of late, until the arrival of Monsieur Le Croch, I had nothing worth the writing unto Your Honour. Before his coming we had so little to hint upon that we did nothing but pass our time in feasts, banquetting, masking, and running at the ring, and such like. He brought with him such a number of letters, and such

abundance of news, that, for the space of three days, we gave ourselves to nothing else but to reading of writings and hearing of
tales, many so truly reported that they might be compared to any
that ever Luciane did write *de veris narrationibus*. Among all his
tidings, for the most assured, I send this unto Your Honour as an
undoubted truth, which is, that the Cardinal of Lorraine, at his being with the Emperor, moved a marriage between his youngest son,
the Duke of Astruche, and this Queen; wherein he hath so far
travailed that it hath already come unto this point, that if she find
it good, the said Duke will out of hand send hither his ambassador,
and farther proceed to the consummation hereof, with as convenient
speed as may be; and to the intent her mind may be the better
known, Le Croch is sent unto her with this message from the
Cardinal, who hath promised unto the Emperor to have word again
before the end of May; and for this cause Le Croch is ready for his
departnre, and his letters writing both day and night. This Queen
being before advertised of his towardness, by many means hath
sought far off to know My Lord of Murray's mind herein, but would
never so plainly deal with him that he could learn what her meaning is or how she is bent. She useth no man's council but only
this man's that last arrived, and assuredly until the L. of Lidington's return she will do what she can to keep that secret; and because resolution in his absence cannot be taken, she will, for this
time, return Le Croch with request to have longer time to devise;
and after, with the most speed she can, she fully purposeth to advertise him, I mean her uncle the Cardinal, of her mind. Of this
matter the L. of Lidington is made privy. I know not whether by
some intelligence that he had before his departure, or since his arrival in France, divers letters have passed between Her Grace and
him, whereof as much as it imported not greatly the knowledge of
was communicated to some, as much as was written in cypher is
kept unto themselves. Whether also the L. of Lidington hath had
conference with the Spanish ambassador in England of this matter
or any like, I leave it unto Your Honour's good means to get true
knowledge thereof. Guesses or surmizes in so grave matters I would
be loth to write for verities. This also Your Honour may take for
truth, that the Emperor hath offered with his son, for this Queen's
dower, the county of Tyroll, which is said to be worth 30,000 franks
by year. Of this matter also the rhingrave wrote a letter unto
this Queen, out of France not long since. This is all that presently
I can write unto Your Honour hereof; as I can come by farther
knowledge Your Honour shall be informed.

I have received Your Honour's writings by the Scottish man that
last came into these parts; he brought also letters unto this Queen
from the L. of Lidington; their date was old, and contained only
the news of France. I perceive divers ways, that Newhaven is sorre
closed, but I am not so ignorant of their nature but that I know
they will say as much as they dare do, I will not say as the proverb
doth, '*canis timidus fortius latrat.*' From hence I do assure them,
what means somever they make, or how pitiful somever their mone
be, they are like to receive but small comfort for all their long allie.
We stand daily in doubt what friendship we shall need ourself, except we put better order into our misruled Papists than yet we do,

or know how to bring to pass that we may be void of their comber.

To-morrow, the 15th of this instant, the Queen departeth of this town towards Edenborough. If my hap be good, you shall thoroughly hear some merry tidings of the Bp. of St. Andrews; upon Wednesday next he shall be arreigned, and five other priests, for their massing at Easter last. Thus most humbly I take my leave; at St. Andrews the 15th of May, 1563.

No. VIII. (p. 160.)

Letter of Randolph to the Right Honourable Sir William Cecil, Knight, Principal Secretary to the Queen's Majesty.

[10th of April, 1563. Paper office, from the original in his own hand.]

MAY it please Your Honour, the 7th of this instant, Rowlet, this Queen's secretary, arrived here; he reporteth very honestly of his good usage, he brought with him many letters unto the Queen that came out of France, full of lamentation and sorrow. She received from the Queen-mother two letters; the one contained only the rehearsal of her griefs, the other signifying the state of France as then it was, as in what sort things were accorded, and what farther was intended for the appeasing of the discords there, not mistrusting but that if reason could not be had at the Queen of England's hands, but that the realm of France should find her ready and willing to support and defend the right thereof, as by friendship and old alliance between the two realms she is bound.

How well these words do agree with her doings Your Honour can well consider, and by her writings in this sort unto this Queen (which I assure Your Honour is true), you may assuredly know that nothing shall be left undone of her part, that may move debate or controversie between this Queen and our sovereign.

It was much mused by the Queen herself, how this new kindness came about, that at this time she received two long letters written all with her own hand, saying, all the time since her return she never received half so many lines as were in one of the letters, which I can myself testify by the Queen's own saying, and other good assurance, where hitherto I have not been deceived. I can also farther assure Your Honour that this Queen hath sayed that she knoweth now, that the friendship of the Queen's Majesty my sovereign may stand her more in stead than that of her good mother in France, and as she is desirous of them both, so will she not lose the one for the other. I may also farther assure Your Honour that whatsomever the occasion is, this Queen hath somewhat in her heart that will burst out in time, which will manifest that some unkindness hath passed between them that will not be easy forgotten. In talk sometimes with myself, she saith that the Queen-mother might have used the matter otherwise than she hath done, and doth much doubt what shall be the success of her great desire to govern alone, in all things to have her will. Seeing then that presently they stand in such terms one with the other, I tho't it better to confirm her in that mind (this Queen I mean), than to speak any word that might cause her to conceive beter of the other. And yet I am assured she shall receive as friendly letters, and as many good words from this Queen as the others did write unto her. Whether the Queen-mother will speak any thing unto the L. of Lidington of that purpose she did write unto this Queen of, I know not; but if she do, I think it hard if Your Honour can get no favour thereof, at his return, or I perchance by some means here. It may perchance be written only by that Queen, to try what answer this Queen will give, or understand what mind she beareth unto the Queen's Majesty our sovereign. The Queen knoweth now that the Earl Bothwell is sent for to London. She caused a gentleman of hers to inquire the cause; I answered that I knew none other, but that his takers were in controversy who took him, and that it should be judged there. I know that she thinketh much that he is not sent into Scotland. It is yet greatly doubted that if he were here, he would be reserved for an evil instrument. If the Lord of Lidington have not been plain with Your Honour herein, he is in the wrong to those who are his friends here, but most of all to himself. There comes a vulture in this realm, if ever that man come again into credit.

No. IX.   (p. 163.)

The Oration made by William Maitland of Lethington, younger Secretary for the Time, in the Parliament holden by our Sovereign the King's Mother, Queen of this Realm for the Time, the Time of the Restitution of umquile Matthew Earl of Lennox.

My Lords, and others here convened. Albeit, be that it has pleased Her Majesty most graciously to utter unto you, by her own mouth, ye may have sufficiently conceived the cause of this your present assembly; yet having Her Majesty's commandment to supply My Lord Chancellor's place, being presently as ye see deceased, I am willed to express the same somewhat more at large.

Notour it is, how, in Her Highness's minority, a process of forfaltour was decreed against My Lord of Lenox, for certain offences alledged committed by him; specified in the dome and censement of parliament given thereupon; by reason whereof he has this long time been exiled, and absent forth of his native country; how grievous the same has been unto him, it has well appeared by divers his suites, sundry ways brought unto Her Majesty's knowledge, not only containing most humble and due submission, but always bearing witness of his good devotion to Her Majesty, his natural Princess, and earnest affection he had to Her Highness most humble service, if it should please Her Majesty of her clemency to make him able to enjoy the benefit of a subject; many respects might have moved Her Highness favourably to incline to his request, as the anciency of his house and the sirname he bears, the honour he has to appertain to Her Majesty by affinity, by reason of My Lady Margaret Her Highness's aunt, and divers other his good considerations, as also the affectuous request of her good sister the Queen's Majesty of England, whose earnest commendation was not of least moment, besides that of her own natural, Her Majesty has a certain inclination to pity the decay of noble houses, and as we heard, by her own report, has a great deal more pleasure to be the instrument of the uphold, maintenance, and advancement of the ancient blood than to have matter ministred of the decay or overthrow of any good race. Upon this occasion Her Majesty the more tenderly looked upon his request, and her good sister the Queen of England's favourable letter, written for recommendation of his cause, in consideration whereof not only has she granted unto him her letter of restitution, by way of grace, but also licensed him to pursue, by way of reduction, the remedies provided by the law for such as think themselves grieved by any judgment, unorderly led, and to have the process reversed; for examination whereof, it has pleased Her Majesty presently to assemble you the three estates of this her realme, by whose advice, deliberation, and decision at Her Majesty's mind, to proceed forward upon his complaints, as the merits of the cause, laws of the realm, and practice observed in such cases will bear out. The sum of all your proceedings at this time, being, by that we have heard, thus as it were pointed out, I might here end, if the matter we have in hand gave me not occasion to say a few more words, not far different from the same subject, wherein I would extend the circumstances more largely, if I feared not to offend Her Highness, whose presence and modest nature abhors long speaking and adulation, and so will compel me to speak such things as may seem to tend to any good and perfect point; and lest it should be compted to me, as that I were oblivious, if I should omit to put you in remembrance, in what part we may accept this, and the like demonstrations of her gentill nature; whose gracious behaviour towards all her subjects in general, may serve for a good proof of that felicity we may look for under her happy government so long as it shall please God to grant her unto us; for a good harmony to be had in the common weill, the offices between the Prince and the subjects must be reciproque, as by Her Majesty's prudence we enjoy this present peace with all foreign nations, and quietness among yourselves, in such sort that I think justly it may be affirmed Scotland, in no man's age, that presently lives, was in greater tranquillity; so is it the duty of all us her loving subjects to acknowledge the same as a most high benefit, proceeding from the good government of Her Majesty, declaring ourselves thankful for the same, and rendering to Her Majesty such due obedience, as a just Prince may look for at the hands of faithful and obedient subjects. I mean no forced nor unwilling obedience, which I know her nature does detest, but such as proceeds from the contemplation of her modest kind of regiment, will for love and duty sake produce the fruits thereof. A good proof have we all in general had of Her Majesty's benignity these three years, that she has lived in the government over you, and many of you have largely tasted of her large liberality and frank dealing: on the other part Her Highness has had large appearance of your dutiful obedience, so it becomes you to continue, as we have begun, in consideration of the many notable examples of her clemency above others her good qualities, and to abhor and detest all false bruites and rumours, which are the most pestilent evils that can be, in any common weil, and the sowers and inventors thereof. Then may we be well assured to have of her a most gracious Princesse, and she most faithful and loving subjects; and so both the head and the members, being encouraged to maintain the harmony and accord of the politic bodies, whereof I made mention before, as the glory thereof shall partly appertain to Her Majesty, so shall no small praise and unspeakable commodity redound therethrough to you all universally her subjects.

No. X. (P. 166.)

The Perils and Troubles that may presently ensue, and in Time to come follow, to the Queen's Majesty of England and State of this Realm, upon the Marriage of the Queen of Scots to the Lord Darnley.

FIRST, the minds of such as be affected to the Queen of Scots, either for herself, or for the opinion of her pretence to this crown, or for the desire to have change of the forme of religion in this realm, or for the discontentation they have of the Queen's Majesty, or her succession, or of the succession of any other beside the Queen of Scotts, shall be, by this marriage erected, comforted, and induced to devise and labour how to bring their desires to pass : and to make some estimate what persons those are, to the intent the quantity of the danger may be weighed ; the same may be compassed in those sorts either within the realm or without.

The first are such as are specially devoted to the Queen of Scotts, or to the Lord Darley, by bond of blood and alliance ; as first, all the house of Lorrain and Guise for her part, and the Earl of Lennox and his wife, all such in Scotland as be of their blood, and have received displeasure by the Duke of Chatelherault and the Hamiltons. The second are all manner of persons, both in this realm and other countries, that are devoted to the authority of Rome, and mislike of the religion now received ; and in these two sorts are the substance of them comprehended, that shall take comfort in this marriage.

Next therefore to be considered what perils and troubles these kind of men shall intend to this realm.

First, the general scope and mark of all their desires is, and always shall be, to bring the Queen of Scotts to have the royal crown of this realm ; and therefore, though the devisees may vary among themselves for the compassing hereof, according to the accidents of the times, and according to the impediments which they shall find by means of the Queen's Majesty's actions and governments, yet all their purposes, drifts, devices, and practices, shall wholly and only tend to make the Queen of Scotts Queen of this realm, and to deprive our sovereign lady thereof ; and in their proceedings there are two manners to be considered, whereof the one is far worse than the other ; the one is intended by them, that either from malicious blindness in religion, or for natural affection to the Queen of Scotts, or the Lord Darley, do persuade themselves that the the said Queen of Scotts hath presently more right to the crown than our sovereign lady the Queen, of which sort be all their kindred on both sides, and all such as are devoted to Popery, either in England, Scotland, Ireland, or elsewhere ; the other is meant by

T 5

them, which, with less malice, are persuaded that the Queen of
Scotts hath only right to be the next heir to succeed the Queen's
Majesty and her issue, of which sort few are without the realm, but
here within, and yet of them, not so many as are of the contrary,
and from these two sorts shall the perils, devises, and practices proceed. From the first, which imagine the Queen of Scotts to have
perpetually right, are to be looked for these perils. First, it is to
be doubted the devil will infect some of them to imagine the hurt
of the life of our dear sovereign lady, by such means as the devil
shall suggest to them, although it is to be assuredly hoped, that
Almighty God will, as he has hitherto, graciously protect and preserve her from such dangers? Secondly, there will be attempted,
by persuasions, by bruites, by rumours, and such like, to alienate
the minds of good subjects from the Queen's Majesty, and to conciliate them to the Queen of Scotts, and on this behalf the frontiers and the North will be much solicited and laboured. Thirdly,
there will be attempted causes of some tumults and rebellions,
especially in the North toward Scotland, so as thereupon may fol-
lowsome open enterprise set by violence. Fourthly, there will be, by
the said Queen's council and friends, a new league made with
France, or Spain, that shall be offensive to this realm, and a furtherance to their title. And it is also very likely, that they will
set afoot as many practices as they can, both upon the frontiers and
in Ireland, to occasion the Queen's Majesty to increase and continue
her charge thereby, to retain her from being mighty or potent, and
for the attempting of all these things, many devises will be imagined from time to time, and no negligence will therein appear.

From the second sort, which mean no other favour to the Queen
of Scotts, but that she should succeed in title to the Queen's Majesty, is not much to be feared, but that they will content themselves to see not only the Queen's Majesty not to marry, and so to
impeach it, but to hope, that the Queen of Scotts shall have issue,
which they will think to be more pleaseable to all men, because
thereby the crowns of England and Scotland shall be united in one,
and thereby the occasion of war shall cease; with which persuasion
many people may be seduced, and abused to incline themselves to
the part of the Queen of Scotts.

The remedies against these perils.

A DUPLICAT.

[4th of June, 1565. Cott. Lib. Cal. B. 10. fol. 290.]

*A Summary of the Consultation and Advice given by the Lords and
others of the Privy Council. Collected out of the sundry and several
Speeches of the said Counsellors.*

Lord Keeper,	Mr. Comptroller,
Lord Treasurer,	Mr. Vice Chamberlain
Earls of { Derby, Bedford, Leiceste	Mr. Secretary, Cave, Peter,
Lord Admiral,	Mason.
Lord Chamberlain.	

Questions propounded were these two.

1. FIRST, What perils might ensue to the Queen's Majesty, or this realm, of the marriage betwixt the Queen of Scotts and the Lord Darnley.

2. What were meet to be done, to avoid or remedy the same.

To the First.

The perils being sundry, and very many, were reduced by some counsellors into only one.

1. First, That by this marriage, the Queen of Scotts (being not married), a great number in this realm, not of the worst subjects, might be alienated in their minds from their natural duties to her Majesty, to depend upon the success of this marriage of Scotland, as a means to establish the succession of both the crowns in the issue of the same marriage, and so favour all devises and practises, that should tend to the advancement of the Queen of Scotts.

2. Secondly, That considering the chief foundation of them, which furthered the marriage of Lord Darnley, was laid upon the trust of such as were Papists, as the only means left to restore the religion of Rome, it was plainly to be seen, that both in this realm and Scotland, the Papists would most favour, maintain, and fortify this marriage of the Lord Darnley, and would, for furtherance of faction in religion, devise all means and practices that could be within this realm, to disturb the estate of the Queen's Majesty, and the peace of the realm, and consequently to achieve their purposes by force rather than fail. By some other, these perils having indeed many branches, were reduced, though not otherwise, into two sorts, and these were in nature such as they could not be easily severed the one from the other, but were knit and lincked together, naturally for maintaining the one with the other. The first of these sort of perils was, that, by this marriage with the Lord Darnley, there was a plain intention to further the pretended title of the Queen of Scotts not only to succeed the Queen's Majesty, as in her best amity she had professed, but that to occupy the Queen's estate, as when she was in power, she did manifestly declare.

The second was, that hereby the Romish religion should be erected, and increased daily in this realm, and these two were thus knit together, that the furtherance and maintenance of the title staid, in furthering of the religion of Rome within this realm; and in like manner the furtherance of the same religion stood by the title, for otherwise the title had no foundation.

Proves of the first). And to prove that the intention to advance the title to disturb the Queen's Majesty, must needs ensue, was considered that always the intention and will of any person is most manifest, when their power is greatest, and contrary when power is small, then the intention and will of every person is covered and less seen. So that when the Queen of Scott's power was greatest, by her marriage with the Dauphin of France, being afterwards French King, it manifestly appeared of what mind she and all her friends were, using then manifestly all the means that could be de-

vised to impeach and dispossess the Queen's Majesty, first by writing
and publishing herself in all countries Queen of England; by
granting charters, patents, and commissions, with that style, and
with the arms of England, both the French and Scotts, which
charters remain still undefaced; and to prosecute it with effect, it
is known what preparations of war were made, and sent into Scotland; and what other forces were assembled in foreign countries;
yea, in what manner a shameful peace was made by the French
with King Philip, to employ all the forces of France to pursue all
the matters by force, which by God's providence, and the Queen's
Majesty contrary power, were repelled; and afterwards, by her
husband's death, her fortune and power being changed, the intention began to hide itself; and although by the Scottish Queen's
commissaries an accord was made at Edinburgh, to reform all those
titles, and claims, and pretences, yet to this day, by delays and
cavillations, the ratification of that treaty has been deferred.
And so now, as soon as she shall feel her power, she will set the
same again abroad, and by considering of such errors as were committed in the first, her friends and allies will amend the same, and
proceed substantially to her purpose.   By some it was thought
plainly, that the peril was greater of this marriage with the Lord
Darnley, being a subject of this realm, than with the mightiest
Prince abroad, for by this, he being of this realm, and having for
the cause of religion, and other respects, made a party here, should
increase by force with diminution of the power of the realm; in
that whatsoever power he could make by the faction of the Papist;
and other discontented persons here, should be as it were deducted
but of the power of this realm; and by the marriage of a stranger,
she could not be assured of any part here; so as by this marriage
she should have a portion of her own power to serve her turn, and
a small portion of adversaries at home in our own bowels, always
seem more dangerous than treble the like abroad, whereof the examples are in our own stories many, that foreign powers never prevailed in this realm, but with the help of some at home.   It was
also remembered, that seeing how before this attempt of marriage,
it is found, and manifestly seen, that in every corner of the realm,
the faction that most favoureth the Scottish title, is grown stout
and bold, yea seen manifestly in this court, both in hall and chamber, it could not be but (except good heed were speedily given to
it) by this marriage, and by the practice of the fautors thereof, the
same faction would shortly increase, and grow so great and dangerous, as the redress thereof would be almost desperate.   And to this
purpose it was remembered, how of late in perusing of the substance of the justices of the peace, in all the countries of the realm,
scantily a third was found fully assured to be trusted in the matter
of religion, upon which only string the Queen of Scots title doth
hang, and some doubt might be, that the friends of the Earl of
Lennox, and his had more knowledge hereof than was thought, and
thereby made avant now in Scotland, and their party was so great
in England as the Queen's Majesty durst not attempt to contrary
his marriage.   And in this sort, was the sum of the perils declared,
being notwithstanding more largely and plainly set out, and made

so apparent by many sure arguments, as no one of the council could deny them to be but many and very dangerous.

Second Question.

The question of this consultation was what were meet to be done to avoid these perils, or else to divert the force thereof from hurting the realm; wherein there were a great number of particular devises propounded, and yet the more part of them was reduced by some into three heads.

1. The first thought necessary by all persons, as the only thing of the most moment and efficacy, to remedy all these perils and many others, and such as without it no other remedy could be found sufficient, and that was to obtain that the Queen's Majesty would marry, and make therein no long delay.

2. The second was, to advance, establish, and fortify indeed the profession of religion, both in Scotland and in England, and to diminish, weaken, and feeble the contrary.

3. The third was, to proceed in sundry things, either to disappoint and break this intended marriage, or, at the least, thereby to procure the same not to be so hurtful to this realm as otherwise it would be.

The first of these three hath no particular rights in it, but an earnest and unfeigned desire and suit, with all humbleness, by prayer to Almighty God, and advice and council to the Queen's Majesty, that she would defer no more time from marriage, whereby the good subjects of the realm might stay their hearts, to depend upon Her Majesty, and the same issue of her body, without which no surety can be devised to ascertain any person of continuance of their families or posterities, to enjoy that which otherwise should come to them.

Second, concerning the matters of religion, wherein both truth and policy were joined together, had these particulars.

First, whereas of late the adversaries of religion, in the realm, have taken occasion to comfort and increase their faction, both in England, Scotland, and abroad, with a rumour and expectation that the religion shall be shortly changed in this realm, by means that the bishops, by the Queen's Majesty's commandment, have of late dealt strightly with some persons of good religion, because they had forborn to wear certain apparel, and such like things: being more of form and accidents than of any substance, for that it is well known that Her Majesty had no meaning to comfort the adversaries, but only to maintain an uniformity as well in things external as in the substance, nor yet hath any intention to make any change of the religion, as it is established by laws. It was thought by all men very necessary for the suppressing of the pride and arrogancy of the adversaries, indirectly hereby to notify, by her special letters to the two archbishops, that her former commandments was only to retain an uniformity, and not to give any occasion to any person to misjudge of Her Majesty, in the change of any part of religion, but that she did determine firmly to maintain the form of her religion, as it was established, and to punish such as did therein violate her laws. And in these points, some also wished that it might please her archbishops, that if they should see that the adversaries continued in taking occasion to fortify their faction, that in that case they should use a moderation therein, until the next parliament, at which time, some good, uniform and decent order might be devised, and established, for such ceremonies, so as both uniformity and gravity, might be retained amongst the clergy.

The second means was, that the quondam bishops, and others, which had refused to acknowledge the Queen's Majesty's power over them, according to the law, and were of late dispersed in the plague time to sundry places abroad, where it is known they cease not to advance their faction, might be returned to the Tower, or some other prison, where they might not have such liberty to seduce and inveigle the Queen's Majesty's subjects, as they daily do.

The third means was, that where the bishops do complain that they dare not execute the ecclesiastical laws, to the furtherance of religion, for fear of the premunire wherewith the judges and lawyers of the realm, being not best affected in religion, do threaten them, and in many cases lett not to pinch and deface them, that upon such cases opened, some convenient authority might be given them, from the Queen's Majesty, to continue during her pleasure.

The fourth was, that there were daily lewd, injudicious, and unlawfull books in English brought from beyond seas, and are bodily received, read, and kept, and especially in the North, seducing of great numbers of good subjects, the like boldness whereof was never suffered in any other Princess's time, that some streight order might be given to avoid the same, and that it might be considered by the judges what manner of crime the same is, to maintain such books, made directly against Her Majesty's authority, and maintaining a foreign power, contrary to the laws of the realm.

The fifth was, that where a great number of monks, fryars, and such lewd persons are fled out of Scotland, and do serve in England, especially in the North as curates of churches, and all such of them as are not found honest and conformable, may be banished out of the realm, for that it appeareth they do sow sedition in the realm, in many places, and now will increase their doings.

The sixth, where sundry having ecclesiastical livings, are on the other side the sea, and from thence maintain sedition in the realm; that livings may be better bestowed to the commodity of the realm, upon good subjects.

The seventh is that the judges of the realm, having no small authority in this realm, in governance of all property of the realm, might be swore to the Queen's Majesty, according to the laws of the realm, and so thereby they should for conscience sake maintain the Queen's Majesty's authority.

The particulars of the third intention to break and avoid this this marriage, or to divert the perils.

First, to break this marriage, considering nothing can likely do it but force, or fear of force, it is thought by some that these means following might occasion the breach of the marriage.

1. That the Earl of Bedford return to his charge.

2. That the works at Berwick be more advanced.

3. That the garrison be there increased.

4. That all the wardens put their frontiers in order with speed, to be ready at an hour's warning.

5. That some noble person, as the Duke of Norfolk, or the Earl of Salop, or such other, be sent into Yorkshire, to be Lieutenant-general in the North.

6. That preparations be made of a power to be in readiness to serve, either at Berwick, or to invade Scotland.

7. That presently Lady Lennox be committed to some place where she may be kept from giving or receiving of intelligence.

8. That the Earl of Lennox and his son may be sent for, and required to be sent home by the Queen of Scotts, according to the treaty; and if they shall not come then to denounce to the Queen of Scotts the breach of the treaty, and thereupon to enter with hostility; by which proceeding, hope is conceived (so the same be done in deeds and not in shews) that the marriage will be avoided, or at the least that it may be qualified from many perils: and whatsoever is to be done herein is to be executed with speed, whilst she has a party in Scotland that favoureth not the marriage, and before any league made by the Queen of Scotts with France or Spain.

9. Some other allows well of all these proceedings, saving of proceeding to hostility, but all do agree in the rest, and also to these particularities following.

10· That the Earl's lands upon his refusal, or his son's refusing, should be seized, and bestowed in gift or custody, as shall please Her Majesty, upon good subjects.

11. That all manifest favourers of the Earl, in the North, or elsewhere, be inquired for, and that they be, by sundry means, well looked to.

12. That inquiry be made in the North, who have the steward-ship of the Queen's Majesty's lands there, and that no person, deserving mistrust, be suffered to have governance or rule of any of her subjects or lands in the North, but only to retain their fees, and more trusty persons have rule of the same people's lands.

13. That all frequent passages into this realm, to and from Scotland, be restrained to all Scottish men, saving such as have safe conduct, or be especially recommended from Mr. Randolph, as favourers of the Realm.

14. That some intelligence be used with such in Scotland as favour not the marriage, and they comforted from time to time.

15. That the Queen's Majesty's household, chambers and pension, be better seen unto, to avoid broad and uncomely speech used by sundry against the state of the realm.

16. That the younger son of the Earl of Lennox, Mr. Charles, be removed to some place where he may be forthcoming.

17. That considering the faction and title of the Queen of Scott's hath now of long time received great favour, and continued, by the Queen's Majesty's favour herein to the Queen of Scotts and her ministers, and the Lady Catherine, whom the said Queen of Scotts accompted as a competitor unto her in pretence of title, it may please the Queen's Majesty, by some exterior act, to shew some re-

mission of her displeasure to the Lady, and to the Earl of Hartford, that the Queen of Scotts thereby may find some change, and her friends put in doubt of further proceeding therein.

18. That whosoever shall be Lieutenant in the North, Sir Ralph Sadler may accompany him.

19. That with speed the realm of Ireland may be committed to a new governor.

20. Finally, that these advices being considered by Her Majesty, it may please her to choose which of them she liketh, and to put them in execution in deeds, and not to pass them over in consultations and speeches.

For it is to be assured that her adversaries will use all means to put their intention in execution. Some by practice, some by force, when time shall serve, and no time can serve so well the Queen's Majesty to interrupt the perils as now at the first, before the Queen of Scotts purposes be fully settled.

No. XI. (p. 172.)

Randolph to the Earl of Leicester, from Edinburgh, the 31st of July, 1565.

[Cott. Lib. Cal. B. ix. fol. 216. An original.]

MAY it please Your Lordship, I have received your Lordship's letter by my servant, sufficient testimony of your Lordship's favour towards me, whereof I think myself always so assured, that, what other mishap soever befal me, I have enough to comfort myself with; though I have not at this time received neither according to the need I stand, nor the necessity of the service that I am employed in, I will rather pass it, as I may with patience, than trouble Your Lordship to be further suiter for me, when there is so little hope that any good will be done for me. I doubt not but Your Lordship hath heard by such information as I have given from hence, what the present state of this country is, how this Queen is now become a married wife, and her husband, the self-same day of his marriage, made a King. In their desires, hitherto, they have found so much to their contentment that if the rest succeed and prosper accordingly, they may think themselves much happier than there is appearance that they shall be; so many discontented minds, so much misliking of the subjects to have these matters thus ordered and in this sort to be brought to pass, I never heard of any marriage: so little hope, so little comfort as men do talk was never seen, at any time, when men should most have showed themselves to rejoice, if that consideration of her own honour and well of her country had been had as appertained in so weighty a case. This is now their fear, the overthrow of religion, the breach of amitie with the Queen's Majesty, and the destruction of as many of the nobility as she hath misliking of, or that he liketh to pitch a quarrel unto. To see all these inconveniencys approaching, there are a good number that may sooner lament with themselves and complain to their neighbours than be able to find remedie to help them; some attempt with all the force they have, but are too weak to do any good; what is required otherways, or what means there is made, Your

Lordship knoweth; what will be answered, or what will be done therein, we are in great doubt; and though your intent be never so good unto us, yet do we so much fear your delay that our ruin shall prevent your support. When council is once taken, nothing so needful as speedy execution. Upon the Queen's Majesty we wholly depend; in Her Majesty's hands it standeth to save our lives, or to suffer us to perish; greater honour Her Majesty cannot have, than in that which lieth in her Majesty's power to do for us, the sums are not great, the numbers of men are not many that we desire; many will dayly be found, tho' this will be some charge; men grow dayly, though, at this time, I think Her Majesty shall lose but few; her friends here being once taken away, where will Her Majesty find the like? I speak least of that which I think is most earnestly intended by this Queen and her husband, when by him it was lately said that he cared more for the Papists in England than he did for the Protestants in Scotland: if therefore his hopes be so great in the Papist's of England, what may Your Lordship believe that he thinketh of the Protestants there? for his birth, for his nurritour, for the honour he hath to be of kine to the Queen my mistress, if in preferring those who are the Queen's Majesties worst subjects to those that are her best, he declareth what mind he beareth to the Queen's Majesty's self, any man may say it is slenderly rewarded, and his duty evil forgotten; he would now seem to be indifferent to both the religions, she to use her mass, and he to come sometimes to the preaching: they were married with all the solemnities of the Popish time, saving that he heard not the mass: his speech and talk argueth his mind, and yet would he fain seem to the world that he were of some religion: his words to all men, against whom he conceiveth any displeasure how unjust soover it be, so proud and spiteful that rather he seemeth a monarch of the world than he that, not long since, we have seen and known the Lord Darnley: he looketh now for reverence of many that have little will to give it him; and some there are that do give it that think him little worth of it. All honours that may be attributed unto any man by a wife, he hath it wholly and fully; all praises that may be spoken of him he lacketh not from herself: all dignities that she can endue him with, which are already given and granted; no man pleaseth her that contenteth not him; and what may I say more, she hath given over to him her whole will, to be ruled and guarded as himself best liketh; she can as much prevail with him in anything that is against his will as Your Lorpship may with me to persuade that I should hang myself; this last dignity out of hand to have been proclaimed King, she would have it deferred until it were agreed by parliament, or he had been himself 21 years of age, that things done in his name might have the better authority. He would, in no case, have it deferred one day, and either then or never; whereupon this doubt has risen amongst our men of law, whether she being clad with a husband, and her husband not twenty-one years, any thing without Parliament can be of strength that is done between them; upon Saturday at afternoon these matters were long debating. And before they were well resolved upon, at nine hours at night, by three heralds, at sound of the trumpet he was proclaimed King. This was the night before the

marriage; this day, Monday at twelve of the clock, the lords, all
that were in toun, were present at the proclaiming of him again,
where no man said so much as Amen, saving his father, that cried
out aloud God save his Queen ! The manner of the marriage was
in this sort : upon Sunday in the morning between five and six, she
was conveyed by divers of her nobles to the chapell ; she had on her
back the great mourning hood, not unlike unto that she wore the
doulfull day of the burial of her husband ; she was led into the chapell by the Earl of Lennox and Athol, and there was she left untill
her husband came, who was also conveyed by the same lords; the minister priests, two, do there receive them, the bands are asked the
third time, and an instrument taken by a noteur that no man said
against them, or alledged any cause why the marriage should not
proceed. The words were spoken, the rings which were three, the
middle a rich diamond, were put upon her finger ; they kneel together, and many prayers said over them, she tarrieth out the mass,
and he taketh a kiss, and leaveth her there, and went to her chamber, whither within a space she followeth ; and being required according to the solemnity, to cast off her cares and leave aside those
sorrowful garments, and give herself to a more pleasant life, after
some pretty refusall, more I believe for manner sake than grief of
heart, she suffered them that stood by, every man that could approach, to take out a pin, and so being committed to her ladies,
changed her garments but went not to bed, to signify to the world
that it was not lust that moved them to marry, but only the necessity of her country, not, if God will, long to leave it destitute of an
heir. Suspicious men, of such as are given of all things to make
the worst, would that it should be believed that they knew each
other before that they came there ; I would not Your Lordship
should so believe it, the likelihoods are so great to the contrary
that if it were possible to see such an act done I would not believe
it. After the marriage followeth commonly great cheer and danc-
ing ; to their dinner they were conveyed by the whole nobility ; the
trumpets sound ; a largess cried; money thrown about the house in
great abundance, to such as were happy to get any part ; they dine
both at one table, she upon the upper hand ; there serve her these
Earls, Athole sewer, Morton carver, Craufoord cup-bearer; these
serve him in like offices, Earls Eglington, Cassels, and Glencairn;
after dinner they danced awhile, and then retired themselves till
the hour of supper ; and as they dined so did they sup, some danc-
ing there was, and so they go to bed ; of all this I have written to
Your Lordship I am not *oculatus testis*, to this, but of the verity
Your Lordship shall not need to doubt, howsoever I came by it ; I
was sent for to have been at the supper, but like a currish or uncourtly carle, I refused to be there ; and yet that which your Lordship may think might move me much, to have had the sight of my
mistress, of whom these eighteen days by just account I got not a
sight. I am, My Lord, taken by all that sort as a very evil person,
which in my heart I do well allow, and like of myself the better,
for yet can I not find either honest or good that liketh their doings.
I leave at this time further to trouble Your Lordship, craving pardon for my long silence. I have more ado than I am able to discharge, I walk now more abroad by night than by day, and the day

too little to discharge myself of that which I conceive or receive in the night. As your Lordship, I am sure, is partaker of such letters as I write to Mr. Secretary, so that I trust that he shall be to this, to save me of a little labour to write the same again, most humbly I take my leave at Edinburgh, this last day of July, 1565.

No. XII. (p. 174.)

Letter of the Earl of Bedford to the Honourable Sir William Cecil, Knt., Her Majesty's Principal Secretary, and one of Her Highness's Privy Council.

[2d of Sept. 1565. Paper Office, from the original.]

AFTER my hearty commendations, this day at noon Captain Brickwell came hither, who brought with him the Queen's Majesty's letters, containing her full resolution and pleasure for all things he had in charge to give information of, saving that for the aid of the Lords of the Congregation there is nothing determined, or at the least expressed in the same letters, and for that purpose received I this morning a letter, subscribed by the Duke, the Earl of Murray, Glencarne, and others, craving to be holpen with 300 harquebusyers out of this garrison for their better defence. And albeit, I know right well the goodness of their cause, and the Queen's Majesty our sovereign's good will, and care towards them; and do also understand that it were very requisite to have them holpen, for that now their cause is to be in this manner decided, and that it now standeth upon their utter overthrow and undoing, since the Queen's party is at the least 5000, and they not much above 1000; besides that the Queen hath harquebusyers, and they have none, and do yet want the power that the Earl of Arguyle should bring to them, who is not yet joined with theirs; I have thereupon thought good to pray you to be a means to learn Her Majesty's pleasure in this behalf, what and how I shall answer them, or otherwise deal in this matter, now at this their extreme necessity. For, on the one side, lyeth thereupon their utter ruin and overthrow, and the miserable subversion of religion there; and, on the other side, to adventure so great and weighty a matter as this (albeit it be but of a few soldiers for a small time), without good warraunte, and thereby to bring, peradventure, upon our heads some wilful warrs, and in the mean time to leave the place unfurnished (having in the whole but 800), without any grant of new supply for the same; and by that means also, to leave the marches here the more subject to invasion, while in the mean season new helps are preparing; to this know not I what to say or how to do. And so much more I marvel thereof, as that having so many times written touching this matter, no resolute determination cometh. And so between the writing and looking for answer, the occasion cannot pass but must needs proceed and have success. God turn it to his glory; but surely all men's reason hath great cause to fear it. Such a push it is now come unto, as this little supply would do much good to advance God's honour, to continue Her Majesty's great and careful memory of them, and to preserve a great many noblemen and gentlemen. If it be not now helpen it is gone for ever. Your good will and affection that way I do nothing mistrust, and herein shall take such good advice as by any means I can. I received from these lords two papers inclosed, the effect whereof shall appear unto you. For those matters that Captain Brickwell brought, I shall answer you by my next, and herewith send you two letters from Mr. Randolph, both received this day. By him you shall hear that the Protestants are retired from Edenborough, further off. So I hope your resolution for their aid shall come in time, if it come with speed, for that they will not now so presently need them; and so with my hearty thanks commit you to God. From Berwick, this 2d of Sept. 1565.

No. XIII. (Page 174.)

The Queen to the Earl of Bedford.
[12th Sept. 1566. Paper Office.]

UPON the advertizements lately received from you, with such other things as came also from the Lord Scrope and Thomas Randolph, and upon the whole matter well considered, we have thus determined. We will, with all the speed that we can, send to you 3000*l.* to be thus used. If you shall certainly understand that the Earl of Murray hath such want of money, as the impresting to him of 1000*l.* might stand him in stead for the help to defend himself, you shall presently let him secretly to understand that you will, as as of yourself, let him have so much, and so we will that you let him have, in the most secret sort that you can, when the said sum shall come to you, or if you can, by any good means, advance him some part thereof beforehand.

The other 2000*l.* you shall cause to be whole, unspent, if it be not that you shall see necessary cause to imprest some part thereof to the now members of the 600 footmen and 100 horsemen; or to the casting out of wages of such workmen as by sickness or otherwise ought to be discharged. And where we perceive, by your sundry letters, the earnest request of the said Earl of Murray and his associates, that they might have, at the least, 300 [of our soldiers to aid them. And that you also write, that though we would not command you to give them aid, yet if we would but wink at your doing herein, and seem to blame you for attempting such things, as you with the help of others should bring about, you doubt not but things would do well; you shall understand for a truth that we have no intention, for many respects, to maintain any other Prince's subjects to take arms against their sovereign; neither would we willingly do any thing to give occasion to make wars betwixt us and that Prince, which has caused us to forbear hitherto to give you any power to let them be aided with any men. But now, considering we take it, that they are pursued, notwithstanding their humble submission and offer to be ordered and tried by law and justice, which being refused to them, they are retired to Dumfrese, a place near our west marches, as it seemeth there to defend themselves, and adding there-unto the good intention, that presently the French King pretendeth, by sending one of his to join with some one of ours, and jointly to treat with that Queen, and to induce her to forbear this manner of violent and rigorous proceeding against her subjects, for which purpose the French ambassador here with us has lately written to that Queen, whereof answer is daily looked for; to the intent, in the mean time, the said lords should not be oppressed and ruined for lack of some help to defend them, we are content and do authorize, if you shall see it necessary for their defence, to let them (as of your own adventure, and without notifying that you have any direction therein from us) to have the number of 300 soldiers, to be taken, either in whole bands or to be drawn out of all your bands, as you shall see cause. And to cover the matter the better, you shall send these numbers to Carlisle, as to be laid there in garrison, to defend that march, now in this time that such powers are on the other part drawing to those frontiers, and so from thence as you shall see cause to direct of, the same numbers, or any of them, may most covertly repair to the said lords, when you shall expressly advertize, that you send them that aid only for their defence, and not therewith to make war against the Queen, or to do any thing that may offend her person ; wherein you shall so precisely deal with them, that they may perceive your care to be such as if it should otherwise appear, your danger should be so great as all the friends you have could not be able to save you, towards us. And so we assure you our conscience moveth us to charge you so to proceed with them ; for otherwise than to preserve them from ruin, we do not yield to give them aid of money or men : And yet we would not that either of these were known to be our act, but rather to be covered with your own desire and attempt.

No. XIV. (Page 178.)

Randolph to Cecil, from Edinburgh, 7th Feb. 1565-6.

[An original.]

My humble duty considered; what to write of the present state of the country I am so uncertain, by reason of the daily alterations of men's minds, that it maketh me much slower than otherwise I would. Within these few days there was some good hope that this Queen would have shewed some favour towards the lords, and that Robert Melvin should have returned unto them with comfort upon some conditions. Since that time there are come out of France, Clernau by land, and Thorneton by sea; the one from the Cardinal, the other from the Bishop of Glasgow. Since whose arrival neither can there be good word gotten, nor appearance of any good intended them, except that they be able to perswade the Queen's Majesty, our sovereign, to make her heir apparent to the croun of England. I write of this nothing less than I know that she hath spoken. And by all means that she thinketh the best doth travaile to bring it to pass. There is a band lately devised, in which the late Pope, the Emperor, the King of Spain, the Duke of Savoy, with divers Princes of Italy, and the Queen-mother suspected to be of the same confederacy to maintain Papistry throughout Christiandom ; this band was sent out of France by Thorneton, and is subscribed by this Queen, the copy thereof remaining with her, and the principal to be returned very shortlie, as I hear, by Mr. Stephen Willson, a fit minister for such a devilish devise; if the coppie hereof may be gotten, that shall be sent as I conveniently may. Monsieur Rambollet came to this toun upon Monday, he spoke that night to the Queen and her husband, but not long; the next day he held long conferences with them both, but nothing came to the knowledge of any whereof they intreated. I cannot speak with any that hath any hope that there will be any good done for the lords by him, though it is said that he hath every good will to do so to the uttermost of his power. He is lodged near to the court, and liveth upon the Queen's charges. Upon Sunday the order is given, whereat means made to many to be present that day at the mass. Upon Candlemas-day there carried their candles, with the Queen, her husband, the Earle of Lennox, and Earle of Athol; divers other lords have been called together and required to be at the mass that day, some have promised, as Cassels, Montgomerie, Seton, Cathness. Others have refused, as Fleming, Levingston, Lindsay, Huntly, and Bothel; and of them all Bothel is stoutest, but worst thought of; it was moved in council that mass should have been in St. Giles church, which I believe was rather to tempt men's minds than intended indeed: She was of late minded again to send Robert Melvin to negociate with such as she trusteth in amongst the Queen's Majesty's subjects, of whose good willis this way I trust that the bruit is greater than the truth, but in these matters Her Majesty is too wise not in time to be ware, and provide for the worst; some in that country are thought to be privie unto the bands of confederacie of which I have written, whereof I am sure there is some things, tho' perchance of all I have not heard the truth: in this court divers quarles, contentions, and debates, nothing so much sought as to maintain mischief and disorder. David yet retaineth still his place, not without heart-grief to many that see their sovereign guided chiefly by such a fellow; the Queen hath utterly refused to do any good to My Lord of Argyll, and it is said that shall be the first voyage that she will make after she is delivered of being with child; the bruit is common that she is, but hardly believed of many, and of this I can assure you, that there have of late appeared some tokens to the contrary.

No. XV. (Page 183.)

Part of a Letter from the Earl of Bedford and Mr. Tho. Randolph to the Lords of the Council of England from Barwick, 27th of March, 1566. An Original in the Cotton Library, Caligula. fol. 183.

MAY IT PLEASE YOUR HONOURS,

HERING of so maynie matters as we do, and fyndinge such varietie in the reports, we have myche ado to decerne the veritie; which maketh us the slower and loother to put any thing in wrytinge to the entente we wold not that Your Honours, and by you the Queen's Majestie, our sovereigne, should not be advertised but of the verie trothe as we can possible. To this end we thought good to send up Captain Carewe, who was in Edinbourge at the tyme of the last attemptate, who spoke there with diverse, and after that with the Queen's self and her husband, conforme to that which we have learned by others and know by this reporte, we send the same, confirmed by the parties self, that were there present and assysters unto those that were executors of the acte.

This we fynde for certain, that the Queen's husband being entered into a vehement suspicion of David, that by hym some thynge was committed, which was most agaynste the Queen's honour, and not to be borne of his perte, fryste communicated his mynde to George Duglas, who, fynding his sorrowes so great, sought all the means he coulde to put some remedie to his grieff; and communicating the same unto My Lord Ruthen by the King's commandment, no other waye coulde be found then that David should be taken out of the waye. Wherein he was so earnest and daylye pressed the same, that no reste could be had untyll it was put in execution. To this that was found good, that the Lord Morton and Lord Lindsaye should be made privie to th' intente that theie might have their friends at hande, yf neade required; which caused them to assemble so mayny, as theie thought sufficient against the tyme, that this determination of theirs should be put in executione; which was determined the ixth of this instante, 3 daies afore the parliament should begyne, at which time the sayde lordes were assured that the Erles Argyle, Morraye, Rothes and their complyces sholde have been forfeited, yf the King could not be persuaded through this means to be their friends; who for the desyre he hade that this intent should take effect, th' one waye was contente to yielde, without all difficultie, to t'other, with this condition, that theie should give their consents, that he might have the crowne matrimonial. He was so impatient to see these things he saw, and were daylye brought to his eares, that he dayly pressed the said Lord Ruthen, that there might be no longer delaye; and to the intent that myght be manifeste unto the world that he approved the acte, was content to be at the doing of that himself.

Upon Saturdaye at night neire unto viii of the clock the King conveyeth himself, the Lord Ruthen, George Duglass, and two others, throwe his owne chamber by the privy stayers up to the Queen's chamber, going to which there is a cabinet about xii foot square; in the same a little low reposing bed and a table, at the which theyr were sitting at the supper, the Queene, the Lady Argile, and David with his capp upon his head. Into the cabinet there cometh in the King and Lord Ruthen, who willed David to come forth, saying, that was no place for him. The Queen said, that it was her will. Her howsband answerede, that yt was against her honour. The Lord Ruthen said, that he should lerne better his dutie, and offering to have taken him by the arm, David took the Queen by the blychtes of her gown and put himself behind the Queen who wolde gladlee have saved him: But the King having loosed his hand, and holding her in his arms, David was thrust out of the cabinet throw the bed chamber into the chamber of presens, whar were the Lord Morton, Lord Lindsey, who intending that night to have reserved him, and the next day to hang him, so many being about him that bore him evil will; one thrust him into the boddie with a dagger, and after him a great many others, so that he had in his bodie above — wonds. It is told for certayne, that the Kinges own dagger was left sticking in him. Wheather he struck him or not we cannot here for certayn. He was not slayne in the

Queen's presens, as was said, but going down the stayres out of the chamber of presens.

There remained a long tyme with the Queen her howsband and the Lord Ruthen. She made, as we here, great intercession that he shold have no harm. She blamed greatlee her howsband that was the actor of so foul a deed. It is said that he did answer, that David had more companie of her boddie than he for the space of two months; and, therefore, for her honour and his own content-ment he gave his consent that he should be taken away. "It is not" (saythe she) "the woman's part to seek her husband, and therefore in that the fault was his own." He said that when he came, she either wold not, or made herself sick. "Well," saythe she, "you have taken your last of me and your farewell." Then were pity, sayth the Lord Ruthen, he is Your Majesty's husband, and must yield dutie to each other. "Why may I not," saythe she, "leave him as well as your wife did her husband?" Other have done the like. The Lord Ruthen said, that she was lawfully divorced from her husband, and for no such cause as the King found himself greve. Besydes, this man was mean, basse, enemie to the nobilitie, shame to her, and destruction to herself and country. "Well," saith she, "that shall be dear blude to some of you, yf his be spylt." God forbid, sayth the Lord Ruthen; for the more Your Grace showe yourself offended, the world will judge the worse.

Her husband this tyme speaketh litle, herself continually weepeth. The Lord Ruthen being ill at ease and weak, calleth for a drink, and saythe, "This I must do with Your Majesties pardon," and persuadeth her in the best sort he could, that she would pacify her-self. Nothing that could be said could please her.

In this mean time there rose a nombre in the court; to pacify which there went down the Lord Ruthen, who went strayt to the Erles Huntly, Bothwell, and Atholl, to quiet them, and to assure them for the King that nothing was intend against them. These notwithstanding taking fear when theie heard that My Lord of Mur-ray would be there the next day, and Argile meet them, Huntly and Bothwell both get out of a window and so depart. Atholl had leave of the King, with Flysh and Glandores (who was lately called Deysley the person of Owne) to go where they wold, and bring con-corde out of the court by the Lord of Lidington. Theie went that night to such places where they thought themselves in most sauftie

Before the King leaft talk with the Queen, in the hering of the Lord Ruthen, she was contents that he shold lie with her that night. We know not how he ** himself but came not at her, and excused hymself to his friends, that he was so sleepie that he could not wake in due season.

There were in this companie two that came in with the King; the one Andrewe Car of Fawdenside, whom the Queen sayth would have stroken her with a dagger, and one Patrick Balentine, brother to the justice clerk, who also, Her Grace sayth, offered a dag against her belly with the cock down. We have been earnestly in hand with the Lord Ruthen to know the varitie; but he assoureth us of the contrarie. There were in the Queen's chamber the Lord Robert, Arther Arskin, one or two others. They at the first offering to make a defence, the Lord Ruthen drawd his dagger, and 4 mo wear pons then, that were not drawn nor seen in her presens, as we are by this Lord assured.

[The letter afterwards gives an account of the flight to Dunbar Castle, whither resorted unto the Lords Huntly and Bothwell. That the Earl of Morton and Lord Ruthen find themselves left by the King for all his fair promises, bonds, and subscriptions. That he had protested before the council that he was never consenting to the death of David, and that it is sore against his will: "That of the great substance David had there is much spoken, some say in gold to the value of 11m£. His apparel was very good, as it is said, 28 pair of velvet hose. His chamber well furnished, armour, dagger, pystoletts, harquebuses, 22 swords. Of all this nothing spoyld or lacked saving 2 or 3 dagger. He had the custody of all the Queen's letters, which all were delivered unlooked upon. We hear of a juill that he had hanging about his neck of some price that cannot be heard of. He had upon his back when he was slayn, a night gown of damask furred, with a satten dublet, a hose of russet velvet."]

No. XVI. (p. 187.)

Part of a Letter from Randolph to Cecil, Jan. 16, 1565-6.

——I cannot tell what misliking of late there hath been between Her Grace and her husband, he presseth earnestly for the matrimonial crown, which she is loth hastily to grant, but willing to keep somewhat in store, until she know how well he is worth to enjoy such a sovereignty: and therefore it is thought that the Parliament for a time shall be deferred, but hereof I can write no certainty.

From Mr. Randolph's Letter to Secretary Cecil.

(4 April, 1566. Paper Office, from the original.)

The justice-clerk in hard terms, more for his brothers cause than any desert, and as far as I can hear the King of all other in worst, for neither hath the Queen good opinion of him for attempting of any thing that was against her will, nor the people that he hath denied so manifest a matter, being proved to be done by his commandment, and now himself to be the accuser and pursuer of them that did as he willed them. This Scott, that was executed, and Murray that was yesterday arreigned, were both accused by him. It is written to me, for certain, by one that upon Monday last spok with the Queen that she is determined that the house of Lennox shall be as poor in Scotland as ever it was. The Earl continueth sick, sore troubled in mind: he staith in the abby, his son has been once with him, and he once with the Queen, since she come to the castle. The Queen hath now seen all the covenants and bands that passed between the King and the Lords, and now findeth that his declaration, before her and council, of his innocency of the death of

u

David, was false; and grievously offended that, by their means, he should seek to come to the crown matrimonial.

Part of a Letter from Randolph to Cecil, from Berwick, 25 April,
1566.

—— There is continually very much speech of the discord between the Queen and her husband, so far that, that is commonly said and believed of himself, that Mr. James Thornton is gone to Rome to sue for a divorce between them. It is very certain that Malevasier had not spoken with him within these three days. He is neither accompany'd nor looked upon of any nobleman; attended upon by certain of his own servants, and six or seven of the guard; at liberty to do, and to go where and what he will, they have no hope yet among themselves of quietness.

——David's brother, named Joseph, who came this way with Malevasier, unknown to any man here, is become secretary in his brother's place.

No. XVII. (p. 189.)

The Earl of Bedford to Cecil, 3d August, 1566.

The Queen and her husband agree after the old manner, or rather worse. She eateth but very seldom with him, lieth not nor keepeth company with him, nor loveth any such as love him. He is so far out of her books, as at her going out of the castle of Edinburgh, to remove abroad, he knew nothing thereof. It cannot for modesty, nor with the honour of a Queen, be reported what she said of him. One Hickman, an English merchant there, having a water spaniel, which was very good, gave him to Mr. James Melvil, who afterwards, for the pleasure which he saw the King have in such kind of dogs, gave him to the King. The Queen thereupon fell marvellously out with Melvil, and called him dissembler and flatterer, and said she could not trust one, who would give any thing to such a one as she loved not.

The Earl of Bedford to Cecil, Aug. 8.

The disagreement between the Queen and her husband continueth, or rather increaseth. Robert Melvill drawing homewards, within twelve miles of Edinburgh, could not tell where to find the Queen; sith which time, she is come to Edinburgh, and had not twelve horses attending on her. There was not then, nor that I can hear of since, any lord, baron, or other nobleman in her company. The King her husband is gone to Dumfermling, and passeth his time as well as he may; having at his farewell such countenance as would make a husband heavy at the heart.

Sir John Forster to Cecil, 8 Sept. from Berwick.

The Queen hath her husband in small estimation, and the Earl of Lennox came not in the Queen's sight since the death of Davy.

Sir John Forster to Cecil, 11th Dec.

THE Earl of Bothwell is appointed to receive the ambassadors, and all things for the christening are at His Lordship's appointment, and the same is scarcely well liked of the nobility, as is said. The King and the Queen is presently at Craigmillar, but in little greater familiarity than he was all the while past.

Advertisements out of Scotland from the Earl of Bedford.

[August, 1566. Paper Office. From the Original.]

THAT the King and Queen agreed well together two days after her coming from——, and after My Lord of Murray's coming to Edinburgh, some new discord has happened. The Queen hath declared to my Lord of Murray that the King bears him evill will, and has said to her that he is determined to kill him, finding fault that she does not bear him so much company; and in like manner hath willed My Lord of Murray to spiere it at the King, which he did a few nights since in the Queen's presence, and in hearing of divers. The King confessed, that reports were made to him, that My Lord of Murray was not his friend, which made him speak that thing he repented; and the Queen affirmed, that the King had spoken such words unto her, and confessed before the whole house, that she could not be content that either he or any other should be unfriend to My Lord of Murray. My Lord of Murray enquired the same stoutly, and used his speech very modesty, in the mean time the King departed very grieved; he cannot bear that the Queen should use familiarity either with man or woman, and especially the ladies of Arguile, Murray, and Marre, who keep most company with her. My Lord of Murray and Bothwell have been at evil words for the L. of Ledington, before the Queen, for he and Sir James Balfoure had new come from Ledington, with his answer upon such heads or articles as Bothwell and he should agree upon, which being reported to the said Earl in the Queen's presence, made answer, that ere he parted with such lands as was desired, he should part with his life. My Lord of Murray said stoutly to him, that twenty as honest men as he should lose their lives ere he reafte Ledington. The Queen spake nothing, but heard both; in these terms they parted, and since, that I hear of, have not met. The Queen after her hunting came to Edinburgh, and carried the Prince thence to Stirling with her. This last Saturday was executed a servant of the Lord Ruthven's, who confessed that he was in the cabinet, but not of council of the fact. The Queen hath also opened to My Lord of Murray, that money was sent from the Pope, how much it was, and by whom, and for what purpose it was brought.

No. XVIII. (p. 196.)

Part of a Letter from Elizabeth to Mary, Feb. 20, 1569. A copy in-terlined by Cecil. It contains an answer to a complaining letter of Mary's upon the Imprisoning of the Bishop of Ross.

——AFTER this [i.e. Mary's landing in Scotland] how patiently did

I bear with many vain delays in not ratifying the treaty accorded by your own commissioners, whereby I received no small unkindness, besides the manifold causes of suspicion that I might not hereafter trust to any writings. Then followed a hard manner of dealing with me, to intice my subject and near kinsman, the Lord Darnly, under colour of private suits for land, to come into the realm, to proceed in treaty of marriage with him without my knowledge, to conclude the same without my assent or liking. And how many unkind parts accompany'd that fact, by receiving of my subjects that were base runnagates and offenders at home and enhansing them to places of credit against my will, with many such like, I will leave, for that the remembrance of the same cannot but be noysome to you. And yet all these did I as it were suppress and overcome with my natural inclination of love towards you; and did afterwards gladly, as you know, christen your son, the child of my said kinsman, that had before so unloyally offended me, both in marriage of you, and in other undutiful usages towards me his sovereign. How friendly also dealt I by messages to reconcile him, being your husband, to you, when others nourished discord betwixt you, who as it seemed had more power to work their purposes, being evil to you both, than I had to do you good, in respect of the evil I had received. Well I will overpass your hard accidents that followed for lack of following my council. And then in your most extremity, when you was a prisoner indeed, and in danger of your life from your notorious evil willers, how far from my mind was the remembrance of any former unkindness you had shewed me. Nay, how void was I of respect to the designs which the world had seen attempted by you to my crown, and the security that might have ensued to my state by your death, when I finding your calamity to be great, that you were at the pit's brink to have miserably lost your life, did not only intreat for your life, but so threatened some as were irritated against you, that I only may say it, even I was the principal cause to save your life.

No. XIX. (p. 204.)

Letter of Q. Elizabeth to Q. of Scots. Thus marked on the back with Cecil's hand.—Copia Literarum Regiæ Majestatis ad Reginam Scotorum VIIIo Aprilis.

[Paper office.]

MADAME, vous ayant trop moleste par M. de Crocq, je n'eusse eu si peu de consideration de vous fascher de cette lettre, si les liens de charite vers les ruinez, et les prieres des miserables ne m'y contraignassent. Je entens que un édit a été divulgué de par vous, madame, que ung chascun, que veult justifier que ons esté les meurtriers de votre feu mari, et mon feu cousin, viennent à lele faire xiiime de ce mois. La quelle chose, comme c'est plus honorable et nécessaire, qui ne tel cas se pourra faire, ne y estant caché quelque mistére ou finesse, ainsi le père et amis du mort gentelhomme m'ont humblement requis, que je vous priasse de prolongue le jour, pource qu'ilz cognoissent que les iniques se sont combinés par force de faire ce que par droict ils ne pourront pas faire ; partant, je ne puis mais sinon

pour l'amour de vous même, à qui il touche le plus, et pour la consolation des innocens, de vous exhorter le leur concéder cette re-
queste, laquelle, si elle les seroit nié, vous tourneroit grandement
en soupcon, de plus que j'espère ne pensez, et que ne voudriez
volontiers ouyr.   Pour l'amour de Dieu, madame, usez de telle sin-
cérité et prudence en ce cas qui vous touche de si près, que tout le
monde aye raison, de vous livrer comme innocente d'ung crime si
énorme, chose que si ne fistes, seriez dignement esbloyé hors de
rancz de Princesses, et non sans cause faite opprobre de vulgaire, et
plutôt que cela vous avienne, je vous souhaiterois une sépulture
honorable, qu'une vie maculée; vous voiez madame, que je vous
traite comme ma fille, et vous promets, que si j'en eusse, ne luy souhaiterois mieulx, que je vous desire, comme le Seigneur Deu me
porte tesmoignage, à que je prie de bon cœur de vous inspirer à faire
ce que vous sera plus à honneur, et à vos amis plus de consolation,
avec mes très cordialles recommendations comme a icelle à qui se
souhaite le plus de bien, qui vous pourra en ce monde avenir.   De
West. ce 8 jour de Janvier* en haste.

No. XX. (p. 209.)

*Account of the sentence of Divorce between the Earl of Bothwell and
Lady Jean Gordon, his Wife.   From a Manuscript belonging to
Mr. David Falconer, Advocate.   Fol. 455.*

Upon the 29 of Apryle 1567, before the Richt Hon. Mr. Robert
Maitland Dean of Aberdene, Mr. Edward Henryson doctor in the
laws, two of the senators of the college of justice, Mr. Clement
Little, and Mr. Alexander Syme advocatiis, commissers of Edinr;
compeered Mr. Henry Kinrosse, procurator for Jean Gourdoune
Countess of Bothwell, constitute be her pursewing of ane proces of
divorcement intendit by her contra James Erle Bothwell her husband for adultry committed be him with Bessie Crawfurde the pursuer's servant for the time; and sicklyke, for the said Erle, compeared Mr. Edmond Hay, who, efter he had pursued and craved the
pursuer's procurator's oath de calumnia, if he had just caus to pur-
sew the said action, and obtained it, denied the libell, and the said
Mr. Harrie took the morne, the last day of Apryle, to prove the
same pro prima.   The quhilk day, having produced some witnesses,
he took the next day, being the 1 of May, to do farther diligence,
upon the quhilk 1 of May he produced some moe witnesses, and renounced farther probatioune.   After quhilk, he desired a term to
be assigned to pronounce sentence.   To whom the said commissers
assigned Satterday next, the 3 of May, to pronounce sentence
therein, secundum alegata et probata, quilk accordingly was given
that day in favour of the purswar.

At the same time there was another proces intendit be the Erl
of Bothwell contr his lady, for to have their marriage declared nul,
as being contracted against the canons, without a dispensation, and
he and his lady being within degrees defendand, viz., ferdis a kin,
and that wyse for expeding of this proces, there was a commissioune

*A mistake in the date corrected with Cecil's hand VIII. Aprilis.

grantit to the Archbishop of St. Androis to cognosce and determine it, and Robert Bishop of Dunkeld, William Bishop of Dunblane, Mr. Andro Craufurd chanon in Glasgow and parson of Egelshame, Mr. Alexander Criechtoun, and Mr. George Cooke Chancellor of Dunkeld, and to Mr. Johne Manderstoune chanon of Dunbar and prebendar of Beltoune, or any ane of them. This commissione is datit 27th Aprile, 1567, was presented to two of the saids commissioners, viz., Mr. Andrew Crawfurd and Mr. John Manderstoune on Satterday 3 May, by Mr. Thomas Hepburne pastor of Auldhamstocks, procurator for the Erle of Bothwell, who accepted the delegatioune, and gave out their citation by precept, directed Decano Christianitatis de Hadingtoune, nec non vicario seu curato eccle. parochiæ de Chreichtoune seu cuicunq ; alteri capellano debiti requisitis, fer summoning, at the said Erle's instance both of the lady personally if she could be had, or otherways at the parosche kerk of Creichtoune the tyme of service, or at her dwelling place before witnesses, primo, secundo, tertio et peremptorie, unico tamen contextu protuplice edicto. And likeways to be witnesses in the said matter, Alex. Bishop of Galloway, who did marry the said Erle and lady in Halerud-hous kirk, in Feb. 1565, Sir John Bannatyne of Auchnole justice clerk, Mr. Robert Creichtoun of Elliok the Queen's advocate, Mr. David Chalmers provost of Creichtoun and chancellor of Ross, Michael—Abbot of Melross, and to compear before the said judges or any one of them in St. Geil's kirk in Edr on Monday the 5 of May, be thamselves, or their procurators. Upon the said 5 day, Mr. John Manderstoun, one of the judges delegat only being present, compeared the same procurators for both the parties that were in the former proces, Mr. Edmund Hay (articulatlie   *) and some of the witnesses summoned produced, and received for proving the same. The said procurator renounced farder probatioune, and the judge assigned the morne, the 6th of May, and publicandum producta, nempe depositiones ipsorum testium. The quhilk day, post publicatas, depositiones prædictas, Mr. Hen. Kinrosse, procurator for the lady, instanter objecit objectiones juris generaliter, contra producta, insuper renunciavit ulteriori defensioni; proinde conclusa de consensu procuratorum hinc inde causa, judex prædictus statuit crastinum diem pro termina, ad pronunciandum suum sententiam definitivam, ex deductis coram eo, in præsenti causa et processu. Conform hereunto, on Wednesday the 7th of May, the said judge gave out his sentence in favour of the Erle, declaring the marriage to be, and to have been null from the beginning, in respect of their contingence in blood, which hindered their lawful marriage without a dispensation obtained of befoir.

---

* Two words in the parenthesis illegible.

No. XXI.   (p. 211.)

A Letter from England concerning the Murder of King Henry Darnley.

[E. of Morton's Archieves. Bundle B. No. 25.]

HAVING the commodity of this bearer, Mr. Clark, I tho't good to write a few words unto you. I have rec^d some writs from you, and some I have seen lately sent others from you, as namely to the Earl of Bedford of the 16th of May. I have participat the contents thereof to such as I thought meet, this mekle I can assure you; the intelligence given hithere by the French was untrue, for there was not one Papist nor Protestant which did not consent that justice should be done, be the Queen my sov^{ns} aid and support, against such as had committed that abominable ill murder in your country; but to say truth, the lack and coldness did not rise from such as were called to council, but from such as should give life and execution thereunto. And further, I assure you, I never knew no matter of estate proponed as had so many favourers of all sorts of nations as this had; yea, I can say unto you, no man promoted the matter with greater affection, than the Spanish ambassador. And sure I am that no man dare openly be of any other mind, but to affirm that whosoever is guilty of this murder, hand fasted with advoutre, is unworthy to live. I shall not need to tell you, which be our letts, and stayes from all good things here. You are acquainted with them as well as I. Neds I must confess, that, howsoever we omit occasions of benefit, honour, and surety; it behoveth your whole nobility, and namely such as before and after the murder, were deemed to allow of Bodwell, to prosecute with sword and justice the punishment of those abominable acts, though we lend you but a cold aid, and albeit you and divers others, both honourable and honest, be well known to me, and sundry others here, to be justifiable in all their actions and doings; yet think not the contrary but your whole nation is blemished and infamit by these doings which lately passed among you. What we shall do I know not, neither do I write unto you assuredly, for we be subject unto many mutations, and yet I think we shall either aid you or continue in the defence and safeguard of your Prince, so as it appear to us that you mean his safeguard indeed, and not run the fortune of France, which will be your own destruction if you be unadvised. I know not one, no, not one of any quality or estate in this country which does allow of the Queen your sovereign, but would gladly the world were rid of her, so as the same were done without farther slander, that is to say by ordinary justice. This I send to you the 23d of May.

No. XXII. (p. 215.

Part of a Letter from Sir Nicolas Throkmorton to Cecil, 11th of July, 1567, from Berwick.

[An Original. Paper Office.]

——Sir, your letter of the 6th of July, I received the 10th at Berwick. I am sorry to see that the Queen's Majesty's disposition altereth not towards the lords, for when all is done, it is they which must stand her more in stead, than the Queen her cousin, and will be better instruments to work some benefite and quietness to Her Majesty and her realm, than the Queen of Scotland which is void of good fame.

A Letter from Sir Nicolas Throkmorton to Cecil, from Fastcastle, 12th of July, 1567.

[Paper Office.]

Sir, as you might perceive by my letter of the 11th July, I lodged at Fastcastle that night accompanyed with the Lord Hume, the Lord of Ledington, and James Melvin, where I was entreated very well according to the state of the place, which is fitter to lodge prisoners than folks at liberty, as it is very little, so it is very strong. By the conference I have had with the Lord of Ledington I find the lords his associates and he hath left nothing unthought of, which may be either to thir danger or work them suerty, wherein they do not forget what good and harme France may do them, and likewise they consider the same of England; but as farr as I can perceive, to be plain with yow, they find more perril to grow unto them through the Queen's Majesty's dealing than either they do by the French, or by any contrary faction amongest themselves, for they assure themselves the Queen will leave them in the bryers if they run her fortoun, and though they do acknowledge great benefit as well to them, as to the realm of England by Her Majesty's doings at Leith, whereof they say mutually Her Majesty and both the realms have received great fruit : yet upon other accidents which have chanced since, they have observed such things in Her Majesty's doings, as have ended to the danger of such as she hath dealt withal, to the overthrow of your own designments, and little to the suerty of any party ; and upon these considerations and discourses at length, methinketh I find a disposition in them, that either they mind to make their bargain with France, or else to deal neither with France nor yow, but to do what they shall think meet for their state and suerty, and to use their remedys as occasion shall move them ; meaning neither to irritate France nor England, untill such time as they have made their bargain assuredly with one of yow ; for they think it convenient to proceed with yow both for a while pari passu, for that was My Lord of Ledington's terms. I do perceave they take the matter very unkindly, that no better answer is made to the letter, which the lords did send to Her Majesty, and likewise that they hear nothing from yow to their satisfaction. I have answered as well as I can, and have alleged their own proceedings so obscurly with the Queen and their uncertainty hath occationed this that is yet happened, and therefore Her Majesty hath sent me to the end I may inform her throughly of the state of the matters, and upon the declaration of their minds and intents to such purposes as shall be by me proposed on Her Majesty's behalf unto them, they shall be reasonably and resolutely answered.—At these things the Lord of Ledington smiled and shook his head, and said it were better for us you would let us alone than neither to do us nor yourselves good, as I fear me in the end that will prove : So if their be any truth in Ledington, Le Crocq is gone to procure Ramboilet his coming hither or a man of like quality, and to deliver them of their Queen for ever, who shall lead her lite in France in a abbay reclused, the Prince at the French devotion, the realm governed by a council of their election of the Scottish nation, the forts committed to the custody of such as shall be chosen amongst themselves, as yet I find no great likehood that I shall have access to the Queen, it is objected they may not so displease the French, King, unless they were sure to find the Queen of England a good friend ; and when they once by my access to the Queen have offended the French, then they say yow will make your profit thereof to their undoing; and as to the Queen's liberty, which was the first head that I proposed, they said that hereby they did perceive that the Queen wants their undoing, for as for the rest of the matters it was but folly to talk of them, the liberty going before : but said they, is you will do us no good, do us no harm, and we will provide for ourselves. In the end they said, we should refuse our own commodity before they concluded with any other, which I should hear of at my coming to Edinr ; by my next I hope to send yow the band concluded by Hamiltons, Argyll, Huntly, and that faction, not so much to the prejudice of the Lords of Edinr, as that which was sent into France ; thus having no more leisure, but compell'd to leap on horseback with the lords to go to Edinr, I humbly take my leave of from Fastcastle the 12th of July, 1567.

To Sir Nicolas Throkmorton being in Scotland. By the Queen, the 14th July, 1567.

[Paper Office.]

TRUSTY and well beloved, we greet you well, though we think that the causes will often change upon variety of accidents, yet we think for sundry respects, not amiss, that as yow shall deal with the Lords having charge of the young Prince for the committing of him into our realm, so shall yow also do well, in treaty with the Queen, to offer her that where her realm appeareth to be subject to sundry troubles from time to time, and hereby (as it is manifest) her son cannot be free, if she shall be contented that her son may enjoy suerty and quietness within this our realm, being so near as she knows it is ; we shall not faill to yield her as good suerty therein for her child as can be devised for any that might be our child, born of our own body, and shall be glad to show to her therein the trew effect of nature ; and herein she may be by yow rem-

U 5

embered oow much good may ensue to her son to be nourished
and acquainted with our country: and therefore, all things
considered, this occason for her child, were rather to be sought
by her friends of him than offered by us; and to this end we mean
that yow shall so deal with her, both to stay her indeed from
inclining to the French practice, which is to us notorious, to convey
her and the Prince into France, and also to avoid any just offence,
that she might hereafter conceive, if she should hear that we
should deal with the Lords for the Prince.

*Sir Nicolas Throkmorton to Queen Elizabeth, 14th July, 1567, From
Edinburgh.*

[An Original. Paper Office.]

It may please Your Majesty to be advertised, I did signifie unto
Mr. Secretary by my letters of the 11th and 12th of July, the day
of mine entry into Scotland, the causes of my stay, my lodging at
Fastcastle, a place of the Lord Humes's where I was met by the
said Lord and by the Lord Lidington, and what had passed in conference betwixt us, whilest I was at the said Fastcastle. Since
which time, accompanyed with the lords aforesaid, and with 400
horses by their appointment for my better conduct, I came to Edin-
the 12th of this present. The 13th being Sunday appointed
for a solemne communion in this town, and also a solemne fast
being published, I could not have conference with the Lords which
be assembled within this town, as I desired, that is to say the Earls
of Athole and Morton, the Lord Hume, the Lord of Lidington,
Sir James Balfour captain of the castle, Mr. James M'Gill, and the
president of the session.

Nevertheless I made means by the Lord of Lidington that they
would use no protracte of time in mine audience, so did I likewise to the Earle of Morton, whom I met by chance; I was answered by them both, that albeit the day was destined to sacred
exercises, such as were there of the council would consult upon
any moyen touching my access unto them and my conference with
them, and said also, that in the afternoon either they would come
to me, or I should hear from them. About 4 of the clock in the
afternoon, the said 13th day, the Lord of Lidington came to my
lodgings, and declared unto me on behalf of the lords and others,
that they required me to have patience, though they defferred my
conference with them, which was grounded principally upon the
absence of the Earles of Mar and Glencairn, the Lords Semple,
Crighton, and others of the council, saying also that they did consider the matters which I was on your behalf to treate with them
of, were of great importance, as they could not satisfy nor conveniently treate with me, nor give me answer without the advice of the
lords, and others their associates; the Lord of Lidington also said
unto me, that where he perceived, by his private conference with
me in my journey thitherwards, that I pressed greatly to have
speedy access to the Queen their sovereign, he perceived by the
lords and others which were here, that in that matter there was

great difficulty in respects, but especially because they had refused
to the French ambassador the like access, which being granted
unto me might greatly offend the French, a matter which they desired and intended to eschew; for they did not find by your Majesty's dealings with them hitherto, that it behoved them to irritate
the French King, and to lose his favour and good intelligence with
him: I answered, that as to their refusal made unto the French
ambassador, Monsieur de Ville Roye was dispatched forth of France
before these accidents here happened, and his special erraud was
to impeach the Queen's marriage with the Earle of Bothel (for so
indeed since my coming hither I learned his commission tended to
that end, and to make offer to the Queen of another marriage), and
as to Monsieur de Crocq, he could have no order forth of France
concerning these matters since they happened; and therefore they
might very well hold them suspected to have conference with the
Queen, least they might treate of matters in this time without instructions, and so rather do harm then good; but Your Majesty
being advertized of all things which had chanced, had sent me his
ther to treat with them, for the well of the realm, for the conversation of their honours and credit, and for their suerty: and I
might boldly say unto him, that Your Majesty had better deserved
than the French had. He said for his own part, he was much
bound unto Your Majesty, and had always found great favour and
courtesy in England; but to be plain with you, Sir, sayed he, there
is not many of the assembly that have found so great obligation at
the Queen your sovereigns hands, as at the French Kings, for the
Earles of Morton and Glencairn be the only persons which took
benefit by the Queen's Majestys aid at Leith, the rest of the noblemen were not in the action; and we think, said he, the Queens Majesty your sovereign, by the opinion of her own council and all the
world, took as great benefit by that charge as the realm of Scotland,
or any particular person: and not to talk with yow as an ambassador,
but with Sir Nicholas Throkmorton, My Lord Morton, and such as
were in pain for the death of Davie, found but cold favour at the
Queens Majesty's hands, when they were banish'd forth of their
own country; but I would all our whole company were as well wil
ling to accomplish the Queen your sovereign intents and desires as
I am; for mine own part I am but one, and that of the meanest
sort, and they be many noblemen and such as have great interest
in the matter, assure yow shall be assured I will imploy myself to
imploy my credit, and all that I may do, to satisfie the Queen your
mistress, as much as lyeth in me, and for your own part you have
a great many friends in this assembly, with many other good words.
But for conclusion I must take this for an answer to stay untill the
other lords were come, and thereupon I thought meet to advertize
Your Majesty what hath passed, and how far forth I have proceeded; your expectation being great to hear from hence.

And now to advertize Your Majesty of the state of all things, as
I have learned since my coming hither, it may please Your Majesty to understand as followeth:

The Queen of Scotland remaineth in good health in the castle of
Lochlevin, guarded by the Lord Linsay and Lochleven the owner

of the house; for the Lord Ruthven is employed in another commission, because he began to show great favour to the Queen, and
to give her intelligence.   She is waited on with 5 or 6 ladys, 4 or 5
gentlewomen, and 2 chamberers, whereof one is a French woman.
The Earle of Buchan, the Earle of Murray's brother, hath also liberty to come to her at his pleasure; the lords aforesaid, which
have her in guard, doe keep her very straitly, and as far as I can
perceive, their rigour proceedeth by their order from these men,
because that the Queen will not by any means be induced to lend
her authority to prosecute the murder, nor will not consent by any
perswasion to abandon the Lord Bothell for her husband, but
avoweth constantly that she will live and die with him; and saith
that if it were put to her choice to relinquish her crown and kingdom, or the Lord Bothell, she would leave her kingdom and dignity,
to go as a simple damsell with him, and that she will never consent
that he shall fare worse or have more harm than herself.

    And as far as I can perceive, the principall cause of her deten-
tion is, for that these lords do see the Queen being of so fervent affection towards the Earle Bothell as she is, and being put at, as
they should be compelled to be in continuall arms, and to have occasion of many battles, he being with manifest evidence notoriously
detected to be the principall murderer, and the lords meaning prosecution of justice against him according to his merits.

    The lords mean also a divorce between the Queen and him, as a
marriage not to be suffered for many respects, which separation
cannot take place if the Queen be at liberty, and have power in her
hands.

    They do not also forget their own peril, conjoin'd with the danger
of the Prince, but as far as I can perceave, they intend not either to
touch the Queen in suerty or in honor, for they do speak of her
with respect and reverence, and do affirm, as I do learn, that the
conditions aforesaid accomplished, they will both put her to liberty,
and restore her to her estate.

    These lords have for the guard of their town 450 harqubushers
which be in very good order, for the entertainment of which company's untill all matters be compounded, they did sue unto Your
Majesty to aid them with such sum of mony as hath been mentioned to Mr. Secretary by the Lord of Lidingtons writing, amounting as I perceive to ten or twelve thousand crouns of the—

    They were latly advertized that the French King doth mind to
send hither Monsieur de la Chapell dez Ursine, a knight of the
French order, and always well affectionate to the house of Guyse,
and howsoever La Forest, Villaroy, and Du Crocq have used language in the Queens favour and to these lords disadvantage there, to
Your Majesty; La Crocq doth carry with him such matter as shall
be little to the Queen's advantage; so as it is thought the French
King, upon his coming to his presence, will rather satisfie the lords
than pleasure the Queen; for they have their party so well made,
as the French will rather make their profit by them than any other
way.

    Herewith I send Your Majesty the last bond agreed on, and

signed by the Hamilton's, the Earl of Argyll, Huntly, and sundry others at Dumbarton.

Nevertheless, since my coming to this town the Hamiltons have sent unto me a gentleman of their surname, named Robert Hamilton, with a letter from the Bishop of St. Andrew's and the Abbot of Arbroth, the copy whereof I send Your Majesty and mine answer unto them, referring to the bearer the declaration of some things as these did by him unto me.

The Earle of Argyll hath, in like manner, sent another unto me with a letter and credit, I have used him as I did the others, the coppy of both which letters I send Your Majesty also. The Lord Harrys hath also sent me but not written, and I have returned unto him in like sort.

Against the 20th day of this month there is a generall assembly of all the churches, shires, and boroughs towns of this realm, namely, of such as be contented to repair to these lords to this town, where it is thought the whole state of this matter will be handeled, and I fear me much to the Queen's disadvantage and danger; unless the Lord of Lidington and some others which be best affected unto her do provide some remedy; for I perceave the great number, and in manner all, but chiefly the common people, which have assisted in these doings, do greatly dishonour the Queen, and mind seriously either her deprivation or her destruction; I used the best means I can (considering the furie of the world here), to prorogue this assembly, for that appeareth to me to be the best remedy: I may not speak of dissolution of it, for that may not be abiden, and I should thereby bring myself into great hatred and peril. The chiefest of the lords which be here present at this time dare not show so much lenity to the Queen as I think they could be contented, for fear of the rage of the people. The women be most furious and impudent against the Queen, and yet the men be mad enough; so as a stranger over busie may soon be made a sacrifice amongest them.

There was a great bruit that the Hamiltons with their adherents would put their force into the fields against the 24th of this month, but I do not find that intent so true as the common bruit geeth.

The Earle of Argyll is in the Highlands, where there is trouble among his own countrymen.

The Earle of Lennox is by these lords much desired here, and I do believe Your Majesty may so use him, and direct him, as he shall be able to promote your purpose with these men.

The Earle of Argyll, the Hamiltons and he be incompatible.—— I do find amongst the Hamiltons, Argyll, and the company two strange and sundry humours.

Hamiltons do make shew of the liberty of the Queen, and prosecute that with great earnestness, because they would have these lords destroy her, rather than she should be recovered from them by violence; another time they seem to desire her liberty and Bothwell's destruction, because they would compass a marriage betwixt the Queen and the Lord of Arbroth.

The Earle of Argyll doth affect her liberty and Bothwell's destruction, because he would marry the Queen to his brother,

And yet neither of them, notwithstanding their open concurance (as appeareth by their bond), doth discover their minds to each other, nor mind one end; Knox is not here, but in the west parts, he and the rest of the ministers will be here at the great assembly, whose austerity against the Queen I fear as much as any man's.

By some conference which I had with some of this councill, me thinketh that they have intelligence that there is a disposition in the Queen of Scotland to leave this realm and to retire herself either into England or into France, but most willingly into England, for such —— and mislikings as she knoweth hath been, and is meant unto her in France, leaving the regiment either to a number of persons deleagued and authorized by her, or to some one or more.

And it may please Your Majesty, I think it not amiss to put yow in remembrance, that in case the said Queen come into England by your allowance, without the French King's consent, she shall loose her dowery in France, and have little or nothing from hence to entertain her; and in case she do go into France with the King's contentment, she may be an instrument (if she can recover favour, as time will help to cancell her disgrace) either by matching with some husband of good quality, or by some other devise, to work new unquietness to her own country, and so consequently to Your Majesty's.

Therefore it may please Your Majesty to consider of this matter, and to let me know your pleasure with convenient speed, how I shall answer the same, if it be propounded unto me, either by the Queen or by the councill, as a piece of the end and composition. For I am sure, of late, she hath seemed very desirous to have the matter brought to pass that she might go into England, retaining her estate and jurisdiction in herself, though she do not exercise it; and likewise I understand that some of this council which be least affected to her safety do think there is no other way to save her. Thus Almighty God preserve Your Majesty in health, honour, and all felicity; at Edinr the 14th July, 1567.

Sir Nicholas Throkmorton to Queen Elizabeth, the 18th of July, 1567, from Edinburgh.

[An Original. Paper Office.]

It may please Your Majesty, yow might perceave by my letters of the 16th, how far I had proceeded with these lords, and what was their answer; since which time I have spoken particularly with the Earle Morton, the Lord of Lidington, and Sir James Balfour captain of this castle; at whose hands I cannot perceave that as yet access to the Queen to Lochleven will be granted me, staying themselves still by the absence of the lords and others their associates, which (they say) they look for within two days; and for that I find, by likelihood and apparent presumptions, that mine access to the Queen will hardly be granted, I have thought good not to defer this dispatch untill I have a resolute answer in that matter.

May it therefore please Your Majesty, to understand Robert Melvin returned from the Queen in Lochleven to this town, the 6th of July, and brought a letter from her written of her own hand to these lords, which doth contain, as I understand, matter as followeth—A request unto them to have consideration of her health and if they will not put her to liberty, to change the place of restraint to the castle of Stirling, to the end she might have the comfort and company of her son, and if they will not change her from Lochleven, she required to have some other gentle-women about her, naming none.

To have her apothecary, to have some modest minister.——To have an imbroiderer to draw forth such work as she would be occupied about, and to have a varlet of the chamber.——Touching the government of the realm she maketh two offers, which are but generally touched in her letter, the particularitys be not specified, but refered to Robert Melvin's credit, the one is to commit it only and wholly to the Earle of Murray, the other is to the lords whose names ensue, assisted with such others as they shall call unto them, that is to say, the Duke of Chattelrault, the Earls of Morton, Murray, Marr, and Glencairn.

She hath written unto them that I might have access unto her. —— She requireth further, that if they will not treat her and regard her as their Queen, yet to use her as the King their sovereign's daughter (whom many of them knew), and as their Prince's mother.—She will by no means yield to abandon Bothell for her husband, nor relinquish him; which matter will do her most harm of all, and hardeneth these lords to great severity against her.

She yieldeth in words to the prosecution of the murder.

I have the means to let her know that Your Majesty hath sent me hither for her relief.

I have also persuaded her to conform herself to renounce Bothell for her husband, and to be contented to suffer a divorce to pass betwixt them; she hath sent me word that she will in no ways consent unto that, but rather die; grounding herself upon this reason, taking herself to be seven weeks gone with child, by renouncing Bothell, she should acknowledge herself to be with child of a bastard, and to have forfeited her honour, which she will not do to die for it; I have perswaded her to save her own life and her child, to choose the least hard condition.

Mr. Knox arrived here in this town the 6th of this month, with whom I have some conference, and with Mr. Craig also, the other minister of this town.

I have perswaded with them to preach and perswad lenity. I find them both very austere in this conference, what they shall do hereafter I know not, they are furnished with many arguments, some forth of the Scripture, some forth of histories, some grounded (as they say) upon the laws of this realm, some upon practices used in this realm, and some upon the conditions and oth made by their Prince at her coronation.

The Bishop of Galloway, uncle to the Earle of Huntley, hath sent hither to these lords, that his nephew the Earle and some others of that side may, at Linlithgow or at Stirling, have some communication with some appointed on this side, assuring them that there is a good disposition in the lords of the other party to concurre with these, assuring further that they will not dissent for trifles or unnecessary things, and (as I am given to understand) they can be pleased the Queen's restraint be continu'd untill the murder be pursued in all persons, whereby the separation of the Queen and Bothell is implyed, the preservation of the Prince, the security for all men, and a good order taken for the governance of the realm in tranquillity.

Captain Clerk, which have so long served in Denmark and served at Newhaven, did, the 16th of this month (accompanied with one of his soldiers, or rather the soldier as the greater fame goeth) kill one Wilson a seaman, and such a one as had great estimation with these lords, both for his skill, his hardyness, honesty, and willingness in this action; whereupon Clerk hath retired himself; their quarrel was about the ship which took Blacketer, which ship was appointed by these lords to go to the north of Scotland to impeach the passage of the Earle Bothell, in case he went either to the isles, or to any other place; by the death of this man this enterprize was dashed.

The Bishop of Galloway is come to Linlithgow, and doth desire to speak with the Lord of Lidington.

The Abbot of Kilwinning hath sent for Sir James Balfour, captain of the castle, to have conference with him.

As I wrote unto Your Majesty in my last, the Hamiltons now find no matter to disever these lords and them asunder, but would concurr in all things (yea, in any extremity against the Queen) so as that they might be assured the Prince of Scotland were crouned King, and should die without issue, that the Earle of Lenox's son living should not inherit the croun of this realm, as next heir to his nephew.

And although the lords and councelors speak reverently, mildly, and charitably of their Queen, so as I cannot gather by their speech any intention to cruelty or violence, yet I do find by intelligence, that the Queen is in very great peril of her life, by reason that the people assembled at this convention do mind vehemently the destruction of her.

It is a public speech among all the people, and amongst all estates (saving of the counselors) that their Queen hath no more liberty nor privilege to commit murder nor adultery than any other private person, neither by God's laws, nor by the laws of the realm.

The Earl of Bothell, and all his adherents and associates, be put to the horn by the ordinary justice of this town, named the lords of the session; and commandment given to all shirriffs, and all other officers, to apprehend him, and all other his followers and receiptors. The Earl of Bothell's porter, and one of his other servitors of his chamber being apprehended, have confessed such sundry circumstances, as it appeareth evidently that he the said Earl was one of the principal executors of the murder in his one person, accompanyed with sundry others, of which number I cannot yet certainly learn the names but of three of them, that is to say, two of the Ormistons of Tivotdall, and one of Hayborn of Bolton; the lords would be glad that none of the murderers should have any favour or receipt in England, and hereof there desire is, that the officers upon the border may be warned; Bothell doth still remain in the north parts; but the Lord Seaton and Fleming, which have been there, have utterly abandoned him, and do repair hitherwards. The intelligence doth grow daily betwixt these lords, and those which held of; and notwithstanding these lords have sent an hundred and fifty harqubushers to Stirling, to keep the town and passage from surprise; and so have they done in like manner to St. Johnston, which be the two passages from the north and west to this town, I do understand the captain of Dunbar is much busied in fortifying that place. I do mervile the carriages be not impeached otherwise than they be.

Of late this Queen hath written a letter to the captain of the said castle, which hath been surprized; and thereby matter is discovered which maketh little to the Queen's advantage.

Thus, having none other matter worthy Your Majesty's knowledge, I beseech God to prosper Your Majesty with long life, perfect health, and prosperous felicity. At Edinburgh, the 18th of July 1567.

Letter of Sir Nicholas Throkmorton to the Right Honourable the Earl of Leicester, Knight of the order, and one of the Lords of Her Majesty's most Honourable Privy Council.

(24th of July, 1567. Paper Office. From the original.)

By my former dispatches sent to her Majesty and Mr. Secretary, since the 12th of July, Your Lordships might have perceived the state of this country, and to what end these matters be like to come; so as not to trouble Your Lordship with many words : this Queen is like very shortly to be deprived of her royal estate, her son to be crowned King, and she detained in prison within this realm, and the same to be governed in the young King's name by a council, consisting of certain of the nobility, and other wise men of this realm ; so as it is easy to be seen that the power and ability to do any thing to the commodity of the Queen's Majesty, and the realm of England, will chiefly, and in manner wholly, rest in the hands of these lords and others their associates assembled at Edinburgh. Now if the Queen's Majesty will still persist in her former opinion towards the Queen of Scotland (unto whom she shall be able to do no good), then I do plainly see that these lords and all their accomplices will become as good French as the French King can wish to all intents and purposes. And as for the Hamiltons, the Earls of Arguile, Huntlye, and that faction, they be already so far inchanted that way, as there needeth little devise to draw them to the French devotion. Then this is the state of things so come to pass of this country, that France has Scotland now as much conjoined unto them, to all purposes, as ever it was ; and what an instrument the young Prince will prove to unquiet England, I report me to Your Lordships wisdoms ; and therefore, considering the weight of the matter and all the circumstances, I trust your Lordships will well bethink you in time (for 'tis high time) how to advise Her Majesty to leave nothing undone that may bring the Prince of Scotland to be in her possession, or, at the least, to be at her devotion. And, amongst other things that I can imagine for the first degree, nothing is more meet to bring this to effect than to allure this company here assembled, to bear Her Majesty their favour. Some talk hath passed between the Lord of Liddington and me in certain conferences about this matter. By him I find that, when Her Majesty shall have won these men to her devotion, the principal point that will make them conformable to deliver their Prince into England will rest upon the Queen, and the realms enabling him to the succession of the crown of England for fault of issue of the Queen's Majesty's body; some other things will also be required, as the charge of the said Prince and his train to be at the charge of England. I do well perceive that these men will never be brought to deliver their Prince into England without the former condition, for the succession of England; for (saith Liddington) that taking place, the Prince shall be as dear to the people of England as to the people of Scotland; and the one will be as careful of his preservation as the other, Otherwise, he saith, all things considered, it will be reported that the Scottishmen have put their Prince to be kept in safety, as those which commit the sheep to be kept by the wolves. So as for conclusion, Your Lordships may perceive here will be the scope of this matter. As unto the delivering of him upon hostages, he sayeth, let no man think that the condition of the succession not being accomplished, the nobility and the gentry will never consent to leave themselves destitute of their sovereign upon any hostages, neither upon any promises, nor likelihood of good to issue in time to come. It were not good for yourselves (saith he) that the matter were so handled; for then you should adventure all your goods in one ship, which might have a dangerous effect, considering the unwillingness of the Queen your sovereign to consent to establishing any successor to the crown. And then how unmete were it that Her Majesty have in her possession already all such persons as do pretend to it, or be inheritable to the crown, to have our Prince also in her custody. For so there might follow, without good capitulations, a strange and dangerous issue, tho' the Queen your mistress do think that such imaginations could not proceed but from busy heads, as you have uttered unto us on her behalf. What is come to pass since my last despatch, and how far forth things are proceeded, I refer Your Lordship to be informed by my letters sent unto her Majesty at this time. And so I pray Almighty God preserve Your Lordship in much honour and felicity. At Edinburgh, this 24th of July, 1567.

It may please Your good Lordship to make My Lord Stuard partner of this letter.

The Queen to Sir Nicholas Throkmorton. By the Queen.

[6th August 1567.]

TRUSTY and right well-beloved, we greet you well, for as much as we do consider that you have now a long time remained in those parts without expedition in the charge committed unto you, we think it not meet, seeing there hath not followed the good acceptation and fruit of our well meaning towards that state, which good reason would have required, that you should continue there any longer; our pleasure therefore is, that you shall, immediately upon the receipt hereof, send your servant Middlemore unto the lords and estates of that realm that are assembled together, willing him to declare unto them, that it cannot but seem very strange unto us, that you having been sent from us, of such good intent, to deal with them in matters tending so much to their own quiet and to the benefit of the whole estate of their country, they have so far forgotten themselves, and so slightly regarded us and our good meaning, not only in delaying to hear you and deferring your access to the Queen their sovereign, but also, which is strangest of all, in not vouchsafing to make any answer unto us. And altho' these dealings be such, indeed, as were not to be looked for at their hands, yet do we find their usage and proceeding towards their Sovereign and Queen to overpass all the rest in so strange a degree, as we for our part, and we suppose the whole world besides, cannot but think them to have therein gone so far beyond the duty of subjects as must needs remain to their perpetual tauche for ever. And therefore ye shall say, that we have tho't good without consuming any longer time in vain, to revoke you to our presence, requiring them to grant you liscence and passport so to do, which when you shall have obtained, we will that you make your repair hither unto us with as convenient speed as you may. Given, &c.

Indorsed 6th August, 1567.

Throkmorton to the Right Honourable Sir William Cecil, Knight, one of her Majesty's Privy Council and Principal Secretary, give these.

[12th August 1567. Paper Office. From the Original.]

SIR,

WHAT I have learned, since the arrival of My Lord of Murray and Mons. de Linnerol, you shall understand by my letter to Her Majesty at this time. The French do, in their negotiations, as they do in their drink, put water to their wine. As I am able to see into their doings, they take it not greatly to the heart how the Queen sleep, whether she live or die, whether she be at liberty or in prison. The mark they shoot at is, to renew their old league; and can be as well contented to take it of this little King (howsoever his title be), and the same by the order of these lords, as otherwise. Lyneroll came but yesterday, and me thinketh he will not tarry long, you may guess how the French will seek to displease these lords, when they changed the coming of la Chapelle des Oursins for this man, because they doubted that de la Chapelle should not be grateful to them, being a Papist. Sir, to speak more plainly to you than I will do otherwise, me thinketh the Earl of Murray will run the course that those men do, and be partaker of their fortune. I hear no man speak more bitterly against the tragedy, and the players therein, than he, so little like he hath to horrible sins. I hear an inkling that Ledington is to go into France, which I do as much mislike as any thing for our purpose. I can assure you the whole Protestants of France will live and die in these mens quarrels; and, where there is bruit amongst you, that aid should be sent to the adverse party, and that Martigues should come hither with some force; Mons. Baudelot hath assured me of his honour that, instead of Martigues coming against them, he will come with as good a force to succour them: and if that be sent under meaner conduct, Robert Stuart shall come with as many to fortify them. But the constable hath assured these lords, that the King meaneth no way to offend them. Sir, I pray you find my revocation convenient, and speed you to further it, for I am here now to no purpose, unless it be to kindle these lords more against us. Thus I do most humbly take my leave of you, from Edinburgh, the 12th of August, 1567.

Yours to use and command.

The Queen to Nicholas Throkmorton.

TRUSTY and well beloved, we greet you well. We have, within these two days, received three sundry letters of yours, of the 20th, 22d, and 23rd of this month, having not before these received any seven days before; and do find, by these your letters, that you have very diligently and largely advertised us of all the hasty and peremptory proceedings there; which as we nothing like, so we trust in time to see them wax colder, and to receive some reformation. For we cannot perceive that they with whom you have dealt can answer the doubts moved by the Hamiltons, who howsoever they may be carried for their private respects, yet those things which they move will be allowed by all reasonable persons. For if they may not, being noblemen of the realm, be suffered to hear the Queen their sovereign declare her mind concerning the reports which are made of her, by such as keep her in captivity, how should they believe the reports, or obey them, which do report it? and therefore our meaning is, you shall let the Hamiltons plainly understand that we do well allow of their proceedings (as far forth as the same doth concern the Queen their sovereign for her relief) and in such things as shall appear reasonable for us therein to do for the Queen our sister, we will be ready to perform the same. And where it is so required, that upon your coming thence, the Lord Scroope should deal with the Lord Herris to impart their meanings to us, and ours to them; we are well pleased therewith, and we require you to advertize the Lord Scroope hereof by your letters, and to will him to shew himself favourable to them in their actions, that may appear plainly to tend to the relief of the Queen, and maintenance of her authority. And as we willed our secretary to write unto you, that upon your message done to the Earl of Murray, you might return, so our meaning is you shall. And if these our letters shall meet you on the way, yet we will have you advertise both the Lord Scroope and the Hamiltons of our meaning.

Indorsed 29 Aug. 1567.

No. XXIII. (p. 218.)

Sir Nicholas Throkmorton to the Archbishop of St. Andrews and the Abbot of Arbrothe.

(13th Aug. 1567. Paper Office. From a copy which Sir Nicholas sent to the Queen.)

AFTER my good commendations to your good Lordships, this shall be to advertize you that the Queen's Majesty my sovereign having sent me hither her ambassador to the Queen her sister your sovereign, to communicate unto her such matter as she thought meet, considering the good amity and intelligence betwixt them, who being detained in captivity (as your Lordships know) contrary to the duty of all good subjects, for the enlargement of whose person and the restitution of her to her dignity, Her Majesty gave me in charge to treat with these lords, assembled at Edenburgh, offering them all reasonable conditions and means as might be, for the safeguard of the young Prince, the punishment of the late horrible murder, the dissolution of the marriage betwixt the Queen and the Earl of Bodwell, and lastly for their own sureties. In the negociation of which matters I have (as Your Lordships well know) spent a long time to no purpose, not being able to prevail in any thing with those lords to the Queen my sovereign's satisfaction. Of which strange proceedings towards Her Majesty, she (not being minded to bear this indignity) hath given me in charge to declare her further pleasure unto them, in such sort as they may well perceive her Majesty doth disallow of their proceedings, and thereupon hath revoked me. And further hath given me in charge to communicate the same unto Your Lordships, requiring you to let me know, before my departure hence (which shall be, God willing, as soon as I have received answer from you) what you and your confederates will assuredly do, to set the Queen your sovereign at liberty, and to restore her to her former dignity by force or otherwise; seeing these lords have refused all other mediation, to the end the Queen's Majesty my sovereign may concur with Your Lordships in this honourable enterprize.

And in case, through the dispersion of your associates, Your Lordships can neither communicate this matter amongst you, nor receive resolution of them all by that time, it may please you to send me the opinion of so many of you as may confer together within two or three days, so as I may have your answer here in this town by Monday or Tuesday next at the farthest, being the 19th of this August; for I intend (God willing) to depart towards England upon Wednesday following. Thus I most humbly take my leave of Your Lordships at Edenburgh, the 13th of Aug. 1567.

Indorsed the 13th of Aug. 1567.

Sir Nicholas Throkmorton to the Lord Herrys.

(24th Aug. 1567. Paper Office. From a copy which Sir Nicholas sent to Secretary Cecil.)

YOUR good Lordship's letter of the 13th of August I have received the 19th of the same. For answer whereunto it may like Your Lordship to understand that I will signify unto you plainly, how far forth I am already thoroughly instructed of the Queen's Majesty my sovereign's pleasure concerning the detention of the Queen your sovereign, and concerning her relief.

To the first Her Majesty hath given in charge, to use all kinds of persuasion in her name, to move these lords assembled at Edenburgh to desist from this violent and undutiful behaviour, which they use towards their sovereign. And in this part, besides the shew of many reasons, and sundry persuasions of amicable treaty with them, Her Majesty hath willed me to use some plain and severe reproach unto them, tending so far forth as if they would not be better advised, and reform these their outrageous proceedings exercised against their sovereign, that then they might be assured Her Majesty neither would nor could endure such an indignity to be done to the Queen, her good cousin and neighbour.

And notwithstanding these my proceedings with them, they have made proof to be little moved thereby; for as yet neither will they consent to the enlargement, neither suffer me to speak with her. So as it seemeth to me, it is superfluous to treat any more with them after this manner. Whereupon I have advertised the Queen's Majesty my sovereign, expecting daily Her Majesty's further order; and as I shall be advertised thereof, so will not fail to signify the same to Your good Lordship; and in the mean time will advertise Her Majesty also what Your Lordship hath written unto me. Thus with my due commendations to Your good Lordship, I commit the same to Almighty God, resting always to do you the pleasure and service that I can lawfully. At Edenburgh.

Indorsed 24th of August, 1567.

No. XXIV. (p. 223.)

Account of Lord Herries's Behaviour in the Parliament held December 15, 1567.

(Paper Office.)

THE Lord Herrys made a notable harangue in the name of the Duke and himself, their friends and adherents, (the Duke himself, the Earl of Cassilles, and the Abbot of Kilwinning being also present) to persuade the union of the whole realm in one mind. Wherein he did not spare to set forth solemnly the great praise that part of this nobility did deserve, which in the beginning took meanes for punishment of the Earl Bothwell, as also seeing the Queen's inordinat affection to that wicked man, and that she could not be induced by their persuasion to leave him, that in sequestring her person within Lochleven, they did the duty of noblemen. That their honourable doings, which had not spared to hazard their lives and lands, to avenge their native country from the slanderous reports that were spoken of it among other nations, had well deserved that all their brethren should join with them in so good a cause. That he and they, in whose names he did speak, would willingly, and without any compulsion, enter themselves in the same yoke, and put their lives and lands in the like hazard for maintenance of our cause. And if the Queen herself were in Scotland, accompanied with 20,000 men, they will be of the same mind, and fight in our quarrel. He hoped the remainder noblemen of their party, Huntly, Arguile, and others, which had not as yet acknowledged the King, would come to the same conformity, whereunto he would also earnestly move them. And if they will remain obstinate, and refuse to qualify themselves, then will the Duke, he and their friends, join with us to correct them that otherwise will not reform themselves. So plausible an oration, and more advantageous for our party, none of ourselves could have made. He did not forget to term My Lord Regent by the name of Regent (there was no mention at all of the Earl of Murray,) and to call him Grace at every word, when his speeches were directed to him, accompanying all his words with low courtesies after his manner.

No. XXV. (Page 233.)

Queen Mary to Queen Elizabeth.

[Cott. Lib. Cal. i. A copy, and probably a translation.]

MADAM,

ALTHOUGH the necessity of my cause (which maketh me to be importune to you) do make you to judge that I am out of the way; yet such as have not my passion, nor the respects whereof you are persuaded, will think that I do as my cause doth require. Madam, I have not accused you, neither in words, nor in thought, to have used yourself evil towards me. And I believe that you have no want of good understanding to keep you from perswasion against your natural good inclination. But in the mean time I can't chuse (having my senses) but perceive very evil furtherance in my matters since my coming hither. I thought that I had sufficiently discoursed unto you the discommodities which this delay bringeth unto me. And especially that they think in this next month of August to hold a parliament against me and all my servants. And in the mean time, I am stayed here, and yet will you, that I should put myself further into your country (without seeing you,) and remove me further from mine; and there do me this dishonour at the request of my rebels, as to send commissioners to hear them against me, as you wold do to a mere subject, and not hear me by mouth. Now, madam, I have promised you to come to you, and having there made my moan and complaint of these rebels, and they coming thither, not as possessors, but as subjects to answer. I would have besought you to hear my justification of that which they have falsely set forth against me, and if I could not purge myself thereof, you might then discharge your hands of my causes, and let me go for such as I am. But to do as you say, if I were culpable I would be better advised : but being not so, I can't accept this dishonour at their hands, that being in possession they will come and accuse me before your commissioners, whereof I can't like : and seeing you think it to be against your honour and consignage to do otherwise, I beseech you that you will not be mine enemy untill you may see how I can discharge myself every way, and to suffer me to go into France, where I have a dowry to maintain me; or at least to go into Scotland, with assurance that if there come any strangers thither, I will bind myself for their return without any prejudice to you, or if it plies you not to do thus, I protest that I will not impute it to falsehood if I receive strangers in my country without making you any other discharge for it. Do with my body as you will, the honour or blame shall be yours. For I had rather die here, and that my faithful servants may be succoured (tho' you would not so) by strangers, than to suffer them to be utterly undone, upon hope to receive in time to come, particular commodity. There be many things to move me to fear that I shall have to do in this country with others than with you. But forasmuch as nothing hath followed upon my last moan, I hold my peace, happen what may hap. I have as leef to abide my fortune as to seek it, and not find it. Further, it pleased you to give license to my subjects to go and come. This has been refused by My Lord Scroop and Mr. Knolls (as they say) by your commandment, because I would not depart hence to your charge, untill I had answer of this letter, tho' I shewed them, that you required my answer upon the two points contained in your letter.

The one is to let you briefly understand I am come to you to make my moan to you, the which being heard, I would declare unto you mine innocency, and then require your aid, and for lack thereof, I can't but make my moan and complaint to God that I am not heard in my just quarrel, and to appeal to other Princes to have respect thereunto as my case requireth ; and to you, madam, first of all when you shall have examined your conscience before him, and have him for witness.——And the other, which is to come further into your country, and not to come to your presence, I will esteem that as no favour, but will take it for the contrary, obeying it as a thing forced. In mean time, I beseech you to return to me my Lord Herries, for I can't be without him, having none of my counsal here, and also to suffer me, if it please you, without further delay, to depart hence whithersoever it be out of this country. I am sure you will not deny me this simple request for your honour's sake, seeing it doth not please you to use your natural goodness towards me otherwise, and seeing that of mine own accord I am come hither, let me depart again with yours. And if God permit my causes to succeed well, I shall be bound to you for it; and happening otherwise, yet I can't blame you. As for My Lord Fleeming, seeing that upon my credit you have suffered him to go home to his house, I warrant you he shall pass no further, but shall return when it shall please you. In that you trust me I will not (to die for it) deceive you. But *from* [perhaps *for*] Dumbarton I answer not, when my L. Fleeming shall be in the Tower. For they which are within it will not forbear to receive succoour if I don't assure them of yours; no, tho' you would charge me withal, for I have left them in charge; to have more respect to my servants and to my estate than to my life. Good sister, be of another mind, win the heart, and all shall be yours, and at your commandment. I thought to satisfy you wholly, if I might have seen you. Alas! do not as the serpent, that stoppeth his hearing, for I am no enchanter but your sister, and natural cousin. If Cæsar had not disdained to hear or read the complaint of an advertiser, he had not so died; why should Princes ears be stopped seeing that they are painted so long? meaning that they should hear all and be well advised before they answer. I am not of the nature of the basilisk, and less of the chamelion, to turn you to my likeness, and tho' I should be so dangerous and curs'd as men say, you are sufficiently armed with constancy and with justice, which I require of God, who give you grace to use it well with long and happy life. From Carlisle, the 5th of July, 1568.

No. XXVI. (Page 234.)

Part of a Letter from Sir Francis Knollys to Cecil, 8th Aug. 1568, from Bolton.

[An Original. Paper Office]

—But surely this Queen doth seem, outwardly, not only to favour the form, but also the chief article of the religion of the gospel, namely, justification by faith only: and she heareth the faults of papestry revealed by preaching or otherwise with contented ears, and with gentle and weak replys, and she doth not seem to like the worse of religion throw me.

Part of a Letter from Sir Francis Knollys to Cecil, 21 Sept. 1568, from Bolton.

—It came to this Queen's ears of late that she was bruited to be lately turned to the religion of the gospell, to the great disliking of the Papists hereabouts, which thing she herself confessed unto me, and yesterday, openly in the great chamber, when the assembly was full, and some Papists present, she took occasion to speak of religion, and then openly she professed herself to be of the Papist religion, and took upon her to patronize the same more earnestly than she had done a great while afore, altho' her defences and arguments were so weak that the effect of her speech was only to show her zeal; and afterwards to me alone, when I misliked to see her become so confidently backward in religion, Why, said she, would you have me to lose France and Spain, and all my friends in other places, by seeming to change my religion, and yet I am not assured the Queen my good sister will be my assured friend, to the satisfaction of my honour and expectation?

x

No. XXVII.   (p. 234.)

A Letter from My Lord Herries to My Lord Scroop and Sir F. Knollys, Sept. 3d, 1568.

[Cott. Lib. Cal. C.   An original in his own hand.]

MY Lords, pleasit Your Honourable Lordships, I am informed by James Borthwick, lately come from the Queen's Majesty your soverane, that his schawin to Her Highness I shuld have ridden in Crafurdmure, sen my last cuming into this realm, upon the Earl of Murray's dependants. And that I suld have causit, or been of counsall to Scottismen to have ridden in Ingland, to slay or spulzie Her Majesty's subjects.

My Lords, I thought it right needful because Your Lordships is, by your soverane, commanded to attend upon the Queen's Majesty my mistress, so having daily access in thir matters, to declare upon the truth; humbly desiring that Your Lordships will, for God's cause, certificate the Queen your soverane the same.

As God lives, I have neither consented, nor any wise had knowledge of any Scottisman's riding in England, to do the subjects thereof hurt in bodies or goods, sene the siege of Leith; and as I understand it shall be fund true, that gif ony sic open hurt be done, it is by the Queen my sovereign's disobedients, and that I have not ridden nor hurt no Scottisman, nor commanded no hurt to be done to them, sen my coming from the Queen's Majesty of Ingland, it is well kend, for that never ane will complain of me.

I have done more good to Crawfurdmure nor ever the Earl of Murray has done, and will be loather to do them any harm than he will. Except the Queen's Majesty your sovereign, command sic false reports to be tryit, quhereof this is altogidder an inventit leasing, Her Grace sall be trublit, and tyne the hearts of true men here, quhom of sic report sall be made, that baieth would serve hir, and may, better than they unworthy liars.

My Lords, I understand the Queen's Majesty your sovereign is not contented of this bruite, that there should ony Frenchman come in this realm, with the Duke of Chettelherault. Truth it is, I am no manner of way the counsall of their cuming, nor has no sic certainty thereof, as I hear by Borthwick's report, from the Queen's Majesty your sovereign. And gif I might as well say it, as it is true indeed, Her Grace's self is all the wyitt, and the counsall that will never let her take order with my maistress cause. For that our Sovereign havand Her Majesty's promise, be writing, of luff, friendship, and assistance gif need had so requirit, enterit that realm, upon the 16 day of May, sen that time the Queen's Majesty has commanded me diverse times to declare she would accept her cause, and do for her, and to put her in peaceable possession of this realme, and when I required of Her Majesty, in my maistress name, that Her Highness would either do for her, (as her special trust was she wold,) according to her former promises, or otherwise give her counsal, wold not consent, (as I show Her Grace I fand diverse repugnant,) then that she would permit her to pass in France, or to some other Prince to seek support, or failing hereof, (quhilk was agains all reason,) that she would permit her to return in her awin countrie, in sic sempil manner as she came out of it, and said to Her Majesty ane of thir, for her honour, would not be refusit, sceand that she was comed in her realm upon her writings and promises of friendship. And siclike, I said to Her Highness, gif my maistress had the like promise of her nobility and estates, as she had of herself, I should have reprovit them highly, gif they had not condescendit to one of thir three, and so I say, and so I write, that in the warld it shall be maist reprehendable, gif this promise taketh not other good effect, nor yet it does. Notwithstanding, I get gud answer of thir promises of iriendship made to my sovereign, and to put her Grace in this her awin countrie peaceably, we have fund the contrary working by Mr. Middlemore directit from Her Highness to stay the army that cuist down our houses. And alsua, in the proceeding of this late pretendit Parliament, promised twenty days before the time to myself to have caused it been dischargit. And yet contrary to this promise, have they made their pretendit manner of forfaulture of 31 men of guid reputation, bishops, ab-bottis, and baronis, obedient subjects to our sovereign, only for her cause.

They have also disponit, sen our sovereign's cause was taken upon hand be the Queen's Majesty of that realm, an hundred thousand pound Scots worth of her awin true subjects geir, under the color of the law, groundit upon their false, treasonable, stowin, authority.

The murders, the oppressions, the burnings, the ravishing of women, the destruction of policy, both ecclesiastical and temporal, in this mean time, as in my former writings I said it was lament-able to ony Christian man to hear of, except God gif grace, the pro-fession of the evangile of Jesus Christ professit be your Prince, counsall and realme, be mair myndit, nor the auld inamity that has stand betwixt the realms, many of my countrymen will doubt in this article, and their proceedings puttis myself in Sanct Thomas belief.

Now, my Lords, gif the Queen's Majesty of that realm, upon quhais promis and honour my maistress came there, as I have said, will leave all the French writings, and French phrases of writings, quhilks amongis them is over meikle on baith the sides unfit, and plainly, according to the auld true custom of Ingland and Scotland, quherein be a word promist truth was observ'd, promise, in the name of the eternal God, and upon the high honour of that nobill and princely blude of the Kings of Ingland, quhereof she is descendit, and presently wears the diadem, that she will put my maistress in her awin country, and cause her as Queen thereof in her authority and strength to be obeyit, and to do the same will ap-point an certain day within two months at the farthest, as we nu-derstand this to be our weil, sua will we, or the maist part of us all, follow upon it, leaving the Frenchmen, and their evil French phrases togidder. And therefore, and for the true perpetual friend-ship of that realm, will condition, and for our part, with the grace of Almighty God, keep sic heads and conditions of agreement, as noble and wise men can condescend upon, for the weill of this hail island. As I have been partlings declaring to the Queen your sovereign, quhilk I show to your Lordships selfis both in religion, in the punishment of the Earl Bothwile, for the Queen's last husband's slaughter, and for a mutual band of amity perpetually to remain amangis us.

Doubtless, My Lords, without that, we may find sic time and friendly working, as may give us occasion baith to forgette Middlemore and his late pretendit Parliament, we will turn the leaf, leaving our sovereign agains our will to rest where she is, under the promise of friendship, as I have baith said, and will ever affirm, made by your sovereign, quhilk was only cause of Her Grace's coming in that realme, and seek the help and moyen of French, or Spanish, till expulse this treasonable and false pretendit authority, quhilk means to reign above us.

My Lords, I desire Your Lordships consider, that it is he, that maist desires the amity betwixt Ingland and Scotland to continue, and of a poor man best cause has, that writ this.

My brother, the Laird of Skirling, schaws me, that in Your Lordships communing with him, it appearit to him, your mind was we should suffer the Earl of Murray to work, altho' it were agains reason to us, and complain thereof to the Queen's Majesty, and Her Highness wald see it reformit. My Lords, Her Majesty will be over meikle troublit to reform the wranges we have sustainit already. For I am sure, gif reason and justice may have place, our maistress and we her subjects; have received express wrang, far above two hundred thousand pounds sterling, in the time of this unhappy government, seeing the reformation of sa great causes comes, now a days, so slowlie, and the ungodly law of oblivion in the sic matters so meikle practis'd, I think, nowther for the Queen's honour, nor our weil, Your Lordships would sua mean, nor that it is good to us to follow it. And that ye will give your Sovereign sic advertisment thereof, as your good wisdoms shall find in this cause meet. It will be true and frindful working for us, indeed, and nowther French phrases nor boasting, and finding little other effect, that will cause us to hold away the Frenchmen. This is plainly written, and I desire Your Lordships plain answer, for in truth and plainness langest continues gud friendship, quhilk in this matter I pray God may lang continue, and have Your Lordships in his keeping. Off Dumfries, the 3d day of September 1568.

Your Lordships at my power
to command leifully
HERRIS.

Queen Mary to Q. Elizabeth.

[1568. Cott. Lib. Cal. I. An original.]

MADAME ma bonne soeur. J'ay resceu de vos lettres, d'une mesme dete ; l'une, ou vous faites mention de l'excuse de Monsr. de Murra pour tenir son pretendu parlement, qui me semble bien froid, pour obtenir plus de tollèrance que je m'estois persuadée n'avoir par vostre promesse, quant à n'osser donner commission de venir sans un parlement pour leur peu de nombre de noblesse alors, je vous respons

qu'ils n'ont que trois ou quatre d'avantage, qui eussent aussi bien
dit leur opinion hors de parlement, qui n'a esté tenu tant pour cette
effect, mais pour faire ce qu'expressement nous avions requis estre
empeschès, qui est la forfalture de mes subjects pour m'avoir estés
fidelles, ce que je m'assurois, jusques á heir, avoir eu en promesse de
vous, par la lettre écrite à Mi Lord Scrup e Maistre Knoleis vous,
par la lettre ècrite à Mi Lord Scrup e Maistre Knoleis vous induire
à ire contre eulx, voire, à les ensayre resentir; toutefois je vois
que je l'ay mal pris, j'en suis plus marrie, pour ce que sur votre
lettre qu'l, me montrerent, et leur parole, je l'ay si divulguement
assuray que pour vengeance que j'en dèsirasse, si non mettre dif-
férence entre leur faux deportemens, et les miens sincéres.   Dans
vostre lettre aussi dateè du 10me d'Aoust, vous metties ces mots.
" I think your adverse party, upon my sundry former advices, will
" hold no Parliament at all ; and if they do, it shall be only in
" form of an assembly to accord whom to send into this realm, and
" in what sort ; for otherwise, if they shall proceed in manner of a
" Parliament, with any act of judgment against any person, I shall
" not, in any wise, allow thereof ; and if they shall be overseen,
" then you may think the same to be of no other moment,
" than the former proceedures ; and by such their rash manner
" of proceeding, they shall most prejudice themselves ; and be
" assured to find me ready to condemn them, in their doings." Sur
quoy, j'ay contremandè mes serviteurs, les faissant retirer, souffrant
selon vostre commandement d'ètre faussement nommés traitres, par
ceulx, qui le sont de vray ; et encore d'être provoquès par escarmons
dies, et par prinses de mes gens et lettres, et au contraire vous étes
informèe que mes subjects ont èvahis les vostres, Madame, qui a
fait ce rapport n'est pas homme de bien, car Laird de Sesford et son
fils sont et ont estès nies rebelles depuis le commencement ; enquirès
vous, s'ils n'estoient à Donfris aveques eulx, j'avois offri respondre
de la frontière, ce qui m'en devroit asses descharger, neanmoins,
pour vous faire preuve de ma fidèlitè, et de leur falsite, s'il vous
fayte donner ma le mom des coulpables, et me fortifier, je command-
eray mes subjects les pour suivre, ou si vous voulès que ce soit les
vostres, les miens leur ayderont : je vous prie m'en mander vostre
volonté, au reste mes subjects fidelle seront responsables à toutce que
leur sera mis su les contre vous, ni les vostres ni les rebelles, despuisque
me conseillates les faire retirer.   Quant aux Francois, j'escrivis, que
l'on m'en fit nulle poursuite, car j'esperois, tant en vous, que je n'en
aurois besoign,—je nçe seu si le dict aura en mes lettres, mais je
vous jure devant Dieu que je ne scay chose du monde le leur venue
que ce que m'en aves manday, ni n'en ai oui de France mot du
monde, et ne le puis croire pour c'est occacion, et si ils si sont, c'est
sans mon sceu ni consentement.   Pourquoy je vous supplie ne me
condamner sans m'ouire, car je suis prest de tenir tout ce que j'ay
offert a Mester Knoleis, et vous assure que vostre amitè, qu'il vous
plest m'offrir, sera rescue avant toutes les choses du monde, quant
France servit la pour presser leur retour á ceste condition, que
prenies mes affaires en mein, en soeur, et bonne ami, comme ma
Francé est en vous ; mais une chose soule me rende confuse, j'ay tant
d'enemis qu'ont votre oreille, la quelle ne pouvant avoir par parolle,

toutes mes actions vous sont desguisées, et falsement raportées, par quoi il m'est impossible de m'assurer de vous, pour les manteries qu'on vous a fait, pour destruire vostre bonne volonté de moy; par quoy je désirerois bien avoir ce bien vous faire entendre ma sincere et bonne affection, laquelle je ne puis si bien descrire, que mes enemis a tort ne la décoloré. Ma bonne soeur, gagnes moy; envoyés moy querir, n'entrés en jalousie pour faulx raports de celle que ne désire que votre bonne grace; je me remettray sur Mester Knoleis à qui je me suis librement descouverte, et après vous avoir baisée les mains, je prierai Dieu vous donner en santé, longue et heureuse vie. De Boton, ou je vous promets, je n'espère pertir, qu'aveques vostre bonne grace, quoyque les menteur mentent.   Ce 26 d'Aoust.

No. XXVIII. (p. 235.)

Queen Elizabeth to the Earl of Murray.

[Paper Office.   From a copy corrected by Secretary Cecil.]

RIGHT trusty and right well beloved cousin, we greet you well·
Where we hear say, that certain reports are made in sundry parts of Scotland, that whatsoever should fall out now upon the hearing of the Queen of Scotts cause, in any proof to convince or to acquit the said Queen concerning the horrible murder of her late husband our cousin, we have determined to restore her to her kingdom and government, we do so much mislike hereof, as we cannot endure the same to reeeive any credit: and therefore we have thought good to assure you, that the same is untruly devised by the authors to our dishonour.   For as we have been always certified from our said sister, both by her letters and messages, that she is by no means guilty or participant of that murder, which we wish to be true, so surely if she should be found justly to be guilty thereof as hath been reported of her, whereof we should be very sorry, then, indeed, it should behoove us to consider otherwise of her cause than to satisfy her desire in restitution of her to the government of that kingdom.   And so we would have you and all others think, that should be disposed to conceive honourably of us and our actions.
Indorsed 20 Sep. 1568.

No. XXIX. (p. 238.)

Sir Francis Knollys to Cecil, the 9th of October, 1568, from York.

[An Original.   Paper Office.]

MY Lord's Grace of Norfolk sending for me to Bolton, to attend him here Thursday last, I made my repair hither accordingly, meaning to stay here until Munday next; as touching the matters of the commission, that His Grace and the rest have from Her Highness, His Grace hath imparted unto me of all things thereunto appertaining, and what hath hitherto passed, and altho' the matters be too weighty for my weak capacity, to presume to utter any opinion of mine own thereof, yet I see that my Lord Herris for his parte laboureth a reconciliation, to be had without the extremity of odious accusations; My Lord of Ledington also saith to me, that he could wish these matters to be ended in dulce maner, so that it might be done with safety; of the rest you can conceive, by the advertisements and writings sent up by our commissioners.

A Letter from the Bishop of Ross to the Queen of Scots, from York, October, 1568.

[Cott. Lib. Calig. C. 1. A copy.]

PLEIS Your Majesty I conferred at length with A. ane great part of a night, who assurit me that he had reasoned with B. this Saturday C. on the field, who determinate to him that it was D. determinate purpose not to end your cause at this time, but to hold the same in suspence, and did that was in her power, to make the E. pursue extremity, to the effect F. and his adherents might utter all they could to your dishonour, to the effect to cause you come in disdain with the hail subjects of this realm, that ye may be the mair unable to attempt any thing to her disadvantage. And to this effect is all her intention, and when they have produced all they can against you, D. will not appoint the matter instantly, but transport you up in the country, and retain you there till she think time to show you favour, which is not likely to be hastily, because of your uncles in France, and the fear she has of yourself to be her unfriend. And therefore their counsel is, that ye write an writing to to the D. meaning that ye are informit that your subjects which has offendit you.—This in effect that Your Majesty hearing the estate of your affairs as they proceed in York, was informed that Her Majesty was informed of you, that you could not gudely remit your subjects in such sort as they might credit you hereafter, which was a great cause of the stay of this controversy to be ended. And therefore persuading her D. effectually not to trust any who had made such narration. But like as ye had rendered you in her hands, as most tender to you of any living, so prayit her to take na opinion of you, but that ye wald use her counsell in all your affairs, and wald prefer her friendship to all others, as well uncles as others, and assure her to keep that thing ye wald promise to your subjects by her advice. And if D. discredit you, ye wald be glad to satisfy her in that point be removing within her realm in secret and quiet manner, where her G. pleased, until the time her G. were fully satisfied, and all occasion of discredit removed from her. So that in the mean time your realm were holden in quietness, and your true subjects restored and maintained in their own estate, and sic other things tending to this effect. And affirms that they believe that this may be occasion to cause her credit you that ye offer so far; and it may come that within two or three months she may become better-minded to Your Grace, for now she is not well-minded, and will not show you any pleasure for the causes aforesaid.

N. B. The title of this paper is in Cecil's hand; the following key is added in another hand.

> A. The Laird of Lethington.
> B. The Duke of Norfolk.
> C. Was the day he rode to Cawood.

D. The Queen of England.
E. The Queen of Scots commissioners.
F. The Earl of Murray.

No. XXX. (p. 243.)

Deliberation of Secretary Cecil's concerning Scotland, Dec. 21. 1568.

[Paper Office.]

THE best way for England, but not the easiest; that the Queen of Scots might remain deprived of her crown, and the state continue as it is.

The second way for England profitable, and not so hard.—That the Queen of Scots might be induced, by some perswasions, to agree that her son might continue King, because he was crowned, and herself to remain also Queen; and that the government of the realm might be committed to such persons as the queen of England should name, so as for the nomination of them it might be ordered, that a convenient number of persons of Scotland should be first named to the Queen of England, indifferently for the Queen of Scots, and for her son, that is to say, the one half by the Queen of Scots, and the other by the Earle of Lennox, and Lady Lennox, parents to the child; and out of those, the Queen's Majesty of England to make choice for all the officers of the realm, that are, by the laws of Scotland, disposable by the King or Queen of the land.

That until this may be done by the Queen's Majesty, the government remain in the hands of the Earle of Murray as it is, providing he shall not dispose of any offices or perpetuals to continue any longer but in these offered of the premises.

That a Parliament be summoned in Scotland by several commandments, both of the Queen of Scots, and of the young King.

——That hostages be delivered unto England on the young King's behalf, to the number of twelve persons of the Earle of Murray's part, as the Queen of Scots shall name; and likewise on the Queen's behalf, to the like number as the Earle of Murray shall name; the same not to be any that have by inheritance or office cause to be in this Parliament, to remain from the beginning of the summons of that Parliament, untill three months after that Parliament; which hostages shall be pledges, that the friends of either party shall keep the peace in all cases, till by this Parliament it be concluded, that the ordinance which the Queen of England shall devise for the government of the realm (being not to the hurt of the crown of Scotland, nor contrary to the laws of Scotland for any man's inheritance, as the same was before the Parliament at Edinr the——December, 1567) shall be established to be kept and obeyed, under pain of high treason for the breakers thereof.

——That by the same Parliament also be established all executions and judgments given against any person for the death of the late King.

——That by the same Parliament, a remission be made universally from the Queen of Scots to any her contrarys, and also from every one subject to another, saving that restitution be made of lands and houses, and all other things heritable, that have been by either side taken from them which were the owners thereof at the committing of the Queen of Scots to Lochlevin.

That by the same Parliament it be declared who shall be successors to the crown next after the Queen of Scots and her issue; or else that such right as the Duke of Chatelherault had, at the marriage of the Queen of Scots with Lord Darnly, may be conserved and not prejudiced.

That the Q. of Scots may have leave of the Queen's Majesty of England, twelve months after the said Parliament, and that she shall not depart out of England without special licence of the Queen's Majesty.

That the young King shall be nourished and brought up in England, till he be—years of age.

It is to be considered, that in this cause the composition between the Queen and her subjects may be made with certain articles, outwardly to be seen to the world for her honour, as though all the parts should come of her, and yet for the surety of contrarys, that certain betwixt her and the Queen's Majesty are to be concluded.

No. XXXI. (p. 244.)

The Queen to Sir Francis Knolleys, 22nd January, 1568-9.

[Paper Office.]

WE greet you well, we mean not, at this point, by any writing, to renew that which it hath pleased God to make grievous to us and sorryful to yow ; but forbearing the same as unmeet at this point, having occasion to command yow in our service, and you also whilest you are to serve us. We require yow to consider of this that followeth with like consideration and diligence, as hitherto yow have accustomate in our service ; at the time of our last letters written to yow the fourteenth of this month for removing of the Queen of Scots, we had understanding out of Scotland of certain writtings sent by her from thence into Scotland, amongst the which one is found to contain great and manifest untruths touching us and others also, as shall and may plainly appear unto yow by the copy of the same, which likewise we send you and because at the same time we were advertized, that it should be shortly proclaimed in Scotland, though then it was not, we thought good first to remove the Queen, before we would disclose the same, and then expect the issue thereof ; and now, this day, by letters from our cousin of Hudson we are ascertained, that since that time the same matters contained in the writing, are published in diverse parts of Scotland, whereupon we have thought it very meet, for the discharge of our honour, and to confound the falsehood contained in that writing, not only to have the same reproved by open proclamation upon our frontiers, the coppy whereof we do herewith send you, but also in convenient sort to charge that Queen therewith, so as she may be moved to declare the authors thereof, and persuaders of her to write in such slanderous sort such untruths of us; and in the mean sea-

x 5

son, we have here stayed her commissioners, knowing no other whom we may more probably presume to be parties hereunto, than they' untill the Queen shall name some other, and acquit them ; who being generally charged, without expressing to them any particularity, do use all manner of speeches to discharge themselves; wherefore our pleasure is, that ye shall, after ye have well perused the coppy of this writting sent to yow, speedily declare unto her, that we have good understanding given us of divers letters and writtings, sent by her into Scotland, signed by her own hand, amongst which one such writting is sent with her commandment, expressly as now it is already published, as we are much troubled in mind that a Princess as she is having a cause in our hands so implicated with difficultys and calamitys, should either conceave in her own mind, or allow of them that should devise such false, untrue, and improbable matters against us, and our honor, and specially to have the aventure to have the same being known so untrue to be published ; and you shall also say, because we will not think so ill of her, as that it should proceed of her self, but rather she hath been counselled thereunto, or by abuse made to think some part thereof to be true, we require her, even as she may look for any favour at our hands, that she will disburden herself as much as truly she may herein, and name them which have been the authors and perswaders thereof, and so she shall make as great amends to us as the case may require : after you have thus proceeded, and had some answer of her, whether she shall deny the writing absolutely, or name any that have been the advisers thereof, you shall say unto her that we have stayed her commissioners here, untill we may have some answer hereof, because we cannot but impute to them some part of this evil dealing, untill by her answer the authors may be known; and as soon as you can have direct answers from her, we pray you to return us the same ; for as the case standeth, we cannot but be much disquieted with it, having our honour so deeply touched contrary to any intention in us, and for any thing we know in our judgment the Earl of Murray and others named in the same writting, void of thought for the matters, to them therein imputed ; you may impart to the Queen of Scots either he contents of the slanderons letter, or show her the copy to read it, and you may also impart this matter to the Lord Scroop, to join with you there as you shall think meet.

Sir Francis Knollys to Queen Elizabeth, from Wetherby, the 28th January, 1568.

[An original. Paper Office.]

——I will supress my own grieffs, and pass them over with silence, for the present learning of Your Majesty—and for this Queen's answer to the coppie of her supposed letter sent unto Scotland, I must add this unto my brother's letter, sent unto Mr. Secretary yesternight late ; in process of time she did not deny but that the first lines contained in the same copie, was agreeable to a letter that she had sent unto Scotland, which touched My Lord of Murray's promise to deliver her son into Your Majesty's hands, and to avoid that the same should not be done without her consent, made her, she saith, to write in that behalf; she saith also that she wrote that they should cause a proclamation to be made to stir her people to defend My Lord of Murray's intent and purpose, for delivering of her said son, and impunge his rebellious government, as she termed it, but she utterly denyeth to have written any of the other slanderous parts of the said letter touching Your Majesty; she said also, that she suspected that a Frenchman, now in Scotland, might be the author of some Scotch letters devised in her name, but she would not allow me to write this for any part of her answer.

No. XXXII. (p. 248.)

Sir Nicholas Throkmorton to the Right Honourable the Lord of Liddington.

[20th of July, 1569. From the original.]

Your letter of the 3d of July, I have received the 15th of the same. For answer whereunto you shall understand that friends here to my Lord Regent and you do wish such a concurrence in all doings, as in matter and circumstances there arise no dissension, or at the least, no more nor other than the difference of countries doth necessarily require. We here do think convenient that as few delays be used as may be, for the consummation of the matter in hand, which principally to advance your allowance, prosecution, and speedy promotion in Scotland, is most requisite, for you are so wise, and well acquainted with the state of the world, and with all our humours, as you know that some do allow and disallow for reason, some for respect of multitude, some for respect of persons, and so the cause is to go forward as men do like to set it forward. You are not to seek that some will use cautions, some neutrality, some delays, and some will plainly impunge it. And yet all and every of these sorts will alter their doings, when they shall see the Regent and his favourers accord with the best and greatest part there, and agree with the wisest and strongest party here. Tho' the matter has taken its beginning here, upon deep and weighty considerations, for the weil of both the Princes and their realms, as well presently as in time to come, yet it is thought most expedient that the Regent, and realm of Scotland, by you, should propose the matter to the Queen our sovereign, if you like to use convenience, good order, or be disposed to leave but a scar, and no wound of the hurts past. I would be glad that this my letter should come to your hands before the convention, whereat it seems your Queen's restoration and marriage to the Duke of Norfolk shall be propounded, either to wynne in them both allowance or rejection. To which proceedings, because you pray me to write frankly, I say and reason thus, me thinketh you use a preposterous order to demand the consent of such persons, in such matters, as their minds to a good end hath rather been felt or prepared, and therefore there must needs follow either a universal refusal, or factious division amongst you, whereby a bloustering intelligence must needs come to Queen Elizabeth of the intended marriage from thence, which ought to have been secretely and advisedly propounded unto Her Highness; hereby you see then the meaning is, by this dealing, Her Majesty shall be made inexorable, and so bring the matter to such passe, as this which should have wrought surety, quietness, and a stay to both Queens and their realms, shall augment your calamity, and throw us your best friends into divorse with you, and into an unhappy division amongst ourselves; for you may not conjecture that the matter is now in deliberation, but expecteth good occasion for executing; sure I am you do not judge so slenderly of the managing of this matter, as to think we have not cast the worst, or to enter therein so far without the assistance of the nobility, the ablest, the wisest, and the mightiest of this realm, except Queen Elizabeth : from whom it hath been concealed until you, as the fittest minister, might propound it to her, on the behalf of the Regent and the nobility of Scotland. How far Master Woddes defamations do carry them of Queen Elizabeth's affections, and Master Secretary's to assist the Regent and to suppress the Queen of Scots, I know not, nor it is not material; but I do assuredly think that Her Majesty will prefer her surety, the tranquillity of her reign, and the conversation of her people, before any device, which may proceed from vain discourse, or imperfections of passions and inconsiderate affections. And as for Mr. Secretary, you are not to learn that as he liketh not to go too fast afore, so he coveteth not to tarry too far behind, and specially when the reliques be of no great value or power. If I could as well assure you of his magnanimity, and constancy, as of his present conformity, I would say confidently, you may repose as well of him in this matter, as of the Duke of Norfolk, the Earls of Arundel, Pembroke, Leicester, Bedford, Shrewsbury, and the rest of the nobility; all which do embrace, and proteste the accomplishment of this case. I have, according to your advice, written presently to My Lord Regent, with the same zeal and care of his well doing that I owe to him, whom I love and honour. Mr. Secretary hath assured unto him the Queen of Scotland's favour and good opinion, wherewith he seemeth to be well satisfy'd. If your credit be as I trust, hasten your coming hither, for it is very necessary that you were here presently. Q. Elizabeth both doth write to My Lord Regent in such sort, as he may perceive Mr. Wood's discourses of Her Majesty's affection to be vain, and Mr. Secretary otherwise bent than he conjectureth of him, the effect of which Her Majesty's letter you shall understand, by My Lord Leicester's letter unto you at this dispatch. At the Court, 20th July, 1569.

No. XXXIII. (P. 249.)

Part of a Letter from the Earl of Murray to L. B., probably Lord Burleigh.

[1569. Harl. Lib. 37. B. 9. fo. 42.]

——BECAUSE I see that great advantage is taken on small occasions, and that the mention of the marriage between the Queen my sovereign's mother and the D. of Norfolk hath this while past been very frequent in both the realms, and then I myself to be spoken of as a motioner, which I perceive is at the last come to Her Majesty's ears; I will, for satisfaction of Her Highness, and the discharge of my duty towards Her Majesty, manifest unto you my interest, and medling in that matter from the very beginning, knowing whatsoever is prejudical to Her Highness, cannot but be hurtful to the King my sovereign, this his realm, and me. What conferrences was betwixt the Duke of Norfolk, and any of them that were with me within the realm of England, I am not able to declare; but I am no wise forgetful of any thing that passed betwixt him and me, either at that time or since. And to the end Her Majesty may understand how I have been dealt with in this matter, I am compelled to touch some circumstances, before there was any mention of her marriage In York, at the meeting of all the commissioners, I found very — and neutral dealing with the Duke, and others her Highness's commissioners, in the beginning of the cause, as in the making of the others to proceed sincerely, and so forth. During which time, I entered into general speech, sticking at our just defence in the matters that were objected against us, by the said Queen's commissioners, looking certainly for no other thing, but summary cognition in the cause of controversy, with a final declaration to have followed. Upon a certain day the Lord Lithington secretary rode with the Duke to Howard, what purpose they had I cannot say, but that night Lithington returning, and entring into conferrence with me upon the state of our action, I was advised by him to pass to the Duke, and require familiar conference, by which I might have some feeling to what issue our matters would tend. According to which advice, having gotten time and place convenient in the gallery of the house where the Duke was lodged, after renewing our first acquaintance made at Berwick, the time before the assize at Leith, and some speeches passed betwixt us: he began to say to me, how he in England had favour and credit, and I in Scotland had will and friendship of many, it was to be tho't there could be none more fit instruments, to travel for the continuance of the amity betwixt the realms, than we two. And so that discourse upon the present state of both, and how I was entered into that action tending so far to the Queen's dishonour, I was willed by him to consider how matters stood in this, what honour I had received of the Queen, and what inconveniences her defamation in the matters laid to her charge might breed to her posterity. Her respect was not little to the crown of England, there was but one heir. The Hamiltons my unfriends, had the next respect, and that I should esteem the issue of her body would be the more affectionate to me and mine, than any other that could attain to that crown. And so it should be meetest, that she affirmed her dismission made in Lochlevin, and we to abstract the letters of her hand write, that she should not be defamed in England. My reply to that was, now the matter had passed in Parliament, and the letters seen of many, so that the abstracting of the same could not then secure her to any purpose, and yet should we, in that doing, bring the ignominy upon us.— Affirming it would not be fair for us that way to proceed, seeing the Queen's Majesty of Eugland was not made privy to the matter as she ought to be, in respect we were purposely come in England for that end, and for the — of the grants of our cause. The Duke's answer was, he would take in hand to handle matters well enough at the court. After this, on the occasion of certain articles, that were required to be resolved on before we entered on the declaration of the very ground of our action, we came up to the court; where some new commissioners were adjoined to the former, and the hearing of the matter ordained to be in the Parliament-house in Westminster, in presence of which commissioners of the said Queen, and —— through the —— rebuking of the Queen of England's own commissioners, we uttered the whole of the action, and produced such evidences, letters, and probations, as we had, which might move the Queen's Majesty to think well of our cause. Whereupon expecting Her Highness's declaration, and seeing no great likelihood of the same to be suddenly given, but daily motions then made to come to an accord with the said Queen, our matters in hand in Scotland, in the mean season, standing in hazard and danger, we were put to the uttermost point off our wit, to imagine whereunto the matters would tend, tho' albeit we had left nothing undone for justification of our causes, yet appeared no end, but continual motions made to come to some accord with the Queen, and restore her to whole or half reign. I had no other answer to give them, but that I should neither do against conscience or honour in that matter. Notwithstanding this my plain answer wrought no end, nor despatch to us, and that I was informed that the Duke began to mislike of me, and to speak of me, as that I had reported of the said Queen irreverently, calling her —— [probably *adulterer*] and murderer, I was advised to pass to him, and give him good words, and to purge myself of the things objected to me, that I should not open the sudden entry of his evil grace, nor have him to our enemy —— considering his greatness. It being therewithal whispered and showed to me, that if I departed, he standing discontented and not satisfied, I might peradventure find such trouble in my way, as my throat might be cut before I came to Berrick. And therefore, since it might well enough appear to her marriage, I should not put him in utter despair, that my good will could not be had therein. So few days before my departing I came to the park in Hampton Court, where the Duke and I met together, and there I declared unto him that it was come to my ears, how some misreport should be made of me to him, as that I should speak irreverently and rashly of the said queen my sovereign's mother, such words as before expressed, that he might —— [probably *suspect*] thereby my affection to be so alienate from her, as that I could not love her, nor be content of her preferment, howbeit he might perswade himself of the contrary, for as she once was the person in the world that I loved best, having that honour to be so near unto her, and having received such advancement and honour by her, I was not so ungrate or so unnatural ever to wish her body harm, or to speak of her as was untruly reported of me (howsoever the truth was in the self), and as to the preservation of her son now my sovereign, had moved me to enter into this cause, and that her own pressing was the occasion of that was uttered to her —— [probably *dishonour*] whensoever God should move her heart to repent of her by past behaviour and life, and after her known repentance, that she should be separate from that ungodly and unlawful marriage that she was entered in, and then after were joined with such a godly and honourable a personage, as were affectioned to the true religion, and whom we might trust, I could find in my heart to love her, and to shew her as great pleasure, favour, and good will as ever I did in my life; and in case he should be that personage, there was none whom I could better like of, the Queen —— in —— of England being made privy to the matter, and she allowing thereof, which being done, I should labour in all things that I could, to her honour and pleasure, that were not prejudicial to the King my sovereign's estate, and prayed him not to think otherwise of me, for my affection was rather buried and hidden within me, awaiting until God should direct her to know herself, than utterly alienated and abstracted from her; which he seemed to accept in very good part, saying, Earl of Murray, thou thinks of me that thing, whereunto I will make none in England or Scotland privy, and thou hast Norfolk's life in thy hands. So departing, I came to my lodging, and by the way and all night, I was in continual thought and agitation of mind, how to behave myself in that weighty matter, first imagining whereunto this should tend, if it were attempted without the Queen's Majesty of England's knowledge and good will, this realm and I myself in particular having received such favour and comfort at her Highness's hands, and this whole isle such peace and quietness, since God possessed Her Majesty with her crown. And on the other part, seeing the Duke had disclosed him to me, protesting none other were or should be privy to our speech, I tho't I could not find in my heart to utter any thing that might endanger him; moved to the uttermost with these cogitations, and all desire of sleep then removed, I prayed God to send me some good relief and outgate, to my discharge and satisfaction of my troubled mind, which I found indeed; for, upon the morn, or within a day or two thereafter, I entered in conversation with my Lord of Leicester, in his chamber at the court, where he began to find strange with me, that in the matter I made so difficult to him, standing so precisely on conference, and how when I had in my communication with the Duke, come so far —— and there he made some discourse with me, about that which was talke betwixt us, I perceiving that the Duke had —— [probably *disclosed*] the matter to my Lord of Leicester, and thinking me thereby discharged at the Duke's hands, therefore I repeated the same communication in every point to my Lord of Leicester, who desired me to show the same to the Queen's Majesty, which I refused to do, willing him if he tho't it might import Her Highness any thing, that he has one —— by Her Majesty, and for many benefits received at Her Highness's hands is obliged to wish her well, should make declaration of the same to Her Majesty, as I understand by some speech of Her Highness to me, he did. This my declaration to the Duke was the only cause that stayed the violence and trouble prepared for me unexecuted, as I have divers ways understood. The same declaration I was obliged to renew since in writings of —— sent to my servant John Wood. The sum whereof, I trust, he showed the Duke, and something also I wrote to himself for it was tho't this should redeem some time, that the Duke should not suddenly declare him our enemy, for his greatness was oft laid before me, and what friendship he had of the chief of the nobility in England, so that it might appear to the Queen's Majesty of England—so cold towards us, and doing nothing publickly that might seem favourable for us, we had some cause to suspect that Her Highness should not be contrarious to the marriage when it should be proposed to her. The sharp message sent by Her Majesty with the Lord Boyd, who had the like commission from the Duke tending so far to the said Queen's preferment, as it were proposing one manner of conditions from both, gave us to think that Her Highness had been foreseen in the Duke's design, and that she might be induced to allow thereof. But howbeit it was devised in England, that the Lord of Lethington should come as from me, and break the matter to Her Highness, as Her Majesty in a letter declared that she looked for his coming, yet that devise proceeded never of me, nor the noblemen at the convention could no wise accord to his sending nor allow of the matter motioned, but altogether misliked it, as bringing with it the same great inconvenience to the surety and quietness of this whole isle ; for, our proceedings have declared our misliking and disallowance of the purpose from the beginning, and if we had pleased he was ready for the journey. And in likewise it was devised to give consent that the ——— [probably *divorce*] between the said Queen and Bothwell should be suffered to proceed in this realm, as it was desired by the said Lord Boyd, by reason we could not understand what was the Queen's Majesty's pleasure, and allowance in that behalf———And whereas ye mean, that Her Highness was not made privy of any such intention, the fault was not in me. The first motion being declared, as I have written, to my Lord of Leicester, and by him imparted to Her Majesty, so far as I could perceive by some speech of Her Highness's to me, before my departing. Thus I have plainly declared how I have been dealt withal for this marriage, and how just necessity moved me not to require directly, that which the Duke appeared so ——— unto. And for my threatenings, to assent to the same, I have expressed the manner ; the persons that laid the matter before me, were of my own company. But the Duke since hath spoken, that it was his writing which saved my life at that time. In conclusion I pray you persuade Her Majesty, that she let no speeches nor any other thing passed and objected to my prejudice, move Her Majesty to alter her favour—towards me, or any ways to doubt of my assured constancy towards Her Highness ; for in any thing which may tend to her honour and surety, I will, while I live, bestow myself, and all that will do for me, notwithstanding my hazard or danger, as proof shall declare, when Her Majesty finds time to employ me.

No. XXXIV. (p. 254.)

William Maitland of Ledington to my Lord of Leicester, March 20th, 1570, from Ledington.

[An original.]

THE great desolation threatened to this whole realm, be the divisions thereof in dangerous factions, doth press me to frame my letters to Your Lordship, in other sort, than were behovefull for me, if I had no other respect, but only to maintain my private credit; therefore I am driven to furnish them with matter, which I know not to be plausible, whereupon by misconstruing my meaning, some there may take occasion of offence, thinking that I rather utter my own passions, than go about to inform Your Lordship truly of the state; but I trust my plain dealing shall bear record to the sincerity of my meaning; to make the same sensible, I will lay before Your Lordship's eyes that the plat of this country; which first is divided into two factions, the one pretending the maintenance of the King's reign, the other alledging the Queen to have been cruelly dealt withall, and unjustly deprived of her state; the former is composed of a good number of nobility, gentlemen, and principal burroughs of the realme, who shall have, as Mr. Randolph beareth us in hand, the Queen's Majesty your sovereign's allowance and protection; the other hath in it some most principall of the nobility, and therewithall, good numbers of the inferior sort, throughout the whole realm, which also look assuredly that all kings do allow their quarrel and will aid them accordingly. What consequence this division will draw after it, I leave it to Your Lordship's consideration; there is fallen out another division, accidentally, by my Lord Regent's death, which is like to change the state of the other two factions, to increase the one, and diminish the other, which is grounded upon the regiment of the realm. Some number of noblemen aspire to the government, pretending right thereto by reason of the Queen's demission of the croun, and her commission granted at that time for the regiment during the King's minority; another faction doth altogether repine against that division, thinking it neither fit nor tolerable, that three or four of the meanest sort amongst the Earls shall presume to challenge to themselves a rule over the whole realme, the next of the blood, the first in rank, the greatest alway both for the antientry of their houses, degree, and forces, being negleckted; this order they think preposterous, that the meaner sort shall be placed in public function to command, and the greater shall continue as private men to obey; besides that, they think if the commission had in the beginning been valewable (which the most part will not grant,) yet can it not be extended to the present, for that the conditions thereunto annexed are ceased, and so the effect of the whole void; the latter part of this division hath many pretences, for besides the Queen's faction, which is wholly on that side, a great number of these that have heretofore professed the King's obedience, do favour the same, and will not yield to the government of the other, whose preferment for respects they mislike, when the Queen's faction shall be increased, with a part of the King's, and these not of least substance, and yow may judge what is like to ensue ; another incident is like to move men to enter in further discourses, it is given out here in Scotland that the Queen's Majesty is setting forth some forces towards the border, which shall enter this realm, to countenance these that aspire to the regiment, and suppress the contrary faction, and bruits are spread, that the same shall be here out of hand ; these that think themselves of equal force with their contrary faction at home, or rather an overmatch to them, yet not able to encounter with the forces of another Prince rather than yield to their inferiors, will, I fear, take advice of necessity, and evill councillors, and seek also the maintenance of some foreign Prince, whereby Her Majesty (altho' no further inconvenience were to be feared), must be driven to excessive charges, and it would appear there were a conspiracy of all the elements at one time to set us together by the ears, for now, when the rumour of your forces coming towards the border is spread abroad, even at the same time is arrived at Dumbarton, a galzeon with a messenger sent expressly from the King of France, to that part of the nobility that favours the Queen, to learn the state of the country, and what support they lack or desire, either for furtherance of her affairs, or for their own safety ; assuredly this message will be well received, and suffered accordingly, this is the present state of Scotland. Now, if Your Lordship would also know my opinion, how to choice the best, as the case standeth ; I will in that also satisfie Your Lordship I am required from them to deal plainly, and Your Lordship shall judge wither I do so or not; for I think it plain dealing, when I simply utter my judgment, and go not about to disguise my intents. I trust the Queen's Majesty hath a desire to retain at her devotion the realme of Scotland, which she hath gone about to purchase, with bestowing great charges, and the loss of some of her people ; this desire is honourable for Her Highness, profitable for both the countreys, and of none to be disallowed ; especially if it be (as I take it) to have the amity of the whole realm, for it is not a portion of Scotland can serve her turn, nor will it prove commodious for her to suit the friendship of a faction of Scotland, for in so doing, in gaining the best, she may lose the more, and the same would bring all her actions with us in suspicion, if she should go about to nourish factions amongst us, which meaning I am sure never entered into Her Majesty's heart ; then if it be the friendship of the whole she doth demand, let her not, for pleasure of one part, go about to overthrow the remnant, which will not be so faisable, as some may give her to understand ; but rather by way of treaty, let her go about to pacify the whole state, bring the parties to an accord, reduce us all by good means to an uniformity, so shall she give us all occasion to think well of her doings, that she tendeth our wealth, and provoks us universally to wish unto Her Majesty a most prosperous continuance ; by the contrary, if, for the pleasure of a few, she will send forces to suppress these whom they mislike, and so consequently offend many ; men be not so faint hearted, but they have courage to provide for their own safty, and not only will embrace the means partly offered, but will also procure further at the hand of other Princes. This for mine own part I do abhorr, and protest I desire never to see forces of strangers to set foot within this land, yet I know not what point necessity may drive men into, as if men in the middle of the sea were in a ship, which suddenly should be set on fire, the fear of burning would make them leap into the sea, and soon after the fear of the water would drive them to cleive again to the fired ship, so for avoiding present evil, men will many times be inforced to have recourse to another, no less dangerous. Trust me, forces will not bring forth any good fruit to Her Majesty's behove, it must be some way of treaty shall serve the turn, wherein by my former letters Your Lordship doth know already what is my judgement; you see how plainly I do write, without consideration in what part my letters may be taken, yet my hope is that such as will favourably interpret them, shall think that I mean as well to Her Majesty and that realme, as these that will utter other language. I wish the continuance of the amity betwixt the two contrys, without other respect, and will not conceal from Her Majesty taking frank dealings in evil part, I shall from thenceforth forbear; in the mean season, I will not cease to trowble Your Lordship, as I shall have occasion to write, and so I take my leave of Your Lordship.

No. XXXV. (p. 257.)

Letter of Queen Elizabeth to the Earle of Susseks, July 2d, 1570.

(Calderw. MS. History, vol. 2. p. 189.)

RIGHT trusty and well beloved cousin we greet you well; this day we have received your letters of 28 the last month, with all others, sent from Scotland, and mentioned in your letters, whereunto answer is desired to be given before the tenth of this month; which is a very short time, the weightiness of the matters, and the distance of the places considered; nevertheless we have, as the shortness could suffer it, resolved to give this answer following, which we will that yow, by warrand hereof, shall cause to be given in our name to the Earl of Lennox and the rest of the noblemen conveend with him. Where it is by them, in their letters, and writings alledg'd, that for lack of our resolute answer, concerning the establishing of the regiment of the realm, under their young King, great inconvenience, have happened, and therefore they have deferred now at their last convention to determine of the samine, who shall have the place of governour, until the 21st this month, before which time they require to have our advise, in what person or persons the government of that realm shall be established, we accept very thankfull the goodwill and reputation they have of us, in yielding so frankly to require and follow our advise in a matter that toucheth the state of their King, theirselves, and realm so near, wherein as we perceive that by our former forbearing to intermeddle therein, they have taken some discomfort, as though that we would not have regard to their state and surety, so on the other part, they of their wisdoms ought to think that it might be by the whole world evil interpreted in us to appoint them a form of government, or a governour by name, for that howsoever we should mean well if we should do so, yet it could not be without some jealousy in the heads of the estate, nobility, and community of that realm, that the government thereof should be by me specially named, and ordain'd; so as finding difficulty on both parts, and yet misliking most that they should take any discomfort by our forbearing to show our mind therein, we have thought in this sort for to proceed, considering with ourselves how now that realm had been a good space of time ruled in the name of their King, and by reason of his base age, governed heretofore by a very careful and honourable person, the Earle of Murray, untill that by a mischievous person (an evil example) he was murdered, whereby great disorder and confusion of necessity had, and will more follow, if determination be not made of some other speciall person, or persons, to take the charge of governor, or superior ruler speciall for administration of law and justice, we cannot but very well allow the desire of these Lords to have some speciall governour to be chosen; and therefore being well assured that their own understanding of all others is best to consider the state of that realm, and to discern the abilities and qualities of every person meet and capable for such a charge, we shall better satisfie ourselves, whom they by their common consent shall first choose, and appoint to that purpose, then of any to be by us aforehand uncertainly named, and that because they shall perceave that we have care of the person of their King, who by nearness of blood, and in respect to his young years, ought to be very tender and dear to us, we shall not hide our opinion from them, but if they shall all accord to name his grandfather, our cousin, the Earl of Lennox, to be governor alone, or jointly with others, (whom we hear to be in the mean time by their common consent appointed Lieutenant-general) reason moveth us to think that none can be chosen in that whole realm that shall more desire the preservation of the King, and be more meet to have the government for his safety, being next to him in blood of any nobleman of that realm, or elsewhere; and yet hereby we do not mean to prescribe to them this choice, except they shall of themselves fully and freely allow thereof; furthermore we would have them well assured that whatsoever reports of devises are, or shall be spread or invented, that we have already yielded our mind to alter the state of the King or government of that realm, the same are without just cause or ground by us given, for as we have already advertized them, that although we have yielded to hear, which in honour we could not refuse, what the Queen of Scots on her part shall say and offer, not only for her own assurance, but for the wealth of that realm, yet not knowing what the same will be that shall be offered, we mean not to break the order of law and justice by advancing her cause, or prejudging her contrary, before we shall deliberately and assuredly see, upon the hearing of the whole, some place necessary, and just cause to do; and therefore finding that realm ruled by a King, and the same affirmed by laws of that realm, and thereof invested by coronation and other solemnities used and requisite, and generally so received by the whole estates, we mean not by yielding to hear the complaints or informations of the Queen against her son, to do any act whereby to make conclusion of governments, but as we have found it, so to suffer the same to continue, yea not to suffer it to be altered by any means that we may impeshe, as to our honour it doth belong, as by your late actions hath manifestly appeared, untill by some justice and clear cause, we shall be directly induced otherwise to declare our opinion ; and this we would have them to know to be our determination and course that we mean to hold, whereon we trust they for their King may see how plainly and honourably we mean to proceed, and how little cause they have to doubt of us, whatsoever to the contrary they have or shall hear ; and on the other part, we pray them of their wisdoms to think how unhonourable and contrary to all human order it were for us, when the Queen of Scotland doth so many ways require to hear her cause, and doth offer to be ordered be us in the same as well for matters betwixt ourselves and her, as betwixt herself and her son and his party of that realm, against which offers no reason could move us to refuse to give ear, that we should aforehand openly and directly, before the causes be heard and considered, as it were, give a judgment or sentence either for ourselves or for them whom she maketh to be her contraries. Finally ye shall admonish them, that they do not, by misconceiving our good meaning toward them, or by indirect assertions of their adversary, grounded on untruths, hinder or weaken their own cause, in such sort, that our good meaning towards them shall not take such effect towards them as they shall desire, or themselves have need of. All this our answer ye shall cause be given them, and let them know that for the shortness of time, this being the end of the second of this month, we neither could make any longer declaration of our mind, nor yet write any several letters, as if time might have served we would have done. 2d. July 1570.

No. XXXVI. (p. 258.)

The Bishop of Ross to Secretary Lidington from Chattisworth.
[15th June, 1570.]

I HAVE received your letters dated the 26th of May, here at Chattisworth, the 10th of January, but on the receipt thereof I had written to you at length, like as the Queen did with my Lord Levingston, by which you will be resolved of many points contained in your said letter. I writ to you that I received your letter and credit from Thomas Cowy at London, and sent to Leicester to know the Queen of England's mind, whether if you should come here or not. He sent me word that she will no ways have you come as one of the commissioners, because she is yet offended with you ; and therefore it appears good that ye come not hither, but remain where you are, to use your wisdom and diligence, as may best advance the Queen's affairs, for I perceive your weill and safety depends thereon, in respect to the great feid and ennimity born against you by your Scots people, and the great heirship taken of your father's landis ; both were sure demonstrations of their malice. Yet I am encouraged by your stout and deliberate mind. Assure yourself no diligence shall be omitted to procure supports forth of all parts where it may be had. We will not refuse the aid neither of Papist, Jew, nor Gentil, after my advice; and to this end, during this treaty, let all things be well prepared. And seeing my Lord Seaton is desirous to go into Flanders, the Queen thinks it very necessary that he so do, for the Duke D'Alva has gotten express command of the King of Spain to give support, and I am sure that there he shall have aid both of Flanders and the Pope, for it abides only on the coming of some men of countenance, to procure and receive the same. He must needs tarry there, on the preparations thereof, during the treaty, which will be a great furtherance to the same here. The Queen has already written to the Duke D'Alva for this effect, advertizing of his coming: there is certain sums of money coming for support of the Englishmen, as I wrote to you before, from the Pope. Whereupon I would he had a general commission to deal for them, and receive such sums as shall be given. The means shall be found to cause you be answerit of the sums you writ for, to be disposit upon the furnishing of the castle of Edinburgh, so being some honest and true man were sent to Flanders to receive it, as said is, which I would you prepared and sent. Orders shall be taken for the metals as you writ of. We have proponit your avyce in entring to treat with the Queen of England, for retiring of her forces puntyally for lack of aid. Your answers to the Englishmen are tho't very good, but above all keep you weill out of their hands, in that case, estote prudentes sicut serpentes. You may take experience with the hard dealing with me, how ye would be used if ye were here, and yet I am not forth of danger, being in medio nationis pravæ; alway no fear, with God's grace, shall make me shrink from Her Majesty's service. Since the Queen of England has refused that you come here, it appears to me quod nondum est sedata malitia amorreorum, &c. and therefore if Athol or Cathenes might by any means be procured to come, they were the most fit for the purpose. Rothes were also meet, if he and I were not both of one sirname: so the treaty would get the less credit either in Scotland or here. Therefore avys, and sends the best may serve the turn, and fail not Robert Melvil come with them, whoever comes, for so is the Queen's pleasure; in my last packet, with James Fogo, to you, in the beginning of May, I sent a letter of the Queen's own handwriting to him, which I trust ye received. I am sorry ye come not, for the great relief I hoped to have had by your presence, for you could well have handled the Queen of England, after her humour, as you were wont to do. The rest I refer to your good wisdom, praying God to send you health. From Chattisworth the 15th of January.

No. XXXVII. (p. 267.)

The Declaration of John Cais to the Lords of Grange and Lethington zoungare upon the 8th Day of Oct. 1571.

WHEREAS you desire to know the Queen's Majesty's pleasure, what she will do for appeasing of these controversies, and therewith has offered yourself to be at her commandment, touching the common tranquillity of the whole isle, and the amity of both realms; her pleasure in this behalf, that ye should leave off the maintenance of this civil discord, and give your obedience to the King, whom she will maintain to the utmost of her power.

And in this doing, she will deal with the Regent and the King's party to receive you into favour, upon reasonable conditions for security of life and livings.

Also, she says that the Queen of Scotts, for that she has practised with the Pope and other Princes, and also with her own subjects in England, great and dangerous treasons against the state of her own country, and also to the destruction of her own person, that she shall never bear authority, nor have liberty while she lives.

If ye refuse these gentle offers, now offered unto you, she will presently aid the King's party, with men, ammunition, and all necessary things to be had, against you.

Whereupon Her Majesty requires your answer with speed, without any delay.

No. XXXVIII. (p. 272.)

Articles sent by Knox to the General Assembly, August 5th, 1572.

Calderw. MS. History, vol. ii. 356.

FIRST, desiring a new act to be made ratifying all things concerning the King and his obedience that were enacted of before without any change, and that the ministers who have contraveend the former acts be corrected as accordeth.

That sute be made to the Regent's grace and nobility maintaining the King's cause, that whatsoever proceedeth in this treaty of peace they by mindful the kirk be not prejug'd thereby, in any sort, and they especially of the ministers that have been robbed of their possessions within the kirk during the time of the troubles, or otherwise dung and injured, may be restored.

To sute at the Regent, that no gift of any bishoprick or other benefice be given to any person, contrary to the tenor of the acts made in the time of the first Regent, of good memory, and they that are given contrar the said acts, or to any unqualified person, may be revoked and made null be an act of secret council, and that all bishopricks so vacand may be presented, and qualified person nominant thereunto, within a year after the vaking thereof, according to the order taken in Leith be the commissioners of the nobility and of the kirk in the month of January last, and in special to complain upon the giving of bishoprick of Ross to the Lord Methven.

That no pentions or benefices, great or small, be given of simple donation of any Lord Regent without consent of the possessor of the saids benefices having tittle thereto, and the admission of the superintendent or commissioners of the province where this benefice lyeth, or of the bishops lawfully elected according to the said order taken at Leith; and desire an act of council to be made thereupon until the next Parliament, wherein the samine may be specially inacted, with inhibition to the lords of session to give any letters or deceerts, upon such simple gifts of benefices or pentions not being given in manner above rehearsed, and that the kirk presently assembled declare all such gifts null so far as lyeth in their power.

That the first form of presentation to benefices, which were in the first and second Regent's time, be not chang'd as now it is commonly ; but that this clause be contained in the presentation, that if the persons presented make not residence, or be slandrous, or found unworthy either in life or doctrine be the judgment of the kirk (to which alwise he shall be subject) or meet to be transported to another room at the sight of the kirk, the said presentation and all that shall fall thereupon shall be null and of no force nor effect; and this to have place also in the nomination of the bishops.

That an act be made in this assembly that all things done in prejudice of the kirk's assumption of the third, either by papists or others, by giving of fews, liferents, or taks, or any otherwise disponing the said assumed thirds, be declared null with a solemn protestation the whole kirk disassenteth thereto.

That an act be made decerning and ordaining all bishops, admitted to the order of the kirk now received, to give account of their whole rents, and intromissions therewith once in the year, as the kirk shall appoint, for such causes as the kirk may easily consider the same to be most expedient and necessar.

Anent the jurisdiction of the kirk, that the same be determined in this assembly, because this article hath long been postponed to make sute to the Regent and council for remedy against messengers and excommunicate persons.

Last, that order be taken anent the procurers of the kirk, who procure against ministers and ministry, and for sutting of justice of the kirk's actions in the session.

No. XXXIX. (p. 275.)

Declaration of Henry Killigrewe, Esq, upon the Peace concluded the 23d Feb. 1572.

BE it known to all men, by these presents, that I, Henry Killigrewe, Esq. ambassador for the Queen's Majesty of England, Forasmuch as, at the earnest motion and solicitation being made to me, on Her Highness's behalf, there is accord and pacification of the public troubles and civil war within this realm of Scotland agreed and concluded, and the same favourably extended towards the right Honourable George Earl of Huntly, Lord Gordon and Baidzenoch, and the Lord John Hamilton, son to the Duke's Grace of Chastellarault, and commendatour of the abbey of Abirbrothock for the surety of the lives, livings, honours, and goods of them, their kinfolks, friends, servants, and partakers, now properly depending on them ; in treating of the which said pacification, the murders of the late Earl of Murray, uncle, and the Earl of Levenax, grandfather, late Regent to the King's Majesty of Scotland, his realm and lieges, as also an article touching the discharge for the fructis or moveable goods, which the said persons have taken fra personis professing the King's obedience, before the damages done or committed by them, since the 15th day of Junij, 1567, and before the penult day of July last by passed, by reason of the common cause or any thing depending thereupon, being thought by the King's commissaries matteris of such wecht and importance, as the King's present Regent could not conveniently, of himself, remit or discharge the same. Yet in respect of the necessity of the present pacification, and for the weil of the King, and common quietness of this realm and lieges, it is accorded, that the matters of remission of the said murderers, and of the discharge of the said fructis, moveable goods, and other damages, be moved by the persons desiring the said remissions and discharge to the Queen's Majesty my Sovereign, as to the Princess nearest both in blood and habitation to the King of Scots. And whatsoever Her Majesty shall advise and councel touching the said remission and discharge, the said Lord Regent, for the weil of the King and universal quietness of the realm of Scotland, shall perform, observe, and fulfil the same. And in likewise, the said Earl Huntly, and commendatour of Abirbrothock, being urged to have delivered pledges and hostages for observation of the conditions of the said accord and pacification, hath required me in place thereof, in Her Majesty's name, by virtue of my commission, to promise for them, that they shall truly and faithfully observe and keep the said pacification, and all articles and conditions thereof, for their parts, and that it would please Her Majesty to interpose herself, as surety and cautioner for them to that effect, to the King's Majesty of Scotland their sovereign and his said Regent, which I have done and promise to do, by virtue of Her Majesty's commission, as by the honourable and plain dealing of the said Earl and Lord, their intention to peace well appears, the same being most agreeable to the mind of the Queen's Majesty my sovereign, which so long by her ministers hath travelled for the said pacification, and in the end, at her motion and solicitation the same is accorded, knowing her Majesty's godly desire that the same may continue unviolate; and that the noblemen and others now returning the King's obedience shall have sufficient surety for their lives, livings, honours, and goods. Therefore, in her Majesty's name, and by virtue of my commission, I promise to the aforesaid Earl Huntley and commendatour of Abirbrothock, that by her Majesty's good means, the said remission and discharge shall be purchased and obtained to them, their kinfolks, friends, servants, and partakers, now properly depending upon them (the persons specified in the first abstinance always excepted,) as also that the said pacification shall be truly observed to them, and that Her Majesty shall interpose herself as conservatrix thereof, and endeavour herself to cause the same to be truly and sincerely kept in all points and articles thereof accordingly. In witness whereof I have to this present subscribed with my hand, and sealed the same with my own seal, the 13th day of Feb. Anno Domini 1572. And this to be performed by me, betwixt the date hereof and the Parliament which shall be appointed for their restitution, or at the furthest before the end of the said Parliament. Sic subscribitur.

The Bishop of Glasgow's Note concerning the Queen of Scotland's Dowry.

(1576. Cott. lib. Calig. B. 4.)

THE Queen of Scotland, Dowager of France, had for her dowry,

x

besides other possessions, the Dukedom of Turene, which was
solemnly contracted and given to her by the King and Estates of
Parliament; which dukedom she possessed peacefully till 1576, and
then, under the pacification betwixt the King and Mons. his brother, to augment whose appenage this dutchy was given, to which
the Queen of Scotland yielded upon account of Princes who were
her near relations, provided the equivalent which was promised her
should be faithfully performed. So that year, after a great many
solicitations in lieu of that dutchy, she had granted her the county
of Vermandaise, with the lands and bailiwicks of Seuley and
Vetry; tho' 'tis known that county and the other land were not of
equal value with Turene, but was promised to have an addition of
lands in the neighbourhood to an equal value.   Upon this letters
patent were granted, which were confirmed in the courts of Parliament, chamber of accompts, court of aids, chamber of the treasury
and others necessary: upon which she entered into possession of that
county, &c.   Afterwards, by a valuation of the commissioners of
the chamber of accompts, it was found that the revenue of that
county, &c. did not amount to those of Turene, by 3000 livres. But
instead of making up this deficiency according to justice, some of
the privy council, viz. M. de Cheverny, the presidents of Bellievre,
Nicocholay, and St. Bonet, in the name of the King, notwithstanding of her aforesaid losses, did sell and alienate the lands of
Senlis and the dutchy of Estaimpes, to Madam de Montpensier,
from whom the King received money; of which sale the counsellors
aforesaid obliged themselves to be guarantees, which hath hindered
the aforesaid Queen to have any justice done her. So that Madam
de Montpensier hath been put in possession of these lands of Senlis,
contrary to all the declaration, protestation, and assurances of the
King of France to Queen Mary's ambassadors. So that the Queen
of Scotland is dispossessed of her dowry, contrary to all equity,
without any regard to her quality.

No. XL. (p. 277.)

A Letter from the Lord of Lochlevin to the Regent Mortoun.

[3d March, 1577. E. of Mortoun's Archives. Bund. B. No. 19.]

IT will please Your Grace, I received Your Grace's letter, and has
considered the same. The parson of Camsey was here at me before
the receit thereof, directed fra my Lord of Mar, and the master
anent my last written, which was the answer of the writing that
the master sent to me, which I sent to Your Grace, desiring me to
come to Stirling to confer with them. I had given my answer before the receit of Your Grace's letter, that I behuiffit to be besyd
Sanct Androis, at ane friend's tryst, which I might not omit; I
understand by my said cousin, that the King's Majesty is to write
to divers of the nobility to come there, anent Your Lordship's trial,
and that he had written before his departing to my Lord Monthrois,
I understand likewise, he will write to Your Grace to come there
for the same effect, which I tho't good to make Your Grace foreseen
of the same, praying Your Grace, for the love of God Almighty, to
look upon the best, and not to sleep in security, but to turn you

with unfeigned heart to God, and to consider with yourself, that when the King's Majesty was very young, God made him the instrument to divest his mother from her authority, who was natural Princess, for offending of his Divine Majesty, and that there ran no vice in her, but that the same is as largely in you, except that Your Grace condescended not to the destruction of your wife. For as to harlotry and ambition, I think Your Grace has as far offended God, and far more in avaritiousness, which vycis God never left unplagued, except speedy repentance, which I pray God grant to Your Grace, for otherwise Your Grace can never have the love of God nor man. I pray Your Grace flatter not yourself; for if Your Grace believes that ye have the good-will of them that are the King's good-willers, ye deceive yourself; for surely I see perfectly that your own particulars are not contented, lat be the rest and that most principally for your hard dealing. I pray Your Grace, beir with me that I am thus hamlie, for certainly it proceeds from no grudge, but from the very affection of my heart towards Your Grace, which has continued since we were acquainted. And now I see, because the matter stands in Your Grace's handling with the King's Majesty, for certainly if Your Grace fall forth with him now, I see not how ye shall meet hereafter; pray I Your Grace to call to God, and look on the best, and cast from Your Grace both your vices, to wit, ambition and avaritiousness. I am riding this day to Sanct Androis, and trust to return on Wednesday at the farthest. If Your Grace will command me in any offices that are honest, that I may do Your Grace pleasure in at Sterling, advertise of Your Grace's mind, and shall do to my power and knowledge, and this with my heartlie, &c. &c.

To our trusty Cousin the Lord Lochleven.

[From the original. E. of Morton's Archives. Bund. B. No. 31.]

TRUSTY Cousin, after our most hearty commendations, we received your letter of the 3d of March, and as we take your plainness therein in good part, as proceeding from a friend and kinsman, in whose good affection towards us we never doubted, so ye may not think it strange that we purge ourselves so far of your accusation, as in conscience we find ourselves to have offended in. As touching our offence to God, we intend not to excuse it, but to submit us to his mercy; for in our private estate we could, and can live as well contented, as any of our degree in Scotland, without further aspiring. The bearing too the charge of the government of the realm, indeed, mon lead us, or any other that shall occupy that place, not simply to respect ourself, but His Majesty's rowme, which we supply, and therein not transcending the bounds of measure, as we trust, it shall not be found we have done, it ought not to be attributed to any ambition in us. For as soon as ever His Majesty shall think himself ready and able for his own government, none shall more willingly gree and advance the same nor I, since I think never to set my face against him, whose honour, safety, and preservation has been so dear unto me, nor I will never believe to find otherwise at his hand than favour, although all the unfriends I have in the earth were about him, to persuade him to the contrary. As we write unto you, our friendly dealing and confidence in the house of Mar is not thankfully acquit; as we trust yourself considers; but because the ambassadors of England, my Lord of Angus, the chancellor, treasurer, and some noblemen rides west this day to see the King, we pray you heartily address yourself to be there as soon as ye can, and as ye shall find the likelihood of all things, let us be advertized thereof with your own advice, by Alexr Hay, whom we have thought good to send west, seeing my Lord of Angus from Sterling rides to Douglas. And so we commit you in the protection of God. At Holyrood house, the 4th of March, 1577.

For the avaritiousness laid to our charge, indeed it lies not in us so liberally to deal the King's geare, as to satisfy all cravers, nor never shall any sovereign and native born Prince, let be any officer, eschew the disdains of such, as think them judges to their own reward; in many causes I doubt not to find the assistance of my friends, but where my actions shall appear unhonest, I will not crave their assistance, but let me bear my own burthen.

Letter of Walsingham's to Randolph, February 3, 1580-1.

[Cott. Lib Calig. C. 6.]

SIR,

I HAVE received from my Lord Lieutenant the copy of your letter of the 25th of the last directed unto His Lordship, containing a report of your negotiation with the King and his council, in your second audience, wherewith having made Her Majesty acquainted, she seemed somewhat to *mislike* that you should so long *defer to deal for the enlargement of* Empedocles. But I made answer in your behalf that I thought you were directed by the advice of the said Empedocles *friends*, in the soliciting of that cause, who knew what time was fittest for you to take to deal therein, with most effect, and best success, with which answer, Her Majesty did in the end rest very well satisfied, touching that point.

Your putting of us in the hope that D'Aubigny might easily be won at Her Majesty's devotion, was at first interpreted to have been ironie spoke to you. But since it seemeth you insist upon it, I could wish you were otherwise persuaded of the man, or at least kept that opinion to yourself, for considering the end and purpose of his coming into Scotland, as may be many ways sufficiently proved, was only to advance the Queen's liberty, and reception into that government, to overthrow religion, and to procure a foreign match with Villenarius, wherein the inclosed copy, which you may use good purpose there, shall partly give you light; there is no man here can be persuaded that he will change his purpose for so small advantage as he is likely to find by it, and therefore you shall do well to forbear to harp any more upon that string, as I have already written to you. The Prince of Orange sending, I fear will not be in time that it may do any good; for besides that these people are in themselves slow in their resolutions, their own affairs are, at present, so great, their state so confused, and the Prince's authority so small, that he cannot so soon take order in it; and yet for mine own part, I have not been negligent or careless in the matter, having more than three weeks past sent one about it, from whom nevertheless I do yet hear nothing. The letters you desire should be written thither by the French ministers; I have given order to Mr. Killingrew to procure, who, I doubt not, will carefully perform it, so that, I hope, I shall have them to send you by the next. And so I commit you to God. At Whitehall, the 3d of February, 1580.

Your very loving cousin and servant,
FRA. WALSINGHAM.

This letter is an original, and in some parts of it wrote in ciphers and explained by another hand. By Empedocles is understood Morton. By Villenarius, the King of Scots. D'Aubigny is marked thus o   i   o.

3. Feb. 1580.

Sundry Notes gathered upon good Diligence given, and in Time to be better manifested, being now thought meet to be in convenient sort used and laid against D'Aubigny, to prove him abusing the King, the Nobility and that State.

(Cott. Lib. Calig. C. 6. An original.)

FIRST, it hath been informed by credible means, that D'Aubigny was privy and acquainted with La Navé the King's mother's secretary, coming into Scotland, and of his errand there, tending chiefly to persuade the King, to think and esteem it an evil president for Princes that subjects might have power to deprive their lawful sovereigns, as they did his mother, who was not minded, by any mean, to defeat him, either of the present government of that realm, or yet of the possession of the crown and inheritance thereof, but rather to assure the same to him : and that for the accomplishment of that assurance, the King should have been advised and drawn to have governed, for some short time, as Prince, calling D'Aubigny to rule as governor of the Prince, by commission from the Queen his mother, until the King's enemies were suppressed; after which time D'Aubigny should have power given to establish and resign that kingdom to the King, by his mother's voluntary consent, whereby all such, as had before been in action against the Queen or her authority, might be brought to stand in the King's mercy. And for that the King might live in more surety, D'Aubigny should be declared both second person in succession of that crown, and also Lieutenant General of Scotland, and that D'Aubigny before his departure out of France received commission from the King's mother to the effects remembered, or near the same. That in this behalf he had conference with the Bishops of Glasgow, and Ross, and with Sir James Baford, with which persons, and with the Duke of Guise, he had and hath frequent intelligence, and by Sir James Baford he was advised to confer with the Lord John Hamilton before his repair into Scotland, wherein he agreed, and yet afterwards he sent one John Hamilton to the said Lord John to excuse him in this part, alledging, that he did forbear to come to him, lest thereby he should mar or hinder greater effects to be executed by him in Scotland.

That before his coming into that realm, the nobility and country were well quieted and united in good concord, with great love betwixt the King and nobility, and amongst the noblesse, but he hath both drawn the King against sundry of the chiefest of his nobility, that have been most ready, and have expended their blood and possessions to preserve religion, and defend the King's person, his government and estate, and also hath given occasions of great suspicions and offence to be engendered betwixt the King and his nobility, and especially with such as have been in action against the King's mother, and her authority, who by force and means of the said commission and practice should have been brought into most dangerous condition; and who also may find themselves in no small perill while he possesses the King's ear, abuseth his presence, and holdeth such of the principal keys and ports of his realm, as he presently enjoyeth.

That he hath drawn the King not only to forget the great benefits done to him and his realme, by the Queen's Majesty of England, but also to requite the same with sundry signs of great unthankfulness and wounding therewith the honour of Her Majesty, and thereby hath adventured to shake the happy amity long time continued betwixt those Princes.

And whereas these griefs were to be repaired by gentle letters and good offers, to have passed and been done betwixt them; in which respect the King and council having resolved to write to Her Majesty, for Her Highness better satisfaction in the late negotiation of Mr. Alexander Hume of Northberwick, had given order to the King's secretary to frame that letter: He minding to break the bond of amity in sunder, willed the secretary to be sure that nothing should be inserted in that letter whereby the King should crave any thing at her hands, seeking thereby to cut off all loving courtesies betwixt them, as by the declaration of the said secretary may be better learned, and thereupon further approved.

That under the hope and encouragement of D'Aubigny's protection, Alexander King presumed with that boldness to make his lewd harangue, and by his means hath hitherto escaped chastisement and correction, due for his offence.

That Sir James Baford, condemned of the slaughter of the King's father, hath been called into the realm by Lennox, without the privity of the King. And whereas the said Sir James found in a green velvet desk, late the Earl of Bothwell's, and saw and had in his hands the principal band of the conspirators in that murder, and can best declare and witness who were authors and executors of the same; he is drawn by Lennox to suppress the truth, and to accuse such as he himself knoweth to be innocent: and as by order of the law will be so found, if they may have due trial, which, contrary to all justice, is by Lennox means denied.

This is the charge against D'Aubigny, mentioned in the foregoing letter by Walsingham; but by Baford they mean Sir James Balfour.

No. XLII. (p. 298.)

The Copy of the King of France his Directions sent to Scotland with Seineur de la Motte Fenelon. Translated out of the French.

(Calderw. MS. History, vol. iii. p. 208.)

FIRST, on Their Majestys most Christian part, he shall make the most honourable salutation and visiting to the Most Serene King of Scotland, their good brother and little son, that in him is possible.

To give him their letters that are closed, such and such like as they have written to him with their hands, and to show expressly the perfect friendship and singular affection, that Their Majestys bear to him, and to bring back the answer.

To take heed to the things which touch near the most Serene King, to the effect that his person may be in no danger, but that it may be most surely preserved.

And that he be not hindred in the honest liberty that he ought to have, and that no greater or straiter guards be about him than he had before.

And such like, that he be not impeached in the authority, that God hath given to him of King and Prince sovereign above his subjects, to the effect he may as freely ordain and command in his affairs, and in the affairs of his country, with his ordinary council, as he was used to do of before.

That his nobility, barons, and commonalty of his country may have their free liberty to resort to His Serene Majesty without suspicion of greater guards or more armed men about his person than the use was, that they be not affraid and hindered to resort; and further that the Segnieur de la Motte Fenelon sall liberally and freely speak to the said Serene King and council, requiring the re-establishing of that that may or hath been changed or altered.

And that he may know if the principalls of the nobility and other men of good behaviour of the towns and commonality of the contry conveens, and are content with the form of government presently with the said Serene King, to the end that if there be any miscontent he may travaile to agree them together, and that he return not without the certainty of the samine.

And if he may understand that there be any who have not used them so reverently towards the said Serene King their sovereign Lord, as the duty of their obedience required, that he may pray on his behalf of His Majesty Most Christian the said Serene King his good brother, giving him councill wholly to forget the same, and exhorting them to do their duty towards his Majesty, in time coming, in all respects with the obedience and true subjection they ought him.

And if the said Segnieur de la Motte perceves the said Serene King to be in any manner constrained of his person, authority,

liberty, and disposition of his affairs, than he used to be, and not
convenient for his royal dignity, or as the sovereignty of a Prince
doth require, that he use all moyen lawful and honest to place him
in the samine, and that he employ as much as the credit of his
Most Christian Majesty may do toward the nobility and subjects of
that contry, and as much as may his name, with the name of his
crown towards the Scottish nation, the which he loves and confides
in as much as they were proper Frenchmen.

And that he witness to the said Serene King, and his estates, of
his consent, and to all the nobility and principall personages of the
contry, that His Most Christian Majestie will continue on his part
in the most ancient alliance and confederacy, which he hath had
with the said Serene King his good brother, praying his nobility
and contry, with his principall subjects, to persevere in the samine,
in all good understanding and friendship with him : the which, on
his part, he shall do, observing the samine most inviolable.

Further His most Christian Majesty understanding that the·
Serene King his good brother was contented with the Duke of Lenox
and his servise, the said Signieur de La Motte had charge to pray
His Serene Majesty that he might remaine beside him to his contentment, believing that he should more willing intertain the points
of love and confederace, betwixt Their Majestys and their contrys,
because he was a good subject to them both ; and if he might not
remain, without some alteration of the tranquility of his estate,
that he might retire him to his own house in the said contry, in
sureness, or if he pleased to return to France that he might surely
———and if it pleases His Serene Majesty, to cause cease and stay
the impeachments, that are made of new upon the frontiers, to the
effect that the natural Frenchmen may enter as freely into the
contry, as they were wont to do of before.

And that there may be no purpose of diffamation, nor no speech
but honourable of the Most Christian King, in that contry, by such
like as is spoken most honourably of the Serene King of Scotland
in France,

He had another head to propone, which he concealed till a little
before his departure, to wit, that the Queen. the King's mother,
was content to receive her son in association of the kingdom.

No. XLIII. (p. 306.)

Lord Hunsdane to Sir Francis Walsingham, the 14th of August,
1584, from Berwick.

(Calderw. MS. History, vol. iii. p. 374.)

SIR,

ACCORDING to my former letters, touching my meeting with the
Earl of Arran upon Wednesday last, there came hither to me from
the Earle, the justice clerk, and Sir William Stuart Captain of
Dumbarton, both of the King's privie council, to treat with me
about the order of our meeting, referring wholly to me to appoint
the hour, and the number we should meet withal : so as we concluded the place to be Foulden, the hour to be ten o'clock, and the

number with ourselves to be 13 of a side; and the rest of our troops to stand each of them a mile from the town; the one on the one side, the other on the other side, so as our troops were two miles asunder: I was not many horsemen, but I supplied it with footmen, where I had 100 shot on horse, but they were very near 500 horse well appointed: According to which appointment, we met yester-day, and after some congratulations, the Earle fell in the like protestations of his good will and readiness to serve the Queens Majesty, before any Prince in the world, next his sovereign, as he had done heretofore by his letters, and rather more; with such earnest vows, as unless he be worse than a devil, Her Majesty may dispose of him at her pleasure; this being ended, I entered with him touching the cause I had to deal with him, and so near as I could, left nothing unrehearsed that I had to charge the King or him with any unkind dealing toward Her Majesty, according to my instructions, which without any delay he answered presently, as ye shall perceive by the said answers sent herewith; but I replying unto him, he amplified them with many more circumstances, but to this effect: Then I dealt with him touching the point of Her Majesty's satisfaction, for the uttering such practices as has been lately set on foot for the disquieting of Her Majesty and her estate, who thereof made sundry disclosures, what marriages have been offered to His Majestie by sundrie Princes, and by what means the Earle has sought to divert them, and for what causes; the one, for that be marriage with Spain or France, he must also alter his religion, which, as he is sure the King will never doe, so will he never suffer him to hearken unto it, so long at he hath any credit with him; he denys not but the King has been dealt withal be practices to deal against Her Majesty, which he has so far denied and refused to enter into, as they have left dealing therein, but whatsoever the King or he knoweth therein, there shall be nothing hidden from Her Majesty, as Her Majesty shall know very shortly; surely it seems by his speeches, that if the King would have yielded thereunto, there had been no small company of French in Scotland ere now to disquiet Her Majesty.——This being ended, I dealt with him earnestly for the stay of this Parliament, which now approacheth; or at the least that there may be nothing done therein, to the prejudice of these noblemen and others now in England, for the forfaulting of their livings and goods: hereupon he made a long discourse to me, first of the Earl of Angus dealing about the Earl of Morton, then of his going out, notwithstanding of sundrie gracious offers the King had made him, then of the road of Ruthven, how that presently after they had the King's Majesty in their hands, they imprisoned himself, dealt with the King for putting of the Duke out of the realme, the King refused so to do, they told him plainly that if he would not, he should have the Earl of Arran's head in a dish; the King asked what offence the Earle had made? and they answered that it must be so, and should be so; hereupon for the safeguard of Arran's life, the King was content to send away the Duke, and yet Arran afterwards sundrie times in danger of his life; I alledged unto him the King's letter to the

Queen's Majesty, and his acts in council, that they had done nothing but for his servise, and with his good liking and contentment, who answered me, he durst do no otherwise, nor could not do any thing but that which pleased them, with such a number of other their dealings with the King whilest he was in their hands as are too long to be written, and too bad if they were true ; I said the King might have let the Queen's Majesty's ambassador have known his mind secretly, and Her Majesty would have relieved him ; he answered, that the King was not ignorant that the apprehensions, in that manner proceeded from Mr. Bow's practice, and thereby durst not impart so much to him, and yet the King was content, and did give remission to as many as would acknowledge their faults, and ask remission ; and such as would not, he thought fit to banish, to try their further loyalty, in which time they conspired the King's second apprehension, and the killing of the Earle and others, and seduced the ministers to their faction, and yet not satisfied with these conspiracies and treasonable dealings (as he terms them,) are entered into a third, being in England under Her Majesty's protection, to dishonour Her Majesty as far as in them lieth, or at least to cause the King conceive some unkindness in Her Majesty, for the harbouring of them ; I wrote to yow what the conspiracy was, the taking of the King, the killing of the Earle of Arran, and some others, the taking of the castle of Edinx and bringing home the Earles to take the charge of the King; all which (says he) is by Drummond confessed, and by the provost of Glencudden not greatly denied, and the Constable of the Castle thereupon fled; the Earl brought Drummond with him as far as Langton, where he lay, to have confessed the conspiracy before me, but having at his lighting received a blow on his leg with a horse, so as he could bring him no further, I replied that I thought verily they would not work any such practices in respect of the Queen's Majesty, abiding within her realme, and if there be any such practices, they have proceeded from others, and they not privie unto them : and that if it be not apparently proved against them, that it will be thought to be some practice to aggravate the fault, and to make them the more odious to the King. He answered me, that it should be proved so sufficiently, that they should not be able with truth to deny it, for their own hands is to be showed to part of it, and therefore concluded, that if Her Majesty should so press the King for them at this time that would rather hinder this matter of the amity, nor further it, and that since they seek chiefly his life, he could not, in any reason, seek to do them any good ; and besides he assured me, that if he would, he dare not, this last matter being fallen out as it is ; and surely if this matter had not fallen out, I would not have doubted the restoring of the Earl of Mar very shortly, if Her Majesty would have employed me therein, but for the Earl of Angus, I perceive the King is persuaded that both he, and the rest of the Douglasses, have conceived so mortall an hatred against him and the Earl of Arran, about the death of the Earl of Morton, as if they were at home, to-morrow next, they would not leave to practise and conspire the death of them both, and therefore a hard matter to do any thing for him : finally, he concluded and required me to assure Her Majesty from the King, that there shall nothing be hid from her, nor any thing left undone that may satisfie Her Majesty with reason, and that the King shall never do any thing, nor consent to have any thing done in her prejudice, so long as he had any credit with him, or authority under him. Having this far proceeded, he desired to show me his commission, which is under the great seal, to himself only, which is as large as may be, and yet sundrie of the privie councel there with him, but not one in commission, nor present, nor near us all this time, having spent almost five hours in these matters; he presented to me the Master of Gray, who delivered to me a letter from the King in his commendation, whom I perceive the King means to send to Her Majesty, and therefore requires a safe-conduct for his passage, which I pray yow procure, and to send it so soon as you may. I let him understand of the Lord Seaton's negociation with the French King. He swore to me, that Seaton was but a knave, and that it was partly against his will, that he should be sent thither. But his commission and instruction being of no great importance, he yielded the sooner; and if Seaton has gone beyond his instructions, which Arran drew himself, he will make Seaton smart for it. Touching William Newgate and Mark Gulgan, he protested he never heard of any such; he says there was a little poor soul, with a black beard, come thither a-begging, who said he was an enemy to Desmond, to whom he gave a croun, but never heard of him since, and for any Scots man going into Ireland, he says there is no such matter; if there be, there may be some few raskals that he knows not of; and touching the coming of any Jesuits into Scotland, he says it is but the slanderous devise of the King's enemys, and such as would have the world believe the King were ready to revolt in religion, who the world shall well see will continue as constant therein, as what Prince soever professed it most; and the Earle himself dos protest to me, that to his knowledge, he never saw a Jesuit in his life, and did assure me if there was any in Scotland, they should not do so much harm in Scotland, as their ministers would do, if they preach such doctrine as they did in Scotland; and touching one Ballanden, of whom I wrote to yow, I heard from Mr. Colvil, the Earle avows constantly that he knows not, nor hath not heard of any such man, but he would inquire at the justice clerk, and would inform me what he could learn of that: thus I have made yow as short a discourse as I can of so many matters, so long discoursed upon, but these are the principal points of all our talk, so near as I can remember it, and for this time I commit yow to the Almighty. At Berwick the 14th of August, 1584.

The King is very desirous to have my son Robert Carrie to come to him. I pray yow know Her Majesty's pleasure.

Arran's Answers to the Griefs or Articles proposed to the Lord Hunsdane, set down in another Form.

As to the strait and severe persecution of all such, as have been noted to have been well affected to the Queen's Majesty, it cannot

appear they were either from that cause punished, or hardly dealt
with, since His Majesty of late has been so careful and diligent to
choice out good instruments to deal betwixt Her Majesty and him,
as His Majesiy has done in electing of Your Lordship and me : besides that in all their accusations, their good will and affection born
to Her Majesty, was, at no time, laid to their charge, but capital
actions of treason many way tried now be the whole three estates,
and more than manifest to the world.

As for His Majesty inhibiting, by public proclamation, such as
were banished, not to repair in England ; the bruits and whisper-
ings that came to His Majesty's ears of their conspiracies and treasons, which since syn they accomplished, so far as in them lay,
moved His Majesty to inhibit them to repair to any place, so near
His Majesty's realm, lest they should have attempted these things,
which shortly they did attempt, being farther off, and more distant
both by sea and land.

As for reception of Jesuits, and others, Her Majesty's fugitives,
and not delivering them according to his promise, as Your Lordship propones, His Majesty would be most glad, so that it might
fall out by Your Lordship's traviles, that no fugitive of either
realme should be received of either, and when so shall be, it shall
not fail on His Majesty's part, albeit in very deed this time bygone
His Majesty has been constrained to receipt Her Majesty's mean
rebells and fugitives, contrar his good naturall, since Her Majesty
hath receipt, in effect, the whole and greatest rebells and traitors
His Majesty in His own blood ever had ; as for the agreement with
His Majesty's mother anent their association, His Majesty has commanded me, in presence of Your Lordship's servant, to assure Her
Majesty and Your Lordship, in His Majesty's name, that it is altogether false, and an untruth, nor any such like matter done yet.

His Majesty has commanded me to assure Your Lordship, that it
is also false and untrue, that His Majesty has, by any means direct
or indirect, sent any message to the Pope, or received any from
him ; or that His Majesty has dealt with Spain, or any foreigners,
to harm Her Majesty or her realm, which His Majesty could have
no honour to do, this good intelligence taking place, as I hope in
God it shall.

As concerning the contemptuous usage of Her Majesty's ministers
sent unto His Majesty, His Majesty used none of them so, and if
His Majesty had, sufficient cause was given by them, as some of
their own writs do yet testify ; as I more particularly showed Your
Lordship at Foulden at our late meeting.

No. XLIV.   (P. 308.)

*The Scottish Queen's Offers upon the Effect of her Liberty, propounded
by her Secretary Naw, November,* 1534.

(Cott. Lib. Calig. c. viii. A Copy.)

THE Queen my mistress being once well assured of Your Majesty's
amity.

1. Will declare openly that she will (as it is sincerely her meaning) straitly to join unto Your Majesty, and to the same to yield and bear the chief honour and respect, before all other Kings and Princes in Christendom.

2. She will swear and protest solemnly, a sincere forgetfulness of all wrongs which she may pretend to have been done unto her in this realm, and will never in any sort or manner whatsoever, show offence for the same.

3. She will avow and acknowledge, as well in her own particular name, as also for her heirs and others descending of her for ever, Your Majesty for just, true, and lawful Queen of England.

4. And consequently, will renounce, as well for herself as for her said heirs, all rights and pretences which she may claim to the crown of England, during Your Majesty's life, and other prejudice.

5. She will revoke all acts and shews, by her heretofore made, of pretence to this said crown to the prejudice of Your Majesty, as may be the taking of the arms and stile of the Queen of England, by the commandment of King Francis her late lord and husband.

6. She will renounce the Pope's bull for so much as may be expounded to turn in her favour, or for her behoof, touching the deprivation of Your Majesty, and will declare that she will never help and serve herself with it.

7. She will not prosecute, during Your Majesty's life, by open force or otherways, any public declaration of her right in the succession of this realm, so as secret assurance be given unto her, or at the least public promise, that no deciding thereof shall be made in the prejudice of her, or of the King her son, during Your Majesty's life, nor after your decease, until such time as they have been heard thereupon, in publick, free, and general assembly of the parliament of the said realm.

8. She will not practise, directly or indirectly, with any of Your Majesty's subjects, neither within nor out of your realm, any thing tending to war, civil or foreign, against your Majesty and your estate, be it under pretext of religion, or for civil and politick government.

9. She will not maintain or support any of your subjects declared rebels, and convicted of treason against you.

10. She will enter into the association, which was showed her at Wingfield for the surety of Your Majesty's life, so as there be mended or right explicated some clauses which I will show to Your Majesty, when I shall have the copy thereof, as I have beforetime required.

11. She will not treat with foreign Kings or Princes, for any war or trouble against this state, and will renounce, from this time, all enterprises made or to be made in her favour for that respect.

12. Furthermore, this realm being assailed by any civil or foreign war, she will take part with Your Majesty, and will assist you in your defence with all her forces and means, depending of herself and with all her friends of Christendom.

13. And to that effect, for the mutual defence and maintenance of Your Majesty, and the two realms of this isle, she will enter with your Majesty in a league defensive as shall be more particu-

larly advised, and will perswade as much as in her, the King her son to do the like. The leagues with all parts abroad remaining firm, and especially the antient league between France and Scotland, in that which shall not be against this present.

14. She will enter into a league offensive, having good assurance or secret declaration and acknowledgment of her right in the succession of this crown, and promise that happening any breach betwixt France and this realm, (which she prayeth God never to happen,) the just value of her dowry shall be placed for her in lands of the revenue of the crown.

15. For assurances of her promises and covenants, she doth offer to abide herself in this realm for a certain time, (better hostage can she not give than her own person,) which, so as she be kept in the liberty here before propounded, is not in case to escape secretly out of this country, in the sickly state she is in, and with the good order which Your Majesty can take therein.

16. And in case Your Majesty do agree to her full and whole deliverance, to retire herself at her will out of this realm, the said Queen of Scots she will give sufficient hostage for such time as will be advised.

17. If she abide in this realm, she will promise not to depart out of it without your licence, so as it be promised unto her that her state, in such liberty as shall be accorded unto her, shall not be in any sort altered, until after tryall to have attempted against your life, or other trouble of your estate.

18. If she go into Scotland, she will promise to alter nothing in the religion which is now used there, she being suffered to have free exercise of hers, for her and her household, as it was at her return out of France; and further, to pull out every root of new division between the subjects, that none of the subjects of Scotland be sifted for his conscience, nor constrained to go to the service of the contrary religion.

19. She will grant a general abolition of all offences, done against her in Scotland, and things shall remain there as they are at this present, for that respect, saving that which hath been done against her honour, which she meaneth to have revoked and annulled.

20. She will travel to settle a sure and general reconciliation between the nobility of the country, and to cause to be appointed about the King her son, and in his council, such as shall be fit for the entertainment of the peace and quiet of the country, and the amity of the realm.

21. She will do her best to content Your Majesty, in favour of the Scots lords banished and refuged hither, upon their due submission to their Princes, and Your Majesty's promise to assist the said King and Queen of Scotland against them, if they happen to fall into their former faults.

22. She will proceed to the marriage of the King her son, with the advice and good council of Your Majesty.

23. As she will pass nothing without the King her son, so doth she desire that he intervene conjointly with her in this treaty, for

the greater and perfecter assurance thereof; for otherwise any thing can hardly be established to be sound and continue.

24. The said ScotchQueen trusteth, that the French King, her good brother, according to the good affection which he hath always showed her, and hath been afresh testified unto me by Monsr. de Mannissiere for this said treaty, will very willingly intervene, and will assist her for the surety of her promises.

25. And so will the Princes of the House of Lorrain, following the will of the said King, will bind themselves thereunto.

26. For other Kings and Princes of Christendom, she will assay to obtain the like of them, if for greater solemnity and approbation of the treaty if it be found necessary.

27. She doth desire a speedy answer, and final conclusion of the premisses, to the end to meet in time with all inconveniences.

28. And in the mean time, the more to strengthen the said treaty, as made by her of a pure and frank will, she desireth that demonstration be made of some releasement of her captivity.

Objections against the Scottish Queen under Secretary Walsinghame's Hand, November, 1584.

THE Queen of Scots is ambitious, and standeth ill affected to Her Majesty, and therefore it cannot be but that her liberty should bring peril unto Her Majesty.

That her enlargement will give comfort to Papists, and other ill affected subjects, and greatly advance the opinion had of her title as successor.

That as long as she shall be continued in Her Majesty's possession, she may serve as it were a gage of Her Majesty's surety, for that her friends, for fear of the danger she may be thrown into, in case any thing should be done in her favour, dare not attempt any thing in the offence of Her Majesty.

November, 1584. } *What Course were fit to be taken with the Queen of Scots, whether she be enlarged or not.*

(Cott. Lib. Col. 8.)

THE course to be taken with the said Queen may be considered of in three degrees, either,

1. To continue her under custody in that state she now is.
2. To restrain her of the present liberty she now hath.
3. Or to set her at liberty upon caution.

1. Touching the first, to continue her under custody in that state she now is, it is to be considered, that the Princes that favour that Queen, upon the complaint she maketh of hard usage, are greatly moved with commiseration towards her, and promise to do their endeavour for her liberty, for which purpose her ministers solicit them daily.

And to move them the more to pity her case, she acquainteth them with her offers made to Her Majesty, which appeared to be no less profitable than reasonable for Her Majesty, so as the refusal and rejecting giveth her friends and favourers cause to think her hardly dealt withal, and therefore may, with the better ground and reason, attempt somewhat for the setting of her at liberty.

It is also likely that the said Queen, upon this refusal, finding her case desperate, will continue her practice under hand, both at home and abroad, not only for her delivery, but to obtain to the present possession of this crown upon her pretended title, as she hath hitherto done, as appeareth, and is most manifest by letters and plots intercepted, and chiefly by that late alteration of Scotland, which hath proceeded altogether by her direction, whereby a gap is laid open for the malice of all Her Majesty's enemies, so as it appeareth that this manner of keeping her, with such number of persons as she now hath, and with liberty to write and receive letters (being duly considered), is offensive to the Princes, the said Queen's friends; and subject to all such practices as may peril Her Majesty's safety, and therefore no way to be liked of.   •

2. Touching the second, to restrain her in a more straighter degree of the liberty she hath hitherto enjoyed.

It may at first sight be thought a remedy very apt to stop the course of the dangerous practices fostered heretofore by her: for, true it is, that this remedy might prove very profitable, if the realm of Scotland stood in that sort devoted to Her Majesty, as few years past it did; and if the King of that realm were not likely, as well for the release of his mother, as for the advancement of both their pretended titles, to attempt somewhat against this realm and Her Majesty, wherein he should neither lack foreign assistance, nor a party here within this realm: But the King and that realm standing affected as they do, this restraint, instead of remedying, is likely to breed these inconveniences following:

First, It will increase the offence both in him, and in the rest of the Princes her friends, that misliked of her restraint.

Secondly, It will give them just cause to take some way of redress.

Lastly, It is to be doubted, that it may provoke some desperate ill-disposed person, all hope of her liberty removed, to attempt somewhat against Her Majesty's own person (a matter above all others to be weighed), which inconveniency being duly considered, it will appear manifestly that the restraint, in a straighter degree, is likely to prove a remedy subject to very hard events.

The latter degree, whether it were fit to set the said Queen at liberty, ministreth some cause of doubt, touching the manner of the liberty, in what sort the same is to be performed, whether to be continued here within the realm, or to be restored into her own country.

But first, this proposition, before the particularities be weighed, is to be considered in generality.

For it is very hard for a well-affected subject, that tendreth Her Majesty's surety, and weigheth either the nature of the Scottish Queen, being inclined to ambition and revenge, or her former actions, what practices she hath set on foot most dangerous for Her Majesty and this realm, to allow of her liberty, being not made acquainted with such causes, as time hath wrought, to make it less perilous than it hath been, nor with such cautions as may, in some sort, be devised to prevent both her ambition and malice; and therefore, to make this apparent.

It is to be considered, that the danger that was in the mother, is now grown to be in the son. He pretendeth the same title she doth: Such as do affect her, both at home and abroad, do affect him (and he is the more dangerous for that he is unmarried, which may greatly advance his fortune; and that he is a man, whereby he may enter into action in his own person); where she is restrained, he is at liberty; his own realm is now altogether at his devotion, and the party affected to this crown abased; so as the matter duly considered, neither liberty nor restraint doth greatly alter the case for perils towards Her Majesty, unless by such promises as may be made by the way of treaty with her, the danger likely to grow from the King her son be provided for.

But in this behalf it may be objected, that so long as the mother remains in Her Majesty's hands, the King will attempt nothing for fear of his mother's peril.

To this objection it may be answered, first, That they hope that Her Majesty, being a Prince of justice, and inclined to mercy, will not punish the mother for the son's offence, unless she shall be found by good proof, culpable. Secondarily, That men will not be over hasty, considering in what predicament the King standeth touching his expectation of this crown, to advise any thing that in time future may be dangerous to the giver of such council as may reach to his mother's peril.

And lastly, The taking away of his mother, he being strong in the field through both foreign assistance, and a party here within the realm, will appear so weak a remedy (which may rather exasperate both him and her party, to proceed with more courage and heat to revenge, if any such hard measure should be offered unto her) as they will suppose, for the reason above specified, that no such extremity will be used.

It may also be objected, that the setting of her at liberty will greatly encourage the Papists both at home and abroad; but herein, if the provision be duly considered, that may be made by Parliament both here and there, they shall rather find cause of discomfort than otherwise.

These two doubts being resolved, and the perils that was in the mother appearing most manifestly to be seen in the son accompanied with more danger, with due consideration had also of such remedies as may be provided for the preventing of the dangers, that her liberty may minister just cause to doubt of; there will be good cause of hope found, that the same will rather breed benefit than perils.

Now it resteth, in what sort the said liberty shall be performed; if it shall be thought meet she shall be continued within the realm with some limitation, especially in that place where she now resideth, the country round about being so infected in religion as it is, it is greatly to be doubted that will very much increase the corruption, and falling away in that behalf. Besides, she should have commodity, with much more ease and speed, to entertain practices within this realm, than by being in her own country.

If abroad freely without limitation either in Scotland or France, then shall Her Majesty lose the gages of her safety, then shall she be at hand to give advice in furtherance of such practices, as have been laid for to stir trouble in this realm, wherein she hath been a principal party.

For the first, it is answered before, that the respect of any perils that may befal unto her, will in no sort restrain her son. For the other, if it be considered what harm her advice will work unto herself, in respect of the violation of the treaty, and the provision that may be made in Parliament here, it is to be thought, that she will then be well advised, before she attempt any such matter, which now she may do without perill. Besides such Princes, as have interposed their faith and promise for her, cannot with honour assist her, wherein the French King will not be found very forward, who, in most friendly sort, hath lately rejected all such requests, propounded either by her, on her son's ministers, that might any way offend Her Majesty. And so to conclude, seeing the cause of her grief shall be taken away; the French King gratified, who is a mediator for her, and will mislike, that, by any Spanish practice, she should be drawn to violate her faith, that the rest of the Princes shall have no just cause of offence, but rather to think honourably of her Majesty considering the Scottish Queen's carriage towards her, which hath deserved no way any such favour; the noblemen of Scotland shall be restored, who will be a good stay of such counsells as may tend to the troubling of this realm, especially having so good ground of warrant as the Parliament to stand unto; the charges and perils which her practices might have bred to this realm shall be avoided; and lastly, the hope of the Papists shall be taken away, by such good provisions, as in both the realms may be made, whereby the perills that might fall into Her Majesty's own person (a matter of all others to be weighed) shall be avoided, when by the change that may grow by any such wicked and ungodly practice, they shall see their case no way relieved in point of religion.

Reasons to induce Her Majesty to proceed in the Treaty under Secretary Walsingham's Hand.

(Cott. Lib. Cal. c. 8.)

THAT such plots as have of late years been devised (tending to the raising of trouble within this realm) have grown from the Scots Queen's ministers and favourers, not without her allowance and seeking: Or,

That the means used by the said ministers, to induce Princes to give ear to the said plots, is principally grounded upon some commiseration had of her restraint.

That the stay, why the said plots have not been put in execution, hath proceeded, for that the said Princes have, for the most part, been entertained with home and domestic troubles.

That it is greatly to be doubted, that now their realms begin to be quiet, that somewhat will be attempted in her favours by the said Princes.

That it is also to be doubted, that somewhat may be attempted by some of her fautors in an extraordinary sort, to the perill of Her Majesty.

That for the preservation thereof, it shall be convenient for Her Majesty to proceed to the finishing of the treaty, not long sithence begun between her and the said Queen.

No. XLV. (p. 313.)

Letter of Q. Mary to Q. Elizabeth

(Cott. Lib. Coll. B. VIII. fol. 147.   An original.)

MADAME MA BONNE SEUR,

M'ASSEURANT que vous avez eu communication d'une lettre de Gray que vostre homme Semer me livra hier soubz le mon de mon filz y recongnoissant quasi de mot a la mot mesmes raisons que le dit Gray m'escrivit en chifre estant dernierement pres de vous desmontrant la suffisance & bonne intention du personage je vous prieray seulement suivant ce que si devant je vous ay tant instantement importuné que vous me permettiez desclaircir librement et ouvertement ce point de l'association d'entre moy et mon filz et me dessier les mains pour proceder avec lui comme je jugeray estre requis pour son bien & le mien. Et j'entreprendz quoy que l'on vous die & puisse en rapporter de faire mentir ce petit brouillon qui persuadé par aucuns de vos ministres a entrepris cette separation entre moy & mon enfant, & pour y commencer je vous supplie m'octroyer qui je puisse parler a ce justice clerk qui vous a este nouvellement envoyé pour mander par luy a mon filz mon intention sur cela, ce qui je me promis que ne me refuserez, quant ce ne seroit que pour demontrer en effect la bonne intention que vous m'avez asseurée avoir a l'accord & entretien de naturel devoir entre la mere & l'enfant qui dit en bonnes termes estre empesche pour vous me tenant captive en un desert ce que vous ne pourrez mieux desmentir & faire paroitre vostre bon desir a notre union que me donnant les moyens d'y proceder, & non m'en retenir et empescher comme aucune des vos ministres pretendent a fin de laisser toujours lieu a leur mauvais & sinistres practiques entre nous. La lettre porte que l'association n'est pas passée, aussi ne luy ai je jamais dit, bienque mon filz avoit accepté; & que nous en avions convenu ensemble, comme l'acte signé de sa main, & ces lettres tant a moy, que en France en font foy, ayant donné ce meme temoinage de sa bouche propre a plusieurs ambassadeurs et personnes de credit, s'excusant de ne l'oser faire publier par craint de vous soulement, demandant forces pour vous resister d'avant de ce declarer si ouvertement estant journellement persuade au contraire par vos ministres qui luy prometoyent avecque une entreire a Yorck le faire declairer votre heretier. Au surplus Madame quand mon enfant seroit si malheureux que de s'opiniastrer en cette extreme impieté & ingratitude vers moy, je ne puis penser que vous non plus qu'aucum aultre Prince de la Chretienté, le voulissiez cu cela applaudir on meintenir pour luy fayre acquerir ma malediction ains que plutos *introviendrez* pour luy faire recongnoitre la raison trop juste & evidant devant Dieu & les hommes. Helas & encores ne luy vouloier j'en ofter, mays donner avec droit ce qu'il tient par usurpation. Je me suis du tout commise a vous, & fidelement faites si il vous plest que je ne en soye pis qu'aupravant, & que le faulsete des uns ne prevale desvant la verite vers vous, pour bien recevant mal, & la plus grande affliction que me scaurroit arriver a scavoir la perte de mon fils. Je vous supplie de me mander en cas qu'il persiste en cette m'esconnoissance de son devoir, que de luy ou de moy il vous plaist advouer pour legittime Roy ou Royne d'Ecosse, & si vous aves agreable de poursuivre avec moy a part la traité commencé entre nous de quoy je vous requiers sans plus attendre de response de ce mal gouverné enfant vous en requerrant avec autant d'affection que je sens mon cœur oppressé d'ennuy. Pour Dieu souvenez vous de la promesse que m'avez faites de me prendre en votre protection me rapportant de tout a vous & sur ce priant Dieu qu'il vous viueille preserver de touts vos ennemys & dissimulez amys, comme je le desire de me consoler & de me venger de ceulz qui pourchassent un tel malheur entre la mere & l'enfant. Je cesseray de vous troubler, mais non a m'ennuier que je ne recoive quelque consolation de vous & de Dieu encore un coup je le supplie de vous garder de tout peril. Futhbery XII Mars.

Votre fidelement vouée sœur
et obeissant cousine,

A la Reyne d'Angleterre   MARIE Q.
Madame ma bonne sœur &
cousine.

No. XLVI. (p. 318.)

A Testament by Q. Mary.

N. B. The following paper was transcribed by the Rev. Mr. Crawford, late Regius Professor of Church History in the University of Edinburgh. Part of this paper, according to him, is written by Nane, Mary's Secretary, the rest with the Queen's own hand. What is marked (") is in the Queen's hand.

[Cott. Lib. Vespas. L. 16. p. 415.]

CONSIDERANT par ma condition presente l'estat de vie humaine, si incertain, que personne ne s'en peust, ou doibt asseurer, sinnon soubs la grande et infinie misericorde de Dieu. Et me voulant prevaloir d'icelle contre tous les dangers et accidens, qui me pourroient inopinement survenir en cette captivité, mesmes a cause des grandes et longues maladies, ou j'ay eté detenué jusques a present; j'ay advisé tandis que j'ay la commodité, ou raison en jugement, de pourvoir apres ma mort la salut de mon ame, enterrement de mon corps, et disposition de mon bien, estat, & affaires, par ce present mon testament et ordonnance de mon dernier volonté, qin s'ensuyt.

Au nom du Pere, du Filz, et du benoite St. Esprit. Premierement, me recongnoissant indigne pecheresse avec plus d'offences envers mon Dieu, que de satisfaction par toutes les adversites que j'ay souffert ; dont je la loue sa bonté. Et m'appuyant sur la croix de mon Sauveur et Redempteur Jesus Christ, Je recommende mon ame a la benoiste et individue Trinité, et aux prieres de la glorieuse Vierge Marie, et de tous les anges saincts & sainctes de paradis, esperant par leur merites & intercession, estre aydée a obtenir de estre faicte participante avec eulx de felicité eternelle. Et pour m'y acheminer de cueur plus net et entier despouillant des a present tout resentiment des injures, calomnies, rebellions, et aultres offenses, qui me pourroient avoir esté factes durant ma vie, par mes subjets rebelles et aultres ennemis ; J'en retriet la vengeance a Dieu, & le supplie leur pardonner, de mesme affection, que je luy requiers pardons a mes faultes, et a tous ceuls et celles que je puis avoir offensé de faicts ou de parolles.

Je veulx et ordonne, &c. [*The two following paragraphs contain directions concerning the place and circumstance of her burial.*]

Pour ne contrevenir a la gloire, honneur, et conservation de 'Eglise catholique, apostolique et Romaine, en la quelle je veulx vivre et mourir, si le Prince d'Escosse mon filz y puest etre reduiet contre la mauvaise nourriture, qu'il a prise a mon tres grand regret en l'heresie de Calvin entre mes rebelles, je le laisse seul et unique heretier de mon royaume d'Escosse, de droict que je pretende justement en la couronne d'Angleterre et pays qui en dependent, et chacun mes meubles et immeubles qui resteront apres ma mort, et execution de ce present testament.

Si non, et que mon dit filz continue a vivre en la dite heresie, Je cede, transporte, et faicte don "de touts et chacuns mes droicts, "que je pretende & puis pretendre a la couronne d'Angleterre, et "aultres droicts, seigneuries, ou royaulmes en dependantz, au roy "catholique, ou aultre de siens qu'il luy plaira, avesques advis, "consentement de sa saincteté ; taut pour le voyr aujourdhuy le "seul seurs appui de la religion catholique, que pour reconnoissance "de gratuites faveurs que moy, et les miens recommandez par moy, "ont avons receu de luy en ma plus grand necessité ; et resguard "aussi au droict que luy mesme peut pretendre a ces ditz royaulmes "et pays, je le supplie qu'un recompence il preign alliance, de la "maison de Lorraine, et si il ce pleut de celle de Guise, pour me- "moire de la race de laquelle je suis sortie au coste de Mere, n'a "ayant de celuy de mon pere, que mon seul enfant, lequel estant "Catholique j'ay tousjours voué pour une de ses filles, si il luy "plaisoit de l'accepter, ou faillant une de ses niepces mariée comme "sa fille.

"Je laysse mon filz a la protection du Roy, de Prince, et Ducs "de Lorrayne et de Guise, et du Mayne, aux quelz je recommende "et son estat en Escosse, et mon droict en Angleterre, si il est "catholique, et quelle le parlie de cestre royne."

Je faitz don au "Compté de Lenox" de Compté de Lenox tenu par feu son pere, et commande mon filtz, comme mon heretier et successeur, d'obéyr en cest en droit a ma volonté.

Je veulx et ordonne toutes les sommes et deniers, qui se troveront par moys deues, tien mis cause de droict estre faits "a Lohliven" etre promptement payée et acquittés, et tout tort et griefs reparés par les dits executeurs desquelz J'en charge la conscience. Oultre, &c. [*Follow two or three paragraphs concerning particular legacies, and then is added*] Faict au manior de Sheffeld en Angleterre le jour de —— Mil cincq cens soixant & dix sept.

After a large blank page follows in the Queen's hand:

"Si mon filz meurt, au Comte de Lenox, au Claude Hamilton "lequel se montrera le plus fidelle vers moy, et plus constant en "religion, au jugement de —— Ducs de Lorraine et de Guyse, ou je "le rapport sur ce de ceulx a que j'auray donnay la charge de "trayter avesque eux de par moy et ceulx, a condition de ce marrier "ou allier en la dite mayson ou par leur advis."

Follow near two pages of particular legacies.

"Et le remets ma tante de Lenox au droict quelle peut pretendre "a la Conté d'Angous avant l'acort fait par mon commandement "entre ma dite tante de Lenox et le Comte de Morton, ven quil a "esté fait & par le feu Roy mon mary et moy, sur la promesse de sa "fidelle assistance, si luy et moy encourions dangier et besoing "d'ayde, ce qu'il rompit, s'entendant secretement au les nos ennemis "rebelles, qu'attemt prient contre sa vie, et pour cest effect pris les "armes, et ont porté les banieres desploiës, contre nous, je revoque "aussi toute autre don que je luy ay fait de Conté de Morton sur "promesses de ses bons services a advenir, et entends que la dite "Conté soit reunie a la couronne, si ell se trouve y partenir, comme "ses trahisons tant en la mort de mon feu mary, que en mon "banissement, et poursuit de la mien ne l'ont merite. Et defends "a mon filz de ce jamays scrvire de luy pour de luy pour la hayne "qu'il aye a ses parents, la quelle je crains ne s'estende jusques a "luy, le connoisant du tout affectionné aux ennemis de mon droite "en ce royaume, du quel il es penconnaire.

"Je recommende mon nepveu Francois Stuart a mon filz, et luy "commande de tenir pres de luy et s'enservit, et je luy laisse le "bien du Conte de Boduell son oncle, en respect qu'il est de mon "sang, mon filleul, et ma este laissé en lutelle par son pere.

"Je declare que mon frere bastard Robert Abbé de St. Croix "n'a en que par circonvention Orkenay, et que le ne fut jamays "mon intention, comme il apret par la revocation que j'ay fayte "depuys, et été aussi faite d'avant la asge de xxv ans, ce que "j'aimois deliberer si il ne m'eussent prenner par prison de se de "defayre aulx estats je veulx donc que Orkenay soit reune a la "couronne comme une de plus necessaires pour mon filz, & sans "mayson ne pourra etre bien tenue.

"Les filles de Morra ne parvient accessi heriter, ains revient la "Conté a la Couronne, si il luy plest luy donner sa —— ou fille en "marriasge, et il nome l'en sienne ligne."

No. XLVII. (p. 318.)

A Letter from Mr. Archibald Douglas to the Queen of Scotts.

(April.—— Harl. Lib. 37. B. 9. fo. 126)

PLEASE Your Majesty, I received your letter of the date of 12th of Novr, and in like manner has seen some part of the contents of one other of the same date, directed to Monsr. de Movisir, ambassador for his Majesty the most Christian King, both which are agreeable to your princely dignity, as by the one Your Highness desires to know the true causes of my banishment, and offers unto me all favour if I shall be innocent of the heinous facts committed in the person of your husband of good memory, so by the other the said ambassador is willet to declare unto me, if your husband's murder could be laid justly against me, that you could not sollicit in my cause, neither yet for any person that was participant of that execrable fact, but would seek the revenge thereof when you should have any means to do it ; Your Majesty's offer, if I be innocent of that crime, is most favourable, and your desire to know the truth of the same is most equitable ; and therefore that I should, with all my simplicity sincerity, and truth, answer thereunto is most reasonable, to the end that your princely dignity may be my help if my innocence shall sufficiently appear ; and procure my condemnation if I be culpable in any matter, except in the knowledge of the evil disposed minds of the most part of your nobility against your said husband, and not revealing of it ; which I am assured was sufficiently known to himself, and to all that had judgment never so little in that realm ; which also I was constrained to understand, as he that was specially employed betwixt the Earl Morton and a good number of your nobility, that they might with all humility intercede at Your Majesty's hand for his relief in such matters as are more specially contained in the declaration following, which I am constrained for my own justification by this letter to call to Your Majesty's remembrance. Notwithstanding that I am assured, to my grief, the reading thereof will not smally offend your princely mind. It may please Your Majesty to remember that, in the year of God, 1566, the said Earl of Morton, with divers other nobility and gent. were declared rebels to Your Majesty, and banished your realm for insolent murder committed in Your Majesty's own chamber, which they alleged was done by command of your husband, who, notwithstanding, affirmed that he was compelled by them to subscribe the warrant given for that effect ; howsoever the truth of that matter remains amongst them, it appertains not to me at this time to be curious : true it is that I was one of that number that heavily offended against Your Majesty, and passed in France the time of our banishment, at the desire of the rest, to humbly pray your brother the most Christian King to intercede that our offences might be pardoned, and Your Majesty's clemency extended towards us ; albeit divers of no small reputation, in that realm, was of the opinion that the said fact merited neither to be requisite for not yet pardoned. Always such was the careful mind of his Majesty towards the quietness of that realm, that the dealing in that cause was committed to Monsieur de Movisir, who was

directed at that time to go into Scotland to congratulate the happy
birth of your son, whom Almighty God of his goodness may lonl
preserve in happy estate, and perpetual felicity; the careful travai
of the said de Movisir was so effectual, and Your Majesty's mind so
inclined to mercy, that within short space thereafter I was permitted
to repair in Scotland, to deal with Earls Murray, Athol, Bodwel,
Arguile, and Secretary Ledington, in the name and behalf of the
said Earl Morton, Lords Reven, Lindsay, and remanent complesis,
that they might make offer in the names of the said Earl of any
matter that might satisfy Your Majesty's wrath, and procure your
clemency to be extended in their favours; at my coming to them,
after I had opened the effect of my message, they declared that the
marriage betwixt you and your husband had been the occasion already of great evil in that realm; and if your husband should be
suffered to follow the appetite and mind of such as was about him,
that kind of dealing might produce with time worse effects; for
helping of such inconvenience that might fall out by that kind of
dealing, which they had thought it convenient to join themselves
in league and band with some other noblemen, resolved to obey
Your Majesty as their natural sovereign, and have nothing to do
with your husband's command whatsoever, if the said Earl would
for himself enter into that band and confederacy with them,
they could be content to humbly request and ravel by all means
with Your Majesty for his pardon, but, before they could any
farther proceed, they desired to know the Earl's mind herein;
when I had answered, that he nor his friends at my departure
could not know that any such like matter would be proponit, and
therefore was not instructed what to answer therein, they desired that I should return sufficiently instructed in this matter
to Sterling before the baptism of your son, whom God might
preserve; this message was faithfully delivered to me at Newcastle in England, where the said Earl then remained, in presence
of his friends and company, where they all condescended to have no
farther dealing with your husband, and to enter into the said band.
With this deliberation I returned to Sterling, where, at the request
of the most Christian King and the Queen's Majesty of England, by
their ambassadors present, Your Majesty's gracious pardon was
granted unto them all, under condition always that they should remain banished forth of the realm the space of two years, and farther
during Your Majesty's pleasure, which limitation was after mitigated at the humble request of your own nobility, so that immediately after the said Earl of Morton repaired into Scotland to
Quhittingaime, where the Earl of Bodvell and Secretary Ledington
come to him; what speech passed there amongst them, as God shall
be my judge, I knew nothing at that time, but at their departure I
was requested by the said Earl Morton to accompany the Earl Bodvell and Secretary to Edinburgh, and to return with such answer
as they should obtain of Your Majesty, which being given to me by
the said persons, as God shall be my judge, was no other than these
words, "Schaw to the Earl Morton that the Queen will hear no
speech of that matter appointed unto him:" when I craft that the
answer might be made more sensible, Secretary Ledington said,

that the Earl would sufficiently understand it, albeit few or none at that time understand what passed amongst them. It is known to all men, als veill be railing letters passed betwixt the said Earl and Ledingtou when they become in divers factions, as also ane buck sett furth by the ministers, wherein they affirm that the Earl of Morton has confessed to them, before his death, that the Earl Bodvell come to Quhittingaime to prepon the calling away off the King your husband, to the which proposition the said Earl of Morton affirms that he could give no answer unto such time he might know Your Majesty's mind herein, which he never received. As to the abominable murder, it is known too by the depositions of many persons that were executed to the death for the committing thereof, that the same was executed by them, and at the command of such of the nobility as had subscrivit band for that effect; by this unpleasant declaration, the most part thereof known to yourself, and the remainder may be understood by the aforesaid witnesses that was examined in torture, and that are extant in the custody of the ordinary judges in Scotland, my innocency, so far as may concern any fact, does appear sufficiently to Your Majesty. And as for my dealing aforesaid, I can be no otherwise charged therein, but as what would accuse the vessel that preserves the vine from harm for the intemperancy of such as immoderately use the same. As for the special cause of my banishment, I think the same as proceeded upon ane opinion conceived, that I was able to accuse the Earl of Morton of so much matter as they alledge himself to have confessed before he died, and would not be induced, for loss of reputation to perform any part thereof. If this be the occasion of my trouble, as I suppose it is, what punishment I should deserve I remit me to Your Majesty's better judgment, who well knows how careful ever ilk gentleman should be of his fame, reputation and honour, and how far every ilk man should abhor the name of a pultroun, and how indecent it would have been to me to accuse the Earl of Morton, being so near of his kin, notwithstanding all the injuries I was constrained to receive at his hand all the time of his government, and for no other cause but for shewing of particular friendship to particular friends in the time of the last cruel troubles in Scotland. Sorry I be now to accuse him in any matter being dead, and more sorry that being on lyff, be such kind of dealing obtained that name of Ingrate. Always for my own part I have been banished my native country those three years and four months, living in anxiety of mind, my holl guds in Scotland, which were not small, intermittit and disponit upon, and has continually since the time I was relieved out of my last troubles at the desire of Monsieur de Movisir, attend to know Your Majesty's pleasure, and to wait upon what service it should please Your Majesty for to command. Upon the 8th of April inst. your good friend Secretary Walsinghame has declared unto me, that Her Highness tho't it expedient that I should retire myself where I pleased, I declared unto him I had no means whereby I might perform that desire until such time as I should receive it from Your Majesty. Neither knew I where it would please Your Highness to direct me until such time as I should have receeceived further information from you. Upon this occasion, and partly by permission, I have taken the hardress to write this present letter, whereby Your Majesty may understand any part of my troubles past, and straight present. As to my intention future, I will never deny that I am fully resolved to spend the rest of my days in Your Majesty's service, and the King your son's, wheresoever I shall be directed by Your Majesty, and for the better performing thereof, if so shall be Her Majesty's pleasure, to recommend the trial of my innocency, and examination of the verity of the preceding narration, to the King your son, with request that I may be pardoned for such offences as concerned Your Majesty's services, and var common to all men the time of his les aige and perdonit to all, except to me, I should be the bearer thereof myself, and be directed in whatever service it should please Your Majesty for to command. Most humbly I beseech Your Majesty to consider hereof, and to be so gracious as to give order that I may have means to serve Your Majesty according to the sincerity of my meaning, and so expecting Your Majesty's answer, after the kissing your hand with all humility, I take leave from London.

No. XLVIII.   (p. 322.)

A Letter from Sir Amias Pawlett.

(Original.   Cal: C, 9.)

Sir,

I did forbear, according to your direction signified in your letters of the fourth of this present, to proceed to the execution of the contents of Mr. Waade's letters unto you for the dispersing of this lady's unnecessary servants, and for the ceasing of her money, wherein I was bold to write unto you my simple opinion (although in vain as it now falleth out), by my letters of the 7th of this instant, which I doubt not, are with you before this time; but upon the receipt of your letters of the 5th, which came not unto my hands until the 8th in the evening, by reason, as did appear by indorsement, that they had been mistaken, and were sent back to Windsor, after they were entered into the way towards me, I considered, that being accompanied only with my own servant, it might be thought that they would be intreated to say as I would command them; and therefore I thought good, for my better discharge in these money matters, to crave the assistance of Mr. Richard Bagott, who repairing unto me the next morning we had access to this Queen, whom we found in her bed, troubled after the old manner with a defluxion, which was fallen down into the side of her neck, and had bereft her of the use of one of her hands, unto whom I declared, that upon occasion of her former practices, doubting lest she would persist therein by corrupting underhand some bad members of this state, I was expressly commanded to take her money into my hands, and to rest answerable for it when it shall be required ; advising her to deliver the said money unto me with quietness.   After many denials, many exclamations, an and many bitter words against you (I say nothing of her railing against myself), with flat affirmation that Her Majesty might have her body, but her heart she should never have, refusing to deliver the key of the cabinet, I called my servants, and sent for barrs to break open the door, whereupon the yielded, and causing the door to be opened, I found there in the coffers, mentioned in Mr. Waade's remembrance, five rolls of canvass, containing five thousand French crowns, and two leather bags, whereof the one had in gold one hundred and four pounds two shillings, and the other had three pounds in silver, which bag of silver was left with her, affirming that she had no more money in this house, and that she was indebted to her servants for their wages.

Curle can tell you the truth of this matter. Mr. Waade's note maketh mention of 3 rolls left in Curle's chamber, wherein no doubt, he was misreckoned, which is evident as well by the testimonies and oaths of divers persons, as also by probable conjectures; so as in truth we found only two rolls, every of which containeth one thousand crowns, which was this Queen's guifte to Curle's wife at her marriage. There is found in Naw's chamber in a cabinet, a chain worth by estimation one hundred pounds, and in money, in one bag, nine hundred pounds, in a second bag two hundred fourscore and six pounds eighteen shillings. All the aforesaid parcels of money are bestowed in bags, and sealed by Mr. Richard Bagot, saving five hundred pounds of Naw's money, which I reserve in my hands for the use of this household, and may be repayed at London, where Her Majesty shall appoint, out of the money received lately by one of my servants out of the exchequer. I feared lest the people might have dispersed this money in all this time, or have hidden the same in some secret corners; for doubt whereof I had caused all this Queen's family, from the highest to the lowest, to be guarded in the several places where I found them, so as yff I had not found the money with quietness I had been forced to have searched first all their lodgings, and then their own persons. I thank God with all my heart, as for a singular blessing, that that falleth out so well, fearing lest a contrary success might have moved some hard conceits in Her Majesty.

Touching the dispersing of this Queen's servants, I trust I have done so much as may suffice to satisfy Her Majesty for the time, wherein I could not take any absolute course until I heard again from you, partly because Her Majesty, by Mr. Waade's letter doth refer to your consideration to return such as shall be discharged to their several dwellings and countries, wherein, as it seemeth, you have forgotten to deliver your opinion; partly, for that as yet I have received no answer from you of your resolution upon the view of the Scottish family sent unto you, what persons you will appoint to be dismist; only this I have done, I have bestowed all such as are mentioned in this bill, inclosed in three or four several rooms, as the same may suffice to contain them, and that their meat and drink shall be brought unto them by my servants. It may please you to [advertise me, by your next letters, in what sort and for what course I shall make their passports; as also, if they shall say that they are unpaid of their wages, what I shall do therein. Yt

This lady hath good store of money at present in the French ambassador's hands. is said that they have been accustomed to be paid of their wages at Christmas, for the whole year. Her Majesty's charge will be somewhat diminished by the departure of this people, and my charge by this occasion will be the more easy. But the persons, all save Bastian, are such silly and simple souls, as there was no great cause to fear their practices, and upon this ground I was of opinion, in my former letter, that all this dimissed train should have followed their mistress until the next remove, and there to have been discharged upon the sudden, for doubt that the said remove might be delayed, yf she did fear or expect any hard measure.

Others shall excuse their foolish pity as they may; but, for my part, I renunce my part of the joys of heaven, if in any thing that I have said, written, or done, I have had any other respect than the furtherance of Her Majesty's service; and so I shall most earnestly pray you to affirm for me, as likewise for the not seasing of the money by Mr. Manners, the other commissioners, and myself. I trust Mr. Waade hath answered, in all humble duties, for the whole company, that no one of us did so much as think that, our commission reaching only to the papers, we might be bold to touch the money, so as there was no speech of that all to my knowledge, and as you know I was no commissioner in this search, but had my hands full at Tyxall, discreet servants are not hastily to deal in great matters without warrant, and especially where the cause is such as the delay of it carrieth no danger.

Your advertisement of that happy remove hath been greatly comfortable unto me. I will not say, in respect of myself, because my private interest hath no measure of comparison with Her Majesty's safety, and with the quiet of this realm. God grant a happy and speedy yssue to these good and godly counsels; and so I commit you to his merciful protection. From Chartley, the 10th of September, 1586.

No. XLIX. (Page 328.)

Letter from the King of Scots to Mr. Archibald Douglas, his Ambassador in England, October, 1586.

(Cott. Lib. Calig. C. 9. An original in the king's hand.)

RESERVE up yourself na langer in the earnest dealing for my mother, for ye have done it too long; and think not that any your travellis can do goode if hir lyfe be takin, for then adeu with my dealing with thaime that are the special instrumentis thairof; and theirfore, gif ye looke for the continewance of my favour towartis you, spair na pains nor plainnes in this cace, but reade my letter wrettin to Williame Keith, and conform yourself quhollie to the contentis thairof, and in this requeist let me reap the fruictis of your great credit there, ather now or never. Fairwell. Oct. 1586.

Letter to Sir William Keith, Ambassador in England, probably from Secretary Maitlaid, Nov. 27, 1586.

(A copy in the Collect. of Sir. A. Dick. Vol. A. fol. 219.)

BY your letters sent by this bearer (albeit concerning no pleasant subject), His Majesty conceives well of your earnestness and fidelity in your negotiations, as also of Mr. Archibald's activity and diligence, whom you so greatly praise and recommend, I wish the issue correspond to His Majesty's opinion, your care and travell, and his great diligence as you write. His Majesty takes this rigorous proceeding against his mother deeply in heart, as a matter greatly concerning him both in honour and otherwise. His Highnesses actions and behaviour utter plainly not only how far nature prevails, but also how he apprehends of the sequel of that process, and of what moment he esteems it. There is an ambassade shortly to be directed, wherein will be employed an Earl and two counsellors, on whose answer will depend the continuance or dissolution of the amity and good intelligence between the Princes of this isle. In the mean season, if farther extremity be used, and His Majesty's suit and request disdained, His Highness will think himself dishonoured and contemned far besides his expectation and deserts. Ye may perceive His Majesty's disposition by his letter to you, which you shall impart to Mr. Archibald, and both deal according thereto. I need not to recommend to you care, concerning your master's service both in weill and in honour. As you and your colleague shall behave yourself in this behalf, so for my own part will I interpret your affection to your master. I am glad of that I hear of yourself, and I do fully credit that you write of Mr. Archibald, whose friends here make great account of his professed devotion to the Queen, besides the duty he owes to the King's Majesty her son. Farther I am constrained to remit to next occasion, having scarce time to scribble these few lines (which of themselves may bear witness of my haste.) Wishing you a prosperous issue of your negociation, I commit you, &c. Halyrudhouse, Nov. 27th, 1586.

The people, and all eatates here are so far moved by the rigorous proceedings against the Queen, that His Majesty, and all that have credit are importuned, and may not go abroad for exclamations against them, and imprecations against the Queen of England.

.No, L. (p. 330.)

To the King's Majesty, from Mr. Archibald Douglas.

16 Oct. 1586. From the original in the Collect. of Sir A. Dick. Vol. B. Fol. 324.

PLEASE Your Majesty, I received your letter of the date the 28th of September, the 5th of October, which was the same day that I directed Wm. Murray towards Your Highness ; by such letters as he carried, and others of several dates, Your Majesty may perceive that I had omitted nothing so far as my travel might reach unto, anent the performing of the two chief points contained in the said letter befor the receipt thereof, which by these presents I must repeat for answering of the saidis. As to the first, so far as may

concern the interceeding for the Queen Your Majesty's mother her
life I have divers times, and in every audience, travelled with this
Queen in that matter, specially to know what her full determination
must be in that point, and could never bring her to any further
answer, but that this proceeding against her by order of justice was
no less against her mind, than against their will that loved her best:
as towards her life she could give no answer thereunto, untill such
time as the law hath declared whether she was innocent or guilty.
Herewithal it was her pleasure thus far to inform me, that it was
a number of the associats that earnestly pressed her that the law
might proceed against her, giving reasons that so long as she was.
suffered to deal in matters, so long would never this realm be in
quiet, neither her life, neither this state in assurance, and in the
end they used this protestation that if she would not in this matter follow their advice, that they should remain without all blame
whatsoever should fall out; whereupon she had granted them liberty
to proceed, lest such as had made the request might hereafter have
charged herself with inconvenience if any should happen.

And by myself I know this her speech to be true, because both
Papist and Protestant has behaved them, as it hath been her pleasure
to declare, but upon divers respects, the one to avoid suspicion that
otherwise was conceived against them. the other upon zeal, and
care that they will be known to have for preservation of their
sovereign's life and state in this perilous time, upon consideration
whereof, I have been constrained to enter into some dealing with
both, wherewith I made Her Majesty acquainted; the Protestants,
and such as in other matters will be known to bear no small favour
unto Your Majesty's service, hath prayed that they may be excused
from any dealing in the contrary of that, which by their oath they
have avowed, and by their speech to their sovereign requested for,
and that before my coming in this country; if they should now
otherwise do, it would produce no better effect but to make them
subject to the accusation of their sovereign, when it should please
her to do it, of their inconstancy, in giving councell whereby they
might incur the danger of ill councellors, and be consequent worthy
of punishment. Such of the Papists as I did deal with, went immediately, and told Her Majesty what I had spoken to them, who
albeit she understood the matter of before, sent for me, and declared
to me my own speech that I had uttered to them, willing me for
the weil of my maister's service to abstain from dealing with such,
not yf, sufficiently moved to think of my master as she did. I craved
leave of Her Majesty, that I might inform them of Your Majesty's
late behaviour towards her, and the state of this realm, whereunto
with some difficulty she gave her consent. At my late departure
from court, which was upon the 5th of this instant, and the day
after that the lords of this grand jury had taken their leaves of
Her Majesty to go northward Fothringham, it was her pleasure to
promise to have further speech in this matter at the returning of
the said lords, and to give full answer according to Your Majesty's
contentment to the remainder matters, that I had proponit in name
of Your Majesty. As to the second part concerning the association,
and desire that the promise made to the Master of Gray concern-

ing Your Majesty's title may be fulfilled; it appears by the said letter that the very point whereupon the question that bring Your Majesty title in doubt, hath not been rightly at the writing of the said letter considered, which I take to have proceeded for lack of reading of the act of parliament, wherein is fulfilled all the promise made by the Queen to the said Master, and nothing may now cause any doubt to arise against your said tittle, except that an opinion should be conceived by these lords of this Parliament that are so vehement at this time against the Queen Your Majesty's mother, that Your Majesty is, or may be proved hereafter assenting to her proceedings, and some that love Your Majesty's service were of that opinion that too earnest request might move a ground whereupon suspicions might grow in men so ill effected in that matter, which I tho't might be helped by obtaining of a declaration in parliament of Your Majesty's innocence at this time, and by reason that good nature and public honesty would constrain you to intercede for the Queen your mother, which would carry with itself, without any further, some suspicion that might move ill affected men to doubt. In my former letters I humbly craved of Your Majesty that some learned men in the laws might be moved to advise with the words of the association, and the mitigation contained in the act of parliament, and withall to advise what suspicious effects Your Majesty's request might work in these choleric men at this time, and how their minds might be best moved to receive reason; and upon all these considerations they might have formed the words of a declarator of Your Majesty's innocence to be obtained in this parliament, and failing thereof, the very words of protestation for the same effect that might best serve for Your Majesty's service, and for my better information. Albeit this was my simple opinion, I shall be contented to follow any direction it shall please Your Majesty to give; I have already opened the substance hereof to the Queen of this realm, who seems not to he offended herewith, and hath granted liberty to deal therein with such of the parliament as may remain in any doubt of mind. This being the sum of my proceedings in this matter, besides the remainder, contained in other letters of several dates, I am constrained to lay the whole open before Your Majesty, and to humbly pray that full information may be sent unto me what further to do herein; in this middle time, while I shall receive more ample direction I shall proceed and be doing according to such direction as I have already received. And so, most gracious sovereign, wishing unto Your Majesty all happy success in your affairs, I humbly take my leave from London, this 16th of October, 1586. Your Majesty's most humble subject and obed^t servant.

A Memorial for His Majesty by the Master of Gray.

[12th Jan. 1586. An original in his own hand in the Collect. of Sir A. Dick. Vol. A. fol. 222.]

It will please Your Majesty I have tho't meeter to set down all things as they occur, and all advertisements as they came to my cars, then jointly in a lettre.

I came to Vare the 24th of Decer. and sent toWm. Keith and

Mr. Archibald Douglas to advertise the Queen of it, like as they did at their audience. She promised the Queen Your Majesty's mother's life should be spared till we were heard. The 27th they game to Vare to me, the which day Sir Robt. came to Vare, where they showed us how far they had already gone in their negociation, but for that the discourse of it is set down in our general letter, I remit me to it, only this far I will testify unto Your Majesty that W^m. Keith had used himself right honestly and wisely till our coming, repecting all circumstances, and chiefly his colleague his dealing, which indeed is not better than Your Majesty knows already.

The 29th day of Decr. we came to London, where we were no ways friendly received, nor after the honest sort it had pleased Your Majesty use her ambassadors; never man sent to welcome or convey us. The same day we understood of Mr. de Bellievre his leave taking, and for that the custom permitted not we sent our excuses by Mr. George Young.

The 1st day of Jan'ry. W^m. Keith and his colleague according to the custom sent to crave our audience. We received the answer contained in the general letter, and could not have answer till the 6th day, what was done that day Your Majesty has it in the general, yet we was not out of esperance at that time, albeit we received hard answers.

The 8th day we speak with the Earl of Leicester, where our conferrence was, as is set down in the general. I remarked this, that he that day said plainly the detaining of the queen of Scotland prisoner was for that she pretended a succession to this crown. Judge then by this what is tho't of your Majesty, as ye shall hear a little after.

The 9th day we speak with the French ambassador, whom we find very plain in making to us a wise discourse of all his proceedings, and Mr. de Bellievre we thanked him in Your Majesty's name, and opened such things as we had to treat with this Queen, save the last point, as more largely set down by our general.

It is tho't here, and some friends of Your Majesty's advised me, that Bellievre his negociation was not effectual, and that the resident was not privy to it, as indeed I think is true, for since Bellievre his perting, there is a talk of this Chasteauneuf his servants taken with his whole papers and pacquets, which he was sending in France, for that they charge him with a conspiracy of late against the Queen here her life. It is alledged his servant has confessed the matter, but whom I shall trust I know not, but till I see proof I shall account him an honest man, for indeed so he appears, and one (without doubt) who hath been very instant in this matter. I show him that the Queen and Earl of Leicester had desired to speak with me in private, and craved his opinion; he gave it freely that he tho't it meetest, I shew him the reason why I communicate that to him, for that I have been suspected by some of Her Majesty's friends in France to have done evil offices in her service, that he should be my witness that my earnest dealing in this should be a sufficient testimony that all was lies, and that this knave Naué who now had betrayed her, had in that done evil offices; ye desired me, seeing she saw only with other folks eyes, that I should no ways impute it to her, for the like she had done to himself by Nau6 his persuasion. I answered he should be my witness in that.

The 9th day we sent to court to crave audience, which we got the 10th day; at the first, she said a thing long looked for should be welcome when it comes, I would now see your master's offers. I answered, no man makes offers but for some cause; we would, and like Your Majesty, first know the cause to be extant for which we offer, and likewise that it be extant till Your Majesty has heard us. I think it be extant yet, but I will not promise for an hour, but you think to shift in that sort.   I answered, we mind not to shift, but to offer from our sovereign all things that with reason may be ; and in special, we offered as is set down in our general, all was refused and thought nothing.   She called on the three that were in the house, the Earl of Leicester, my Lord Admiral, and Chamberlain, and very despitefully repeated all our offers in the presence of them all.   I opened the last part, and said, Madam, for what respect is it that men deal against your person or estate for her cause.   She answered, because they think she shall succeed to me, and for that she is a Papist ; appearingly said I both the causes may be removed, she said she would be glad to understand it.   If, Madam, said I, all that she has of right of succession were in the King our sovereign's person, were not all hope of Papists removed ?   She answered, I hope so.   Then, Madam, I think the Queen his mother shall willingly demit all her rights in his person.   She answered, she hath no right, for she is declared unhabil.   Then I said, if she have no right, appearingly the hope ceases already, so that it is not to be feared that any man attempt for her.   The Queen answered, but the Papists allow not our declaration ; then let it fall, says I, in the King's person by her assignation.   The Earl of Leicester answered, she is a prisoner, how can she demit ?   I answered, the demission is to her son, by the advice of the friends she has in Europe, and in case, as God forbid, that any attempt cuttis the Queen here away, who shall party with her to prove the demission or assignation to be ineffectual, her son being opposite party, and having all the princes her friends for him, having bonded for the efficacy of it with His Majesty of before ?   The Queen made as she could not comprehend my meaning, and Sir Robt. opened the matter again, she yet made as tho' she understood not.   So the Earl of Leicester answered that our meaning was, that the King should be put in his mother's place.   Is it so, the Queen answered, then I put myself in a worse case than of before : by God's passion, that were to cut my own throat, and for a dutchy or earldom to yourself, you or such as you would cause some of your desperate knaves kill me. No, by God, he shall never be in that place.   I answered, he craves nothing of Your Majesty but only of his mother.   The Earl of Leicester answered, that were to make him party to the Queen my mistress.   I said, he will be far more party, if he be in her place through her death.   She would stay no longer, but said she would not have a worse in his mother's place   And said, tell your King what good I have done for him in holding the crown on his head

z 5

since he was born, and that I mind to keep the league that now stands between us, and if he break it shall be a double fault, and with this minded to have bidden vs a farewell ; but we achevit [i. e. finished arguing upon this point.] And I spake craving of her that her life may be spared for 15 days; she refused. Sir Robt. craved for only eight days ; she said, not for an hour ; and so geid her away. Your Majesty sees we have delivered all we had for offers, but all is for nothing, for she and her councel has laid a determination that they mind to follow forth, and I see it comes rather of her council than herself, which I like the worse; for without doubt, Sir, it shall cut off all friendship ye had here. Altho' it were that once they had meaned well to Your Majesty, yet remembering themselves, that they had medled with your mother's blood, good faith they cannot hope great good of yourself, a thing in truth I am sorry for; further Your Majesty may perceive by this last discourse of that I proponit, if they had meaned well to Your Majesty they had used it otherwise than they have done, for reason has bound them. But I dare not write all. I mind something to speak in this matter, because we look shurly our letters shall be trussit by the way.

For that I see private credit nor no means can alter their determination, altho' the Queen again and the Earl of Leicester has desired to speak with me in particular : I mind not to speak, nor shall not ; but assuredly shall let all men see that I in particular was no ways tyed to England, but for the respect of Your Majesty's service. So albeit, at this time I could not effectuate that I desired, yet my upright dealing in it shall be manifested to the world. We are, God willing, then to crave audience, where we mind to use sharply our instructions, which hitherto we have used very calmly ; for we can, for your honour's cause, say no less for Your Majesty, than the French ambassador has said for his master.

So I pray your Majesty consider my upright dealing in your service, and not the effect ; for had it been doable [i. e. possible to be done] by any I might have here had credit ; but being I came only for that cause, I will not my credit shall serve here to any further purpose. I pray God preserve Your Majesty, and send you a true and sincere friendship. From London this 12th of Jan. 1586.

I understand the Queen is to send one of her own to Your Majesty.

To the Right Hon. my Lord Vice-Chancellor and Secretary to His Majesty, from the Master of Gray.

[21th Jan, 1586. An original in the Collect. of Sir A. Dick. Vol. A. fol. 179.]

Mr Lord, I send you these lines with this inclosed to His Majesty, whereby Your Lordship shall understand how matters goes on here. And before all things I pray Your Lordship move His Majesty to respect my diligence, and not the effect in this negotiation, for I swear if it had been for the crown of England to myself I could do no more, and let not unfriends have advantage of me, for the world shall see that I loved England for His Majesty's service only. I look shortly to find Your Lordship friend as ye made promise, and by God I shall be to you if I can. Wm. Keith and I devyset, if matters had gone well, to have run a course that Your Lordship might have been in credit and others disappointed, but now I will do for you as for myself; which is to care for no credit there, for in conscience they mean not honestly to the King our sovereign, and if they may, he will go the get his mother is gone, or shortly to go, therefore My Lord, without all kind of scruple I pray you to advise him the best is not this way. They say here, that it has been said by one who heard it from you, that ye desired not the King and England to agree, because it would rack the noblemen, and gave an example of it by King James the Fourt. I answered in your name that I was assured you never had spoken it. Mr. Archibald is the speaker of it, who I assure Your Lordship has been a poison in this matter, for they lean very mickle to his opinion. He cares not he says, for at length the King will be fain to deal this way, either by fair means or necessity, so that when he deals this course he is assured to be welcome; to set down all that is past of the like purposes, it would consume more paper than I have here, so I defer it to meeting. There is a new conspiracy alledged against the Queen to have been intended, for the French ambassador resident three of his men taken, but I think in the end it shall prove nothing. Mr. Stafford, who is ambassador for this Queen in France, is touched with it, his brother is taken here, always it has done this harm in our negotiation, that all this council would not move this Queen to medle with the Queen of Scotland's blood, till this invention was found forth. I remit all other things to the inclosed. We minded to have sent to His Majesty a discourse, which we have set down of all our proceedings since our hither coming, but we are surely advertized that the bearer is to be trussed by the way for our pacquets, so that we defer it till our own coming; this I have put in a privy part beside the pacquet. We shall, I think, take leave on Fryday the 13th day, where we mind exactly to follow the rigour of our instructions for it cannot stand with the King's honour that we say less than the French ambassador, which was, Le roy mon maistre ne peult moins faire que se resentir. So that about the 24th I think we shall, God willing, be at home, except that some stay come which we look not for. The Queen and the Earl of Leicester has desired to speak with me. I refused save in presence of my colleagues, by reason I see a determination which particular credit cannot help, and I crave no credit but for that cause. It will please Your Lordship retire the inclosed from His Majesty and keep it. So after my service commended to yourself and bed fellow, I commit you to God. From London the 12th of Jan. 1586.

To the King's Majesty, from Sir Robert Melvil.

[12th Jan. 1586. An original in his own hand, in the collect. of Sir A. Dick. Vol. A. fol. 181.]

It may please Your Majesty, since the direction of our former letters, we had audience, and Her Majesty appeared to take our overtures in good part in presence of her council; albeit no offers could

take place with them, having taken resolution to proceed with extremity, not the less it pleased Her Majesty to desire us to stay for
two days on taking our leave, until she had advised upon our propositions; since which time, Her Majesty is become more hard by
some letters (as we are informed) has come from Scotland, making
some hope to believe that Your Majesty takes not this matter to
heart, as we know the contrary in effect, and had of before removed
the like opinion out of Her Majesty's mind, which by sinister information was credited, their reports has hindered our commission,
and abused this Queen, fearing in like manner we shall be stayed
until answer come from Scotland by such person as they have intelligence of. And albeit that it will be well enough known to all
men how heavily Your Majesty takes this proceeding to heart, the
truth is, that they have by this occasion so persuaded the Queen,
that it is like to hinder our negotiation. As also Alchinder (i.e.
Alexander) Steward is to be directed in their party, by our knowledge, who has awantyt more of his credit, than I believe he may
perform, and we willed him to desist from this dealing, saying it
does harm, and he is not meet for that purpose, remitting to Your
Majesty's good discretion to take order herein as we shall be answerable to Your Majesty not to omit any point we have in charge,
as the truth is, the Master of Grhaye has behaved himself very up-
rightly and discreetly in this charge, and evil tayne with be divers
in these parts who were of before his friends. We have been be-
halding to the menstrals who has born us best company, but has
not been troubled with others. Wylzeme Kethe hath left nothing
undone that he had in charge. As for master Archibald he has
promised at all times to do his dewoyr, wherein he shall find true
report made to Your Majesty, craving pardon of Your Majesty that
I have been so tedious, after I have kissed Your Majesty's hand I
humbly take my leave. Praying God to grant your Majesty many
good days and happy, in whose protection I commit Your Majesty
at London, the 20th of Jan. 1586.

SIR.

ALBEIT Master George has not been in commission, he is not inferior in his service to any of us, as well by his good advice and
diligent care he takes for the advancement of your service, wherein
we have not been a little furthered.

*To the King's Majesty, from the Master of Gray and
Sir Robert Melvil.*
[21st Jan. 1586, An original in the collect. of Sir A. Dick.
Vol. A. fol. 180.]

PLEASE it Your Majesty in the last audience we had, since our last
advertisement by Wm. Murray, we find Her Majesty at the re-
suming our offers something mitigated, and inclined to consider
more deeply of them, before we got our leave, at our reasoning,
certain of the council, namely, my Lord of Leicester, Sir Chris-
topher Haton, my Lord Hunsdon, and my Lord Hawart being present
in the chamber, gave little show of any great contentment to have
her from her former resolution, now cassin in perplexitie what she

should do always we left her in that state, and since have daily pressed conference with the whole council, which to this hour we have not yet obtained. This day we have sent down to crave ou leave. The greatest hinder which our negotiation has found hitherto is a persuasion they have here that either Your Majesty deals superficially in this matter, or that with time ye may be moved to digest it, which when with great difficulty we had expugnit, we find anew that certain letters written to them of late from Scotland has found some place of credit with them in our contrare. So that resolving now to clear them of that doubt by a special message, they have made choice of Sir Alexander Stewart to try Your Highness's meaning in it, and to persuade Your Majesty to like of their proceedings, wherefrom no terror we can say out unto him, is able to divert him, he has given out that he has credit with Your Majesty and that he doubts not to help this matter at Your Highness's hand. If he come there that errand, we think Your Majesty will not oversee the great disgrace that his attempts shall give us here, if he be not tane order with before that he be further heard, and if so be that any other be directed (as our intelligence gives us there shall) our humble suit is to Your Majesty, that it may please Your Highness to hear of us what we find here, and at what point we leave this matter with Her Majesty, before that they find accidence, the causes whereof remitting to our private letters. We commit Your Majesty for the present to God's eternal protection. From London this 21st of Jan. 1586.

No. LI. (p. 333.)

Copy of a Letter from the Earls of Shrewsbury and Kent, &c. touching their Proceedings with Regard to the Death of the Scottish Queen to Her Majesty's Council.

It may please Your Honble good Lordships to be advertised, that, on Saturday the 4th of this present, I Robert Beale came to the house of me the Earl of Kent, in the county of——, to whom Your Lordship's letter and message was delivered, and Her Majesty's commision shown; whereupon I the Earl forthwith sent precepts for the staying of such hues and cries as had troubled the country, requiring the Officers to make stay of all such persons, as should bring any such warrants without names, as before had been done, and to bring them to the next justice of peace, to the intent that upon their examination, the occasion and causes of such seditious bruites might be bolted out and known. It was also resolved that I the said Earl of Kent should, on the Monday following, come to Lylford to Mr. Elmes, to be the nearer and readier to confer with my Lord of Shrewsbury. Sunday at night, I Robert Beale came to Fotheringay, where after the communicating the commission, &c. unto us Sir Amice Pawlet and Sir Drue Drury, by reason that Sir A. Pawlet was but late recovered, and not able to repair to the Earl of Shrewsbury, being then at Orton, six miles off; it was thought good that we Sir Drue Drury and Robert Beale should go unto him, which we did on —— morning; and together with the delivery of Her Majesty's commission, and

Your Lordship's letter imparted unto him what both the Earl of
Kent and we thought meet to be done in the cause, praying His
Lordship hither the day following, to confer with me the said Earl,
concerning the same ; which His Lordship promised. And for the
better colouring of the matter, I the said Earl of Shrewsbury sent
to Mr. Beale, a justice of peace of the county of Huntingdon next
adjoining, to whom I communicated that warrant, which Robert
Beale had under Your Lordship's hands, for the staying of the hues
and cries, requiring him to give notice thereof to the town of Peterborough, and especially unto the justices of peace of Huntingdon-
shire, and to cause the pursuers and bringers of such warrants to be
stayed, and brought to the next justice of peace ; and to bring us
word to Fotheringay Castle on Wednesday morning what he had
done, and what he should in the mean time understand of the
authors of such bruites. Which like order, I also Sir Amias Pawlet had taken on Monday morning in this town, and other places
adjoining. The same night the sheriff of the county of Northamp-
ton upon the receipt of Your Lordship's letter came to Arundel,
and letters were sent to me the Earl of Kent of the Earl of Shrewsbury's intention and meeting here on Tuesday by noon ; and other
letters were also sent with their Lordships assent to Sir Edward
Montagu, Sir Richard Knightly, Mr. Tho. Brudenell, &c. to be
here on Wednesday by eight of the clock in the morning, at which
time it was thought meet that the execution should be. So upon
Tuesday, we the Earls came hither, where the sheriff met us ; and
upon conference between us it was resolved, that the care for the
sending for the surgeons, and other necessary provision should be
committed unto him against the time. And we forthwith repaired
unto her, and first in the presence of herself and her folks, to the
intent that they might see and report hereafter that she was not
otherwise proceeded with than according to law, and the form of
the statute made in the 27th year of Her Majesty's reign, it was
thought convenient that Her Majesty's commission should be read
unto her, and afterwards she was by sundry speeches willed to prepare herself against the next morning. She was also put in remembrance of her fault, the honorable manner of proceeding with her,
and the necessity that was imposed upon Her Majesty to proceed
to execution, for that otherwise it was found that they could not
both stand together ; and however, sithence the Lord Buckhurst's
his being here new conspiracies were attempted, and so would be
still ; wherefore since she had now a good while since warning, by
the said Lord and Robert Beale, to think upon and prepare herself
to die, we doubted not but that she was, before this, settled, and
therefore would accept this message in good part. And to the effect that no Christian duty might be said to be omitted, that might
be for her comfort, and tend to the salvation both of her body and
soul in the world to come, we offered unto her that if it would
please her to confer with the Bishop and Dean of Peterborough,
she might ; which Dean, we had, for that purpose, appointed to be
lodged within one mile of that place. Hereto she replied, crossing
herself in the name of the Father, the Son, and the Holy Ghost,
saying that she was ready to die in the Catholic Roman faith, which

her ancestors had professed, from which she would not be removed. And albeit we used many persuasions to the contrary, yet we prevailed nothing; and therefore, when she demanded the admittance of her priest, we utterly denied that unto her. Hereupon, she demanded to understand what answer we had touching her former petition to Her Majesty, concerning her papers of accounts, and the bestowing of her body. To the first we had none other answer to make, but that we thought if they were not sent before, the same might be in Mr. Waade's custody, who was now in France, and seeing her papers could not any wise pleasure Her Majesty, we doubted not but that the same would be delivered unto such as she should appoint. For, for our own parts, we undoubtedly thought that Her Majesty would not make any profit of her things, and therefore (in our opinions) she might set down what she would have done, and the same should be imparted unto Her Majesty, of whom both she and others might expect all courtesy. Touching her body, we knew not Her Majesty's pleasure, and therefore could neither say that her petition should be denied, or granted. For the practice of Babington, she utterly denied it, and would have inferred it that her death was for her religion; whereunto it was eftsoons by us replied, that for many years she was not touched for religion, nor should have been now, but this proceeding against her was for treason, in that she was culpable of that horrible conspiracy for destroying Her Majesty's person; which she again denied, adding further that albeit she for herself forgave them that were the procurers of her death, yet she doubted not but that God would take vengeance thereof. And being charged with the depositions of Nauè and Curle to prove against her, she replied, that she accused none, but that hereafter when she shall be dead, and they remain alive, it shall be seen how indifferently she had been dealt with, and what measures had been used unto her; asked whether it had been heard before this, that servants had been practised to accuse their mistress, and hereupon also required what was become of them, and where they remained.

Upon our departure from her, for that it seemed by the commission, that the charge of her was in the disposition of us the Earls, we required S. Amias Pawlet and S. Drue Drurie to receive for that night the charge which they had before, and to cause the whole number of soldiers to watch that night, and that her folks should be put up, and take order that only four of them should be at the execution, remaining aloof of and guarded with certain persons so as they should not come near unto her, which were Melvil her steward, the physician, surgeon, and apothecary.

Wednesday morning, after that we the Earls were repaired to unto the castle, and the sheriff had prepared all things in the hall for the execution, he was commanded to go into her chamber, and to bring her down to the place where were present we which have signed this letter, Mr. Henry Talbot, Esq., Sir Edward Montague, Knt., his son and heir apparent, and William Montague, his brother, Sir Richard Knichtly, Knt., Mr. Thomas Brudenell, Mr. Beuill, Mr. Robert and John Wingfield, Mr. Forrest, and Rayner, Benjamin Piggot, Mr. Dean of Peterborough, and others.

At the stairfold, she paused to speak to Melvil in our hearing, which was to this effect : " Melvil, as thou hast been an honest servant to me, so I pray thee continue to my son, and commend me unto him.   I have not impugn'd his religion, nor the religion of others, but wish him well.   And as I forgive all that have offended me in Scotland, so I would that he should also ; and beseech God, that he would send him his Holy Spirit, and illuminate him." Melvil's answer was, that he would so do, and at that instant he would beseech God to assist him with his Spirit.   Then she demanded to speak with her priest, which was denied unto her, the rather for that she came with a superstitious pair of beads and a crucifix.   She then desired to have her women to help her, and upon her earnest request, and saying that when other gentlewomen were executed, she had read in chronicles that they had women allowed unto them, it was permitted that she should have two named by herself, which were Mrs. Curle and Kenedy.   After she came to the scaffold, first in presence of them all, Her Majesties commission was openly read ; and afterwards Mr. Dean Peterborough, according to a direction which he had received, the night before from us the Earls, wou'd have made a godly admonition to her, to repent and die well in the fear of God and charity to the world.   But at the first entry, she utterly refused it, saying that she was a Catholiqe, and that it were a folly to move her being so resolutely minded, and that our prayers would little avail her.   Whereupon, to the intent it might appear that we, and the whole assembly, had a Christian desire to have her die well, a godly prayer, conceived by Mr. Dean, was read and pronounced by us all. " That it would please Almighty God to send her his Holy Spirit and grace, and also, if it were his will, to pardon all her offences, and also of his mercy to receive her into his heavenly and everlasting kingdom and finally to bless Her Majesty, and confound all her enemies ;" whereof Mr. Dean, minding to repair up shortly, can show your Lordships a copy.

This done, she pronounced a prayer upon her knees to this effect, " to beseech God to send her his Holy Spirit, and that she trusted to receive her salvation in his blood, and of his grace to be received into his kingdom, besought God to forgive her enemies, as she forgave them ; and to turn his wrath from this land, to bless the Queen's Majestie, that she might serve him.   Likewise to be merciful to her son, to have compassion of his church, and altho' she was not worthy to be heard, yet she had a confidence in his mercy, and prayed all the saints to pray unto her Saviour to receive her." After this (turning to her servants) she desired them to pray for her that her Saviour would receive her.   Then, upon petition made by the executioners, she pardoned them ; and said, that she was glad that the end of all her sorrows was so near.   Then she disliked the whinning and weeping of her women, saying that they rather ought to thank God for her resolution, and kissing them willed them to depart from the scaffold, and farewell.   And so resolutely kneeled down, and having a kerchief banded about her eyes, laid down her neck, whereupon the executioner proceeded.   Her servants were incontinently removed, and order taken that none should approach unto her corps, but that it should be embalmed by the surgeon appointed. And further her crosse, apparel, and other things are retained here, and not yielded unto the executioner for inconveniences that might follow, but he is remitted to be rewarded by such as sent him hither.

This hath been the manner of our dealings in this service, whereof we have thought good to advertise Your Lordships, as particularly as we could, for the time, and further have thought good to signify unto Your Lordships besides, that for the avoiding of all sinister and slanderous reports that may be raised to the contrary, we have caused a note thereof to be conceived to the same effect in writing, which we the said Lords have subscribed, with the hands of such other there the knights and gentlemen above named that were present at the action. And so beseeching Almighty God long to bless Her Majesty with a most prosperous reign, and to confound all his and her enemies, we take our leaves. From Fotheringay Castle, the 8th of February, 1586, in haste.

Your Lordships at commandment.

N. B. This, as well as several other papers in this Appendix, is taken from a collection made by Mr. Crawford of Drumsoy, historiographer to Queen Anne, now in the library of the Faculty of Advocates. Mr. Crawfurd's transcriber has omitted to mention the book in the Cott. Lib. where it is to be found.

No. LII. (p. 336.)

The objections against Mr. Davison, in the Cause of the late Scottish Queen, must concern Things done either, 1. *Before her Trial at Fotheringay.* 2. *During that Session.* 3. *After the same.*

(Cott. Lib. Cal. C 1.)

1. Before her trial, he neither is, nor can be charged to have had any hand at all in the cause of the said Queen, or done any thing whatsoever concerning the same directly or indirectly.

2. During that session, he remained at court, where the only interest he had therein, was as Her Majesty's secretary, to receive the letters from the commissioners, impart them to Her Highness, and return them her answers.

3. After the return thence, of the said commissioners, it is well known to all her council.

1. That he never was at any deliberation or meeting whatsoever, in parliament, or council, concerning the cause of the said Queen, till the sending down of Her Majesty's warrant unto the commissioners, by the Lords and others of her council.

2. That he was no party in signing the sentence passed against her.

3. That he never penned either the proclamation publishing the same, the warrant after her death, nor any other letter, or thing whatsoever concerning the same. And,

That the only thing which can be specially and truly imputed to him, is the carrying up the said warrant unto Her Majesty to be signed. She sending a great counsellor unto him, with her pleasure to that end, and carrying it to the great seal of England, by her own special direction and commandment.

For the better clearing of which truth, it is evident,

1. That the letter, being penned by the Lord Treasurer, was delivered by him unto Mr. Davison, with Her Majesty's own privity, to be ready for to sign, when she should be pleased to call for it.

2. That being in his hands, he retained it at the least five or six weeks unpresented, nor once offering to carry it up, till she sent a great counsellor unto him for the same, and was sharply reproved therefore by a great peer, in Her Majesty's own presence.

3. That having signed it, she gave him an express commandment to carry it to the seal, and being sealed to send it immediately away unto the commissioners, according to the direction. Herself appointing the Hall of Fotheringay for the place of execution, misliking the court-yard, in divers respects, and in conclusion absolutely forbad him to trouble her any further, or let her hear any more hereof, till it was done. She, for her part, having (as she said) performed all that, in law or reason, could be required of her.

4. Which directions notwithstanding, he kept the warrant sealed all that night, and the greatest part of the next day in his hands, brought it back with him to the court, acquainted Her Majesty withal, and finding Her Majesty resolved to proceed therein, according to her former directions, and yet desirous to carry the matter so, as she might throw the burthen from herself, he absolutely resolved to quit his hands thereof.

5. And hereupon went over unto the Lord Treasurer's chamber, together with Mr. Vice-chamberlain Hatton, and in his presence restored the same into the hands of the said Lord Treasurer, of whom he had before received it, who from thenceforth kept it, till himself and the rest of the council sent it away.

Which, in substance and truth, is all the part and interest the said Davison had in this cause, whatsoever is, or may be pretended to the contrary.

Touching the sending down thereof unto the commissioners, that it was the general act of Her Majesty's council (as is before mentioned) and not any private act of his, may appear by,

1. Their own confession. 2. Their own letters sent down therewith to the commissioners. 3. The testimonies of the Lords and others to whom they were directed. As also, 4. of Mr. Beale, by whom they were sent. 5. The tenor of Her Majesty's first commission for their calling to the star-chamber for the same, and private appearance and submission afterward instead thereof before the Lord Chancellor Bromley. 6. The confession of Mr. Attorney-General in open court confirmed. 7. By the sentence itself upon record. 8. Besides a common act of council, containing an answer to be verbally delivered to the Scottish ambassador then remaining here, avowing and justifying the same.

Now where some suppose him to have given some extraordinary furtherance thereunto, the former may evidently appear by,

1. His former absolute refusal to sign the band of association, being earnestly pressed thereunto by his Majesty's self.

2. His excusing of himself from being used as a commissioner, in the examination of Babington and his accomplices, and avoiding the same by a journey to the Bath.

3. His being a mean to stay the commissioners from pronouncing of the sentence at Fotheringay, and deferring it till they should return to her Majesty's presence.

4. His keeping the warrant in his hands six weeks unpresented, without once offering to carry it up, till His Majesty sent expressly for the same to sign.

5. His deferring to send it away after it was sealed unto the commissioners, as he was specially commanded, staying it all that night, and the greatest part of the next day, in his hands.

6. And finally his restoring thereof into the hands of the Lord Treasurer, of whom he had before received the same.

Which are clear and evident proofs, that the said Davison did nothing in this cause whatsoever, contrary to the duty of the place he then held in Her Majesty's service.

Cal. C 9.

This seems to be an original. On the back is this title:

The innocency of Mr. Davison in the cause of the late Scottish Queen.

No. LIII. (Page 380.)

Letter from O to His Majesty King James.

(From the original. Bibl. Fac. Jur. Edin. A. 1. 34. No. 4.)

Most worthy Prince, the depending dangers upon your affectionates, have been such, as hath inforced silence in him, who is faithfully devoted to your person, and in due time of trial, will undergo all hazards of fortune for the maintenance of the just legal rights, that, by the laws divine, of nature and of nations, is invested in your royal person. Fall not then, most noble and renowned Prince, from him whose Providence hath in many dangers preserved you, no doubt to be an instrument of his glory, and the good of his people. Some secrets, I find, have been revealed to your prejudice, which must proceed from some ambitious violent spirited person near Your Majesty in council and in favour; no man in particular will I accuse, but I am sure it hath no foundation from any, with whom, for your service, I have held correspondence; otherwise, I had, long since, been disabled from performance of those duties, that the thoughts of my heart endeavoureth; being only known to this worthy nobleman bearer hereof, one noted in all parts of Christendom for his fidelity to your person and state, and to Mr. David Fowlis your most loyal servant, my first and faithful correspondent; and unto James Hudsone, whom I have found in all things that concern you, most secret and assured. It may, therefore, please Your Majesty, at the humble motion of O, which, jargon I desire to be the indorsement of your commands unto me, that, by some token of your favour, he may understand in what terms you regard his fidelity, secrecy, and service. My passionate affection to your person (not as you are a King, but as you are a good King, and have just title, after my sovereign, to be a great King) doth transport me to presumption. Condemn not, most noble Prince, the motives of care and love, altho' mixed with defects in judgment.

1. I, therefore, first beseech Your Majesty, that for the good of those whom God, by Divine Providence, hath destined to your charge, that you will be pleased to have an extraordinary care of all practicers, or practices, against your person ; for it is not to be doubted, but that in both kingdoms, either out of ambition, faction, or fear, there are many that desire to have their sovereign in minority, whereby the sovereignty and state might be swayed by partiality of subalternate persons, rather than by true rule of power and justice. Preserve your person, and fear not the practices of man upon the point of your right, which will be preserved and maintained against all assaults of competition whatsoever. Thus I leave the protection of your person and royal posterity to the Almighty God of Heaven, who bless and preserve you and all yours in all regal happiness, to his glory.

2. Next to the preservation of your person, is the conservation and secret keeping of your councils, which, as I have said, are often betrayed and discovered, either out of pretended zeal in religion, turbulent faction, or base conception, the which Your Majesty is to regard with all circumspection, as a matter most dangerous to your person and state, and the only means to ruin and destroy all those that stand faithfully devoted to Your Majesty's service. Some particulars, and persons of this nature, I make no doubt have been discovered by the endeavours of this nobleman, the bearer hereof, of whom Your Majesty may be further informed.

3. The third point considerable is that Your Majesty by all means possible, secure yourself of the good affection of the French King and states, by the negotiation of some faithful secret confident ; the French naturally distasting the union of the British islands under one monarch. In Germany, I doubt not, but you have many allies and friends, but by reason of their remote state they do not so much importe this affair, which must by guided by a quick and sudden motion.

4. When God, by whose providence the period of all persons and times is determined, shall call to his kingdom of glory Her Majesty (although I do assuredly hope that there will not be any question in competition, yet for that I hold it not fitting to give any minute entrance into a cause of so high a nature), I do humbly beseech Your Majesty to design a secret, faithful and experienced confident servant of yours, being of an approved fidelity and judgment, continually to be here resident, whose negotiation, it were convenient Your Majesty should fortifie, with such secret trust and powers, as there may not need 14 days respite to post for authority, in a cause that cannot endure ten hours respite, without varieties of danger.

In the which it is to be considered, that all such as pretend least good to your establishment, will not in public oppugn your title, but out of their cunning ambition will seek to gain time by alledging their pretence of common good to the state, in propounding of good conditions for disburthening the common weal, of divers hard laws, heavy impositions, corruptions, oppressions, &c., which is a main point to lead the popular, who are much disgusted with many particulars of this nature. It were therefore convenient, that these motives, out of Your Majesty's providence should be prevented, by your free offer in these points following, viz :—

1. That Your Majesty would be pleased to abolish purveyors and purveyance, being a matter infinitely offensive to the common people, and the whole kingdom, and not profitable to the Prince.

2. That Your Majesty would be pleased to dissolve the court of wards, being the ruin of all the ancient families of this realm, by base matches, and evil education of their children, by which no revenue of the crown will be defrayed.

3. The abrogating the multiplicity of penal laws, generally repined against by the subject, in regard of their uncertainty, being many times altered from their true meaning, by a variety of interpretation.

4. That Your Majesty will be pleased to admit free outport of the native commodities of this kingdom, now often restrained by subalternate persons for private profit, being most prejudicial to the commerce of all merchants, and a plain destruction to the true industry and manufacture of all kingdoms, and against the profit of the crown.

These, being by Your Majesty's confidents in the point of time propounded, will assuredly confirm unto Your Majestie the hearts and affections of the whole kingdom, and absolutely prevent all insinuations and devices of designing patriots, that out of pretext of common good would seek to patronize themselves in popular opinion and power, and thereby to derogate from Your Majesty's bounty and free favour by princely merit of your moderation, judgment, and justice.

Your Majesty's favour, thus granted to the subject, will no way impeach the profits of the crown, but advance them. The disproportionable gain of some chequer officers, with the base and mercenary profits of the idle unnecessary clerks and attendants, will only suffer some detriment ; but infinite will be the good unto the kingdom, which will confirm unto Your Majesty the universal love and affection of the people, and establish your renown in the highest esteem to all posterity.

The Lord preserve Your Majestie, and make you triumphant over all your enemies.

My care over his person, whose letters pass in this pacquet, and will die before he leave to be yours, shall be no less than of mine own life, and in like esteem will I hold all your faithful confidents, notwithstanding I will hold myself reserved from being known unto any of them, in my particular devoted affections unto Your Majesty, only this extraordinary worthy man, whose associate I am in his misfortune, doth know my heart, and we both will pray for you, and if we live you shall find us together.

I beseech Your Majesty burn this letter, and the others; for altho' it be in an unusual hand, yet it may be discovered.

Your Majesty's most devoted

and humble servant,

O.

James Clark, Printer, Aberdeen.

A CATALOGUE

OF

NEW AND CHEAP PUBLICATIONS

Handsomely bound in cloth, gilt,

SOLD BY

W. MILNER, HALIFAX :—G. CLARK & SON, ABERDEEN :—

AND

J. M. BURTON, IPSWICH.

LIFE ON THE OCEAN, or TWENTY YEARS AT SEA: being the Personal Adventures of the Author, by G. LITTLE.

TRAVELS IN MEXICO, by ALBERT M. GILLIAM.

MORRIS' TRAVELS in Turkey, Greece, Egypt, &c.

SELF-CONTROL : by MRS. BRUNTON.

JOHNSON'S COMPLETE ENGLISH DICTIONARY, 8vo.

BEAUTIES of the REV. JOHN WESLEY, containing the most interesting passages in his Works.

WILBERFORCE'S PRACTICAL VIEWS of CHRISTIANITY.

MASON on SELF-KNOWLEDGE.

BUCHAN'S DOMESTIC MEDICINE.

CULPEPER'S BRITISH HERBAL.

The RECLUSE of NORWAY, by MISS PORTER.

The LAKE of KILLARNEY, by do.

Adventures of DON QUIXOTE.

LOUISA EGERTON, or Castle Herbert.

The BACHELOR'S CHRISTMAS, or Castle Dismal.

CAPTAIN KYD, or the Wizard of the Sea.

The REGENT'S DAUGHTER, by ALEXANDRE DUMAS.

Lives of Eminent NAVAL HEROES, demy 18mo.

BUFFON'S NATURAL HISTORY, 100 cuts.

BAXTER'S SELECT WORKS.

PAUL REDDING, or the Wanderer Restored.

WONDERS of the WORLD in Nature and Art.

JACK MALCOLM'S LOG, or Sea Adventures.

LIFE of NAPOLEON BONAPARTE.

LIFE of VISCOUNT NELSON.

YOUNG MAN'S OWN BOOK.

BYRON'S SELECT POEMS.

THIRTY YEARS from HOME, or a VOICE from the MAIN
DECK.

The Life of the Rev. JOHN WESLEY.

The VICAR of WAKEFIELD.

OLD ENGLISH BARON, and the CASTLE of OTRANTO.

BUNYAN'S PILGRIM'S PROGRESS.

COMPLETE LETTER WRITER.

YOUNG WOMAN'S COMPANION.

DOMESTIC COOKERY, illustrated with numerous cuts.

CŒLEBS in SEARCH of a WIFE, by H. More.

Jenks' FAMILY DEVOTIONS, demy 18mo.

Hervey's MEDITATIONS and CONTEMPLATIONS, demy
18mo.

MEMOIRS of Mrs. A. Rogers, demy 32mo. gilt edges.

Fleetwood's LIFE of CHRIST, 32mo.

Lowson's COMPLETE HORSE and CATTLE FARRIER.

The MODERN CABINET of ARTS, 18mo.

FLOWERS of POETRY.

POPULAR GEOGRAPHY.

Stories for YOUNG PERSONS, by Miss Sedgwick.

Robertson's HISTORY of SCOTLAND.

BURNS' complete WORKS and LIFE, by Dr. Currie.

PETER PINDAR'S WORKS.

Johnson's LIVES of the POETS.

Boswell's LIFE of JOHNSON.

Goldsmith's HISTORY of ENGLAND.

———— HISTORY of GREECE.

The ROMANCE of REAL LIFE, by Miss Smith.

The VICTORIA SCRAP BOOK; in Poetry and Prose.

BURNS' POEMS, with a splendid Frontispiece.

BAXTER'S SAINTS' EVERLASTING REST.